Introduction to
LAW
ENFORCEMENT

David H. McElreath
Daniel Adrian Doss
Carl J. Jensen, III
Michael Wigginton, Jr.
Ralph Kennedy
Kenneth R. Winter
Robert E. Mongue
Janice Bounds
J. Michelle Estis-Sumerel

CRC Press
Taylor & Francis Group
Boca Raton London New York

CRC Press is an imprint of the
Taylor & Francis Group, an **informa** business

CRC Press
Taylor & Francis Group
6000 Broken Sound Parkway NW, Suite 300
Boca Raton, FL 33487-2742

Printed on Acid-free paper
Version Date: 20130111

International Standard Book Number-13: 978-1-4665-5623-2 (Hardback)

This book contains information obtained from authentic and highly regarded sources. Reasonable efforts have been made to publish reliable data and information, but the author and publisher cannot assume responsibility for the validity of all materials or the consequences of their use. The authors and publishers have attempted to trace the copyright holders of all material reproduced in this publication and apologize to copyright holders if permission to publish in this form has not been obtained. If any copyright material has not been acknowledged please write and let us know so we may rectify in any future reprint.

Library of Congress Cataloging-in-Publication Data

Introduction in law enforcement / David H. McElreath ... [et al.].
     p. cm.
   Includes bibliographical references and index.
   ISBN 978-1-4665-5623-2 (hbk. : alk. paper)
   1. Law enforcement--United States. 2. Police--United States. I. McElreath, David.

HV8139.I58 2013
363.20975--dc23   2012037623

**Visit the Taylor & Francis Web site at
http://www.taylorandfrancis.com**

**and the CRC Press Web site at
http://www.crcpress.com**

Dedication

This textbook is dedicated to the men and women whose dutiful and tireless efforts and contributions enhance the safety of communities throughout the nation. Their relentless commitment to honor their law enforcement oaths of office and to render service to their fellow man is appreciated by these authors. Some may pursue a lifetime of law enforcement service, whereas others leave the field to pursue other endeavors. Regardless of their currency in the profession, time in service, grade, position, location, or future endeavors, these authors offer a heartfelt "thank you" for their sacrifices and services.

Many officers who pursue careers in law enforcement become disabled or die in the line of duty. Others experience illness that interrupts their careers. This textbook is dedicated to those officers whose service resulted in death, or involves disability or illness. Again, these authors offer a heartfelt "thank you" for such service and sacrifice.

We also realize that law enforcement officers have positively and meaningfully impacted countless lives. For those readers whose lives have been bettered because of the contributions of a law enforcement officer (or officers), we ask you to remember their service, and to say "thank you" to the individual(s) who influenced your life. We also challenge you to be a positive influence in the lives of others.

We also dedicate this book to the families, friends, and colleagues of law enforcement officers, whether alive or deceased. Because of the work requirements, lengthy hours, stresses, dangers, sacrifices, and surprises of life that are associated with law enforcement careers, your commitment, assistance, understanding, and support are much appreciated. Once again, we offer a heartfelt "thank you."

Finally, this text would not have been possible with the support from those who are most important in our lives: Leisa, Boo, Emily, Bethany, Kate, and Brent; Janice; Brenda, Genevieve, and Elyse; Margaret and Caleigh; Denise; Stephanie and Zachary; Jennifer and Jill; and Lisa.

Contents

Preface

Throughout the nation, law enforcement officers patrol the streets of small towns, rural areas, and urban settings. They walk among our streets, secure our courtrooms and schools, drive through our neighborhoods and among our roadways, patrol our waterways and skies, and bolster the security of our public events. Their personal backgrounds and individual situations are diverse; regardless, they all have a common attribute—each one answered a calling to serve their locales as peace officers.

They may perform innocuous services as members of police bands or may endanger their lives when answering calls for assistance. They may experience the viciousness of natural disasters or the comforts of beach patrols. Their responsibilities are tremendous, and their fiduciary obligation to render public service is often misunderstood and unappreciated. Regardless, their chosen occupation and calling are rife with complexity and represent the continuing of a sacred trust and responsibility.

Within American society, law enforcement officers share a rich history and tradition of maintaining societal order and deterring crime. This legacy continues through contemporary times. Law enforcement has changed drastically since the beginning of American society. Throughout history, it has been viewed from a variety of perspectives including vocational and professional, and as both a science and an art. Although technologies, laws, people, geographic boundaries, and society have changed since the founding of the United States, one thing is unchanged—time after time, someone, somewhere heeds the call to serve others as a member of the law enforcement community.

Modern perspectives of law enforcement are both complex and diverse. They integrate functions of management and statistical analysis; functions of public and business administration; applications of psychology and natural science; applications of physical fitness and marksmanship; theories of education, organizational behavior, and economics; tenets of law and public policy; and many others. Modern law enforcement is a blend of both theoretical knowledge and applied practice that continuously changes through time.

Other facets of change permeate the law enforcement and criminal justice domains. During the latter period of the nineteenth century, the concept of fingerprinting was introduced, and it revolutionized the criminal justice domain. Today, fingerprinting is a common attribute of the law enforcement domain. Over a century ago, the concept of night vision was inconceivable. Today, it embellishes the operations of various special weapons and tactics teams during nocturnal duties. Over a century ago, the act of communicating was performed manually consisting primarily of written and oral words and phrases. Today, it is instantaneously facilitated through numerous electronic devices and radio waves.

Throughout the tumultuous periods of change that have affected the law enforcement and criminal justice domains, one attribute of humanity remains unchanged, that is, human nature. Humans have the potential for ethical, moral behavior and unethical, immoral behavior. Humans have the potential for performing both good and evil deeds. Humans have the capacity for conducting themselves within the boundaries of the law or committing acts of crime. All human actions have the potential for impacting the lives of others either positively or negatively. All law enforcement officers are human, and their cumulative service to American society is beneficial despite their susceptibility to the fallibility of human nature.

Throughout the history of the United States, a primary theme has permeated the justice domain: Law enforcement personnel contribute toward the deterring of crime and the maintaining of societal order. During modern times, they still continue to attain these goals. This textbook serves as an introduction to the perspectives of law enforcement personnel and organizations that daily and unceasingly benefit American society with respect to this theme.

Within the pages of this text are discussions of the history of American law enforcement and its contemporary issues. This text introduces the relationships that exist between the served community and the law enforcement organization, and the relationships that exist between and within law enforcement organizations. The discussions also consider the science and art of the law enforcement domain, ranging from the tangible characteristics of forensic endeavors to the intangible characteristics of personal difficulties experienced by law enforcement officers during the course of their careers.

This textbook considers the effects of change through time that have influenced the law enforcement domain. From the origins of law enforcement within American society to the modern period, law enforcement has experienced much change legally, technologically, operationally, managerially, administratively, organizationally, economically, politically, and governmentally. Such considerations are contained within the discussions of this textbook.

This textbook introduces the history of American law enforcement; recent demographics of crime within American society and the United States; the agencies that comprise international, federal, state, local, and tribal law enforcement organizations; private law enforcement and security organizations; and law enforcement administration and management. It discusses the dangers of law enforcement and the types of policing that permeate law enforcement organizations. Additional discussions include types of patrols and specialized assignments, concepts of investigations, and forensics. Certainly, this textbook incorporates considerations of law enforcement ethics, the United States Constitution, and the justice system.

The preceding notions highlight the attributes of change that have permeated law enforcement within the United States and the issues of modern law enforcement. This textbook culminates in a discussion of the future of law enforcement. No one can predict the future with certainty and complete exactness. However, one thing is certain—change will continue to impact and influence the law enforcement domain. The final discussions of this textbook encompass areas of research and development that have the potential to impact the futures of both law enforcement and American society.

These discussions contribute toward a foundation for understanding and appreciating the service that is rendered by all law enforcement officers, regardless of their organization, location, position, or time in service. After reading this textbook, we hope that readers will have gained a robust view of the law enforcement domain and its goals from a variety of perspectives. Whether the reader desires to enter a law enforcement career or is merely curious about the justice domain, we hope that reading this textbook will provide meaningful benefits.

Authors

David H. McElreath, PhD, is a professor in the Department of Legal Studies at the University of Mississippi. His background includes service as professor and chair, Department of Legal Studies, University of Mississippi; professor and chair, Department of Criminal Justice, Washburn University; associate professor, Southeast Missouri State University; colonel, United States Marine Corps; and law enforcement and corrections positions with the Oxford, Mississippi Police and Forrest County, Mississippi Sheriff's departments. His education and training include a PhD in adult education and criminal justice, University of Southern Mississippi; a Master Strategic Studies from the United States Army War College; a Master of Criminal Justice from University of Mississippi; and a Bachelor of Public Administration from University of Mississippi. McElreath is also a graduate of the United States Army War College. He has served as a consultant, including working on projects for the United States Department of State. He is the author of numerous publications on the criminal justice and homeland security systems.

Daniel Adrian Doss, PhD, is an assistant professor, College of Business Administration, University of West Alabama; assistant professor, Belhaven College; adjunct assistant professor, Embry-Riddle Aeronautical University; and chair of graduate business and management, University of Phoenix (Memphis). His professional career has consisted of software engineering and analytical positions in both the defense and commercial industries. Corporate entities included full-time and contract positions with Federal Express and uMonitor.com, and contract positions via Data Management Consultants, with Loral Corporation (formerly IBM Federal Systems) and Lockheed Martin. Additional credentials include lieutenant colonel, Mississippi State Guard; graduate of the Lafayette County Law Enforcement Academy (Oxford, Mississippi); and graduate of the Law Enforcement Mobile Video Institute. He has also coauthored a variety of peer-reviewed journal articles and conference proceedings. His education consists of a PhD in business administration from Northcentral University; a Master of Criminal Justice in homeland security from the University of Mississippi; an MA in computer resources and information management from Webster University; an MBA from Embry-Riddle Aeronautical University; a graduate certificate in forensic criminology from the University of Massachusetts (Lowell); a graduate certificate in non-profit financial management from the University of Maryland (Adelphi); and a BS in computer science with a mathematics minor from Mississippi State University. He is currently pursuing additional doctoral studies in police science through the University of South Africa.

Carl J. Jensen, III, PhD, is the director of the University of Mississippi's (UM) Center for Intelligence and Security Studies. He also is a member of UM's Department of Legal Studies and serves in an adjunct capacity as a senior behavioral scientist with the RAND Corporation. Dr. Jensen served as a special agent with the Federal Bureau of Investigation

(FBI) for 22 years; his FBI career included service as a field agent, a forensic examiner in the FBI Laboratory, and an instructor and assistant chief of the Behavioral Science Unit. He has been published extensively and lectured throughout the world. Dr. Jensen received a BS from the U.S. Naval Academy, an MA from Kent State University, and a PhD from the University of Maryland.

Michael Wigginton, Jr., PhD, is an assistant professor of criminal justice and director of the University of Mississippi Master of Criminal Justice Executive Cohort Program, Department of Legal Studies; former assistant professor, Southeast Louisiana University; adjunct professor at Tulane University; senior special agent, United States Customs Service; special agent, United States Drug Enforcement Administration; detective and state trooper, Louisiana State Police; police officer, New Orleans Police Department; and United States Air Force security police dog handler with service in Vietnam. His education and training include a PhD in criminal justice from the University of Southern Mississippi; an MS from the University of New Orleans; an MS from the University of Alabama; and a BA from Loyola University of New Orleans. He is also the author of numerous publications on the criminal justice system.

Ralph Kennedy, MEd, is an instructor of criminal justice at the University of Mississippi; former adjunct instructor at the National Center for Biomedical Research and Training, Academy of Counter-Terrorist Education, Louisiana State University; a retired special agent for the U.S. Secret Service; a former rotational instructor/course developer and U.S. Secret Service representative at the Federal Law Enforcement Training Center (FLETC); the former deputy director, Law Enforcement Training Center, U.S. Department of Veterans Affairs; a former police officer and academy instructor in the Memphis Police Department; and a U.S. Marine Corps Reserve military police officer. His education includes a BS and an MEd from the University of Memphis. He is a U.S. Department of Homeland Security/ Office for State and Local Government Coordination and Preparedness certified trainer. He has also authored several articles for educational and law enforcement professional publications.

Kenneth R. Winter, MSCJ, is an instructor of legal studies at the University of Mississippi and an instructor of criminal justice at Delta State University. He currently serves as the executive director of the Mississippi Association of Chiefs of Police and a contract investigator at the United States Department of Homeland Security. He is the former director of the Mississippi Crime Laboratory; former director of the Mississippi Delta Law Enforcement Academy; former chief of police of Indianola, Mississippi; former forensic scientist at the Wisconsin State Crime Laboratory; and police officer/chief of detectives of Greenville, Mississippi. His education and training include an MS in criminal justice from Delta State University; graduate work in continuing adult vocational education from the University of Wisconsin–Madison; a BA in human relations–criminal justice from the University of Alabama; an AA in law enforcement from Northwest Mississippi Junior College; graduate of 153rd Session-FBI National Academy; and he is a Certified Latent Fingerprint Examiner and Certified Senior Crime Scene Analyst by the International Association for Identification.

Robert E. Mongue, JD, is an assistant professor of legal studies at the University of Mississippi and was an adjunct instructor of criminal law and paralegal studies at Andover College in Maine. A graduate of the University of Maine School of Law, he has over 30 years of experience as a trial and appellate attorney in both state and federal courts, including work as both a prosecutor and a defense attorney. He is the author of three books and several articles. Other presentations by Mongue include seminars and workshops on understanding court systems, litigation, litigation case management, trial preparation, and trial tactics. He is the co-chair of the Scholarly Journal Committee of the American Association for Paralegal Education and is a member of the Advisory Council of the Organization of Legal Professionals.

Janice Bounds, MBA, is an associate professor of legal studies and has been involved in legal studies and taught at the University of Mississippi for 36 years. Bounds has extensive experience with the court system at both the state and federal levels, having previously taught court reporting and worked with the court system. In addition to her teaching experience, she has worked in the U.S. Attorney's Office for the Northern District of Mississippi. Bounds received her undergraduate degree from Georgia Southwestern College, Americus, Georgia, and her master's degree from the University of Mississippi. Additionally, she has achieved numerous certifications in criminal justice.

J. Michelle Estis-Sumerel, MS, is a coordinator of e-learning instruction at Itawamba Community College, and an adjunct instructor in the department of legal studies at the University of Mississippi. She is a candidate for a PhD in community college leadership at Mississippi State University; and has earned an MS in sociology with an emphasis in criminology at Mississippi State University; and a BS in sociology at the University of North Alabama. She is also the creator of several courses in law enforcement, corrections, and homeland security.

Crime in the United States

1

> Short of war, our society is faced with no more important problem than crime.[1]
>
> **O. W. Wilson (1950)**

Learning Objectives

The objectives of the chapter are to

- Explain the differences between civil and criminal law
- Explain the Uniform Crime Report and other sources of crime data
- Identify the categorization of crime
- Recognize the trends of crime affecting the United States
- Define the concept of recidivism
- Define the societal impacts of crime

Introduction

One thing is certain: we shall always have crime and will always need dedicated and honest individuals who are willing to place themselves in harm's way in the struggle to make our communities a safer place for us all to live. Across the United States, crime and criminal behavior continues to be a pervasive problem that receives considerable attention from the media, law enforcement, and social science researchers. Crime touches every segment of our society. In 2008, there were over 14 million crimes that came to the attention of law enforcement officials.[2]

Crime can be defined as any act that is punishable by law. Typically, criminal behavior is considered to be acts that our society does not condone. As a society, we feel strongly that some behavior is so unacceptable that it should be prohibited by law. To make this happen, elected officials vote to make something punishable by criminal law; each of our 50 states and the federal government have developed statutes that describe what behaviors are considered illegal and what the punishments for these behaviors should be.

Deviant behavior also comes to the attention of the police but is different from criminal behavior in that it is not against the law. Behavior that our society labels as deviant includes any behavior that does not conform to the expectations of society. This could be as simple as deviant forms of dress to a group becoming too loud in a public place. Depending on the situation and how disruptive the group becomes, this deviant behavior can quickly turn into criminal behavior such as disorderly conduct. Although deviant behavior can be troublesome to a community, as it applies to law enforcement, it is not the primary focus of resources. It is behavior that has been defined as violating a law or ordnance that will be the focus for police and law enforcement professionals.

Crimes can be divided into categories based on their seriousness. The first two categories are misdemeanors and felonies. Misdemeanors are crimes that are less serious and punishable with a range of sentences from fines to incarceration in a jail for up to a year. Examples of misdemeanors include disorderly conduct, vandalism, and trespassing. Felonies are more serious crimes that carry a penalty ranging from a year or more in prison to the most extreme sentence of death. Examples of felonies include aggravated assault, rape, and murder.

Status offenses are a third category of crime that applies only to individuals who are under a certain age. These behaviors are typically not against the law for an adult but hold a special status for juveniles. Examples of these offenses include truancy, drinking alcohol, curfew violations, and smoking. Most states have specific age limits set for each offense.

Criminal Law and Civil Law

Law in the United States can be classified either as criminal law or civil law. Criminal law is concerned with behaviors that are considered to be harmful to society as well as the victim. These laws have been codified at the local, state, and federal level. Criminal law identifies the behavior and the associated punishment with that crime. Because criminal law is considered to include behavior that is harmful to society, the state prosecutes an individual who has violated a criminal law.

Civil law, on the other hand, includes actions that are not criminal. These usually involve disputes between individuals or private organizations, and the remedy sought typically includes monetary or property compensation. Law enforcement is rarely involved in civil law, with the exception of serving court papers that deal with civil cases.

The same act can constitute both a crime and a civil wrong. For example, when a person steals an item, the government is entitled to prosecute the offender for the crime of theft and the victim is entitled to bring a civil action against the thief for the tort of conversion. These actions proceed separately. The government seeks the appropriate fine, jail sentence, or other penalty for the harm to society, in general, and to deter future criminal conduct. The victim seeks return of the stolen object or monetary compensation for the value of the item.

Measuring Crime

Information about crime in the United States is gathered from several sources and published in many different formats. We look at a few of these sources for information about criminal offending and victimization as well as specific crimes and variations in crime trends over time in the United States. Specifically, we look at the Uniform Crime Report (UCR), National Incident-Based Reporting System (NIBRS), National Crime Victimization Survey (NCVS), and self-report surveys.

One of the most widely used official sources of crime data is the UCR. The UCR contains data that has been collected, analyzed, and published annually by the Federal Bureau of Investigation (FBI) since 1930.[3] There are over 17,000 law enforcement agencies that voluntarily contribute arrest incident data to the FBI for compilation and dissemination. As of 2003, approximately 93% of the nation's agencies were participating in the program.[4]

The primary goal of the UCR is to provide a consistent and reliable set of crime statistics for law enforcement professionals and researchers.

From the data collected by the UCR, the FBI produces a comprehensive report, *Crime in the United States*, which is published annually, including several crimes that have been divided into Part I and Part II crimes. Part I crimes are also referred to as index crimes and include eight of the most serious crimes that are the most likely to come to the attention of the police. Part I crimes are further divided into violent crimes against persons and property crimes. Violent crimes include murder, rape, assault, and robbery. Property crimes include burglary, motor vehicle theft, larceny-theft, and arson. Part II crimes include all other crimes reported that are not listed as part of the index crimes. Examples of these crimes include gambling, drug violations, and vandalism.[5]

The *Crime in the United States* publication reports information on crimes cleared and arrest characteristics, including the offender's age, sex, and race. Information is available on the number of law enforcement personnel as well as on the number of sworn officers killed or assaulted each year. There is detailed information on homicides included in this report. Although characteristics are available for arrestees of other crimes, information on the crime of homicide includes the age, sex, and race of both the victims and the offenders. Information is also collected on the victim–offender relationship, weapons used, and other circumstances surrounding this crime.[6]

To increase the reliability of data on the crimes being reported by individual departments, the FBI provides standardized definitions for the offenses. The definition for criminal homicide includes murder and nonnegligent manslaughter, which is the willful killing of one human being by another. Manslaughter by negligence is the killing of another person through gross negligence. Robbery is the taking or attempted taking of anything of value from the care, custody, or control of a person or persons by force or threat of force or violence and/or by putting the victim in fear. Aggravated assault is an unlawful attack by one person upon another for the purpose of inflicting severe or aggravated bodily injury. Burglary is the unlawful entry of a structure to commit a felony or a theft. Larceny-theft is the unlawful taking, carrying, leading, or riding away of property from the possession of another. Motor vehicle theft is the theft or attempted theft of a motor vehicle. Arson is any willful or malicious burning or attempt to burn, with or without intent to defraud, a dwelling house, public building, motor vehicle or aircraft, or the personal property of another (Table 1.1).

As with any source of crime data, there are some precautions that law enforcement professionals need to take into consideration. The data collected in the UCR include crimes that have been reported to police and do not include crimes that fail to come to the attention of law enforcement. This phenomenon is referred to as the "dark figure of crime." The dark figure of crime is the actual number of crimes committed in the United States of which we do not have an accurate count. This number fluctuates depending on the seriousness of the crime, relationship between the offender and the victim, and attitudes toward law enforcement within a community.

Citizens are more likely to report crimes that are more serious. There also appears to be a relationship in how often crimes are reported and the victim–offender relationship. We tend to find that victims are less likely to report crimes such as theft and assault when a family member or close acquaintance is responsible. Finally, there appears to be an association between a citizen's reluctance to report crime and his or her views of the police department within their community. When community residents have low levels of trust

Table 1.1   Offense Summaries

	Part I Offenses
Criminal homicide	(a) Murder and nonnegligent manslaughter: the willful (nonnegligent) killing of one human being by another. Deaths caused by negligence, attempts to kill, assaults to kill, suicides, and accidental deaths are excluded. Justifiable homicides are classified separately and the definition is limited to (1) the killing of a felon by a law enforcement officer in the line of duty or (2) the killing of a felon, during the commission of a felony, by a private citizen. (b) Manslaughter by negligence: the killing of another person through gross negligence.
Forcible rape	Penetration, no matter how slight, of the vagina or anus with any body part or object, or oral penetration by a sex organ of another person, without the consent of the victim.
Robbery	The taking or attempting to take anything of value from the care, custody, or control of a person or persons by force or threat of force or violence and/or by putting the victim in fear.
Aggravated assault	An unlawful attack by one person upon another for the purpose of inflicting severe or aggravated bodily injury. This type of assault usually is accompanied by the use of a weapon or by means likely to produce death or great bodily harm.
Burglary	The unlawful entry of a structure to commit a felony or a theft.
Larceny/theft	The unlawful taking, carrying, leading, or riding away of property from the possession or constructive possession of another.
Motor vehicle theft	The theft or attempted theft of a motor vehicle. A motor vehicle is self-propelled and runs on land surface and not on rails.
Arson	Any willful or malicious burning or attempt to burn, with or without intent to defraud, a dwelling house, public building, motor vehicle or aircraft, personal property of another, and so on.

Source: Federal Bureau of Investigation[7]

in law enforcement, they tend to be more reluctant to report crime. This may be from a fear of law enforcement, the belief that the police will not respond or will not act in a manner to resolve the issue for the citizen.

Additionally, an area of inconsistency to consider is the method through which crimes are reported by law enforcement agencies. For example, when multiple crimes are committed by one person or multiple individuals commit one crime, there are differences in the way these crimes are reported to the UCR. The hierarchy rule is used when a single offender commits several crimes during one incident. In this case, only the most serious crimes will be reported. This reporting results in the overall crime rate being changed by underreporting the actual number of crimes.[8] Finally, there are issues with the type of data that is collected and its limited nature. Arrest data is restricted to the age, sex, and race of the offender for most of the crimes that are reported.

As a reaction to these deficiencies and a growing need to better understand crime, the FBI has developed a second reporting system, the NIBRS. This system was developed to capture the changing nature of crime and to provide a more in-depth look at criminal offenders and victims. Participation was voluntary, and in 2004, over 5000 law enforcement agencies were participating.[9] Data were collected for two categories of crime: Group A and Group B. Group A offenses were divided into 22 categories made up of 46 crimes, and Group B offenses were made up of 11 categories. Group B offenses gathered arrest data only, while Group A offenses collected detailed information about the offense, the victim, the offender, and the arrestee (Table 1.2).[10]

Table 1.2   NIBRS Group A Offense Categories

Arson	Homicide offenses
Assault offenses	Kidnapping/abduction
Bribery	Larceny/theft offenses
Burglary/breaking and entering	Motor vehicle theft
Counterfeiting/forgery	Pornography/obscene material
Destruction/damage/vandalism of property	Prostitution offenses
Drug/narcotic offenses	Robbery
Embezzlement	Sex offenses, forcible
Extortion/blackmail	Sex offenses, nonforcible
Fraud offenses	Stolen property offenses
Gambling offenses	Weapon law violations

Source: Nation Archive of Crimi.. . justice Data[11]

The NIBRS addresses the differential reporting procedures used in the UCR by reporting each incident separately and not following the hierarchy rule. The goal of this system is not only to address problems of the UCR, but also to provide more accurate data that are more reflective of our changing society. One of the daunting tasks for researchers is keeping up with the dynamic nature of our world and the consequential changing nature of criminal offenders. Definitions of the crimes have been updated to reflect these changes. There are several benefits of utilizing this system, including the expansion of the crimes with which law enforcement is faced. This system includes white-collar crime, hate crimes, elderly abuse, gang activities, pornography, and child pornography, which are absent from the previous reporting system. Although NIBRS is generally considered to be superior to the UCR, it also places a larger burden on the police to accurately record greater amounts of data. For this reason, some law enforcement agencies have been reluctant or unable to switch over to NIBRS.

Although these two reporting systems record crimes that come to the attention of the police, as discussed earlier, not all crime is reported by citizens. To tap into crimes that are not reported to the police and gather additional information about the characteristics of criminal victimization, the NCVS has been collecting data since 1973. This survey is administered by the U.S. Census Bureau (sponsored by Bureau of Justice Statistics) twice a year. It samples around 49,000 households, which generates data on approximately 100,000 residents. Residents are asked directly about their victimization.

Offense categories are divided into personal and property crimes. Information gathered on this survey includes the type of crime, when and where the crime occurred, and the relationship between the victim and the offender. This survey includes questions that tap into the characteristics and behaviors of the offender, such as the offender's use of weapons, drugs, and alcohol. The survey also measures any self-protective actions taken by the victim during the incident and the results of those actions. The NCVS provides more detailed information about all components of crime by asking the respondent to describe the incident in detail.[12] Respondents are additionally asked whether the crime of which they were a victim was reported to the police and reasons for reporting or not reporting.[13] This information is very valuable in trying to uncover the causes for the dark figure of crime.

Criticisms of the NCVS include sampling error, inaccuracy of the respondents, and problems created by interviewer interaction. Sampling error occurs when a sample of the population is used to represent generalized findings about the population as a whole.[14] This is a problem that cannot be addressed unless the entire population is surveyed, which is not economically feasible nor an efficient use of resources. It is simply a source of error that must be taken into consideration when viewing crime statistics generated from the NCVS. Respondent error occurs when a victim erroneously defines a crime or telescopes the time frame in which the crime has occurred. For example, a respondent may define a burglary as a robbery, which categorizes the crime as a violent crime instead of a property crime.

An example of telescoping occurs when a respondent is asked about being the victim of a crime in the last 6 months but includes a crime that occurred 8 months ago.[15] This unnecessarily inflates the crime rates of the time period. Interviewer interactions occur when a respondent adjusts his or her answers to a survey question based on interactions with the person who is conducting the interview. This could take the form of a respondent not providing a truthful answer out of embarrassment or shame; just as victims of crime are reluctant to call the police if the offender is a friend or family member, they are less likely to report these same offenses on victimization surveys.

The fourth source of crime data comes from self-report surveys. These surveys are typically administered to juveniles and are an instrument designed to uncover crime that has not been reported to the police and, in some instances, may be unknown to the victim. The basic approach of this method is to ask respondents if they have engaged in any deviant or criminal behavior and to what extent.[16] Self-report surveys experience many of the same weaknesses as victimization surveys such as sampling error and respondent inaccuracy. There may be reluctance by juveniles or other respondents to report crimes or deviant behavior that have not come to the attention of law enforcement or other school authorities. There is a fear that their responses will be used against them. There is also the tendency for juveniles to exaggerate their criminal offending by reporting crimes that they did not commit (Table 1.3).

Table 1.3 Crime Measurements

Measurement	Method	Strength	Weakness
Uniform Crime Report	Crimes reported to police	High level of participation by departments	Does not address crime that does not come to the attention of law enforcement
NIBRS (National Incident-Based Reporting System	Crimes reported to police	More detailed information	Low level of voluntary participation by departments
NCVS (National Crime Victimization Survey)	Crimes reported by victims	Taps into unreported crimes	Inaccuracy of respondent's information (telescoping)
Self-report survey	Crimes reported by offenders	Gains information about deviant and criminal behavior	Inaccuracy of respondent's information

Crime Trends in the United States

Crime data is presented to the public in terms of rates, percentage changes, and total numbers. A rate is expressed as the number of offenses per 100,000 inhabitants in a specified area for a given year. For example, the violent crime rate for 2008 was estimated to be 454.4 violent crimes per 100,000 inhabitants for the entire United States. Percentage changes address how this rate changes from year to year and assess trends in crime data. For example, violent crime decreased by 1.9% from 2007 to 2008.

Crime may also be expressed as the absolute number of crimes. In 2008, there were 1,382,012 violent crimes and 9,767,915 property crimes recorded in the United States. It is important to understand these differences and how the media, researchers, and politicians use such statistics to present crime data. Presenting a percentage change between rates is a more accurate reflection of how crime fluctuates from year to year because the population is controlled. Crime data that present percentage changes in absolute numbers is not as accurate because population fluctuates from year to year.

Violent and property crime rates as measured by the UCR are generally used to present an overview of crime trends in the United States. These crimes are used because it is thought that the serious nature of these offenses makes them more likely to be reported by victims and therefore more accurate. There is some debate on how representative this data is of the true level of crime in the United States, but it appears to be generally agreed that these measurements provide us with a good indication of crime trends over time. The trends reported by the UCR, the NCVS, and self-report studies tend to show similar increases and decreases in crime rates over time, even if the absolute numbers vary from measurement to measurement.

Because violent and property crime data have been systematically collected by the UCR since 1930, these data are subjected to analysis of long-term trends regardless of the measurement criticisms. Overall, crime in the United States appears to have declined over the last 20 years. This finding seems to be consistent with data from the UCR as well as data from the NCVS. Data also suggest that serious violent crime committed by juveniles (offenders 12–17 years of age) has declined by over 60% from 1993 to 2005.[17] In 2005 and 2006, there was a slight increase in the rate of violent crime; however, that rate dropped both in 2007 and 2008 and continues the downward overall trend. The current violent crime rate is the lowest it has been since before 1980.[18] Figures 1.1 and 1.2 depict these observations.

When we look more closely at the offenses that make up the violent crime rate, we see that murder has declined by 4.4% from 2007 to 2008 according to the FBI's UCR. Preliminary statistics also suggests that this percentage change will double from 2008 to 2009. Other violent crimes such as rapes were at the lowest level they have been in 20 years with an estimated number of 89,000 in 2008. This is a decrease of 1.6% from 2007. Robbery rates also dropped in 2008 by an estimated 1.5%. These specific crimes suggest a continued downward trend in violent crime.

Property crimes include burglary, larceny-theft, motor vehicle theft, and arson. There were an estimated 9.7 million property crimes reported in the United States during 2008. This resulted in a rate of 3,212.5 offenses per 100,000 residents, which is a 1.6% decline from the rate in 2007. This again confirms a continued downward trend of property crimes in the U.S. with an 8.6% decrease from 2004 and a 14.2% overall decrease from 1999.

Taking a look at the specific offenses that make up property crimes, larceny-theft comprised over two-thirds of all property crime and burglary made up over 22%. Motor vehicle theft experienced the sharpest decline in 2008 with a 12.7% decrease from 2007. The rate for

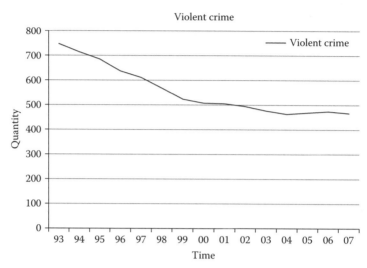

Figure 1.1 Juvenile violent crime. (From the U.S. Bureau of Justice Statistics, Key Facts at a Glance. Retrieved May 16, 2010, from http://bjs.ojp.usdoj.gov/content/glance/cv2.cfm.)

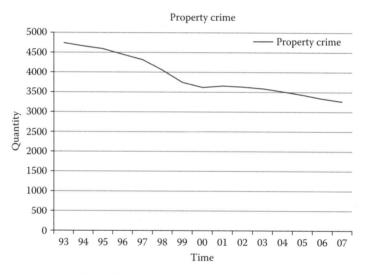

Figure 1.2 Property crime. (From U.S. Department of Justice, Federal Bureau of Investigation, Crime in the United States in 2007. Retrieved May 16, 2010, from http://www.fbi.gov/ucr/cius2007/index.html.)

motor vehicle theft was 314.7 offenses per 100,000 inhabitants, and more than 6.4 billion dollars were lost to this type of property crime. Almost three-fourths of all motor vehicle thefts were of automobiles. Looking at property crimes as a whole, it is estimated that over 17 billion dollars were lost as a result of property crime in the United States during 2008 (Figure 1.3).[20]

Victim Characteristics

Data gathered from the NCVS report many of the same trends in the overall decrease of violent and property crimes over time. According to the NCVS, the violent crime victimization rate has declined over 40% in the last 10 years, while the property crime victimization

The Crime Wave That Isn't

According to a 2009 Gallup Poll, three quarters of all Americans believe crime is getting worse, despite clear evidence to the contrary: as the tables on property and violent crime show, both have decreased steadily over the past several years. What explains this great disparity between perception and reality? Sociologists and criminologists cite a variety of reasons, although no one knows for sure. In the first place, Americans are inundated with depictions of crime on a regular basis, from the local news, to reality shows such as "Cops" and "America's Most Wanted," to such popular fare as "Criminal Minds." Politicians also use crime to their advantage, pontificating about how their "soft" adversaries are to blame for "out of control" criminals. In addition, horrific but unusual events, such as the Virginia Tech and Fort Hood massacres, create the illusion that violent events are an everyday part of our lives. Whatever the reason, fear of crime is a big seller; gun dealers often do great business after a murderous rampage.

Figure 1.3 Synopsis of Crime Gallup Poll Description. (From Keohane, J. 2010. The crime wave in our heads. Retrieved January 30, 2011, from http://www.dallasnews.com/opinion/sunday-commentary/20100326-Joe-Keohane-The-crime-wave-762.ece.)

rate has declined by 32%. The violent crime victimizations in 2008 were the lowest they have been since 1973 when victimization data first began to be recorded. Looking at more recent changes, the violent victimization rates went unchanged from 2007 to 2008, and property victimization rates declined slightly during the same time period.

Victims who respond to this survey are residents in the United States and are age twelve and older. There are several characteristics of the victims themselves that we tend to see associated with crime. For example, women are less likely to be the victim of crime when compared to men, with the exception of rape and sexual assault. When comparing victimization by race, blacks are more likely than whites to be the victim of a violent crime in all categories except simple assault. When compared to racial groups other than whites, blacks are still more likely to be the victim of a crime.

While we tend to find elevated victimization rates among blacks, individuals who self-identify as being of more than one race are two to three times more likely to be the victim of a crime when compared to blacks, whites, and other races. This multirace group made up only 1% of the population in 2008; however, the victimization rate for this group is significantly higher. Looking at differing victimization rates among ethnic groups, non-Hispanic groups are more likely to be the victim of a violent crime when compared to Hispanics with the exception of robbery. There is a strong relationship between victimization and age. The age distribution of victims tends to cluster at the younger and older ends of the continuum. Individuals between the ages of 15 and 24 are more likely to be victims of crime, and individuals older than 50 are the least likely to be victims.

In 2008, there was also a relationship between elevated property crimes and lower levels of annual household income of the victims. Overall, differences in property crime rates were distributed at opposite ends of the income scale. Households that earned less than $7500 per year were one and half more times likely to experience a property crime than households that earned over $75,000, and more specifically, these same households were three times more likely to experience a burglary. Property crime victimization rates were also associated with the size of the household. Households that had six or more members were more than twice as likely to be the victim of a property crime.[21]

Victimization data can also give us additional information about the relationship between the victim and offender. In 2008, women (70%) were much more likely than men (49%) to be victimized by someone they knew. "Known offender" includes a person intimate with the victim, family member, friend, or acquaintance. Violence between intimates also results in women being the victim more often than men in 20% of the cases. An intimate is considered to be a person who is a current or former spouse or girlfriend/boyfriend.

Information is also collected concerning the use of firearms in the commission of a crime in the victimization survey. Firearms were used in 7% of all violent crimes in 2008, which mirrors the rate for 2007. Ten-year trends show that firearm use during the commission of a crime has been declining from a rate of 2.5 per 1,000 persons to 1.4.

As we discussed earlier in this chapter, crimes are differentially reported to police. The NCVS collects data from respondents on whether they reported the crime that they were a victim of and reasons why or why not. Results of this survey show that there are certain offenses that are more likely to be reported to police than others. Robbery and aggravated assault are more likely to be reported to police than sexual assault/rape and simple assault. Of all crimes, both violent and property crimes, motor vehicle theft (80%) is the most likely to be reported than any other crime. Overall, the number of crimes reported to police has not fluctuated greatly over a 10-year period.

When looking at characteristics of the victims of crime and differences in whether they are more or less likely to report an offense, we find that women are more likely than men to report violent crimes. Black females were more likely to report violent crimes than white females and slightly more likely than females of other races. There does not appear to be a significant difference in the reporting trends of Hispanics as compared to non-Hispanics. Property crimes tended to be reported at the same rate, regardless if the household was headed by a male or a female. Black female–headed households were more likely to report property crime when compared to all other households. Male Hispanic households were the only ethnic group that was less likely to report property crimes when compared to all other groups.[22]

The relationship between the victim and the offender can have great ramifications for whether a crime gets solved. Some 40 years ago, for example, the rate at which homicides were "cleared," or solved, exceeded 90%. In those days, murders were generally between individuals who knew one another; hence, the police had a ready list of suspects to question. In recent years, however, homicide clearance rates have fallen to around 63%. Some criminologists attribute this to the rise in "stranger-on-stranger" murders that result from drug deals gone bad or other types of criminal activity. In those cases, the police have few, if any, suspects to pursue.[23]

Offender Characteristics

Arrest data collected within the UCR give us access to information about the characteristics of offenders. In 2008, there were over 14 million arrests for crimes committed in the United States. Looking at overall trends, more arrests were made for drug offenses than for any other crime category (12.2%). The arrest rate for violent crime was 198.2 per 100,000 inhabitants, and the arrest rate for property crime was 565.2 per 100,000 inhabitants in the same year.

These rates indicate a slight decrease in violent crime arrests but a 5.6% increase in property crime arrests. Arrests for juveniles decreased by 2.8% from 2007 to 2008. The majority of arrests for both violent and property crimes were of males, with over 75% of violent crime arrests and over 65% of property crime arrests. In 2008, almost 70% of all persons arrested were white, while over 28% were black and the remaining 2.4% were of other races.

Crimes Encountered

The diversity of crimes encountered by law enforcement personnel is amazing. Offenses ranging from the most minor to the most shocking victimize our communities. Why does crime occur? One might argue that for every offense and offender, something, in some way was unique to those offenders that influenced the decision to commit the crime.

Drugs and Crime

Drug use, selling and manufacturing of illegal drugs, and additional crimes associated with drug abuse continue to be a social problem for our society. In 2007, federal, state, and local law enforcement agencies made more than 1.8 million drug-related arrests in the United States. In September 2008, over half of federal prisoners were incarcerated for drug offenses, resulting in nearly 100,000 inmates in federal prisons convicted and sentenced for drug offenses.

More than 35 million individuals used illegal drugs or abused prescription drugs in 2007. In 2006, more than 1 million individuals entered drug treatment services looking for assistance with their addiction to illicit or prescription drugs. As staggering as these numbers are, what is more disturbing is that more than 1000 children were injured, killed, or removed from homes or areas where methamphetamine laboratories were located from 2007 through September 2008. We can see from these statistics that drug use in the United States affects more than the user and has consequences for families, children, law enforcement, and corrections.

When we look at specific drugs in the United States, we find that cocaine is the leading drug threat to our society. Methamphetamine use and manufacturing is quickly rising in its level of seriousness and is currently the second leading drug threat. This is followed by marijuana, heroin, pharmaceutical drugs, and ecstasy.

Looking more closely at the methamphetamine problem in the United States, methamphetamine manufacturing levels are projected to surpass the levels in 2007. This is a shift from earlier trends depicted in methamphetamine laboratory seizure data that illustrate that methamphetamine production in the United States decreased each year from 2003 through 2007. This current increase may be a result of the changes in the flow of methamphetamine from Mexico. Many users and distributors have been forced to begin producing the drug again because of this decreased flow.[24]

Many states have passed tougher laws concerning the sale and possession of key elements used in the manufacturing of methamphetamine. Some of these ingredients include pseudoephedrine, anhydrous ammonia, and red phosphorus. These may seem like complex chemical compounds found in chemistry laboratories, but these chemicals are found in everyday items such as over-the-counter cold medicines, fertilizer, and matches.[25] To circumvent state and federal laws that restrict the purchase of some of these drugs like pseudoephedrine and ephedrine, individuals as well as criminal groups are making numerous small-quantity product purchases from multiple stores. This purchasing method is known as "smurfing." There are some reports that pseudoephedrine brokers have established "smurfing" networks that pay several individuals to make purchases on their behalf.[26]

Methamphetamine use and manufacturing continue to be a problem requiring specialized training for law enforcement for the foreseeable future. Officers need to know how to recognize clandestine laboratories, how to effectively handle meth users, and how to coordinate services with the community and local agencies to deal with the destruction and cleanup of these laboratories and protect any children or elderly persons found near these areas.

Turning our discussion to marijuana, the level of use and cultivation of this drug continues to be high in the United States, and data from the domestic indoor and outdoor cannabis eradication assessment illustrate that the number of cannabis plants eradicated has increased dramatically from 2004 to 2008. In 2004, 2,996,225 plants outdoors and 203,896 plants indoors were destroyed. This increased to the destruction of 7,562,322 plants outdoors and 450,986 plants indoors in 2008. As we can see from these numbers, the majority of plants are eradicated from outdoor sites, and this number increased by over 150% from 2004 to 2008.[27]

Prescription drug abuse is also a pervasive problem in our society. Levels are very high and individuals are able to obtain these drugs from several sources. Many individuals use traditional diversion methods such as doctor-shopping and prescription fraud. The Internet has been a growing source for purchasing large quantities of certain prescription drugs such as Vicodin, Xanax, and Valium. Law enforcement has also reported that prescription drug distribution by gangs has increased since 2004.[28]

As noted earlier, the majority of arrests in the United States are for drug offenses. Over 82% of these arrests are for the possession of an illegal substance, leaving over 17% of drug arrests for the sale or manufacturing of an illegal substance. The majority of arrests for the possession of drugs were for marijuana, while heroin and cocaine were the top drugs for sale and/or manufacturing. Arrests for the production and sale of synthetic or manufactured drugs, such as methamphetamine, were almost double in Southern states as compared to other regions of the United States. This finding appears to support other findings that methamphetamine is a problem facing many rural communities.[29]

Hate Crimes

Hate crimes include any victimization of a person on the basis of his or her race, religion, sexual orientation, ethnicity or national origin, or disability. The UCR collects information on hate crimes in the United States. In 2008, there were 7783 criminal incidents involving 9168 offenses that were reported as a result of bias or prejudice. Of the over 7000 incidents, information shows that 51.3% were motivated by a racial bias, 19.5% were motivated by a religious bias, 16.7% were motivated by a sexual orientation bias, and 11.5% were motivated by an ethnicity or national origin bias. One percent involved a bias against disability.

The majority of violent hate crimes consisted of intimidation, whereas approximately one-third were simple assaults. The remaining crimes were aggravated assaults and only one homicide was classified as a hate-biased murder. Unlike crime trends for general crimes, where there are more property crimes compared to violent crimes, we find the opposite when we talk about hate crimes. Among hate crimes, 5542 were violent crimes and 3608 were property crimes. The majority of the property crimes (82.3%) were acts of destruction, damage, or vandalism. The remaining 17.7% consisted of robbery, burglary, larceny-theft, motor vehicle theft, arson, and other offenses. When looking at the characteristics of perpetrators of hate crimes, we find that there were 6927 known offenders. Of these offenders, 61.1% were white and 20.2% were black. The race was unknown for 11.0%, and other races accounted for the remaining known offenders.

Victims of race hate crimes were most often the victim of an offender's anti-black bias. Other victims of race crimes varied, with over 15% being the victims of an anti-white prejudice followed by less than 4% who were targeted because of an anti-Asian/Pacific Islander bias. Finally, 1.3% of victims were targeted because of an anti-American Indian/Alaskan Native prejudice, and the remaining 5.6% were victims because of a bias against a group of individuals in which more than one race was represented.

Anti-religious offenses also made up a significant number of hate crimes in 2008. There were 1732 victims of anti-religious hate crimes. Of these crimes, two-thirds were targeted because of an offender's anti-Jewish bias. Other religions that were the root of anti-religious hate crimes were anti-Islamic, anti-Catholic, anti-Protestant, and anti-Atheist/Agnostic bias.

An additional source for hate crimes were based on sexual orientation. Offenders targeted 1706 victims because of a bias based on sexual orientation. Of those, 57.5% were victims of an offender's anti-male homosexual bias, 27.3% were victims because of an anti-homosexual bias, 11.6% were victims because of an anti-female homosexual bias, 2.0% were victims because of an anti-heterosexual bias, and 1.6% were victims because of an anti-bisexual bias.[30]

Gangs and Crime

Gang activity is a constant concern for law enforcement in all communities. There were approximately one million gang members belonging to more than 20,000 gangs that were criminally active in the United States as of September 2008. According to data from the National Drug Threat Survey, almost 60% of state and local law enforcement agencies reported criminal gang activity in their jurisdictions in 2008. This is an increase from the 45% that was reported by state and local agencies in 2004. A trend that many local agencies must be aware of is the migrating movement of some gangs from urban to suburban and rural communities. This is expanding the gangs' influence in most regions and catching many agencies by surprise in those regions where training in dealing with gang activity is somewhat limited. There are a variety of reasons why this is taking place, including expanding drug territories, recruitment of new members, diversion from law enforcement, and moving to escape from other gangs.

The result of the increase of gang activity in these suburban and rural communities is increases in gang-related crime and violence because of expanding gang influence. This is typical of criminal gangs as it has been estimated that they commit as much as 80% of the crime in many communities. Typical gang-related offenses include alien smuggling, armed robbery, assault, auto theft, drug trafficking, extortion, fraud, home invasions, identity theft, murder, and weapons trafficking. Many gangs actively use the Internet to recruit new members and to communicate with members in other areas of the United States and in foreign countries.[31]

Cyber Crime

The modern age presents a new genre of crime: cyber crime. The prevalence of information technologies and digital technology provides a virtual medium through which crime may be facilitated. This type of crime parallels crimes that occur in physical reality. For example, many states illegalize gambling. Gambling may occur physically or may be conducted via online gambling websites. Other cyber crimes involve the use of digital devices. The introduction of computing environments was soon followed by malicious software.

Such software includes a myriad of viruses, worms, and so on, that often steal credit card numbers, bank account information, and other data from unsuspecting individuals. This stolen information may then be used to commit the crime of credit fraud.

Illegally accessing secure computing environments is another form of virtual crime. According to Bantavani,[32] in Charlotte, North Carolina, "A former Bank of America (BOA) computer programmer was sentenced to 27 months in federal prison... to be followed by 2 years of supervised release for unauthorized access to the financial institution's protected computers." The punitive actions also included mandatory restitution in the "amount of $419,310.90."[32] Although many vendors, government agencies, and commercial entities implement firewalls and proprietary software to dissuade such invasions, no system or software product is impervious to infiltration.

Another characteristic of virtual crime is its anonymity. Criminal factions may reside anywhere and may attempt to enact crimes against entities that need not be located within the same geographic proximity. For example, through spoofing Internet addresses, a criminal could reside in China and could access computer systems that are physically located within the United States. Such scenarios occur frequently because of the presence of networked computing devices. All a criminal requires is a working network connection to facilitate acts of crime.

Some aspects of cyber crime involve corporate espionage. Given the advent and proliferation of globalism, such crimes are not uncommon. Recently, a significant crime occurred against the Ford Motor Company. According to Balaya,[33] a former employee of Ford Motor Company, "Xiang Dong Yu, a.k.a. Mike Yu, 49, of Beijing, China, was sentenced today to 70 months in federal prison and ordered to pay a fine of $12,500 as a result of having pleaded guilty in federal court to two counts of theft of trade secrets." Balaya[33] summarizes this account as follows:

> According to the plea agreement in this case, Yu was a Product Engineer for the Ford Motor Company from 1997 to 2007 and had access to Ford trade secrets, including Ford design documents. In December 2006, Yu accepted a job at the China branch of a U.S. company. On the eve of his departure from Ford and before he told Ford of his new job, Yu copied some 4000 Ford documents onto an external hard drive, including sensitive Ford design documents. Included in those documents were system design specifications for the Engine/Transmission Mounting Subsystem, Electrical Distribution System, Electric Power Supply, Electrical Subsystem, and Generic Body Module, among others. Ford spent millions of dollars and decades on research, development, and testing to develop and continuously improve the design specifications set forth in these documents. The majority of the design documents copied by the defendant did not relate to his work at Ford. On December 20, 2006, the defendant traveled to the location of his new employer in Shenzhen, China, taking the Ford trade secrets with him. On January 2, 2007, Yu emailed his Ford supervisor from China and informed him that he was leaving Ford's employ.

Virtual crime also provides a means for both terrorist organizations and organized crime entities to gain funding. This type of crime is not uncommon globally. According to the U.S. Department of Justice,[34] a crime ring, involving fraud, was discovered and broken up during 2011. This organization perpetrated crimes of copyright infringement, counterfeiting, and conspiracy.[34] The DOJ highlighted the sentencing of these individuals as follows:[34]

Mamadou Sadio Barry, 40, was sentenced to 60 months in prison; Moussa Baradji, 29, was sentenced to 50 months in prison; Sedikey Sankano, 42, was sentenced to 24 months in prison; and Won Ahn, 69, was placed on probation for 1 year. Barry, Baradji, and Sankano also were ordered to serve 3 years of supervised release following their prison terms. Barry and Baradji were ordered to pay $70,894 in restitution and Sankano was ordered to pay $3867 in restitution. The court found that these defendants were responsible for distributing illegal copies of products that, if legitimate, would have been valued at more than $2 million.

Virtual crime threatens every facet of American society. Annually, untold millions are either directly or indirectly the victims of such crimes. Because of the anonymous nature of this type of crime, determining its origins is a daunting task, and there are times when such crimes are perpetrated with complete anonymity, ensuring that perpetrators are never found. Regardless, both organizations and individuals should be mindful of the threats that exist among virtual environments.

Investigations and Suspects

The investigation of criminal activity involves varying forms of crime and suspects. A suspect is defined as someone who is "regarded or deserving to be regarded with suspicion."[35] The acts of managing investigations and suspects involve both significant time and collaboration. According to the Bureau of Justice Statistics,[36] Tables 1.4 and 1.5 show various attributes of managing the suspects of federal investigations that occurred during the period between 2004 and 2009.

These tables show a variety of crime types that affect American society and the quantities of suspects that were managed by federal agencies during the examined period. Although these tables present only federal characteristics, similar attributes are manifested among the many regional, state, local, and tribal law enforcement entities that serve American society. Regardless of whether a location is rural or urban, crime exists. All cities, communities, and rural areas are comprised of humans. Human nature is imperfect, and humans are capable of committing acts of crime for a variety of reasons—anger, profit, jealousy, personality disorder, covetousness, peer pressure, greed, and many others.

Table 1.4   Offense Types and Suspects

Offense Type	FY 2004–2009 Suspects in Investigations Initiated					
	2004	2005	2006	2007	2008	2009
Violent offenses	5715	5373	5011	5366	5356	5270
Property offenses	24,956	24,862	25,008	25,421	25,063	26,701
Drug offenses	37,501	37,215	35,210	35,810	34,529	35,465
Public-order offenses	21,278	20,616	20,158	21,779	21,977	22,625
Weapon offenses	14,398	13,304	12,321	11,713	11,631	11,096
Immigration offenses	35,858	35,109	34,894	37,691	78,986	85,950
Missing/unknown	1509	1111	1333	630	1028	1234
Total	141,215	137,590	133,935	138,410	178,570	188,341

Source: Bureau of Justice Statistics.[36]

Table 1.5 FY 2004–2009 Suspects in Investigations Initiated[36]

Offense	2004	2005	2006	2007	2008	2009
Murder	701	661	502	700	912	923
Negligent manslaughter	0	0	0	0	0	0
Assault	1470	1533	1311	1299	1125	1065
Robbery	2421	2025	2067	1986	1934	1888
Sexual abuse	665	586	583	929	960	869
Kidnapping	244	291	267	230	217	250
Threats against the President	214	277	281	222	208	275
Fraud	17,342	17,355	17,400	18,078	18,146	19,520
Forgery	969	1376	1172	928	768	973
Counterfeiting	491	452	460	448	409	379
Burglary	45	36	27	36	38	38
Larceny-felony	1314	1068	1130	1037	881	815
Motor vehicle theft	360	406	375	459	450	393
Arson and explosives	694	645	565	625	538	531
Transportation of stolen property	51	61	50	63	53	53
Embezzlement	3380	3169	3556	3429	3488	3601
Other property offenses	310	294	273	318	292	398
Drug possession	691	752	850	786	796	880
Drug trafficking	36,605	36,284	34,185	34,847	33,635	34,479
Other drug offenses	205	179	175	177	98	106
Agriculture	9	8	2	62	24	58
Antitrust	32	32	49	30	11	33
Food and drug	115	240	163	177	135	137
Transportation	316	273	236	251	268	221
Civil rights	1374	1147	837	1061	870	763
Communications	62	25	23	45	32	22
Customs laws	190	126	109	167	208	243
Postal laws	169	164	141	163	172	127
Other regulatory offenses	2693	3083	2928	3214	3426	4014
Weapon offenses	14,398	13,304	12,321	11,713	11,631	11,096
Immigration felonies	35,858	35,109	34,894	37,691	78,986	85,950
Tax law violations	947	973	981	938	1015	1072
Bribery	282	290	308	300	283	258
Perjury, contempt, and intimidation	587	510	512	446	446	382
National defense	721	647	716	733	899	799
Escape	2293	2102	1837	1630	1729	1724
Racketeering and extortion	3419	3416	2922	3288	3261	3509
Gambling	81	114	122	119	85	89
Liquor offenses	27	9	22	22	44	11
Nonviolent sex offenses	3011	2778	2957	3795	3936	3840
Obscene material	43	30	43	55	56	49
Traffic offense	212	175	182	200	150	142
Wildlife offense	515	479	452	525	489	446
Environmental offenses	8	15	9	6	14	7
Conspiracy/aiding and abetting	2779	2715	3419	3671	3512	3819

Table 1.5   (*Continued*) FY 2004–2009 Suspects in Investigations Initiated[36]

Offense	2004	2005	2006	2007	2008	2009
All other offenses	1393	1265	1188	881	912	860
Missing/unknown	1509	1111	1333	630	1028	1234
Total records	141,215	137,590	133,935	138,410	178,570	188,341

Source: Bureau of Justice Statistics.[36]

Table 1.6   Chronological Listing

Month the Matter Was Received	FY 2004–2009 Suspects in Investigations Initiated					
	2004	2005	2006	2007	2008	2009
October	12,066	10,783	10,936	11,654	13,695	16,268
November	9851	10,772	10,455	10,783	12,195	12,696
December	10,482	9382	9529	9137	9978	13,281
January	11,933	12,007	12,113	11,631	14,976	15,376
February	12,574	12,164	11,536	11,826	15,271	16,611
March	14,518	13,896	12,878	13,388	17,127	18,946
April	12,568	11,874	10,640	12,017	18,545	17,150
May	11,429	11,645	11,642	12,692	16,322	14,984
June	11,914	11,741	12,009	11,591	15,819	16,483
July	11,373	10,231	10,152	10,818	15,511	15,693
August	11,776	12,386	11,671	12,156	14,549	15,211
September	10,731	10,709	10,374	10,717	14,582	15,642
Missing/unknown	0	0	0	0	0	0
Total	141,215	137,590	133,935	138,410	178,570	188,341

Source: Bureau of Justice Statistics.[36]

Crime does not cease. It is continuous and permeates all periods of the year. Table 1.6 shows the monthly characteristics of crime and quantities of suspects that were managed federally during the examined period.[36]

Federally, a variety of entities are involved with the managing of suspects. Collaboration often occurs among a variety of government entities. According to the Bureau of Justice Statistics, during the examined period between 2004 and 2009, the agencies mentioned in Table 1.7 managed suspects among a myriad of federal investigations.[36]

Although the data contained within Table 1.7 are primarily indicative of federal agencies and investigations, it must be noted that collaboration often occurs between federal entities and commercial entities to pursue investigations and manage suspects. For example, during the recent cyber-attack against Lockheed Martin an opportunity for collaboration between the federal government and Lockheed Martin occurred.[37] This attack involved the breaching of corporate computer systems and defense-related environments.[37] The perpetrators "breached security systems designed to keep out intruders by creating duplicates to 'SecurID' electronic keys from EMC Corp's RSA security division," thereby potentially facilitating the theft of materials related to "sensitive data on arms that are under development as well as technology used by U.S. forces in Iraq and Afghanistan."[37] This incident shows the seriousness of virtual crime and the collaboration that may occur between federal agencies and corporate entities.

Table 1.7   Agencies Managing Suspects: 2004–2009

Investigating Department, Authority	FY 2004–2009 Suspects in Investigations Initiated					
	2004	2005	2006	2007	2008	2009
Dept. of Agriculture	651	639	573	594	901	841
Dept. of Commerce	90	83	65	99	105	74
Dept. of Defense	3882	4015	4948	5142	4285	4903
Dept. of Education	127	113	144	113	85	88
Dept. of Energy	21	19	14	17	21	36
Dept. of Health and Human Services	691	778	640	766	722	738
Dept. of Homeland Security	64,746	63,359	62,590	66,281	107,395	114,654
Dept. of Housing and Urban Development	19	48	40	51	15	11
Dept. of Interior	2316	2135	2213	2236	2265	2,2977
Dept. of Justice	44,824	44,312	41,778	41,411	40,478	42,449
Dept. of Labor	353	377	466	352	404	373
Dept. of State	1205	1053	959	789	558	643
Dept. of Treasury	2351	2369	2208	2443	2426	2670
Dept. of Transportation	181	215	105	105	78	97
Federal/state task force	4438	3993	3730	4042	3679	4047
Independent federal agencies	459	342	335	390	367	390
State/local authorities	613	376	473	440	545	496
Other	13,935	12,985	12,476	12,832	13,605	12,586
Missing/unknown	313	379	268	307	276	268
Total	141,215	137,590	133,935	138,410	178,570	188,341

Source: Bureau of Justice Statistics.[36]

Notable Incidents

Crime can occur anywhere, anytime, and be perpetrated by anyone. Further, anyone may be the victim of crime. Many prominent individuals have been accused, tried, and convicted of crimes. These incidents range from the activities of well-known athletes to those of members of the U.S. Congress.

James "Jim" Traficant was a U.S. Congressman from Ohio. He served as a member of the U.S. Congress between 1985 and 2002. According to CNN, Traficant was found guilty "on all counts against him, covering charges of taking bribes, filing false tax returns, racketeering, and forcing his aides to perform chores at his farm in Ohio and on his houseboat in Washington."[38] Traficant served a prison term following his conviction and was released in 2009 (Figure 1.4).[39]

During 1986, Federal District Judge Walter L. Nixon, Jr. of Mississippi was sentenced to a prison term of 5 years. This incarceration resulted from the crime of perjury. Specifically, Nixon was found guilty of "lying to a special Federal grand jury in July 1983 when he denied discussing a drug-smuggling case involving a businessman's son with a prosecutor and with the businessman."[40] This case shows that even members of the justice community are not immune to criminal activity and prosecution.

Figure 1.4 Jim Traficant. (From "Dirty Politics: Political Scandals Involving Sex, Money, Drugs & Lies," *New York Daily News*, 2012. Retrieved from http://www.nydailynews.com/news/politics/scandalous-side-politics-sex-money-drugs-lies-gallery-1.14714?pmSlide=28.)

William J. Jefferson, a former Congressman from Louisiana, was sentenced to an imprisonment of 13 years. This incarceration resulted from criminal charges of corruption. According to Boyce,[41] these charges included "crimes of bribery, money laundering and racketeering." Boyce[41] further indicates that "The former nine-term Congressman who served from 1991 to 2009 had planned, according to prosecutors, to use the money in order to bribe the vice president of Nigeria who was at the time, in Washington D.C. Jefferson had hoped the money would help pave the way for a telecommunications deal that would have been lucrative for the congressman's family, prosecutors said."

Billy Cannon, a famous football player from Louisiana State University who won the 1959 Heisman Trophy, was incarcerated for the crime of counterfeiting. Cannon and his associates "manufactured more than $6 million in $100 bills" and circulated "several hundred thousand dollars."[42] Further, "Cannon buried the rest of the fake money in Igloo coolers."[42] This crime represented the "seventh largest counterfeiting scheme in U.S. history."[42] Cannon was denoted as the leader of the organization. Cannon confessed to this crime and served a period of imprisonment.

Another Heisman Trophy winner, who later became a famous criminal, was O.J. Simpson. Simpson is currently serving a "9 to 33 year" prison sentence that resulted from a conviction of "leading an armed raid on a sports memorabilia dealer to recover prop-erty he said was his."[43] The charges involved "seven felony offences: conspiracy to com-mit kidnapping; conspiracy to commit robbery; first-degree kidnapping with use of a deadly weapon; burglary with a deadly weapon; robbery with a deadly weapon; assault with a deadly weapon; and coercion with a deadly weapon."[43] Misdemeanor offenses included conspiracy to commit a crime.[43] Previously, during 1997, a "wrongful death judgment" was levied against Simpson regarding the case of Ron Goldman and Nicole Brown Simpson.[43]

Although these events involve famous individuals, an array of innumerable criminal events occurs daily both openly and clandestinely. One needs to look no further than the pages of their local newspaper or to view their local television station for the accounts of such incidents. Small towns and communities are rife with crime. Examples of such crimes often involve events of drug trafficking.

According to the *Northeast Mississippi Daily Journal*,[44] Jeremy Young, a man in Holly Springs, Mississippi, received a sentence of incarceration for 10 years in prison in associa-tion with "federal drug and gun charges." Further, Young "was indicted in March 2010 on four counts that he distributed crack cocaine and possessed a firearm in furtherance of drug trafficking," and also "faced up to life in prison and up to a $1 million fine on the original charges."[44] The town of Holly Springs has a population of approximately 7871 indi-viduals and is located in rural Mississippi.[45]

Another small-town incident involved the recent shooting of a father by his daugh-ter. During 2011, according to KOMO News,[46] a teenage girl, aged 15 years, shot her father "in the torso with a hunting bow" because he had confiscated her cellular tele-phone as a "disciplinary measure." After being wounded, the girl refused to allow him to use the cellular telephone to call for assistance.[46] As a result, the wounded man was forced to crawl "to a neighbor's home to phone 911."[46] The father was airlifted to a medi-cal center where he was classified as a serious case. The daughter fled their residence with the "bow and at least 35 arrows, but was later found by a SWAT team in the woods behind her house."[46] She was apprehended without incident. [46] This incident occurred in Tahuya, Washington. The town of Tahuya has a population of approximately 6069 individuals.[47]

Such acts of crime are representative of crimes that are perpetrated among the small communities of the United States. However, larger, populous areas also manifest acts of crime. Kori Lanard, a former NFL Falcons cheerleader, is currently incarcerated for her involvement with a chop-shop operation in Georgia.[48] She and her sister were apprehended when "fleeing into some woods after they were found with stolen vehicles."[49] At the time of the authoring of this textbook, this case was being processed in the criminal justice system. Only time will tell the outcome of this incident.

These examples are also indicative of another concept: one individual is not better than another. Within the criminal justice system, allegations and charges may be brought against anyone. Regardless of whether someone is famous or is the member of a small community, charges may be levied, arrests may occur, court hearings and trials are imple-mented, and appropriate outcomes are manifested in due time: The cases of Traficant and Cannon show that even those at the forefront of American society can be prosecuted and serve a period of incarceration. The incidents of Holly Springs and Tahuya also involve the same concepts of justice. Regardless of the individual, all may be held accountable with respect to the tenets of law.

Juveniles

The connotations of crime often invoke mental images of adults who either perpetrate or are the victims of criminal events. However, much crime also involves juveniles. According to the Office of Juvenile Justice and Delinquency Prevention (OJJDP), of the Office of Justice Programs, recent years have witnessed a "historic low" regarding juvenile issues.[50] The "juvenile Violent Crime Index arrest rate reached a historic low in 2004, down 49% from its 1994 peak."[50] However, this decline of juvenile activity was succeeded by a "12% increase over the next 2 years and then a 3% decline between 2006 and 2008."[50] The 2008 year manifested a total of "288 arrests for Violent Crime Index offenses for every 100,000 youth between 10 and 17 years of age."[50] The OJJDP summarizes its findings via observing that "If each of these arrests involved a different juvenile (which is unlikely), then no more than 1 in every 345 persons aged 10–17 was arrested for a Violent Crime Index offense in 2008, or less than one-third of 1% of all juveniles aged 10–17 living in the U.S."[50] The OJJDP arrest rates, regarding violent crime, are shown in Figure 1.5.

Property crimes are also committed by juveniles. During 2008, "for every 100,000 youth in the U.S. aged 10–17, there were 1323 arrests of juveniles for Property Crime Index offenses."[51] Such an observation contrasts greatly with the observations regarding juvenile trends in violent crime. According to the OJJDP, the "relatively stable juvenile arrest rate trend between 1980 and the mid-1990s for Property Crime Index offenses stands in stark contrast to the Violent Crime Index arrest rate trend."[51] Despite this contrast, the "2008 juvenile Property Crime Index arrest rate was 49% less than the 1991 peak."[51] The OJJDP arrest rates, regarding property crime, are shown in Figure 1.6. Juveniles also commit a variety of other offenses. Examples include drunk driving, drug crime, disorderly conduct, curfew violations, running away, weapons infractions, vandalism, simple assault, and a variety of other crimes.[52] According to the OJJDP, "the juvenile arrest rate for simple assault increased by 156% between 1980 and 1997, declined slightly through 2002, then rose again through 2006. The rate dropped by 7% in the last 2 years to a level 10% less than the 1997 peak."[52] The OJJDP also notes an interesting observation regarding the trends in simple

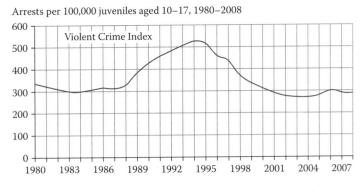

Arrests per 100,000 juveniles aged 10–17, 1980–2008

Note: Rates are arrests of persons aged 10–17 per 100,000 persons aged 10–17 in the resident population. The Violent Crime Index includes the offenses of murder and nonnegligent manslaughter, forcible rape, robbery, and aggravated assault.

Figure 1.5 Juvenile arrest rates for Violent Crime Index offenses, 1980–2008. (Courtesy of the U.S. Department of Justice Office of Juvenile Justice and Delinquency Prevention [OJJDP]. *Juvenile arrest rate trends, violent crime.* Retrieved from http://www.ojjdp.gov/ojstatbb/crime/JAR_Display.asp?ID=qa05201.)

Arrests per 100,000 juveniles aged 10–17, 1980–2008

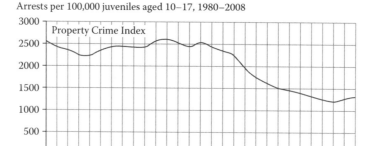

Note: Rates are arrests of persons aged 10–17 per 100,000 persons aged 10–17 in the resident population. The Property Crime Index includes the offenses of burglary, larceny-theft, motor vehicle theft, and arson.

Figure 1.6 Juvenile arrest rates for Property Crime Index offenses, 1980–2008. After years of decline, the juvenile arrest rate for Property Crime Index offenses increased 9% between 2006 and 2008. (Courtesy of the U.S. Department of Justice Office of Juvenile Justice and Delinquency Prevention [OJJDP]. *Juvenile arrest rate trends, property crime.* Retrieved from http://www.ojjdp.gov/ojstatbb/crime/JAR_Display.asp?ID=qa05206.)

Arrests per 100,000 juveniles aged 10–17, 1980–2008

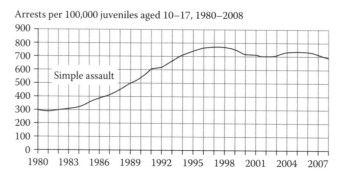

Note: Rates are arrests of persons aged 10–17 per 100,000 persons aged 10–17 in the resident population.

Figure 1.7 Juvenile arrest rates for simple assault, 1980–2008. (Courtesy of the U.S. Department of Justice Office of Juvenile Justice and Delinquency Prevention [OJJDP]. *Juvenile arrest rate trends, property crime, simple assault.* Retrieved from http://www.ojjdp.gov/ojstatbb/crime/JAR_Display.asp?ID=qa05211.)

assault versus aggravated assault. According to the OJJDP, "unlike the trend for simple assault, the juvenile aggravated assault arrest rate declined steadily since the mid-1990s, falling by 43% between 1994 and 2008."[52] Further, the OJJDP indicates that "the 2008 juvenile arrest rate for simple assault was substantially greater than the 1980 rate for most racial groups."[52] The OJJDP arrest rates regarding simple assault are shown in Figure 1.7.

Juvenile offenses must be seriously considered. Youths endanger their future by committing criminal offenses during their formative years. No solitary cause may be identified as the sole catalyst for the committing of crimes by juveniles. Parenting, home conditions, peer pressure, gang involvement, esteem issues, mental disorders, economic issues, and a host of other factors influence the committing of juvenile crimes. Roberts (2011) provides some interesting observations regarding the criminal justice system and the attributes of juvenile offenders:

The juvenile justice system is a complex web of people and agencies that processes about a quarter of a million youths annually at a cost exceeding $1 billion. To understand the system requires baseline knowledge of the statistical trends during the past decade that have shaped the system's ability to function and the roles played by the various components of the system. Academic experts have long recognized that crime is a young man's game. The typical criminal is a male who begins his career at 14 or 15, continues through his mid-20s, and then tapers off into retirement. Three statistics demonstrate the disproportionate impact of those under the age of 18 on criminal activity; while comprising roughly one-sixth of the nation's population, they make up a full one-quarter of all people arrested and account for nearly one-third of the arrests for the seven crimes in the uniform crime index (homicide, forcible rape, robbery, aggravated assault, burglary, vehicle theft, and larceny).[53]

The financial costs associated with juvenile crime are staggering. Such costs are indicative of the economic allocation of resources that are necessary to diminish juvenile crime and to process offenders. There is no ultimate solution that will completely and utterly cease the committing of crimes by juveniles. However, instances of juvenile crime may be diminished through the use of appropriate punitive measures, counseling programs, and interventions.

Recidivism

Recidivism is defined as a "tendency to relapse into a previous condition or mode of behavior."[54] Two prominent studies investigated issues of recidivism within the United States. One study occurred in 1989, whereas the other was conducted during 2002.[55] One of these studies examined "108,580 state prisoners released from prison in 11 states in 1983," whereas the other examined "272,111 prisoners released from prison in 15 states in 1994."[55] For each respective year, these quantities of released prisoners represented "two-thirds of all the prisoners released in the United States for that year."[55] The outcomes of these studies showed that within 3 years of release, over two-thirds of these individuals were arrested again.[55]

These recidivism studies involved some interesting observations. According to the Bureau of Justice Statistics,[55] "67.5% of prisoners released in 1994 were rearrested within 3 years, an increase over the 62.5% found for those released in 1983." Further, 51.8% of those released were again in prison within 3 years of their initial release.[55] Recidivism increases among various types of crimes were also noticed. These increases involved the following observations:[55]

- Property offender rates increased from 68.1% to 73.8%.
- Drug offender rates increased from 50.4% to 66.7%.
- Public-order offender rates increased from 54.6% to 62.2%.
- Violent offender rates increased from 59.6% to 61.7%.

The reconviction rates associated with such recidivism were relatively unchanged between 1983 and 1994. For the years 1983 and 1994, these rates involved the following observations:[55]

- Property offender rates were, respectively, 53.0% and 53.4%.
- Drug offender rates were, respectively, 35.3% and 47.0%.
- Public-order offender rates were, respectively, 41.5% and 42.0%.
- Violent offender rates were, respectively, 41.9% and 39.9%.

Recidivism represents a serious problem for society. Many individuals may lack the social, vocational, and professional skills that are necessary for their reintegration into a free society; some may have become accustomed to the lifestyle that was experienced during the period of incarceration; and some may not have supportive environments during their release and succumb to the temptations that led to their initial incarceration. Certainly, many other causes may be identified. Such issues must be dealt with in an attempt to reduce rates of recidivism.

The problem of recidivism is neither unnoticed nor ignored by the federal government. During 2011, the U.S. Attorney General, Eric Holder, announced the implementation of a reentry council for the purpose of identifying and advancing "effective public safety and prisoner reentry strategies."[56] This initiative involves both short-term and long-term collaborations among federal agencies. The primary goals of the organization involve improving the safety of communities via the reduction of "recidivism and victimization"; assisting released prisoners in becoming "productive, tax-paying citizens"; and saving tax dollars through "lowering the direct and collateral costs of incarceration."[56]

The Second Chance Act is another resource designed to diminish recidivism. This legislation became law on April 9, 2008. It "authorizes federal grants to government agencies and nonprofit organizations to provide employment assistance, substance abuse treatment, housing, family programming, mentoring, victims support, and other services that can help reduce recidivism."[57] Through the Act, communities may receive grant funding to sponsor a variety of activities that facilitate the transition of convicts within society. Examples include drug counseling programs, substance abuse treatment programs, or skills training programs (Figure 1.8).

Figure 1.8 President George W. Bush signs into law the Second Chance Act. (From Soyfer, M., 2011, *Penn Political Review*. Retrieved from http://pennpoliticalreview.org/2011/11/and-the-thrilling-conclusion/.)

Although recidivism affects individual communities, it also affects the whole of society. The costs of incarcerating convicts again are expensive and are indicative of the resources that are necessary to process such individuals within the justice system and to provide their sustenance after they are again incarcerated. The costs of their repeated criminal acts are also significant considerations because victims may necessitate medical care and treatment, and they may experience the loss of money or other items of value. Recidivism is demonstrative of repeated acts of crime. Analogous with the committing of an initial crime, there is no perfect solution to eliminate recidivism. However, communities may facilitate a variety of programs to assist offenders upon their release and facilitate their societal integration.

Summary

Many media reports would like us to believe that crime in the United States is rapidly rising and is out of control. As we have seen, we are currently experiencing a continued downward trend in violent and property crime rates in the United States for the last 20 years. It is important to recognize crime trends in the United States and local communities in order to better understand ways to help the community in preventing crime and protect its citizens. It is equally important for professionals in law enforcement to remember that society and criminals change and that police and other agencies should continue to train to effectively meet the needs of the communities they serve.

Crime is everywhere; it is unceasing. Every American community is affected by crime. Anyone can be the victim of a crime, and anyone can commit a crime. Although much effort is garnered toward the diminishing of crime and the preserving of order, crime persists within society. Because of the imperfections of humans and the temptations of human nature—greed, malice, envy, jealousy, and an array of other temptations—crime shall never cease. Therefore, society must determine and implement the highest and best strategies possible for countering and dissuading acts of crime.

Both small communities and urban areas are subject to crime. Acts may be perpetrated by individuals or small groups, or they may be conducted as components of significant organized crime entities. Both famous individuals and the members of localities may perpetrate crime or be the victims of crime. Regardless of the instance, all citizens are accountable for their actions and deeds and may be prosecuted accordingly within the criminal justice system.

Figure 1.9 shows declining violent crime rates nationally throughout the last few years.

Although violent crime rates have fallen, there is no guarantee that other forms of crime have diminished commensurately or that quantities of all forms of crime will increase in the future. Both communities and their law enforcement organizations must remain vigilant to contribute toward the goals of maintaining societal order and deterring crime.

Juveniles have the capacity to commit acts of crime. Age is not a restriction when committing crimes. Youthful offenders, under the age of 18, commit a variety of criminal offenses, ranging from vandalism to robbery. These criminal acts are analogous to those crimes committed by adult offenders. No one solitary cause may be identified as the only catalyst for the committing of juvenile crimes.

Recidivism affects not only individual communities, but the whole of American society. Within 3 years, most offenders are arrested again for acts of crime. The costs of recidivism are also significant—society must pay to again provide sustenance for such individuals, and victims also experience losses. The Second Chance Act is a legislative tool that facilitates resources that may be assistive when integrating released convicts into free society.

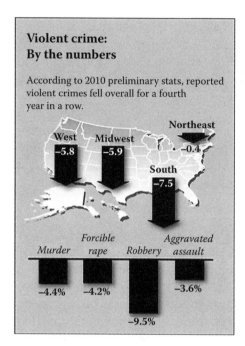

Figure 1.9 Diminishing of violent crime. (Courtesy of the FBI. Retrieved from http://www.fbi
.gov/news/stories/2011/may/crimes_052311/image/crime-in-the-u.s.)

Crime changes to accommodate the wonders of modern technologies. Given the proliferation and devising of electronic technologies, crime now exists intangibly. This form of crime is known as cyber crime or virtual crime. Generally, these forms of crime have counterpart activities within physical reality. Regardless, the effects of virtual crime are devastating, and virtual crimes may be untraceable. Figure 1.10 is a reminder of the existence of virtual crime.

Terminology

Adult offender
Arson
Assault
Bureau of Justice Statistics
Civil law
Collaboration
Conviction
Crime
Crime mapping
Criminal law
Cyber crime
Department of Justice
Federal agency
Forecasting
Fraud
Gang
Hate crime

Figure 1.10 A modern McGruff. (Courtesy of the State of Vermont Office of the Chief Information Officer. Retrieved from http://itsecurity.vermont.gov/sites/security/files/mcgruff_cybercrime.jpg.)

Homicide
Incarceration
Investigation
Juvenile offender
Larceny
Measurement of crime
Organized crime
Prostitution
Recidivism
Reentry council
Robbery
Sex crimes
Statistic
Suspect
Trafficking
Trend
Uniform Crime Reports
Victim
Violence
Virtual crime

Discussion Questions

1. This chapter examines numerous facets of crime and law enforcement. Given the contents of the discussions and the genres of crime, please substantively respond to the following queries: What is law enforcement, and what is its historical purpose and function? Further, within the response, please consider the current environments and public markets that host law enforcement entities. Do you believe that modern law enforcement entities adhere to the historical foundations of law enforcement, or has time changed the overall perceptions and functions of law enforcement regarding the satisfaction of the primary tenets of its historical purposes and functions?

2. This chapter examines a variety of historical and contemporary issues that affect law enforcement entities. These issues range from drug crimes to Congressional crimes. Perform some independent research, select a criminal event of your choice, and provide a critical analysis of the control, leadership, organization, planning, and coordination facets of the law enforcement response(s) to your selected event. Within your analysis, please also consider an analysis of alternatives—do you believe that a different approach of law enforcement should have been pursued regarding your selected criminal event?

3. Recidivism affects the whole of American society both qualitatively and quantitatively. Based on the discussions of this chapter, explore local or state programs in your area that exist to diminish recidivism. Provide a discussion that highlights the salient aspects of these programs. What improvements can you offer to diminish the rates of recidivism? Further, within the discussion, please consider whether these programs are effective and efficient.

4. Some argue that juvenile crime rates are not increasing and are remaining relatively static through time. Further, these arguments include the notion that the basic needs and wants of modern youths are identical to those of previous generations. However, society may perceive that juvenile crime is increasing because of the social habits, lack of respect for elders and authority figures (e.g., not saying "sir" or "ma'am" and making direct eye contact), and modes of dress that are manifest within modern youth culture. State whether you either agree or disagree with this concept, whether you believe juvenile crime is increasing, and provide a substantive discussion that justifies your opinions.

References

1. Wilson, O. W. (1963). *Police Administration*. New York, NY: McGraw-Hill.
2. Federal Bureau of Investigation. *Uniform Crime Reports: Crime in the United States, 2008*. Retrieved May 7, 2010, from http://www.fbi.gov/ucr/cius2008/data/table_29.html
3. Federal Bureau of Investigation. *a Word about the UCR Data*. Retrieved May 7, 2010, from http://www.fbi.gov/ucr/word.htm
4. Federal Bureau of Investigation. *UCR Summary Reporting, Frequently Asked Questions*. Retrieved May 7, 2010, from http://www.fbi.gov/ucr/ucrquest.htm
5. Federal Bureau of Investigation. *Uniform Crime Reports: Crime in the United States, 2004*. Retrieved May 9, 2010, from http://www.fbi.gov/ucr/cius_04/appendices/appendix_02.html
6. Federal Bureau of Investigation. *Uniform Crime Reports: Crime in the United States, 2004*. Retrieved May 9, 2010, from http://www.fbi.gov/ucr/cius_04/appendices/appendix_04.html

7. Federal Bureau of Investigation. *Uniform Crime Reports: Crime in the United States, 2007.* Retrieved May 9, 2010, from http://www.fbi.gov/ucr/cius2007/about/offense_definitions.html

8. Federal Bureau of Investigation. *UCR Summary Reporting, Frequently Asked Questions.* Retrieved May 15, 2010, from http://www.fbi.gov/ucr/ucrquest.htm

9. Federal Bureau of Investigation. *UCR Summary Reporting, Frequently Asked Questions.* Retrieved May 15, 2010, from http://www.fbi.gov/ucr/ucrquest.htm

10. U.S. Department of Justice. *National Incident-based Reporting System.* Retrieved May 9, 2010, from http://www.fbi.gov/ucr/nibrs/manuals/v1all.pdf

11. National Archive of Criminal Justice Data. *NIBRS Concepts.* Retrieved May 9, 2010, from http://www.icpsr.umich.edu/NACJD/NIBRS/concepts.html

12. Bureau of Justice Statistics. *National Crime Victimization Survey.* Retrieved May 9, 2010, from http://bjs.ojp.usdoj.gov/content/pub/pdf/ncvs104.pdf

13. National Archive of Criminal Justice Data. *National Crime Victimization Resource Guide.* Retrieved May 9, 2010, from http://www.icpsr.umich.edu/NACJD/NCVS/

14. National Archive of Criminal Justice Data. *Accuracy of NCVS Estimates.* Retrieved May 9, 2010, from http://www.icpsr.umich.edu/NACJD/NCVS/accuracy.html

15. National Archive of Criminal Justice Data. *Methodological Issues in the Measurement of Crime.* Retrieved May 9, 2010, from http://www.icpsr.umich.edu/NACJD/NCVS/#Methodological_Issues

16. Thornberry, T., & Krohn, M. *The Self-report Method for Measuring Delinquency and Crime.* Retrieved May 16, 2010, from http://www.ncjrs.gov/criminal_justice2000/vol_4/04b.pdf

17. Bureau of Justice Statistics. *Key Facts at a Glance.* Retrieved May 16, 2010, from http://bjs.ojp.usdoj.gov/content/glance/cv2.cfm

18. U.S. Census Bureau. *Crimes and Crime Rates by Type of Offense: 1980 to 2007.* Retrieved May 16, 2010, from http://www.census.gov/compendia/statab/2010/tables/10s0295.pdf

19. U.S. Department of Justice. *Crime in the United States in 2007.* Federal Bureau of Investigation. Retrieved May 16, 2010, from http://www.fbi.gov/ucr/cius2007/index.html

20. Federal Bureau of Investigation. *Uniform Crime Reports: Crime in the United States, 2008.* Retrieved May 16, 2010, from http://www.fbi.gov/ucr/cius2008/offenses/property_crime/index.html

21. Bureau of Justice Statistics. *Criminal Victimization 2008.* Retrieved May 16, 2010, from http://bjs.ojp.usdoj.gov/content/pub/pdf/cv08.pdf

22. Bureau of Justice Statistics. *Criminal Victimization 2008.* Retrieved May 16, 2010, from http://bjs.ojp.usdoj.gov/content/pub/pdf/cv08.pdf

23. Riedel, M., & Jarvis, J. (1999). The decline of arrest clearances for criminal homicide: Causes, correlates, and third parties. *Criminal Justice Policy Review, 9*(3), 279–306.

24. U.S. Department of Justice. *National Drug Threat Assessment, 2009.* Retrieved May 24, 2010, from http://www.justice.gov/dea/concern/18862/ndic_2009.pdf

25. U.S. Department of Justice. *Diversion, Meth Resources.* Retrieved May 24, 2010, from http://www.methresources.gov/diversion.html

26. U.S. Department of Justice. *National Drug Threat Assessment, 2009.* Retrieved May 24, 2010, from http://www.justice.gov/dea/concern/18862/ndic_2009.pdf

27. National Drug Intelligence Center. *Domestic Cannabis Cultivation Assessment 2009.* Retrieved May 24, 2010, from http://www.justice.gov/ndic/pubs37/37035/national.htm#Top

28. U.S. Department of Justice. *National Drug Threat Assessment, 2009.* Retrieved May 24, 2010, from http://www.justice.gov/dea/concern/18862/ndic_2009.pdf

29. Federal Bureau of Investigation. *Uniform Crime Reports: Crime in the United States, 2008.* Retrieved May 24, 2010, from http://www.fbi.gov/ucr/cius2008/arrests/index.html

30. Federal Bureau of Investigation. *Uniform Crime Reports: Crime in the United States, 2008.* Retrieved May 24, 2010, from http://www.fbi.gov/ucr/hc2008/victims.html

31. Federal Bureau of Investigation. *Uniform Crime Reports: Crime in the United States, 2008.* Retrieved May 24, 2010, from http://www.fbi.gov/publications/ngta2009.pdf

32. U.S. Department of Justice. *Computer Programmer Sentenced to Federal Prison for Unauthorized Computer Access.* Retrieved May 24, 2010, from http://www.justice.gov/criminal/cybercrime/press-releases/2011/caverlySent.pdf

33. Balaya, G. *Chinese National Sentenced Today for Stealing Ford Trade Secrets.* Retrieved May 24, 2010, from Department of Justice. http://www.justice.gov/opa/pr/2011/December/11-crm-1696.html

34. U.S. Department of Justice. *Four CD and DVD Counterfeiters and Suppliers in Atlanta Sentenced to Prison.* Retrieved May 24, 2010, from http://www.justice.gov/opa/pr/2011/February/11-crm-241.html

35. Suspect. *Merriam-Webster Dictionary.* Retrieved May 24, 2010, from http://www.merriam-webster.com/dictionary/suspect

36. Bureau of Justice Statistics. Suspects in investigations initiated. *Database Query.* Retrieved May 24, 2010, from http://bjs.ojp.usdoj.gov/fjsrc/var.cfm?ttype=trends&agency=EOUSA&db_type=CrimMatrs&saf=IN

37. Lockheed Martin hit by cyber incident. *Newsmax.* Retrieved June 1, 2011, from http://www.newsmax.com/US/LockheedMartin/2011/05/28/id/398127

38. Traficant found guilty of bribery, racketeering. *CNN News.* Retrieved June 1, 2011, from http://articles.cnn.com/2002-04-11/justice/traficant.trial_1_traficant-guilty-verdict-bribery?_s=PM:LAW

39. Disgraced Fmr. Rep. James Traficant released from prison. *ABC News.* Retrieved June 1, 2011, from http://abcnews.go.com/Politics/james-traficant-ohio-congressman-released-prison/story?id=8474242

40. Around the nation: Federal judge sentenced to 5 years for perjury. *The New York Times.* Retrieved May 24, 2011, from http://www.nytimes.com/1986/04/01/us/around-the-nation-federal-judge-sentenced-to-5-years-for-perjury.html

41. Boyce, G. Former LA congressman William J. Jefferson is sentenced to 13 years in prison. *The Examiner.* Retrieved May 25, 2011, from http://www.examiner.com/progressive-in-new-orleans/former-la-congressman-william-j-jefferson-is-sentenced-to-13-years-prison

42. Thompson, W. The redemption of Billy Cannon. *ESPN.* Retrieved May 22, 2011, from http://sports.espn.go.com/espn/eticket/story?page=091030BillyCannon

43. Weir, T. O.J. Simpson can't gain ground in court. *USA Today.* Retrieved May 23, 2011, from http://content.usatoday.com/communities/gameon/post/2011/05/oj-simpson-appeal-denied-prison/1

44. Holly Springs man sentenced to 10 years in prison. *Northeast Mississippi Daily Journal.* Retrieved June 1, 2011, from http://www.nems360.com/view/full_story/13515064/article-Holly-Springs-man-sentenced-to-10-years-in-prison?instance=home_news_2nd_left

45. Holly Springs. *CityData.* Retrieved May 28, 2011, from http://www.city-data.com/city/Holly-Springs-Mississippi.html

46. Police: Teen shot father with hunting bow after he took cell phone. *KOMO News Channel 4.* Retrieved May 28, 2011, from http://shelton.komonews.com/news/crime/police-teen-shot-father-hunting-bow-after-he-took-cell-phone/643603

47. Tahuya, Washington. *CityData.* Retrieved May 29, 2011, from http://www.city-data.com/city/Tahuya-Washington.html

48. Swartz, K. Former Falcons cheerleader linked to elaborate chop-shop operation. *Atlanta Journal-Constitution.* Retrieved June 1, 2011, from http://www.ajc.com/news/former-falcons-cheerleader-linked-958927.html?cxtype=rss_news_128746

49. Johnson, J. Charges in chop-shop case are snowballing. *Athens Banner-Herald.* Retrieved June 1, 2011, from http://onlineathens.com/stories/052511/new_834389983.shtml

50. Office of Juvenile Justice and Delinquency Prevention. *Juvenile Arrest Rate Trends, Violent Crime.* Retrieved May 29, 2011, from http://www.ojjdp.gov/ojstatbb/crime/JAR_Display.asp?ID=qa05201

51. Office of Juvenile Justice and Delinquency Prevention. *Juvenile Arrest Rate Trends, Property Crime.* Retrieved May 29, 2011, from http://www.ojjdp.gov/ojstatbb/crime/JAR_Display.asp?ID=qa05206

52. Office of Juvenile Justice and Delinquency Prevention. *Juvenile Arrest Rate Trends, Property Crime, Simple Assault*. Retrieved May 29, 2011, from http://www.ojjdp.gov/ojstatbb/crime/JAR_Display.asp?ID=qa05211

53. Roberts, C. *Juvenile Delinquency: Cause and Effect*. Retrieved June 1, 2011, from Yale University. http://www.yale.edu/ynhti/curriculum/units/2000/2/00.02.05.x.html

54. Recidivism. *Merriam-Webster Dictionary*. Retrieved May 22, 2011, from http://www.merriam-webster.com/dictionary/recidivism

55. Bureau of Justice Statistics. *Reentry Trends in the U.S.* Retrieved June 1, 2011, from http://bjs .ojp .usdoj.gov/content/reentry/recidivism.cfm

56. U.S. Department of Justice. *Attorney General Eric Holder Convenes Inaugural Cabinet-Level Reentry Council*. Retrieved June 1, 2011, from http://www.justice.gov/opa/pr/2011/January/11-ag-010.html

57. Council of State Governments. *Second Chance Act*. Retrieved June 1, 2011, from http://www .nationalreentryresourcecenter.org/about/second-chance-act

Bibliography

Balaya, G. *Chinese National Sentenced Today for Stealing Ford Trade Secrets*. Retrieved April 12, 2011, from Department of Justice. http://www.justice.gov/opa/pr/2011/December/11-crm-1696.html

Bureau of Justice Statistics. *Criminal Victimization 2008*. Retrieved May 17, 2010, from http://bjs.ojp .usdoj.gov/content/pub/pdf/cv08.pdf

Bureau of Justice Statistics. Suspects in Investigations Initiated. *Database Query*. Retrieved May 25,2011, from http://bjs.ojp.usdoj.gov/fjsrc/var.cfm?ttype=trends&agency=EOUSA& db_type=CrimMatrs&saf=IN

Bureau of Justice Statistics. *Key Facts at a Glance*. Retrieved May 17, 2010, from http://bjs.ojp .usdoj.gov/content/glance/cv2.cfm

Bureau of Justice Statistics. *National Crime Victimization Survey*. Retrieved May 17, 2010, from http://bjs.ojp.usdoj.gov/content/pub/pdf/ncvs104.pdf

Bureau of Justice Statistics. *Reentry Trends in the U.S.* Retrieved May 17, 2010, from http://bjs .ojp.usdoj.gov/content/reentry/recidivism.cfm

Federal Bureau of Investigation. *Uniform Crime Reports: Crime in the United States, 2008*. Retrieved May 9, 2011, from http://www.fbi.gov/ucr/cius2008/arrests/index.html

Federal Bureau of Investigation. *Uniform Crime Reports: Crime in the United States, 2008*. Retrieved May 9, 2011, from http://www.fbi.gov/ucr/cius2008/data/table_29.html

Federal Bureau of Investigation. *Uniform Crime Reports: Crime in the United States, 2008*. Retrieved May 9, 2011, from http://www.fbi.gov/ucr/hc2008/victims.html

Federal Bureau of Investigation. *Uniform Crime Reports: Crime in the United States, 2008*. Retrieved May 9, 2011, from http://www.fbi.gov/publications/ngta2009.pdf

National Archive of Criminal Justice Data. *Accuracy of NCVS Estimates*. Retrieved May 18, 2010, from http://www.icpsr.umich.edu/NACJD/NCVS/accuracy.html

National Archive of Criminal Justice Data. *Methodological Issues in the Measurement of Crime*. Retrieved May 16, 2010, from http://www.icpsr.umich.edu/NACJD/NCVS/#Methodological_Issues

National Archive of Criminal Justice Data. *National Crime Victimization Resource Guide*. Retrieved May 18, 2010, from http://www.icpsr.umich.edu/NACJD/NCVS/

National Archive of Criminal Justice Data. *NIBRS Concepts*. Retrieved May 16, 2010, from http:// www.icpsr.umich.edu/NACJD/NIBRS/concepts.html

National Drug Intelligence Center. *Domestic Cannabis Cultivation Assessment 2009*. Retrieved May 28, 2010, from http://www.justice.gov/ndic/pubs37/37035/national.htm#Top

Suspect. *Merriam-Webster Dictionary*. Retrieved May 26, 2011, from http://www.merriam-webster .com/dictionary/suspect

Thornberry, T., & Krohn, M. *The Self-report Method for Measuring Delinquency and Crime.* Retrieved May 20, 2011, from http://www.ncjrs.gov/criminal_justice2000/vol_4/04b.pdf

U.S. Census Bureau. *Crimes and Crime Rates by Type of Offense: 1980 to 2007.* Retrieved May 9, 2011, from http://www.census.gov/compendia/statab/2010/tables/10s0295.pdf

U.S. Department of Justice. *Crime in the United States in 2007.* Retrieved May 24, 2010, from Federal Bureau of Investigation. http://www.fbi.gov/ucr/cius2007/index.html

U.S. Department of Justice. *National Incident-based Reporting System.* Retrieved May 24, 2010, from http://www.fbi.gov/ucr/nibrs/manuals/v1all.pdf

U.S. Department of Justice. *Computer Programmer Sentenced to Federal Prison for Unauthorized Computer Access.* Retrieved May 19, 2011, from http://www.justice.gov/criminal/cybercrime/press-releases/2011/caverlySent.pdf

U.S. Department of Justice. *Four CD and DVD Counterfeiters and Suppliers in Atlanta Sentenced to Prison.* Retrieved February 24, 2011, from http://www.justice.gov/opa/pr/2011/February/11-crm-241.html

The History of Law Enforcement in the United States

2

The police are the public and the public are the police; the police being only members of the public who are paid to give full time attention to duties which are incumbent on every citizen in the interests of community welfare and existence.[1]

Robert Peel

Learning Objectives

The objectives of this chapter are to

- Discuss the origins and heritage of American law enforcement
- Explain the history of civilian law enforcement
- Review the history of military law enforcement
- Describe the maturation of federal, state, local, and tribal agencies

Introduction

Law enforcement in the United States is composed of thousands of agencies that perform their duties daily with integrity and dedication. Challenging and exciting as a career field, law enforcement serves the citizens in our nation as one of a series of first responders entrusted to serve, in the words of Chief William Parker of the Los Angeles Police Department, as that "thin blue line": a barrier protecting our citizens from those that would exploit them.

Across the nation, a myriad of police academies and training programs graduate new classes of police officers each month. Upon their respective graduations, these graduates become brethren among the ranks of a timeless fraternity of individuals whose sacrifices provide their societal peers with both tangible and intangible benefits. Many of these individuals will die in the performance of the duties, some will enjoy a lifelong career in law enforcement, and some will depart the profession for a variety of reasons. However, in all cases, these individuals continue a tradition of service that has benefited the United States since its origin.

The United States is well over 200 years old. Although this period of time is less than the life span of some other nations, its modern police forces are highly trained, effective, and motivated. Modern policing now spans the entirety of the nation and encompasses both civilian and military settings. The humble beginnings of American law enforcement have matured into global influences during modern times.

The entities that comprise modern law enforcement are the products of change. Throughout its history, the United States has experienced societal change that drastically influenced its law enforcement organizations and activities. Furthermore, these changes

Figure 2.1 Uniformed military police escort Erich Gimpel, right foreground, and William C. Colepaugh, background, walking into court at Governors Island, N.Y., March 3, 1945. Both were subsequently convicted as Nazi spies and sentenced to die by hanging. (Courtesy of U.S. Army/AP Photo. Retrieved from http://abcnews.go.com/Blotter/spy-files-nazi-plot-us-blown-drunkeness-idiocy/story?id=13292849.)

are also representative of the maturing of the nation from its humble origin, through the period of manifest destiny, through the War Between the States, and throughout the technological developments and national entanglements of the twentieth century. Doubtlessly, law enforcement will also continue to be influenced by societal change here in the twenty-first century.

Law enforcement in the United States is composed of thousands of different departments, agencies, and organizations operating in our society at the local, tribal, state, federal, and private level. Diverse and yet comprehensive, law enforcement and the regulatory functions it performs impact all aspects of our lives. To better understand the profession of today, it is important to examine the historical foundations of the discipline (Figure 2.1).

The British Heritage, Colonial America, and the First Generation of Law Enforcement in the United States

Much of the historical foundations for law enforcement in the United States are drawn from the British. Since the earliest days of colonialization of North America, the influence of the European powers, especially the British, has been significant in the development of the nation that would become the United States. Beginning with the small colonial settlements, many of which would grow into some of the most dynamic cities of our nation, day and night watches, city marshals, police, constables, and sheriffs served our communities. Most of these positions have roots that extend into Britain.

The origin of the sheriff is found in early England. Drawn from the terms shire reeve, the sheriff was a strong, traditionally British law enforcement official and was easily adopted into North America. One of the most striking characteristics of the American sheriff was his rapid community acceptance once the position was created. As early as 1632, the office of the sheriff replaced such legal officers as the "provost marshal," "marshal general," or "marshal of the colony" in Virginia. The duties of the sheriff in the English Colonies included the collection of taxes and fees owed by the governor. Formal qualifications for the position of the sheriff rarely reached beyond age, residence, citizenship, and electoral status. Today, the position of the sheriff is common across the nation, with an estimated 3,500 individuals serving in that position. Clearly, the position of the sheriff has proven over the last 300 years to provide effective community service within the United States.

Though drawn from the French, the constable is similar to the sheriff in many respects. Although not as powerful, the constables have served in both the urban and rural settings. A town constable was responsible for guarding the town by day; apprehending the drunks, disorderly persons, and vagrants; catching the criminals; and commanding the watch. In addition, many communities expected the constable to be responsible for items affecting the health and well-being of the citizens including duties such as monitoring and reporting the condition of the streets, sidewalks, and privies.[2]

Most of the towns and small communities in America relied on some form of day or night watch to provide security. Town after town set up a night watch system and frequently staffed the watch with citizens who often served on an unpaid basis. As in England, the early day and night watches were anything but effective, but they provided a basic security service. In some communities, citizens were expected to serve and in those communities, they rotated the responsibility among themselves. Like their counterparts in England, and in earlier American cities, some citizens hired substitutes to serve in their place. In some communities, it was common for a court to sentence a man guilty of a minor misdemeanor to be a watchman as punishment.

As American cities grew, significant changes in policing and police operations were needed. It is difficult today to grasp the nature of policing in this era. The officers worked long hours, walked their beats, and performed their duties as they defined those duties, working with limited to no communications capability, oversight, or supervision. Graft and corruption were common. Until the twentieth century, many officers earned many times more money through graft and corruption than from their salaries.

The political spoils system flourished with appointments to public positions of employment including police service. In England, similar problems were being experienced. Stepping forward to enact change was the Home Secretary of England, Sir Robert Peel. Sir Robert Peel established the Royal Irish Constabulary in 1812, and it had proved to be a great success. Peel realized the English police were in great need of reform. To Peel, it was obvious that something similar to the Irish force was needed. As a result, the foundation for Peel's vision of a professional police service for England was established with the enactment of the Metropolitan Police Act of 1829. This Act provided for paid constables who were accountable to the public. Peel visualized professional police forces across the cities of England, who were professional, well trained, and accountable for their actions. By September 1829, the new officers, called "Bobbies" or "Peelers" by the public, were on the streets. Colonel Charles Rowan, an army officer, and Sir Richard Mayne, an attorney, were appointed as Justices of the Peace in charge of the force. The early years of the new force were difficult, but the force proved to be the foundation of the modern police force in Britain and the United States[3] (Figure 2.2).

Figure 2.2 Sir Robert Peel, Home Secretary of England, whose efforts led to the creation of the London Metropolitan Police Department in 1829. (Retrieved from http://hua.umf.maine.edu/ Reading_Revolutions/pictures/CornLaws/SirRobertPeel.jpg.)

Boston, Philadelphia, New York, and the Birth of Urban Policing

In the United States, people, events, and politics influenced the birth and shaped the evolution of law enforcement, especially urban policing. Many of the issues that led to London creating a full-time police department were the same issues that would lead the growing cities in the United States to also establish urban policing structured along the British model visualized by Peel.

In the growing cities, the split watches had outlived their effectiveness. For years, New York, Boston, and Philadelphia were some of the largest cities in the nation. Boston made significant contributions to the development of urban policing. In 1801, Boston became the first city in the United States to require by statute the establishment and maintenance of a permanent night watch.[4] The years that followed proved to be a learning period for the watch. By 1821, Boston issued revised instructions for the night watchmen. They were no longer allowed to walk or talk together on their streets. They were to make their rounds and return to the box where they were to remain until their next rounds. This was very basic police service, oriented more toward cost than public need. As the city continued to grow, the existing service soon came to an end.[5]

In Philadelphia, little had been done toward the adoption of a modern urban enforcement model until the death of Stephen Girard, one of its prominent citizens. The terms of the estate of Stephen Girard required the city to introduce some form of policing. His estate covered one-half of the cost of the new police.[6] In response, the city administration mandated that an organized, 24-hour service be available. At the time, the most effective approach to enforcement was the adoption of a day and night watch, each with its own service mission and separate organizational structure.

On December 26, 1833, a formal 24-hour policing came into existence when Philadelphia adopted a day watch and a night watch. The Philadelphia approach character-ized the belief that the control of two separate organizations was more efficient than one. This belief received wide acceptance by other cities. Boston set up a similar organization on May 21, 1838, and Cincinnati in 1842.

Though other cities experimented with changes, it was New York City that earned the distinction of organizing the first modern police department designed along the lines of Peel's London police. Between 1820 and 1845, significant increases in population, crime, disorder, and vice in New York City served as the catalyst for a comprehensive police agency. The growing crime problem in the city was too much for the existing law enforce-ment. The "leatherheads" of the period were inefficient as suggested by the popular saying of the time "lazy as a leatherhead."[7]

In 1844, the New York State Legislature authorized communities to organize 24-hour police forces. The Legislature also provided special funds to the cities for this police service. A plan was presented by several New York police magistrates to completely revamp the existing police system. One of those who presented the plan was George W. Matsell, who became chief of police in 1845. The proposed ordnance abolished the watch department, dock masters, health wardens, and other municipal functionaries. Members of the new police department assumed these duties. In addition to the policemen concerned with the prevention of crime, the plan provided for an additional 40 "police officers." Their duties supported the various courts for the service of civil process. Tenure for both groups was to be for good behavior thus, in theory, ending political patronage from the selection process.[8]

But the policemen heeded the wishes of the politicians who, they realized, retained control of appointments, promotions, and assignments within the police department itself. The command structure of the police force was often staffed by individuals who owed their rank and assignment to the politicians. In this system, a protective father image often developed around the politician who, in turn, was protected by his people. In this set-ting, many officers were genuinely enthusiastic partisans at elections and fully supported the politicians. The outcome of the elections determined who would control the political machine and directly influence social issues. The control of drinking, prostitution, and gambling meant financial gain for many. Control of the city provided a legal framework for extortion of money from those operating along the fringes of legal parameters.

Saloon keepers, prostitutes, and gamblers regarded bribery as a normal operating expense to ensure the smooth delivery of services demanded by the public. Graft and cor-ruption formed a partnership. It was a partnership formed on the expected economic gain attained from cooperation with all of the forces controlling the city government. It went all the way down to the average policemen walking the beat as well as tolerance in vice enforcement. The criminals were not the only persons who benefitted from the mainte-nance of a favored status with the men who controlled the local government. The officers who had political security guarantees protecting their positions often worked all day at another job and slept all night on their police job. The code of the day was to avoid trouble. The less work the officers did, the fewer chances they had to become involved in trouble.

During the early 1850s, American urban police officials were addressing the issue of placing the police in uniforms and arming them. At first, urban departments resisted the adoption of pistols for the individual officer. They did so more on the grounds of the cost of the weapons than on a moral or ethical issue. However, the nature of the work of early urban police officers was dangerous. The men walked their beats alone with no handcuffs, no signal boxes for communication, and no wagons for the escorting of prisoners. The urban police officers were normally only armed with a club or, as the early Boston police, with a borrowed saber. Departments began to experience the first fatalities of police officers. Thus, urban police officers began joining the ranks of rural officers, sheriffs, and United States Marshals who had carried guns since their earliest days.

As the cities grew, they realized that exclusive reliance on foot patrols had limitations. Urban departments began limited use of various transportation methods including the purchase of horses and wagons to fulfill the transportation needs of the police departments.

But even within this setting, professionals emerged to lay the foundation for the future. In 1857, John A. Kennedy, an innovator with outstanding foresight, became the head of the New York City Police. He held this position for 10 years and recognized the value of the technological developments of the period. His foresight led to the use of the camera, enhancing the effectiveness of the "Rogues' Gallery" pioneered in Boston by Francis Tukey. Kennedy also formed a detective force, a harbor police, and a special "Broadway Squad," selected for their size and appearance. The Broadway Squad personnel had beats in the most prominent areas of the city where they protected the most influential citizens. Following the lead of the New York City Police Department, St. Louis set up a detective bureau in 1867. These officers, known as "The Street Service Bureau," had the responsibility of conducting criminal investigations.

Until the end of the century, countless cities created their own police departments. Most of these departments were small, but they provided the basic enforcement services as needed. By the turn of the century, many cities struggled with the effects of the political spoils system and the corruption it inspired. In New York, the efforts to expose police corruption led to the Lexow Commission, which uncovered within the police department extensive corruption and brutality. In the wake of the investigation, officers were dismissed and new leadership was appointed to "cleanse" the department. While cities were struggling with the impact of corruption, efforts were underway to establish a foundation of law enforcement professionalism with the formation in Chicago in 1893 of the National Chiefs of Police Union, primarily to apprehend and return wanted persons who flee local jurisdictions. Soon the Union was renamed the International Association of Chiefs of Police. Chief Richard Sylvester of the Washington, D.C. Police Department served as the Association's third president. Under his direction, the Association established itself as the premier law enforcement professional organization in the nation.

State-Level Law Enforcement

The development of law enforcement on the state level was a slow process. The sheriff on the county level, the constable, town marshal, and later city police fulfilled most law enforcement needs. In an emergency, the local or state militia could always be called to arms. As the population continued to increase, governmental organizations became more sophisticated. States gradually established basic law enforcement organizations designed to be responsive to state authorities (see Figure 2.3 through Figure 2.5).

The first attempt at state-level law and order dates back to the Revolutionary War. The Virginia Assembly dispatched elements of its own militia through the Cumberland Gap into its frontier counties west of the Appalachians, an area known as "Kantuckee." The

Figure 2.3 Patch of the Mississippi Highway Patrol. (Retrieved from http://www.quickerbuy
.com/products/mississippi-highway-patrol-patch-434184844.)

Figure 2.4 Patch of the Alabama Highway Patrol. (Retrieved from http://www.patchgallery
.com/main/displayimage.php?album=69&pid=25793.)

Figure 2.5 Patch of the California Highway Patrol. (Retrieved from http://www.chp.ca.gov/
html/uniforms.html.)

militia protected the settlers from local law breakers and organized their defense to counter the threat of Indian attack. To support the effort of the militia, some of the frontiersmen were recruited into small companies of "patrollers" and commissioned to track down those who posed a threat to the settlers.

As state enforcement organizations emerged, the following two distinct patterns developed: a rural model and an urban model. A rural model is a reflection of a loosely controlled organization, such as the Texas Rangers. An urban model, as characterized by the Pennsylvania State Police, was based upon a formal military structure, and developed later into the traditional state police/highway patrol model.

The Texas Rangers are recognized as the first state-level law enforcement organization in the United States, even though Texas, at the time of the creation of the Rangers, was a republic rather than a state. It could be argued that during this period, the Texas Rangers were the national police of the Republic of Texas rather than a true state force.

In 1823, Stephen F. Austin commissioned 10 men to "range about" in order to discourage Indian raids and marauders, deal with outlaws, and settle disputes through the administration of "seat-of-the-pants" "on-the-scene" justice. In 1835, the provisional government of Texas placed three Ranger companies under the command of R. M. Williamson. Their actions were subject to the direction of the military authorities with the intent to patrol the Mexican border. This function of border patrol persisted for many years although general police work, including criminal investigation, ultimately became their primary function. After the War Between the States, Texas abolished the Rangers and replaced them with a State Police. The Texas State Police unfortunately proved ineffective and were disbanded, only to be replaced by the reestablishment of the Texas Rangers. Since that time, the Texas Rangers have established a long and distinguished history of service.

Other states took steps to establish state police forces. On May 16, 1865, Massachusetts Governor John A. Andrews created a "State Constabulary," which was empowered with statewide police powers to suppress commercialized vice and was controversial when established. Within 10 years, the duties and responsibilities of Massachusetts State Constabulary were redefined as the Legislature changed the force into the State Detective Force. The department later became part of the Department of Public Safety in 1919.

In 1887, California created the State Capital Police and tasked them with providing security on state property. In 1903, Connecticut set up a small state force, assuming the duties formerly exercised by the Law and Order League, a quasipublic organization. The Connecticut force was modeled after the Massachusetts District Police. Like the Massachusetts Police, the Connecticut force was to combat commercialized vice, with emphasis on the enforcement of the liquor and gambling laws. They also performed various inspection duties and investigated suspicious fires. The Connecticut force was so small that any system of regular patrols was impractical. After many changes, the Connecticut force became a state detective force operating under the control of an administrative board, until the extensive reorganization of 1920.[9]

Though states were experimenting with various state-level law enforcement models, it was Pennsylvania that established the first true urban state police force. On July 1, 1905, Governor Pennypacker offered the appointment of Superintendent of the newly created State Police to Captain John C. Groome. Groome was an outstanding selection by the Governor. A member of the National Guard for more than 23 years, Groome believed the only organizational model that could ensure success for this new state police was an organization patterned along military lines. Groome followed this philosophy in his selection of personnel.

The Pennsylvania State Police became the state police pattern followed by the majority of states as they established their organizations over the next 40 years. As state police organizations assumed traffic-related duties and adopted motorcycles and automobiles into their equipment inventories, the highway patrol so common today was born.

One of the most sensational cases that involved state police organizations of the period was the kidnapping and death of Charles A. Lindbergh, Jr. In 1932, the son of Charles Lindbergh was kidnapped from the family's home in New Jersey. Charles Lindbergh, Sr. was a world famous aviator who had achieved fame as the first person to fly nonstop alone across the Atlantic. The kidnapping and subsequent death of the child was primarily investigated by the New Jersey State Police with assistance from the Federal Bureau of Investigation (FBI). Using extensive resources from the emerging field of forensic science and countless hours investigating leads, a suspect, Bruno Richard Hauptmann, was arrested for the crime in 1934. Prosecuted, convicted, and later executed, the impact of the kidnapping led to federal legislation making kidnapping a federal offense, falling under the jurisdiction of the FBI.

World War II affected state enforcement organizations. The loss of personnel from the state organizations forced many enforcement organizations to operate below authorized strength levels. Many states created auxiliary forces to supplement the state agencies. With the conclusion of World War II, thousands of veterans returned to civilian life with an interest in law enforcement after exposure to military police or shore patrol duty. State enforcement agencies welcomed home these veterans. By 1950, 36 states had established state police organizations with full law enforcement authority and 12 established state agencies with authority restricted to enforcement of traffic laws or to crimes committed on state highways.[10]

State governments began to reassess their policing responsibilities. Many states created new agencies to fill the void existing between comprehensive state and local enforcement including investigative agencies, wildlife enforcement, medical examiner resources, criminal laboratories, alcohol and drug enforcement agencies, investigative divisions within attorney general offices, and numerous other enforcement and regulatory organizations within the states. These agencies play a key role in the enforcement of laws and the enhancement of public safety.

State enforcement agencies took the lead in the advancement of highway safety-related issues. In 1948, radar was introduced for traffic enforcement. As early as 1952, Col. George Mingle, the Superintendent of the Ohio State Police, began to promote the use of the safety belt by all highway patrol personnel. In February 1956, he issued specifications including two safety belts in the front seats of all new highway patrol cars. By 1987, a total of 25 states had implemented mandatory use laws and 15 states had pending legislation on similar statutes for seat belts. Eventually, all states required the use of safety belts. Other issues addressed by state enforcement agencies included reduction of the speed limit on interstate highways, use of cell phones while driving, enhancement of drinking- and driving-related enforcement, and general motor vehicle safety. State enforcement has also been very involved in various drug trafficking intervention initiatives, in an attempt to impact the flow of illegal drugs across our nation using the highway system.

Federal Enforcement

Provisions for the establishment and maintenance of law enforcement and the judiciary on the federal level of government were vague. Article III, Section 1 of the Constitution provided the authority for the creation of the United States Supreme Court and all lesser courts deemed necessary, but this clause of the Constitution did not set guidelines for the organization or structure of the Court. Initially, few criminal laws had been enacted on the federal level. Treason and counterfeiting, the major concerns for any new nation, were addressed in the Constitution, but no provisions existed for the enforcement of federal laws or for the creation of federal enforcement agencies. The responsibility for law enforcement rested with the local governments. As time would show, states were unprepared to handle the full responsibility for order maintenance.

The first criminal statute enacted by Congress on April 30, 1790, defined treason and made provision for its punishment. It also defined and prescribed the penalty for murder in a fort, arsenal, dockyard, or any place under the jurisdiction of the United States. Penalty for each offense was death by hanging. Section 31 of this first legislation abolished the traditional English opportunity for certain persons charged with a felony to claim the benefit of clergy and be tried in ecclesiastical courts.

Soon after the adoption of the United States Constitution, the United States Marshals were created under the authority of the Judiciary Act of 1789. This Act authorized the appointment of a marshal for each of the 11 states that had ratified the Constitution.

At the conclusion of the Revolutionary War, the Colonial Navy was disbanded. Recognizing the need of a force to enforce customs laws in the ports and along the coast, the federal government created the Revenue Marine Service under the authority of the Tariff Act of 1790. The Revenue Marine, which eventually evolved into the United States Coast Guard, served as the nation's naval force until the reestablishment of the United States Navy in 1798.

The United States Marshals Service and the Revenue Marine Service gave the federal government limited ability to exert its will without calling upon the military. As the years of the nineteenth century rolled by, the nation faced new demands and challenges. The expansion of federal enforcement would be a natural by-product of the growth of the nation.

Throughout the 1800s, the need for additional federal level investigative and enforcement assets increased. The need to protect the United States Mail, provide support for customs and revenue collection, and by the 1860s, a great need to protect the nation's currency, all led to the formation of new federal enforcement agencies. With the establishment of the United States Secret Service in 1865, the government now had an agency in addition to the United States Marshals to enforce the growing list of federal crimes. Early in their history, the Secret Service concentrated much of its efforts upon the protection of the nation's currency.

With the assassination of President McKinley in 1901, the Secret Service assumed the responsibility of the protection of the President. In the almost 150-year history of the Secret Service, the agency has built a long and distinguished record. In 2002, the Department of Homeland Security was established with the passage of Public Law 107-296. One aspect of this legislation transferred the United States Secret Service from its traditional home in the Department of the Treasury to its new home in the Department of Homeland Security effective March 1, 2003.

Figure 2.6 An FBI officer. (Retrieved from http://www.fbi.gov/news/photos/image/people/nyswat.jpg.)

By the early 1900s, federal enforcement was on the edge of major growth. The turn of the century saw the Secret Service serving as the primary federal level investigative agency, but political controversies including the successful investigation, prosecution, and conviction of several influential politicians led to a restriction of their ability to conduct wide ranging investigations. In 1908, this restriction led to the decision by United States Attorney General Charles J. Bonaparte to authorize the creation of FBI. Over the next 100 years, the FBI became one of the most famous law enforcement agencies in the world. Its most famous Director, J. Edgar Hoover, led the agency for almost 50 years. During his tenure, the FBI became a leader in law enforcement training, criminal and scientific investigation, and domestic espionage and threat investigation (Figure 2.6).

Over the next several decades, federal enforcement expanded with the creation of a wide range of agencies with law enforcement, regulatory, or administrative support responsibilities such as the Federal Bureau of Narcotics, Federal Bureau of Prohibition, Drug Enforcement Administration, United States Border Patrol, Naval Criminal Investigative Service, Federal Emergency Management Agency, and Transportation Security Administration, just to name a few agencies.

Private Security and Enforcement

Free enterprise, service demands, and potential profits from untapped markets led to the development of private enforcement organizations. Driven by profit and linked to cost-effective service, the private security organizations filled a wide void created by inefficient public enforcement. Private security or private enforcement did not begin in the United States.

History is full of examples of private forces employed to provide protection. Human nature has been to protect acquired property. In Japan, the Samurai provided security and protection for those who employed them. In China, the elite classes utilized private security to protect themselves and their property from the encroaching Mongol Hordes. Throughout the world, people with power and influence paid to protect themselves, families, and property.

During the nineteenth century, there was a definite need for private enforcement organizations. Rural law enforcement and in many cases incompetent and corrupt urban law enforcement organizations failed to cope with the increasing service demands of their growing communities. As a result, the void existing between law enforcement capabilities and community-related law enforcement needs was soon filled by an emerging private security industry.

Entrepreneurs recognized the opportunities presented by the demand for contracted security. In Boston, as early as 1821, a private guard service provided contract service to local merchants. By the late 1840s and early 1850s, private detectives emerged in the United States. In June 1845, one of New York City's ex-constables, Gil Hays, set up his "Independent Police." This action was a response to the reorganization of the police system in New York City. This "Independent Police" was one of the first private detective agencies in the United States.[11]

The most famous and efficient private agency of the era was the internationally renowned "Pinkertons," founded by Allan Pinkerton as the Pinkerton National Detective Agency in Chicago in 1851. Legend has it that Pinkerton began his career as a detective in Chicago in July 1847 when H. E. Hunt, the owner of the general store in Dundee, Illinois, asked Pinkerton to help in the investigation and arrest of John Craig. Craig, a counterfeiter, had been passing ten dollar bills in Dundee. Pinkerton's success in the Craig case inspired the founding of Pinkerton's private detective agency in Chicago in 1851.

The "Pinkertons" became the premier national "enforcement organization" of their time, possessing greater capabilities than any federal, state, or local law enforcement agency. The Pinkertons advanced the profession and made strides in areas including criminal investigation and identification. By 1880, there were no federal, state, or local agencies organized or equipped better than the Pinkertons.

Though private security agencies and private detectives increasingly offered their services across the nation, the Pinkertons dominated the industry throughout the 1800s and well into the 1900s. By the late 1960s, just after the name of the enterprise became Pinkerton's Inc. and the corporate headquarters moved to California, it had 70 branch offices (including central offices in Chicago and New York), about $75 million in annual revenues, and some 13,000 full-time employees worldwide. In the mid-1970s, the company had about 800 employees in the Chicago area. By the end of the century, the enterprise founded a century and a half earlier had become a subsidiary of a large Swedish corporation called Securitas.[12]

In 1909, the William J. Burns Detective Agency was formed in New York City and soon challenged the Pinkertons for industry domination. Although the Burns agency was primarily engaged in detective and investigative work, in 1910, Burns convinced the American Bankers Association to award his company the security contract previously held by the Pinkertons to protect the 12,000 member banks.

William Burns (1861–1932) from time to time returned to government service and left interim control of the agency to his two sons, Raymond and William Burns. Reflecting its rapid growth, in 1913, the agency changed its name to Burns International Detective Agency. William Burns professionally continued to move in and out of the ranks of federal service. He directed the Bureau of Investigation from 1921 to 1924. By the time of Burns's death, the Burns Detective Agency became the second largest agency of its type in the United States.

Throughout the twentieth century, private security and enforcement servicers provided diverse services, driven by the market demand, ranging from visible security to undercover operations. By 2010, private security organizations and operations were extremely diverse. Ranging from retail security to contractors providing security services in Afghanistan and Iraq, the field had proven to be multibillion dollar industry. Within the industry, there are a variety of security forces. Typically, private enforcement can be categorized as contract forces or in-house forces. Contract forces, as the name suggests, provide their services for a fee. Services provided under contract can range dramatically and include guard, investigative, protection, or alarm services. In-house services may include retail loss prevention or corporate protection.

Today, the United States has more than 10,000 private security companies that bring in revenue of more than $15 billion each year. Those employed by private security companies far outnumber public police employees, and the number of private security guards employed in the United States is expected to continue to increase in the future.[13]

Breaking Barriers

It is difficult to imagine the struggle that led to the shattering of sexual and ethnic barriers. These barriers had long limited or eliminated the opportunities for individuals other than a Caucasian male to get a job in a law enforcement agency. Cities used women in the role of "matrons" for years, assigning them limited duties typically involving juveniles and adult women. Though rare, opportunities in the profession were slowly presenting themselves. Though Marie Owens served as a member of the Chicago Police Department from 1893 as a detective, records suggest Lola Baldwin was the first woman to have police powers in the United States when she served in Portland, Oregon, in 1905. The first woman awarded the title of policewoman in the United States was Alice Stebbins Wells when Los Angeles appointed her to that position on September 13, 1910. Her appointment was the subject of much publicity, both positive and negative. Wells proved to be a leader. In 1915, Wells organized and served as the first president of the International Association of Policewomen (Figure 2.7).

Figure 2.7 Alice Stebbins Wells. (Retrieved from http://en.wikipedia.org/wiki/Alice_Stebbins_Wells.)

Slowly, cities added women to their police forces. By 1915, 16 cities in the United States employed at least one policewoman on a full-time basis. The typical salary of a police-woman was between $800 and $1200 per year, much less than her male counterpart. On January 24, 1916, Miss Laura Kindead became the first policewoman for St. Louis where she was expected to focus her efforts upon juvenile cases and wife and child abandonment. In 1920, 56 cities had 164 policewomen.[14]

World War I provided an unexpected boom to the movement for the adoption of women into enforcement positions. The mobilization effort for the war drew men from all career areas. Expanding industrial demands provided employment opportunities in urban areas. There were many drawbacks for these pioneers. Women continued to receive lower salaries than their male counterparts, had stricter appointment standards than males, and promotions were slower. Despite this, advances did occur. In 1918, the Welfare Bureau of the New York City Police Department came under the direction of Mrs. Ellen O'Grady, who was appointed as a Deputy Police Commissioner, earning the distinction of becom-ing the first woman in the nation to be in an executive position in a police department. In 1919, Indianapolis created a Bureau of Policewomen. During its first year of operation, it handled more than 5,000 cases and helped to set up a policewoman's house for misde-meanants and destitute women.

In 1919, the Commissioner of Police in New York City, Richard Enright, said women officers were a necessity in policing his city. In 1920, the New York State Legislature offi-cially set up the position of policewoman in New York City. In 1921, New York City gave its first Civil Service Examination for the position of policewoman. Following shortly was the creation of a Bureau of Women, under the direction of Mary Hamilton. When first organized, the Bureau of Women was separate from traditional police station houses and was located in an abandoned stationhouse. With few resources, the policewomen turned their new headquarters into a haven for troubled women and children. The policewomen received patrol duty, though most often in plain clothes rather than uniform.

Normally tasked with enforcement attention directed toward women, girls, and chil-dren, the early policewomen were more social workers than enforcement officers. The use of females as enforcement personnel slowly gained acceptance across the nation. In 1925, a survey of 210 cities in the country revealed the employment of 355 police matrons, 395 policewomen, and 22 women who performed both functions. Salary ranged from $780 to $2460 per year. Most frequently, the female officers were assigned to look after runaway, truant, and delinquent children and to check amusement parks, dance halls, and disor-derly houses.[15]

Over the next 85 years, female members of the profession entered the ranks of depart-ments across the nation, serving on all levels of government and in the private sector. Still a profession dominated by men, agencies actively recruited females into the ranks (Figure 2.8).

Early Advancements in Science, Investigations, and Technology

Science and technology have proven essential to effective law enforcement. Transportation and communications benefited from technological advancement. In the 1920s, the main-stay of the police department's patrol capability was the walking beat officer. The officer was likely to encounter a variety of crimes such as robbery, burglary, theft, and assault. Investigations of crimes were straightforward and basic for the street officer. With limited

Figure 2.8 Firearms instruction is an important part of law enforcement training in the United States. (Retrieved from http://www.fbi.gov/news/photos/image/people/fbiagentsgun.JPG.)

technology, the police officer depended on his knowledge of the people of the neighborhood to solve crimes. In the rural areas of the nation, law enforcement typically relied upon horses for transportation, as did the early state level agencies. With the development of affordable automobiles, motorcycles, boats, and even aircraft, law enforcement began recognizing the value of mobility.

Early in the century, some departments began acquiring automobiles, motorcycles, and bicycles for limited patrol and emergency response needs. Many sources suggest the first use of an automobile in police service in the United States occurred in Akron, Ohio, in 1899 when an electric car patrolled the streets of the city. Other cities soon followed. At least as early as 1903, St. Louis placed into service a "St. Louis," a locally manufactured automobile. Berkeley, California, under the leadership of Chief August Vollmer used bicycles, motorcycles, and automobiles during the first two decades of the twentieth century.

Departments experimented with communications systems. Early night watches and police officers discovered that a distinctive sound could occur when the police baton stuck the bricks in the street. Police whistles were developed. Many cities employed "call box" systems, initially placing telegraphs and later telephones on the beat from which the officer walking the street could call the department and learn of new requests for service.

From the early 1900s, visionaries sought ways to incorporate radio communications into law enforcement. In the 1920s, more departments incorporated radios into their departments. Some departments, including the Chicago Police Department, worked with their local commercial radio stations such as WGN in Chicago, which agreed to interrupt its radio entertainment to broadcast messages from headquarters to patrol cars with car radios.

In May of 1924, at an amateur radio show held in Los Angeles, Police Chief R. Lee Heath observed a contest demonstrating home-built automobile-mounted radio receivers potentially suitable for police use. He was impressed with the results, and the following year, at the National Radio Exposition, Heath organized a demonstration of an airplane with an officer aboard following a "suspect's" car, radioing its movements to listeners below on 305-m radio station KRCA.[16]

Figure 2.9 Technology in police vehicles. (Retrieved from http://www.ci.buffalo.mn.us/police/technology/technology.htm.)

Though we are not sure of the first police department to broadcast, some of the earliest departments to broadcast included the Berkeley Police Department, which received a police radio license in 1928. The St. Louis Police Radio Station KGPC began transmitting from the top floor of police headquarters serving the police fleet of 30 scout cars and detective cruisers in 1930, and in 1931, the Los Angeles Police Department began broadcasting. In 1930, Galvin Manufacturing Corporation introduced its Motorola brand car radio, one of the first commercially successful car radios. The radio was intended for the public, but soon police departments and city governments across the United States ordered radios for public safety use. Motorola dominated the law enforcement market for decades.

During the twentieth century, advancements in all areas of law enforcement equipment, recruitment, training, education, planning, procedures, and tactics would reflect greatly upon the professional status achieved by the discipline. Law enforcement personnel had evolved into a well-trained and typically well-led profession (Figure 2.9).

Law Enforcement in the First Half of the Twentieth Century

For urban policing, 1900 marked the beginning of a century of change. The large cities of the nation found themselves dealing with the challenges of urbanization, rising crime, and an increased demand for social services. Although the large cities captured attention, the vast majority of Americans lived in a rural or small-town setting. For those in rural America, the sheriff continued to play the role of the primary law enforcer. In small towns, many were served even at the turn of the century by city marshals, night watches, or very small police departments. For most of these small departments, service demands were limited, with minor offenses taking the majority of their time.

With the political spoils system seeing police positions as a welcome prize to award as favors, it was very difficult for even the officers who wanted to advance by merit to do so.

The New York Police Scandal of 1895 and the subsequent Lexow Commission investigation revealed the deep corruption present in the nation's largest police department, which included as common practice officers "buying" promotions. But New York was not alone in the struggle to contend with corruption, political interference, inefficiency, payoffs, kickbacks, and brutality.

On the national level, federal law enforcement experienced a century marked by expansion. Agencies including what would be known as the FBI, the Federal Bureau of Narcotics, and the Bureau of Prohibition were just three of the many agencies that were established.

Within this setting, the seeds of professionalism had been planted. Two of the most influential leaders in the profession were Washington, D.C. Police Chief Richard H. Sylvester (1860–1930) and Berkeley, California Police Chief August Vollmer (1876–1955). Sylvester served as the third President of the International Association of Chiefs of Police. Under his guidance, the Association advanced the discipline by providing training and assistance to police departments. Sylvester retired from the Washington, D.C. Police Department in 1915; his influence and leadership, especially in the evolution of the International Association of Chiefs of Police, were significant.

Possessing limited formal education, Vollmer was remarkable, and his work overshadowed Sylvester and emerged to dominate the area of police operations and administration in the early 1900s. Under Vollmer's leadership, advancements occurred in officer recruitment, training, education, and accountability. Vollmer incorporated technology in every aspect of police operations possible including advancements in criminal detection and investigation. He led advancements in officer transportation and communications. He worked to break both racial and gender barriers. In the early 1920s, Vollmer accepted a leave of absence and accepted the position of police chief in Los Angeles. Though his tenure with that department was not long, he did work to introduce into the Los Angeles Department many of the innovations that had proven so successful in Berkeley. Throughout his career, Vollmer served as a consultant, educator, and author. Many of those who contributed significantly to the advancement of the profession in the 1930s–1960s began their careers under the influence of Vollmer on the West Coast.

As Vollmer's influence extended across the nation, by the 1920s, many cities continued to struggle with urban corruption, made even more complex with the dynamics of prohibition. In 1920, the United States adopted prohibition of alcohol as the law of the land. This legislation opened the door to a new wave of criminal activity, fueled by profits unimagined just a few years before. No city was immune. Combined with the economic collapse of the 1930s, the United States experienced criminal activity that overwhelmed the ability of law enforcement to respond.

Some cities, responding to the public dissatisfaction of increasing criminal activity, looked outside the ranks of their department for leadership. For Philadelphia, Smedley Darlington Butler (1881–1940), a 42-year-old United States Marine Corps officer and two-time winner of the Medal of Honor, appeared to be the ideal choice. Butler's reputation proclaimed a high moral character beyond the reproach of graft and corruption, no matter the personal gain. He had commanded the military occupational force placed in Haiti and the United States Mail Guards. His background appeared perfect, his reputation untarnished. In 1924, Butler was asked to accept the position of Director of Public Safety for Philadelphia. Serving in the position for almost two years, Butler sought to sever political influence in the department, advance officers based upon merit, enforce the law equally, and regain the respect of the public. Butler's efforts drew praise from the public but did not retain the support of many of the major business leaders or politicians in the city. As a result, he left the city frustrated, and many of the changes he instituted in the department were soon abandoned.

New York City continually struggled with the issues of political influence and police professionalism. As the largest department in the nation, the scales of its activities were unmatched. The ranks of the New York Police Department have always been filled with dedicated professionals. One of those was Lewis J. Valentine. Valentine joined the New York Police Department in 1903 and rose through the ranks. He was promoted to sergeant in 1913, lieutenant in 1917, and captain in 1926. In 1934, he was named police commissioner, a position he held for 11 years.[17] Upon his retirement, Valentine was credited with providing leadership within the department making it one of the most professional and efficient in the nation.

One of the most significant events to occur during this period pertaining to police labor was the Boston Police Strike. The Boston Police Department was recognized as one of the finest departments in the nation under the leadership of Chief Stephen O'Meara, but working conditions were difficult and pay was viewed as inadequate. O'Meara led the department from 1906 until his death in 1918. Upon O'Meara's death, efforts were made within the department for higher pay, reduced work weeks, and increased benefits. It was very common for police officers across the nation to work long hours with little pay and no benefits.

In 1919, Boston police officers earned $1400 a year and had not received a pay raise in years. The officers worked an average of 87 hours per week under deplorable conditions. Promotions were based solely on political considerations. The officers demanded a raise of $200 a year. The city's police commissioner rejected the officers' demand. Tensions increased and attempts at compromise failed. After a series of events, an estimated 1117 police officers in Boston decided to strike. With only about 400 officers remaining available for duty, the city stood on the edge of disaster. Edwin Curtis, the police commissioner for Boston, decided to crush this labor action by breaking the back of the police labor organization. Curtis refused to address the labor concerns held by the officers, though the mayor later agreed to the officers' demands. Soon it was too late for compromise. The city dismissed all striking officers and replaced them with new personnel. The action in Boston effectively halted any organized labor effort in law enforcement for decades.

The 1920s and 1930s witnessed criminal activity related to prohibition that swept the nation. It was a period of gangsters and "Tommy guns," and a period that made some of the offenders gain an almost folk-hero status. It was a period of growth in organized crime, a wave of violence including bank robbery, drug abuse, kidnapping, and motor vehicle theft. Offenders including John Dillinger, Baby Face Nelson, Ma Barker, Pretty Boy Floyd, Bonnie and Clyde, Machine Gun Kelly, and Al Capone captured headlines and the imagination of the public. Local law enforcement needed assistance.

The 1920s and 1930s were a period in which most states created their state police or highway patrols. Federal enforcement was expanded, new agencies were formed, and many of the existing agencies witnessed an expansion of their enforcement responsibilities. On the federal level, leaders emerged. J. Edgar Hoover (1895–1972) of the FBI, Harry Anslinger (1892–1975) of the Federal Bureau of Narcotics, and Frank J. Wilson (1887–1970) of the United States Secret Service each led their agencies into this period of expanded enforcement. The FBI directed much of its efforts on bank robbery, kidnapping, and motor vehicle theft. The Federal Bureau of Narcotics not only responded to illicit drug production and trafficking, but also made the most significant advancements in combating organized crime. The Secret Service not only worked to protect the President, but also worked to protect the nation's currency. It was Wilson whose work led to the successful prosecution and conviction of Al Capone on charges of income tax violations in 1931.

The most notable and remembered examination of crime and the justice system of this period was the National Commission on Law Observance and Enforcement. Published in January 1931 as a series of 14 volumes compiled after an investigation that lasted almost two years, the Wickersham Commission examined important national justice issues. These issues were police, causes of crime, cost of crime, lawlessness in law enforcement, crime and the foreign born, penal institutions, probation and parole, criminal procedure, the federal court, child offenders and the federal system, deportation laws, prosecution, criminal statistics, prohibition, and the preliminary report of the overall study.

George W. Wickersham, former Attorney General of the United States from 1909 to 1913 during the administration of President Taft, was the chairperson of the study. Wickersham had the opportunity to work with some of the most outstanding professionals of the period. This study was an exposé of conditions of the entire criminal justice system. It addressed national problems and proposed broadly applicable solutions to these problems.

The economic depression of the 1930s led many highly qualified individuals into the law enforcement profession. As World War II ended, millions of Americans left service, thousands of whom were drawn to the law enforcement profession.

Law Enforcement in the Second Half of the Twentieth Century

Law enforcement in the second half of the twentieth century was shaped by countless events: the Red Scare of the McCarthy Era of the 1950s, the Civil Rights Movement, the national unrest resulting from the conflict in Vietnam, the drug revolution, the urban unrest of the 1980s, cyber and financial crimes, and finally the impact of terrorism. As the nation started this period, World War II had recently ended. Veterans filled the ranks of law enforcement agencies that found not only their ranks, but also their duties and responsibilities expanding. Leaders in the profession during this period included J. Edgar Hoover, Orlando Wilson, and William Parker.

The leaders of the profession of this era shaped the discipline. J. Edgar Hoover's control of the FBI was unquestioned. Capturing the imagination of the public, the FBI was world renown. Though the latter period of his directorship of the Bureau is controversial, few can debate the value to local and state enforcement provided by FBI agents assigned to provide training to officers, in the absence of comprehensive law enforcement training academies. Hoover led the Bureau until his death in 1972.

Orlando Winfield Wilson (1900–1972), a protégé of Vollmer, began his distinguished career in Berkeley, California. By the 1950s, he was considered one of the authorities in the field of police administration. Wilson, who led the departments in Fullerton, California; Wichita, Kansas; and Chicago, Illinois also distinguished himself as an author, educator, and, during World War II, a military police officer. Like Vollmer before him, Wilson influenced the careers of countless officers who followed in his steps.

On the West Coast, the Los Angeles Police Department achieved a national reputation for excellence under the guidance of William Henry Parker III (1902–1966). Parker received an appointment to the Los Angeles, California, Police Department in 1927 and served the department for 39 years. In 1950, he was appointed Chief of Police, a position he held until his death in 1966. Under his guidance, the Los Angeles Police Department was recognized as one of the finest in the nation; departments across the country emulated the Los Angeles Police Department.

Throughout the 1950s and the early 1960s, the law enforcement profession was on the edge of a major leap forward. In the 1960s, President Johnson called for an examination of the justice system and from that examination, the submission of recommendations for improvement. The examination, known as the President's Commission on Law Enforcement and the Administration of Justice, determined that the profession needed increased resources, more qualified applicants, and further research to discover more effective approaches to the administration of justice.

Responding to the report, a major effort was mounted to financially stimulate law enforcement. In 1968, Congress passed the Omnibus Crime Control and Safe Streets Act as a result of intensifying public concern about the ability of state and local criminal justice agencies to cope with the soaring crime rates. The Act created the Law Enforcement Assistance Administration (LEAA) as the principal federal agency to deal with the problem of crime at the state and local levels.

The LEAA had a troubled existence. The LEAA intended to function in five ways as follows: (1) to support statewide planning in the field of criminal justice through the creation of statewide planning agencies; (2) to supply the states and localities with block grants of federal funds to improve their criminal justice systems; (3) to make discretionary grants to special programs in the field of criminal justice; (4) to develop new devices, techniques, and approaches in law enforcement through the National Institute of Law Enforcement and Criminal Justice, the organization's research arm; and (5) to supply money for the training and education of criminal justice personnel.[18] Critics accused the administration of waste and mismanagement. But in spite of the waste, law enforcement agencies benefited in countless ways, not the least of which was recruitment of college- and university-educated officers, academically trained in criminal justice programs created with funding provided under LEAA grants. Billions of dollars in funds and resources were injected into the system by the federal government. As a result, by the 1990s, American policing little resembled the law enforcement of the 1960s. The new generation of law enforcement officer was better trained and educated than ever before.

Even before the LEAA, a movement begun on the state level to establish minimum training standards for the officers. Prior to the establishment of minimum standards, many law enforcement officers received little formal training; some received none at all. Early efforts to establish training guidelines occurred in California and New York; police officer standards and training (POST) legislation was enacted in 1959. By 1968, 31 states had enacted similar laws. By 1985, all states had established minimum training hour requirements.

Specialized training and innovation to operations captured the imagination of law enforcement administrators. Investigators and traffic officers had been in action for decades. Another specialization, Special Weapons and Tactics (SWAT), became popular across the nation in the 1960s. In 1964, the Philadelphia Police Department created a SWAT team in response to the growing number of bank robberies throughout the city. About the same time, the police department in Delano, California created a high-risk team in response to the civil unrest lead by the United Farm Workers. However, it was not until 1967 that the Los Angeles Police Department established what is widely recognized as the first all-purpose SWAT team that was armed and trained to respond to any situation beyond the capability of regular patrol units.

Other cities formed SWAT teams through the 1960s and 1970s, generally in response to riots and similar disturbances. Billions of dollars in funds and resources were injected into the system by the federal government. As a result, by the 1990s, American policing little resembled the law enforcement of the 1960s. The new generation of law enforcement officer was better trained and educated than ever before. In 1966, the Los Angeles Sheriff's Department introduced an innovative approach to the service of the country. Under the funding provided by a federal grant, the Los Angeles Sheriff's Department introduced Project Sky Knight, a patrol experiment centered on the use of helicopters, patrolling over the city at an altitude of 500 to 700 feet.

In 1983, the Los Angeles Police Department created the Antiterrorist Division and the Los Angeles Task Force on Terrorism as full-time units for the purpose of combating terrorism. The Task Force on Terrorism was staffed with personnel from the Antiterrorist Division, the Los Angeles Sheriff's Department, and the FBI.

Experimentation in policing styles led to experiments in preventive patrol, directed patrol, aggressive patrol, team policing, and community policing. The Kansas City Preventive Patrol Experiment, which became the most famous study of the use of officers during the period, found that different approaches to patrol appeared to have no effect on the crime rate; in other words, 60% of patrol time was wasted effort. Police Chief Clarence Kelley responded by shifting officers from routine patrol to community-related policing.

Though great advancements were achieved during this period, law enforcement agencies continually found themselves responding to challenges. In the 1960s and 1970s, violence shook many cities as urban unrest exploded into riots as people responded to civil rights and the conflict in Vietnam. In many of these riots, law enforcement resources were overwhelmed and military assistance was called to reestablish order. Additionally, some cities experienced scandals pertaining to corruption or abuse of power in the law enforcement ranks. New Orleans, New York, Miami, Denver, and Los Angeles were just a few of the departments impacted by scandal, but each emerged as a stronger and more professional agency.

The policing of 1950 hardly resembled the policing of 2000. Technology, diversity, science, training, education, and the challenges of global crime redefined law enforcement and public safety. By 2010, new officers were drawn from college and university campuses across the nation. Department leadership was well trained and prepared to lead their agencies. Political interference in the operations of police agencies reached an all-time low.

But all was not perfect in law enforcement. Demands for services strained budgets. Aggressive enforcement and prosecution resulted in an explosion in the inmate population. The demand for drugs fueled global violence, especially in Mexico. The Global War on Terrorism also reduced agency isolationism.

Law Enforcement and the U.S. Military

Although the focus of this chapter has primarily been upon civilian law enforcement, it is important to note that the military also has a need for policing. This need is satisfied through the military police. During modern times, each respective service demonstrates the characteristics of organized policing and law enforcement. Analogous with the societal histories of its civilian counterparts, modern military policing matured from humble beginnings during the American Revolution.

The need for policing and law enforcement within the military has been evident since the founding of the nation. Regardless of the conflict in which the military has been engaged, the need for policing, law enforcement, discipline, and investigation has existed. The concept of American military policing originates with the Marechaussee Corps. This organization was authorized by Congress on May 27, 1778 and was "assigned by General George Washington to perform those necessary police functions required in camp and in the field."[19] The writings of General George Washington demonstrate an example of the uses of the Marechaussee Corps. The comments of General Washington, which were directed to General Howe, are given as follows:

> The scarcity of cavalry has obliged me to divert the Marechaussee Corps of horse from the proper occupation, and put them upon ordinary field duty. Enclosed you have a letter under a flying seal for General Glover, directing him to repair immediately to Springfield, and superintend forwarding the drafts from Massachusetts Bay. Should not General Glover be arrived at West Point, you will be pleased to forward the letter immediately to him. I have written to General Heath, desiring him to order all the officers, who were upon the recruiting service in Massachusetts, to repair to Springfield, and march the drafts from thence. As they arrive they are to be distributed in proportion to the several regiments of the State, so as to keep them as nearly as possible upon a level.[20]

The first organization of American military police consisted of "1 captain, 4 lieutenants, 1 clerk, 1 quartermaster sergeant, 2 trumpeters, 2 sergeants, 5 corporals, 43 provosts, and 4 executioners. Reflecting the unit's special requirements for speed and equipment, the corps was mounted and accoutered as light dragoons."[21] This unit was also organized commensurately with the structuring of a "regular Continental Army company."[22]

General Washington appointed Captain Bartholomew Von Heer as the provost marshal of the Continental Army and the commander of the Marechaussee Corps. Captain Von Heer and his personnel performed the task of patrolling the encampment and "its vicinity in order to detain fugitives and arrest rioters and thieves."[23] During periods of combat, the unit patrolled "behind the Army's so-called second line where it would secure the rear by rounding up stragglers and preventing desertions."[24] It also guarded against rear attacks. The Marechaussee Corps also supplemented logistical function through the supervising of "relations with the sutlers, the merchants who supplied the Army," and it also was responsible for the "collection, security, and movement of prisoners of war."[25] During 1779, another larger military police organization was necessitated to administer the Charlottesville prisoner-of-war compound. This unit was organized by the Commonwealth of Virginia and secured the "British and German soldiers captured at Saratoga."[26] The Marechaussee Corps did not endure the cessation of the American Revolution and was disbanded in 1783.

The personnel who comprised the Marechaussee Corps rendered a variety of services. These soldiers assisted in the maintaining of order and the safeguarding of the rights of soldiers. They provided protection of military supplies among encampments, during periods of combat, and during transit between locations. They also assisted with the capturing of spies and the enforcement of military discipline.[27]

The 1800s manifested a loose approach to military law enforcement until the beginning of the War Between the States. Until the outbreak of this conflict, commanders often appointed and "detailed certain officers and men to perform similar functions" which were indicative of the military police duties.[28] This method of policing endured through the "War of 1812, the Mexican War, and frequent clashes with Indian tribes along the frontier."[29] This period also represented American expansionism with respect to the concept of Manifest Destiny. The basic tenets of Manifest Destiny involved the notion that the American nation would expand westward to the Pacific Ocean. The basic premise of Manifest Destiny demanded "that the United States should own the entire Pacific Northwest all the way to the southern border of Alaska."[30] Such expansionism often involved disputes among settlers and altercations with Indian tribes. The U.S. Military was often relied upon as a provider of law, order, and discipline throughout this period.[31]

The war between the states necessitated the organizing of the military police. Brigadier General Irvin McDowell, a Union field commander, instituted organized policing among the Union force. This structuring of police was comprised of "a commissioned officer as regimental provost marshal along with a permanent guard of ten enlisted men."[32] This instituting of the military police was a measure to diminish instances of both marauding and property destruction and to arrest offenders within the military. Clear distinctions were made between military personnel and civilians. Civilians were not to be arrested by this organization, and it was to not interfere with local law enforcement among civilian towns.

Although this initial attempt to manifest a police organization provided some order and discipline, problems persisted between the ranks of soldiers and the citizenry of Washington, D.C. General McClellan was displeased with the activities of military personnel who were "in the habit of frequenting the streets and hotels of the city."[33] General McClellan tasked Colonel Andrew Porter with keeping military personnel within their camps unless they were provided a "special pass."[34] Colonel Porter oversaw approximately 1,000 personnel and was responsible for the suppression of "gambling, marauding, and looting in the capital area and to intercept stragglers and fugitives from nearby Army units."[35] The formation of such military police units was a pivotal point regarding the philosophies of law enforcement and policing that pervaded the military. It was from these origins that the "gradual extension of the jurisdiction of provost marshals" slowly matured "from responsibility for maintaining law and order within the military to include the protection and, to some extent, the control of the civilian population."[36]

The harshness of war necessitated the act of conscription within the United States. The Office of the Provost Marshal General of the Army was created by the U.S. Congress on March 3, 1863. Congress also appointed Colonel James Fry to this position. Colonel Fry was tasked with "overseeing the administration and enforcement of military recruitment and conscription along with a number of other quasimilitary police duties associated with the war effort."[37] Colonel Fry was also empowered with the ability to essentially arrest anyone who attempted to avoid conscription or impeded any conscription activities.[38] During 1866, with the conclusion of the War Between the States, the Office of Provost Marshal General was dissolved.

The manpower requirements of military policing were vast during the War Between the States. During 1863, the U.S. Congress also created and authorized the Invalid Corps. This organization was comprised of soldiers who were deemed unfit for service among the front lines of battle. Such personnel had been wounded during battle or were "weakened by illness and judged unfit for further frontline service."[39] The duties of this organization included tasks as provost guards, prisoner escorts, and railroad guards.[40] However, during the 1864 raid against Washington, D.C., the Invalid Corps were engaged in combat among rear areas.[41]

It was not until World War I that any significant investment was made in the establishment of a permanent military police organization within the military. After the conclusion of the War Between the States, the Provost Marshal General's Bureau remained static until the "American Expeditionary Forces entered France during World War I in 1917."[42] The increase of American forces necessitated a greater quantity of military police personnel and services. During October 1917 the establishment of the Military Police Corps occurred. This organization performed a variety of policing tasks including security and escort services for prisoners of war, logistics security, and supply operations. Furthermore, a need for investigative services also existed given increases of crime rates.[43]

Crime was not ignored by the higher echelons of the Army. During 1918, General John Pershing authorized the "Provost Marshal General of his American Expeditionary Forces to organize a criminal investigation division within the Military Police Corps for the purpose of detecting and preventing crimes within the territory occupied by the American Expeditionary Forces."[44] This investigation division became the Criminal Investigation Division (CID). The CID was first led by an officer who "served as the CID advisor to the Provost Marshal General on all matters (administrative and technical) pertinent to criminal investigation."[45] The Provost marshals individually retained operational control of the CID. This initial version of the CID manifested "no central control of investigative efforts" and its investigative personnel were impeded because of poor training and inexperience.[46] The CID personnel were chosen from "military police units within each command."[47]

The reporting of crimes occurred through methods that were analogous to those of a civilian police force. Such crimes were committed by "American soldiers or other nationals against the Allies."[48] The personnel of the CID unit performed as detectives when investigating crime or suspected crime.[49] Despite its shortcomings, the CID generated effective outcomes regarding the recoveries of both "government and personal" property.[50] Although the CID demonstrated some amount of effectiveness, it never reached its full potential during World War I. After the end of World War I, the U.S. Army experienced a reduction in size to manifest a peacetime organizational strength. As a result, there was little necessity for the CID unit.

World War I, during its final phases, heralded much discussion regarding the permanency of the military police. On October 15, 1918, the U.S. Congress officially authorized the establishment of the Military Police Corps, but rejected the concept of a permanent organization.[51] Later, during 1920, within the National Defense Act, Congress ratified the "permanent organization of military police units."[52] These legislative acts ensured the survival of military policing after the conclusion of World War I (Figure 2.10).

World War II again necessitated a revival of military policing. The Military Police Service School was created at Arlington Cantonment, Fort Myer, Virginia, on December 19, 1941. Again, a military police organization was instituted to maintain order, "watch over new soldiers entering the military," perform security tasks regarding prisoners of war, perform combat operations, and provide security for logistics and supply operations.[53]

"We were split up two and two and sent around to various villages to do the town constable act.
I cannot recall our coming ever being received with cheers"

Figure 2.10 Depiction of a military police unit arriving in Europe during World War I. (Retrieved from http://www.oldmagazinearticles.com/pdf/WW1_Military-Police.pdf.)

Additional duties involved protecting designated buildings, public works, and localities of special importance from pillage, sabotage, and damage; supervising and controlling the evacuation and repatriation of civilian populations; assisting in the enforcement of gas defense, passive antiaircraft measures, and blackouts; and performing security investigations and other general measures for security and secrecy.[54]

The new structuring of military police included "three new battalions and four separate companies of military police from already existing assets."[55] Any existing unit that had analogous responsibilities and duties was transferred into a new organization. The military police organization grew steadily, and the quantity of military police units had grown to 17 battalions by the middle of 1942.[56] The Corps of Military Police commenced with approximately 2000 personnel and manifested approximately 200,000 personnel before the conclusion of World War II.[57]

The endangerments of subversion and hostile aliens were not ignored during World War II. In addition, the bulk of American aircraft manufacturing was located within California. Around the United States, a variety of ports, factories, rivers, naval yards, and segments of the oil industry were significant resources for the prosecution of war. These resources were susceptible to the threats of saboteurs or direct attacks. An example of such relevancy and endangerment is as follows:[58]

On 23 February 1942, a Japanese submarine shelled the Ellwood oil refinery near Santa Barbara, California. These were the first enemy shells to strike the continental United States since 1814. The second attack came on the night of 21 June 1942 when a submarine surfaced and fired on Fort Stevens along Oregon's Columbia River. The third attack came on 9 September 1942 when a floatplane from a submarine dropped an incendiary bomb on a mountain near Brookings, Oregon. In November 1944, the Japanese began releasing balloons equipped with antipersonnel and incendiary bombs. Although a total of 9000 were sent toward the United States between November 1944 and April 1945, only 285 are known to have landed. Seven people were killed, and a number of balloon-related forest fires started in the Pacific Northwest.[59]

Internal locations of the United States were also attractive targets. Therefore, the continental United States was designated as the Zone of Interior (ZI). The attractiveness of targets is described as follows:[60]

While U-boats were searching for merchant ships in June 1942, a new threat emerged. On 13 June, a German submarine off-loaded four enemy agents on the beach at Amagansett, Long Island, New York. Four days later, four more agents were put ashore on Ponte Vedra Beach near Jacksonville, Florida. The saboteurs were ordered to destroy the dams at Muscle Shoals, Alabama, seriously damage the railways from New York to Chicago to St. Louis, and poison the New York City water supply. While the agents on Long Island were discovered quickly, the ones in Florida evaded discovery for over 24 hours—all eight were eventually captured.[61]

A total of 51 military police battalions were created to service the ZI land mass. They were tasked with roles as "mobile defense forces that would respond to civil disturbances (such as riots and labor strikes) which would hamper the war industry," and were tasked with protecting national infrastructure.[62] Within the ZI, military police units were responsible for protecting the following assets:[63]

- Telegraph and telephone lines
- Wharves and docks
- Important bridges
- Government plants
- Storage depots
- Terminals
- Government agencies
- Transportation facilities
- Trains and railroads
- Prisoners of war
- Manufacturing resources

The termination of World War II witnessed the stationing of American military police units among the conquered territories. These units served to enforce law, maintain order, and prevent the formation of militant and new military groups.[64] During the aftermath of World War II, the quantity of military police personnel was reduced to approximately 20,000 soldiers. Once again, the United States military was downsized to represent the organizational structuring of a peacetime organization. Plans for reorganizing the Army excluded the Military Police Corps.[65]

Two unintended results of World War II impacted American law enforcement. First, the law enforcement profession experienced an influx of war veterans that had served as military police during the war or became interested in law enforcement as a career after their military discharge. Second, many thousands of former service personnel used the GI Bill to attend college after the war and then decided to enter the law enforcement profession upon graduation. This World War II generation laid the foundation for post–World War II law enforcement.

The Korean War again necessitated the services of military police units. In 1950, within the Army Reorganization Act, the U.S. Congress facilitated the revival of the Military Police Corps.[66] The Korean War instigated change within the military police. The economic conditions of Korea facilitated a thriving black market, and the responsibilities of controlling and eradicating these activities were tasked to the military police. Wright indicates that

> the destruction caused by military operations and the usual local shortages of supplies in occupied territories created an extensive demand for items such as cigarettes, gasoline, food, weapons, and vehicles[;] the Department of the Army called on the military police, subject to the Uniform Code of Military justice, to detect and apprehend military personnel and civilians participating in black-marketing.[67]

The military police also rendered valuable services behind the lines of the United Nations. According to Edwards, military police functions included "protecting roads and junctions, installations, equipment, and supplies" as well as preventing crime, absentee apprehension, preventing accidents, and investigation.[68] During the Korean War, military police units were strongly utilized among prisoner-of-war camps. Edwards indicated that captured communist prisoners totaled approximately 150,000 personnel and that prison disturbances among these prisoners were not uncommon.[69] Military police units were used to manage and control these facilities and prisoners. In addition, Edwards indicated that military police units were used to perform "search-and-kill missions against North Korean guerillas."[70]

The Korean War did not technically end; instead, the cessation of hostilities was instigated via the signing of a cease-fire agreement. This agreement remains effective in modern times. After its signing, various military police units have served near the demilitarized zone, between North and South Korea, for over half of a century.

Military police units also provided significant services during the Vietnam War. Westheider indicated that military police units performed the expected acts of policing, maintaining law and order, traffic control, and security.[71] However, given the nature of the war in Vietnam, military police units also performed duties as "tunnel rats and patrolled the jungles and villages near Long Binh and in other areas throughout Vietnam and engaged the enemy in firefights."[72] Wright provided similar observations and indicated that military police units also "secured highways and bridges against both local subversives and North Vietnamese regulars"; "supervised the movement of refugees and the control of political detainees"; and "became frontline fighters during the successful effort to repel the North Vietnamese during the Tet offensive in 1968."[73]

During the period between the Vietnam War and the Gulf War, military police units experienced a variety of endeavors. Such events included the operations in Grenada; providing security for the Olympic Games in Seoul, Korea; serving during the aftermath of Hurricane Hugo; and serving in Panama during the years of 1989 and 1990.[74] Throughout this period and its operations, military police units served to maintain order and prevent crime.

The next significant conflict involving American forces was the Gulf War. Once again, military police units rendered valuable services during this conflict. For the first time, female soldiers were utilized "in harm's way performing a variety of military occupational specialties such as transportation and military police."[75] Before this war, only "female nurses were near the front lines."[76] Once again, military police units performed roles and tasks that were similar to those of their predecessors during America's previous conflicts. Thousands of prisoners were processed by military police units during the Gulf War, and military police units also facilitated combat support operations.[77]

Figure 2.11 U.S. Army Specialist Brandon Mudek waits to be inspected by his squad leader at Camp Echo, Iraq, November 4, 2006, prior to a mission into Diwaniyah, Iraq. Mudek is assigned to 1st Squad, 3rd Platoon, 984th Military Police, Police Transition Team. (U.S. Air Force photo by Technical Sergeant Dawn M. Price. Retrieved from http://www.defense.gov/ HomePagePhotos/LeadPhotoImage.aspx?id=1434)

The events of September 11, 2001 drastically impacted American society and mobilized the nation against a formidable enemy whose characteristics were unlike those of the previous wars. The military police performs a variety of functions during the current conflict. Such functions occur both domestically and overseas. An example of domestic functions includes "defense support to civilian authorities" through the provision of a quick reaction force (QAF) that is capable of responding to emergencies.[78] One example of overseas functions is "the training of fledgling Iraqi Police force."[79]

The history of the military police is both important and fascinating. Its history is one of defending American interests, both domestically and internationally, since the founding of the United States. Military police have guarded against enemy attacks and sabotage, facilitated the transfer and housing of an innumerable quantity of prisoners, provided combat support, and served among a myriad of humanitarian operations. Military police units are now a permanent fixture of the American military and provide essential services and fulfill important roles with respect to the security of the United States, its citizenry, and its interests (Figure 2.11).

Landmark Cases

A series of federal court decisions directly impacted police procedures. The 14th Amendment served as the cornerstone for criminal defendant protections such as the 1961 Mapp case restricting warrantless searches and the 1966 Miranda decision giving suspects the right to remain silent and the right to legal aid. Although these two cases are often considered mainstays of modern policing, an array of other legal decisions have influenced law enforcement activities. Examples of such cases are given as follows:

- In the monumental case of *Miranda v. Arizona*, 384 U.S. 436 (1966), the United States Supreme Court ruled that an individual, while in custody or in some other manner deprived of freedom of action in any way, must, before interrogation, be informed of his or her constitutional rights.[80]
- In 1968, in the case of *Terry v. Ohio*, 392 U.S. 1, the United States Supreme Court held that a "frisk" may be justified when its purpose is to "discover guns, knives, clubs, or other hidden instruments for assault of the police officer," when a reasonably prudent man in the circumstances would be warranted in the belief that his safety or the safety of others is in danger.[81]
- In the 1969 case of *Chimel v. California*, 395 U.S. 752, the United States Supreme Court held that a search incident to a lawful arrest in a home must be limited to the area into which the arrestee might reach to grab a weapon or other evidentiary items.[82]
- The 1985 Supreme Court decision *Tennessee v. Garner*, 471 U.S. 1, helped to establish a national standard that allows police to shoot only when lives are endangered. In determining whether a shooting is justified, many departments consider not only the split second decision to fire but also how the officer got into the situation that left him no choice.[83]

Post-9/11: The Explosion of Homeland Security

In the wake of the attacks upon Oklahoma City, New York, and Washington, D.C. and the impact of hurricanes such as Katrina, the roles of law enforcement and the collective body of first responders were redefined. Although homeland security will be discussed in greater depth later in this text, the formation of the Department of Homeland Security; the continued struggle against drug production; trafficking, and abuse; the Global War on Terrorism; the debate over illegal immigration, collection, processing, and distribution of intelligence; border security issues; and the violence linked to it has led to the realization that the service demands of our nation upon law enforcement had radically redefined themselves. Today, law enforcement is engaged globally with training, conducting investigations, providing security including executive protection, and working in both traditional and nontraditional roles to make Americans safer both at home and abroad.

Homeland security is a paramount concern of the United States. During modern times, it is not uncommon for agencies to perform activities of antiterrorism and counterterrorism. The events of September 11, 2001 thrust the United States into a war against terrorism. This war necessitates the involvement of both civilian and military police forces to facilitate the safety and security of the American populace. During 2007, the U.S. Marine Corps implemented a plan to hire approximately 1200 civilian police officers. This plan provides a policing expansion as a method of reducing the "operational stress on Marine Corps Military Police" and embellishes "security and police services across the Marine Corps."[84] At the end of 2009, approximately 900 police offers were "serving alongside their Marine Military Police counterparts at Marine Corps Installation Provost Marshal Offices across the United States"[85] (Figure 2.12).

With these changes, the opportunities for employment and advancement have never been better. Agencies, both public and private, are constantly in search of quality personnel. One need not have a background in policing, the military, law, or criminal justice to

Figure 2.12 A Marine Corps Police Academy graduating class. (Retrieved from http://www
.usmccle.com/training.htm.)

pursue a career in law enforcement. In fact, many backgrounds are welcomed to provide a
robust array of skill sets and areas of knowledge among law enforcement agencies.

Homeland security requires much collaboration among law enforcement entities. The
sharing of resources, information, and intelligence often occurs among multiple agencies.
Internationally, Interpol may cooperate with American federal agencies to pursue investigations. Local law enforcement agencies may collaborate with other local agencies or may
collaborate with federal or tribal entities. Regardless of the scenario, cooperation is imperative to protect American society.

During 1993, the initial attack against the World Trade Center (WTC) inflicted much
damage on the infrastructure of the facility. The attack was perpetrated through the use of
a rented Ryder truck that contained "approximately 1200 to 1500 pounds of a homemade
fertilizer-based explosive."[86] The resulting explosion destroyed five stories and produced
a crater of approximately 150 feet.[87] More than 1000 individuals were injured during the
explosion and 6 others died as a result of the attack[88] (Figure 2.13).

After the attack, collaboration occurred between the FBI and the New York Joint
Terrorism Task Force. This effort involved approximately 700 personnel.[89] Further analysis
divulged an additional plot to destroy concurrently numerous New York landmarks that
included the "U.N. building, the Holland and Lincoln Tunnels, and the federal plaza."[90]
The investigation yielded the arrests of Islamic terrorists whose intent was to completely
destroy these landmarks and the WTC. Over time, it was determined that the responsible individuals included Ramzi Yousef, Mohammed Salameh, Abdul Yasin, Mahmoud
Abouhalima, Ahmed Ajaj, Nidal Ayyad, and Eyad Ismoil.

The collaboration that occurred led to the swift arresting or detaining of individuals.
It acted as a force multiplier regarding the efforts to investigate the causes of the event and
to determine the responsible individuals. Through collaboration, law enforcement entities increased their ability to improve the efficiency and effectiveness of the investigation.
Further, through such investigation, methods of improving the operational security of the

Figure 2.13 The aftermath of the 1993 terrorist attack against the WTC. (Courtesy of the FBI. Retrieved from http://www.fbi.gov/news/stories/2008/february/tradebom_022608.)

WTC were crafted and improvements in the sharing of resources and information among law enforcement entities occurred.

During modern times, the sharing of law enforcement resources and information is of paramount importance among practitioners of homeland security. Tips may be submitted by both organizations and individuals regarding suspicious activities that they may observe. Through collaboration, a greater scope of investigation may occur that leverages the highest and best use of resources both domestically and internationally.

Summary

Law enforcement in the United States has had a rich history. The profession is a dynamic field that continues to grow and offer challenges and excitement to those who enter its ranks. Many of those who enter the profession in the first decades of the twenty-first century will become the agency leaders of the future. What we know is that society will continue to need the services provided by the profession. Thus, it is up to those who are in the field to strive to provide the most professional, responsive, and cost-effective service possible to the society we are sworn to protect.

American society has changed drastically during the preceding centuries. Accordingly, law enforcement entities have changed with the times and have incorporated modern technologies within the performance of duty. Furthermore, the profession incorporates women and minorities, thereby demonstrating the breaking of traditional barriers. Despite such changes through the centuries, one aspect of law enforcement has remained constant: law enforcement officers are human and have the same strengths and weaknesses that were manifested by their predecessors.

Historically, the primary mission of American law enforcement entities has been to preserve order and to deter crime. Regardless of whether a law enforcement entity is federal, state, local, or tribal, this mission is common. However, given the myriad of law enforcement entities that permeate American societies, the abilities of each individual organization are unique.

Within the United States, law enforcement occurs within both the civilian and military populations. Both forms of law enforcement originated with the founding of the United States. Until World War II, military policing was not a permanent fixture within the American military. After World War II, military police units became permanent assets of the U.S. Military. Military police units have served during every conflict in which the United States was involved since the founding of the country.

Terminology

Arrest
Chimel v. California
Civil law
Constabulary
Criminal law
Detain
Federal law enforcement
Fingerprints
Global War on Terrorism
Intelligence
Local law enforcement
Marine Corps Police Academy
Marechaussee Corps
Military police
Miranda v. Arizona
Rural policing
State law enforcement
Technology
Tennessee v. Garner
Terrorism
Terry v. Ohio
Thin blue line
Tribal law enforcement
Urban policing
Wickersham Commission
Zone of Interior

Discussion Questions

1. This chapter highlighted the salient points of American policing history. Through the history of American policing, technology has changed drastically, whereas the human aspect of policing is unchanged. Based on the technological advancements that have occurred within the last two centuries, please substantively discuss your opinions regarding which three advancements are the most influential regarding modern policing.

2. This chapter focused on the origins of both military law enforcement and its civilian counterparts. Based on the notions of military versus civilian policing,

substantively discuss the similarities and differences that exist between the two paradigms. Given the basis of your opinion, further discuss substantively whether you believe the relationship between these two paradigms is unchanging, diverging, or converging.

3. An Internet search of the phrase "emerging technologies" yields numerous results representing a myriad of domains and applications. Conduct an Internet search using the phrase "emerging technologies," and select the three technologies that you believe are promising resources for future law enforcement practices. Substantively discuss why you believe these technologies are appropriate for use among law enforcement entities.

4. This chapter indicated that American law enforcement has a British heritage. Over the last two centuries, both Britain and America have matured nationally and their respective law enforcement organizations have changed accordingly through time. Substantively compare and contrast the modern differences and commonalities that exist between American and British law enforcement entities. Based on the arguments contained within your discussion, substantively discuss whether you believe both nations share commonalities and dissimilarities among their modern law enforcement practices.

5. Historically, the United States has expressed both tenets of criminal law and civil law. There is a difference between civil law and criminal law. Provide a definition of both concepts and discuss examples of each concept. Based on the differences between these types of law, substantively discuss how law enforcement activities are affected by both categories.

References

1. Peel, R. Police quotes. *BrainyQuote*. Retrieved from http://www.brainyquote.com/quotes/keywords/police_9.html
2. Johnson, D. (1981). *American Law Enforcement: A History*. Saint Louis, MO: Forum Press.
3. Bloy, M. (2002). Sir Robert Peel (1788–1859). *The Victorian Web*. Retrieved from http://www.victorianweb.org/history/pms/peel/peel10.html
4. Bopp, W. J., & Schultz, D. O. (1971). *A Short History of American Law Enforcement*. Springfield, IL: Charles C. Thomas Publisher.
5. Savage, E. H. (1873). *Boston by Daylight and Gaslight*. Boston, MA: John P. Dale & Company.
6. Bopp, W. J., & Schultz, D. O. (1971). *A Short History of American Law Enforcement*. Springfield, IL: Charles C. Thomas Publisher, and Johnson, D. (1981). *American Law Enforcement: A History*. Saint Louis, MO: Forum Press.
7. Sante, L. (2003). *Low Life: Lures and Snares of Old New York* (p. 237). New York, NY: Farrar, Straus, and Giroux.
8. Dempsey, J. S., & Forst, L. S. (2011). *An Introduction to Policing*. Mason, OH: Cengage Learning.
9. Smith, B. (1940). *Police Systems in the United States*. Franklin Square, NY: Harper and Brothers.
10. Sutherland, E. H., & Cressey, D. R. (1970). *Criminology*. Philadelphia, PA: Lippincott.
11. Johnson, D. (1981). *American Law Enforcement: A History*. Saint Louis, MO: Forum Press.
12. Wilson, M. R. (2005). *Pinkerton National Detective Agency*. The Electronic Encyclopedia of Chicago. Retrieved from http://encyclopedia.chicagohistory.org/pages/2813.html
13. Carson, C. (2009). *The History of Private Security*. Retrieved from http://www.ehow.com/about_5418822_history-private-security.html
14. Sutherland, E. (1924). *Principles of Criminology*. Chicago, IL: University of Chicago Press.
15. Feinman, C. (1980). *Women in the Criminal Justice System*. New York, NY: Praeger Publishing.

16. Marnell, H. (2010). *An Unofficial History of the Los Angeles Police Department's Communications Division.* Retrieved from http://harrymarnell.net/kma367.htm

17. Fogelson, R. (1977). *Big City Police* (p. 143). Cambridge, MA: Harvard University Press.

18. U.S. National Archives and Records Administration (1995). *423.1 Administrative History. Records of the Law Enforcement Assistance Administration [LEAA].* Retrieved from http://www.archives.gov/research/guide-fed-records/groups/423.html#423.1

19. Wright, R. (1992). *Army Lineage Series: Military Police. Center of Military History—United States Army.* Washington, DC. Retrieved from http://www.history.army.mil/books/lineage/mp/mp.htm

20. Ibid, p. 5.

21. Ibid, p. 1.

22. Ibid.

23. Ibid.

24. Ibid.

25. Ibid.

26. Ibid.

27. Military Police (2011). Military police corps. *GlobalSecurity.Org.* Retrieved from http://www.globalsecurity.org/military/agency/army/mp.htm

28. Ibid.

29. Wright, R. (1992). *Army Lineage Series: Military Police. Center of Military History—United States Army* (p. 5). Washington, DC. Retrieved from http://www.history.army.mil/books/lineage/mp/mp.htm

30. University of Houston, TX (2011). *Manifest Destiny. Digital History: Using New Technologies to Enhance Teaching and Research.* Retrieved from http://www.digitalhistory.uh.edu/database/article_display .cfm?HHID311

31. Wright, R. (1992). *Army Lineage Series: Military Police. Center of Military History—United States Army.* Washington, DC. Retrieved from http://www.history.army.mil/books/lineage/mp/mp.htm

32. Ibid, p. 5.

33. Ibid.

34. Ibid.

35. Ibid.

36. Ibid.

37. Ibid, p. 6.

38. Ibid.

39. Ibid, p. 5.

40. Ibid.

41. Ibid.

42. History. *U.S. Army Criminal Investigation Command.* Retrieved from http://www.cid.army.mil/history.html

43. Ibid.

44. Ibid.

45. Ibid.

46. Ibid.

47. Ibid.

48. Ibid.

49. Ibid.

50. Ibid.

51. Wright, R. (1992). *Army Lineage Series: Military Police. Center of Military History—United States Army.* Washington, DC. Retrieved from http://www.history.army.mil/books/lineage/mp/mp.htm

52. Ibid, p. 9.

53. Green, M. (2000). *Military Police.* Mankato, MN: Capstone Press.

54. Wright, R. (1992). *Army Lineage Series: Military Police. Center of Military History—United States Army*, p. 10. Washington, DC. Retrieved from http://www.history.army.mil/books/lineage/mp/mp.htm

55. Ibid.

56. Ibid.

57. Green, M. (2000). *Military Police*. Mankato, MN: Capstone Press.

58. Craig, R. (2010). Army MP and Homeland Defense in World War II. CBS Interactive Business Network. Retrieved from http://findarticles.com/p/articles/mi_m0IBW/is_2002_March/ai_86128061/

59. Ibid.

60. Ibid.

61. Ibid.

62. Ibid.

63. Ibid.

64. Green, M. (2000). *Military Police*. Mankato, MN: Capstone Press.

65. Craig, R. (2010). Military Police Units in the Korean War. CBS Interactive Business Network. Retrieved from http://findarticles.com/p/articles/mi_m0IBW/is_2_19/ai_70378764/

66. Ibid.

67. Wright, R. (1992). *Army Lineage Series: Military Police. Center of Military History—United States Army*, p. 11. Washington, DC. Retrieved from http://www.history.army.mil/books/lineage/mp/mp.htm

68. Edwards, P. (2006). *The Korean War: Daily Life Through History*, p. 116. Westport, CT: Greenwood Press.

69. Ibid.

70. Ibid.

71. Westheider, J. (2007). *The Vietnam War*. Westport, CT: Greenwood Press.

72. Ibid, p. 78.

73. Wright, R. (1992). *Army Lineage Series: Military Police. Center of Military History—United States Army*, p. 12. Washington, DC. Retrieved from http://www.history.army.mil/books/lineage/mp/mp.htm

74. Military Police (1992). *Military Police*. Washington, DC: U.S. Government Printing Office.

75. Kentucky National Guard (2011). *Kentucky National Guard in the Persian Gulf War 20th Anniversary History Now Available for Viewing*. Retrieved from http://kentuckyguard.wordpress.com/2011/04/08/kentucky-national-guard-in-the-persian-gulf-war-20th-anniversary-history-now-available-for-viewing/

76. Ibid.

77. Ibid.

78. 49th Military Police Brigade (2011). *49th Military Police Brigade*. California National Guard. Retrieved from http://www.calguard.ca.gov/49mp/Pages/default.aspx

79. Ibid.

80. Waldron, R., Quarles, C. L., McElreath, D. H., Waldron, M., & Milstein, D. (2009). *The Criminal Justice System*. Tulsa, OK: K&M Publishers.

81. Germann, A. C. (1973). *Introduction to Law Enforcement and Criminal Justice*, p. 129. Springfield, IL: Charles C. Thomas Publisher.

82. Ibid.

83. Gaines, L., & Kappeler, V. (2011). *Policing in America* (7th ed.). Waltham, MA: Anderson Publishing.

84. MCCP (2011). *Marine Corps Civilian Police. U.S. Marine Corps*. Retrieved from http://www.usmccle.com/civLawHome.htm

85. Ibid.

86. Turner, M.T. (2003). *World Trade Center 1993*. The Turner Network. Retrieved from http://turnernetwork.com/online/documents/wtc1993.shtml

87. Ibid.
88. Ibid.
89. FBI (2008). *FBI 100*. Federal Bureau of Investigation. Retrieved from http://www.fbi.gov/news/stories/2008/february/tradebom_022608
90. Ibid.

Bibliography

Beirne, P. (1987). Adolphe Quetelet and the origins of positivist criminology. *American Journal of Sociology*, *92*(5), 1140–1169.

Bloy, M. (2002). Sir Robert Peel (1788–1859). *The Victorian Web*. Retrieved from http://www.victorianweb.org/history/pms/peel/peel10.html

Castillo, F. (2007). Criminal forensics - MO vs signature - how to tell the difference between a crook's various actions. Retrieved from http://ezinearticles.com/?Criminal-Forensics---MO-vs-Signature---How-to-Tell-the-Difference-Between-a-Crooks-Various-Actions&id=652849

Craig, R. (2010). Army MP and homeland defense in World War II. *CBS Interactive Business Network*. Retrieved from http://findarticles.com/p/articles/mi_m0IBW/is_2002_March/ai_86128061/

Inciardi, J. (1984). *Introduction to Criminal Justice*. Orlando, FL: Academic Press.

Kakalik, J. S., & Wildhorn, S. (1971). *Private Police in the United States: Findings and Recommendations*. Santa Monica: The Rand Institute.

Kennedy, A. (n.d.). Police quotes. *BrainyQuotes.com*. Retrieved from http://www.brainyquote.com/quotes/keywords/police.html

Sparks, J. (1835). *The Writings of George Washington Being His Correspondence, Addresses, Messages, and Other Papers, Official and Private, Selected and Published from the Original Manuscripts; With a Life of the Author, Notes, and Illustrations*. (Vol. 3). Boston Russell, Odiorne, and Metcalf, and Hilliard, Gray.

Vollmer, A. (1919, August). Revision of the Atcherley modus operandi system. *Journal of the American Institute of Criminal Law and Criminology*, *10*(2), 229–274.

World. (2003). World Trade Center 1993. *The Turner Network*. Retrieved from http://turnernetwork.com/online/documents/wtc1993.shtml

Local and Tribal Enforcement in the United States

3

> The world is a dangerous place, not because of those that do evil, but because of those who look on and do nothing.
>
> **Albert Einstein**

Learning Objectives

The objectives of this chapter are to

- Examine the local and tribal law enforcement systems within the United States
- Discuss the demographics of local police agencies
- Explain the demographics of local sheriff's departments
- Identify the attributes of tribal agencies
- Recognize the contributions of local law enforcement agencies to society

Introduction

Law enforcement in the United States is highly effective, and it is well respected internationally. However, the composition of law enforcement in the United States is among the most complex in the world. The early modern police departments in the United States were modeled after their predecessors in England. United States law enforcement agencies adopted the mission of crime prevention and control, the idea of preventive patrol, and the quasimilitary organizational structure, which had been the model in early London. Other important concepts borrowed from England were the ideas of local control of police agencies and limits on authority given to governments and police.[1]

Unlike many other Western nations, the United States does not have a national police agency. In the United States, law enforcement is fundamentally controlled by the executive branch of the government at the following four judicial levels: municipal, county, state, and federal. Although the majority of United States law enforcement agencies are found at the municipal level, each jurisdiction has a variety of law enforcement agencies responsible for enforcing its laws. Because of the issue of local governmental control of police agencies, there is little uniformity among the nearly 18,000 federal, state, and local law enforcement jurisdictions regarding names, organizational structure, function, and authority, particularly at the city and county levels. In addition, local control contributes to the widespread disparity in United States law enforcement in terms of quality of services, professional standards, and budget expenditures.

One product of the fragmented nature of United States policing is variety: Agency responsibilities and roles can be very different at each level. In addition, within each category, there is much variation.[2] For example, enforcing the law and keeping the peace in a small suburban city may be the primary responsibility of a municipal law enforcement agency, however, a county sheriff's department may also be active in that community. In addition, there are numerous other state police and federal law enforcement agencies whose jurisdiction and authority may be involved. Furthermore, all branches of the American military involve some facet of law enforcement.

In fact, most communities in the United States have several levels of police authority. Their jurisdictions and responsibilities often overlap, and virtually no two police agencies are structured alike or function in exactly the same way. The result is a very complex system of law enforcement. Regardless of the type of law enforcement agency or its organizational role, the primary goals and objectives of all law enforcement entities are to maintain order and to prevent crime. Historically, such notions have pervaded law enforcement organizations, roles, and responsibilities. This notion remains applicable during modern times. Chapters 3, 4, and 5 will distinguish the various levels of law enforcement authority and provide general details about major agencies and their duties and responsibilities.

Demographics of Local (and State) Law Enforcement

The Bureau of Justice Statistics (BJS), Office of Justice Programs (OJP), within the United States Department of Justice (DOJ) periodically publishes a local police census report every four years. This report, Census of State and Local Law Enforcement Agencies (CSLLEA), contains the most highly reliable data on state and local personnel available in the United States.

The 2008 CSLLEA was published in July 2011. The 2012 CSLLEA occurred during the time of this authorship, however, its results will not be published until sometime in 2013 or later. Therefore, the most recent data sets available are from the period between 2004 and 2008. The 2008 version of the CSLLEA exhibited the following characteristics:[3]

- 12,501 local police departments
- 3063 sheriffs' offices
- 50 primary state law enforcement agencies
- 1733 special jurisdiction agencies
- 638 other agencies, primarily county constable offices in Texas

Based on the 2008 census, the following changes were noted regarding the state and local agencies:[4]

- State and local law enforcement agencies employed about 1,133,000 persons on a full-time basis in 2008, including 765,000 sworn personnel.
- Local police departments were the largest employer of sworn personnel, accounting for 60% of the total. Sheriffs' offices were next, accounting for 24%.
- About half (49%) of all agencies employed fewer than 10 full-time officers. Nearly two-thirds (64%) of sworn personnel worked for agencies that employed 100 or more officers.

- State and local law enforcement agencies employed more than 1.1 million persons on a full-time basis, including about 765,000 sworn personnel (defined as those with general arrest powers).
- Agencies also employed approximately 100,000 part-time employees, including 44,000 sworn officers.

The 2008 census showed that there were 373 full-time state and local law enforcement employees per 100,000 residents nationwide, compared to 367 per 100,000 in 2004. The 2008 values equate to approximately one sworn officer to represent approximately every 400 residents nationally.[5] Such quantities are shown in Figure 3.1.

The 2008 census also considers changes that occurred during its examined period between 2004 and 2008. The census observations regarding state and local law enforcement agencies are as follows:[6]

- From 2004 to 2008, state and local agencies added a net total of about 33,000 full-time sworn personnel.
- From 2004 to 2008, overall full-time employment by state and local law enforcement agencies nationwide increased by about 57,000 (5.3%). Sworn personnel increased by about 33,000 (4.6%) and nonsworn employees by about 24,000 (6.9%).
- From 2004 to 2008, state and local law enforcement agencies added about 9500 more full-time sworn personnel than during the previous four-year period.
- The number of full-time sworn personnel per 100,000 residents increased from 250 in 2004 to 251 in 2008.
- Fifteen of the 50 largest local police departments employed fewer full-time sworn personnel in 2008 than in 2004. The largest declines were in Detroit (36%), Memphis (23%), New Orleans (13%), and San Francisco (10%).

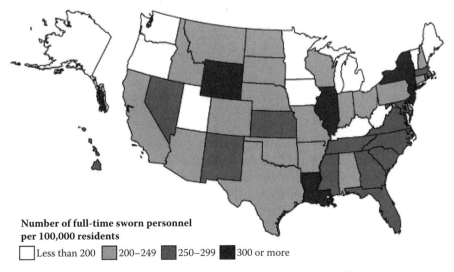

Figure 3.1 Ratio of law enforcement personnel to residents nationally in 2008. (From Reaves, B. A., U.S. Bureau of Justice Statistics, 2008, *Census of State and Local Law Enforcement Agencies*. Retrieved from http://bjs.ojp.usdoj.gov/content/pub/pdf/csllea08.pdf.)

- Ten of the 50 largest local police departments reported double-digit increases in sworn personnel from 2004 to 2008. The largest increases were in Phoenix (19%), Prince George's County, Maryland (17%), Dallas (15%), and Fort Worth (14%).
- Local police departments added the most officers, about 14,000. Sheriffs' offices and special jurisdiction agencies added about 8000 officers each.

A review of the 2008 data shows that local police departments were the largest employers of full-time state and local law enforcement personnel with approximately 593,000 (or 52%) of the more than 1.1 million employees nationally.[7] Sheriffs' offices represented employment of approximately 353,000 (31%).[18] Special jurisdiction agencies (those that served a special geographic jurisdiction or had special enforcement or investigative responsibilities) and the 50 primary state law enforcement agencies each make up approximately 8% of the total.[9]

Approximately 461,000 sworn state and local law enforcement employees (60%) were local police officers, whereas sworn sheriff's personnel accounted for about 183,000 (24%).[10] The special jurisdiction agencies employed about 57,000 (7%), and the 50 primary state law enforcement agencies employed roughly 61,000 (8%).[11] Local police departments accounted for 36% of the 369,000 full-time civilian personnel nationwide, and sheriffs' offices accounted for 46%.[12] With regard to civilians, almost half (48%) of the full-time employees in sheriffs' offices were civilians as compared to 35% in state law enforcement agencies and 22% in local police departments.[13]

Tables 3.1 and 3.2 show the observations of the 2008 study regarding the demographics of state and local law enforcement organizations nationally.

Furthermore, approximately 1200 state and local law enforcement agencies (7%) employed 100 or more full-time sworn personnel and 83 of those agencies employed 1000 or more officers.[14] The agencies with 1000 or more officers included a total of 49 local police departments, 20 state law enforcement agencies, 13 sheriffs' offices, and 1 special jurisdiction agency.[15] The agencies with 100 or more officers employed 64% of all full-time sworn personnel, and those with 1000 or more officers employed 29%.[16]

Agencies with less than 10 full-time sworn personnel employed less than 5% of all full-time officers, but also employed 50% of all part-time law enforcement officers.[17] Approximately 8800 state and local law enforcement organizations (49% of the total)

Table 3.1   State and Local Law Enforcement Employees Demographics, by Type of Agency, 2008

Type of Agency	Agencies	Full-Time Employees			Part-Time Employees		
		Total	Sworn	Nonsworn	Total	Sworn	Nonsworn
All agencies	17,985	1,133,915	765,246	368,669	100,340	44,062	56,278
Local police	12,501	593,013	461,063	131,950	58,129	27,810	30,319
Sheriff's office	3063	353,461	182,979	170,482	26,052	11,334	14,718
Primary state	50	93,148	60,772	32,376	947	54	893
Special jurisdiction	1733	90,262	56,968	33,294	14,681	4451	10,230
Constable/marshal	638	4031	3464	567	531	413	118

Source: Reaves, B. A., U.S. Bureau of Justice Statistics, 2008, *Census of State and Local Law Enforcement Agencies.* Retrieved from http://bjs.ojp.usdoj.gov/content/pub/pdf/csllea08.pdf.
Note: Excludes agencies employing less than one full-time officer or the equivalent in part-time officers.

Table 3.2 Full-time Personnel Demographics, 2008

Size of Agency*	Agencies	Full-Time Employees		
		Total	Sworn	Nonsworn
All agencies	17,985	1,133,915	765,246	368,669
1,000 or more officers	83	326,197	230,759	95,438
500–999	89	94,168	60,124	34,044
250–499	237	133,024	83,851	49,173
100–249	778	174,505	115,535	58,970
50–99	1300	136,390	89,999	46,391
25–49	2402	124,492	83,349	41,143
10–24	4300	98,563	67,132	31,431
5–9	3446	32,493	23,107	9386
2–4	3225	11,498	9470	2028
0–1	2125	2585	1920	665

Source: Reaves, B. A., U.S. Bureau of Justice Statistics, 2008, *Census of State and Local Law Enforcement Agencies*. Retrieved from http://bjs.ojp.usdoj.gov/content/pub/pdf/csllea08.pdf.

Note: Excludes agencies employing less than one full-time officer or the equivalent in part-time officers.

* Based on number of full-time sworn personnel.

employed fewer than 10 full-time sworn personnel, whereas approximately 5400 (30%) employed less than 5 officers.[18] Among the small organizations, approximately 2100 (12%) had just one full-time officer or had part-time officers.[19] Organizations that employed at least 1000 full-time sworn personnel represented less than 1% of all part-time officers nationally.[20]

Municipal

Approximately 52% of all peace officers in America are employed at the municipal level.[21] Municipal officers accomplish most law enforcement because more crime is committed in the population-dense areas of metropolitan regions, cities, and towns. The municipal police department is the most common peacekeeping unit in the United States. Although state laws regulate all institutions, there is still a large commitment to the concept of *home rule*, an age-old penchant toward local autonomy. Chiefs of police are still elected in some jurisdictions, but the majority of chiefs are appointed by a mayor, board of aldermen, or the city council. The chief's relationship with his or her political boss will then set the tone for the type of law enforcement commitment of the municipality.

There are more municipal police agencies in the United States than any other type of police agency. In fact, municipal police departments are the backbone of United States policing. The 12,766 municipal police departments (including tribal police) range widely in size, but most are relatively small agencies. However, the majority of local officers work for larger agencies. Departments with fewer than 10 full-time officers make up 55% of all agencies, but employ just 6% of all officers. About 600 (4.7%) local police agencies employ 100 or more full-time sworn officers. About 60% of all local police officers are employed by these agencies.[22]

The largest local police departments in the United States are the New York Police Department (36,023 officers), the Chicago Police Department (13,354 officers), the Los

Angeles Police Department (9727 officers), the Philadelphia Police Department (6624 officers), and the Houston Police Department (5053 officers). The larger police departments generally do not hire part-time sworn officers.[23]

Historically, the basic goals of local law enforcement have included enforcing laws, peacekeeping, crime prevention, providing services, and protecting civil rights and civil liberties.[24] Uniform officers, who are considered the backbone of policing in the United States, carry out the majority of these activities. In terms of day-to-day activities, research indicates uniform police officers spend about as much time on non-police-related activities as they do on police-related mobile patrol.[25] Basic training for municipal police departments usually consists of attending a municipal or possibly a state police-training academy, which typically has an extensive basic law enforcement training curriculum. These curriculums often differ in format, training requirements, and length of time that is necessary to satisfy specific organizational and legal mandates regarding officer training.

County

An elected sheriff heads most county law enforcement agencies. The sheriff is a unique figure in United States law enforcement in terms of status and role. Sheriffs exercise significant political control and influence and are directly involved in partisan politics. Aside from the political anomaly, the sheriffs' offices are very similar to many municipal police departments. However, they are organized at the county level and usually exercise their functions within unincorporated areas. In addition, sheriffs' offices often have other duties besides law enforcement, such as operating a county jail, collecting taxes, serving process, and providing court security.

In 2008, a total of 3063 sheriffs' offices employed at least one full-time sworn officer or the equivalent in part-time officers.[26] When compared with the 2004 values, the reduced quantity of reported 2008 offices occurred because of consolidation among various law enforcement agencies.[27] States that exhibited the highest quantities of sheriffs' offices are as follows:[28]

Texas (254)
Georgia (159)
Kentucky (120)
Missouri (114)
Kansas (104)
Illinois (102)
North Carolina (100)

The 2008 census shows various demographic changes that occurred between 2004 and 2008. Between 2004 and 2008, total full-time personnel among sheriffs' offices increased by 27,000 employees (8.2%) to approximately 353,000.[29] The quantity of full-time sworn personnel increased by 8000 (4.5%) to about 183,000 during this period.[30] The quantity of civilian employees increased by 19,000 (12.5%) to approximately 170,000.[31]

The 2008 census showed that roughly all (96%) sheriffs' offices performed traditional law enforcement functions such as providing patrol services, responding to citizen calls for service, and traffic law enforcement.[32] A similar percentage performed court-related duties such as serving process (98%) and providing court security (96%).[33] In addition, approximately 75% of sheriffs' offices were responsible for operating at least one jail.[34] Nationally, sheriffs' offices had the equivalent of 59% of their full-time sworn personnel assigned to law enforcement operations, 23% to jail operations, 12% to court operations, and 6% to other responsibilities.[35]

Also, the findings of the 2008 census indicated that a total of 13 sheriffs' offices employed 1000 or more full-time sworn officers, accounting for 18% of the full-time sworn personnel employed by sheriffs' offices nationally.[36] It also showed that a total of 378 (12%) sheriffs' offices employed at least 100 officers, accounting for 66% of sworn personnel.[37] The Los Angeles County Sheriff's Department, California, represented the largest department in the United States and employed 9461 full-time sworn personnel.[38] The Cook County Sheriff's Department, Illinois, represented the second largest department and employed 5655 sworn personnel.[39]

Table 3.3 shows the 2008 demographics of sheriff's departments nationally.

Almost 30.3% of all peace officers in America are employed at the county level,[40] either in a county police department or as deputy sheriffs. Although the early American sheriff did not patrol his jurisdiction in the traditional sense, he nonetheless had arrest authority over those who transgressed. His was a reactive role, responding to citizen complaints and investigating crimes that had already occurred. For many decades, sheriffs were not salaried, rather, they received fees for the number of summons they served.

In many states, sheriffs were also tax collectors and received approximately 10% of the gross county tax revenue as salary and expense account. In a wealthy county or a large county, this was a lucrative public office and many sheriffs' were the political kingpins or "Boss Hogs" of their county. Although many modern sheriffs' departments now provide full-range patrol and crime-prevention services, many rural departments are still essentially process servers, jailers, and bailiffs. Today, however, 97% of all sheriffs' offices claim to provide some form of "preventative patrol operations and reactive investigation services,"[41] in addition to their traditional roles of judicial, correctional, and court-related responsibilities.

Table 3.3   National 2008 Sheriff's Office Demographics

Size of Agency*	Agencies	Full–Time Employees		
		Total	Sworn	Nonsworn
All agencies	3063	353,461	182,979	170,482
1,000 or more officers	13	59,981	32,897	27,084
500–999	27	34,348	17,184	17,164
250–499	98	64,704	34,743	29,961
100–249	240	68,265	36,085	32,180
50–99	327	44,772	23,037	21,735
25–49	573	40,988	20,084	20,904
10–24	910	30,121	14,196	15,925
5–9	569	8485	3901	4584
2–4	261	1615	822	793
0–1	45	182	30	152

Source: Reaves, B. A., U.S. Bureau of Justice Statistics, 2008, *Census of State and Local Law Enforcement Agencies.* Retrieved from http://bjs.ojp .usdoj .gov/content/pub/pdf/csllea08.pdf.

Note: Excludes agencies employing less than one or the full-time officer or the equivalent in part-time officers.

* Based on number of full-time sworn personnel.

The states of Alaska, Connecticut, Hawaii, and Rhode Island do not possess any local sheriffs' departments.[42] Instead, among these states, the court-related duties typically performed by the local sheriffs' offices are performed by state agencies.[43] The District of Columbia also does not have a sheriff's department, but the duties traditionally performed by such a department are performed by the U.S. Marshals Service.[44]

Tribal

More than 200 police departments operate in Native American tribal lands, serving an even larger number of tribal communities. These departments range in size from only 2 or 3 officers to more than 200 officers. The communities they serve are as small as the Grand Canyon-based Havasupai Tribe (with a population of only 600) and as large as the Navajo Nation (with a population of more than 250,000 and a land area larger than the State of Connecticut).[45]

It is somewhat unclear if the tribal police community should be considered state, county, or local police. Tribal police agencies are actually a federal entity within the U.S. Department of Interior, Bureau of Indian Affairs (BIA).

The United States has "a unique legal and political relationship with the American Indian tribes and Alaska Natives entities as provided by the Constitution of the United States, treaties, court decisions, and federal statutes."[46] Law enforcement authority in Indian country, which encompasses more than 46 million acres of tribally owned land; 10 million acres of individually owned land; and 440,000 acres of federally owned land, is widely dispersed among 564 recognized tribes in 31 states. Jurisdiction over offenses occurring on tribal land may lie with federal, state, or tribal agencies depending upon the particular offense, the offender, the victim, and the offender location.[47]

The federal government through the BIA's Office of Law Enforcement Services and Federal Bureau of Investigation (FBI) investigate crimes and directly enforce the law on tribal land. In addition, the Indian Self-Determination and Education Assistance Act of 1975 affords tribes, through federal grants and contracts, the opportunity to provide for their own police departments. The various tribal councils appoint tribal police. Among the tribes' inherent law enforcement powers is the authority to exercise criminal jurisdiction over all tribal members and the authority to arrest and detain non-Indians for delivery to state or federal authorities for prosecution. Tribal police have general arrest authority, but their powers are typically limited to the reservations. However, almost all (99%) of the tribal police officers have cross-deputy agreements with another tribal or public agency, thereby creating reciprocity with local and state authorities for crimes committed on and off tribal land.[48]

The BIA's Office of Law Enforcement Services works cooperatively with tribal authorities at the Indian reservations to enforce law on the reservations. Where reservations do not have tribal police, the BIA has complete charge of law enforcement services. Where there is a combination of BIA-employed police and tribal police, the BIA-employed police have general supervision of the tribal police and are responsible for the training and direction.[49]

The BIA's headquarters offices are located in Washington, D.C., and Albuquerque, New Mexico. There are also 12 area offices and 83 agency offices located throughout the United States.[50] In 2004, tribal police employed 2490 sworn officers.[51]

The most common administrative arrangement for police departments in Indian country is organization under the auspices of the Indian Self-Determination and Education Assistance Act of 1975. Also known as Public Law 93–638 (PL 93–638), this law gives tribes the opportunity to establish their own government functions by contracting with the BIA.[52]

Special Jurisdiction Agencies

In general, the special jurisdiction agencies perform functions similar to municipal police. However, special jurisdiction agencies serve special geographic jurisdictions or have special enforcement or investigative responsibilities. In addition, sworn special jurisdiction police may conduct criminal records checks, reference checks, background investigations, and driving record checks of applicants for sworn positions.

In 2008, more than 1700 state and local law enforcement agencies served a special geographic jurisdiction or had special enforcement or investigative responsibilities.[53] These agencies employed approximately 90,000 personnel full time that included 57,000 sworn personnel.[54] More than two-thirds of special jurisdiction law enforcement agencies served public buildings and facilities and employed more than 21,000 sworn personnel.[55] Similar to the 2004 census, these entities represented an array of sectors ranging from transportation to academia. Table 3.4 shows the basic demographic characteristics of the 2008 census regarding personnel quantities of the special jurisdiction segment.

Campus law enforcement organizations, representing universities and colleges, were also considered within the special jurisdiction segment of the 2008 census. The 2008 census showed that over 500 campus police departments served four-year public institutions and employed approximately 11,000 sworn personnel.[56] Another 253 campus departments served two-year public colleges and employed more than 2600 full-time sworn personnel.[57] In addition, a total of 18 agencies served medical campuses and employed more than 700 full-time personnel.[58]

Within the natural resources segment, a total of 246 agencies employed approximately 15,000 full-time sworn personnel.[59] Some of the largest natural resources law enforcement organizations were operated by state agencies and departments. Based on the 2008 census, examples included the following entities:

- California Department of Parks and Recreation (645 personnel)
- Florida Fish and Wildlife Conservation Commission (626 personnel)
- Texas Parks and Wildlife Department (480 personnel)
- Ohio Department of Natural Resources (394 personnel)
- California Department of Fish and Game (330 personnel)

State-level resources were also considered regarding natural resources enforcement. The New York City Department of Environmental Protection, which employed 168 full-time police officers to protect the city's watershed and water infrastructure, represented the largest local-level agency within this category.[60]

The transportation sector was included within the 2008 demographics. During 2008, 167 law enforcement agencies were tasked with specific transportation-related jurisdictions, and they employed approximately 11,500 full-time personnel.[61] The largest organization was the Port Authority of New York and New Jersey Police Department, employing 1667 officers.[62] Other characteristics of the transportation category included the following observations regarding personnel quantities:[63]

- New York State Metropolitan Transportation Authority (694 personnel)
- Los Angeles World Airports (577 personnel)
- Maryland Transportation Authority (456 personnel)

Table 3.4   Special Jurisdiction Law Enforcement Agencies and Full-Time Sworn Personnel, by Type of Jurisdiction, 2008

Type of Special Jurisdiction	Agencies	Full-Time Sworn Personnel
Total	1733	56,968
Public buildings/facilities	1126	21,418
4-year university/college	508	10,916
Public school district	250	4764
2-year college	253	2648
State government buildings	29	1138
Medical school/campus	18	747
Public hospital/health facility	48	715
Public housing	13	250
Other state-owned facilities	7	240
Natural resources	246	14,571
Fish and wildlife conservation laws	56	5515
Parks and recreational areas	124	4989
Multi-function natural resources	16	2926
Boating laws	10	461
Environmental laws	7	368
Water resources	18	185
Forest resources	9	65
Levee district	6	62
Transportation systems/facilities	167	11,508
Airports	103	3555
Mass transit system/railroad	18	3214
Transportation—multiple types	5	2000
Commercial vehicles	12	1320
Harbor/port facilities	25	876
Bridges/tunnels	4	543
Criminal investigations	140	7310
State bureau of investigation	22	3527
County/city investigations	66	2006
Fraud investigations	13	636
Fire marshal/arson investigations	21	478
Tax/revenue enforcement	6	177
Other/multiple types	12	486
Special enforcement	54	2161
Alcohol/tobacco laws	22	1280
Agricultural laws	12	387
Narcotics laws	5	233
Gaming laws	10	231
Racing laws	5	30

Source: Reaves, B. A., U.S. Bureau of Justice Statistics, 2008, *Census of State and Local Law Enforcement Agencies.* Retrieved from http://bjs.ojp.usdoj.gov/content/pub/pdf/csllea08.pdf.

Note: Excludes agencies employing less than one full-time officer or the equivalent in part-time officers.

- Washington, D.C. Metropolitan Area Transit Authority (442 personnel)
- Metropolitan Atlanta Rapid Transit Authority (MARTA) (309 personnel)

Regional Policing and Police Task Forces

Small police departments are limited in their efficiency and are quite expensive to maintain on a 24-hour-a-day basis. Nine-one-one systems (911) are expensive to operate, and the radio dispatcher position is a 24-hour-a-day job, supplementing the patrol response units of the department. Even if only one officer is on duty in a small department, there must still be one civilian employee on duty at the same time, unless the agency relies entirely on cell phones to receive calls from an in-service patrol officer. If you add up the cost of a central radio dispatch unit, the costs of maintaining a separate jail, and the personnel costs, the total tax drain is increased exponentially.

Some cities are operating cooperative 911 efforts and have centralized radio dispatching arrangements, regional jails, and often even contractually available detective units from a larger city, the county sheriff, or the state police. Central police purchasing authorities can mitigate other expenses. The small city can purchase a new patrol vehicle, fully equipped with radio and safety equipment, for the approximate cost per vehicle at which a state police unit could purchase 100 car lots.

There are very few regional policing efforts in the United States, although the concept was used both in Great Britain and throughout Europe. Regional police departments were created to serve more than one county or city. Occasionally, the regional department might cross a county or a state line.

There are fewer police departments than there were a decade or two ago. Many small departments over the last 40 years were consolidated or eliminated because of training and liability insurance expenses. Most one- and two-person police agencies were absorbed into more viably efficient units. In Connecticut, state police officers are contracted to the city. In Los Angeles County, California, the sheriff contractually provides deputies to police cities within the sheriff's jurisdiction. The city pays for their cost plus expenses but does not have to hire and fire, and train and retrain. The contracting agency manages all of these arrangements and insures a high-quality enforcement and prevention effort.

Properly administered multiagency task forces also increase police efficiency. For example, take the case of a drug dealer running a sale operation at the juxtaposition of a three- or four-state boundary. If the dealer walks 5 feet, he or she can be in another jurisdiction, minimizing arrest opportunities. In other instances, the dealer might be in another city or another county. Regional task forces often have city, county, state, and federal officers, and often these officers can be sworn in on the state or federal level. They do not have to stop at a county line, a city limit, or a state jurisdiction anymore. The criminals cannot hide in another venue because the officer has jurisdiction, and even if he or she did not hide, the "fresh pursuit" doctrine would apply if the officer observed a crime being committed.

Most regionalization efforts within a state include multicounty units jointly supporting and financing drug examination laboratories and police academies. Sometimes multiple county or city contracts also include regional 911 centers and jails.

Other Agencies

The CSLLEA (2008) listed 638 other agencies and indicated that the county constable offices were the primary agencies in this category.[64] In the United States, the office of constable developed during the colonial period from its English predecessor. Today, the constable is a statewide, constitutional, elected or appointed county public official and peace officer under the statutes of many states; however, the duties and responsibilities of the office of constable vary widely from state to state. In many states, the office is an integral part of the law enforcement community involved in the delivery of justice. In other states, constables are not active in patrols or preventive policing. In these states, the office is relatively obscure to the public. In addition, a number of states have completely abolished the use of the office.[65]

Although there is no consistent use of the office of constable nationwide, the following are some general duties and responsibilities often performed by a constable: keeping and preserving the peace within the county; carrying out court orders of the minor courts, including executing and returning criminal warrants and civil processes; providing security for the minor courts; being available to assist the needs of the county sheriff and local police departments (if requested); posting delinquent tax notices and other services for county commissioners; carrying specimens for the county coroners; transporting defendants and prisoners to and from the county prison and the offices of the minor courts; and issuing traffic and nontraffic citations. Although constables possess broad criminal and civil powers, in most jurisdictions, serious criminal matters are left to the local police department or sheriffs' offices.

In states using the office of the constable, the counties are usually required to provide their constables with uniforms, a marked motor vehicle, and a blue flashing light for use on official duty. Some states mandate limited initial and in-service training requirements for constables to include firearms and safety training. State law enforcement training divisions often provide this training.[66]

Reserve Police

Volunteer officers make up the police reserves. The main purpose of reserve officers is to provide volunteer support to augment the various units of a law enforcement agency on a daily basis and to serve as a ready-trained "reserve force" that could be mobilized on short notice in case of natural disasters, civil disorders, or terrorist attacks. In addition, many police reserve programs provide agencies with a trained pool of officers from which the agency may recruit full-time officers.

The concept is used extensively throughout the United States by various local police agencies. Reserve program standards vary from agency to agency. In some instances, the reserve officer's authority is restricted to performing nonenforcement duties, for example, helping in various types of police education programs, administrative duties, search and rescue, and so on.

In other cases, reserve officers are required to gain certification according to state law enforcement training requirements and are duly sworn officers with full law enforcement authority (while on duty). As such, they may be called upon to work alongside a regular police officer or to perform many of the traditional duties and responsibilities of regular officers. In addition, they wear identical uniforms and badges to those of regular officers while on duty. Because these officers have the same powers of arrest as regular officers, they are required by law to meet the same hiring, background, medical, and psychological standards as a regular officer including basic, in-service, and firearms training. Reserve training programs are generally held on weekends and nights over an extended period so as not to conflict with a reserve officer candidate's full-time work.[67]

In most cases, reserve police officers are usually required to work a specified number of hours per month (usually ranging from 8 to 24) at times that do not interfere with their primary careers. Reserve officers generally do not receive compensation and many are required to purchase their own uniforms and equipment. For many, the real benefit of being a police reserve is simply the sense of accomplishment and the civic pride achieved by performing a valuable serve to their communities. For others, the police reserve program allows an opportunity for individuals to experience law enforcement work prior to seeking a full-time law enforcement career.

Police agency management, which recognizes the financial and service benefits of having nonpaid "force multipliers," often welcomes reserve officers, however, some controversy may also accompany the use of reserve officers. Regular officers and police unions may not always welcome the use of the reserve police concept. For them, the idea of a police reserve may appear to slow recruitment and hiring of needed additional full-time, professional police officers. The use of reserve police officers may also reduce the paid overtime opportunities for regular officers. In addition, the public may not always be supportive of the reserve police concept because they may fear that the reserve officers are not as well trained and competent as regular officers.

Perished in the Line of Duty

On May 17, 1792, New York City Deputy Sheriff Isaac Smith was the first recorded local law enforcement officer killed in the line of duty. In 1916, Anna Hart, a jail matron employed by the Hamilton County (OH) Sheriff's Office, became the first female law enforcement officer killed in the line of duty. To date, more than 2300 deputy sheriffs have died in the line of duty.[68]

Sadly, law enforcement officers continue to perish in the line of duty. Their lives are sacrificed for the betterment and protection of society. According to the Officer Down Memorial, during 2011, a total of 166 American law enforcement officers perished in the line of duty. The cause of death varied from heart attack to stabbing. Based on Officer Down data, the causes of death of these officers and the related quantities of deceased personnel are as follows:[69]

Aircraft accident: 1
Animal-related: 1
Assault: 5
Automobile accident: 34
Drowning: 4
Duty-related illness: 7
Explosion: 1
Gunfire: 67
Gunfire (accidental): 5

Heart attack: 11
Heat exhaustion: 1
Motorcycle accident: 5
Stabbed: 2
Struck by vehicle: 4
Training accident: 1
Vehicle pursuit: 4
Vehicular assault: 12
Weather/natural disaster: 1

These causes of death and their related quantities demonstrate the dangerousness of the law enforcement occupation (Figure 3.2). All law enforcement officers are potential

Figure 3.2 Like other public safety professions, those serving in the ranks of law enforcement face a wide variety of dangers. (From the Officer Down Memorial Page, http://www.odmp.org/pdfs/odmp_psa_three_top_killers-8x11.pdf.)

targets of offenders and their associates, and they risk their lives daily to serve their communities. Periodic line-of-duty deaths are a reality of the law enforcement occupation. Based on the 2011 Officer Down data, 155 of these deceased officers were male and 11 were female.[70] The average age of the deceased officers was 41 years.[71] The average tour of duty was 12 years and 9 months.[72] No law enforcement officer is impervious to the threats of the occupation. All law enforcement officers must be mindful of officer safety concerns.

The Officer Down Memorial presents an online testament to the services of these deceased law enforcement officers. Further data may be obtained via the Officer Down website at http://www.odmp.org/search/year?year=2011#ixzz1t6uBQ1Ux.

Case Consideration: August Vollmer

The history of American law enforcement exhibits numerous events that influenced the maturing of the law enforcement domain and boasts notable events that shaped both private and public law enforcement entities. These events range from the incidents that occurred during the westward expansion of the nation and the contributions of technological and methodical advancements that improved the effectiveness and efficiency of law enforcement organizations. A variety of individuals contributed to the development and maturation of the law enforcement domain.

Among localities, law enforcement officers work long hours, often receive low wages, and serve their respective communities faithfully. Some are volunteers who receive no financial payment for their services. Many local law enforcement officers may receive national fame for their actions, whereas others are remembered and honored because their service necessitated the sacrificing of their lives. History is also replete with examples of law enforcement personnel whose services were both honorable and dishonorable. Regardless of the characteristics of their careers and servitude, at some point in their lives, they decided to undertake the duties of law enforcement.

From the perspective of local law enforcement, the most influential officer was probably August Vollmer, who has been deemed the father of American policing (Figure 3.3). Before entering law enforcement, Vollmer served in the U.S. Army during the Spanish–American War.[73] Vollmer served as a U.S. Marshal from 1905 to 1909 and was the Berkeley, California Chief of Police from 1909 to 1931.[74] From 1932 to 1937, he was a police administration professor at the University of California (Berkeley).[75] After entering the law enforcement occupation, Vollmer successfully crafted and implemented an array of police reforms that continue to reverberate among modern law enforcement organizations.

When Vollmer commenced his law enforcement career, officers were notorious for corruption and brutality and both "gambling and opium parlors operated openly in Berkeley because the owners paid off city officials."[76] During this period in Berkeley, incidents of crime were so prevalent that the "Southern Pacific transcontinental trains refused to stop at the stations."[77] After assuming his law enforcement duties and during the course of his career, Vollmer profoundly impacted the policing methods of the period and addressed the issues of corruption that pervaded the local police department and community. His actions greatly decreased the corruption and crime that threatened Berkeley society, and they contributed toward Berkeley becoming recognized as the "most crime-free city in America" until his demise.[78]

Figure 3.3 Chief August Vollmer (1876–1955). (Retrieved from http://content.cdlib.org/ark:/ 13030/tf258005b0/.)

Vollmer's police reforms were visionary. According to the City of Berkeley, California, some of the notable reforms that Vollmer incorporated included the following items:[79]

- 1906: Installed a basic records system, which was one of the first in the United States.
- 1906: Installed the first Modus Operandi (MO) System.
- 1907: First used scientific investigation in a criminal case (Kelinschmidt case— analysis of blood, fibers, and soil).
- 1907: Established the department's police school, which included instruction from professors on such subjects as the law and evidence procedures. This was the first school of its kind in the world and had a far-reaching effect on law enforcement.
- 1911: Organized the first police motorcycle patrol.
- 1913: Increased to the use of automobiles as a means of patrolling the streets of Berkeley.
- 1916: Established the first School of Criminology at the University of California, Berkeley. Chief Vollmer became a strong advocate of college-educated police officers.
- 1918: Began using intelligence tests when recruiting police officers.
- 1920: Utilized the first lie detector instrument developed at the University of California.
- 1921: Began using a psychiatric screening in recruitment.
- 1923: Established the first junior traffic police program.
- 1924: Established one of the first single fingerprint systems.
- 1925: Established our first crime prevention division and hired the first female police officer.

Vollmer's accomplishments included other notable endeavors. His additional contributions to the policing domain included the following items:[80]

- 1910: Implemented bicycle patrols.
- 1914: Was the first to use radio communications between officers.
- 1914: Formed the first juvenile division in the United States.
- 1919: Hired one of the nation's first African-American officers.

Many of Vollmer's protégés experienced tremendous success during the course of their careers. They eventually "became leading police chiefs, forensic scientists, criminal justice educators, lawyers, politicians, and military leaders."[81] Before the end of the 1940s, a total of 25 American police chiefs had served with Vollmer at some point during their careers.[82]

The scope of his influence was unconstrained to the locality of Berkeley. During the 1930s, he and his colleagues authored "several comprehensive reports that were published as parts of the Illinois Crime and Wickersham Commissions."[83] He also served as a faculty member with the University of Chicago, authored four books, and published a variety of magazine and journal articles.[84] He also consulted on and assisted with the reforming of numerous law enforcement agencies domestically and internationally. Examples include periods with law enforcement organizations in Los Angeles (where he served as Chief of Police from 1921 to 1922), Dallas, Chicago, and Havana (Cuba).[85] During the Hoover administration, Vollmer was tasked with leading the National Commission on Law Observance and Enforcement.[86] Internationally, he visited "Scotland Yard, the Surete, and dozens of other European and Asian police departments."[87] He also founded the American Society of Criminology.[88]

During his golden years of retirement, Vollmer was diagnosed with both cancer and Parkinson's Disease.[89] He did not wish to hinder others because of his ailments,[90] so in 1955, Vollmer committed suicide "by shooting himself with his service revolver."[91]

Vollmer's lifetime of achievements positively impacted society by eliminating much of the corruption that existed among law enforcement organizations and within the local society of Berkeley. His educational pursuits heralded the origins of police science and criminology within academia. His visionary utilization of innovative policing practices introduced concepts that improved the efficiency and effectiveness of law enforcement operations.

These innovations continue to influence modern society. Throughout the nation, myriad local law enforcement organizations utilize fingerprinting, bicycle patrols, motorcycle patrols, automobiles, radio communications, and advocate educational and other quality requirements for entry into the law enforcement occupations. His hiring of females and African-Americans was unprecedented and reverberates among modern law enforcement agencies. Although his death was tragic, the accomplishments of his life were testaments to his unselfish servitude for the protection and betterment of the society through the improvement of American policing and law enforcement.

Summary

Local law enforcement organizations and personnel are the mainstays of policing among communities throughout the nation. These entities often involve a combination of full-time, part-time, and reserve officers whose shared goals involve the deterring of crime and the maintaining of societal order. They function unceasingly each day of the year and throughout each hour of the day. Some positions may involve financial compensation, whereas others may be completely unpaid via the contributions of volunteer goodwill.

The demographics of local policing fluctuate throughout the nation and reflect the characteristics of communities served. Therefore, some local law enforcement organizations may be better suited for urban policing, whereas others are suited for rural incidents. Certainly, resources may vary among departments depending upon need and financial resources. For example, some agencies may boast helicopters, automobiles, boats, and bikes, whereas others may only afford or need automobiles and bike patrols.

Regardless of the locale, the personnel of local law enforcement organizations experience dangers that may be fatal. Numerous individuals perish in the line of duty each year from a variety of causes ranging from heart attacks to gunshot wounds. No law enforcement officer is insusceptible to the threats posed by this occupation. Figure 3.4 is a

Figure 3.4 Safety must always remain a primary concern of those serving our communities. (Retrieved from http://below100.com/wp-content/uploads/2011/11/Below-100_BreakingUp_8.5x11 .pdf.)

reminder of the dangerousness of policing and serves as a warning to all officers regarding their mortality.

Modern law enforcement organizations are the products of their respective histories. At some point in time, someone, somewhere acted as the first peace officer within a locale and influenced local policing. Some individuals earned national and timeless notoriety and fame, whereas others may have served quietly without experiencing serious incidents. Historically, one of the most notable figures in American law enforcement was August Vollmer.

Each of these fellows served as a local law enforcement officer. However, in most cases, their actions had a national impact during their respective periods. Not all of them originally desired to enter the law enforcement profession, and some did so for economic and financial reasons. However, after entering the profession, they served their respective communities to the best of their abilities. One must not underestimate the impact of local law enforcement organizations and personnel. Their services are essential for maintaining societal order and deterring crime throughout locales nationally. Although there may be many differences among local organizations and personnel, they all share the common policing theme of maintaining societal order and deterring crime.

Discussion Questions

1. Examine the characteristics of your local county (or parish) law enforcement agency and a nearby city law enforcement agency. Compare and contrast the duties, organizational structures, and personnel differences that permeate these organizations. Within your discussion, also include a consideration of how these agencies are complementary entities, and the types of collaboration and cooperation that exist between them.

2. Daryl Gates served as Chief of the Los Angeles Police Department (California) between the years 1978 and 1992. During his tenure with this police department, he experienced the Los Angeles riots that occurred during the early 1990s. Please describe his handling of the riots and the resulting repercussions that ensued during the aftermath of the rioting. Discuss whether you believe he was an effective chief with respect to his handling of the Los Angeles riots.

3. At the time of the writing of this text, Joe Arpaio is the sheriff of Maricopa County, Arizona. His leadership has spawned national controversy regarding his unique approaches to deterring crime and maintaining order. Please discuss whether you believe he is an effective leader with respect to the deterring of crime and the maintaining of societal order within his locale.

4. Examine the demographics of your local police or sheriff's department. Compare and contrast your findings with national observations contained within the 2008 CSLLEA. Within your discussion, please delineate how your local agency differs from the national observations.

References

1. Law Library—American Law and Legal Information. *Police: History—"Modern" Policing in America*. Retrieved from http://law.jrank.org/pages/1641/Police-History--Modern-policing-in-America.html.

2. Samuel, W., & Katz, C. M. (2010). *The Police in America* (p. 59). New York, NY: McGraw-Hill.

  3. U.S. Bureau of Justice Statistics (2008); *Census of State and Local Law Enforcement Agencies* (pp. 1–2). Washington, DC: U.S. Government.
  4. Ibid.
  5. Ibid.
  6. Ibid.
  7. Ibid.
  8. Ibid.
  9. Ibid.
 10. Ibid.
 11. Ibid.
 12. Ibid.
 13. Ibid.
 14. Ibid.
 15. Ibid.
 16. Ibid.
 17. Ibid.
 18. Ibid.
 19. Ibid.
 20. Ibid.
 21. U.S. Bureau of Justice Statistics. *Census of State and Local Law Enforcement Agencies* (p. 2). Washington, DC: Government Printing Office.
 22. U.S. Bureau of Justice Statistics (2007). *Census of State and Local Law Enforcement Agencies, 2004*. Washington, DC: Government Printing Office.
 23. U.S. Bureau of Justice Statistics (2007). *Census of State and Local Law Enforcement Agencies, 2004* (p. 4). Washington, DC: Government Printing Office.
 24. Hess, K. M. (2009). *Introduction to Law Enforcement and Criminal Justice* (p. 117). Belmont, CA: Wadsworth.
 25. *The Kansas City Preventive Patrol Experiment.* Retrieved from http://www.policefoundation .org/docs/kansas.html/
 26. U.S. Bureau of Justice Statistics (2008). *Census of State and Local Law Enforcement Agencies* (pp. 1–2). Washington, DC: U.S. Government.
 27. Ibid.
 28. Ibid.
 29. U.S. Bureau of Justice Statistics (2008). *Census of State and Local Law Enforcement Agencies* (pp. 1–2). Washington, DC: U.S. Government.
 30. Ibid.
 31. Ibid.
 32. Ibid.
 33. Ibid.
 34. Ibid.
 35. Ibid.
 36. Ibid.
 37. Ibid.
 38. Ibid.
 39. Ibid.
 40. U.S. Census Bureau. *Statistical Abstract of the United States: A National Data Book* (Vol. 122, 2nd ed.), Census of state and local law enforcement agencies (p. 196). Washington, DC: Government Printing Office.
 41. Hickman, M., & Reaves, B. *Local Police Departments: 2003* (2006). (p. 63). Washington, DC: Bureau of Justice Statistics.
 42. U.S. Bureau of Justice Statistics (2008). *Census of State and Local Law Enforcement Agencies* (pp. 1–2). Washington, DC: U.S. Government.

43. Ibid.
44. Ibid.
45. *Tribal Law Enforcement*. Retrieved from http://www.tribal-institute.org/lists/enforcement.htm
46. *Services Overview*. Retrieved from http://www.bia.gov/
47. *Bureau of Indian Affairs—Law Enforcement*. Retrieved from http://www.financingstimulus.org/summary/100001082.2007.html/
48. U.S. Bureau of Justice Statistics (2002). *Census of Tribal Justice Agencies in Indian Country, 2002*. Washington, DC: Government Printing Office.
49. Federal Law Enforcement Training Center. *Orientation to Federal Law Enforcement Agencies*. Unpublished manuscript.
50. U.S. Office of Management and Budget. *Bureau of Indian Affairs—Law Enforcement*. Retrieved from http://www.financingstimulus.org/summary/10001082.2007.html
51. U.S. Bureau of Justice Statistics (2007). *Census of State and Local Law Enforcement Agencies, 2004*. Washington, DC: Government Printing Office.
52. *Tribal Law Enforcement*. Retrieved from http://www.tribal-institute.org/lists/enforcement.htm.
53. U.S. Bureau of Justice Statistics (2008). *Census of State and Local Law Enforcement Agencies* (pp. 1–2). Washington, DC: U.S. Government.
54. Ibid.
55. Ibid.
56. Ibid.
57. Ibid.
58. Ibid.
59. Ibid.
60. Ibid.
61. Ibid.
62. Ibid.
63. Ibid.
64. U.S. Bureau of Justice Statistics (2008). *Census of State and Local Law Enforcement Agencies* (pp. 1–2). Washington, DC: U.S. Government.
65. National Constables Association. *What is a Constable?* Retrieved from http://www.angelfire.com/la/nationalconstable/personal.htm.
66. Mississippi Code of 1972, As Amended. *SEC. 19-19-5 General Duties of Constables; Training Program*. Retrieved from http://mscode.com/free/statutes/19/019/0005.htm/
67. Los Angeles County Sherrif's Department. *What is a Reserve Deputy Sherriff?* Retrieved from http://lasdreserve.org/reserve_program.html
68. National Law Enforcement Officers Memorial Fund. *Important Dates in Law Enforcement History*. Retrieved from http://www.nlemf.com/facts/enforcement/impdates.html
69. Officer Down Memorial Page. *Honoring Officers Killed in 2011*. Retrieved from http://www.odmp.org/search/year?year=2011
70. Ibid.
71. Ibid.
72. Ibid.
73. Bennett, C. *Legendary Lawman August Vollmer*. Retrieved from http://www.officer.com/article/10232661/legendary-lawman-august-vollmer
74. Dinkelspiel, F. Remembering August Vollmer, the Berkeley Police Chief who created modern policing. *Berkeleyside*. Retrieved from http://www.berkeleyside.com/2010/01/27/remembering-august-vollmer-the-berkeley-police-chief-who-created-modern-policing/
75. A brief guide to police history. *North Carolina Wesleyan College*. Retrieved from http://faculty.ncwc.edu/mstevens/205/205lect04.htm
76. Dinkelspiel, F. Remembering August Vollmer, the Berkeley Police Chief who created modern policing. *Berkeleyside*. Retrieved from http://www.berkeleyside.com/2010/01/27/remembering-august-vollmer-the-berkeley-police-chief-who-created-modern-policing/

77. Bennett, C. *Legendary Lawman August Vollmer*. Retrieved from http://www.officer.com/article/10232661/legendary-lawman-august-vollmer

78. Boren, K. *August Vollmer: The Great Innovater*. Retrieved from http://www.prospector-utah.com/vollmer.htm

79. City of Berkeley, California. *Our History*. Retrieved from http://www.ci.berkeley.ca.us/police/history/history.html

80. Dinkelspiel, F. Remembering August Vollmer, the Berkeley Police Chief who created modern policing. *Berkeleyside*. Retrieved from http://www.berkeleyside.com/2010/01/27/remembering-august-vollmer-the-berkeley-police-chief-who-created-modern-policing/

81. Fisher, J. *Pioneer Cop: A Half Century Ahead of His Time*. Edinboro University of Pennsylvania. Retrieved from http://jimfisher.edinboro.edu/forensics/vollmer.html

82. Ibid.

83. Ibid.

84. Ibid.

85. Boren, K. *August Vollmer: The Great Innovater*. Retrieved from http://www.prospector-utah.com/vollmer.htm

86. Ibid.

87. Fisher, J. *Pioneer Cop: A Half Century Ahead of His Time*. Edinboro University of Pennsylvania. Retrieved from http://jimfisher.edinboro.edu/forensics/vollmer.html

88. Bennett, C. *Legendary Lawman August Vollmer*. Retrieved from http://www.officer.com/article/10232661/legendary-lawman-august-vollmer

89. Fisher, J. *Pioneer Cop: A Half Century Ahead of His Time*. Edinboro University of Pennsylvania. Retrieved from http://jimfisher.edinboro.edu/forensics/vollmer.html

90. Ibid.

91. Ibid.

State Law Enforcement in the United States

4

In the year 1903, when I assumed the office of Chief Executive of the State, I found myself thereby invested with supreme executive authority. I found that no power existed to interfere with me in my duty to enforce the laws of the State, and that, by the same token, no conditions could release me from my duty so to do. I then looked about to see what instruments I possessed wherewithal to accomplish this bounden obligation—what instruments on whose loyalty and obedience I could truly rely. And I perceived three such instruments—my private secretary, a very small man, my woman stenographer, and the janitor. So, I made the State Police.

Pennsylvania Governor Samuel Pennypacker

Learning Objectives

The objectives of this chapter are to

- Compare the history and development of early state law enforcement agencies
- Describe the significance of state law enforcement
- Explain the organizational facets of state law enforcement agencies
- Discuss the various state law enforcement agencies

Introduction

The development of state-level law enforcement was a slow process. In the early days of our country, the sheriff on the county level, town constable, town marshal, and later city police fulfilled most law enforcement needs. In an emergency, the local or state militia could always be called to arms, but as time passed on and populations not only increased but also became mobile, the need for state-level enforcement agencies became apparent.

As state enforcement organizations emerged, two distinct patterns developed: a rural model and an urban model. An example of a rural model is the Texas Rangers. An example of an urban model is the Pennsylvania State Police, both of which will be discussed later in this chapter.

Over the years, state law enforcement agencies have evolved into efficient and effective organizations. They are found throughout the nation, with the exception of Hawaii, and perform a variety of missions. No two state law enforcement entities are identical. Instead, they uniquely reflect the needs of their respective citizenries with respect to missions, organizations, personnel, and resources.

State Enforcement

The Bureau of Justice Statistics, *Census of State and Local Law Enforcement, 2004*, indicated that there were 49 primary state police agencies (one for each state with the exception of Hawaii). The Hawaii Department of Public Safety was classified as a special jurisdiction agency. In addition, there were numerous other state-level agencies with full police powers in the various states.

The 49 primary state law enforcement agencies in the United States employed 89,265 full-time employees. Of that number, 58,190 were full-time sworn personnel. Most of the sworn officers were working in the area of field operations, where they provided direct services related to traffic, patrol, investigations, and special operations. Many of the civilian employees worked in the area of technical support, including occupations such as dispatching, record keeping, data processing, and other positions related to communications, fleet management, and training.

In addition to traditional law enforcement duties, many state police agencies are responsible for the operation of training academies, forensic laboratories, and special units. Some state agencies also have some responsibilities related to emergency medical services, civil defense, or homeland security responsibilities.

Nineteen of the 49 state law enforcement agencies employed at least 1000 full-time officers. The California Highway Patrol (CHP) was the largest with 7085 full-time sworn officers. The New York State Police (4667), Pennsylvania State Police (4200), Texas Department of Public Safety (3437), and New Jersey State Police (2768) followed the CHP. The smallest state police agencies were the North Dakota Highway Patrol (135), South Dakota Highway Patrol (154), and Wyoming Highway Patrol (188).[1]

Some state police agencies have general police jurisdiction and others have restricted jurisdiction. The Pennsylvania State Police and the Michigan State Police are examples of state agencies that are empowered with general police jurisdiction to enforce all the laws of their state. The Mississippi Highway Patrol and the CHP are examples of state police agencies having restricted jurisdictions. Both are restricted primarily to traffic enforcement but have full jurisdiction within the right of way of any state highway.[2] In either case, the state police agencies usually do not work within municipal or county jurisdictions unless requested.[3]

Other examples of general state law enforcement agencies or investigative agencies are those associated with a tax collection function, such as an Alcohol Beverage Commission, agencies charged with the enforcement of drug and narcotics laws, and so on. Some state agencies such as the Florida Bureau of Law Enforcement or the Tennessee Bureau of Investigation (TBI) have general jurisdiction throughout the state and may conduct independent investigations and assist local law enforcement agencies upon request (Figure 4.1).

Nineteenth Century Experiments

The first attempt at state-level law and order dates back to the Revolutionary War. The Virginia Assembly dispatched elements of its own militia through the Cumberland Gap into its frontier counties west of the Appalachians, an area known as "Kantuckee." The militia protected the settlers from local law breakers and organized their defense to counter

Figure 4.1 Mississippi Highway Patrol officers. (Courtesy of the Mississippi State Troopers Association. Retrieved from http://mstroopers.com/2009/04/troopers-take-national-award/.)

the threat of Indian attack. To support the effort of the militia, some of the frontiersmen were recruited into small companies of "patrollers" and commissioned to track down renegade whites and Indians who posed a threat to the settlers.

With little training for the job, the patrollers performed well. Often unfamiliar with the uncharted frontier, the militia had proved to be ineffective as an enforcement body in western Virginia. The patrollers, on the other hand, acquired a reputation for fearlessness and efficiency. Their area of responsibility often consisted of 30 square miles of wilderness to be patrolled by one man on horseback.

With the admission of Kentucky to the Union in 1792, the state retained the militia and the patroller systems until the harsh life of the frontier faded and traditional forms of enforcement such as the justice of the peace, sheriff, constables, and other locally selected authorities were adopted to replace them.

The Texas Rangers are recognized as the first state-level law enforcement organization in the United States, even though Texas, at the time of the creation of the Rangers, was a Republic rather than a state. It could be argued that the Texas Rangers, during this period, were the national police of the Republic of Texas, rather than a true state force.

The creation of the Texas Rangers emerged from the necessities of frontier life. Settler conflicts with the American Indian, the threat of attack by Mexican bandits or the Mexican Army, and the actual struggle for power and survival during the early days of settlement justified their existence. Violence that occurred in the sparsely populated areas of Texas led to the demand for a reliable force that would be independent of local political pressures. These and related considerations provided the basis for the organization of the first state-level "law enforcement."

In 1823, Stephen F. Austin commissioned ten men to "range about," discouraging Indian raids and marauders, dealing with outlaws, and settling disputes through the administration of "seat-of-the-pants" "on-the-scene" justice. In 1835, the provisional government of Texas placed three Ranger companies under the command of R. M. Williamson. Their actions were subject to the direction of the military authorities with the intent to patrol the Mexican border. This function of border patrol persisted for many years, although general police work, including criminal investigation, ultimately became their primary function.

In 1840, the patrolling of the Mexican border began. During the Mexican War, the Texas Rangers served as military companies fighting against the Mexican forces. During the United States' occupation of Mexico City, General Scott dismissed most of the Texas Rangers under his command after several incidents of violence toward the Mexican citizens. With the conclusion of the war, the Rangers reassumed their role on the frontier, coping with enforcement demands. The work included such tasks as combating highway robbery and capturing runaway slaves. The acceptance of these missions forced the Rangers to be more involved in general police work. By the 1860s, the Rangers had firmly established themselves and their reputation as a part of Texas culture.

Though little of the War Between the States took place in Texas itself, members of the Texas Rangers not only served in, but also organized and commanded southern units. Many of these units participated in some of the bloodiest battles of the war. Colonel Benjamin Terry commanded his unit, Terry's Texas Rangers, and staffed it with many former Rangers. With the conclusion of the War Between the States, the new Texas Reconstruction government viewed the Rangers as a symbol of the past and a threat to the future. In 1865, the new Reconstruction government, concerned about their ability to maintain control of the state, disbanded the Texas Rangers. A state police replaced the Rangers.

The Reconstruction efforts to provide internal security for Texas culminated in 1870 with the formation of the new state police. Few agencies of law enforcement in the west ever provoked such unpopular public responses as this group. Regardless of the actual purpose, the majority of Texans clearly regarded the new state police as an arm of tyranny and oppression directly serving what the citizens viewed as an occupational government. To some degree, the state police certainly earned their unpleasant reputation. One of the captains, Jack Helms, was dismissed for misconduct. The director of the agency, James Davidson, embezzled over $30,000 and fled to Europe to avoid prosecution.

Although authorized strength totaled 257, the new state police never attained its full complement of men. Blacks and whites were almost equally represented in the ranks of the organization. Several counties openly resisted the new authority and soon found themselves under martial law enforced by the state police. The new agency continually suffered the broadside of major scandals and the open hate of much of the public. However, the agency actually seemed to concern itself most frequently with arrests for such routine crimes as gambling, assault, and theft. Most Texans felt that the officers were in truth political spies permitted to search without warrant, disrupt peaceful meetings, and even murder those opposed to Reconstruction domination.

Around 1872, Governor Richard Coke and the newly elected legislature abolished the state police. By 1874, enactments permitted reestablishment of the Texas Rangers. The "New Rangers" were similar to their earlier counterparts. The new Rangers were formed with two divisions: one known as the "Special Forces," under the command of Captain L. H. McNelly, and the other known as the "Frontier Battalion," under the command of Major John B. Jones. The Special Forces had the mission of providing police service to Southwest Texas and the Mexican border. The Frontier Battalion's mission was to counter the Indian threat. The Texas Rangers once more rode the plains.

Rangers were not necessarily full-time professional peace officers. A great number held special and temporary commissions. These men sometimes composed minute companies, ready to serve in unusual circumstances or to represent private interests. The great bulk of writing on the Ranger service ignored such members, instead concentrating on the more spectacular and better reported activities of the regular detachments.

During the Las Cuevas War, a force of 30 Rangers, led by Captain McNelly, invaded Mexico and attacked the main staging area for rustling operations directed against the Texas border area. The Rangers fought a force of about 450 and forced the return of 75 stolen cattle.

Texas's unique mounted force faced three major problems in the generation after the War Between the States: law enforcement on a developing frontier, continued threats from the American Indians, and a simmering international border. The Ranger's role evolved gradually from being used to react to Indian threats to the acceptance of the solid mission of providing the primary law enforcement on the frontier while still providing security along the Rio Grande River. The Rangers continued to collect taxes, protect courts and prisoners, chase Mexican cattle thieves, maintain order at elections, escort strike breakers, assist local posses, and arrest a wide variety of suspects. The Rangers quelled riots, such as those in El Paso in 1877 and Brownsville in 1906. Some of their unusual assignments included preventing illegal prizefights, providing medical assistance in small pox epidemics, and rescuing dogs: in essence, any task desired by the state government.

The early Rangers were by no means an organized or well-disciplined force functioning within solid, well-defined rules. As the Texas frontier came to an end, so did the traditional missions of the Rangers. By 1900, when it became obvious that the traditional Texas Rangers could no longer meet the full demands of the state of Texas, the legislature created a department of public safety, similar to the agencies organized under the Pennsylvania model. The Texas model was not a failure, for it was very responsive to the demands for service that developed in such a sparsely populated land. Other states with similar populations and geographical structures adopted the Texas model (Figure 4.2).

Figure 4.2 The Texas Rangers, Frontier Battalion, Company B, around 1880. (From Cox, M., *Texas Ranger Hall of Fame and Museum*, 2009. Retrieved from http://www.texasranger.org/history/BriefHistory1.htm.)

From 1901 until 1910, Arizona maintained a state organization similar to the Texas Rangers, which it entitled the Arizona Rangers.[4] In 1905, the state of New Mexico established the New Mexico Mounted Police. Both provided border patrol forces and both were abandoned within a few years, having apparently become involved in state politics. In 1917, Colorado established the Colorado Rangers in response to the national push for defense. The Colorado Rangers were disbanded in 1923 after finding themselves as a major issue in the gubernatorial election of 1922.[5]

Massachusetts State Police: An Experiment

The earliest state police forces came into existence without clear direction or understanding of mission. On May 16, 1865, Governor John A. Andrews created a "State Constabulary" for Massachusetts. With general statewide police powers to suppress commercialized vice, it was born into controversy and linked to ethnic prejudices. Native-born Americans in Massachusetts loathed the Irish Catholic fondness for hard liquor. They believed that drunkenness was sinful and criminal, and they were concerned about the fact that the laws against drunkenness were not enforced. Enforcement of these laws was just one of the tasks visualized for the new state police organization. The new body was basic in its conception and organization and soon found itself to be the subject of recurrent legislative revision.[6]

A formal statement made by the governor of Massachusetts over 100 years ago is still so apt in its current application as to bear repetition. In his inaugural address, delivered on January 4, 1867, Governor Alexander H. Bullock recognized that a conflict existed between local and state authority. Primarily because of local influence, he declared:

The state constabulary, which was created, has demonstrated that the representative of the power of the Commonwealth commands a respect and attains results which the municipal officer, embarrassed by local influences and associations, has failed to secure. I regret that the local police have not, in all cases cordially, cooperated with the constabulary of the state; and that in some instances they have manifested a disposition to impede rather than to assist this department of the executive power.[7]

On February 13, 1875, the state constabulary passed into history, as the Legislature renamed it the State Detective Force. In 1879, the continual legislative revisions culminated in the establishment of the Massachusetts District Police, a state detective unit. This department later became part of the Department of Public Safety created by the Constitutional Convention of 1919. On May 27, 1921, Governor Channing H. Cox signed a legislative act that created a Massachusetts State Patrol to police the rural communities, particularly where there was no organized protection.

In 1869, New Hampshire lawmakers were presented with a petition "... praying that the Legislature enact a law providing for a state police to more adequately enforce the laws of the State." At that time, it was hoped that a state police force would focus on the liquor laws of New Hampshire, which the local constables hesitated to enforce for political reasons. Unfortunately, the petition did not become law.

Other states recognized that a void existed in the area of state-level law enforcement. In 1887, California created the State Capitol Police and tasked them with providing security on state property. In 1903, Connecticut set up a small state force. With the powers and duties formerly exercised by the Law and Order League, a quasipublic organization, the new force was modeled after the Massachusetts District Police of that day. Like the Massachusetts Police, the Connecticut force was to more effectively suppress commercialized vice, with emphasis on the enforcement of the liquor and gambling laws. They also performed certain inspection duties and investigated suspicious fires. The Connecticut force was so small that any system of regular patrols was impractical. The organizational structure mandated by the state of Connecticut was loose and ill-defined. After many changes, the Connecticut force became a state detective force operating under the control of an administrative board, until the extensive reorganization of 1920.[8]

Until after the turn of the twentieth century, most states were wholly dependent upon the county sheriff and the local constables to provide police protection for their large rural populations. Since county government was based on a combined system of political patronage and election, the sheriff and his deputies were frequently unqualified to serve as law enforcement officers.

A New Model for Urban State Policing: Pennsylvania

Labor unrest in the coal industry and the subsequent violence that erupted pushed the Governor of Pennsylvania to lead the effort to create a state-level enforcement agency. In 1902, the labor violence reached new levels. In what became to be known as the Great Anthracite Coal Strike, the labor unrest resulted in a nation-wide coal shortage. The nation's concern about the events in Pennsylvania were so great that President Theodore Roosevelt intervened.

The Governor of Pennsylvania, Samuel Pennypacker, found the violence unaccept-able, but he found few assets at his disposal that could be called upon in an emergency. As a result, Pennypacker pushed for the creations of what became the Pennsylvania State Constabulary. Three needs inspired the creation of the organization. First, the need for a law enforcement agency within the executive arm of the state. Second, the need to contend with the conditions in the coal and iron regions and the demonstrated inability of the local organized police forces generally to deal with the conditions successfully. Third, the need to provide adequate police protection after the sheriff–constable system had broken down and exposed the rural districts to the danger of inadequate police protection.

Recognition of these conditions in Pennsylvania had an important bearing upon later state police developments. The rural protection aspect focused the attention where it was needed and influenced state police management in many parts of the country. Agencies responsible for maintaining peace and for protecting life and property evolved from the sheriffs, constables, city police, and the case of the earlier state police forces. Consistent with the view of Governor Pennypacker, the Pennsylvania force was "made," and in the making, whether from accident or from design, there was a sharp break from established tradition. Pennypacker later recounted:

> In the year 1903, when I assumed the office of Chief Executive of the State I found myself thereby invested with supreme executive authority. I found that no power existed to interfere with me in my duty to enforce the laws of the State, and that, by the same token, no conditions

could release me from my duty so to do. I then looked about to see what instruments I possessed wherewithal to accomplish this bounden obligation—what instruments on whose loyalty and obedience I could truly rely. And I perceived three such instruments—my private secretary, a very small man, my woman stenographer, and the janitor. So, I made the State Police.[9]

This new body ignored the traditional models of organization and control, which had become embedded in accepted police practice. On May 2, 1905, Governor Pennypacker signed the act creating the Department of State Police of Pennsylvania. The law was written in the same loose, nonspecific manner as the legislation sponsored by Sir Robert Peel in his efforts to create a police service for England. Governor Pennypacker was faced with the same dilemma faced by Sir Robert Peel 80 years before.

On July 1, 1905, Governor Pennypacker offered the appointment of Superintendent of State Police to Captain John C. Groome, commander of the First City Troop of Philadelphia. Groome was an outstanding selection by the Governor. He had been a member of the National Guard for over 23 years, having joined the famous "First Troop, Philadelphia City Cavalry" in 1881. In 1896, as a lieutenant, Groome became commander of the troop. During the next several years, Groome's spirit and discipline enhanced his public standing. He believed the only organizational model that could ensure success for this new state police was an organization patterned along military lines. Groome followed this philosophy in his selection of personnel.

A total of 193 men survived the rigid selection process for appointment to the Pennsylvania State Police. They were a diverse group with individuals claiming 19 different states as home. All officers appointed to a position of rank by Groome had National Guard or regular Army experience, and of those men who served in ranking positions, 90% had one to three tours in the service. Groome sought men who displayed physical stamina, devotion to duty, unquestioned loyalty, and reckless bravery; not one appointment had the faintest political flavor. When the uniforms, arms, and equipment arrived on March 1, 1906, the new state police force was ready for active duty.

Groome decided that four troops would be strategically located in the state. Furthermore, the force would be horse mounted, and finally, the nonrated officers would live in barracks with a salary of $725 a year.

The model adopted and developed by Groome proved to be extremely successful, far exceeding the initial expectations of advocates and critics. The governor now had a standing force with which he could use as he desired. The state police imposed order on the mining districts. Labor and management could no longer use force to settle problems. Management in mining found out that their police could no longer use violence either. This was the first time Pennsylvania's state government used its power to maintain peace. In 1923, the Pennsylvania State Police installed the first point-to-point radio telegraph between their headquarters and the various state police posts throughout the state.

The Formative Years: 1908–1940

The period of 1908 through 1940 witnessed the formation of state-level law enforcement agencies in the majority of states. Initially, the primary opposition to the creation of state police was from organized labor, which feared the state police would be used as strike breakers.[10] Initially, the concerns of labor were well founded. In 1908, Nevada lawmakers organized the Nevada State Police to counter miners' strikes in Goldfield and Tonopah. The law enforcement personnel, after quieting the unrest in those two towns, were transferred to Rawhide and then to Carson City. In October 1912, when a miners' strike in White Pine County resulted in the deaths of two strikers, the state dispatched a force of five Nevada State Police officers and 104 reserves to restore order. The record of the Nevada State Police shows the diversity of its enforcement. In 1908, it exercised its authority in the suppression of opium use in Reno.[11]

The need to establish state-level enforcement to fill the gap between local enforcement and federal enforcement became even more apparent as technological advancements, especially in the area of transportation, and the need for effective criminal investigations changed the nature of local policing. The New York State Police was organized in 1917, largely through the efforts of two women, Miss Katherine Mayo and Miss M. Moyca Newell. A foreman working for Miss Newell was killed during a holdup attempt in a rural area of the state. Newell and Mayo were outraged that no effort was made to apprehend the four assailants. Along with other influential New Yorkers, they formed a "Committee for a State Police."

Governor Charles Whitman agreed that there was a need for a state constabulary to give the rural areas of the state the same crime protection afforded to the cities. On April 17, 1917, Whitman signed into law a bill creating the Department of State Police.[12] In 1921, the New York State Police patrolled one and one half million miles, recovered 257 automobiles and $188,116 worth of property, seized $892,500 worth of intoxicating liquors, and made 12,664 arrests, of which over half were for violation of traffic laws.[13]

In 1917, Michigan set up its state police in response to the strong patriotic feelings of the period. In 1919, the state legislature made the force permanent.

The West Virginia Department of Public Safety, commonly known as the West Virginia State Police, was established by a Special Session of the West Virginia Legislature on March 24, 1919. Major Jackson Arnold, a veteran of World War I and a major in the West Virginia National Guard, was appointed by Governor Cornwell as the first Superintendent with orders that he form and staff a state police organization by June 24, 1919. The original force of 125 men was organized into two companies. The Troopers wore World War I army uniforms with campaign hats. Their standard weapons were the 45 caliber revolver and the 1903 Springfield rifle. For transportation, they were required to provide their own horse.

Employment as a member of a state police organization was quite demanding during the prohibition and depression years. In the tradition of the Texas Rangers and the Pennsylvania State Police, potential state police recruits committed themselves to a formal enlistment contract, for up to 3 years.

In 1920, the average number of arrests per member of the Pennsylvania State Police was 50, with 95% convicted. The average for the members of the New York Police Department during the same period was 24, with 80% convicted.[14]

On July 1, 1921, H. Norman Schwarzkopf, a graduate of the United States Military Academy at West Point, was appointed as the first Superintendent of the New Jersey State Police. He subsequently organized the first training class later that year (Figure 4.3).

The original transportation for the New Jersey State Police consisted of 61 horses, 20 motorcycles, 1 car, and 1 truck. The horse remained the principle means of transportation until the late 1920s.

Figure 4.3 New Jersey governor A. Harry Moore and state police superintendent H. Norman Schwarzkopf. (Retrieved from http://njspmuseum.blogspot.com/2009/11/snake-bite.html.)

The Delaware State Police were created in 1923 from an existing force of traffic officers employed by the State Highway Commission. On June 27, 1923, the first 11 officers were hired at a monthly salary of $115. Although they had the authority to enforce all laws, the primary emphasis of these motorcycle officers was the enforcement of traffic laws. Many of the state officers killed between the 1920s and 1940s died as a result of motorcycle accidents.

By 1929, nine states had state police organizations similar to the Pennsylvania model. Following the pattern established by the state of Pennsylvania in the creation of the Pennsylvania State Police, the State of Missouri established the Missouri State Highway Patrol by an act of the 56th General Assembly in 1931 with an authorized strength of 125 members. However, because of limited appropriations, only 55 patrolmen were trained for active duty at the St. Louis Police Department Academy. On November 24, 1931, the original force of Missouri Highway Patrolmen began patrolling the highways of the state to enforce the traffic laws and to promote traffic safety.

In Mississippi, the lack of a state-level law enforcement agency led Governor Hugh White to take some desperate action to break up the criminal activities of the Mississippi Gold Coast in 1936. The governor, after receiving numerous complaints of gambling, alcohol, and prostitution, asked Thomas B. Birdsong, the chief of police of Clarksdale, Mississippi, to assume command of the Mississippi National Guard's Riot Section and clean up the coast. Birdsong trained the force and used them to suppress the vice. The National Guard's Riot Section later participated in the trial and hanging of three convicted rapists, the trial and hanging of another man who killed a husband and wife, and numerous manhunts.

Finally, recognizing the need for a state-level law enforcement agency to replace the Mississippi National Guard's Riot Section, the Mississippi Highway Safety Patrol began on April 1, 1938, with a nucleus of 53 troopers, each paid $125 per month. By 1939, every state except for Wisconsin and Vermont had a state police force. Soon the state enforcement administrators found themselves faced with the organizational problems that had traditionally plagued local enforcement agencies. These problems were personnel selection, organizational structure, control, and training. From early on, state police administrators supported the principle of succession from the ranks.

The Vermont Department of Public Safety was created on July 1, 1947, after a Bennington College student disappeared while hiking the Long Trail. After a month long investigation, no trace of the girl was found. It was then that it became evident that the 14 county sheriff's departments were inadequate in dealing with statewide law enforcement problems. The Vermont Department of Public Safety began with 27 highway patrol officers who transferred from the Department of Motor Vehicles and 30 probationary troopers. These officers had statewide police jurisdiction.

General Butler's View

In March 1931 United States Marine Corps Major General Smedley Darlington Butler suggested a further, much more structured view of the organization of the state police model. General Butler was the former Director of Public Safety for Philadelphia and was a contributor to the organization of the Oregon State Police. He had experienced firsthand the difficulties of trying to introduce honesty, efficiency, and professionalism into a politically corrupt system. General Butler, frustrated and angry over his Philadelphia experience, proposed his solution to the question of how to stop political influence. His solution was to introduce an organizational structure designed along strict military guidelines.

General Butler proposed the elimination of local police agencies and the creation of a state police force. This new force would be similar to the military in recruitment, selection, assignment, organization, and discipline. Butler proposed the selection of unmarried young men for 4-year assignments. The men would live in a barracks and could not marry, thus ensuring that they would be undistracted.

General Butler provided for the marriage of officers and noncommissioned officers assigned and posted to duty. Butler's proposal was much more acceptable during the 1930s than today. During the 1930s, with the nation in the grips of the Great Depression, young men were more inclined to accept the enlistment and barracks life Butler proposed. General Butler once told a New Jersey audience that he thought the best way to control crime was to shoot criminals on sight and make jails so unbearable that criminals would never want to return (Figure 4.4).

Traffic Regulation and Enforcement

For many Americans, state-level law enforcement means highway patrol and traffic safety and enforcement. It is true that traffic safety and enforcement have been and remain major aspects of state law enforcement. Many notable events highlight the history of traffic regulation and enforcement. In 1836, well before the development of the automobile, Tennessee enacted a law requiring driving on the right side of the road.

It became clear during the first two decades of the twentieth century that the automobile would assume a major role in American society. With increased automobiles, the nation's roads slowly began to transition into the highway system of today. In 1900, there was one auto for every 10,000 people, and in 1930, practically every family owned a car. It was natural for the states to assume the responsibility for automobile registration

Figure 4.4 United States Marine Corps Major General Smedley D. Butler, who served as director of public safety for Philadelphia in the 1920s. (Courtesy of the Marine Corps Association and Foundation, http://www.mca-marines.org/files/imagecache/full_page_image/ Smedley%20Butler.jpg.)

and the enactment, regulation, and enforcement of traffic and related issues. In 1906, the Commonwealth of Virginia began registration of motor vehicles. Over 4,500 motor vehicles were registered at a fee of $2 each between 1906 and 1910. The first motor vehicle to be registered in Virginia was a 1906 Oldsmobile.[15]

Highway construction commenced with the Lincoln Highway in 1912, which linked New York with Chicago and San Francisco. The Federal Aid Road Act of 1916 encouraged further highway development and provided funds for construction. During the Great Depression of the 1930s, countless roads, highways, and bridges were constructed as projects funded by federal depression recovery initiatives. On October 1, 1940, the super-highway era began with the opening of the first 160 miles of the Pennsylvania Turnpike. Though road construction lagged during World War II, after the war, a new emphasis was placed on the highway system. The Interstate Highway Act of 1956 providing funding to improve older roads and up to date with the creation of 41,000 miles of interstate highways.

As the road system of the nation improved and the number of cars in the nation increased, the highways gave criminals new flexibility. Images of gangsters and fast automobiles robbing banks or bootleggers hauling whiskey across state lines captured the imagination of many Americans. This new wave of mobile criminals created new challenges to law enforcement authorities.

Improved roads and the introduction of faster automobiles increased the need for public highway safety awareness. As speed limits on the roads increased, the nation witnessed an increase in traffic accidents. Steps were taken to implement speed enforcement

Figure 4.5 Traffic safety and enforcement remains a major mission of highway patrols. Here, Kansas Department of Transportation workers change a speed limit sign after the 55 mph mandate of 1974. (Courtesy of the Kansas Department of Transportation, http://www.ksdot .org/interstate50th/KsStory_Ihistory1970_3.asp.)

and highway safety initiatives. By the mid-1960s, a total of 45 states allowed the use of radar in traffic enforcement. In addition to enforcement efforts, safety features were developed and incorporated into new automobiles. The introduction of safety glass and seat belts and the reduction of speed limits on some highways have saved tens of thousands of lives (Figure 4.5).

Growth and Expansion: 1940–1960

World War II greatly affected state enforcement organizations. The loss of personnel from the state organizations forced many enforcement organizations to operate below authorized strength levels. Many states created auxiliary forces to supplement state agencies. With the conclusion of the war, thousands of veterans returned to civilian life with an interest in law enforcement after exposure to military police or shore patrol duty. State enforcement agencies welcomed these veterans home.

By 1950, the police agencies in 36 states had substantially full law enforcement authority, whereas 12 states were restricted to enforcement of traffic laws or to crimes committed on state highways.[16]

State governments began to reassess their policing responsibilities in the late 1950s. States created new agencies to fill the void existing between comprehensive state and local enforcement. In 1951, Tennessee created the Tennessee Bureau of Criminal Identification (TBI) as a component of the Department of Safety. The TBI provided investigative assistance to the various district attorney generals across the state. As a result of the scandals of the administration of Governor Ray Blanton in 1980, the Tennessee Bureau of Criminal Identification was renamed the TBI. It also became a separate department within the state government.

As early as 1952, Colonel George Mingle, the superintendent of the Ohio State Police, began to promote the use of the safety belt by all highway patrol personnel. In February 1956, he issued specifications to include two safety belts in the front seats of all new highway patrol cruisers. By 1987, a total of 25 states had implemented mandatory use laws and 15 states had pending legislation on similar statutes for seat belts.

With the improvement of local law enforcement, many states would concentrate their state police and state highway patrol resources on traffic enforcement.

The Modern Era: 1960 to Present

Highly trained and determined to do a professional job, state law enforcement led the efforts to increase the level of law enforcement training nationwide.

Civil rights marches became frequent occurrences in the South during the 1960s. Often, the local law enforcement found itself overwhelmed, and state enforcement agencies, supported by state and federal military forces, were called upon to reestablish social order. In the fall of 1962, the Mississippi Highway Patrol was called to support the racial integration of the University of Mississippi.

In 1962, the Illinois State Police were rocked with a scandal when it was discovered that officers in two state police districts had received payoffs from about 90 trucking firms since about 1945. After an extensive investigation, the Illinois State Director of Public Safety announced that 40 of the 60 state police assigned to one of the districts had signed confessions admitting they had taken payoffs. These men were promptly suspended with their commander. A total of 20 additional officers were suspended as the investigation continued. The next year, another scandal shook Illinois. In November 1963, a total of 23 state policemen were suspended on charges of accepting kickbacks from tow truck operators.

State law enforcement agencies continued to respond to changing service demands. The functions of the Arizona Highway Patrol, the Enforcement Division of the Department of Liquor Licenses and Control, and the Narcotics Division of the Arizona Department of Law were consolidated by Executive Order on July 1, 1969, into the Arizona Department of Public Safety. Under the Arizona Department of Public Safety, a central state criminal records repository, a criminal investigation organization, a crime laboratory, air rescue services, a statewide communications network, a certified law enforcement officer training program, and motor carrier functions were established.

The New York Drug Enforcement Task Force, founded in 1970, is the largest and most formally structured task force sponsored by the Drug Enforcement Administration. It was created to curtail the illicit sale and distribution of narcotics and dangerous drugs through investigative and prosecutorial action directed against the middle and upper echelons of the narcotics traffickers with New York City.

One of the benefits of the 1972 Equal Employment Opportunity Act was the opening of the ranks of law enforcement agencies to women and minorities. The period of the late 1960s and 1970s witnessed the reduction of employment barriers, which had reduced or prevented the opportunity for females and minorities to obtain an appointment with a state enforcement agency. In 1972, Pennsylvania became the first state to employ women on a state level and assign them the same duties as their male counterparts. By 1978, it was estimated that 2.7% of the personnel employed in state-level enforcement agencies were female.

During the fall of 1979, the New Jersey State Police embarked on an experimental program to recruit, select, and train an all-female class in a concerted effort to increase the number of female state troopers. This special class, a first in the nation, was a one-time infusion of women into the New Jersey State Police. Thirty females completed the course and were sworn in as troopers in June 1980.

In November 1991, allegations of illegal wiretapping by the Missouri State Highway Patrol extended to the top three officials. The investigation revealed that wiretaps were placed at patrol headquarters and one suburban station to gather information about employees. An internal disciplinary panel recommended that a major and a lieutenant be dismissed and a captain be demoted.

Today's typical highway patrol or state police handle a wide variety of additional tasks, which include support services to other police agencies, safety education, motor vehicle inspection, commercial vehicle inspection, blood and transplant organ deliveries, search and rescue operations, 24-hour public information service on road conditions, and security for the governor and others so designated for executive protection.

State-Level Resources and Their Role with Homeland Security

State-level agencies have a much broader role with homeland security efforts than just aiding in the struggle against terrorism. In fact, as events such as Hurricane Katrina in Mississippi and Louisiana so clearly revealed, state level agencies, including law enforcement, serve as key partners with homeland security before, during, and after the event. State agencies must be involved in planning for contingency-related operations including, but not limited to, area evacuation, search and rescue, repair, and reestablishment of damaged infrastructure. Additionally, state-level enforcement may find itself a bridge between federal level support and local jurisdictional needs.

In addition to law enforcement resources, each state maintains, with the support of federal assets, National Guard commands. Since the attacks of September 11, 2011, the state National Guards, among other missions, have been tasked with the formation, organization, and training of CBRNE response units, also known as homeland response force units. The units are regional forces that will cross state lines when needed. They are part of a restructuring of the nation's chemical, biological, radiological, nuclear, and high-yield explosive (CBRNE) consequence management enterprise. One unit will be based in each of the 10 Federal Emergency Management Agency regions. The units are scheduled to have 570 guard members, and each will have a medical team, a search and extraction team, a decontamination team, and very robust command and control capabilities.[17]

State Wildlife Enforcement

Emphasizing wildlife enforcement provides states with resources to deter crimes associated with poaching or the misuse of lands. For the most part, each state possesses some form of state wildlife enforcement organization. Generally, wildlife enforcement officers are described as follows:[18]

> The position of a wildlife officer requires diverse skills and knowledge. It is one of the most demanding in the wildlife and law enforcement field; opportunities are limited and competition for openings is intense. The wildlife officer is quite often the only contact the public has with the Division of Wildlife. The acceptance of conservation programs and of regulations can often be enhanced by the actions of the wildlife officer. Therefore, it is imperative that individuals with a high work ethic, outstanding knowledge of the job, and of unquestionable character be selected for these positions.[19]

State wildlife law enforcement is not an isolated domain. Instead, it often collaborates with a variety of peer agencies both locally, regionally, and nationally. Examples of such partnerships include collaborations with "city and county law enforcement entities, state parks, Department of Natural Resources Enforcement, NOAA, U.S. Fish and Wildlife Service, Tribes, Homeland Security, and U.S. Coast Guard."[20]

Although state wildlife enforcement officers must complete state training and certification requirements to satisfy entry into the law enforcement occupation, they may also complete federal training regimens. For example, in North Carolina, a wildlife officer "recently completed FBI National Academy training in law enforcement techniques."[21] Additional training provides state wildlife law enforcement officers with continuing education and increased skill sets.

Other forms of training include opportunities with the Law Enforcement Mountain Operations School (LEMOS). The LEMOS represents a collaborative project between the U.S. and Canada through which wildlife enforcement officers may undergo a variety of training experiences.[22] The LEMOS is located in Priest Lake, Idaho. Examples of training courses include instruction in "day and night land navigation, cold weather survival skills, emergency medical procedures, and team operations planning."[23] In some instances, the entirety of the outdoor training may be accomplished using only snowshoes as footwear.[24] This situation may occur when learning to evacuate heavy victims from simulated circumstances involving "deep snow and heavy timber."[25]

State wildlife officers encounter a variety of dangers when performing their duties. These dangers may originate from both natural and man-made sources. For example, in Greenville, Mississippi, a wildlife officer was bitten by an alligator during an alligator relocation activity.[26] Wildlife officers in Colorado consistently experience the dangers of wild animal attacks involving bears, and sometimes must kill the animals to protect society.[27] During March 2012, Floridian wildlife officers subdued a "15-foot, 3-inch Burmese Python."[28] Another Florida incident involved the shooting of an escaped tiger that was owned by an actor who had played the movie role of Tarzan.[29] The wildlife officer was attacked by the animal during a recovery operation and had no choice but to kill the animal.[30]

Man-made threats and crimes (both misdemeanors and felonies) are also encountered by state wildlife officers and are not uncommon within America. In North Carolina, state wildlife officers arrested three poachers for uprooting endangered Venus flytrap plants without proper permission.[31] The Venus flytrap is rather innocuous and has a large

Figure 4.6 Florida Forest Service rangers Jean Bernard Tarrete (left), Dave Gravitt (center), and Florida Fish and Wildlife officer Chris stretch out a 15-foot, 3-inch Burmese python caught by Tarrete and another ranger on March 21, 2012 in Picayune State Forest. (Courtesy of *The Valdosta Daily Times*, http://valdostadailytimes.com/archive/x684083506.)

return-on-investment when it is sold on the black market. Although the offenders anticipated selling approximately 200 uprooted plants for 10 cents per plant, "they can sell for as much as $15 each at roadside stands and on Internet sites."[32]

The occupation as a state wildlife and enforcement officer is often deadly. During 2010, in Pennsylvania, Officer David Grove died in the line of duty when he was "investigating a poaching incident in a wooded area."[33] During 2007, in Texas, Game Warden Justin Hurst was killed in a shootout in which he was "reportedly shot at least twice by a rifle, with bullets striking his upper torso and legs."[34] Hurst had suspected that his assailant was illegally hunting from a roadway.[35] Monty Carmikle, a wildlife officer in Arkansas, died in the line of duty in helicopter accident in 2008 while "patrolling for violators of a ban on deer hunting at night."[36] In Mississippi, in 2002, Michael Andrews perished while "responding to a report of poachers headlighting deer near Tylertown in Walthall County."[37]

State wildlife officers represent a different aspect of law enforcement whose primary concentrations focus upon nature. Wildlife enforcement officers are just as legitimate law enforcement personnel as are city police or county sheriffs. They encounter a wide range of situations ranging from the relatively benign illegal uprooting of plants to losing their lives in the line of duty while attempting to apprehend criminals. Their training is not easy; instead, it is rigorous and may sometimes exceed the rigors of typical law enforcement academies (e.g., the LEMOS simulations involving snowshoes). Regardless, state law enforcement officers provide a valuable resource through which both wildlife and society are protected from both natural and man-made threats (Figure 4.6).

Specialized State Enforcement and Investigations

States, in order to ensure the safety of their citizens, have created various enforcement and investigative agencies and departments, with functions including executive protection, bureaus of investigation and narcotics, juvenile and family service, health, and public defense.

Each of the states has some entity that is dedicated to providing investigative services. For example, the Oklahoma State Bureau of Investigation (OSBI) provides investigative services to support the investigating of law enforcement cases. These services include "collecting and preserving evidence at crime scenes, participating in undercover investigations to obtain information and evidence, interviewing witnesses, and apprehending criminals."[38] A variety of investigation types benefit from the services of the OSBI. Examples of these types of investigations include "oil field theft, auto theft, homicide, rape, insurance fraud, political corruption, official misconduct, and other white collar crimes."[39] The personnel of the OSBI represent a diverse set of skills and credentials. The types of personnel comprising the OSBI include "pilots, polygraph experts, forensic computer experts, and experts in crime scene investigations, certified public accountants, forensic child interviewers, forensic video analysts, forensic artist[s], and others with special skills, which provide many avenues to solve and prevent crime."[40]

Among the remaining states, the individual investigative entities are similar. For example, the Mississippi Bureau of Investigation (MBI) is tasked with general powers of policing per the Mississippi Code.[41] The MBI investigates reports and prevents criminal activities; coordinates activities between federal, state, and local authorities that are involved in crime prevention and criminal investigations; and performs other related tasks as may be assigned.[42] Its services encompass protective services, special operations, salvage inspection, victim assistance, and intelligence.[43]

Another perspective on specialized units among the states involves the implementing of special weapons and tactics (SWAT) groups and organizations. The CHP contains a SWAT component. Within California, SWAT teams are used to resolve or mitigate high-risk or potentially hazardous incidents occurring at state facilities.[44] They also serve as a rapid deployment force and provide counter-assault team support to the Dignitary Protection Section and the Governor's Protective Detail upon request.[45] Tactical training is an additional responsibility of the SWAT team.[46]

New Jersey has a special law enforcement unit that addresses issues of cyber crime. Within its Special Investigations Section, the Cyber Crimes Unit (CCU) exists as a resource that is "composed of State Police enlisted detectives, civilian analysts, and task forces from other police agencies."[47] The CCU possesses two investigative squads and other personnel that are committed to the FBI Regional Computer Forensic Laboratory.[48] The mission of CCU is to "conduct and assist in investigations where computers, networks, telecommunication devices, and other technological instruments are the vehicle or target for the commission of criminal acts against network resources critical to the function of corporate or government entities."[49] Successfully completing this mission involves investigations that range from cases of cyber-terrorism to identity theft in the virtual environment.[50]

Within the state of Montana, both fire and police focuses are contained within its Investigations Bureau. Specifically, in Montana, the Investigations Bureau contains the "Fire Prevention and Investigation Section, the Major Case Section, the Medicaid Fraud Control Section, and the Special Investigations Section, which includes the Computer Crimes Unit, the Sexual or Violent Offender Registry, the Sex Offender Compliance Unit, the Internet Crimes Against Children Unit, and the Financial Crimes Unit."[51] Analogous with its peer entities throughout the nation, the Montana Investigations Bureau performs a wide array of investigations ranging from Medicaid fraud and elder abuse to sex crimes and cyber crimes.[52]

The Investigation Division of the Nevada Department of Public Safety emphasizes the countering of narcotics crimes. Specifically, it "concentrates on organizing joint narcotic task forces in rural communities; participating in major narcotic and gang investigations with federal agencies; providing major crime investigative services to local, county, and state law enforcement; is involved in international investigations through its INTERPOL State Liaison Office; and is currently the lead state agency in Homeland Security intelligence matters."[53] This description shows the distinctiveness of the narcotics focus of the agency and demonstrates its support of investigations concentrating upon other issues.

Within the state of Florida, a different organizational emphasis is exhibited by the Bureau of Criminal Investigations. This organization "conducts investigations into auto theft, commercial vehicle and cargo theft, heavy equipment theft, identity theft, driver's license fraud, title fraud, odometer fraud, and other criminal activity related to the DHSMV function."[54] This description presents a vehicular focus within the investigative department.

Similarly, the remaining American states each possess some type of specialized investigative or enforcement organization. Because of the different types of societies and crimes represented among the states, many of these organizations each have a different emphasis, may have differing organizational structures and resources, and fulfill different missions. Regardless, they each share a common bond with respect to the prevention of crime and the maintaining of societal order.

Notable Aspects of State Law Enforcement Entities

Many state law enforcement organizations contribute toward maintaining the safety of their respective citizenries throughout America. Although many state agencies are similar, each state agency represents a unique entity. Regardless, all state agencies share the common goals of deterring crime and maintaining societal order. Below are examples of the primary agencies that serve some of the individual states.

Alabama

The Alabama Highway Patrol was formed in 1935 and consisted of an initial quantity of 74 officers. It commenced operations in 1936 and had an immediate impact among the roadways of Alabama. Before the end of its first year, it had completed "615,335 miles patrolling on motorcycles and 583,756 miles in automobiles. They inspected 8951 vehicles for defective lights and brakes, issuing courtesy cards to call a motorist's attention to defects. They weighed more than 3200 trucks and made some 7000 arrests in enforcing Alabama's highway regulations. In addition, the officers began a continuing practice of assisting motorists, rendering aid to 5269 that first year."[55]

The Alabama Highway Patrol also was among the first of the state law enforcement organizations nationally to use sports cars as operational tools. During the early 1970s, it operated the Javelin AMC within its fleet of patrol cars. This usage highlighted Alabama as the first state to deploy the "first pony car officially used by a major police organization in the USA."[56]

The Alabama Highway Patrol has matured through time to demonstrate both ground and aerial capabilities for law enforcement tasks. It also participates during state emergencies (e.g., hurricanes and other forms of disaster, etc.), helping to facilitate the safety and well-being of Alabamians. Its modern organizational structuring now provides services ranging from aerial speed enforcement and chaplaincy to construction zone traffic enforcement and honor guards (Figure 4.7).[57]

Figure 4.7 Alabama Highway Patrol Javelin. Alabama was the first state to use "pony cars" as an operational component of its highway patrol. (Courtesy of the Alabama Department of Public Safety, http://dps.alabama.gov/Home/wfContent.aspx?ID=70&PLH1=plhInformation-JavelinPatrolCar.)

Missouri

When the Missouri Department of Corrections experienced prison unrest during the 1950, the Missouri Highway Patrol was leveraged as a resource through which order was established within the rioting environments. The most serious of these incidents occurred on September 22, 1954, in which a riot occurred at the men's state penitentiary. The inmates obtained a set of keys and became unruly by burning vehicles and buildings and hurling bricks, and were holding guards hostage.[58] All available highway patrolmen were dispatched to "quell the riot."[59] Approximately 500 inmates rioted.[60] Before midnight, "285 patrolmen in 202 cars were on the scene" in conjunction with approximately 100 St. Louis police officers. These officers took positions atop buildings, opened fire, and seriously wounded many inmates.[61] Additional personnel were required to quell the rioting. By mid-morning, approximately "2000 police officers and National Guardsmen were on duty at the prison."[62]

The fires were visible to the inmates of the Algoa Reformatory and Women's Prison nearly 20 miles away.[63] As a result, the inmates of this facility staged a separate riot. Although these additional facilities were minimally damaged by rioting, "only cell houses and buildings equipped with sprinklers survived" at the primary prison facility.[64] A total of five buildings were destroyed completely and two were "partially destroyed."[65] Over $10 million in damages occurred to state properties.[66] A total of 21 inmates were wounded during this incident, resulting in three deaths; eight prisoners were harmed and injured by fighting among themselves; and one prisoner "was murdered by stabbing and beating."[67]

This incident shows the necessity of leveraging highway patrol and state police forces during periods of unrest that occur within incarceration settings. State law enforcement was a critical aspect of responding to the rioting. Although guards were present within the prison during the time of the riots, Missouri leveraged its state law enforcement personnel as first responders towards quelling the incident. The use of state law enforcement personnel was essential in nullifying the effectiveness of the riot.

Texas

One of the most notable Texas incidents occurred during the late 1960s. This incident involved the 1969 kidnapping of Trooper James Kenneth Crone by Robert Dent and Ila Fae

Figure 4.8 Police vehicles converge during a chase through southeast Texas on May 2, 1969, involving the kidnapping of trooper James Kenneth Crone by Robert Dent and Ila Fae Holiday. (From Colburn, T., 2011, *The Houston Chronicle*. Retrieved from http://blog.chron.com/bayoucityhistory/2011/02/obituary-james-kenneth-crone-69/.)

Holiday. This incident was the basis of the 1974 movie titled *The Sugarland Express*.[68] This event is summarized as follows:

> In May 1969, Ila Fae Holiday assisted her husband Robert Dent to escape from the Beauford H. Jester Prison Farm in Texas, because she feared their son would be placed in the care of her mother. During their flight, they overpowered and kidnapped Texas Department of Public Safety trooper Kenneth Crone, holding him hostage in a slow-moving caravan, along with reporters in news vans and helicopters. The Dents and Crone travelled through Port Arthur, Houston, Navasota, and finally Wheelock, Texas. … The Dents brought Crone to the home of Ila Fae's mother, where they encountered numerous officers. An FBI agent and county sheriff shot and killed Robert Dent and later arrested Ila Fae. Trooper Crone was unharmed. Ila Fae spent five months in a women's correctional facility; she died in 1989.[69]

This pursuit covered approximately 300 miles and occurred over a 5-hour period.[70] Although many may perceive the duties of state law enforcement officers primarily as roles of traffic and roadway enforcement, this incident shows the dangerousness of performing the duties that are affiliated with employment as a state law enforcement officer (Figure 4.8).

Summary

Within the United States, the use of state law enforcement agencies has involved many origins and influences. Uniqueness is exhibited among the histories of each individual state agency that contributes toward maintaining order and preventing crime. Some agencies may have storied and famous events touted within their histories, whereas others may be relatively unassuming and bland. Regardless, each state law enforcement organization contributes a meaningful contribution toward its served populace.

State law enforcement organizations are as diverse as each of the states. There is no national consensus regarding the qualifications and certifications that are necessary for entering law enforcement as a state officer. Instead, each state may mandate its own requirements that may vary distinctively from the requirements of other states.

Each individual state law enforcement organization must fulfill some mission with respect to maintaining societal order and deterring crime. Some state law enforcement organizations involve a focus upon addressing the issues of organized crime, whereas others may have a greater ability to address issues of narcotics. These missions are commensurate with the attributes of crime that impact states and their citizenries.

Across the nation, departments of public safety may encompass a variety of organizational structures. Therefore, they may contain separate organizational components that are dedicated to the functions of fire safety, law enforcement, investigation, search and rescue, and so on. Certainly, these entities collaborate to provide citizens with effective and efficient services.

Although some may identify state law enforcement agencies with the concepts of traditional policing, specialized concentrations often exist among state law enforcement agencies. State wildlife enforcement officers address felony and misdemeanor issues that arise in nature from both man-made and natural threats. Further, the dangers faced by state wildlife law enforcement personnel range from the risks of being shot by poachers to injurious altercations with wildlife.

Discussion Questions

1. Has local control of state and local police agencies and the lack of a national police agency adversely affected the effectiveness of law enforcement in the United States? Explain your answer. Give examples.
2. What are the basic duties of a municipal law enforcement agency? County law enforcement? State law enforcement? Compare and contrast these duties with those of federal law enforcement agencies.
3. Do some research regarding Indian lands. What is the basis for tribal policing? Who provides police services on Indian land? What types of relationships exist between tribal police and federal agencies?
4. What are special jurisdiction agencies and what policing responsibilities do they generally have? Give examples.

References

1. U.S. Bureau of Justice Statistics (2004). *Census of State and Local Law Enforcement Agencies.* Washington, DC: Government Printing Office.
2. Waldron, R., Quarles, C., McElreath, D., Waldron, M., & Milstein, D. (2009). *Introduction to Criminal Justice* (p. 137). Tulsa, OK: K & M Publishers, Inc.
3. U.S. Bureau of Justice Statistics. (1987). *Profile of State and Local Enforcement Agencies.* Washington, DC: Government Printing Office.
4. Sifakis, C. (1982). *Encyclopedia of American Crime.* New York, NY: Facts on File.
5. Smith, B. (1940). *Police Systems in the United States.* New York, NY: Harper & Brothers.
6. Ibid.

7. Bullock, Alexander H. (1886). *Address of His Excellency Alexander H. Bullock to the Two Branches of the Legislature of Massachusetts, January 6, 1866*. Boston, MA: Wright & Potter.

8. Ibid.

9. Ibid.

10. Sutherland, E. H., & Cressey, D. R. (1970). *Principles of Criminology*. Philadelphia, PA: Lippincott.

11. Nevada Department of Public Safety. *A Brief History of the N.H.P.* Retrieved April 1, 2012, from http://nhp.nv.gov/history.shtml

12. New York Division of State Police. *Serving the Public Since 1917*. Retrieved April 3, 2012, from http://www .troopers.ny.gov/Introduction/History/

13. Sutherland, E. H. (1924). *Principles of Criminology*. Chicago, IL: University of Chicago Press.

14. Ibid.

15. Virginia State Police. *Virginia State Police History*. Retrieved May 1, 2012, from http://www.vsp .state.va.us/history.shtm

16. Sutherland, E. H., & Cressey, D. R. (1970). *Principles of Criminology*. Philadelphia, PA: Lippincott.

17. Garamone, J. *Dod and Guard Establish Eight Homeland Response Units*. Retrieved May 3, 2012, from http://www.nationalguard.com/news/2010/jul/14/dod-guard-establish-eight-homeland-response-force-units

18. State of Ohio. *Planning a Wildlife Career: Wildlife Law Enforcement*. Retrieved April 21, 2012, from http://www.dnr.state.oh.us/Home/wild_resourcessubhomepage/about_the_division_landingpage/employemploye/employcadet/tabid/5727/Default.aspx

19. Ibid.

20. Washington Department of Fish & Wildlife. *Enforcement*. Retrieved April 12, 2012, from http://wdfw.wa.gov/enforcement/careers/

21. North Carolina Wildlife Resources Commission. *Conserve & Protect: The Blog of the N.C. Wildlife Resources Commission*. Retrieved April 21, 2012, from http://www.ncwildlife.org/News/Blogs/NCWRCBlog/tabid/715/EntryId/54/Wildlife-Enforcement-Officer-Completes-FBI-Training.aspx

22. U.S. Department of Justice. *Law Enforcement Coordinating Committee*. Retrieved April 21, 2012, from http://www.justice.gov/usao/wae/programs/lecc.html

23. Yuasa, M. (2012). State fish and wildlife enforcement officers keeping busy in the woods and on the water. *The Seattle Times*. Retrieved April 21, 2012, from http://seattletimes.nwsource.com/html/reeltimenorthwest/2017723811_state_fish_and_wildlife_enforc_2.html

24. Ibid.

25. Ibid.

26. The Associated Press. Alligator Bites Wildlife Enforcement Officer in Greenville, Miss. Retrieved April 21, 2012, from http://www.nola.com/environment/index.ssf/2011/06/alligator_bites_wildlife_enfor.html

27. State of Colorado, Division of Wildlife. *Aspenites Urged to Learn to Live with Bears*. Retrieved April 12, 2012, from http://dnr.state.co.us/newsapp/press.asp?pressid=7624

28. Staats, E. (2012). Near-record python snagged by southwest Florida rangers. *The Valdosta Daily Times*. Retrieved April 21, 2012, from http://valdostadailytimes.com/todays-top-stories/x1451005321/Near-record-python-snagged-by-southwest-Florida-rangers

29. Associated Press. Officer Kills Escaped Tiger After Daylong Search in Florida. Retrieved April 12, 2012, from http://articles.boston.com/2004-07-14/news/29208952_1_steve-sipek-tarzan-in-b-movies-tiger

30. Ibid.

31. Associated Press. 3 Poachers arrested for Uprooting Rare N.C. Venus Flytraps. Retrieved April 12, 2012, from http://www.usatoday.com/news/nation/environment/story/2012-01-25/endangered-venus-flytrap-arrests/52790430/1

32. Ibid.

33. The Associated Press. Wildlife conservation officer David L. Grove killed a year ago. *The Herald-Mail*. Retrieved on April 21, 2012 from http://www.herald-mail.com/news/tristate/hm-trial-begins-in-shooting-death-of-pa-game-warden-20120924,0,3200273.story

34. North American Wildlife Enforcement Officers Association. *Justin Hurst, Texas, United States*. Retrieved April 21, 2012, from http://www.naweoa.org/FallenOfficersJ15/usmemorial.php?primarykey=74

35. Ibid.

36. North American Wildlife Enforcement Officers Association. *Monty Carmikle, Arkansas, United States*. Retrieved April 12, 2012, from http://www.naweoa.org/FallenOfficersJ15/usmemorial.php?primarykey=96

37. North American Wildlife Enforcement Officers Association. *Michael Anthony Andrews, Mississippi, United States*. Retrieved April 21, 2012, from http://www.naweoa.org/FallenOfficersJ15/usmemorial.php?primarykey=47

38. Oklahoma State Bureau of Investigation. *Investigative Division*. Retrieved April 21, 2012, from http://www.ok.gov/osbi/Investigative/index.html

39. Ibid.

40. Ibid.

41. Mississippi Department of Public Safety. *Bureau of Investigation*. Retrieved April 21, 2012, from http://www.dps.state.ms.us/crime-investigation/bureau-of-investigation/

42. Ibid.

43. Ibid.

44. California Highway Patrol. *Protective Services Division*. Retrieved April 12, 2012, from http://www.chp.ca.gov/depts_divs_offs/psd.html

45. Ibid.

46. Ibid.

47. State of New Jersey, Department of Law & Public Safety. *Cyber-Crime Unit*. Retrieved April 21, 2012, from http://www.njsp.org/divorg/invest/cyber-crimes-unit.html

48. Ibid.

49. Ibid.

50. Ibid.

51. Montana Department of Justice. *Investigations Bureau*. Retrieved April 21, 2012, from https://doj.mt.gov/enforcement/investigations-bureau/

52. Ibid.

53. Nevada Department of Public Safety. *A Brief History—Department of Public Safety, Investigation Division*. Retrieved April 12, 2012, from http://dps.nv.gov/id/History.shtml

54. Florida Department of Highway Safety and Motor Vehicles. *Bureau of Criminal Investigations (BOI)*. Retrieved April 21, 2012, from http://www.flhsmv.gov/fhp/BuOfIn/

55. Alabama Department of Public Safety. *Department of Public Safety History: 1935–1990*. Retrieved April 21, 2012, from http://dps.alabama.gov/Home/wfContent.aspx?ID=0&PLH1=plhInformation-History

56. The National AMC Police Car Registry Home Page. *Javelin AMX*. Retrieved April 21, 2012, from http://www.javelinamx.com/javhome/copcar/index.htm

57. Alabama Department of Public Safety. *Welcome Message*. Retrieved April 21, 2012, from http://dps.alabama.gov/Home/Default.aspx

58. Missouri Department of Public Safety. *Annex M – Civil Disorder*. Retrieved April 21, 2012, from http://sema.dps.mo.gov/docs/programs/Planning,%20Disaster%20&%20Recovery/State%20of%20Missouri%20Hazard%20Analysis/2011%20State%20Hazard%20Analysis/Anne_M_Civil_Disorder.pdf

59. Ibid.

60. Ibid.

61. Ibid.

62. Ibid.

63. Ibid.
64. Ibid.
65. Ibid.
66. Ibid.
67. Ibid.
68. Ibid.
69. Trooper of 'Sugarland Express' fame dies at 70. *The Police News*. Retrieved April 21, 2012, from http://thepolicenews.net/screenprint.aspx?newsletterid=26094
70. Hearst Communications (2011). Obituary: James Kenneth Crone, 69. *The Houston Chronicle*. Retrieved April 21, 2012, from http://blog.chron.com/bayoucityhistory/2011/02/obituary-james-kenneth-crone-69/

Bibliography

North American Wildlife Officers Association. Kansas man charged with poaching 14-point buck. Retrieved April 12, 2012, from http://naweoa.org/joomla15/index.php?option=com_cont ent&view=article&id=250:kansas-man-charged-with-poaching-14-point-buck&catid=1: naweoa-news&Itemid=82

Rhodes, G. Man, woman arrested and charged with illegal hunting, possession of firearms and unlawfully shot game. Retrieved April 21, 2012, from http://www.dnrec.delaware.gov/News/ Pages/Man,-woman-arrested-and-charged-with-illegal-hunting,-weapons-possession.aspx

Federal and International Law Enforcement

5

And so every one of us in the FBI, I don't care if it's a file clerk someplace or an agent there or a computer specialist, understands that our main mission is to protect the public from another September 11, another terrorist attack.

Robert Mueller

Learning Objectives

The objectives of this chapter are to

- Understand the law enforcement system within the United States
- Recognize the significance of federal, state, local, and tribal agencies
- Define organizational facets of law enforcement agencies
- Explain the duties and responsibilities of the major federal law enforcement agencies
- Compare the relationship between law enforcement and homeland security
- Discuss the role of international law enforcement
- Explain the concept of authority and jurisdiction

Introduction

In the United States, law enforcement is a function of the executive branch of the government. Unlike many other Western nations, the United States does not have a national police agency, but rather, the nation is served by a wide range of agencies, each with a primary area of responsibility.

Federal law enforcement and law enforcement are in a constant state of change. Agencies are created, combined, and in some cases, divided or disbanded. Since the 1970s, agencies such as the Drug Enforcement Administration (DEA), Bureau of Alcohol, Tobacco, Firearms and Explosives, the Secret Service, and the Coast Guard have been formed, reorganized, or moved within the federal government.

During the early years of the Republic, there was limited need for federal level enforcement. Few laws limited the ability to communicate over long distances and the initial reluctance by the states to surrender too much power to the national government initially resulted in slow growth in federal enforcement. As the role and power of the federal government increased over the decades, federal enforcement also expanded.

In the United States, the federal government has jurisdiction over crimes that are national in nature (e.g., national security, operations of the government, customs and immigration matters, regulatory matters, interstate commerce, and federal taxes). In addition, the federal government plays a critical role in maintaining the safety and security of federal property, employees, and the public. Federal enforcement also has a significant international role. Crime does not recognize international boundaries. Threats to the nation from the dangers of terrorism, drug trafficking, cyber crimes, maritime piracy, human trafficking, intellectual property crime and counterfeiting, financial crimes, crimes against children, international organized crime, and international fugitives require federal law enforcement to be engaged internationally.

The first two federal agencies with clear enforcement responsibilities were the United States Marshal Service (USMS) and the Revenue Cutter Service, which is today the United States Coast Guard (USCG). These agencies, which have been serving the nation for over 200 years, have been joined by a wide range of other organizations.[1]

Federal law enforcement agencies have been established in response to new laws and expanding jurisdiction for federal investigators and police officers. In response to the September 11, 2001, terrorist attacks against the United States, a major reorganization of the federal government occurred in 2002. Pursuant to the Homeland Security Act, many federal law enforcement roles and responsibilities were restructured into the following two departments: the Department of Homeland Security (DHS) and the Department of Justice (DOJ). Today, a majority (79%) of the major federal LEOs are found within the DHS and DOJ.[2]

In 2006, the U.S. Governmental Accounting Office (GAO), in *Federal Law Enforcement: Survey of Federal Civilian Law Enforcement Functions and Authorities*, defined a federal LEO, both criminal investigator or uniform police officer, as individuals "authorized to perform at least one of the following four law enforcement functions: conduct criminal investigation, execute search warrants, make arrests, or carry firearms" (p. 2). In 2006, there were over 104 civilian federal law enforcement agencies employing 137,929 sworn LEOs.[2,3]

These officers work in the areas of criminal investigation, police patrol, security and protection, court operations, and corrections. The authority for these agencies to perform law enforcement functions is primarily found in federal statutes or federal regulations, rules, or procedures. Other sources of authority may be found in memoranda of understanding (MOU), presidential directives, internal directives and orders, and delegation of authority from other federal agencies.[2]

As previously stated, there are many federal law enforcement agencies. This chapter highlights some of the famous and familiar agencies that protect American society and contribute to international law enforcement.

U.S. Department of Justice

The mission of the U.S. DOJ is

> to enforce the law and defend the interests of the United States according to the law; to ensure public safety against threats foreign and domestic; to provide federal leadership in preventing and controlling crime; to seek just punishment for those guilty of unlawful behavior; and to ensure fair and impartial administration of justice for all Americans.[4]

With this broad mission, the department is staffed by thousands who perform wide and diverse duties.

The DOJ is directed by the United States Attorney General, who is appointed by the President. The Office of the Attorney General was created by the Judiciary Act of 1789, ch. 20, sec. 35, 1 Stat. 73, 92–93 (1789). Originally a one-person part-time position, the Attorney General was to be "learned in the law" with the duty

> to prosecute and conduct all suits in the Supreme Court in which the United States shall be concerned, and to give his advice and opinion upon questions of law when required by the President of the United States, or when requested by the heads of any of the departments, touching any matters that may concern their departments.[5]

The actual DOJ was created almost 100 years later. In 1870, after the post-Civil War increase in the amount of litigation involving the United States necessitated the very expensive retention of a large number of private attorneys, a concerned Congress passed the Act to Establish the Department of Justice, ch. 150, 16 Stat. 162 (1870) setting it up as "an executive department of the government of the United States" with the Attorney General as its head. Since 1870, the DOJ has served the nation. Over fifty agencies are part of the DOJ, and some of the major enforcement agencies are discussed herein.

U.S. Marshals Service

The U.S. Marshals Service (USMS), created by the first U.S. Congress in 1789, is the oldest federal law enforcement agency (Figure 5.1). President George Washington appointed a U.S. Marshal for each of the 13 legal districts to represent federal interests at the local level. The early U.S. Marshals' tasks included enforcement and control of all legal decisions made by the federal judiciary, the Congress, and the President. Among these were "collection of

Figure 5.1 For the commemoration of the Bicentennial of the Marshal Service, a larger-than-life bronze sculpture titled *Frontier Marshal* was created by Dave Manuel of Joseph, Oregon. (Courtesy of the U.S. Marshals Service. Retrieved from www.usmarshals.gov/history/frontier/)

taxes, organization of the census, security for federal courts and the judges, searching for convicts, escaped slaves and deserters, as well as arresting them and taking them to the appropriate Sheriff's Office, as well as special tasks."[1]

Today, each of the 94 federal judicial districts has a U.S. Marshal. The USMS executes all civil and criminal processes issued by the federal courts and provides physical security for federal courtrooms and personal protection for certain witnesses, juries, and others as directed by the Attorney General. Other major activities of the USMS include the federal fugitive program and custody and transfer of federal prisoners. In addition, the Marshals' Special Operations Group (SOG) is a specially trained, rapidly deployable unit for response to national emergencies, civil disturbances, and terrorists' actions.[6] The USMS also operates the federal Witness Protection Program, which relocates individuals who testify in high-risk criminal prosecutions.

Historically, Marshals have served bravely, often in situations involving great risk. U.S. Marshal Robert Forsyth was the first federal LEO killed in the line of duty. On January 11, 1794, Marshal Forsyth was mortally wounded by a gunshot while attempting to serve civil process in Augusta, Georgia. Since that time, an additional 231 members of the USMS have lost their lives in the performance of their duties—more than any other federal law enforcement agency.[7]

Federal Bureau of Investigation

The Federal Bureau of Investigation (FBI) may well be the most famous of the federal enforcement agencies. Although it has grown into an agency with an international reputation and international role, the FBI had humble beginnings.[8]

In May 1908, after Congress enacted a law prohibiting the DOJ from engaging Secret Service operatives to conduct investigations, the foundation was laid for the creation of a new agency. In July 1908, Attorney General Charles Bonaparte appointed 10 former Secret Service operatives and a number of DOJ peonage investigators as special agents of a newly organized unit in the DOJ. Previous law enforcement experience or a legal background was desirable because the early Bureau did not provide any formal training for new agents. This new unit, which was simply referred to as the "special agent force," served as the foundation of what would later become the FBI.[8]

For over 40 years, the FBI was under the leadership of the very controversial J. Edgar Hoover. Hoover set the tone of the Bureau, shaping the agency and effectively capturing the imagination of the public, especially during the 1930s and 1940s. As a result, during this period, many outstanding men were attracted into the ranks of the agency.

Today, the FBI is the principal investigative arm of the DOJ. Its mission is

> to protect and defend the United States against terrorist and foreign intelligence threats, to uphold and enforce the criminal laws of the United States, and to provide leadership and criminal justice services to federal, state, municipal, and international agencies and partners.[9]

The FBI investigates over 200 violations of federal law with the exception of those assigned to other agencies. Some of its major investigative areas include terrorism, espionage, sabotage, other domestic security matters, kidnapping, extortion, bank robbery, cyber crime, public corruption, white-collar crime, interstate transportation of stolen property, civil rights matters, fraud against the government, and assaulting or killing the President or a federal officer (Figures 5.2 and 5.3).[10]

Figure 5.2 The FBI's Evidence Response Teams (ERTs) are located in all FBI field offices. These highly trained and equipped teams operate at a high level of competence to ensure that evidence is collected in such a manner that it can be introduced in court. (Courtesy of the FBI. Retrieved from http://www.fbi.gov.)

Figure 5.3 The FBI's headquarters in Washington, DC. (Courtesy of the FBI. Retrieved from http://www.fbi.gov/stats-services/publications/facts-and-figures-2010-2011/headquarters-field-offices.)

In 1932, the FBI opened one of the nation's first forensic crime laboratories. Today, the FBI Laboratory conducts thousands of examinations for federal, state, local, and tribal police agencies every year. In addition, the FBI's Identification Division maintains the national fingerprint database.

Over the last several decades, the FBI has gained an international reputation as a leader in the science of criminal investigative analysis (often called "behavioral profiling") with its Behavioral Science Unit. Since the 1970s, the FBI has worked to more systematically apply the insights of psychological science to criminal behavior.[11]

The Bureau has been very involved in investigations related to terrorism, including attacks upon United States interests internationally. Some of its more famous investigations related to international terrorism include the downing of Pan Am Flight 103 over Scotland, the attack on the USS Cole in Yemen, the attacks on United States embassies in Africa, and the attacks of September 11, 2001 on Washington, D.C. and New York. In addition, the Bureau runs more than 100 Joint Terrorism Task Forces (JTTFs) that bring together federal, state, and local LEOs to investigate suspected terrorists.

The FBI is headquartered in Washington, D.C. It maintains 56 field offices located in major cities throughout the United States, over 400 resident agencies in smaller cities across the nation, and more than 60 international offices called "legal attaches" in United States embassies worldwide.[9] As of 2012, the FBI had a total of 35,664 employees, which included 13,778 special agents and 21,886 support professionals.[12]

Drug Enforcement Administration

The Drug Enforcement Administration (DEA) traces its origin to the early twentieth century. Federal drug law enforcement began in 1915 with the Bureau of Internal Revenue. In the decades that followed, several additional agencies were given drug law enforcement responsibilities. In 1930, the Federal Bureau of Narcotics (FBN) was established; led for over thirty years by Harry Anslinger, the Bureau was one of the first law enforcement agencies in the nation to acknowledge the existence of organized crime in the United States.

By the 1960s, the two agencies formally charged with drug law enforcement were the Bureau of Drug Abuse Control (BDAC), Department of Health, Education, and Welfare (HEW) and the FBN, Department of the Treasury. In 1968, the two agencies were combined to form the Bureau of Narcotics and Dangerous Drugs (BNDD), DOJ. The BNDD was the predecessor of the DEA.[13]

The DEA was created in 1973 to combat the nation's growing drug problems. It is charged with enforcement of all federal narcotics and dangerous drug laws. DEA special agents conduct domestic and international investigations of major drug traffickers, concentrating efforts at the illicit source of supply or diversion. The DEA also regulates the legal trade in narcotic and dangerous drugs. Today, the DEA has field offices throughout the United States and 87 foreign offices in 63 countries. The DEA also works cooperatively with U.S. state and local agencies and foreign governments on programs designed to reduce the availability of illicit drugs on the U.S. market through nonenforcement methods such as crop eradication, crop substitution, and training drug agency counterparts.[14] More than 6000 LEOs serve in this agency.

One of the greatest challenges facing the DEA today is the drug trafficking and violence occurring in Mexico, as drug cartels struggle to increase their power. Since 2006, when Mexican President Felipe Calderón began a major effort to suppress the drug cartels, it is estimated that over 50,000 people have been killed in drug-related violence. This violence has devastated much of the Mexican economy and has contributed to the flow of immigrants into the United States from south of the border.

The DEA is also engaged internationally in efforts with other nations to stem the flow of both illegal drugs and prescription medicines that have been diverted from legal use. These efforts include the struggle against various elements of international organized crime, both traditional crime syndicates as well as the continually evolving drug cartels. Finally, the DEA helps support the efforts of the Department of State and the Rule of Law initiatives to assist in developing the infrastructure within evolving nations to combat drug problems within their borders. As an example, the DEA is involved in both Afghanistan and Iraq, assisting those nations in the establishment of their own drug enforcement efforts. The agency also assists internationally with laboratory resources and, in many nations, the establishment of drug courts.

Bureau of Alcohol, Tobacco, Firearms, and Explosives

The Bureau of Alcohol, Tobacco, Firearms, and Explosives (ATF) is another agency whose origin coincided with the beginning of the nation. The oldest tax-collecting Treasury agency, the ATF traces its roots back nearly 200 years to when Congress imposed a tax on imported spirits to help pay the Revolutionary War debt in 1789. At that time, administration of duties was within the Treasury Department. In 1862, Congress created an Office of Internal Revenue, also within the Treasury Department. Throughout much of its history, Treasury agents carried out taxation and regulatory functions with regard to the increasing number of firearms, tobacco, and alcohol laws that were passed by the Congress. In 1968, the Alcohol, Tobacco, and Firearms Division of the Internal Revenue Service (IRS) was created; in 1972, the ATF became an independent organization within the Treasury Department.

In January 2003, as a part of the reorganization of federal law enforcement, the law enforcement function of the ATF was transferred from the Department of the Treasury to the DOJ. Its tax and trade functions remained in the Department of the Treasury with the newly created Alcohol and Tobacco Tax and Trade Bureau. The agency's name was changed to the Bureau of Alcohol, Tobacco, Firearms, and Explosives (ATF) to reflect its new mission in the DOJ. The ATF is responsible for enforcing and administering laws related to "the illegal use and trafficking of firearms, the illegal use and storage of explosive, acts of arson and bombings, acts of terrorism, and the illegal diversion of alcohol and tobacco products."[15] More than 3000 LEOs serve in this agency.

U.S. Department of Homeland Security

The U.S. DHS was created following the attacks of September 11, 2001. Initially, the DHS was tasked with overseeing the national strategy to protect the United States against terrorism.[16] However, its mission has expanded as perceived threats against the nation have increased. By Congressional action, the DHS became an independent department in November 2002, and became fully operational on March 1, 2003.[17] The following sections detail some of the salient DHS organizations that involve a law enforcement focus.

U.S. Coast Guard

The USCG is one of the oldest organizations of the federal government. The first Congress created it as the Revenue Cutter Service in 1790 "to enforce tariff and trade laws and to prevent smuggling." The USCG received its present name in 1915 when the Revenue Cutter

Figure 5.4 The U.S. Coast Guard Cutter *Bertholf*. (Courtesy of Unofficial Networks, 2012. Retrieved from http://gcaptain.com/u-s-coast-guard-awards-northrop/?20690.)

Service merged with the Life-Saving Service (Figure 5.4). Today, the USCG is the primary maritime law enforcement agency of the U.S. government. Federal statutes provide it with general law enforcement powers, which authorize its personnel to make searches, seizures, and arrests on the high seas and waters under U.S. jurisdiction.[18]

The Coast Guard cooperates extensively with other law enforcement agencies in such areas as counterterrorism and drug enforcement; it also enforces conservation and marine environmental laws such as the 200-mile fishery conservation zone and investigates the harmful discharge of oil offshore.

In times of war, the USCG serves as a branch of the armed forces under the Navy. Otherwise, it is a service within the DHS employing more than 4000 LEOs, 200 investigative service personnel, and 4000 maritime law enforcement boarding officers.

U.S. Secret Service

The U.S. Secret Service (USSS) was created in 1865 as a bureau of the Department of the Treasury. In those days, its primary function was to suppress the counterfeiting of U.S. currency, which was a major problem following the Civil War. The newly created agency made an immediate impact by closing down over 200 counterfeiting operations within a year. By 1867, counterfeiting had been brought under control and the public had regained confidence in the nation's currency.[19]

Afterwards, the government needed investigators to combat other types of crime. Since the USSS was already in existence and had a cadre of skilled investigators, other departments of the government naturally called upon its agents to investigate a variety of other crimes. In 1867, Congress broadened the responsibilities of the USSS to include "detecting persons perpetrating fraud against the government."[20] Until 1907, the USSS was the only general investigative agency within the federal government. In 1901, after the assassination of President William McKinley, Congress also gave the USSS the responsibility of protecting the President of the United States (Figure 5.5).[20]

Figure 5.5 President Barack Obama and First Lady Michelle Obama surrounded by Secret Service agents during the inaugural parade in 2009. (Courtesy of the U.S. Secret Service, 2012. Retrieved from http://www.secretservice.gov/photo_gallery_enlarge.shtml#photo_of_Inaugral_Parade4.)

In 1907, at the urging of the Attorney General, Congress barred the USSS from conducting investigations outside the Department of the Treasury.[8] However, two notable exceptions to the ban were subsequently made: one involving national security (a German sabotage plot in 1918) and the other involving high-level public corruption (the Teapot Dome oil scandal in the 1920s). After the successful investigation of both of these cases, congressional restrictions were again imposed and the USSS went back to investigating counterfeiters and forgers.[21]

Since its early days, the USSS mission has greatly changed and expanded. Today, the USSS fights crime on a global scale through its field offices located in the United States, Canada, Mexico, South America, Europe, Africa, and Asia. The agency has a unique, dual mission that includes investigations as well as protection. In January 2003, the USSS was transferred from the Department of the Treasury to the newly created DHS. Protecting the president and vice president, visiting foreign heads of state, and others remained the agency's highest profile mission. In addition to investigating counterfeit currency violations, the USSS investigative authority includes "financial institution fraud, access device fraud, computer crimes, credit card fraud, fraudulent government and commercial securities, fictitious financial instruments, telecommunications fraud, false identification and identity theft."[22]

In 1930, the White House Police was integrated into the USSS. The name was later changed to the Uniformed Division (UD). The UD is responsible for "security at the White House Complex; the vice president's residence; the Department of the Treasury (as part of the White House complex); and foreign diplomatic missions in the Washington, D.C. area." The UD officers carry out their protective responsibilities using fixed security posts and various forms of patrol including foot, bicycle, vehicular, and motorcycle. In addition, the UD provides support to the USSS protective mission through the following special programs: Countersniper Support Unit, Canine Explosive Detection Unit (K-9), Emergency Response Team (ERT), and magnetometers.[23] Over 5000 LEOs and special agents serve in this agency.

Customs and Border Protection

The Customs and Border Protection (CBP) was established as a part of the Homeland Security Act of 2002. With 53,000 employees serving in domestic and international assignments, CBP is the largest law enforcement agency within the DHS. It has many responsibilities that include detecting and apprehending foreign nationals attempting to enter the United States illegally; stopping the flow of contraband and illegal drugs; protecting U.S. agricultural and economic interest from harmful diseases and pests; protecting U.S. businesses from theft of their intellectual property; and enforcing U.S. trade laws, regulating and facilitating international trade, and collecting import duties. In addition, a priority mission after 9/11 has been to prevent terrorists and terrorists' weapons from entering United States borders. CBP's primary law enforcement and critical workforce include the Border Patrol, CBP Officers, CBP Air and Marine, CBP Agriculture Specialists, and CBP Import Specialist.[24]

Border Patrol

Mounted watchmen or guards of the former U.S. Immigration Service have patrolled the southern border of the United States on an irregular basis since 1904. In 1924, Congress officially created the Border Patrol as part of the Labor Appropriation Act (Figure 5.6).[25] Today, the Border Patrol agents protect 1900 miles of the U.S. border with Mexico and 5000 miles of the U.S. border with Canada. Their mission "is the detection and apprehension of illegal aliens and smugglers of aliens at or near the land border."[25] Agents patrol the border in vehicles, boats, aircraft, and on foot. Due to the

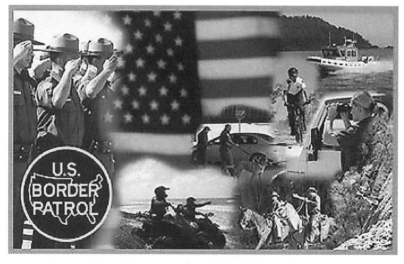

Figure 5.6 The U.S. Border Patrol. (Courtesy of the U.S. Department of Homeland Security. Retrieved from http://www.cbp.gov/xp/cgov/border_security/border_patrol/.)

terrain, agents even use horses, all-terrain motorcycles, bicycles, and snowmobiles.[26] Over 12,000 LEOs serve in this agency.

Customs and Border Protection Officers

The primary responsibility of CBP officers is to detect and prevent terrorists' entry into the United States and enforce laws against smuggling, money laundering, undocumented entry of individuals, weapons trafficking, and numerous other customs violations, while facilitating the orderly flow of legitimate trade and travelers. This mission is carried out at over 300 U.S. ports of entry and includes performing physical checks of travelers, cargo, vehicles, and luggage. CBP officers may also gather intelligence and work with the DEA, FBI, and other federal law enforcement agencies in suspected terrorism and smuggling investigations.[24] Over 18,000 LEOs serve in this agency.

Customs and Border Protection Air and Marine

In 2006, CBP consolidated separate air and marine divisions into the Office of CBP Air and Marine (Figure 5.7). This consolidation created the world's largest aviation and maritime law enforcement agency.[27] The mission of Air and Marine interdiction agents is "to detect, interdict, and prevent acts of terrorism and the unlawful movement of people, illegal drugs, and other contraband toward or across U.S. borders."[28] CBP Air and Marine have 290 aircraft and 225 marine vessels operating from 79 locations throughout the nation.[27]

Figure 5.7 The Office of Air and Marine (OAM) uses a diverse fleet in the performance of its enforcement duties.

Recently, the Border Patrol added air surveillance capabilities and deployed unmanned aerial vehicles (UAV).[26] Interdiction agents patrol oceans, lakes, and rivers to prevent illegal entry of undocumented aliens; interdict illegal drugs; and confiscate illegal weapons. In addition, Air and Marine interdiction agents play a lead role in CBP's critical antiterrorism mission.[24] Over 800 LEOs serve in this agency.

Customs and Border Protection Agriculture Specialists

Serving at the over 300 U.S. ports of entry, the primary mission of the agriculture specialists includes work "to curtail the spread of harmful pests and plant and animal diseases that may harm America's farms and food supply, and to avert bio- and agro-terrorism."[24]

Customs and Border Protection Import Specialists

The primary mission of the import specialists includes "detecting and preventing violations of U.S. customs laws and import/export regulations, and curtailing the entry of illegal drugs and other prohibited goods." In addition, import specialists help prevent terrorists, terrorist weapons, and weapon components from entering the United States.[24]

Immigration and Customs Enforcement

Immigration and Customs Enforcement (ICE) is the largest investigative agency in the DHS. The 2003 reorganization of federal law enforcement resulted in the consolidation of the United States Immigration and Naturalization Service and the United States Customs Service into a single agency whose mission was to enforce the nation's immigration and customs laws. Today, ICE has two operational divisions: Homeland Security Investigations (HSI) and Enforcement and Removal Operations (ERO).[28]

HSI was formerly known as the ICE Office of Investigations (OI). In mid-2010, the agency was realigned to better reflect its mission. HSI is responsible for investigating a wide range of cases "including immigration crime, human rights violations, national security threats, financial and smuggling violations (including illegal arms exports), financial crimes, commercial fraud, human trafficking, narcotics smuggling, child pornography/exploitations, and immigration fraud." HSI has more than 10,000 employees, including 6700 special agents, who are assigned to more than 200 cities throughout the U.S. and 47 countries around the world.[31] Over 6000 LEOs serve in this agency. ERO identifies and apprehends removable aliens, detains when necessary, and removes illegal aliens from the United States.[30]

Since its creation in 1978, the ICE Homeland Security Investigations Forensic Laboratory (HSI-FL), formerly known as the Forensic Document Laboratory, has been the only U.S. crime laboratory specializing in the scientific authentication and research of travel and identity documents and related issues. The HSI-FL provides a broad range of document and latent print-related forensic, intelligence, and investigative support services for ICE, DHS, and many other U.S. and foreign law enforcement agencies. The HSI-FL reference library, the most extensive of its kind in the United States, contains thousands of travel and identity documents and reference materials.[32]

Transportation Security Administration

The Transportation Security Administration (TSA) was created in response to the September 11, 2001 terrorist attacks; initially, it was part of the Department of

Transportation. The TSA's mission is to strengthen the security of U.S. transportation systems while ensuring the freedom of movement for people and commerce. In March 2003, the TSA was transferred from the Department of Transportation to the newly created DHS.[33]

Office of Law Enforcement/Federal Air Marshal Service

The Federal Air Marshal Service (FAMS) is the primary law enforcement agency within the TSA. However, the history of the FAMS precedes the tragic events of 9/11. In 1970, the Customs Air Security Officers Program (more familiarly known as the "Sky Marshal Program") was created to thwart terrorist hijackers on U.S. flights. Although it was very successful, the program ceased operations in 1974 when X-ray technology was introduced in U.S. airports. In 1985, in response to the increased threat of aircraft hijacking, the Department of Transportation in cooperation with the State Department was directed by President Reagan to explore the expansion of the armed Sky Marshal program aboard international flights for U.S. carriers. Congress subsequently passed the International Security and Development Cooperation Act, which provided the statutes that served as the foundation for the current FAMS.[33]

On September 11, 2001, the FAMS consisted of fewer than 50 armed personnel who, by statute, flew only on international flights by U.S. air carriers. The events of 9/11 demonstrated the need for expanded aircraft security onboard U.S. air carriers.

Today, the mission of the FAMS is "to detect, deter, and defeat hostile acts targeting U.S. air carriers, airports, passengers, and crews." The federal air marshals (FAMs) receive special training including investigative techniques, terrorist behavior recognition, firearms, aircraft specific tactics, and close quarters defense measures to protect the flying public.[33]

The role of FAMs in homeland security continues to expand, and they work closely with numerous other law enforcement agencies. FAMS personnel are assigned staff positions at different organizations such as the National Counterterrorism Center, the National Training Center, and the FBI's JTTFs. In addition, the FAMS is assigned liaison assignments with other law enforcement and homeland security agencies during periods of heightened alert or special national events.[34] (The number of LEOs was not available.)

U.S. Department of State

The mission of the Department of State is to shape and sustain a peaceful, prosperous, just, and democratic world and foster conditions for stability and progress for the benefit of the American people and people everywhere. To accomplish this mission, members of the Department of State are engaged worldwide. The nature of the role of the Department of State, engaged globally, makes Department employees and their families potential targets to those who might like to strike the United States. In addition, the Department assists with international police training throughout the world.

Bureau of Diplomatic Security

The Bureau of Diplomatic Security (DS) is the security and law enforcement arm of the Department of State. The DS is responsible for providing a safe and secure environment

Figure 5.8 Great Britain's Prince Harry aboard a USCG vessel.

for domestic and international departmental personnel, property, and information; the agency is a world leader in international investigations, threat analysis, cyber security, counterterrorism, and security technology. U.S. diplomatic missions around the world operate under a security program designed and maintained by the DS (Figure 5.8).[35]

The Bureau of Diplomatic Security protects the Secretary of State and all high-ranking foreign dignitaries and officials visiting the United States. (Note: The USSS protects visiting foreign heads of state.) In addition, the DS investigates passport and visa fraud and conducts personnel security investigations. In cooperation with other U.S. government agencies, such as the FBI and the CIA, the DS investigates the activities of foreign intelligence agencies directed against Department employees. In addition, upon request, the DS assists in apprehending fugitives who have fled the United States. As a global agency, the DS has offices in 25 U.S. cities and 159 foreign countries.[35]

Bureau of International Narcotics and Law Enforcement Affairs

The Bureau of International Narcotics and Law Enforcement Affairs (INL) advises the President, Secretary of State, other bureaus in the Department of State, and other departments and agencies within the U.S. government on the development of policies and programs to combat international narcotics and crime. INL programs support two of the Department's strategic goals: (1) to reduce the entry of illegal drugs into the United States, and (2) to minimize the impact of international crime on the United States and its citizens. Counternarcotics and anticrime programs also complement counterterrorism efforts, both directly and indirectly, by promoting modernization of and supporting operations by foreign criminal justice systems and law enforcement agencies charged with the counterterrorism mission.

U.S. Department of the Treasury

The Department of the Treasury was established as an executive department by the First Session of Congress in 1789. Alexander Hamilton served as the first Secretary of the Treasury from 1789 to 1795. Hamilton suggested government revenues be based upon customs duties.

Internal Revenue Service Criminal Investigations

In 1919, six U.S. Postal Inspectors were transferred to the IRS to establish the IRS Intelligence Unit. Their mission was to investigate suspected widespread tax fraud in the United States. The Intelligence Unit formed the foundation that would eventually become Criminal Investigations (CI), and these agents "are recognized as the finest financial investigators in the world."[36]

The Intelligence Unit gained public acclaim in the 1930s during the investigation resulting in the arrest and conviction of public enemy number one, Al Capone, for income tax evasion. The Intelligence Unit was also involved in solving the Lindbergh kidnapping. In subsequent years, the Intelligence Unit expanded and continued to investigate tax evasion cases involving other notorious criminals, as well as ordinary citizens, high-profile businesspersons, and government officials.[36]

In 1978, the Intelligence Unit's name was changed to CI. Since its creation, its investigative mission has also changed significantly. CI remains the primary investigative arm of the IRS. However, in addition to its traditional responsibility of investigating tax fraud cases, the jurisdiction of CI now includes other complex financial crimes such as money laundering, narcotics, organized crime, and public corruption.[36]

Alcohol and Tobacco Tax and Trade Bureau

The Alcohol and Tobacco Tax and Trade Bureau was created on January 24, 2003, when the Homeland Security Act of 2002 was passed. This legislation divided the functions of the Bureau of Alcohol, Tobacco, and Firearms (ATF) into two new organizations. The Alcohol and Tobacco Tax Trade Bureau (TTF) operates within the Department of the Treasury, and the law enforcement functions of the ATF were shifted to the DOJ.[37]

The Alcohol and Tobacco Tax and Trade Bureau collects federal excise taxes on alcohol, tobacco, firearms, and ammunition and assures compliance with federal tobacco permitting and alcohol permitting, labeling, and marketing requirements to protect consumers. Agents investigate alcohol and tobacco permits for distilleries, wineries, breweries, and tobacco manufactures; monitor importers and exporters; work in the enforcement of regulations of the alcohol and tobacco industries; work to prevent misleading labeling or advertising of alcohol beverages; conduct laboratory analysis of alcohol and tobacco products; and collect alcohol and tobacco excise taxes.

U.S. Forest Service

The U.S. Forest Service (USFS) is an entity of the Department of Agriculture that is responsible for managing public lands in the nation's 155 national forests and 20 national grasslands that cover more than 193 million acres of public land. The agency also oversees

80 experimental forests and ranges, 5 research and development stations, and 18 job corps centers. The USFS maintains and cultivates these lands for public use and national interests through various activities ranging from scientific research and development to firefighting, recreation maintenance, wilderness and wildlife protection, ecosystem management, and timber production.

U.S. Forest Service Law Enforcement and Investigations

The USFS Law Enforcement and Investigations unit (LEI), headquartered in Washington, D.C., is responsible for enforcement of federal laws and regulations governing national forest lands and resources. The USFS law enforcement personnel patrol using a wide range of vehicles including ATVs, horses, foot patrols, snowmobiles, automobiles, and aircraft.[38]

U.S. Postal Service and Postal Inspection Service

In 1772, Postmaster Benjamin Franklin created the position of Surveyor to assist in regulating and auditing the Colonial Postal System. These surveyors have evolved into today's Postal Inspection Service (PIS). The PIS is one of the older United States law enforcement agencies. Congress empowered the Postal Service "to investigate postal offenses and civil matters relating to the Postal Service."[39] Today, the PIS is responsible for protecting the U.S. mail, postal personnel, property, and funds, and for investigating violations of postal laws. Robberies, burglaries, thefts of mail, mail fraud, bombs (whether directed against postal property or transmitted through the mail), assaults on postal employees, and embezzlement of official funds are representative examples of PIS investigations.[10]

To assist in carrying out its duties, the PIS maintains a security force staffed by uniformed postal police officers who are assigned to critical postal facilities throughout the United States. The uniformed officers provide perimeter security, escort high-value mail shipments, and perform other essential protective functions[39] (2584 LEOs in 2006/1715 inspectors and 869 uniformed officers).

Office of Inspector General

Many federal agencies have an Office of Inspector General (OIG). Each head OIG is appointed by the President, by and with the advice and consent of the Senate. The OIG conducts, coordinates, and provides policy direction for audit and investigation activities relating to programs and operations of the department to which they are assigned. The OIG investigates criminal violations and also prevents and detects waste, fraud, and abuse related to federal programs, operations, and employees. In addition, OIGs are responsible for keeping established heads and Congress informed of any problems and deficiencies relating to programs and operations and the necessity for and progress of corrective action.[10]

In 2004, there were 57 statutory OIG components within the federal government. Twenty-seven OIG components employed criminal investigators with arrest and firearm authority. These agencies employed 2867 LEOs in the 50 states and the District of Columbia. The five largest OIGs with LEOs include the Department of Health and Human Services (374), the Treasury Inspector General for Tax Administration (330), the Department of Defense (326), the Social Security Administration (279), and the Department of Housing and Urban Development (213). Other OIGs employing LEOs include the Department of Agriculture, Department of Labor, DHS, DOJ, Department of Veterans Affairs, Department of Transportation, Department of Education, Department of the Interior, National Aeronautics and Space Administration, Environmental Protection Agency, General Services Administration, Department of Energy, Federal Deposit Insurance Corporation, Small Business Administration, Office of Personnel Management, Department of State, Department of the Treasury, Nuclear Regulatory Commission, U.S. Railroad Retirement Board, Department of Commerce, Agency for International Development, and Government Printing Office.[40]

In addition to the primary federal law enforcement agencies found in the DHS, DOJ, and other departments of government, many other federal agencies provide specialized criminal investigative services or provide primarily physical security and/or basic police services to designated federal personnel, property, and facilities.

U.S. Department of the Interior

The United States Department of the Interior (DOI) is responsible for the management and conservation of most federal lands and natural resources and the administration of programs relating to Native Americans, Alaska Natives, Native Hawaiians, territorial affairs, and to insular areas of the United States.

U.S. Department of the Interior, National Park Service—U.S. Park Police

The U.S. Park Police is another of the nation's oldest law enforcement agencies that employs over 600 LEOs. The Park Watchmen originated in 1791 and were created by President George Washington to protect federal property only in the District of Columbia.[41] Today, the Park Police is a component of the National Park Service, DOI. The Park Police serves "designated areas within the National Park Service (primarily the Washington, D.C., New York City and San Francisco, California metropolitan areas)."[42] Furthermore, the mission of the Park Police includes providing highly trained and professional police officers to prevent and detect criminal activity, conduct investigations, apprehend individuals suspected of committing offenses against federal, state, and local laws, provide protection to the President of the United States and visiting dignitaries, and provide protective services to some of the most recognizable monuments and memorials in the world (Figure 5.9).[43]

Protecting American icons is a daunting task. Accomplishing this goal successfully necessitates a variety of modalities of enforcement and numerous resources. The Park Police contains several units such as aviation, canine, intelligence, motor, equine, and special weapons and tactics (SWAT).[44] The operational capacity of the Park Police incorporates various districts nationally. Its CI operations encompass several domains ranging from environmental crimes to narcotics and vice.[45]

Like many federal agencies, the Park Police sponsors a college internship program. The goal of the internship program is to provide students with a "learning experience and to have an opportunity to work with all of the operational units that support the United States Park Police mission of providing law enforcement services to designated areas of the National Park Service."[46]

Figure 5.9 U.S. Park Police performing security duties during the funeral of President Ronald Reagan. (Courtesy of the U.S. National Park Service. Retrieved from http://www.nps.gov/uspp/photpag.htm.)

U.S. Department of the Interior, National Park Service—Park Rangers

Over 1500 federal park rangers serve to ensure the safety of our nation's national parks. The National Park Service describes its park rangers as follows:

> Park Rangers carry out various tasks associated with forest or structural fire control; protection of property; gathering and dissemination of natural, historical, or scientific information; development of interpretive material for the natural, historical, or cultural features of an era; demonstration of folk art and crafts; enforcement of laws and regulations; investigation of violations, complaints, trespass/encroachment, and accidents; search and rescue; and management of historical, cultural, and natural resources, such as wildlife, forests, lakeshores, seashores, historic buildings, battlefields, archaeological properties, and recreation areas. They also operate campgrounds, including such tasks as assigning sites, replenishing firewood, performing safety inspections, providing information to visitors, and leading guided tours. Differences in the exact nature of duties depend on the grade of position, the site's size and specific needs.[47]

Park rangers may be assigned to both urban and rural settings. Although the concept of working in a national park may be attractive and seem innocuous, it is a dangerous endeavor. National parks are attractive targets for terrorist organizations because of their symbolic value.[48] They also experience a variety of illegal activities ranging from drug smuggling operations to human trafficking. Between 2007 and 2009, park rangers "arrested and indicted 385 felony smugglers, seized 40,000 lbs. of marijuana, and intercepted 3800 illegal aliens" in Arizona's Organ Pipe Cactus National Monument park alone.[49] Park rangers also encounter dangerous animals. For example, in Florida's Everglades National Park, Burmese pythons represent a danger to both wildlife and humans (Figure 5.10).[50] During the last decade, park rangers were 12 times more likely to be assaulted injuriously or fatally than were FBI personnel.[51]

Figure 5.10 A U.S. Park Ranger in the Florida Everglades. (Courtesy of the U.S. National Park Service. Retrieved from http://www.nps.gov/ever/naturescience/Burmese-Pythons-in-the-Everglades.htm.)

Training

The Federal Law Enforcement Training Center (FLETC) is located on the northwestern edge of Brunswick, Georgia, and serves as the headquarters facility for the FLETC (Figure 5.11). The training center is situated on 1600 acres with modern conventional facilities such as classrooms, dormitories, and administrative and logistical support structures, including a dining hall capable of serving more than 4000 meals per day. Many federal agencies send their personnel to train at the FLETC. Others, like the FBI and the DEA, maintain separate training facilities.

In addition, the FLETC has 18 firearms ranges, including a state-of-the-art indoor range complex with 146 separate firing points and 8 highly versatile semienclosed ranges with 200 additional firing points. Other training assets include a sprawling complex of driver training ranges, a physical techniques facility, an explosives range, a fully functional mock port of entry, and numerous other structures that support the entire training effort. In all, FLETC provides law enforcement training for 88 federal agencies.

International Policing

Crime is a global concern. National borders mean very little to criminals and criminal organizations. The struggle to combat international crime and criminal activity has always been a challenge to the law enforcement agencies within the international community, and this struggle increased dramatically with the end of the Cold War and the opening of borders between historic adversaries. In addition, new sophisticated criminal organizations

Figure 5.11 Homeland Security Secretary Napolitano speaking at the Federal Law Enforcement Training Center in Glynco, GA. (Courtesy of the U.S. Department of Homeland Security. Retrieved from http://blog.dhs.gov/2010/03/fletc.html.)

such as MS-13, and violent terrorist organizations like al Qa'ida, have emerged over the past few decades.

To combat these threats, efforts are made to increase international cooperation among nations to include their law enforcement and intelligence services. In the United States, many domestic agencies provide assistance to and rely upon foreign agencies to successfully conduct their operations and fulfill their missions. It is not uncommon for American agencies to share information and resources with the law enforcement agencies of other nations. The following agencies are some of the salient entities that impact international law enforcement.

Europol

Europol is the European Union (EU)'s criminal intelligence agency. Formed in 1992 by the Treaty on European Union (TEU), Europol started limited operations in 1994 and became fully functional in 1999. The headquarters of Europol is located in the Hague, the Netherlands.

Europol's mission is to improve the effectiveness and cooperation between member countries by sharing and pooling intelligence to prevent and combat international organized crime. Europol has no executive powers and serves in a supportive role for law enforcement agencies in the EU. Europol support includes information exchange, intelligence analysis, and training resources.

The agency has a staff of about 100 and uses its unique information capabilities and expertise to identify and track the criminal and terrorist organizations in Europe. The greatest security threats facing the European community include terrorism, international drug trafficking, money laundering, organized fraud, counterfeit Euro currency, and human trafficking.[52]

Financial Action Task Force

The Financial Action Task Force (FATF) was established by the Group of Seven (G-7) Summit held in Paris in 1989, based on the threat posed to the banking system and to financial institutions. The G-7 is an international organization established in 1985 to facilitate economic cooperation among the world's largest industrial nations such as Canada, France, Germany, Great Britain, Italy, Japan, and the United States. The FATF also develops and promotes national and international policies to combat money laundering and the financing of terrorism. In essence, the FATF is a "policy making" body that works to guarantee the necessary political will to bring about legislative and regulatory reforms related to its mission.[53]

International Criminal Police Organization

In 1923, a group of European police officials who wanted to prevent and suppress international crime created the International Criminal Police Organization (INTERPOL). Today, it is the world's largest international police organization. It consists of 188 member nations around the world, which assist each other in answering and executing foreign law enforcement and investigative requirements (nonpolitical, religious, racial, and military). It maintains databases on known international criminals and wanted persons, terrorists, missing persons, stolen and lost passports and travel documents, stolen vehicles, and other law enforcement information. In addition, it furnishes member countries with studies, reports, and intelligence on international criminal matters.[54] INTERPOL personnel have no powers of arrest and the organization does not employ any field agents.[55]

The INTERPOL headquarters (General Secretariat) is in Lyon, France (Figure 5.12). The head of INTERPOL is the secretary general, who, with the aid of a 13-member executive committee, supervises operations. The General Secretariat operates 24 hours a day, 365 days a year:

> Officials from more than 80 countries work side-by-side in any of the organization's four official languages: Arabic, English, French, and Spanish. The General Secretariat has seven regional offices located in Argentina, Cameroon, Cote d'Ivoire, El Salvador, Kenya, Thailand,

Figure 5.12 INTERPOL headquarters in Lyon, France. (Courtesy of the Hong Kong Police Force. Retrieved from http://www.police.gov.hk/offbeat/907/eng/n14.htm.)

and Zimbabwe. In addition, INTERPOL has Special Representatives at the United Nations in New York City and at the European Union in Brussels.[54]

Each member nation has a National Central Bureau (NCB) that is usually aligned with that country's national police agency or investigation service. The NCB is the designated contact point for the General Secretariat, regional offices, and other member countries. As such, the NCB coordinates requests received and sent by that nation. The United States NCB (USNCB) is an office under the control and direction of the DOJ and is comanaged by the DOJ and the DHS. It is comprised of permanent DOJ employees and rotational staff detailed from other federal and state agencies for specific periods. Agents are assigned to work in divisions dedicated to specific investigative divisions.[54]

Summary

Throughout its period of over 200 years of service to the nation, federal law enforcement has proven up to the task of facing the crime-related threats to the nation. By 2012, there were over 18,000 state and local law enforcement agencies responsible for enforcing local and state laws. In addition, there were over 100 federal law enforcement agencies charged with enforcing laws at the federal level.

Although the various agencies often work cooperatively and effectively on matters of mutual importance, there is widespread fragmentation and nonconformity in terms of agency names, authority, function, and organizational structure, particularly at the state and local levels. This is primarily the result of local government control of law enforcement, a concept borrowed from England.

Federal law enforcement agencies have jurisdiction over crimes that are national in scope. In addition, some federal law enforcement agencies are charged with maintaining the safety and security of federal property, employees, and the public. The USMS was the first federal law enforcement agency, created in 1789 by the first Congress of the United States. Since that time, many additional federal law enforcement agencies have been established in response to new laws and expanding jurisdictions.

In response to the 2001 terrorist attacks against the United States, a major reorganization of federal law enforcement occurred. Pursuant to the Homeland Security Act of 2002, many federal law enforcement roles and responsibilities were restructured into the DOJ and the newly created DHS. Today, a majority of major federal law enforcement agencies are found within these two departments. Other federal law enforcement agencies are spread throughout various departments and bureaus of the government. Examples of major federal law enforcement agencies include the USCG; PIS, USSS; FBI: IRS, CI; Bureau of Alcohol, Tobacco, Firearms, and Explosives; DEA; CBP; ICE; Transportation Security Agency; Bureau of Diplomatic Security; and Office of Inspectors General.

INTERPOL is the best known large-scale international police organization. It consists of 188 member nations around the world, which assist each other in facilitating foreign law enforcement and investigative requirements. INTERPOL personnel have no powers of arrest and it does not employ any field agents. Member nations have access to INTERPOL's vast databases, which contain information on international criminals and wanted persons, terrorists, missing persons, stolen and lost passports and other travel documents, stolen vehicles, and various other types of law enforcement information. INTERPOL's constitution prohibits any involvement of a political, military, religious, or racial nature. Each member nation has a NCB, which is the designated point of contact for INTERPOL's General Secretariat, regional offices, and other member countries.

The seven federal civilian law enforcement agencies with the largest number of LEOs are as follows:

- Office of Probation and Pretrial Service (Administrative Office of the U.S. Courts)—4.01% or 5528 LEOs
- DEA (DOJ)—4.05% or 5581 LEOs
- OI (DHS, ICE)—4.17% or 5754 LEOs
- Border Patrol (DHS, CBP)—8.52% or 11,758 LEOs
- FBI (DOJ)—9.3% or 12,824 LEOs
- Office of Field Operation (DHS, CBP)—12.77% or 17,618 LEOs
- Federal Bureau of Prisons (DOJ)—24.8% or 34,200 LEOs

The remaining 97 components represent 32.38% or 44,666 LEOs.[2]

Having a far less complex law enforcement role, the federal civil law enforcement community is relatively small compared to the nation's state and local law enforcement effort. However, federal law enforcement is nonetheless complex and also difficult to put into perspective. Many federal law enforcement agencies' duties and responsibilities are limited. They primarily provide physical security and/or basic police services to designated federal personnel, property, and facilities. Jurisdiction and law enforcement duties may be confined to an agency's actual property. Although a few of these agencies employ a large number of sworn LEOs, their impact on the larger law enforcement community is minimal because of their restricted jurisdiction. For example, the Bureau of Prisons (BOP) employs the largest number of federal LEOs (24.8% or 34,200), but BOP's jurisdiction is restricted to providing a safe and secure living environment for the inmates of the federal prison system.

Other federal agencies, even though they may employ far fewer sworn personnel, have a wider impact on the United States and international law enforcement community because of the nature and range of their authority and responsibilities.

Discussion Questions

1. What were the first two federal law enforcement agencies?
2. Park rangers have law enforcement responsibilities. How do ranger duties differ from those of the law enforcement agents of other national agencies?
3. Select three federal law enforcement agencies of your choice. Compare and contrast these agencies. What similarities and differences exist regarding your selected agencies?
4. What is the role of federal law enforcement agencies in the United States?
5. What federal agencies do you find most interesting? What are the duties and responsibilities of those agencies?
6. Contrast the roles of the United States DOJ and the United States DHS in combating terrorism in the United States.
7. What is the OIG? What are its duties and responsibilities?
8. What is INTERPOL? Who created INTERPOL and when? What role does INTERPOL play in international law enforcement?

Notes

1. *U.S. Marshals, the Oldest Law Enforcement Agency of the Nation*. Retrieved from http://www.green-card.com/us-marshals-the-oldest-law-enforcement-agency-of-the-nation
2. U.S. Government Accountability Office (2006). *Survey of Federal Civilian Law Enforcement Functions and Authorities*. Washington, DC: Government Printing Office.
3. Excluded from the total number of federal law enforcement officers is the number of Transportation Security Administration Federal Air Marshals, which is Sensitive Security Information. In addition, the total number of all federal law enforcement officers excluded contract services, civilian law enforcement officers and investigators, and inspector generals within the Department of Defense, and the U.S. Attorneys.
4. U.S. Department of Justice. *About the DOJ*. Retrieved from http://www.justice.gov/about/about.html
5. U.S. Department of Justice. *Statutory Authority*. Retrieved from http://www.justice.gov/about.html
6. *U.S. Marshals Service, History Fact Sheet*. Retrieved from http://www.usmarshals.gov/duties/factsheets/index.html
7. *Federal Law Enforcement Fatalities Approach 1000*. Retrieved from http://www.nleomf.org/officers/stories/federal-law-enforcement.html/
8. *History of the FBI*. Retrieved from http://www.fbi.gov/about-us/history/brief-history
9. FBI. *Quick Facts*. Retrieved from http://www.fbi.gov/about-us/quick-facts/quickfacts
10. Federal Law Enforcement Training center. *Orientation to Federal Law Enforcement Agencies* (Unpublished).
11. FBI. *Behavioral Science Unit*. Retrieved from http://www.fbi.gov/about-us/training/bsu
12. FBI. *Quick Facts*. Retrieved from http://www.fbi.gov/about-us/quick-facts
13. *DEA History Book, 1970–1975*. Retrieved from http://www.deamuseum.org/dea_history_book/1970–1975.html
14. *DEA History*. Retrieved from http://www.justice.gov/dea/about/history.shtml
15. *ATF—Bureau of Alcohol, Tobacco, Firearms and Explosives*. Retrieved from http://www.atf.gov/about/history/
16. U.S. Department of Homeland security. *Department Creation*. Retrieved from http://www.dhs.gov/creation-department-homeland-security
17. Ibid.
18. *Coast Guard History*. Retrieved from http://www.uscg.mil/history/
19. Harry Edward Neal. (1971). *The Story of the Secret Service* (p. 20). New York, NY: Grosset & Dunlap.
20. *Secret Service History—Timeline*. Retrieved from http://www.secretservice.gov/history.shtml
21. Harry Edward Neal. (1971). *The Story of the Secret Service* (p. 25). New York, NY: Grosset & Dunlap.
22. U.S. Secret Service. (August 2007). *The Secret Service Story*. Washington, DC.
23. *Uniformed Division*. Retrieved from http://www.secretservice.gov/whoweare_ud.shtml
24. *We Are CBP*. Retrieved from http://www.cbp.gov/xp/cgov/career/customs_careers/we_are_cbp.xml/
25. *Border Patrol History*. Retrieved from http://www.cbp.gov/xp/cgov/border_security/border_patrol/border_patrol_ohs/history.xml
26. *Border Patrol Overview*. Retrieved from http://www.cbp.gov/xp/cgov/border_security/border_patrol/border_patrol_ohs/overview.xml
27. *World's Largest Aviation and Maritime Law Enforcement Organization Marks Anniversary*. Retrieved from http://www.cbp.gov/xp/cgov/about/history/current_events/oam_anniversary.xml
28. U.S. Immigration and Customs Enforcement. *About ICE*. Retrieved from http://www.ice.gov/about/overview/

29. ICE. *Homeland Security Investigations*. Retrieved from http://www.ice.gov/about/offices/homeland-security-investigations/

30. ICE. *Enforcement and Removal Operations*. Retrieved from http://www.ice.gov/about/offices/enforcement-removal-operations/

31. *DHS, ICE, OI—About Us*. Retrieved from http://www.ice.gov/about/offices/homeland-security-investigations/

32. *Homeland Security Investigations Forensic Laboratory*. Retrieved from http://www.ice.gov/hsi-fl/

33 *Our Mission*. Retrieved from http://www.tsa.gov/about-tsa/mission-vision-and-core-values

34. *Federal Air Marshals*. Retrieved from http://www.tsa.gov/about-tsa/federal-air-marshals

35. U.S. Department of State. *Bureau of Diplomatic Security*. Retrieved from http://www.state.gov/m/ds/

36. U.S. Internal Revenue Service. *Criminal Enforcement*. Retrieved from http://www.irs.gov/uac/Criminal-Enforcement-1

37. *Alcohol and Tobacco Tax and Trade Bureau*. Retrieved from http://www.allgov.com/departments/department-of-the-treasury/alcohol-and-tobacco-tax-and-trade-bureau?agencyid=7258

38. *United States Forest Service*. Retrieved from http://www.allgov.com/departments/department-of-agriculture/united-states-forest-service?agencyid=7277

39. U.S. Postal Inspection Service. *Mission Statement*. Retrieved from https://postalinspectors.uspis.gov/aboutus/mission.aspx

40. U.S. Bureau of Justice Statistics (2004). *Federal Law Enforcement Officers, 2004*. Washington, DC: Government Printing Office.

41. U.S. National Park Service. *United States Park Police*. Retrieved from http://www.nps.gov/uspp/

42. Ibid.

43. Ibid.

44. Ibid.

45. Ibid.

46. U.S. National Park Service. *The United States Park Police Student Internship Program*. Retrieved from http://www.nps.gov/uspp/interpag.htm

47. U.S. National Park Service. *Park Rangers*. Retrieved from http://www.nps.gov/personnel/rangers.htm

48. National Parks Conservation Association. *Perilous Parkland: Homeland Security and the National Parks*. Retrieved from http://www.npca.org/news/media-center/fact-sheets/security.html

49. Ibid.

50. U.S. National Park Service. *Burmese Pythons: Management*. Retrieved from http://www.nps.gov/ever/naturescience/npspythonmanagement.htm

51. Environment News Service. *U.S. Rangers, Park Police Sustain Record Levels of Violence*. Retrieved from http://www.ens-newswire.com/ens/sep2004/2004-09-01-02.asp

52. EUROPOL. *History*. Retrieved from https://www.europol.europa.eu/content/page/history-149

53. *Financial Action Task Force*. Retrieved from http://www.fatf-gafi.org/pages/0,2987,en_32250379_32235720_1_1_1_1_1,00.html

54. INTERPOL. *About INTERPOL*. Retrieved from http://www.interpol.int/About-INTERPOL/Overview

55. Shaw, W. (September 1980). *INTERPOL, Law and Order* (p. 6).

Private Enforcement

6

The private security industry is a crucial component of security and safety in the United States and abroad. Today, private security is responsible not only for protecting many of the nation's institutions and critical infrastructure systems, but also for protecting intellectual property and sensitive corporate information.

Kevin Strom, et al.,
"The Private Security Industry: A Review of the Definitions, Available Data Sources, and Paths Moving Forward," 2010.

Learning Objectives

The objectives of this chapter are to

- Explain the role of the private enforcement and security system within the United States
- Identify the need for private law enforcement and security
- Discuss the significance of private law enforcement and security
- Distinguish between the organizational facets of private law enforcement and security agencies
- Compare various private security and law enforcement agencies
- Describe the relationship between private law enforcement and homeland security

Introduction

Private security is a major industry in the United States. Across the nation and internationally, companies rely heavily on private security for a wide range of functions, including protecting employees and property, conducting investigations, performing preemployment screening, providing information technology security, and many other functions.[1]

Although private security guard forces, such as guards, investigators, patrolmen, armored-car guards, and those who are contracted to respond to alarms, perform a variety of security services that are typically complementary to public law enforcement, the industry is much broader that just those duties.[2]

During recent years, Customs and Border Protection (CBP) detected a marked increase in counterfeit software products. Between fiscal years 2004 and 2005, CBP seizures increased by approximately 185%.[3] These seizures included the traditionally pirated items of "laptop computers, notebook computers, chips, keyboards, monitors and other standard items."[4] However, the increase also included items representing "counterfeit interface cards, switchers, routers, and other components needed for local and wide-area networks, memory sticks, memory modules, and flash drives."[5]

Such items pose a variety of risks ranging from the ability to insert rogue software (e.g., viruses, worms, monitoring programs) into the most sensitive of corporate areas to posing risks of fire hazards when used among computer systems. Through the use of rogue software, intruders may gain access to confidential documents and data sets. They may also possess the ability to erase data and information or to control computer systems inside corporate or government entities. Among many organizations, the use of private security and enforcement protects against the theft and illegal copying of software and hardware products.

One of the earliest recorded examples of private security forces being utilized dates back to the thirteenth century BC. Egyptian Pharaoh Ramses II hired nonmilitary entities to complement Egyptian's own military and security forces. The history of private and public policing is intertwined. In England, it is likely that private policing both preceded and necessitated the introduction of public police.[6] Within the United States, the origins of private security and enforcement are found within the logistics of railroads and various investigative services. Throughout history, the use of private security and enforcement entities has benefitted both individuals and organizations. This notion is unchanged during modern times. Private security and enforcement has matured into a significant business model that protects both individuals and organizations from a large array of threats.

What Is Private Security?

Private security in the United States is big business and clearly a recognized industry. The annual revenue for private security firms is estimated to range from $19 billion to $34 billion. American Society for Industrial Security (ASIS) International, the largest association of private security professionals in the United States, has defined private security as the nongovernmental, private-sector practice of protecting people, property, and information, conducting investigations, and otherwise safeguarding an organization's assets.[7]

History of Private Enforcement and Security in the United States

Although there has always been a need for privately employed day and night watchmen, the momentum for private police development primarily occurred immediately during and after the War Between the States and the westward expansion of the population. Jesse James and other gangs of outlaws began to rob stagecoaches and railroad trains. Gold and silver shipments were also being targeted before, during, and after delivery to public transport. Responding to the need, stage-line, train, and mining companies built their own security forces and hired detective agencies to track down outlaws and predators.

In 1850, Henry Wells and William Fargo formed American Express, operating east of Missouri, and, two years later, Wells Fargo and Company served the country west of Missouri. Gradually, the railroads began their own security police programs instead of using the private firms for protection.

The railroad special agent was a colorful part of the old Wild West. Being able to shoot fast and ride hard were important skills in the late 1800s. In addition to train robbers, there were also station holdup crooks, pickpockets, con men, and bootleggers to contend with. Because of his mission in countering such problems, the railroad special agent of the Old West was considered nearly a duly commissioned law enforcement officer as his modern-day counterpart.

The most famous of all the private security agents or executives continues to be Allan Pinkerton, the son of a Scottish police officer. Pinkerton was appointed as a deputy sheriff in Cook County, Illinois, after he discovered and reported a counterfeiting operation. In 1843, he was appointed Chicago's first detective, even before a full-service Chicago police department was formed. In 1850, he resigned his public position and went into private business. His first two clients were the Rock Island and the Illinois Central Railroad. One year later, he formed the Pinkerton National Detective Agency, with the slogan, "We Never Sleep." Pinkerton's agency logo was an open eye. The eye was painted on every Pinkerton office entrance door in America. This logo probably led to the common use of the term "private eye" as referenced in future textbooks and novels describing private policing. [8]

Since many public agencies lacked jurisdiction or were woefully inadequate, Pinkerton's men stalked the most notable criminals in the United States. During the 1860s and 1870s, his men were writing reports, sending telegraphs to other agents throughout the South and West, and apprehending America's most wanted criminals. Additionally, Pinkerton also protected President Abraham Lincoln against an assassination attempt while he was traveling to his inauguration.[9] The relationship with President Lincoln continued through the War Between the States, during which Pinkerton's agency was tasked with numerous assignments including military intelligence that involved the infiltrating of Confederate encampments (Figure 6.1).[10]

Figure 6.1 Allan Pinkerton and President Abraham Lincoln. (Courtesy of the Library of Congress. Retrieved from http://memory.loc.gov/service/pnp/cwpb/04300/04326v.jpg.)

Additionally, security services like Holmes Protection, Inc., established by Edwin Holmes in 1858, advanced the burglar and robbery alarm businesses, and Washington Perry Brink established a delivery service the same year. In 1891, Brink started protecting the movement of payrolls and bank cash. As early as 1917, Brink began armor-plating his delivery vehicles.

During the 1950s, American federal organizations were encouraged to procure private security services among Department of Defense (DOD) installations.[11] Because of concerns regarding the use of private security organizations, the DOD was discouraged and prohibited from securing private security services in 1982.[12] The permanency of this prohibition was mandated in 1987 via the Defense Authorization Act.[13] Despite the prohibition, the Defense Authorization Act contained some exceptions: "(1) when the contract is to be performed overseas, (2) when the contract is to be performed on a government-owned but privately operated installation, and (3) when the contract (or renewal of the contract) is for the performance of a function already under contract as of September 24, 1983."[14]

The events of September 11, 2001, heralded the repealing of the prohibitions regarding private security among DOD installations. The following statements summarize the saliency of this reconsideration of private security:[15]

> In 2003, the prohibition was temporarily lifted for three years, in response to the greater need for installation protection after 9/11 combined with the unavailability (and/or inappropriateness of using) active duty or reserve military personnel to meet the increased base security requirements. Contract security services could only be acquired by installations to supplement existing DOD security personnel already on duty. Realizing that the need for greater installation security (primarily at access control points) would be permanent, DOD soon requested permanent authority to contract for security guard services. Despite this request from DOD, Congress has extended authority only through 2012. In addition, Congress mandated an annual 10% decrease in total contract personnel to ensure that by 2012 there will be 50% of the number of contract security guards as there were in 2006.

Today, the private security industry employs far more personnel than public policing agencies at the city, county, state, and national level, and private security is a viable and integral component in the fight against crime in the United States. Modern security companies act as force multipliers that complement existing ranks of police officers throughout American society. Through the use of private security and enforcement services, a vast array of individuals and organizations reduce the potential of acts of crime occurring against them and diminish the risks of threats that may endanger them.

Significance of Private Security and Enforcement

The significance and importance of organizational security must not be understated for a variety of reasons. Individuals and organizations employ private security personnel as resources through which they protect themselves and their assets. The use of this form of private protection varies greatly from the provision of services for community leaders to the protection of well-known celebrities. Regardless, the use of private security and enforcement provides a committed resource that is dedicated to the needs of the employing individual or organization.

Corporations have a valid need for security. If a rogue entity gains the blueprints of confidential products or possesses the ability to pirate counterfeit products, then the financial impacts are enormous for legitimate corporations, market consumers, and other stake-holders. If a rogue entity gains operational control of organizational assets, then the out-comes could be disastrous for the organization and its stakeholders. Any number of threats may breach organizational security. Examples range widely from disgruntled employees to acts of corporate espionage that are conducted by market competitors. The use of private security entities diminishes the risks of such events impacting an organization negatively.

Another perspective of private security and enforcement involves a complementary view with respect to the roles of traditional law enforcement agencies and private security organizations. Law enforcement organizations are not necessarily tasked with any specific security function, despite their mission of deterring crime and maintaining societal order. Certainly, when necessary, they may provide security (e.g., escorting a gubernatorial procession) resources and services. However, law enforcement organizations are ill suited to provide customized services among the individual businesses and residential areas that comprise their serviced localities. Instead, their responsibilities are geared towards benefitting the whole of society. In contrast, private security organizations may be hired to fulfill a specific purpose for the hiring entity and have a fiduciary obligation to dedicate sufficient resources towards servicing the needs of their client(s).

Personal security is a salient consideration of private security organizations. For example, perhaps an elderly couple may be fearful because of increases of crime within their neighborhood. Such a scenario may entail the purchasing and installing of a residential alarm system within their home. The presence of such a system may deter potential robbers from committing a crime at the residence and may provide peace of mind for the family. Further, such a security system may contain both audio and video recording capabilities to continuously monitor the family home and may be used to alert and summon law enforcement or medical personnel should an emergency situation occur. These types of security systems and their affiliated services may be purchased and contracted from private security firms.

A financial perspective may be considered within the context of private security. Bank transactions and facilities must be secure to protect the assets of investors, to protect the clientele of the bank, and to ensure the integrity of banking personnel. It is not uncommon to observe security guards patrolling banking institutions or to observe armored cars transporting deliveries of money and other valuable assets. Guard services and armored vehicles may be procured from private security organizations.

Further, private security guards may be observed among an array of businesses and government facilities. They may be employed among schools, hospitals, hotels, restaurants, stores, malls, factories, industrial parks, and many other venues. Their hours may vary from overnight shifts to uninterrupted patrols around the clock (including holidays). Approximately 1.2 million private security guards are employed by somewhere between 11,000 and 15,000 private security organizations.[16] This number of private security personnel is approximately twice the number of police officers.[17]

Private security and enforcement personnel act as complements to the law enforce-ment officers who serve society nationally. They act as a force multiplier through their availability and deployment among both private and public settings. Although private security personnel may not necessarily have powers of arrest, they often may detain indi-viduals who are suspected of committing acts of crime (e.g., shoplifters). Further, the pres-ence and visibility of a uniformed and armed private security officer may act as a deterrent to criminal activity.

Private security and enforcement personnel may be retained for the purpose of personal protection. For example, individuals may employ private security organizations and personnel to protect themselves, their families, their homes, and other assets. Clients range from corporate executives to movie actors. This form of personal protection may be employed by anyone who can afford such services. In some states, such as Florida, this form of private security is used to enforce protective or restraining orders issued within the court system. The protective services of this type of personal security include performing "premises–venue threat assessments," examinations of offices and sports areas for threats and forms of surveillance, and examining "other facilities for improvised explosive devices, electronic surveillance devices, and other hidden people threats."[18] Within this perspective, private security personnel act as preventive and protective resources.

Private investigation is within the domain of private security and enforcement. Investigators who are employed among law enforcement organizations may often investigate concurrently numerous cases that demand their attention. As a result, their cases may become backlogged and may be given low priorities. Often, they are unable to dedicate their full attention to any single case. In contrast, a private investigative service may be procured to investigate a case that may otherwise be slowly investigated by traditional law enforcement agencies. The use of private investigators may encompass a variety of investigations ranging from murder and missing persons to insurance fraud and marital infidelity.

The preceding examples and scenarios demonstrate a plethora of applications that involve the use of private security and enforcement personnel. These considerations are significant because they show that private security and enforcement is accessible to ordinary members of the general public (provided that they can afford the financial expense) as well as to the notable members of society, business, and government. In all cases, the use of private security and enforcement represents a protective and preventive resource that safeguards the hiring organization or individual(s) from a variety of threats.

Private Security: The Scope of Work

During the post-9/11 era, private security guards have a more critical role in homeland security and public safety than ever before. Every day, they are responsible for the protection of critical infrastructure, intellectual property, and millions of lives. The scope of private security encompasses a wide array of applications ranging from investigative services to personal protection. Some of the more prevalent uses of private security organizations are discussed further.

Private Investigations

The term *investigate* is defined as the observation of or studying of "by close examination and systematic inquiry."[19] Investigations may be performed by both traditional law enforcement entities and by private security and enforcement organizations. Private investigators and detectives perform a variety of duties and functions. Examples include finding facts and analyzing information regarding personal, financial, and legal situations.[20] Specific investigative activities and services involve an array of different responsibilities. Examples include background investigations, personal protection, and criminal and civil investigations.[21]

In 2008, around 45,500 private detectives and investigators were employed in the United States by such organizations as private detective agencies, state and local governments, department stores, financial institutions, insurance agencies, and employment security services.[22] Private investigators are hired to collect information through observation and interviews to solve noncriminal cases, including missing persons, medical malpractice, domestic or marital issues, and product liability.[23] Additionally, private corporations or organizations may hire private investigators for criminal cases such as credit card fraud, internal theft, insurance fraud, and, in some cases, corporate intelligence and industrial espionage.[24]

The future of private investigations has the potential for solid growth. In fact, this occupation is expected to grow "faster than the average for all occupations."[25] Employment opportunities for private investigators and detectives are anticipated to increase "21% from 2010 to 2020."[26] This expected increase arises from a societal need to "protect confidential information and property of all kinds" as well as considerations of security for both individuals and organizations.[27] During 2010, the annual median salary for private investigators was $42,870.[28]

Generally, private investigators have some college education and experience much of their learning through on-the-job training.[29] The qualifications necessary to enter the private investigation occupation vary among the states. For example, in Mississippi, there is no licensing requirement for entry into the private investigation occupation.[30] However, in Oklahoma, potential investigators must complete "approved and mandated training."[31] Alabama requires no state licensure for entry into the private investigation occupation, but does require city licensure of private investigators in Birmingham and Mobile.[32] Further, Alabama requires that any private investigation business have appropriate business licensure.[33]

Florida private investigators must be licensed and are regulated by the Florida Department of Agriculture and Consumer Services.[34] Idaho has no licensure requirement for private investigators.[35] Missouri has stronger licensure requirements. In Missouri, candidates for the private investigation occupation must complete a written examination (although individuals who have completed Peace Officer Standards and Training are excluded), undergo "background checks, fingerprinting, and submission of documentation and photograph," and obtain "$250,000 general liability insurance."[36]

Similar differences are manifested among the state licensure laws and regulations of the remaining states. Given these differences, it is apparent that what may be acceptable as valid qualifications for private investigator licensure in one state may be completely unacceptable in another state. Further, given these observations, it is apparent that no consensus exists nationally regarding the qualifications of private investigators. Therefore, if one is willing to move to a state in which licensure is unnecessary, one may enter the private investigation occupation rather quickly and easily.

Training opportunities exist for those who desire to enter the private investigation occupation or who must obtain continuing education credit. The Detective Training Institute (San Juan Capistrano, California) offers a training program that encompasses 31 areas of investigative study that range from insurance fraud investigations to surveillance and bounty hunting.[37] This institute is properly licensed as a California educational institution by the California Bureau for Private Postsecondary Education.[38] Ashworth College (Norcross, Georgia) offers a training program that leads to private investigator credentialing.[39] Ashworth College is accredited by the Distance Education and

Figure 6.2 Private detectives and investigators perform computer searches when researching a crime or conducting a background check. (Courtesy of the U.S. Bureau of Labor Statistics. Retrieved from http://www.stats.bls.gov/ooh/Protective-Service/Private-detectives-and-investigators.htm.)

Training Council and is authorized appropriately by the Georgia Nonpublic Postsecondary Education Commission.[40] Such programs are not necessarily academic from a traditional university perspective, but they provide legitimate vocational training through which candidates may gain entry-level credentials to enter the private investigation occupation.

Many individuals may leave public service to enter the occupation of private investigation. These individuals often possess significant investigate training, education, and experience that spans decades. For example, the Bearden Investigative Agency (Dallas, Texas) has origins that are affiliated with well-known cases and scandals involving "Watergate, the Sharpstown Scandal, Abscam, Brilab, the Cullen Davis criminal case, as well as numerous other high profile civil and criminal cases."[41] Over the last three decades, this agency has expanded its scope of operations to encompass "investigations in all 50 states and approximately 42 foreign countries."[42]

The Bearden example shows a highly successful and experienced organization. Not all private investigators or private investigation agencies will experience such success. Not all private investigation agencies will attract an array of investigators whose credentials and backgrounds manifest cases of national prominence or other notoriety and significance. However, the private investigator occupation is a respectable and necessary aspect of society. Although private investigators may not be deemed as traditional police entities, they do contribute toward the deterring of crime and the maintaining of societal order (Figure 6.2).

Protection of Critical Infrastructure

One of the major roles of private security companies today is the protection of critical infrastructure. Critical infrastructure includes industry and manufacturing, utilities, and transportation. Agriculture and medical care are also aspects of the critical national infrastructure. In the United States, the vast majority of critical infrastructure is owned and operated by the private sector.[43]

Because of numerous integrations among the sectors of the national critical infrastructure, any attack or natural disaster that destroys or impedes any component of the critical infrastructure has the potential of disrupting not only the incident area, but also the entirety of the nation. Therefore, private security organizations and personnel have a daunting and necessary task with respect to the protection of critical national infrastructure (Figure 6.3).

Private security organizations and their personnel are civilians. However, these civilians are entrusted with protecting critical national infrastructure, and fulfilling a range of duties encompassing foot patrols to video monitoring of camera systems. Their powers are less than those of traditional law enforcement, despite their contributions to protecting critical national infrastructure.[44] Because they are civilians, their ability to arrest suspects is limited depending upon jurisdictional laws.[45] This notion is salient because private security personnel may be subject to the consequences and liabilities of false arrest.[46]

Although the powers of private security personnel may be limited, their responsibilities of protecting critical infrastructure, which range from conducting vehicle inspections to manual patrols of national assets, are dangerous.[47] The use of private security to protect critical infrastructure is perceived as a necessary aspect of addressing potential threats of

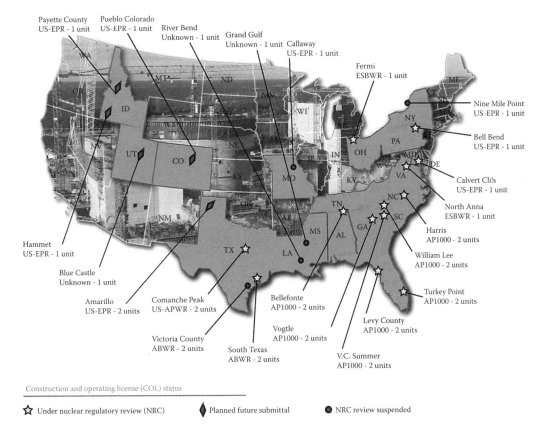

Figure 6.3 Planned expansion of nuclear power infrastructure to provide American energy. Nuclear power is an important component of the critical national infrastructure. (Courtesy of the U.S. Department of Energy. Retrieved from http://www.ne.doe.gov/np2010/neScorecard/images/map_2010_01_lg.jpg.)

terrorism.[48] Further, it also acts as a supplementary force for existing law enforcement organizations, whose resources may be insufficient to perform their traditional missions, and assumes the additional responsibilities of protecting the critical national infrastructure.[49]

Security Consulting

Security consultants work in diverse fields, including engineering, security management, crisis management, and computer security. The services that consulting firms offer may include designing security systems and developing specifications for technological and physical security measures, conducting security training, administering polygraph and psychological stress evaluations, and providing expert advice on loss prevention and risk management.[1]

Some security consulting organizations have received national recognition. For example, during the last decade, the former Blackwater Corporation experienced an incident that garnered much public exposure. During 2007, a total of 17 Iraqi civilians were shot and killed by Blackwater personnel. It was determined that 14 of these shootings were unjustified and "violated deadly force rules in effect for security contractors."[50]

Other perceptions of security consulting entities are not quite as negative and provide benefit for organizations that solicit and procure their offered services. They are often used to expose security weaknesses regarding both tangible and intangible assets. For example, during 2011, famous computer hacker Kevin Mitnick demonstrated the easiness of hacking cell phones by using his own phone as a model of how corporate assets may be attacked and infiltrated.[51] This example is not uncommon because many well-known organizations employ security consulting firms to determine weaknesses in their security regimens.

Security consulting is an important endeavor. Both government agencies and corporations often rely upon objective, external security consulting organizations to test their security environments to determine whether defects exist and to recommend solutions through which weaknesses may be rectified. Even if weaknesses are not apparent, security consulting firms may provide recommendations for improvement that bolster security mechanisms that may be deemed as adequate.

Relationships between Organizations and Private Security

Public and private organizations have a need for stringent security to maintain the integrity and confidentiality of intellectual property and to secure their tangible and intangible resources from intrusion and damages. Security is also necessary for maintaining organizational integrity and performance. Organizational security is concerned with a variety of attributes that encompass numerous domains. Examples include the following:

- Client lists and associated client data
- Customer lists and associated customer data
- Trade secrets
- Operations plan
- Intellectual properties
- Marketing plans
- Confidential financial and economic data sets

- R&D blueprints for new technologies
- Data regarding existing products
- Electronic networks, software, and hardware
- Growth and expansion plans
- Materials regarding joint ventures
- Materials regarding strategic plans
- Materials regarding legal and regulatory issues
- Meeting minutes, telephone conversations, and electronic communications
- Videoconferencing and audio conferencing
- Human resources records and various personnel assignments
- Production processes
- Blueprints and details of physical infrastructures
- Logistics and routing information
- Exercising of human resources actions (e.g., escorting fired personnel off-site)

Certainly, many other examples can be identified. However, a breach of security may compromise the competitiveness of an organization or may negatively impact its ability to supply the needs and wants of market consumers. Security breaches may also impede the ability of an organization to develop and offer new products or services. Government organizations may jeopardize national security when breaches occur. Security breaches may also impede the ability of an organization to function strategically, tactically, or operationally.

Absolutely no organization is invulnerable to tangible or intangible intrusion. Absolutely no organization is invulnerable to the temptations of betrayal among its own personnel or affiliated, partnering components. From the largest of government entities and well-known global corporations to the smallest of organizations, lackluster security may endanger any organization and its stakeholders.

Organizations are susceptible to physical intrusion that may originate either internally or externally. Internal threats may arise when employees become dissatisfied with their employer and are tempted to endanger the organization. For example, one may be demoted, fired, or subjected to some other form of disciplinary action. Other cases may be associated with perceptions of discrimination within the workplace, thereby causing feelings of animosity and resentfulness. External threats may originate from a variety of sources. Examples include the actions of corporate espionage among market competitors or the actions of nations to gain an international strategic advantage.

Given these notions, many organizations implement security forces and private enforcement to strengthen the integrity of their infrastructures. These forces may be internal or external to an organization. Internal forces consist of personnel who are employees of the organization, whereas external forces may be contracted through security firms or may act as independent contractors. Regardless, their primary function is to provide a resource through which the security and integrity of organizations are strengthened.

The need for private security is emphasized by numerous examples of security breaches that have occurred globally. Incidents between American and Chinese firms often involve security breaches involving intellectual properties. Factions of the American government are concerned with both the tangible and the intangible aspects of security that bolster national security and defense. Incidents of corporate and industrial espionage compromise the integrities of both for-profit and nonprofit organizations and may have significant financial and economic consequences when discovered. Although all such events cannot be predicted or prevented, the use of private security and enforcement may act as a deterrent to avoid cataclysmic situations from occurring, which disrupt organizational functioning or impact society. The following example cases show the shortcomings of various organizational environments and the affiliated security needs.

Counterfeit Products and Enforcement

Product counterfeiting is a multibillion-dollar industry, a global crime, and a serious threat to the industries producing the legitimate product and to the consumer who may unknowingly purchase and use the item. The range of goods counterfeited is broad and often appeals to the consumer who is in search of a bargain. Counterfeit items such as high-demand toys, sports memorabilia, handbags, apparel, DVDs, software, building products, and watches are just a few of the items frequently encountered by investigators. The production, distribution, and sale of counterfeit products are international problems. Attempts to combat these problems require the cooperative efforts of public and private investigators. Figure 6.4 highlights the impacts of counterfeit products and services.

A recent incident of software theft involved events between American Superconductor Corporation (AMSC) and the Chinese Sinovel Wind Group Company (SWGC). During 2011, AMSC personnel investigated the malfunctioning of some wind turbines that were located within the Gobi Desert.[52] Despite the issuing of a software command to terminate turbine operations weeks earlier, the examined turbine had not responded correctly and was continuing to operate.[53] The AMSC personnel copied the software that was operating the turbine and sent it to Austria for analysis. The outcome of the analysis showed that the turbines were running a stolen copy of AMSC's software and that "Beijing-based Sinovel had

Figure 6.4 Warning concerning counterfeit goods and products. (Courtesy of the White House. Retrieved from http://www.whitehouse.gov/sites/default/files/imagecache/embedded_img_full/image/image_file/numbers_dvds.jpg.)

complete access to AMSC's proprietary source code."[54] Because of these revelations, it was obvious that AMSC had become immaterial to Sinovel. This notion is highlighted as follows:[55]

> ... in March 2011, Sinovel abruptly and inexplicably began turning away AMSC's shipments at its enormous turbine assembly factory in Liaoning province. On April 5, AMSC had no choice but to announce that Sinovel—now its biggest customer, accounting for more than two-thirds of the company's $315 million in revenue in 2010—had stopped making purchases. Investors fled, erasing 40% of AMSC's value in a single day and 84% of it by September. The company's stock chart looks like the electrocardiogram of a person rushing toward white light.

AMSC responded by filing four suits within the Chinese court system that sought approximately $1.2 billion in damages.[56] Sinovel filed a countersuit alleging that AMSC owed it approximately "$207 million for problems including defective equipment."[57] AMSC also sued for the illegal cancellation of contracts by Sinovel.[58] Because of the incident, AMSC's stock price fell approximately 80% and it laid off approximately 40% of its personnel.[59]

AMSC developed its firmware and technological components within the United States and then forwarded them to Asia.[60] Its software development occurred in Austria and used computers that were unconnected with the Internet.[61] The source of the stolen software was eventually determined to be Dejan Karabasevic—a former AMSC employee.[62] Sinovel recruited Karabasevic energetically during 2010. By the middle of 2011, Karabasevic had provided Sinovel with a functional copy of the software system.[63] Karabasevic received "one year in jail and two years probation for passing proprietary turbine control software" to the Chinese firm.[64] He was also ordered to compensate AMSC the amount of $270,000.[65]

This incident shows the vulnerability of organizations to human temptations. Karabasevic made a conscious decision to assist Sinovel, thereby compromising the confidentiality of AMSC. A forensic analysis of Karabasevic's computer revealed "hundreds of messages about the code exchanged between Karabasevic and three Sinovel employees, including one e-mail in which the engineer sent AMSC's source code to his Sinovel counterpart."[66] The forensic analysis also showed that Karabasevic had accessed his e-mail account from Chinese locations.[67]

Many companies randomly review and examine the contents of organizational e-mail messages that are both transmitted from or received by their corporate mail servers. If AMSC had the ability to analyze the e-mail messages of its personnel, then it could have possibly averted its painful and disastrous experience with Sinovel. However, reviewing any suspicious messages necessitates human intervention to determine whether the contents of the electronic discussions necessitate investigation. Based on the experiences of AMSC, the use of internal or externally contracted security and enforcement personnel, for the purposes of electronic and information security, could prove beneficial when attempting to protect the integrity of organizational environments.

NASA Security Example

Another recent example of the danger of poor organizational security involves security breaches that occurred within the National Aeronautics and Space Administration (NASA) infrastructure. Although NASA is a government organization, the concept of maintaining stringent security permeates both public and private organizations. During 2012, it was announced that a NASA laptop computer was stolen during 2011. This computer contained the unencrypted "command and control codes for the International Space Station."[68]

This missing laptop was only one of 48 NASA computers that were stolen between 2009 and 2011.[69] Additionally, during 2011 NASA was targeted 47 times for electronic intrusion purposes.[70] A total of 13 of these attacks were successful.[71] Such attacks resulted in the interjecting of malware and "unauthorized intrusions" that cost NASA approximately $7 million between 2010 and 2011.[72]

The financial costs are significant but may be only a small representation of the overall costs—both financial and otherwise—that impact NASA and its stakeholders. The success of the security breaches allowed rogue entities the ability to perform the following actions:[73]

- Modify, copy, or delete sensitive files
- Add, modify, or delete user accounts for mission-critical systems
- Upload hacking tools to compromise other NASA systems
- Modify system logs to maintain the anonymity of the breaches

The origins of such attacks are varied. Some attackers have been identified as having Chinese and Romanian locations, whereas others represent factions of organized crime or individuals desiring to test their hacking skills.[74] According to NASA Inspector General Paul Martin, with respect to a 2011 incident involving the Jet Propulsion Laboratory that indicated a Chinese origin, the attack resulted in the attacker having "full functional control" regarding the targeted NASA networks.[75]

Some organizations have strict security protocols that disallow the transporting of computer equipment from their premises. However, this form of protection does not guard against any memorized materials that depart an organization. Other organizations may allow the removal of such equipment from the immediate work site but incorporate various forms of tracking and monitoring software and unique identification systems within their mobile assets. Some organizations may allow the removal of mobile resources without any identifying or tracking methods. In the case of machines that are connected to the Internet, any number of methods may be used to compromise security. In short, when considering electronic domains, organizations are susceptible to the loss of electronic materials that may endanger not only the organization, but also its stakeholders.

Many organizations implement the physical searching of persons leaving or entering work sites by using private security and enforcement personnel. Although using personnel to conduct such searches is expensive, it has an unequalled "detection or deterrent value."[76] However, this form of security cannot protect organizations from the removal of any sensitive materials that are memorized. Regardless, private security or enforcement personnel are important resources through which organizations may implement the searching of persons and their belongings.

Corporate and Industrial Espionage Examples

Industrial and corporate espionage pose significant threats to both for-profit and nonprofit organizations. Recently, such an incident occurred that involved the rivals Hilton Hotels and Starwood Hotels & Resorts. Starwood levied accusations against Hilton regarding "using stolen trade secrets to launch a niche brand called Denizen Hotels" and to embellish "other Hilton lines such as its Waldorf Astoria Collection."[77] Some Hilton executives were accused of the theft of confidential documentation regarding Starwood's W chain of hotels that it intended to use to embellish the development of its Denizen hotel brand.[78]

A lawsuit was filed by Starwood that resulted in a cash settlement of approximately "$75 million to Starwood" and the awarding of an additional "$75 million in hotel management contracts" to Starwood.[79] The settlement favorably benefitted Starwood regarding the loss of intellectual property. In addition to the financial outcomes of the lawsuit, Hilton was prohibited from pursuing or furthering any "lifestyle hotels" for a period of 2 years.[80] Hilton was also subjected to the monitoring of its operations, by court appointed observers, to ensure that it complied with the terms of the settlement agreement.[81]

Another example involves an incident in which corporate trade secrets were stolen from Ford Motor Company. Between 1997 and 2007, Xiang Dong Yu worked for Ford as an engineer. Following his employment with Ford, Yu began working for the Beijing Automotive Industry Corporation. Upon leaving Ford, Yu stole approximately 4000 Ford documents that included "sensitive Ford design documents about engine-transmission and electric power supply systems."[82] This action resulted in millions of dollars of damages to Ford.[83] Yu was ordered to pay a fine of $12,500, sentenced to 70 months in federal prison, and ordered to be deported from the United States upon the completion of the period of incarceration.[84]

These scenarios present instances of corporate and industrial espionage. Annually, corporate and industrial espionage have a significant financial and economic impact among American corporations and consumers. These forms of espionage may originate from internal or external sources that seek to collect intelligence regarding corporate entities. The collecting of this information may yield long-term, strategic advantage for the acquiring entity while simultaneously damaging the performance of the targeted organization. Corporate espionage is defined as follows:[85]

> Economic espionage occurs when an actor, knowing or intending that his or her actions will benefit any foreign government, instrumentality, or agent, knowingly (1) steals or, without authorization, appropriates, carries away, conceals, or obtains by deception or fraud a trade secret; (2) copies, duplicates, reproduces, destroys, uploads, downloads, or transmits that trade secret without authorization; or (3) receives a trade secret knowing that the trade secret had been stolen, appropriated, obtained, or converted without authorization (Section 101 of the EEA, 18 USC Section 1831).

Similarly, industrial espionage is defined as follows:[86]

> Industrial espionage, or theft of trade secrets, occurs when an actor, intending or knowing that his or her offense will injure the owner of a trade secret of a product produced for or placed in interstate or foreign commerce, acts with the intent to convert that trade secret to the economic benefit of anyone other than the owner by (1) stealing or, without authorization, appropriating, carrying away, concealing, or obtaining by deception or fraud information related to that secret; (2) copying, duplicating, reproducing, destroying, uploading, downloading, or otherwise transmitting that information without authorization; or (3) receiving that information knowing that the information had been stolen, appropriated, obtained, or converted without authorization (Section 101 of the EEA, 18 USC Section 1832).

Various estimates of financial and economic losses associated with industrial and economic espionage range from $2 billion to $400 billion annually.[87] Regardless, corporate and industrial espionage are dangerous activities that endanger American organizations and market consumers. Such scenarios often prompt organizations to employ the services of private intelligence firms to "collect business intelligence on matters ranging from employee activities, terrorist threats, market trends, and the business dealings of rival companies."[88]

The use of private firms may be advantageous for organizations that seek to improve their organizational integrity and confidentiality. These private entities are often composed of individuals who possess significant government services experience within the intelligence community.[89] The services provided by these private organizations range greatly among application domains. Examples include the administering of polygraph examinations to corporate employees and gathering intelligence regarding competitors or other threatening market entities.[90]

The use of private intelligence organizations is not riskless. Although organizations desire to maintain strong, secure environments, they may be subjected to the actions of private intelligence firms that seek to gain information on behalf of their competitors. To detect potential weaknesses and threats internally, these private intelligence firms may be employed to determine the sources of various shortcomings within an organization. Regardless, the legal and ethical use of private intelligence firms is a salient consideration when guarding against corporate and industrial espionage.

Considerations of the Relationship

A relationship exists between organizations and private security. Government agencies are resourceful tools through which the American economy and its component entities are protected against threats that may originate both domestically and internationally. However, government law enforcement is constrained by a myriad of factors ranging from manpower quantities to legal limitations. Traditional law enforcement agencies are entities that organizations and individuals may contact during the committing of a crime or after a crime has been committed.

These notions facilitate the concept of private enforcement and security. Private organizations may fulfill security requirements that are not satisfied by traditional law enforcement agencies. Private security and enforcement entities may be contracted to represent the interests of their hiring organization, whereas law enforcement organizations must serve the whole of society. Private security and enforcement entities may dedicate specific resources solely for the purposes of the hiring organization, whereas traditional law enforcement agencies must share resources simultaneously among a variety of cases, investigations, and other duties.

When private enforcement and security entities fail to perform adequately or become too expensive, they may be discharged from further services. The hiring organization may examine replacement security firms from among several market competitors that provide private enforcement and security services. In contrast, traditional law enforcement agencies are static entities whose personnel are public servants and whose costs are satisfied through taxation and other forms of public revenue. Private security and enforcement organizations are generally businesses whose decisions are guided by motives of fiduciary service to their hiring organization and profitability through time. In contrast, traditional law enforcement organizations are not motivated by profitability, but are committed to deterring crime and maintaining order within society.

Regardless, the use of private enforcement and security entities is a valid form of safeguarding against a variety of threats that endanger an array of organizations. Although these private entities are not necessarily always commissioned law enforcement organizations, they are organizations that share similar duties, roles, responsibilities, and functions that permeate traditional law enforcement environments. Through retaining the services of a private enforcement and security entity, organizations gain the benefit of having a dedicated organization that is committed to providing the highest and best forms of security possible in the best interests of the hiring organization.

Modern Times: The FedEx Private Police

Federal Express (FedEx) is the world's largest cargo airline and the globe's largest express transportation entity.[91] Its headquarters is in Memphis, Tennessee, and the airline was founded in 1973.[92] FedEx's annual revenues are approximately $35 billion, and it has over 140,000 personnel globally.[93] It serves over 375 airports around the world that encompass 220 countries and territories.[94] During its daily operations, FedEx processes approximately 3.4 million packages and possesses a global lift capacity of 26.5 million pounds.[95] Within the United States, FedEx vehicles drive over 2.7 million miles daily.[96] FedEx experiences approximately 63 million electronic communications and over 500,000 calls daily.[97] Because of its vast corporate infrastructure, global scope, and widespread destinations security risks are a paramount concern of FedEx. Numerous opportunities exist for security breaches to occur.

During 1994, Auburn Calloway, a FedEx employee, hijacked FedEx Flight 705 in the hope of committing suicide by crashing the aircraft after it had reached its cruising altitude. Calloway's motivations were related to financial indebtedness, familial obligations, and corporate disciplinary measures involving the loss of his job because he had lied on his employment application.[98] Although he attempted to destroy the aircraft, the aircrew fought against and overcame Calloway in a gruesome struggle.[99] Calloway's hijacking attempt was unsuccessful, and the aircraft returned to Memphis, where he was arrested and taken into custody by law enforcement. The attack resulted in the disabling of the aircrew in such severity that they were unable to continue their careers as aviators.

The enormity of cargo airline operations necessitates an enhanced need for security that permeates the cargo airline industry. During 2010, it was discovered that two bombs were being transported via the UPS cargo airline from Yemen to the United States. If the packages had exploded during the course of the flight, these shipments would have endangered not only the aircraft and its crew, but also the residents of the eastern United States.[100] Certainly, the intended destinations of the bomb packages were also endangered. Such incidents show the weakness of cargo airline security through which rogue entities may interject explosive or other weapons within the global logistics framework.

Given its own history and the dangerousness of the modern cargo industry, FedEx recognized the need for enhanced security within the last few years. Although the corporation has implemented security guards and leveraged the services of traditional law enforcement agencies historically, it now manifests its own private police force as a method of bolstering corporate security. This type of private police force provides FedEx with the capacity to conduct a variety of law enforcement operations and investigations independently without reliance upon any other state or federal assistance.

The FedEx private police force has "full law enforcement powers to protect the world's largest cargo airline from terrorism or other threats."[101] The creation and commissioning of this police force resulted from the actions of the Tennessee legislature.[102] The Tennessee legislature amended and altered statutes that authorized a police force in conjunction with the Tennessee Valley Authority, thereby including airlines that were headquartered in Tennessee.[103] This action created the FedEx private police as a legitimate police force that is authorized and recognized by the state of Tennessee. The FedEx private police force primarily functions as an investigative entity.[104] However, it consults with or notifies traditional law enforcement agencies when it suspects that a crime may be occurring that merits significant resources.[105]

Because the force is composed of commissioned police officers, it participates in the regional terrorism task force in conjunction with the Federal Bureau of Investigation.[106] Personnel within the FedEx private police force must experience training that is identical to any law enforcement training that is mandated for law enforcement officer qualifications within the state of Tennessee.[107] Although these personnel are law enforcement officers, they are unsupervised by state agencies.[108] Instead, supervision and liability occur directly through FedEx.[109] Regardless, the primary function of this private entity is to provide an enhanced level of protectiveness and security for FedEx and its stakeholders.

The FedEx case is indicative of the need to protect a segment of the critical national infrastructure. FedEx represents a significant component of the logistics, aviation, trucking, and transportation resources of American society. Just as important are the types of materials that flow through the FedEx distribution and transportation systems. FedEx often processes medical supplies, human organs, electronics, foodstuffs, chemicals, and a variety of other materials that contribute to the functioning of society. FedEx also processes a vast quantity of financial and legal documents that contribute toward the functioning of the American economy. Many organizations do not possess their own distribution networks because of a variety of reasons (e.g., costs, feasibility, etc.) and rely upon FedEx as a significant component of their business models and supply chains.

These concepts are not limited solely to FedEx. They apply to all major ground and air carriers of cargo. By crafting a unique private police force, FedEx demonstrates a law enforcement model that is committed to the benefit of the sponsoring organization and its stakeholders. Through enacting its own private police force, FedEx proactively demonstrated the actions necessary for safeguarding its organizational capacity to fulfill its service obligations and to provide benefit for its stakeholders. Further, because the FedEx private police is a legitimate, state-authorized police entity, it becomes privy to a greater amount and detail of law enforcement information regarding potential threats than would be normally disseminated among corporations.[110] Because the FedEx private police force is a relatively young entity, time will reveal a greater determination of its efficiency and effectiveness. Regardless, the leveraging of a private police force shows a commitment to the preventive and proactive safeguarding of the organization and its stakeholders.

The Business of Private Security

The use of private security and enforcement resources represents an agency relationship in which a private security entity is hired to represent the interests of and to fulfill the obligations of fiduciary duties to the hiring and sponsoring entity. In essence, the hiring of a private security entity creates a principal–agency agreement and relationship between the client (i.e., the hiring organization) and the private security agency. Within the context of this relationship, the private security organization acts on behalf of the hiring organization and renders decisions and performs actions that are in the best interests of the sponsoring client. These duties may range from performing marital infidelity investigations to large-scale operations of protecting corporate infrastructures.

Such relationships constitute the foundations of business models that permeate the private security and enforcement services industry. Regardless of the size of the clientele or the size of the private security agency, a business relationship exists between the client and the private security organization. This notion is unconstrained globally. Wherever and whenever a private security organization agrees to undertake, represent, and act on the behalf of a client, a business relationship is established. Normally, monetary exchange is the primary method of compensation rendered by the client to the hired security agency.

The private security and enforcement business has experienced rapid and substantial growth during the preceding decades. Private security businesses may be found among small cities or globally. They may represent governments and multinational corporations or they may represent individuals or families who are engaged in legal struggles ranging from divorce proceedings to home security alarm systems. Regardless, the use of private security organizations represents the exercising of a business model and the establishing of a business relationship.

Global Contexts and Markets

Private security and enforcement represents a significant industry within the United States. This industry contains domains that consist of guard services, alarm monitoring, investigation, armored transport, correctional facilities management, systems integration and management, security consulting, personnel screening, and information security.[111] Markets for these domains include critical infrastructure, commercial entities, institutional settings, residential settings, and government entities.[112]

Services provided within the private security and enforcement industry are expected to grow phenomenally during the coming years. By the year 2016, one estimate of the growth rate is anticipated to be approximately 17%.[113] In some states, growth rates currently exceed this future estimate of industry growth. Within Arizona, California, and Nevada, the current growth rate exceeds 22%, and positional backlogs may be unfilled for several years.[114] Other estimates indicate a much smaller national rate of growth, which represents approximately 4.9% per year through 2014.[115] This estimate indicates that "guarding and alarm monitoring will remain the largest segments, while pre-employment screening, systems integration and management, and consulting" will demonstrate the quickest rates of growth.[116] Private security and enforcement services are a salient aspect of financial and economic activity within the American economy.

This concept is not limited solely to American boundaries. During recent years, the global private security services industry was estimated to represent a value of $150 billion.[117] This growth rate of this worldwide market was anticipated to be approximately 7.5%, representing a valuation of $200 billion before the beginning of 2012.[118] North America and Western Europe represent the largest markets for private security services.[119] These locations demonstrate approximately 42% and 26% market shares, respectively.[120] The Asia-Pacific region represents approximately 12%–13% of the global private security market share.[121]

Within Europe, the Confederation of European Security Services represents 18 European Union member states and 25 countries.[122] Cumulatively, this amalgamation consists of approximately 50,000 private security companies composed of approximately 1.8 million private security personnel.[123] The European valuation of private security yields an annual amount of "approximately €35 billion."[124]

The war in Iraq necessitates the use of private security and enforcement. The U.S. Department of State anticipated expenditures of approximately $3 billion to "hire a security force," for the purpose of protecting "diplomats in Iraq," after American troops were withdrawn from Iraq.[125] Cumulatively, during 2008, some estimates showed that the United States expended an amount that exceeded $6 billion for private security within Iraq.[126]

Ocean shipping and transportation necessitates robust security to guard against piracy and other acts of crime. Before the end of 2011, it was estimated that approximately half of the maritime vessels that traversed the Indian Ocean carried some form of security guards during their voyages.[127] Organizations expended approximately $1 billion to provide such services and their affiliated resources.[128] Although these costs may seem excessive, it was observed that "armed private security guards also had a 100% success rate in protecting ships."[129]

The United States–Mexico border is tumultuous. Corporations pursuing Mexican business opportunities are susceptible to a variety of risks ranging from the lethal effects of drug war hostilities to burglary. Both private entities and the Mexican government have invested funding to procure private security services. Within Mexico, the quantity of "armed private security firms" has doubled to represent expenditures ranging from approximately "$1.7 billion in 2005 to more than $12 billion in 2011."[130]

The nation of India represents a large market for private security and enforcement services. This market represents approximately $2 billion annually and anticipates the addition of "a million employees this year, even as other industries lay-off workers while the economy cools."[131] Currently, the Indian private security industry employs approximately "5 million people, 1.3 million more than India's police and armed forces combined."[132] These private security organizations guard against a variety of threats ranging from ocean piracy to preventing terrorism.

Within South Africa, the citizenry may not consider the police force an adequate safeguard from crime.[133] Since 2001, the number of South African private security officers and companies increased, respectively, by 111.30% and 66.7%.[134] Much of these increases is attributed to social problems, urbanization and modernization, and concurrent patrolling of sectors by both police forces and private organizations.[135]

The concepts of private security and enforcement are debated within Great Britain. Contract bids for private security are being explored as alternatives to the traditional police presence within the regions of West Midlands and Surrey.[136] Such an option represents the largest consideration of police privatization in Great Britain and represents a "potential value of £1.5bn over 7 years, rising to a possible £3.5bn depending on how many other forces get involved."[137] A similar contract for private security currently exists within Great Britain. This contract involves a £200m relationship between the region of Lincolnshire and the private G4S security firm.[138] This contractual relationship involves approximately half of the civilian police personnel joining the ranks of the G4S organization, and the erecting and operating of a police station.[139]

South American nations also have a need for private security. Brazil is a prime example of the growth of the South American private security industry. During recent years, approximately $20 billion was expended annually within Brazil to procure services including safety and security equipment.[140] The Brazilian growth rate of the private security industry recently fluctuated annually between 10% and 15%.[141]

China represents a large economy with an increasingly consistent need for security. The use of private security firms demonstrates a paradox regarding Chinese legalities. These notions are expressed as follows:[142]

> Private security as an industry was banned in China eleven years ago but the ban served only to drive firms deeper underground. In 2009, some 2800 companies were offering such services illegally in an industry worth 7.9 billion yuan ($1.22 billion) a year, China's Ministry of State Security said. More than two million security guards are now on duty, according to media reports, many of whom are still illegal. In January 2010, the ministry passed new laws allowing Chinese companies to offer private security services but only if the founder has at least five years experience in the police, the army, a justice department, or security guard service management.

These examples show the global necessity and use of private security organizations. The privatization of security firms represents the crafting and developing by many nations of businesses whose primary function is the provision of security. Globally, police forces are incapable of providing a dedicated security function for the purposes of securing local, national, and international business and government activities. However, increases in globalization and economic integration contribute to the demand and need for private security organizations to fulfill this dedicated function.

Globalization increases the risks of conducting business transactions and activities among nations. Globalization stresses the capacities of logistics networks and supply chains and increases the difficulties of recovery when disruptions occur.[143] Any disruption of a global supply chain has the potential of severely impacting corporate revenues and market consumers. Disruptions may occur because of ocean piracy, terrorism, product theft, natural disaster, sabotage, acts of organized crime, logistics constraints, and may other considerations. The use of private security firms provides a resource through which global logistics networks and supply chains may be safeguarded from such impediments.

Acts of crime exist among all nations whether their innate businesses participate in global trade. Within nations, black markets exist for any number of products and services ranging from counterfeit apparel to the illegal smuggling of humans and narcotics. Organizations of all nations are susceptible to acts of revenge that may be perpetrated by disgruntled employees as well as acts of corporate espionage. Shipments of legal products may be hijacked and stolen among logistics networks. Certainly, many other examples may be identified that threaten organizations globally, internationally, and nationally.

It is inconceivable that traditional policing and law enforcement can accommodate the activities that are necessary to prevent such a vast range of threats from occurring globally, internationally, or nationally. Fulfilling the security requirements of the modern world is a daunting task for which traditional law enforcement is often an inappropriate resource. After all, a primary goal of law enforcement is to enforce the law while simultaneously deterring crime and maintaining societal order. However, it is not necessary to provide security functions for organizations.

These notions are not unrealized among organizations. Instead of relying upon law enforcement entities as a security resource, organizations opt to procure security resources and services from private entities or craft and develop security functions internally. Regardless of the option selected, the use of private security entities provides organizations with dedicated resources through which organizational security is embellished.

Organizational Contexts

Both proprietary and contracted security and enforcement services exist among the aforementioned private security domains and their compositional segments. Proprietary applications include security services that are sponsored internally by organizations. Within the proprietary context, organizations may opt to hire personnel whose duties are dedicated to the functions of security. In such instances, the organization may also procure and supply the resources (e.g., vehicles, radios) that are necessary for conducting security functions. The FedEx private police represents an example of the instantiation of proprietary internal security and enforcement.

Contracted security and enforcement services are generally obtained from entities that are external to an organization. In such cases, an organization may procure specific services and resources from a separate vendor whose specialty is private enforcement. Examples may include the installing and maintaining of alarm and monitoring security systems in conjunction with vendors such as the Brinks or ADT security companies. This form of obtaining private security and enforcement services is analogous with the common business practice of outsourcing.

Private security and enforcement entities are often incorporated as business organizations. Their sizes may range from small security firms that serve a single city to security organizations that have an international focus (e.g., defense-related security). Their missions may differ with respect to their served markets. For example, perhaps a small security firm desires only to provide night watchmen to patrol the grounds of a single, local factory or storage business, whereas a larger security firm may operate and manage prisons throughout the United States. Regional security businesses may provide a different scope of operations (e.g., a tri-state area or portion of a state).

An example of a small security firm involves Total Security of Spokane, Washington. This security firm provides residential monitoring systems for citizens of the community. Total Security sells, installs, and implements alarm monitoring systems that alert fire, medical, and law enforcement personnel when the homeowner enters the relevant electronic code within the security system to summon assistance.[144] These systems also alert emergency responders when break-ins occur.[145]

Another example is the Alarm Club of South Florida. This entity provides security services within the Florida counties of Broward, Martin, and Palm Beach.[146] Specifically, Alarm Club offers security services ranging from smartphone video monitoring systems to medical response systems.[147] Because it offers services among multiple counties, it may be viewed as a regional entity.

A larger security corporation that provides armored car services is the Loomis Corporation. Loomis has an international scope of operations that consists of "over 400 operating locations in the United States and in 11 western European countries."[148] Domestically, the corporation "operates an electronically linked service network of nearly 200 operating locations, employs over 8000 teammates, and utilizes a fleet of approximately

3000 armored and other vehicles to provide secure armored transport, automated teller machine (ATM) services, cash processing, and outsourced vault services for banks, other financial institutions, commercial and retail businesses."[149] Certainly, Loomis may be viewed as an international security organization.

These organizations differ greatly in their scopes of operations and their offered products and services. Their missions and clienteles also differ greatly with respect to their served markets. Regardless, these organizations are demonstrative of the different organizational contexts through which private security and enforcement services may be procured. In all cases, they share a common theme: the provision of dedicated, private security for the benefit of their hiring entities.

Training, Licensure, and Certification

Training, licensing, certification, and regulation vary widely from state to state. All but nine states have requirements that either private security companies or private security officers be licensed in some manner.[150] Some states require all security officers to be licensed, while others require only contract security officers or only those carrying firearms on the job to have licenses. At the company level, 33 states require only contract security firms to be licensed, while proprietary companies with their own security force are not required to be licensed.

Private security organizations are also affiliated with environments that are related to national defense and national security. The U.S. Army employs private security organizations to provide various and sundry services. The following statements indicate the training requirements that are expected of Army contractors who provide security services:[151]

> The Department of Army's Regulation for *The Army Civilian Police and Security Guard Program* (AR 190-56 subchapter 4–2 {Initial training and certification policy} subparagraph (d)(2) states: "(2) DA Civilian Guard POs (085) will be required to successfully complete an 80-hr (Field Training Program) FTP structured as above specifically tailored to the guard mission." Whereas the Performance Work Statements currently being used in the Army's contract guard contracts stipulates: "C.6.2. Training and Instruction. C.6.2.1. The Contractor shall furnish fully trained and qualified personnel to accomplish all work identified in the PWS. The Contractor shall establish a core curriculum of at least 120-hr of initial training, provided by the contractor, plus up to 40-hr additional of Installation Specific Training."

The training of private security personnel differs among the states. In some states, training may be quite rigorous, while it may be practically nonexistent among others. For example, assuming that one has no prior New York law enforcement training, the state of New York requires 47 hr of firearms training, 16 hr of on-the-job training, and 8 hr of pre-assignment training as components of its security guard basic training.[152] Its annual training consists of 8 hr of in-service training.[153] Appropriate licensure of firearms must also be accomplished in conjunction with this training regimen.[154]

However, the requirements within the state of Arizona are quite different. Title 32 of the Arizona Revised Statutes indicates that "an agency licensee shall provide 8 hr of pre-assignment training for all persons employed as security guards before the employee acts in the capacity of a security guard" and that "at least 16 hr of initial firearms instruction and 8 hr of annual continuing firearms instruction in the use of the weapon used by the security guard is required if a firearm is used within the scope of employment."[155] Obviously, these requirements are significantly different from those of New York.

Evaluating the Arizona and New York requirements reveals differences in the types of training and the number of training hours that are necessary for entering the private security occupation within these two states. Notable differences concerning occupational requirements are also found when comparing and contrasting the requirements of the remaining states. Given these notions, there is no consensus regarding a universal qualification with respect to the private security and enforcement occupation. Each state may mandate its own personnel qualifications for initial entry and retention within the private security domain.

Critics argue that there is a lack of training and education standards in the private security industry. ASIS International has written voluntary training guidelines that are intended to provide regulating bodies with consistent standards for security services. These guidelines recommend that security guards receive 48 hr of training within the first 100 days of employment. The guidelines also suggest that security guards pass a written or performance examination covering topics such as information sharing with law enforcement, crime prevention, evidence handling, the use of force, court testimony, report writing, communication skills, and emergency response. In addition, ASIS International recommends annual refresher training and additional firearms training for armed officers.[156]

Privately Operated Correctional Facilities

Over the last few decades, the private security industry has moved into the correctional market. With contracts ranging from the total operation of correctional facilities to the providing of specific services such as food, medical, transportation, and dental support, the private security industry has found a new and exciting market within the field of criminal justice.

A prominent example of private corrections is the Corrections Corporation of America (CCA). The private corrections management industry originated with CCA over a quarter of a century ago.[157] CCA also contributed toward the specification of industry standards that have influenced corrections management services.[158] Further, CCA "specializes in the design, construction, expansion, and management of prisons, jails, and detention facilities, as well as inmate transportation services."[159] The corporation has its headquarters in Tennessee and employs approximately 17,000 personnel.[160] The CCA is a publically traded organization, and its stock symbol is CXW.[161]

The scope of operations manifested by CCA is large and encompasses "75,000 offenders and detainees in more than 60 facilities, 44 of which are company-owned, with a total bed capacity of more than 80,000."[162] Collaboration is a significant aspect of CCA's business model. It collaborates with "all three federal corrections agencies (The Federal Bureau of Prisons, the U.S. Marshals Service, and Immigration and Customs Enforcement), nearly half of all states, and more than a dozen local municipalities."[163]

During the fourth fiscal quarter of 2011, CCA announced its financial status as follows: "Total management revenue for the fourth quarter of 2011 increased to $438.3 million from $430.8 million during the fourth quarter of 2010. For the fourth quarter of 2011, CCA generated net income of $40.5 million, or $0.41 per diluted share, compared with net income of $43.7 million, or $0.39 per diluted share, for the fourth quarter of 2010" (Figure 6.5).[164]

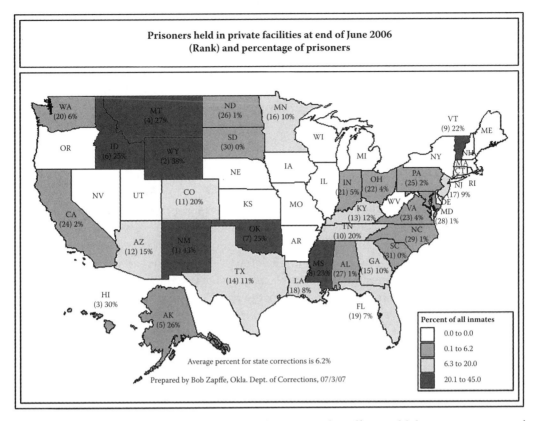

Figure 6.5 Incarcerations and private prisons. (Courtesy of Zapffe, B., Oklahoma Department of Corrections. Retrieved from http://www.doc.state.ok.us/field/private_prisons/maps/PRIVMY06 .png.)

Private prisons can represent considerable economic activity for a region. For example, in Pima County, Arizona, near Tucson, the construction of a 5000-bed private prison was debated within the last few years.[165] This facility was projected to supply approximately 900 jobs within the local community.[166] It was also estimated to contribute approximately "$3.9 million in taxes every year, with $2 million going to Sunnyside Unified School District."[167]

These observations show that private prisons and corrections facilities complement state-sponsored corrections infrastructures. They house prisoners and are responsible for their care, punitive enforcement, and rehabilitation. They are also protective mechanisms because the justice system protects society from offenders via incarceration in private correctional institutions. Because they are often for-profit organizations, they are motivated by the maximizing of shareholder wealth. Therefore, a financial motive underlies their business models and operations. Regardless, private corrections facilities represent a significant industry and are a considerable aspect of the justice system.

National Insurance Crime Bureau

The National Insurance Crime Bureau (NICB) represents a private, nonprofit organization that contributes significantly toward the deterring of various criminal activities that are associated with insurance fraud. The NICB boasts that it is the sole "organization in the

United States that convenes the collective resources needed to prevent, detect, and deter these crimes."[168] Accomplishing these tasks often necessitates close cooperation with law enforcement organizations throughout the nation. Analogous with traditional law enforcement organizations, the NICB leverages "information analysis, investigations, training, and public awareness" to accomplish its goals and fulfill its mission.[169]

The origin of the NICB integrated the Insurance Crime Prevention Institute (ICPI) and the National Automobile Theft Bureau (NATB) in 1992.[170] The ICPI primarily acted as an investigative entity whose investigations emphasized insurance fraud, whereas the NATB "managed vehicle theft investigations and developed vehicle theft databases for use by the insurance industry."[171] The current instantiation of the NICB boasts approximately 1100 insurance companies that focus upon casualty and property insurance, various rental car agencies, self-insured entities, providers of parking services, and transportation organizations.[172] The personnel of the NICB collaborate "with law enforcement agencies, technology experts, government officials, prosecutors, international crime-fighting organizations, and the public" to detect and prevent crimes related to insurance fraud.[173] This observation demonstrates an instance of a private organization cooperating with public law enforcement organizations to detect, investigate, and diminish criminal activities that are associated with insurance fraud.

During its history, an instance of this collaboration occurred when the NATB (a predecessor of the NICB) collaborated with the Nashville Police Department and the Tennessee Department of Revenue to perform a sting operation regarding vehicle theft in East Tennessee.[174] The investigative facets of this operation involved gathering intelligence; infiltrating "auto auctions, salvage yards, and junk yards"; and purchasing stolen vehicles.[175] This sting operation recovered 72 stolen automobiles representing a retail value of approximately $475,000.00.[176] The operation was credited as "what can be accomplished when the public and private sectors join forces against crime."[177]

The organizational structure of the NICB consists of the following components: (1) data analytics, (2) field operations, (3) training, (4) communications, and (5) government affairs. These components provide both law enforcement and private entities with intelligence that may be used to detect, investigate, and deter acts of crime involving insurance fraud. Activities of the data analytics section include the following:[178]

- Providing weekly strategic, case, and law enforcement alerts
- Creating and managing useful online databases (clinic inspections, cloned vehicles, etc.)
- Supporting NICB members with analytical training and services
- Researching and publishing studies regarding insurance fraud topics
- Conducting extensive crime trend analysis

The field operations section represents the only national entity that emphasizes a "multicarrier approach to fraud and theft investigations."[179] The field operations section consists of approximately 160 investigators spanning 10 offices nationally, and it supports both criminal and civil litigation.[180] These agents participate in task forces across the nation in conjunction with law enforcement entities.[181] The primary activities of the field operations section include the following:

- Medical fraud
- Commercial fraud
- Vehicle fraud

The training section is of paramount importance because of the scope and depth of personnel skills that are necessary to conduct investigations. Robust, well-skilled, and knowledgeable agents are necessary for detecting and investigating "fraudulent insurance claims" and discovering "potentially large-scale criminal conspiracies."[182] The activities of the training section include the following:

- Standardized and customized classroom fraud identification and prevention training at member locations
- Classroom-based training academies for fraud investigators
- Print and electronic educational programs, publications, and training guides
- Online educational resources through the National Insurance Crime Training Academy

The act of communicating with peer organizations and the public is an essential aspect of combating insurance fraud. Specifically, the mission of the communications section is to "educate and inform the public, the news media, NICB member companies, and their policyholders on insurance fraud and crime issues through effective communication using all forms of media."[183] Both tangible and intangible media are used to influence and elicit public supportiveness regarding the detection and prevention of insurance fraud.[184]

The government affairs component is responsible for promoting "statutes, regulations, and policies at all levels of government to help serve member interests in preventing, detecting, and defeating insurance fraud and vehicle theft."[185] Through its government affairs efforts, the NICB pursues the following activities in conjunction with peer organizations:

- Influencing legislation and regulations that affect insurance fraud and vehicle theft
- Tracking fraud and theft legislation
- Promoting a strong anti-fraud environment nationwide

The NICB also maintains two databases that emphasize fraud detection and reduction methods nationally. The first database system is termed Hot Spots and is a collection of high-crime areas within the United States regarding vehicle theft. The second database system is termed "Hot Wheels" and is a collection of preferred vehicle characteristics that are attractive to offenders presented on a per-state basis. Figures 6.6 and 6.7 represent both types of database constructs.

Insurance fraud represents a significant aspect of crime nationally, involving both individuals and organizations. Insurance fraud results in approximately $80 billion being paid fraudulently in claims compensation annually.[186] Healthcare fraud, when considered as a solitary category, costs Americans approximately $54 billion annually.[187]

Within the United States, most of the states maintain multifaceted insurance fraud bureaus. The states that do not maintain such entities are Alabama, Illinois, Indiana, Maine, Michigan, Oregon, Vermont, Wisconsin, and Wyoming.[188] According to the Coalition Against Insurance Fraud, some combined 2007 insurance fraud statistics, obtained from individual states that support multifaceted fraud investigation units, include the following:[189]

Budget: $147,738,214
Employees: 1694
Referrals: 115,062

Cases opened: 31,654

Arrests: 4848

Presentations to prosecutors: 5936

Convictions: 4228

Civil actions: 7672

Restitution ordered: $179,036,100

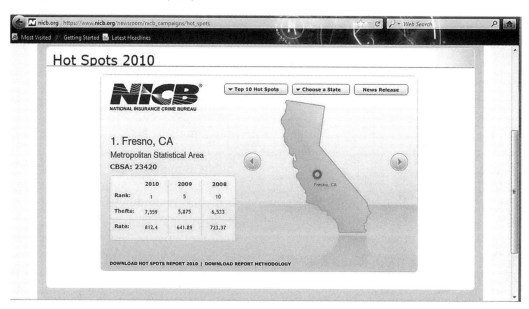

Figure 6.6 Example of the Hot Spots database system. (Courtesy of the National Insurance Crime Bureau. Retrieved from https://www.nicb.org/newsroom/nicb_campaigns/hot_ spots.)

Figure 6.7 Example of the Hot Wheels database system. (Courtesy of the National Insurance Crime Bureau. Retrieved from https://www.nicb.org/newsroom/nicb_campaigns/ hot%E2%80%93wheels.)

These quantities are staggering. Insurance fraud represents a criminal activity that impacts both individuals and organizations and that contributes toward increases of insurance rates nationally, regionally, and locally. Such considerations are indicative of the saliency and importance of the mission of the NICB and its relationships with law enforcement organizations throughout the country. Insurance fraud exists among all states and impacts the residents of all localities either directly or indirectly. Through its efforts and collaborations with law enforcement organizations, the NICB contributes toward the discovery, investigation, and deterrence of insurance fraud.

Through marketing and advertising campaigns, the NICB disseminates a variety of fact sheets that inform the public, the insurance industry, law enforcement organizations, and peer agencies of the dangers, symptoms, and consequences of insurance fraud. Maintaining effective relationships between the NICB and law enforcement agencies facilitates a methodical approach to combating insurance fraud. The NICB may be contacted anonymously to report suspected or known incidents of insurance fraud. Figures 6.8 and 6.9 show sample fact sheets disseminated by the NICB, which highlight various facets of insurance fraud, appropriate fraud reporting methods, and NICB's relationship with law enforcement organizations.

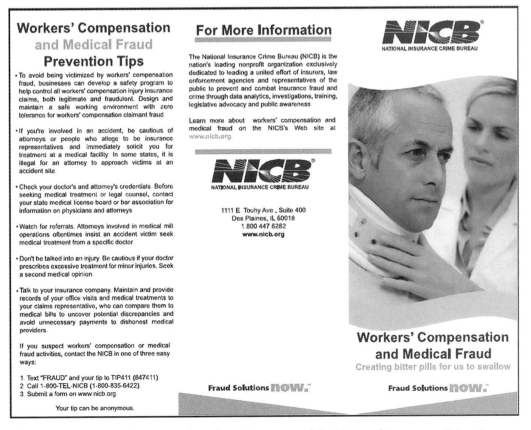

Figure 6.8 Example of an NICB fact sheet. (Courtesy of the National Insurance Crime Bureau. Retrieved from https://www.nicb.org/theft_and_fraud_awareness/brochures.)

Figure 6.9 Example of a fact sheet detailing NICB and law enforcement relationships. (Courtesy of the National Insurance Crime Bureau. Retrieved from https://www.nicb.org/theft_and_fraud_awareness/brochures.)

International Contractors

Since the end of the Cold War, a wide range of private military companies, private security companies, defense contractors, and firms in adjacent sectors that play growing roles in support of state defense and multilateral reconstruction strategies have been formed and operate worldwide. From weak states to emerging markets, these types of firms are also critical in raising and maintaining levels of security in unstable but economically important areas of the world.[190] Companies such as the former Blackwater secured major international contracts, providing a wide range of services not only domestically, but also in support and stability operations in areas including the Middle East, Asia, South America, and Africa. Services include, but are not limited to, a wide range of duties such as air, ground, and maritime surveillance, security and aviation, protective security services, security consultancy, security training and mine action services, fraud investigations, commercial intelligence gathering, security consulting, anticorruption consulting, strategic advice, and other business risk solutions.

Relationship between Private and Public Entities

Private security and law enforcement entities must neither be perceived nor viewed as competitors that seek to replace traditional forms of law enforcement organizations. Instead, they must be considered as complements that support traditional law enforcement organizations and that act as force multipliers with respect to the deterrence of crime and the maintenance of societal order. The preceding NICB discussion highlights the relevancy of this complementary relationship between private security entities and public law enforcement organizations.

Certainly, the NICB and public law enforcement entities share a variety of services and resources ranging from databases and intelligence analysis to training and investigative resources. However, these characteristics of the NICB example are not the only consideration of collaboration and cooperativeness that exists between private and public security and enforcement organizations. Establishing and maintaining a viable, open relationship between private and public entities is essential with respect to any collaborative effort of preventing crime and maintaining order.

If a relationship is established between private and public entities, it will either experience success or failure. Based on the observations of the U.S. Department of Justice, the following factors influence the success of the relationship between public and private security and law enforcement organizations:[191]

- *Strong support from organizational leaders*: This consideration includes a commitment from both public and private sector leadership to facilitate a working relationship.
- *Shared leadership and power*: Successful partnerships show members that the public and private sectors are sharing leadership and power. All members feel they have the opportunity to provide input and be heard.
- *Benefits to all participants*: Partnership members have to find benefits and utility in being a member. Partnerships need to offer much more than "feel-good" events; everyone is too busy to waste time on meetings or systems that do not result in meaningful exchanges of important information.
- *Acceptance and trust*: Both the public and private sector members in the partnership must feel accepted mutually and demonstrate trustfulness so that the relationships can be supportive and informative.
- *Tangible products*: Successful partnerships show results in terms of crimes prevented, cases closed, or solved.
- *Sustaining structure and resources*: Partnerships necessitate the presence of an established structure and its affiliated resources to sustain the organization.
- *Publicity and recognition*: Successful LE-PS partnerships report that a key to success has been partnership publicity and recognition, which provide legitimacy and prestige, making members proud of being associated with a meaningful partnership.
- *Flexibility to adapt to changing environments*: Relationships must be flexible and adaptable to accommodate changing environments regarding the priorities of the participants.
- *Rewarding those responsible for the partnership*: Private security and law enforcement management must be viably considered when promotion and pay issues arise.

In some cases, failed or strained relationships may exist between private and public entities. Based on the observations of the U.S. Department of Justice, the following characteristic are indicative of such relationships:[192]

- *Failure to address or solve joint problems*: If no successful work is accomplished, then there exists little reason or justification to continue the partnership.
- *Changes in leadership*: Leaders, founders, managers, "drivers," or staff coordinators may resign, be reassigned, or retire.

- *Inadequate resources*: In some cases, funding is inadequate or conditioned on unacceptable terms or the partnership may lack support staff to carry out or communicate its activities.
- *Lack of innovation*: Meetings may bore participants by failing to bring in interesting speakers or conduct meaningful activities. It is a challenge to find highly qualified trainers and training topics that appeal to both law enforcement and private security audiences. A key challenge is keeping businesses involved after a crisis passes.
- *Time constraints of executives and managers*: If high-level private security and law enforcement executives do not dedicate sufficient time or organizational resources, partnerships suffer and may fail.

It is not uncommon for private security and enforcement entities to enjoy fruitful relationships with their public counterparts within the realm of traditional law enforcement. In some cases, such as natural disasters, such relationships may be necessary to facilitate the common good of society. Other events may include large-scale sporting events, public events, or holiday festivities (e.g., parades, fireworks shows, concerts).

When NASCAR racing events are held in the state of Delaware, the population may increase by approximately 100,000 individuals in the area of the race.[193] This quantity of people exceeds the ability of local law enforcement entities to perform crowd control duties in addition to performing their normal services.[194] During such events, NASCAR hires private security organizations and personnel to "work under the supervision of Dover police."[195]

During 2011, unprecedented flooding affected numerous towns, cities, and rural areas within states that bordered the Mississippi River. In some cases, flood water levels either equated or surpassed flooding that occurred during the 1920s and 1930s. Because of the seriousness, scope, and magnitude of flooding, both private security entities and public law enforcement entities were among the responders to this form of natural disaster.[196] To facilitate the common welfare and public good, effective relationships had to be forged between private security and public law enforcement agencies (as well as with other responding entities).

These examples and the characteristics of success are indicative of the 4C approach regarding flourishing relationships between private security and public law enforcement entities. This approach encompasses the attributes of communication, cooperation, coordination, and collaboration.[197] According to the U.S. Department of Justice, these attributes are described as follows:[198]

- *Communication*: the exchange of information and ideas is the first step in establishing a relationship between two organizations.
- *Cooperation*: involves partners undertaking a joint project or operation such as the sharing of personnel.
- *Coordination*: achieved when the partners adopt a common goal, for instance, to reduce crime in a certain neighborhood.
- *Collaboration*: occurs when partners understand that their missions overlap and adopt policies and projects designed to share resources, achieve common goals, and strengthen the partners. The goal of public–private partnership, described in greater detail later, is to achieve collaboration.

No guarantee exists that any established relationship between private security and public law enforcement will be successful and mutually beneficial through time. Various factors contribute to the failure of such relationships. Without trust and openness, relationships will experience failure at some point. Misunderstandings and mistrust may occur among the factions of leadership and personnel that deteriorate and impede the foundational characteristics of the relationship. Rivalries between private security and public law enforcement entities also contribute to the diminishing of trust and openness.

Additional considerations of stressful relationship factors also include the following tensions between private and public entities:[199]

- Some law enforcement entities may have little confidence in the employment screening, training regimens, personnel certification, and licensing and regulatory standards of private security personnel.
- Some law enforcement entities perceive that private security personnel represent individuals who were unsuccessful in entering an occupation within the law enforcement domain.
- Some law enforcement entities have a poor understanding of the roles, responsibilities, and services that are provided by private security entities.
- Some private security personnel perceive law enforcement personnel as having an elitist attitude.

Despite this negativity, there is increasingly a greater range of partnerships and collaborations between private security and public law enforcement organizations. The events of September 11, 2001, ushered in the necessities of new partnerships and collaborations between the public and private sectors. Although these two factions represent separate domains of security and enforcement, they both contribute toward the deterrence of crime and the maintenance of societal order. Both entities are complementary with respect to man-made and natural disasters. Both entities are complementary with respect to civil and criminal matters. Both entities attempt to contribute positively toward the common welfare and public good of their served populaces. Given these notions, the separate domains of private security and public law enforcement cannot afford to ignore each other and must strive to establish and maintain meaningful relationships (Figure 6.10).

Accomplishments of Private Security and Enforcement

Private security and enforcement entities have influenced American history at both the national and local level. The most notable of these events is the Watergate incident of the 1970s. Other incidents have impacted communities and localities throughout the United States in recent times.

During 1972, a burglary at an office complex, which housed the Democratic National Committee in Washington, D.C., eventually contributed toward the downfall and resignation of President Richard Nixon. This event revealed the Watergate scandal that impacted American politics by infusing an "enduring skepticism about the federal government" within American society.[200] This incident also resulted in the appointing of "special prosecutors to investigate allegations of presidential wrongdoing" through future administrations.[201]

The initial appearance of this burglary may have seemed somewhat ordinary despite its eventual national impact. Frank Wills, the person who discovered this burglary, was

Figure 6.10 Private security and public law enforcement personnel. Bangor, ME police officer George Spencer (center) surveys Pickering Square after talking with several Bangor Area Transit bus drivers and George Edwards (left), a Seaboard Security guard at the parking garage. Officers responded to a gunshot fired on a BAT Community Connector bus as it made its way from downtown Bangor to the Old Town-Orono area. One of the passengers was showing off a revolver to other passengers when it discharged. Edwards said he left work about a half hour before the incident occurred. (From Russ, J. C., Bangor Daily News, 2010. Retrieved from http://bangordailynews.com/2010/03/04/news/bangor/bat-driver-recalls-hearing-gunshot-fired-inside-bus/.)

rather ordinary. Wills was a security guard with General Security and was the lone night watchman at the Watergate building.[202] During his rounds, Wills discovered that someone had taped open a lock on a basement door.[203] Wills removed the tape and continued his rounds through the building.[204] It was not uncommon for maintenance workers to tape the doors open when they were working.[205] However, after an hour, Wills sensed that something was amiss, and he examined the door again.[206] It was again taped open, thereby prompting him to inform his supervisor and the local police.[207]

This discovery led to the initial Watergate arrests of "James McCord, Bernard Barker, Eugenio Martinez, Frank Sturgis, and Virgilio Gonzales."[208] When arrested, these men possessed "tear gas guns, bugging devices, and thousands of dollars in consecutively numbered $100 bills."[209] They also possessed telephone numbers to the White House.[210] This incident, which initially appeared as a low-key oddity, quickly became a national political struggle that eventually led to the downfall of the President of the United States. It was discovered by a private security guard—Frank Wills (Figure 6.11).

Other incidents have demonstrated the relevance of private security personnel among localities. During 2005, a shooting incident occurred at Red Lake High School (Red Lake, Minnesota), which claimed the life of a private security guard. Derrick Brun was employed as a temporary unarmed security guard when the incident occurred.[211] Jeff Weise, the shooter, was 16 years old and was armed with three guns.[212] In an attempt to confront Weise, Brun became a victim of the high school shooting. Weise killed nine people, including himself.[213] Brun's fatal confrontation with Weise, which lasted only seconds, provided a sufficient amount of time for others to escape and live.[214] When it

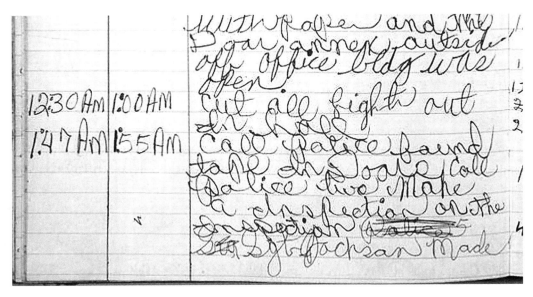

Figure 6.11 Security log that was key to the Watergate investigation. (Courtesy of the U.S. National Archives and Records Administration. Retrieved from http://www.archives.gov/exhibits/american_originals/willentr.jpg.)

occurred, this shooting was deemed as the worst school shooting since the attack at Columbine High School in Colorado.[215]

In 2010 in Panama City, Florida, another shooting incident occurred. This incident involved a former convict committing suicide after firing his weapon at the members of a local school board during its meeting.[216] Mike Jones, a retired police officer serving as a school security guard, attended the meeting in the event any "security questions" arose.[217] Clay Duke, the attacker, was seeking revenge because his wife had been fired by the school district.[218] Jones and Duke engaged in a shootout that resulted in Duke committing suicide.[219] None of the school board members were wounded during the incident.[220] Duke actions were sudden, vengeful, and horrific. However, Jones provided a distraction while people in the meeting room could escape or obtain cover to protect themselves during the attack.

The personnel of private enforcement and security firms often risk their lives to provide some measure of security for their employers or contracted sponsoring entities. Therefore, any perception that the occupation is riskless is false. Private enforcement and security personnel have risked themselves for others since the earliest forming of the private security concept and continue to do so during modern times. Their roles and functions must not be downplayed as immaterial within the contexts of modern enforcement methods.

The lives of others are often dependent upon the actions of private enforcement and security personnel. The smallest of actions by private enforcement and security personnel have the potential of affecting many others both locally and nationally. Frank Wills contributed toward strengthening the integrity of the national political domain. Although Derrick Brun sacrificed his life, others are alive and well because of his actions. Mike Jones selflessly engaged an enraged attacker, thereby providing a distraction that allowed others to survive the incident. Each of these men performed his duties without reservation or hesitance.

Summary

Through history, there is recorded a need for security services that spans centuries. A common theme is demonstrated historically: a need to protect an organization, a group, or an individual from a perceived threat. Within the United States, visionary individuals crafted private agencies that spawned the American private security industry. Notable examples include the actions of Allan Pinkerton.

The need for private security–related services continues to expand, not just in the United States, but globally. Private security and enforcement services are anticipated to grow rapidly worldwide. With an increase of globalization, both nations and their respective businesses and corporations have a vested interest in security. The use of private security and enforcement organizations lends itself to a variety of applications. For example, private security may be used to diminish the risks of ocean piracy and to provide additional manpower that is necessary for protecting logistics systems and physical resources.

The use of private security and enforcement organizations is unconstrained regarding government and commercial applications. Individuals may also procure such services for a variety of reasons. In such cases, private security agencies may be employed to enforce court-mandated restraining orders or to protect personal residences from threats of burglary. Therefore, the scope of private security ranges from small applications to global endeavors.

Private security personnel are found in a variety of settings. They may act as security guards for schools, banks, and hospitals. They may be employed among defense installations and locations that host components of the critical national infrastructure. In any case, their very presence may be deterrents to acts of crime.

There is no consensus regarding the qualifications and licensures of private security personnel and organizations within the United States. Each individual state may mandate its unique qualifications and licensing standards. Therefore, qualifications and licensures that are appropriate within the boundaries of one state may be completely inappropriate within a different state.

The functions and responsibilities of private security vary greatly depending upon different situations, markets served, and organizational missions. One private security organization may provide global security consulting services, whereas another organization may limit its operations to the provision of home burglar alarm systems. Regardless, all private security organizations share a common interest in providing protective services that are in the best interests of their clientele.

Private security is a business—big business. The CCA demonstrates large profits through its existence as a for-profit, publically traded corporation. Around the world, markets exist in practically every nation for private security organizations to provide services of every type and application. Given the proliferation of globalization, much opportunity exists for existing security organizations to expand their businesses into new markets.

Private security has the potential of impacting the nation as well as communities. For example, a lone security guard, Frank Wills, discovered a taped door that unleashed a series of events that led to the downfall and resignation of President Richard Nixon. Among communities, the actions of Mike Jones and Derrick Brun spared the lives of others during separate incidents. Although Jones survived his experience, Brun died in the line of duty.

A common theme that is shared among all private security organizations involves the rendering of services that are in the best interests of their respective clients. They also act as supplements to traditional law enforcement organizations and provide additional manpower with respect to the deterrence of crime and the maintenance of societal order. Therefore, private security is a valid and legitimate endeavor that impacts governments, societies, commercial entities, and individuals.

Discussion Questions

1. The case of the FedEx private police shows its commitment to safeguarding the organization and its stakeholders against a variety of threats. Do some research to determine whether other corporations have developed a private police force that is similar to the FedEx model. Discuss how these private enforcement entities are leveraged for the benefit of the organization and its stakeholders.
2. Private security is a business. Examine a local private security organization that serves your community. Determine the salient aspects of its business model and discuss whether you believe it is successful. Within your discussion, consider the types of services that are offered by your selected security organization.
3. This chapter highlighted the history of American private security and enforcement. Select a different nation, do some research, and discuss the history of private security and enforcement within your chosen nation. Within your discussion, compare and contrast your findings with the events that transpired in American history.
4. Nationally, there is no consensus regarding the licensure qualifications of private security and enforcement personnel. Determine the qualifications and licensure standards that are appropriate for your state. Compare and contrast your findings with the licensure and qualifications standards that are mandated by a state that borders your state.

References

1. Strom, K., Berzofsky, M., Shook-Sa, B., Barrick, K., Daye, C., Horstmann, N., & Kinsey, S. (2010, December). *The Private Security Industry: A Review of the Definitions, Available Data Sources and Paths Moving Forward.* U.S. Department of Justice. Retrieved March 1, 2012 from https://www.ncjrs.gov/pdffiles1/bjs/grants/232781.pdf
2. Kakalik, J. S., Wildhorn, S., & the U.S. Department of Justice (1971, December). *Private Police in the United States: Findings and Recommendations.* Vol. 1. Retrieved March 15, 2012, from http://www.rand.org/pubs/reports/2006/R869.pdf
3. Sarkar, D. Customs agents are seizing record amounts of pirated IT hardware. *Federal Computer Week.* Retrieved April 8, 2012, from http://fcw.com/articles/2006/05/08/customs-agents-are-seizing-record-amounts-of-pirated-it-hardware.aspx
4. Ibid.
5. Ibid.
6. Nalla, M. K. *Police: Private Police and Industrial Security—Scope of Security Work, Nature of Security Work, Legal Authority, Public vis-a-vis Private Police.* Retrieved March 30, 2012, from http://law.jrank.org/pages/1691/Police-Private-Police-Industrial-Security.html#ixzz1rE9Lh7f5

7. ASIS International (2009). *International Glossary of Security Terms*. Retrieved March 30, 2011, from http://www.asisonline.org/library/glossary/index.xml

8. Gough, T.W. (1977, February). *Railroad Crime: Old West Train Robbers to Modern-Day Cargo Thieves, FBI Law Enforcement Bulletin*, pp. 16–25.

9. Travers, J. (2005). *Introduction to Private Investigation: Essential Knowledge and Procedures for the Private Investigator* (2nd ed.). Springfield, IL: Charles C. Thomas Publishers.

10. Kentucky Special Investigations Unit. *History of Private Investigation*. Retrieved April 19, 2012, from http://www.ksiu.org/history

11. National Association of Security Companies. (2009). *The Use of Contract Security at DOD Installations*. Washington, D.C.: NASCO.

12. Ibid.

13. Ibid.

14. Ibid.

15. Ibid.

16. Private Officer News Network (2010). *Private Security Industry Sees Continued Steady Growth*. Retrieved April 18, 2012, from http://privateofficernews.wordpress.com/2010/05/12/private-security-industry-sees-continued-steady-growth-www-privateofficer-com/

17. Ibid.

18. Ibid.

19. Investigation. *Merriam-Webster*. Retrieved April 19, 2012, from http://www.merriam-webster.com/dictionary/investigation

20. U.S. Department of Labor (2012). *Private Detectives and Investigators*. Retrieved April 19, 2012, from http://bls.gov/ooh/Protective-Service/Private-detectives-and-investigators.htm

21. Ibid.

22. Editors of McGraw-Hill and the U.S. Department of Labor, Bureau of Labor Statistics (Eds.). *The Big Book of Jobs* (2007–2008 ed.). New York, NY: McGraw-Hill.

23. Cunningham, W. C., Taylor, T. H., & Hallcrest Systems, Inc. (1985). *Private Security and Police in America: The Hallcrest Report I*. Boston, MA: Butterworth-Heinemann.

24. Dempsey, J. S. (2008). *Introduction to Private Security*. Belmont, CA: Thomson Wadsworth.

25. U.S. Department of Labor (2012). *Private Detectives and Investigators*. Retrieved April 19, 2012, from http://bls.gov/ooh/Protective-Service/Private-detectives-and-investigators.htm

26. Ibid.

27. Ibid.

28. Ibid.

29. Ibid.

30. PI Licensing. *Pursuit Magazine*. Retrieved April 19, 2012, from http://pursuitmag.com/resources/investigator-licensing/

31. Ibid.

32. Ibid.

33. Ibid.

34. Ibid.

35. Ibid.

36. Ibid.

37. Detective Training Institute. *School Catalog*. Retrieved April 19, 2012, from http://www.detectivetraining.com/Catalog.asp

38. Ibid.

39. Ashworth College. *Private Investigation Training*. Retrieved April 19, 2012, from http://www.ashworthcollege.edu/programs/career-diploma/private-investigation/

40. Ibid.

41. Bearden Investigative Agency. *About the Bearden Investigative Agency*. Retrieved April 19, 2012, from http://www.picompany.com/about_bia.html

42. Ibid.

43. Law Enforcement-Private Security Consortium (2009). *Operation Partnership: Trends and Practices in Law Enforcement and Private Security Collaborations*. Washington, DC: U.S. Department of Justice, Office of Community Oriented Policing Services.

44. Parfomak, P. (2004). *Guarding America: Security Guards and U.S. Critical Infrastructure Protection*. Washington, D.C.: U.S. Government.

45. Ibid.

46. Ibid.

47. Ibid.

48. Ibid.

49. Ibid.

50. Johnston, D., & Broder, J. F.B.I. says guards killed 14 Iraqis without cause. *The New York Times*. Retrieved April 19, 2012, from http://www.nytimes.com/2007/11/14/world/middleeast/14blackwater.html?_r=1

51. Reuters shows how to hack phones 'like a News of the World reporter' (2011). *The Huffington Post*. Retrieved April 19, 2012, from http://www.huffingtonpost.com/2011/08/29/reuters-how-hack-phones-news-of-the-world_n_940966.html

52. Riley, M., & Vance, A. China corporate espionage boom knocks wind out of U.S. companies. *Bloomberg*. Retrieved April 9, 2012, from http://www.bloomberg.com/news/2012-03-15/china-corporate-espionage-boom-knocks-wind-out-of-u-s-companies.html

53. Ibid.

54. Ibid.

55. Ibid.

56. Ibid.

57. Ibid.

58. Groom, N. Wind energy dispute may test U.S.-China IP resolve. *Reuters*. Retrieved April 9, 2012, from http://www.reuters.com/article/2012/01/09/us-amsc-sinovel-idUSTRE8081RT20120109

59. Stevens Law Group. Test of IP rights protection in China. Retrieved April 12, 2012, from http://www.stevenslawgroup.com/california-legal-news/IP_Rights_in_China

60. Riley, M., & Vance, A. China corporate espionage boom knocks wind out of U.S. companies. *Bloomberg*. Retrieved April 9, 2012, from http://www.bloomberg.com/news/2012-03-15/china-corporate-espionage-boom-knocks-wind-out-of-u-s-companies.html

61. Ibid.

62. Ibid.

63. Ibid.

64. Ailworth, E., & Freund, E. Engineer guilty in software theft. Retrieved April 9, 2012, from http://articles.boston.com/2011-09-24/business/30198685_1_wind-turbine-software-theft-austria

65. Ibid.

66. Riley, M., & Vance, A. China corporate espionage boom knocks wind out of U.S. companies. *Bloomberg*. Retrieved April 9, 2012, from http://www.bloomberg.com/news/2012-03-15/china-corporate-espionage-boom-knocks-wind-out-of-u-s-companies.html

67. Ibid.

68. Liebowitz, M. Stolen NASA laptop contained space station control codes. *MSNBC News*. Retrieved April 8, 2012, from http://www.msnbc.msn.com/id/46591964/ns/technology_and_science-security/t/stolen-nasa-laptop-contained-space-station-control-codes/#.T4HvmNV0lnE

69. Ibid.

70. Ibid.

71. Ibid.

72. Ibid.

73. Ibid.

74. Ibid.

75. Ibid.

76. Walker, P. (1998). *Electronic Security Systems* (3rd ed.). Woburn, MA: Newnes.
77. Hilzenrath, D., & Douglas, D. Hilton, starwood settle corporate espionage lawsuit on trade secrets. *The Washington Post*. Retrieved April 8, 2012, from http://www.washingtonpost.com/wp-dyn/content/article/2010/12/22/AR2010122205827.html
78. Lattman, P. Hilton and Starwood settle dispute. *The New York Times*. Retrieved April 8, 2012, from http://dealbook.nytimes.com/2010/12/22/hilton-and-starwood-settle-dispute/
79. DeLollis, B. Hilton and Starwood settle lawsuit over trade secrets. *USA Today*. Retrieved April 8, 2012, from http://travel.usatoday.com/hotels/post/2010/12/breaking-news-hilton-and-starwood-settle-lawsuit/136005/1
80. Ibid.
81. Ibid.
82. Ex-Ford engineer sentenced for trade secrets theft (2011). *Reuters*. Retrieved April 10, 2012, from http://www.reuters.com/article/2011/04/13/us-djc-ford-tradesecrets-idUSTRE73C3FG20110413
83. Ibid.
84. Ibid.
85. Office of the National Counterintelligence Executive (2011). *Foreign Spies Stealing U.S. Economic Secrets in Cyberspace: Report to Congress on Foreign Economic Collection and Industrial Espionage, 2009–2011*. Washington, D.C.: U.S. Government.
86. Ibid.
87. Ibid.
88. Lee, A. (2012). Corporate governance: Boardrooms fret over corporate espionage and federal guidance regimes. *Reuters*. Retrieved April 10, 2012, from http://blogs.reuters.com/financial-regulatory-forum/2012/03/12/corporate-governance-boardrooms-fret-over-corporate-espionage-and-federal-guidance-regimes/
89. Ibid.
90. Ibid.
91. FedEx Express. *FedEx Facts*. Retrieved April 9, 2012, from http://www.fedex.com/ag/about/facts.html
92. Ibid.
93. Ibid.
94. Ibid.
95. Ibid.
96. Ibid.
97. Ibid.
98. Price, J., & Forrest, J. (2009). *Practical Aviation Security: Predicting and Preventing Future Threats*. Burlington, MA: Elsevier.
99. Mickolus, E., & Simmons, S. (1997). *Terrorism, 1992–1995: A Chronology of Events and Selectively Annotated Bibliography*. Westport, CT: Greenwood.
100. Burns, J. F. (2010). Yemen bomb could have gone off at east coast. *The New York Times*. Retrieved April 8, 2012, from http://www.nytimes.com/2010/11/11/world/europe/11parcel.html
101. Baird, W. (2004). South Wire: Not content with security guards, FedEx hires its own police force. *The Florida Times-Union*. Retrieved April 8, 2012, from http://jacksonville.com/tu-online/apnews/stories/022804/D81020V00.shtml
102. Ibid.
103. Ibid.
104. Ibid.
105. Ibid.
106. Ibid.
107. Ibid.
108. Ibid.
109. Ibid.

110. Joh, E. (2006). The forgotten threat: Private policing and the state. *Indiana Journal of Global Legal Studies, 13*, 357–389.
111. Strom, K., Berzofsky, M., Shook-Sa, B., Barrick, K., Daye, C., Horstmann, N., & Kinsey, S. (2010). *The Private Security Industry: A Review of the Definitions, Available Data Sources, and Paths Moving Forward*. Research Triangle Park, NC: RTI International.
112. Ibid.
113. Private Officer News Network (2010). *Private Security Industry Sees Continued Steady Growth*. Retrieved April 18, 2012, from http://privateofficernews.wordpress.com/2010/05/12/private-security-industry-sees-continued-steady-growth-www-privateofficer-com/
114. Ibid.
115. The Freedonia Group (2010). *Private Security Services to 2014—Market Research, Market Share, Market Size, Sales, Demand Forecast, Market Leaders, Company Profiles, Industry Trends*. Retrieved April 18, 2012, from http://www.freedoniagroup.com/Private-Security-Services.html
116. Ibid.
117. Associated Chambers of Commerce and Industry of India (2009). *Private Security Industry: Opportunities and Challenges*. Retrieved April 12, 2012, from http://www.google.com/url?sa=t&rct=j&q=billion%20%22private%20security%22%20europe&source=web&cd=5&ved=0CD4QFjAE&url=http%3A%2F%2Fwww.assocham.org%2Fevents%2Frecent%2Fevent_574%2Fmr.-rituraj-kishore-sinha-chief-operation-officer-coo-sis-india-ltd..pdf&ei=EkeOT9jyGoam8QSt0_n9DQ&usg=AFQjCNH-40L6qrgbdiDpiU6nQbYM1n1hOg&cad=rja
118. Ibid.
119. Ibid.
120. Ibid.
121. Ibid.
122. *Confederation of European Security Services*. Retrieved April 12, 2012, from http://www.coess.org/
123. Ibid.
124. Ibid.
125. Hodge, N. U.S. plans private guard force for iraq: state department prepares to hire 5,100-strong security detail and take over military hardware for after army leaves. *The Wall Street Journal*. Retrieved April 8, 2012, from http://online.wsj.com/article/SB10001424052702304906004576369801913947130.html
126. Jelinek, P. (2008). Iraq's private security has cost over $6 billion, U.S. auditors say. *The Huffington Post*. Retrieved April 18, 2012, from http://www.huffingtonpost.com/2008/10/30/iraqs-private-security-ha_n_139203.html
127. Apps, P. (2008). Higher speeds, hired guns drive somali piracy cost. *Reuters*. Retrieved April 18, 2012, from http://arabia.msn.com/news/world/152255/higher-speeds-hired-guns-drive-somali/
128. Ibid.
129. Ibid.
130. Mexico, the next private contracting boom? *Homeland Security News Wire*. Retrieved April 18, 2012, from http://www.homelandsecuritynewswire.com/dr20120201-mexico-the-next-private-contracting-boom
131. Mahbubul, A. Private security: Our positing vis a vis the global perspective. *The Independent*. Retrieved April 18, 2012, from http://theindependentbd.com/weekly-independent/100043-private-security-our-position-vis-a-vis-the-global-perspective.html
132. Ibid.
133. Maritz, N. (2012). The private security industry in South Africa. *Elite SA—MyPressPortal*. Retrieved April 18, 2012, from http://pressportal.co.za/industry-and-real-estate/item/6026-the-private-security-industry-in-south-africa.html

134. Ibid.
135. Ibid.
136. Travis, A., & Williams, Z. (2012). Revealed: Government plans for police privitisation. *The Guardian*. Retrieved April 18, 2012, from http://www.guardian.co.uk/uk/2012/mar/02/police-privatisation-security-firms-crime
137. Ibid.
138. Ibid.
139. Ibid.
140. Massachusetts Office of International Trade & Investment (2007). *Brazil Security Industry*. Retrieved April 18, 2012, from http://www.moiti.org/pdf/Brazil%20Security%20Industry.pdf
141. Ibid.
142. Bodyguard industry booming as China prospers. *Want China Times*. Retrieved April 12, 2012, from http://www.wantchinatimes.com/news-subclass-cnt.aspx?id=20110517000004&cid=1103
143. Whiting, R. (2006). Globalization increasing risk of supply chain disruptions: Survey. *Information Week*. Retrieved April 19, 2012, from http://www.informationweek.com/news/193101249
144. Roy, A. Local security company sees business boost. *KXLY News*. Retrieved April 18, 2012, from http://www.kxly.com/news/spokane-news/Local-security-company-sees-business-boost/-/101214/9401884/-/fndnirz/-/index.html
145. Ibid.
146. Alarm Club. *Alarm Club Mission Statement*. Retrieved April 18, 2012, from http://www.alarmclub.com/about.html
147. Ibid.
148. Loomis. *About Loomis US*. Retrieved April 18, 2012, from http://www.loomis.us/about-loomis/Pages/default.aspx
149. Ibid.
150. Strom, K., Berzofsky, M., Shook-Sa, B., Barrick, K., Daye, C., Horstmann, N., & Kinsey, S. (2010, December). *The Private Security Industry: A Review of the Definitions, Available Data Sources and Paths Moving Forward*. United States Department of Justice. Retrieved March 1, 2012, from https://www.ncjrs.gov/pdffiles1/bjs/grants/232781.pdf
151. National Association of Security Companies (2009). *The Use of Contract Security at DOD Installations*. Washington, D.C.: NASCO.
152. New York Division of Criminal Justice Services. *Security Guard Training*. Retrieved April 18, 2012, from http://www.criminaljustice.ny.gov/ops/sgtraining/
153. Ibid.
154. Ibid.
155. *Arizona Revised Statutes, Title 32 Professions and Occupations, Section 32–2632 Duty of Licensee to Provide Training of Security Guards; Records; Firearms Training*. Retrieved April 19, 2012, from http://law.onecle.com/arizona/professions-and-occupations/32-2632.html
156. ASIS International (2009). *Standards and Guidelines*. Retrieved July 30, 2010, from http://www.asisonline.org/guidelines/guidelines.htm
157. Corrections Corporation of America. *About CCA*. Retrieved April 19, 2012, from http://www.cca.com/about/
158. Ibid.
159. Ibid.
160. Ibid.
161. Ibid.
162. Ibid.
163. Ibid.
164. Corrections Corporation of America (2012). *CCA Announces 2011 Fourth Quarter and Full-Year Financial Results*. Retrieved April 19, 2012, from http://ir.correctionscorp.com/phoenix.zhtml?c=117983&p=irol-newsArticle&id=1658614

165. Herreras, M. (2010). Prison problems. *Tucson Weekly*. Retrieved April 19, 2012, from http://www .tucsonweekly.com/tucson/prison-problems/Content?oid=2205888

166. Ibid.

167. Ibid.

168. National Insurance Crime Bureau. *Our Story*. Retrieved April 23, 2012, from https://www.nicb .org/about-nicb/our_story

169. National Insurance Crime Bureau. *Disaster Fraud 2008*. Retrieved April 23, 2012, from https:// www.nicb.org//newsroom/news_archive/disaster-fraud-2008

170. National Insurance Crime Bureau. *Our Story*. Retrieved April 23, 2012, from https://www.nicb .org/about-nicb/our_story

171. Ibid.

172. Ibid.

173. Ibid.

174. Marx, G. The interweaving of public and private police undercover work. In C. Shearing, & P. Stenning, *Private Policing*. Sage Publications 1987. Retrieved April 23, 2012, from http://web .mit.edu/gtmarx/www/private.html#note6

175. Ibid.

176. Ibid.

177. Ibid.

178. National Insurance Crime Bureau. *Data Analytics*. Retrieved April 23, 2012, from https://www .nicb.org/our_departments/data-analytics

179. National Insurance Crime Bureau. *Field Operations*. Retrieved April 23, 2012, from https:// www.nicb.org/our_departments/field_operations

180. Ibid.

181. Ibid.

182. National Insurance Crime Bureau. *Training*. Retrieved April 23, 2012, from https://www.nicb .org/our_departments/training

183. National Insurance Crime Bureau. *Public Awareness*. Retrieved April 23, 2012, from https:// www.nicb.org/our_departments/communications-and-membership/public_awareness

184. Ibid.

185. National Insurance Crime Bureau. *Government Affairs*. Retrieved April 23, 2012, from https:// www.nicb.org/our_departments/government_affairs/public_awareness

186. Louisiana State Police. *Insurance Fraud Statistics*. Retrieved April 23, 2012, from http://www .lsp.org/ifu.html#stats

187. Ibid.

188. Coalition Against Insurance Fraud. *Go Figure: Fraud Data*. Retrieved April 23, 2012, from http://www.insurancefraud.org/statefraudbureaus.htm

189. Ibid.

190. *Private Military Companies*. Retrieved March 15, 2012 from http://www.privatemilitary.org/

191. U.S. Department of Justice. (2005). *Operation Partnership: Trends and Practices in Law Enforcement and Private Security Collaborations*. Washington, D.C.: U.S. Government.

192. Ibid.

193. Ibid.

194. Ibid.

195. Ibid.

196. Levees, floodwalls require round-the-clock watch. *CBS News*. Retrieved April 24, 2012, from http://www.cbsnews.com/2100-201_162-20063153.html

197. U.S. Department of Justice. (2005). *Engaging the Private Sector to Promote Homeland Security: Law Enforcement–Private Security Partnerships*. Washington, D.C.: U.S. Government.

198. Ibid.

199. Hess, K. (2009). *Introduction to Private Security* (5th ed.). Mason, OH: Cengage Publishing.

200. Nixon resigns. *The Washington Post*. Retrieved April 10, 2012, from http://www.washingtonpost.com/wp-srv/politics/special/watergate/part3.html
201. Ibid.
202. Woo, E. (2000). Frank Wills; guard discovered Watergate break-in. *Los Angeles Times*. Retrieved April 10, 2012, from http://articles.latimes.com/2000/sep/29/local/me-28706
203. Ibid.
204. Ibid.
205. Ibid.
206. Ibid.
207. Ibid.
208. Ibid.
209. Ibid.
210. Ibid.
211. Moreno, S. (2005). Slain guard called a hero for actions at Minn. school. *The Washington Post*. Retrieved April 10, 2012, from http://www.washingtonpost.com/wp-dyn/articles/A61586-2005Mar23.html
212. Ibid.
213. Ibid.
214. Ibid.
215. Ibid.
216. Omer, S. and the Associated Press (2010). School security guard: 'I'm not a hero, folks.' *MSNBC*. Retrieved April 10, 2012, from http://www.msnbc.msn.com/id/40701074/ns/us_news-crime_and_courts/t/school-security-guard-im-not-hero-folks/#.T4T5U9V0lnF
217. Ibid.
218. Ibid.
219. Ibid.
220. Ibid.

Bibliography

Hess, K. (2009). *Introduction to Private Security* (5th ed). Mason, OH: Cengage Publishing.

Ethics

7

The only thing necessary for evil to triumph is for good men to do nothing.

Edmund Burke

Learning Objectives

The objectives of this chapter are to

- Explain the difference between morals and ethics
- Describe the process of decision making within the context of ethics
- Outline the ethics of law enforcement
- Explain the concept of officer discretion
- Discuss officer behavior within the context of ethics

Introduction

Police corruption is the abuse of police authority for personal gain. It is one of the oldest and most persistent problems in American policing. In fact, for as long as there have been police, there has been police corruption and misconduct.[1] Corruption may be seen in the form of police officers accepting gratuities or bribes, protection of illegal activities, direct criminal activities, internal corruption, excessive use of force, violence, and so on. Ethics is at the heart of these and similar problems.

Police officers are held to a higher ethical standard by society because they are stewards of the public trust and are empowered to apply force and remove constitutional privileges when lawfully justified. They take an oath of office. Therefore, they are expected to comply with professional codes of ethics and are subject to various laws, rules, and regulations. Each day, police officers decide and act while balancing competing and conflicting values and interests, frequently with incomplete or inaccurate information, often in highly emotional and dynamic circumstances, and typically under pressure.[2]

Police professionals cannot simply think ethically; they must also act ethically. Anything less can lead to the public's distrust of law enforcement professionals. The nineteenth-century British statesman and Home Secretary Sir Robert Peel, the father of modern law enforcement, is credited with the concept that the police depend on citizen cooperation in providing services in a democratic society. Therefore, the detrimental aspects of police misconduct or corruption cannot be overstated. The public trust is absolutely essential for effective law enforcement.

Ethics

Many people tend to equate ethics with their feelings. But being ethical is clearly not a matter of following one's feelings. A person following his or her feelings may recoil from doing what is right. In fact, feelings frequently deviate from what is ethical. Neither should one identify ethics with religion. Most religions, of course, advocate high ethical standards. Yet, if ethics was confined to religion, then it would apply only to religious people. But ethics applies as much to the behavior of the atheist as to that of the saint. Religion can set high ethical standards and can provide intense motivations for ethical behavior. Ethics, however, cannot be confined to religion, nor is it the same as religion.

Being ethical is also not the same as following the law. The law often incorporates ethical standards to which most citizens subscribe. But laws, like feelings, can deviate from what is ethical. Our own pre-Civil War slavery laws and the apartheid laws of South Africa are grotesquely obvious examples of laws that deviate from what is ethical.

Finally, being ethical is not the same as doing "whatever society accepts." In any society, most people accept standards that are, in fact, ethical. But standards of behavior in society can deviate from what is ethical. An entire society can become ethically corrupt. Nazi Germany is a good example of a morally corrupt society.

Moreover, if being ethical is doing "whatever society accepts," then to find out what is ethical, one has to find out what society accepts. To decide what one should think about abortion, for example, one would have to take a survey of American society and then conform one's beliefs to whatever society accepts. But no one tries to decide an ethical issue by doing a survey. Further, the lack of social consensus on many issues makes it impossible to equate ethics with whatever society accepts. Some people accept abortion, but many others do not. If being ethical is doing whatever society accepts, then one has to find an agreement on issues that does not, in fact, exist.

Ethics is two things. First, ethics refers to well-based standards of right and wrong that prescribe what humans ought to do, usually in terms of rights, obligations, benefits to society, fairness, or specific virtues. Ethics, for example, refers to those standards that impose reasonable obligations to refrain from rape, stealing, murder, assault, slander, and fraud. Ethical standards also include those that enjoin virtues of honesty, compassion, and loyalty. And ethical standards include standards relating to rights, such as the right to life, the right to freedom from injury, and the right to privacy. Such standards are adequate standards of ethics because they are supported by consistent and well-founded reasons.

Second, ethics refers to the study and development of one's ethical standards. As mentioned previously, feelings, laws, and social norms can deviate from what is ethical. So it is necessary to constantly examine one's standards to ensure that they are reasonable and well-founded. Ethics also means the continual effort of studying our own moral beliefs and our moral conduct and striving to ensure that we, and the institutions we help to shape, live up to standards that are reasonable and solidly based (Figure 7.1).

Figure 7.1 Ethical behavior is one of the key elements of law enforcement professionalism. (Courtesy of the U.S. Marines. Retrieved from http://community.marines.mil/unit/hqmc/hr/Pages/EMAS_Conduct.aspx.)

Living Ethically

The law enforcement profession does not allow individuals the luxury of acting one way professionally, yet living a different personal life. The definition of integrity is the same in public as in private. For anyone in law enforcement, this means much more than one may first believe. Officers are expected to treat individuals with dignity at all times, not just when in the public eye. Integrity is one of the most important characteristics of anyone seeking a career in the policing profession. In 1957, the International Association of Chiefs of Police (IACP) adopted its Code of Ethics and Oath of Honor as a statement of the values viewed important if the field of law enforcement would truly evolve into a profession.[3]

CODE OF ETHICS

As a law enforcement officer, my fundamental duty is to serve the community; to safeguard lives and property; to protect the innocent against deception, the weak against oppression or intimidation, and the peaceful against violence or disorder; and to respect the constitutional rights of all to liberty, equality, and justice.

I will keep my private life unsullied as an example to all and will behave in a manner that does not bring discredit to me or to my agency. I will maintain courageous calm in the face of danger, scorn, or ridicule; develop self-restraint; and be constantly mindful of the welfare of others. Honest in thought and deed both in my personal and official life,

I will be exemplary in obeying the law and the regulations of my department. Whatever I see or hear of a confidential nature or that is confided to me in my official capacity will be kept ever secret unless revelation is necessary in the performance of my duty.

Figure 7.2 All law enforcement officers must be mindful of ethical behavior. (Courtesy of the FBI. Retrieved from http://www.fbi.gov/stats-services/publications/law-enforcement-bulletin/may_2011/law_enforcement_professionalism.)

I will never act officiously or permit personal feelings, prejudices, political beliefs, aspirations, animosities, or friendships to influence my decisions. With no compromise for crime and with relentless prosecution of criminals,

I will enforce the law courteously and appropriately without fear or favor, malice or ill will, never employing unnecessary force or violence, and never accepting gratuities. I recognize the badge of my office as a symbol of public faith, and I accept it as a public trust to be held so long as I am true to the ethics of police service.

I will never engage in acts of corruption or bribery, nor will I condone such acts by other police officers. I will cooperate with all legally authorized agencies and their representatives in the pursuit of justice. I know that I alone am responsible for my own standard of professional performance and will take every reasonable opportunity to enhance and improve my level of knowledge and competence.

I will constantly strive to achieve these objectives and ideals, dedicating myself before God to my chosen profession... law enforcement (Figure 7.2).

IACP Oath of Honor

Police officers take risks and suffer inconveniences to protect the lives, defend civil liberties, and secure the safety of fellow citizens, and they endure such risks and tolerate such inconveniences on behalf of strangers. Consequently, police work is one of the most noble and selfless occupations in society. Making a difference in the quality of life is an opportunity that policing provides and that few other professions can offer.

A public affirmation of adhering to an Oath of Honor is a powerful vehicle demonstrating ethical standards. To be successful at enhancing integrity within an organization, leaders must ensure that the oath is recited frequently and displayed throughout the organization as well as ensure that ethical mentoring and role modeling are consistent, frequent, and visible.

The following Law Enforcement Oath of Honor is recommended by the IACP as a symbolic statement of commitment to ethical behavior:[4]

On my honor, I will never betray my badge,[1] my integrity, my character, or the public trust. I will always have the courage to hold myself and others accountable for our actions. I will always uphold the constitution[2] my community[3] and the agency I serve.

Before any officer takes the Law Enforcement Oath of Honor, it is important that he or she understands what it means. An oath is a solemn pledge someone makes when he or she sincerely intends to do what he or she says.

Honor means that one's word is given as a guarantee.
Betray is defined as breaking faith with the public trust.
Badge is the symbol of your office.
Integrity is being the same person in both private and public life.
Character means the qualities that distinguish an individual.
Public trust is a charge of duty imposed in faith toward those you serve.
Courage is having the strength to withstand unethical pressure, fear, or danger.
Accountability means that you are answerable and responsible to your oath of office.
Community is the jurisdiction and citizens served.[2]

Policing with Character

Actions of officers that are inconsistent, incompatible, or in conflict with the values established by an agency negatively affect its reputation and that of its officers. Such actions and inactions thereby detract from the agency's overall ability to effectively and efficiently protect the public, maintain peace and order, and conduct other essential business. Therefore, the policy of a law enforcement agency should be that officers conduct themselves at all times in a manner that reflects the ethical standards consistent with the following rules:

Accountability is a primary requirement for ethical conduct in law enforcement. Accountability means the duty of all officers to truthfully acknowledge and explain their actions and decisions when requested to do so by an authorized member of their agency without deception or subterfuge.

The following is a breakdown of a model policy addressing the general conduct standards expected within a law enforcement organization:[5]

1. *Obedience to Laws, Regulations, and Orders*
   a. Officers shall not violate any law or any agency policy, rule, or procedure.
   b. Officers shall obey all lawful orders.
2. *Conduct Unbecoming an Officer*
   Officers shall not engage in any conduct or activities on- or off-duty that reflect discredit on the officers, tend to bring this agency into disrepute, or impair its efficient and effective operation.
3. *Accountability, Responsibility, and Discipline*
   a. Officers are directly accountable for their actions through the chain of command to the agency's chief executive officer.
   b. Officers shall cooperate fully in any internal administrative investigation conducted by this or other authorized agency and shall provide complete and accurate information in regard to any issue under investigation.
   c. Officers shall be accurate, complete, and truthful in all matters.
   d. Officers shall accept responsibility for their actions without attempting to conceal, divert, or mitigate their true culpability nor shall they engage in efforts to thwart, influence, or interfere with an internal or criminal investigation.

    e. Officers who are arrested, cited, or come under investigation for any criminal offense in this or another jurisdiction shall report this fact to a superior as soon as possible.

4. *Conduct Toward Fellow Employees*

    a. Officers shall conduct themselves in a manner that will foster cooperation among members of this agency, showing respect, courtesy, and professionalism in their dealings with one another.

    b. Employees shall not use language or engage in acts that demean, harass, or intimidate another person. (Members should refer to this agency's policy on "Harassment and Discrimination in the Workplace" for additional information on this subject.)

5. *Conduct Toward the Public*

    a. Officers shall conduct themselves toward the public in a civil and professional manner that connotes a service orientation and that will foster public respect and cooperation.

    b. Officers shall treat violators with respect and courtesy, guard against employing an officious or overbearing attitude or language that may belittle, ridicule, or intimidate the individual, or act in a manner that unnecessarily delays the performance of their duty.

    c. While recognizing the need to demonstrate authority and control over criminal suspects and prisoners, officers shall adhere to this agency's use-of-force policy and shall observe the civil rights and protect the well-being of those in their charge.

6. *Use of Alcohol and Drugs*

    a. Officers shall not consume any intoxicating beverage while on duty unless authorized by a supervisor.

    b. No alcoholic beverage shall be served or consumed on police premises or in vehicles owned by this jurisdiction.

    c. An officer shall not be under the influence of alcohol in a public place, whether on- or off-duty.

    d. No officer shall report for duty with the odor of alcoholic beverage on his or her breath.

    e. No officer shall report to work or be on duty as a law enforcement officer when his or her judgment or physical condition has been impaired by alcohol, medication, or other substances.

    f. Officers must report the use of any substance, before reporting for duty, that impairs their ability to perform as a law enforcement officer.

    g. Supervisors shall order a drug or alcohol screening test when they have reasonable suspicion that an employee is using and/or under the influence of drugs or alcohol. Such screening shall conform to this agency's policy on employee drug-screening and testing.

7. *Use of Tobacco Products*

While on duty, a police officer shall not use a tobacco product unless in a designated area and while not conducting police business. Additionally, officers are not permitted to use tobacco products in a vehicle owned or maintained by this agency.

8. *Abuse of Law Enforcement Powers or Position*

    a. Officers shall report any unsolicited gifts, gratuities, or other items of value that they receive and shall provide a full report of the circumstances of their receipt if directed.

    b. Officers shall not use their authority or position for financial gain, for obtaining or granting privileges or favors not otherwise available to them or others except as a private citizen, to avoid the consequences of illegal acts for themselves or for others, to barter, solicit, or accept any goods or services (to include gratuities, gifts, discounts, rewards, loans, or fees) whether for the officer or for another.

c. Officers shall not purchase, convert to their own use, or have any claim to any found, impounded, abandoned, or recovered property or any property held or released as evidence.

d. Officers shall not solicit or accept contributions for this agency or for any other agency, organization, event, or cause without the express consent of the agency chief executive or his or her designee.

e. Officers are prohibited from using information gained through their position as a law enforcement officer to advance financial or other private interests of themselves or others.

f. Officers who institute or reasonably expect to benefit from any civil action that arises from acts performed under color of authority shall inform their commanding officer.

9. *Off-Duty Police Action*

a. Officers shall not use their police powers to resolve personal grievances (e.g., those involving the officer, family members, relatives, or friends) except under circumstances that would justify the use of self-defense, actions to prevent injury to another person, or when a serious offense has been committed that would justify an arrest. In all other cases, officers shall summon on-duty police personnel and a supervisor in cases where there is personal involvement that would reasonably require law enforcement intervention.

b. Unless operating a marked police vehicle, off-duty officers shall not arrest or issue citations or warnings to traffic violators on sight, except when the violation is of such a dangerous nature that officers would reasonably be expected to take appropriate action.

10. *Prohibited Associations and Establishments*

a. Arresting, investigating, or custodial officers shall not commence social relations with the spouse, immediate family member, or romantic companion of persons in the custody of this agency.

b. Officers shall not knowingly commence or maintain a relationship with any person who is under criminal investigation, indictment, arrest, or incarceration by this or another police or criminal justice agency and/or who has an open and notorious criminal reputation in the community (e.g., persons whom they know, should know, or have reason to believe are involved in felonious activity), except as necessary to the performance of official duties or where unavoidable because of familial relationships.

c. Except in the performance of official duties, officers shall not knowingly enter any establishment in which the law of that jurisdiction is regularly violated.

d. Officers shall not knowingly join or participate in any organization that advocates, incites, or supports criminal acts or criminal conspiracies.

Public Statements, Appearances, and Endorsements

1. Officers shall not, under color of authority,

a. Make any public statement that could be reasonably interpreted as having an adverse effect upon department morale, discipline, operation of the agency, or perception of the public.

    b. Divulge or willfully permit to have divulged, any information gained by reason of their position, for anything other than its official, authorized purpose.

    c. Unless expressly authorized, make any statements, speeches, or appearances that could reasonably be considered to represent the views of this agency.

2. Endorsements:

Officers may not, under color of authority, endorse, recommend, or facilitate the sale of commercial products or services. This includes but is not limited to the use of tow services, repair firms, attorneys, bail bondsmen, or other technical or professional services. It does not pertain to the endorsement of appropriate governmental services where there is a duty to make such endorsements.

Political Activity

Officers shall be guided by state law regarding their participation and involvement in political activities. Where state law is silent on this issue, officers shall be guided by the following examples of prohibited political activities during working hours, while in uniform, or otherwise serving as a representative of this agency:

    a. Engage in any political activity.

    b. Place or affix any campaign literature on city- or county-owned property.

    c. Solicit political funds from any member of this agency or another governmental agency of this jurisdiction.

    d. Solicit contributions, signatures, or other forms of support for political candidates, parties, or ballot measures on property owned by this jurisdiction.

    e. Use official authority to interfere with any election or interfere with the political actions of other employees or the general public.

    f. Favor or discriminate against any person seeking employment because of political opinions or affiliations.

    g. Participate in any type of political activity while in uniform.

Expectations of Privacy

1. Officers shall not store personal information or belongings with an expectation of personal privacy in such places as lockers, desks, departmentally owned vehicles, file cabinets, computers, or similar areas that are under the control and management of this law enforcement agency. While this agency recognizes the need for officers to occasionally store personal items in such areas, officers should be aware that these and similar places may be inspected or otherwise entered—to meet operational needs, internal investigatory requirements, or for other reasons—at the direction of the agency chief executive or his or her designee.

2. No member of this agency shall maintain files or duplicate copies of official agency files in either manual or electronic formats at his or her place of residence or in other locations outside the confines of this agency without express permission (Figure 7.3).

What Causes Corruption in Policing?

Many factors negatively influence police integrity. Recognizing some of the key factors involved is an essential first step in efforts to strengthen the foundation of police ethics. These factors include the following:

Figure 7.3 State of Illinois Executive Ethics Commission bestows the New Abraham Lincoln Ethics Award on state correction guards. (Courtesy of the State of Illinois Executive Ethics Commission. Retrieved from http://www2.illinois.gov/eec/Pages/ALEthicsaward06.aspx.)

Changing Moral Standards of a Contemporary Society

Many observers believe that the moral standards of contemporary society have fallen far below those of the past. They do not see this as just a nostalgic longing for imaginary good old days. Rather, they perceive that the social environment in which we live today reflects a significant and continuing decline in moral and ethical standards in many areas of life.

This is not to say that the history of police in the United States is free from charges of and documented instances or periods of corruption, brutality, and inefficiency, but that they have just recently shown a general decline. Early reforms of the twentieth century were replete with efforts to bring police under some reasonable form of political and community accountability in an effort to deter corruption. Findings of numerous administrative and political investigations of police misconduct over the past 60 years—such as the Wickersham, Kerner, and Knapp Commissions, among others—have made it all too clear that police can and have failed to adhere to ethical standards. What is being said, however, is that the fabric of American society (if not Western culture) in many important respects has undergone a change of values that has diminished the importance of such things as personal and social responsibility, virtue, honesty, civility, and general adherence to standards of conduct based on traditionally honored moral codes.

Americans "lack a moral consensus" according to one authority and are essentially "making up their own rules and laws."[1] A survey conducted by the same source found that only 13% of all people believe in the Ten Commandments and that nine out of ten lie regularly. Of course, surveys of this type may reflect an actual change or simply that people are more honest in answering survey questions, while those answering previous surveys engaged in a higher level of hypocrisy.

Whether social standards have lowered is open to debate. However, there is no doubt that unethical conduct has been and continues to be a significant factor in our society. In some places and at some times, such conduct seems to be normal. From Tammany Hall and the Teapot Dome scandal to Enron and recent Wall Street dealings, dishonesty is not only common but almost expected in politics and in business. Drug use is expected. Cheating is expected. Sexual misconduct is expected. Violence is expected. Many citizens seem not to have a sense of outrage, or even surprise, regarding such things. As a culture, the United States is often numb to the widespread use of drugs, corruption of politicians, and violence in our streets. When these behaviors become so commonplace in the eyes of the community, participation in them takes on a semblance of acceptability and, as such, carries far less social stigma as immoral. Some in this environment even come to feel bad about being honest. According to Gary Edwards, Executive Director of the Ethics Resource Center in Washington, D.C., "people come to feel like suckers if they are honest, if companies they are competing against are not."[2]

Another significant phenomenon is the environment in which law enforcement officers work, an environment that focuses on criminals, people who reject responsibility for their own actions. The perpetrators of crimes are often outraged when they are called upon to accept the consequences of their acts. Typically, they blame their actions upon other people and other things—never upon themselves. Lacking any feeling of personal responsibility, they proceed to repeat the behavior again and again, each time denying personal accountability. Unfortunately, there is a perception that this atmosphere is perpetuated by many of our political and social institutions including a legal system that often fails to assign guilt or impose punishment upon the perpetrator, instead blaming the perpetrator's upbringing or environment or a host of other alleged causes of and purported excuses for the misconduct. There is significant doubt whether this perception is valid. For example, the crime rate has decreased significantly since its high rate in 1991.[6] However, as long as the perception exists that society does not set defined boundaries on behavior and call wrongdoers to task for their bad or illegal acts, many Americans feel little inclination to avoid unethical or immoral behavior. They are not required to accept the consequences of their unethical or immoral acts, and thus do not see themselves as bearing any responsibility for them.

The combination of these two factors—the perception of low or moral standards and the failure of individuals to accept responsibility for the consequences of their own acts—produce a "What's wrong with that?" mentality across a broad spectrum of U.S. society. The abnormal seems normal; the immoral seems commonplace. Obviously, the police are not to blame for this state of affairs; it is a phenomenon of modern society as a whole. However, it would be naive to believe that the police are not directly and drastically affected by it. It is much more difficult for police officers, as well as others in our society, to hold strong to ethical standards while so many around them—particularly those who hold positions that should serve as examples to all—are compromising or failing to adhere to the same code of conduct.

One of the effects upon the police is very simple and very obvious: Police officers' attitudes inevitably reflect the environment in which they were raised and in which they work. This is first apparent in the recruiting process. Applicants for police careers are a cross-section of our society, and, in general, they reflect the moral tone of that society. Fortunately, many police applicants are ethical, moral, dedicated individuals of high integrity, but it is only realistic to expect that, as a class, police applicants bring to their work attitudes of the culture in which they grew up and live.

Figure 7.4 Police arresting a woman for acts of prostitution. (From *Urban Christian News,* 2010. Retrieved from http://www.urbanchristiannews.com/ucn/2010/01/dallas-police-aim-to-help-not-jail-prostitutes.html.)

In addition, once they become police officers, police personnel are affected by and may adhere to the values of the environment in which they perform their police duties. They may not—and often do not—understand or accept the idea that regardless of what they see going on around them, they as police officers hold a position of trust, a very special position in society, a position that demands high ethical and moral standards precisely because of its unique nature (Figure 7.4).

The Officer's Working Environment

Another of the major factors that negatively affect the moral standards of the police is the very high degree of frustration being experienced by today's police officers. Frustration often leads to disillusionment, cynicism, and anger, and these, in turn, can result in reduced performance, corruption, and, all too often, brutality.

These frustrations arise from many sources. For example, many, if not most, officers perceive the legal system as being weighted far too heavily against law enforcement and in favor of the criminal. Further, police officers far too often see other individuals or segments of society—criminals, criminal lawyers, politicians, and so on—defying the law and getting away with or even being rewarded for it, while the honest cop labors year after year in a relatively low-paid and often dangerous and thankless job.

Of course, there are other causes of job frustration that may or may not contribute in some manner to the deterioration of police ethics or integrity. Slow promotion, inadequate pay scales, departmental infighting, low morale, domestic strains caused by police work, constant danger or threat of danger, frequent temptations, and all the other stressors of modern police work can take a heavy toll. All of these are familiar subjects that have been explored in other publications, and no attempt will be made to discuss them here.

However, there is another, seldom-mentioned factor that contributes significantly to police frustration and a downward spiral of declining ethical standards, and it needs to be understood and addressed if significant changes are to occur: the expectations that are held about police ethics (Figure 7.5).

Figure 7.5 Police work may involve long hours and various types and amounts of public interaction. Policing involves a variety of stressors. (From *NBC News*, "Police: Blood Draws Will Help Stop Drunk Drivers," 2009. Retrieved from http://www.msnbc.msn.com/id/32824729/ns/us_news-crime_and_courts/t/police-blood-draws-will-help-stop-drunk-drivers/#.TlGtX6isOSo.)

Organizational Expectations of the Police

Our society has certain perceptions, images, and expectations of the police, not all of which are realistic or accurate. Failure of the public and political and community leaders to gain a clear and realistic conception of the role and capabilities of the police has had serious consequences for law enforcement in the United States. Misinformed or conflicting perceptions of the proper role of the police and conflicting expectations about what is or should be expected from the police often contribute to an environment of confusion built on mixed or even conflicting goals and objectives. This directly affects the working environment of police, their morale, and their susceptibility to corruption and brutality.

For example, the public—the same public that is itself so often lacking in moral and ethical standards or a feeling of responsibility for its own actions—generally expects higher standards of the police. Whatever they may think or do themselves, individuals expect police to adhere to high norms. Even the perpetrators of the foulest crimes are often contemptuous or even indignant when a police officer fails to follow the rules or otherwise displays a lack of integrity in some manner. Police are held to a higher standard by the public, and any failure to meet these public expectations usually arouses the scorn of the public and leads to calls for punishment or reform. Police are expected to be better than everyone else—to be, in effect, superhuman. This puts incredible pressure on the individual officer, which some officers simply cannot overcome. When it comes to police transgressions, there often appears to be little in the way of understanding or forgiveness on the part of the public, the media, and others.

Ironically, in attempting to address the problem of police integrity, some agencies may complicate the problem if they send mixed signals to their personnel. Most police agencies place great emphasis on or attach great importance to making arrests, issuing traffic citations, or other enforcement matters. This is an issue of great political and social significance and is understandable in isolation. The problem comes when law enforcement agencies fail to clearly draw the legal, ethical, and moral lines—in the form of clear policies and procedures, training, supervision, and discipline—that must be followed in order to meet these enforcement objectives. This often becomes even more acute in communities that are experiencing high and/or growing crime rates and are placing greater pressure on their police agency to do something about it. In an effort to do something about crime and also to meet implied or formal agency performance criteria, some officers may feel compelled to bend the rules of due process in order to fulfill their perceived mission. Unfortunately, overzealous enforcement has played a significant role in many cases of alleged police brutality or excessive use of force. Likewise, informal police practices that bend, circumvent, or even overlook personal due process requirements in order to make a case can collectively establish an environment in which such irregularities are condoned, ignored, or even accepted under the theory that the means are justified by the ends (e.g., reduced crime). Carried to its extreme, such an environment can inadvertently support the notion among some officers that they are justified in pursuing criminal activity no matter what they have to do and that they are justified in protecting one another in any instances of legal rule bending or rule breaking. These are environments in which police corruption can grow or even flourish.

In the above situation, the agency inadvertently set in motion a working environment where, on the one hand, it demands strict adherence to legal procedure and the police code of conduct but establishes other conflicting or even contradictory roles. In an environment in which many officers feel that the courts are working against their interests and the interests of law and order and a community that generally does not understand or appreciate their job, one can come to appreciate the organizational dynamics that often lead to confusion, conflict, cynicism, and, in some cases, corruption.

Because of standards of the culture in which most officers were raised, the environment in which they work, and the fact that police officers are, after all, only human, these departmental pressures may merely add to the frustration level of officers who are trying to do a difficult job in a complex world, where the realities of the street are far different than the ideals that departmental personnel are expected to meet. This is not an excuse for police lack of integrity; it is merely one of the unpleasant realities that one must understand if efforts to improve the ethical standards of police departments are to succeed.

Members of law enforcement are faced with ethical decisions regarding whether to report misconduct and criminal behaviors. A recent example of reporting police corruption involves the case of Sergeant James DeLorenzo, a 28-year veteran of the New Jersey State Police (NJSP). DeLorenzo "reported mismanagement and waste within the State Police's Solid Hazardous Waste Unit in 2006."[7] DeLorenzo recently filed a lawsuit against the NJSP citing that he was being "retaliated against for reporting financial waste."[8]

"I'm sensing confidence, boldness, and moral sensibility.
You're not going to turn out to be a whistleblower, are you?"

Figure 7.6 Reporting internal misconduct involves integrity. (Courtesy of CSL Cartoonstock. Retrieved from http://www.cartoonstock.com/directory/i/interview.asp.)

Another example involves the St. Louis, Missouri Police Department. Margaret Lin Owens worked in the "drug section of the department's crime lab for 25 years until she was fired on May 21, 2010."[9] According to Mann,[9] "Owens alleges that on two occasions in 2008, a fellow chemist did not follow proper testing procedures and failed to detect benzylpiperazine in pills that came into the lab. The first case concerned a plastic container of 49 round blue tablets embossed with the graphic of a lounging lady. The second involved a plastic bag filled with two round pink tablets marked with an apple." This case is currently ongoing. Only time will determine its outcome.

Those officers with high and strong integrity may opt to report such indiscretions and criminality. Although the reporting of fellow officers is an act of integrity, such reporting involves risk. Fears of retaliation are not unfounded, given the potential of unofficial blacklisting, personal injury, or the destruction of careers (Figure 7.6).

Role of the Police in a Democratic Society

The root causes of corruption in police agencies should also be understood from the perspective of misunderstandings about the role of the police in American society. Unfortunately, it is not just the public who misunderstands this role; often, the police misunderstand it as well.

Public Perceptions

The public misunderstands several things about the role of the police in modern society. In some instances, these views are more a matter of sociopolitical attitudes than true misunderstandings. For example, some segments of the population see the police as an instrument of oppression, maintained by the establishment to crush all opposition or dissent. This viewpoint has been present in virtually every culture in the past; fortunately, it is not presently a majority view in our own society. However, this perception of the nature of the police function can be a serious problem in a given community and cannot be ignored by law enforcement agencies in that community. In the context of the present discussion, this hostile view may be broadened and strengthened when a lack of police integrity in a community leads to overt police misconduct, especially the use of excessive force against a group or individual members of a group. Lack of ethical behavior by police almost inevitably leads to increased brutality; when this view is perceived by the public as being directed at one segment of the community, serious results can ensue. We have had numerous examples of these consequences in recent years, particularly in urban areas.

Another perception about the police that is held by the vast majority of the public is that the prevention and detection of crime, the apprehension of criminals, and the protection of the public from criminal activity are the sole responsibility of the police. The belief by the public that crime is the province of the police alone and that the public, in general, has no responsibility to take part in this process places an impossible burden upon law enforcement.

This public perception is, of course, totally erroneous. No matter how much the public (and often the police themselves) may wish it to be true, the police alone cannot eradicate crime. Practice and research clearly show that most crime is solved through information provided by or gathered through a cooperative public. Without such cooperation and assistance, police would be ineffective. Until the public (1) is educated to understand this basic reality, (2) accepts the fact that they as well as other elements of the criminal justice system (e.g., courts and prison systems) share responsibility for public safety, and (3) is brought into a constructive partnership with the police in efforts to control crime, people will continue to expect more of the police than the police can possibly provide. The disparity between expectation and reality will continue to generate a downward spiral of disappointment, discontentment, and outright hostility toward the police even among many law-abiding citizens, which will fuel the belief among many officers that they are neither understood nor appreciated by the public (Figure 7.7).

Police Self-Perceptions

Police officers themselves do not always fully understand their own roles and their own capabilities. Often law enforcement personnel, from chief to new recruit, do not accept the fact that even the best police force, however brave, diligent, and skillful its personnel may be, cannot eradicate crime without community cooperation and must not be expected to do so.

Unfortunately, the law enforcement community has to a large extent fostered both the public perception that the police are solely responsible for eradicating crime and the perception of the police themselves that eradicating crime is their sole province and their sole responsibility. Upper-level police executives sometimes quite naturally wish to emphasize to the community and the community's governing body the role of their department in dealing with crime and their success in doing so. Further, at all departmental levels, police officers tend to feel that they should have the sole responsibility for combating crime. Encouraged by political rhetoric about "the war on crime" and the "the war on drugs,"

Figure 7.7 Public demonstrations often show public disgruntlement with law enforcement agencies and personnel. (From *News One*, "Top 5 Worst NYPD Brutality Moments," 2008. Retrieved from http://newsone.com/nation/casey-gane-mccalla/top-5-worst-nypd-brutality-moments/.)

officers often come to believe that, as the "soldiers" in the front lines of this "war," only they have the capability to do the "fighting," and they resent any implication that other segments of the community can or should have some of that responsibility.

The result is that the police themselves often encourage the public to expect the police to do the impossible. Again, frustration results, both on the part of the public and on the part of the police. With frustration comes discouragement, cynicism, and at times, eventually the feeling among officers that "everybody else does it, so why shouldn't I get in on some of the action too?"

The public must understand that it is not just the police, but the community as well, who bear the responsibility for combating crime. Not only must the community understand the true role of the police, but the police themselves must understand it as well. Only then can the misunderstandings and frustrations described previously be resolved.

This redefinition of the police role includes the requirement that police officers understand what they must be and what they must do both individually and as police officers. This, in turn, requires a clear understanding of what is expected and, in fact, necessary in terms of police ethics and conduct.

There are many different views as to what the role of the police is or should be today. In the context of police ethics, it is clear that no matter how it may be defined by politicians, sociologists, and so on, the police role includes certain elements that must be articulated and understood by both the public and the police.

To begin with, everyone concerned must understand both the meaning of and the need for law and order. Unfortunately, the term "law and order" has become a synonym for oppression by the "establishment," with the police serving as the instrument of that oppression. This attitude must be addressed and refuted. Notwithstanding the fulminations of the demagogues, no society can survive unless it is governed by law. But the laws must be just laws, and they must be administered in a manner that maintains order while preserving the individual rights and freedoms upon which our country was founded.

For there to be "law and order" and justice in our society, there must be what has been termed a "social compact" between the public and the police, a mutual obligation in which both perform their parts. In addition, there must also be a similar social compact among the police themselves—a realization by all departmental personnel of the need to fulfill their role in a manner that contributes to law and order rather than endangering it. Adhering to principles of due process for the accused cannot be regarded as an abstract principle to be employed when convenient or dismissed when deemed irrelevant, troublesome, or cumbersome. To deny these rights or employ them only when convenient is inconsistent with a democracy and counter to the very principles that police officers are sworn to uphold. To act otherwise is to bring law enforcement down to the same level as the wrongdoer. One may be better able to achieve conformance with the law by removing all restrictions on the police, but these very restrictions are what separates the democracy from the totalitarian state.

Ethics, morality, integrity, and personal responsibility are important standards of behavior for police. Police officers must realize that they occupy a position of unique trust and that whatever the norms of the society in which they work may be, the police officer who fails to maintain appropriate standards of behavior violates his or her responsibilities both to the public and to fellow members of the law enforcement community. Police personnel must clearly understand that unethical or immoral police behavior at any level endangers the social compact, thus reducing respect for the police and severely damaging the ability of the police to fulfill their role in upholding the law and maintaining a safe and orderly society (Figure 7.8).[3]

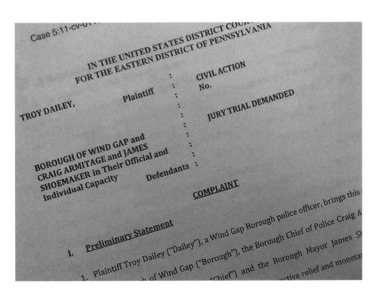

Figure 7.8 Court proceedings often involve officers. This picture shows paperwork regarding an actual Pennsylvania lawsuit. A Wind Gap police officer, Troy Dailey, sued Wind Gap Borough, along with the borough police chief and mayor, and claimed he was a whistleblower who was targeted for retaliation because he spoke out about questionable practices. Law enforcement agencies and police personnel are often the subject of lawsuits. (Retrieved from http://www .lehighvalleylive.com/slate-belt/index.ssf/2011/06/wind_gap_police_officer_troy_d.html)

Corruption and Ethical Challenges

Corruption within the criminal justice system may have roots from different beginnings. Delattre offers four hypotheses regarding the causes of corruption in policing:

- **The Society-at-Large Hypotheses:** Corruption occurs as a result of expectations or practices of the citizens or the community.
- **The Structural or Affiliation Hypotheses:** Corruption occurs as a result of the environment to which the officers are subjected.
- **The Rotten Apple Hypotheses:** Corruption occurs because the individual did not possess character and integrity in the beginning. Once put in a situation to act unethically, it came naturally.
- **Slippery Slope** is a term used by Delattre to describe officers' actions that started petty in nature—such as "acts of omission" in conducting day-to-day responsibilities, such as following departmental policy—and gradually eased into more serious unethical conduct or "acts of commission," such as violation of rights and accepting bribes as a way of doing business (Figure 7.9).[10]

The Ideal of Noble Cause Corruption

Can any action that is unethical be known as "noble cause"? Delattre uses this term to address the actions of police that are considered wrong yet are done for a good reason. For example, an officer lying to a suspect to gain a confession of a crime or the use of excessive force to gain valuable evidence or information that may be used to save human lives.

The question is this: Is this actually corruption or defiant behavior, and are there ever situations in which such actions are justified in the criminal justice profession? As a standard, there is no such thing as "corruption for noble cause." A corrupt act is wrong regardless of the reason behind the act. The idea that suggests that the "ends justify the means" in

Figure 7.9 New Orleans, LA Police Department former captain Michael Roussel. He was convicted of corruption charges involving an illegal kickback scheme during the aftermath of Hurricane Katrina. (From *The Times-Picayune*, "Former New Orleans Police Capt. Michael Roussel Gets a Just Sentence for His Corruption: An Editorial." 2011. Retrieved from http://www .nola.com/crime/index.ssf/2011/03/new_orleans_police_officers_co.html and http://www.nola .com/opinions/index .ssf/2011/04/new_orleans_police_capt_michae.html.)

policing is not a standard that should be applied on a regular basis. This is not to say that this ideology cannot be applied, because if the proper guidelines are applied ethically in the decision-making process, then a good outcome will result.

Howard Cohen offers four standards that must be met for an end to justify the means:[11]

1. The end itself must be good.
2. The means must be a plausible way to achieve the end.
3. There must be no alternative, better means to achieve the same end.
4. The means itself must not undermine some other equal or greater end.

This simple four-point test, when appropriately applied, is a successful guide in the use of discretion and decision making.

Discretion in Policing

Discretion is defined as freedom or authority to make decisions and choices. Discretion allows officers great latitude in meeting the demands placed upon them in today's society. Officers are expected to make decisions that are best for both the community and the citizens they serve while operating within the confines of policy, the law, and good ethical standards.

O.W. Wilson's "Square Deal Code" of Wichita, Kansas, addressed this in a unique way by establishing the policy of never to arrest if a summons will suffice; never to summons if a warning would be better.[12] One might say that this limits the ability to apply discretion. On the contrary, it provides the officer with the freedom to make a decision yet provides a standard philosophy that it is usually better to apply the least means (Figure 7.10).

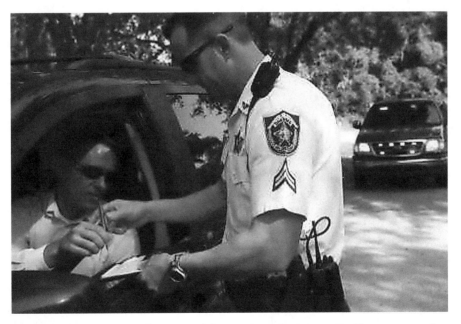

Figure 7.10 Officers often use discretion when making decisions. Traffic stops are often prime examples of such discretion. (From O'Rourke, S., 2009, *Tampa Bay Times*. Retrieved from http://www.tampabay.com/news/publicsafety/article1023956.ece.)

Figure 7.11 Reno, NV police officers receive training in critical thinking. Called the Reno Model, this program recognizes the importance of problem-solving skills in training a successful police officer. The Reno Model focuses on adult learning methods and other learning constructs to create a positive experience for the trainee and trainer. (Courtesy of the City of Reno, NV, 2011. Retrieved from http://www.ci.reno.nv.us/index.aspx?page=1090.)

Dilemmas in Policing

In policing, as in society in general, we are not always going to be able to have "win–win" situations. As a matter of fact, more often than not, the options an officer has may not be in the best interest of anyone. So, how does an officer come to rectify such a situation? This is when an officer must look for a solution that presents the greatest amount of good with the least amount of harm to the fewest people. Again, these actions must occur within the boundaries set by policy and the law.

Critical thinking is one avenue for successful resolution of dilemmas faced by police officers. Albanese sets four steps to properly address an issue:

1. Begin with an open mind (no preconceptions).
2. Isolate and evaluate the relevant facts on both sides.
3. Identify the precise moral question to be answered.
4. Apply ethical principles to the moral question based on an objective evaluation of the facts, only then drawing a conclusion (Figure 7.11).[13]

Deterring Corruption

Numerous methods of deterring corruption exist among American law enforcement agencies and municipalities. Both punitive and reward systems may be leveraged as tools through which aberrant behaviors are deterred among law enforcement entities. In many cases, reports may be filed anonymously when individuals believe that they will be the victim of negative repercussions for reporting misconduct or criminal behaviors among fellow officers.

Punitive measures often range anywhere from suspension or dismissal to periods of incarceration. When corruption is present within a law enforcement organization, imprisonment may result from the actions of corrupted officers. During the last few decades, the New Orleans Police Department has witnessed various cases of police corruption that necessitated imprisonment. According to Lengel,[6] such cases included the following incidents:

- In the 1990s, in an FBI probe called "Operation Shattered Shield," about 12 New Orleans cops went to prison for participating in a cocaine trafficking ring.
- In 1994, a 13-year police veteran went off to prison for shooting an unarmed man in a bar.

New Orleans is not the only city that experienced police corruption or that currently manifests some amount of corruption within its law enforcement infrastructure. During 2011, federal authorities collaborated with the Baltimore, Maryland, police to "unravel a towing scheme involving 17 police officers" during a sting operation.[14] The Glendale, California Police Department relieved from duty several officers after they used a "patrol car for a personal trip to Las Vegas.[5]" Certainly, many other examples may be identified and discussed regarding police indiscretion and corruption. No law enforcement agency is impervious to the potential of corruption.

The visibility of such incidents and their associated punitive measures may curb aberrant behavior among police personnel. They serve as warnings regarding the extremity of punitive measures that may be taken against corrupt officers. Once a former officer is incarcerated, he may become the victim of acts of revenge within the prison system, thereby endangering his life.

Rewards may be leveraged to control officer behavior and deter corruption. Polinsky and Shavel[10] indicate that reward mechanisms may deter "corruption by paying rewards to enforcement agents for reporting violations. Such rewards can partially or completely mitigate the problem of bribery, but they encourage framing." These rewards may range from financial compensation to allowances of personal time.

Many organizations exist through which quality control is monitored among law enforcement agencies. One such entity is the New York Commission to Combat Police Corruption (CCPC). This entity describes itself as follows:[1]

CCPC was created in 1995 as a permanent board to monitor and evaluate the anticorruption programs, activities, commitment, and efforts of the New York City Police Department. The commission is completely independent of the NYPD and is presently comprised of six commissioners appointed by the mayor who advise a full-time staff of attorneys.

Such organizations are independent of the law enforcement agency. They often conduct quantitative and qualitative studies to investigate reports of corruption among law enforcement entities. Because they are not directly related to law enforcement entities, their analysis is hoped to be objective without the biases that may exist within the law enforcement organization. The independent status and goal of objectivity contribute to strengthening the analysis of the law enforcement organization. Once the analysis is completed, its findings and conclusions may be used to adjust the functioning of the examined law enforcement agency, thereby influencing organizational quality.

Figure 7.12 Example of a hotline advertisement. (Courtesy of the San Francisco Bay Area InfraGard Chapter, 2009. Retrieved from http://www.sfbay-infragard.org/blogs/news_events/ 2009/02/fbi-bay-area-public-corruption.html.)

Other methods of deterring corruption include the use of telephone "hotlines" for reporting incidents of corrupt behavior. Following severe corruption within the Philadelphia, Pennsylvania, Police Department, a hotline was installed as a method of reporting corrupt police officers and activities.[15] Within the District of Columbia, the Metropolitan Police Department also implemented a hotline for reporting corruption.[16] Similarly, many such hotlines are in use throughout the United States.

Regardless of the method used to deter and diminish acts of police corruption, it shall never be eliminated. Police officers are human and are subject to human weaknesses, temptations, and failures. However, through the use of reward and punitive systems, corruption may be countered, to some degree, among law enforcement agencies. Through using hotlines, corruption may be reported anonymously, thereby contributing toward the diminishment of police corruption (Figure 7.12).

Summary

As discussed in this chapter, ethics refers to well-based standards of right and wrong that prescribe what humans ought to do, usually in terms of rights, obligations, benefits to society, fairness, or specific virtues. Ethical standards include virtues of honesty, compassion, and loyalty. And ethical standards include standards relating to rights, such as the right to life, the right to freedom from injury, and the right to privacy. Such standards are adequate standards of ethics because they are supported by consistent and well-founded reasons.

Additionally, ethics refers to the study and development of one's ethical standards. As mentioned previously, feelings, laws, and social norms can deviate from what is ethical. So it is necessary to constantly examine one's standards to ensure that they are reasonable and well-founded. Ethics also means the continual effort of studying our own moral beliefs and our moral conduct and striving to ensure that we, and the institutions we help to shape, live up to standards that are reasonable and solidly based.

The law enforcement profession does not allow individuals the luxury of acting one way professionally yet living a different personal life. Officers are expected to treat individuals with dignity at all times, not just when in the public eye. Integrity is one of the most important characteristics of anyone seeking a career in the policing profession.

No law enforcement agency is insusceptible to the potential of corruption among its ranks. Corruption affects both large and small law enforcement organizations. Reward systems, punitive measures, and hotlines may be used to deter and diminish corruption among law enforcement agencies. However, the greatest gains in establishing higher ethical standards within policing will likely involve executive leadership, which assures increased scrutiny in recruiting and selecting candidates. In addition, it is imperative that police executives set the tone for agencies and lead by example, always stressing unyielding ethics and never choosing the easy route in lieu of the ethical one. Executive leadership must also ensure more quality training resources and greater involvement with ethics training at all levels of the agency.

In order to live up to the high ethical standards expected of a professional law enforcement officers, they must readily recognize an ethical problem or dilemma, identify various options to address the particular issue involved, make a rational and ethically sound choice of which option to choose, take prompt action based upon that choice, and accept responsibility for the outcome. To maintain the public trust, executive leadership must then demonstrate the courage to expeditiously and affirmatively deal with the officers who fall short of ethical expectations (Figure 7.13).

Figure 7.13 Graduation day for police academy recruits at the Southern Desert Regional Police Academy at the College of Southern Nevada. (From Shimada, K., 2009, *Las Vegas Sun*. Retrieved from http://www.lasvegassun.com/news/2009/mar/12/thirty-five-police-recruits-graduate-academy/.)

References

1. Dempsey, J. S., & L. S. Forst. (2012) *An Introduction to Policing*. Clifton Park, NY: Delmar, Cengage Learning. 218.
2. Gleason, T. Ethics training for police. *Police Chief Magazine*, Retrieved April 14, 2012, from http://www.policechiefmagazine.org/magazine/index.cfm?fuseaction=display_arch&article_id=1054&issue_id=112006
3. Wilson, O.W. 1963. *Police Administration*. New York, NY: McGraw-Hill.
4. IACP (2001). *Ethics Tool Kit*. Alexandria, VA: International Association of Chiefs of Police. Retrieved from http://www.theiacp.org/PoliceServices/ProfessionalAssistance/Ethics/tabid/140/Default.aspx
5. Ibid.
6. United States Crime Rates (1960–2009). *The Disaster Center*. Retrieved March 23, 2011, from http://www.disastercenter.com/crime/uscrime.htm
7. Megerian, C. (2010). Suspended N.J. State Police sergeant files whistleblower lawsuit. *New Jersey Real-Time News*. Retrieved August 22, 2011, from http://www.nj.com/news/index.ssf/2010/08/suspended_nj_state_police_serg.html
8. Ibid.
9. Mann, J. (2011). Fired St. Louis police chemist files whistle-blower suit. *STLToday.com*. Retrieved August 22, 2011, from http://www.stltoday.com/news/local/crime-and-courts/article_f091612c-86f5-11e0-8f67-0019bb30f31a.html
10. Delattre, E. (2006). *Character and Cops* (5th ed.). Washington DC: AEI Press.
11. Ibid.
12. Ibid.
13. Albanese, J. S. (2006). *Professional Ethics in Criminal Justice—Being Ethical When No One is Looking*. Boston, MA: Pearson.
14. Fenton, J., Hermann, P., & Scharper, J. (2011). More than 30 Baltimore police officers charged, suspended in towing scheme: Federal authorities say cops allegedly got kickbacks from towing operator. *The Baltimore Sun*. Retrieved February 23, 2011, from http://articles.baltimoresun.com/2011-02-23/news/bs-md-towing-corruption-20110223_1_edwin-javier-mejia-majestic-auto-repair-shop-medallion-towers
15. Odom, V. (2010). Philly seeks stronger recruits amid police woes. *ABC 6 News*.
16. MPD (2011). Metropolitan Police Department Directory. District of Columbia.

Bibliography

City of New York (2011). New York Commission to Combat Police Corruption. Retrieved August 21, 2011, from http://www.nyc.gov/html/ccpc/html/home/home.shtml

City of Reno, Nevada (2011). The Reno Model. Retrieved August 21, 2011, from http://www.ci.reno.nv.us/index.aspx?page=1090

Delattre, E. (2006). *Character and Cops* (5th ed.).Washington, DC: AEI Press.

Fenton, J., Hermann, P., & Scharper, J. (2011). More than 30 Baltimore police officers charged, suspended in towing scheme: Federal authorities say cops allegedly got kickbacks from towing operator. *WXIN Fox 59 News*. Retrieved August 21, 2011, from http://www.fox59.com/news/crime/bs-md-towing-corruption-20110223,0,5863859.story?page=2

IACP (2001). *Ethics Tool Kit*. Alexandria, VA: International Association of Chiefs of Police. Retrieved from http://www.theiacp.org/PoliceServices/ProfessionalAssistance/Ethics/tabid/140/Default.aspx

KTLA (2011). Officers fired after taking patrol car to Vegas: Six Glendale police officers have been put on administrative leave. *KTLA News*. Retrieved August 21, 2011, from http://www.ktla.com/news/landing/ktla-glendale-police-misconduct,0,1011170.story

Lengel, A. (2010). Scandal-ridden New Orleans police at crossroads. *AOL News*. Retrieved August 21, 2011, from http://www.aolnews.com/2010/07/16/scandal-plagued-new-orleans-police-at-crossroads/

Mann, J. (2011). Fired St. Louis police chemist files whistle-blower suit. *STLToday.com*. Retrieved August 22, 2011, from http://www.stltoday.com/news/local/crime-and-courts/article_f091612c-86f5-11e0-8f67-0019bb30f31a.html

MPD (2011). Metropolitan Police Department Directory. *District of Columbia*. Retrieved August 21, 2011, from http://mpdc.dc.gov/mpdc/cwp/view,a,1230,q,537848,mpdcNav_GID,1523,mpdcNav,|31417|.asp

Odom, V. (2010). Philly seeks stronger recruits amid police woes. *ABC 6 News*. Retrieved August 21, 2011, from http://abclocal.go.com/wpvi/story?section=news/crime&id=7593700

Polinsky, A., & Shavell, S. (2001). Corruption and optimal law enforcement. *Journal of Public Economics, 81*, 1–24.

Wilson, O.W. (1963). *Police Administration*. New York: McGraw-Hill.

Types of Policing

8

The primary object of an efficient police is the prevention of crime: the next that of detection and punishment of offenders if crime is committed. To these ends all the efforts of police must be directed. The protection of life and property, the preservation of public tranquility, and the absence of crime, will alone prove whether those efforts have been successful and whether the objects for which the police were appointed have been attained.

Sir Richard Mayne
Commissioner of Metropolitan Police, 1829

Learning Objectives

The objectives of this chapter are to

- Discuss special organizational functions and roles
- Understand specialized policing among air, land, and maritime modalities
- Explain the supporting roles of specialized organizations
- Understand the use of intelligence among special agencies
- Understand the training of special units
- Discuss the benefit of special organizations

Introduction

Historically, American policing has maintained order and prevented crime. However, subsequent to the terrorist attacks of September 11, 2001, American law enforcement has taken on the additional responsibility of protecting homeland security.

The American police mission originated with the British citizen Sir Robert Peel, who founded the London Metropolitan Police Department in 1829. Because of Peel's influence, the British ascribe to a version of law enforcement that involves police working both with the community and as a part of the community.[1] The practice of responding to calls for service originated in the early days of policing and has since become a mainstay in British and American policing. During the formative years of Anglo-American policing, police received calls to perform a sundry of duties including firefighting, maintenance and control of sanitation, issuance and regulation of municipal licenses, building inspections, collection of taxes, and a host of other tasks.[2] When he established the London Metropolitan Police Department, Peel emphasized "service" as a significant part of the overall police mission. Modern police officers devote approximately 10% to 15% of their effort to fighting crime and the remaining time is spent responding to calls for service. Even though the prevention of crime or the absence of crime is a highly desirable aspect of police duty, it is only a small part of the overall police mission.

Since the introduction of American policing, five primary styles of policing have evolved in the United States: traditional policing, community policing, problem-oriented policing (POP), zero-tolerance policing, and homeland security policing. Over the years, American law enforcement has served as a "first responder" to critical incidents such as the 1995 Oklahoma City bombing and the events surrounding 9/11, as well as natural and man-made disasters. Subsequent to 9/11 and Hurricane Katrina, American law enforcement adopted a truly all-hazards approach to their newly acquired homeland security mission. This chapter explains and analyzes the aforementioned styles of policing and highlights each style's contributions to American law enforcement.

Community Defined

Before we can discuss the nuts and bolts of community policing, we must define community. Community is defined as forming a "smaller social unit within a larger one, and sharing common interests such as work, identity, location etc." Flynn (1998) believes that some people regard a community as a residential neighborhood, whereas others regard it as a city, county, or region. Flynn adds "ethnic, cultural and racial groups often refer to themselves as communities (the Latin American, African-American, or Asian community), and groups with common interests consider their commonality as community (the business, academic, or law enforcement community)."[3]

On the other hand, police define "community" in terms of geographical boundaries. According to the Bureau of Justice Assistance, police officers need to be mindful that ethnicity, social factors, and shared interests also play a part in defining community.[4] It should be noted that community policing strategies vary depending on the needs and responses of the communities involved. Therefore, police administrators must be able to adopt crime prevention/problem solving strategies that are suitable to the needs of a specific community.

A major concern of police administrators when attempting to implement the community policing strategy is the willingness of the community to participate. According to Skogan, "research on the social and geographical distribution of opportunities to participate in organized group activity indicates that they are least common where they appear to be most needed—in low income, heterogeneous, deteriorated, high turn-over areas." Skogan added that community organizations that focus on crime are more common in "better-off" neighborhoods "while poorer areas characterized by high levels of fear, fatalism, mutual distrust, and despair are less well served."[5]

Traditional Policing

The traditional style of policing in the United States originated during the reform or professional era of policing (1900–1970). The reform era of policing relied heavily upon new technology such as radios, 911 emergency telephone systems, and automobile patrols to respond to calls for assistance from citizens.[6] During this era, police concentrated solely on crime and other community problems such as urban decay, leaving such responsibilities as blighted housing and abandoned vehicles to other municipal agencies.

The traditional style of policing has often been described as a reactive style of policing. In this context, reactivity implies that police respond to calls after a crime occurs or after the need for service arises. Ratcliffe refers to the traditional style as "fire brigade" policing, "where once the fire is put out, the case is dealt with and then the police withdraw to await the next incident that requires attention."[7]

The traditional style of policing exemplifies a bureaucratic management model. The bureaucratic management model theoretically resembles a pyramid, with the police chief positioned at the top and the line officer situated at the bottom. The traditional style of policing and the bureaucratic management model both have a clear-cut chain of command with a line of communication that flows from the top toward the bottom of the organization. Rarely does communication flow from the bottom to the top of the pyramid; line officers have little to say in the department's decision-making process.

In traditional policing, the police structure is highly centralized, which drastically reduces the officers' contact with the local populace. Moreover, traditional policing advocates preventative patrol and a rapid response to calls for service as primary methods of crime control. Historically, traditional policing has not focused on the "root causes" of crime and has not involved the general public in any crime prevention processes, as the police consider themselves the single authority on crime. Traditional policing focuses primarily on law enforcement, property, and violent crimes; as a consequence, the underlying causes of crime go unabated. The success of traditional policing has always depended upon the number of arrests, clearance rates, summons, and traffic citations that the department issues on an annual basis.

Former Houston Police Chief Lee Brown cites the following elements as characteristics of a traditional style of policing:[8]

- Police *react* to incidents. The organization responds to calls for police service.
- *Information* from and about the community is limited.
- Planning efforts focus on internally generated police data.
- *Planning* is narrow in its focus and centers on internal operations such as policies, procedures, rules, and regulations.
- *Recruitment* focuses on the officer's spirit of adventure rather than their spirit of service.
- *Police officers* are restrained in their role. They are not encouraged or expected to be creative in addressing problems and are not rewarded for undertaking innovative approaches.
- *Training* is geared toward the law enforcement role of policing even though officers spend only 15% to 20% of their time on such activities.
- *Management* uses an authoritative style and adheres to the military model of command and control.
- *Supervision* is control oriented as it reflects and reinforces the organization's management style.
- *Rewards* are associated with officers' participation in daring events rather than their roles in conducting service activities.
- *Performance* evaluations are based not on outcomes but on activities. The number of arrests made and the number of citations issued are of paramount importance.
- Agency effectiveness is based upon data, particularly crime and clearance rates, from the Federal Bureau of Investigation's (FBI's) Uniform Crime Reports.
- *Police departments* operate as entities unto themselves with few collaborative links to the community.

The traditional style of policing served the public well.[9] It signaled a great improvement over the political style of policing that it replaced. The political style of policing is characterized by negative political control and widespread corruption.[10] Despite the improvement it provides, the traditional style of policing has also received criticism for failing to address the root causes of crime and for neglecting input from the citizenry regarding the causes of crime, their fear of crime, and quality of life issues. In essence, the traditional style of policing has failed to prevent crime.

Community Policing

During the turbulent 1960s, the United States endured serious social change (Figure 8.1). American law enforcement faced numerous outbreaks of civil disobedience throughout the country. The federal government created commissions to investigate the causes of the violent civil disorder and to analyze the police response to these instances of civil disobedience. President Lyndon B. Johnson's National Advisory Commission on Civil Disorders, established in 1967, served as one of the government's most important fact-finding commissions. The commission, commonly known as the Kerner Commission, ascertained possible causes of the civil disorders and recommended solutions.[11] Disorder is defined as "incivility, boorish and threatening behavior that disturbs life, especially urban life."[12] One of the commission's most significant findings concerning the causes of the riots included a historical pattern of racism among whites directed toward other ethnicities in America.[13]

Most of the rioting that transpired in our nation's streets occurred in opposition to the Vietnam War. However, social issues such as civil rights, education, jobs, women's rights, police abuse, and the environment also led to the outbreaks of civil disobedience. Several government commissions reported that the police were not always equipped to handle such problems, thereby leading the officers to occasionally overreact to demonstrators. Furthermore, commissions found that police were generally unaware of the underlying causes of such violent activity by the American public; the police had suffered a large disconnect from the public.

To illustrate this disconnect between the police and the public during the turbulent 1960s, the police coined the term "thin blue line." The term referred to the police, usually dressed in blue, which became the fine line between law-abiding citizens and anarchy. To bridge the gap between police and the community, many metropolitan police departments established community relations units whose missions enhanced the police image and established rapport with the community and its leaders. The idea of establishing a community relations unit, however, had little to no effect on the line officers who believed

Figure 8.1 1960s police patrol car. (Courtesy of the City of Pasadena, CA. Retrieved from http://www.ci.south-pasadena.ca.us/events/adam_12.JPG.)

community relations did not qualify as real police work. Instead, many of the police officers regarded community relations as social work.

In an attempt to reconnect with the public during these times of civil unrest, police
administrators developed the strategy of team policing. Team policing originated in the
United Kingdom, and it emphasizes the delivery of round-the-clock decentralized police
services by a team of officers usually led by a sergeant or lieutenant in a specific geographical area. In addition, team leaders are held accountable for conditions in their area of
responsibility. Even though team policing ultimately failed, three of the team policing
strategies survived: storefront police stations, foot patrol, and community crime watch.[14]
Team policing is considered to be the forerunner to community-oriented policing (COP).

Fleissner and Heinzelmann claim that the technology of the traditional style of policing such as the 911 communications system "was viewed as a poor use of resources because
it allowed too little time for in-depth investigations."[15] Furthermore, the police patrol car
replaced the "foot beat" and consequently removed police from the public. The foot beat
was an important law enforcement tactic because it helped reduce the fear of crime and
contributed to the public's perceived safety.[16]

Use of the patrol car allows police to cover a larger geographical area in less time and
to respond to calls for service faster, but the benefits of the patrol car are accompanied by
several drawbacks. Motor patrols tend to isolate "officers from the citizens they serve" and
may contribute to "reactive, rather than proactive styles of dealing with crime."[17] Finding
the patrol car to be an inadequate solution to law enforcement, many police administrators
continued their search for a better way to conduct business.

Moreover, during the 1960s and 1970s, American cities experienced a "white flight"
phenomenon when white populations of major U.S. cities moved to the suburbs, leaving
municipalities behind to face a depleted tax base and social problems that accompany urban
decay. The combination of these factors contributed to a major spike in crime and disorder
across the nation. As a consequence, police administrators realized that they should embrace
community policing as a strategy to prevent crime and to help solve problems plaguing their
community. Police executives came to recognize that crime prevention required community participation and cooperation for the community policing paradigm to succeed.

> Community policing is a philosophy that promotes organizational strategies, which support
> the systematic use of partnerships and problem solving techniques, to proactively address the
> immediate conditions that give rise to public safety issues such as crime, social disorder and
> fear of crime.[18]

More simply, community policing is defined as "a policing strategy that attempts to
harness the resources and residents of a given community in stopping crime and maintaining order."[19] It should be noted that community policing is often misunderstood as
a program or set of programs such as Drug Abuse Resistance Education (DARE), foot
patrols, bike patrols, or police. Many of these COP techniques work as part of a broader
strategic community policing plan; these techniques alone do not constitute community
policing. Another perspective indicates that "community policing is an overarching philosophy that informs all aspects of police business."[20]

The philosophy of COP consists of two core components: community partnership and
problem solving. Traditionally, the police have always been considered the primary crime
fighters. The reality of the situation, however, is that the police cannot prevent crime alone.
Crime prevention requires a partnership between the police, the community, the private

sector, and the government (Figure 8.2). According to Fuller, "Good policing requires citizen cooperation. If people do not report crimes, do not provide information to the police, and are unwilling to testify in court, then the police cannot effectively fight crime."[21]

The partnership between the police and the community is based upon "trust."[22] The Bureau of Justice Assistance states:

> [T]rust is the value that underlies and links the components of community partnership and problem solving. A foundation of trust will allow police to form close relationships with the community that will produce solid achievements. Without trust between police and citizens, effective policing is impossible.[23]

Police conduct has a major impact on the level of community trust. If a law enforcement agency is physically and verbally abusive to the community, then it will be extremely difficult for the agency to forge a working relationship with the general public. In addition, corruption not only has a debilitating effect on the department, but it impacts the community as well. If a department has been described as being "corrupt," then in all probability the community will not trust the police. Scheider contends that "citizens who do not trust the police are less likely to report crime and participate in developing solutions to problems. They are also more likely to place blame for increases in crime on the shoulders of the police."[24]

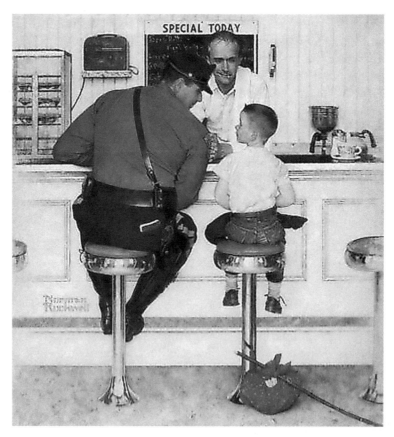

Figure 8.2 Community-oriented policing necessitates trust and interaction with the populace. (Courtesy of the Town of Vernon, CT. Retrieved from http://gis.vernon-ct.gov/police/images/runaway.jpg.)

Figure 8.3 Crafting relationships with the public. (Courtesy of the City of Pittsburgh, PA. Retrieved from http://www.pittsburghpa.gov/police/images/mast/cop.jpg.)

The second component of COP is problem solving. Historically, the police have been mostly responsible for identifying community problems that have led to increases in crime. In the COP paradigm, citizens of various neighborhoods identify problems that in their opinion adversely affect the quality of life in their communities. Often times what seems important to the police is not important to the community and vice versa. COP affords the community an opportunity to participate in the crime prevention process (Figure 8.3). Based on the writings of Vitto, Walsh, and Kunselman, the following five characteristics summarize community policing:[25]

1. An admission that the police alone cannot solve the problem and that direct participation by citizens is also required.
2. A shift in the focus of problem definition to a customer orientation and corresponding concentration on those problems identified by the citizens themselves as being of greatest concern.
3. An emphasis on proactive, rather than reactive, policing, replacing a total preoccupation with 911 calls with efforts targeted at particular problems.
4. The identification and implementation of a range of nontraditional approaches.
5. The redirection of officers from their cruisers into more direct contact with the community along with the delegation of decision-making authority to the patrol officer.

Transforming the Police Agency

In addition to attempting to gain the confidence of the community in the community policing paradigm, police administrators must also sell this crime prevention strategy to the line officers and especially the middle managers of the department (Figure 8.4). In the traditional style of policing, police managers tend to be micromanagers. This situation is not the case with community policing. Because of the foundational concepts of COP, line officers assigned to COP are given greater latitude in the decision-making process, thus reducing the amount of supervision line officers usually require. In addition, officers are encouraged to develop creative problem-solving approaches.[26]

Figure 8.4 Regardless of rank, all supervisors and subordinates contribute to effective community-oriented policing. (Courtesy of the City of Bay City, MI. Retrieved from http://cityofbaycity.org/images/pages/SC141/100_0708.JPG.)

Another important element of COP is fixed geographical responsibility. In essence, this term means that under the COP paradigm, line officers should be assigned to a specific geographical area for an extended period of time.[27] The term geographical accountability refers to "administrative arrangements in which one officer is fully responsible for the police-related conditions (e.g., crime, fear, victimization, disorder, quality of life) within a single geographic area."[28] Moreover, MaGuire and Gantley claim that geographical responsibility has two defining characteristics: "responsibility for a distinct area and the autonomy to design solutions to problems in that area."[29] The end result of geographical responsibility is that the patrol officer will be most familiar with the needs and strengths of their communities. This situation allows the officer the best position to forge close ties with the community and will lead to effective solutions to local problems.[30]

Supervisors in COP act as facilitators; they are required to provide the COP officers with all of the necessary tools required to get the job done and solve the problem. Convincing police middle managers to accept the COP philosophy is not an easy task. Traditionally, police officers have strongly resisted change and have been fairly well entrenched in the traditional style of policing. Goldstein suggests that police supervisors can help facilitate the transition to the COP paradigm by encouraging team building, raising morale, and emphasizing their role as a coach and mentor to the line officers assigned to COP.[31] Engel claims that the "ultimate goal for supervisors in the COP paradigm is to develop subordinates by emphasizing problem solving skills, sound judgment, and creativity."[32]

It is widely believed that the failure to convince police middle managers (captains and lieutenants) to accept a more community-related police strategy resulted in the complete failure of the team policing concept. As a result, it is incumbent upon the top police executive to convince the rank and file of the department that the COP paradigm attacks the root causes of crime.

Police agencies that plan on utilizing the COP strategy must be prepared to enhance their ability to communicate with the public. In community policing, information flow must occur between the police and the community they serve. According to Snipes and Katz, "successful community policing requires considerable sharing of information in both directions—from the public to police and from police to the public."[33]

When implementing the COP strategy, police executives must reorganize their department to achieve success. Deputy Chief Ramsey of the Chicago Police Department strongly suggested that police agencies must change their organizational structure in the following ways if community policing is to be sustained in the future:[34]

- The organizational structure must be decentralized, flattened, and streamlined.
- The organizational culture must change, but this will take several years to accomplish.
- The concept of community policing must be institutionalized in the department so every officer is doing community policing, not just community policing officers assigned to a specialized unit.
- Nonpatrol roles must be redefined, including a movement toward generalization and removing specialized units.

Various factors affect the successfulness of community policing. According to Trojanowicz, for any community policing effort to be successful in both the short and long term, police chiefs must have support of the following five main groups, each of which has its own priorities and concerns:[35]

1. The police department
2. The community
3. Elected officials
4. Community agencies
5. The media

It takes a total commitment from the police, government, private sector, and community to make COP a success. It should be noted, however, that COP is not a panacea to all of the social problems that plague our communities. Rather, it should be used as a tool to help prevent crime and improve the quality of life in our nation's communities.

Broken Windows Theory

This concept was introduced by criminologists George Kelling and James Q. Wilson. Kelling and Wilson developed their theory following a human nature experiment conducted by Stanford University psychologist Phillip Zimbardo. In 1967, Zimbardo abandoned two similar automobiles in different neighborhoods—one in the heart of Bronx County, New York, and the other in an affluent neighborhood in Palo Alto, California. Zimbardo removed the license plates and left the hoods open.[36]

In the Bronx, it took about 10 minutes for people to begin stripping the vehicle and within three days, the vehicle was stripped of all valuable parts.[37] In Palo Alto, however, the situation was completely different. The vehicle sat untouched for approximately one week. In an attempt to solicit a response, Zimbardo took a sledgehammer and demolished a section of the abandoned automobile. Shortly after, passersby began to strike the vehicle with the sledgehammer. After a few hours, the vehicle was resting on its roof, completely destroyed.[38]

Kelling and Wilson compared the Zimbardo human nature experiment to a building with a broken window. The premise of theory is that "if a window in a building is broken and is left unrepaired, all of the rest of the windows will soon be broken."[39] The broken windows theory applies to crime. If small crimes (misdemeanors) such as vagrancy, public drunkenness, abandoned vehicles, prostitution, and vandalism are left unchecked in a particular neighborhood, they will eventually lead to more serious offenses (felonies).

Former New York City (NYC) Mayor Rudy Giuliani was a major advocate of the broken windows theory. He used the theory to implement a zero-tolerance policing strategy to address the spiraling crime rate in NYC. According to the Giuliani Archives, Mayor Giuliani stated:[40]

> If a climate of disorder and lack of mutual respect is allowed to take root, incidences of other, more serious anti-social behavior will increase. There's a continuum of disorder. Obviously, murder and graffiti are two vastly different crimes. But they are part of the same continuum, and a climate that tolerates one is more likely to tolerate the other.

Kelling and Wilson believed that serious crime flourishes in areas in which disorderly behavior goes unabated.[41]

Problem-Oriented Policing

POP is a strategy that is closely related to COP. One perspective contends that POP greatly expands the role of the police officer from one of reaction to one of proactive problem solving. Even though COP and POP are closely related, they are fundamentally different. Clark claims that "COP strengthens relationships with communities and engages their assistance in the fight against crime. POP on the other hand, like situational crime prevention, is mostly directed to reducing opportunities for crime through environmental changes and criminal or civil enforcement."[42] Unlike COP, POP does not require community participation in the problem solving process.[43]

Herman Goldstein, a Professor Emeritus at the University of Wisconsin Law School and the father of POP, strongly believed that the traditional reactive style of policing was an ineffective strategy in crime prevention.[44] Goldstein further believed that the police should focus on problems as opposed to incidents.[45] In the context of POP, problems may be recognizable as a "collection of incidents related in some way (if they occur at the same location, for example) or as underlying conditions that give rise to incidents, crimes, disorder, and other sustentative community issues that people expect the police to handle."[46] The rationale for this philosophy is that by focusing on problems rather than incidents, the police will be able to concentrate more on the cause of crime rather than just the mere symptoms (Figure 8.5).[47]

In 1983, the Newport News, Virginia Police Department was one of the first law enforcement agencies to develop and implement a problem-oriented approach to policing. Their goal was to reassess their traditional reactive style of policing and to fundamentally change the way they do business. As a result of their reassessment, the Newport News

Figure 8.5 Drug-related activities are problematic crimes that impact American communities. This image depicts the aftermath of a drug arrest. (Courtesy of the State of Florida. Retrieved from http://www.flhsmv.gov/fhp/html/photogallery/Kingdrugarrest.jpg.)

Police Department developed a four-step problem solving methodology commonly known as SARA. The Center for POP has documented the SARA model as follows:[48]

- Scanning:
  - Identifying recurring problems of concern to the public and police
  - Identifying the consequences of the problem for the community and police
  - Prioritizing those problems
  - Developing broad goals
  - Confirming that the problems exist
  - Determining how frequently the problem occurs and how long it has been taking place
  - Selecting problems for closer examination
- Analysis:
  - Identifying and understanding the events and conditions that precede and accompany the problem
  - Identifying relevant data to be collected
  - Researching what is known about the problem type
  - Taking inventory of how the problem is currently addressed and the strengths and limitations of the current response
  - Narrowing the scope of the problem as specifically as possible
  - Identifying a variety of resources that may be of assistance in developing a deeper understanding of the problem
  - Developing a working hypothesis about why the problem is occurring

- Response:
  - Brainstorming for new interventions
  - Searching for what other communities with similar problems have done
  - Choosing among alternative interventions
  - Outlining a response plan and identifying responsible parties
  - Stating specific objectives for the response plan
  - Carrying out the planned activities
- Assessment:
  - Determining whether the plan was implemented (a process evaluation)
  - Collecting pre- and postresponse qualitative and quantitative data
  - Determining whether broad goals and specific objectives were attained
  - Identifying any new strategies needed to augment the original plan
  - Conducting ongoing assessment to ensure continued effectiveness

The scanning process involves the police identifying problems. According to Peak,[49] "it initiates the problem solving process by conducting a preliminary inquiry to determine whether a problem really exists and whether further analysis is needed." Police usually identify problems by analyzing police incident reports, utilizing crime analysis, and collecting observations of police officers. Eck and Spelman suggest that information about problems should also be collected from businesses, other government agencies, and private citizens.[50]

Analysis is considered to be the most important and most difficult step in the SARA problem-solving model. According to Ortmeier, "the analysis must address the underlying causes rather than just the symptoms of the problem."[51] Swanson, Territo, and Taylor suggest that the analysis process examines offenders, victims, the social and physical environment, and any previous responses to the problem. The goal of this step is to understand the scope, nature, and causes of the problem and to formulate a variety of options for its resolution.[52]

In the response process, the information obtained through the analysis step is used by police officers (problem solvers) to implement solutions. Peak points out that the solution to a specific problem might require the assistance of more than one government agency; it might take multiple municipal agencies to resolve a problem. For example, a neighborhood bar may be the source of nuisance crimes such as public urination, fights, and disorderly conduct. The problem solver might seek the assistance of the state Alcohol Beverage Control Agency to certify state and local licenses. The Department of Public Health might be requested to inspect the premises for health or sanitation issues. The state Fire Marshal's office and building inspectors could be utilized to inspect for any fire or building code violations. These agencies, acting in concert, could successfully resolve the public nuisance and improve the quality of life for that particular neighborhood.[53]

This example illustrates the need for police officers to network or make contacts with people and organizations outside the police agency. Networking will enable police officers to discover what they can accomplish by working with other agencies and encourage the officers to take a broader, more informed view of the problems they must handle.

The final step of the SARA model is assessment. The assessment process should incorporate qualitative as well as quantitative means to determine whether the response to the problem was a success or failure. This process can be accomplished through the use of surveys of residents of the community where the problem originated as well as the personal observations of beat officers. Personal interviews of business owners or community residents could also assist in determining whether or not the problem has been solved or if police officials must reevaluate their initial response to the problem.

The success of POP is measured "by the police officer's ability to solve problems, reduce the impact of the problem, or potentially to displace and disperse the problem from a concentrated area."[54] The police should be mindful of the fact that they are unable to solve every social problem. Social problems such as urban decay, poor education, and unemployment are issues that the police attempt to resolve.

Zero-Tolerance Policing

Zero-tolerance policing is a strategy that is based on the broken windows theory, and it calls for the police to primarily focus on disorder, minor crime, and the appearance of crime (Figure 8.6).[55] The premise of this police strategy is that if misdemeanor offenses are left unattended, the offenders will later commit more serious offenses. Zero-tolerance policing has been described as heavy-handed policing, meaning that the police normally utilize aggressive tactics while engaging in this enforcement activity. Zero-tolerance policing is also known as order-maintenance policing and quality of life policing. It is widely believed that zero-tolerance policing is an intensification of the traditional style of policing. Like the traditional style of policing, the success of zero-tolerance policing is gauged by the number of arrests, field stops, and summons issued.

There is a difference between zero-tolerance policing and other policing strategies. First, community policing and POP are based on the notion that the police should focus on crime prevention, whereas zero-tolerance policing focuses on a crime attack model."[56]

Figure 8.6 Law enforcement has no tolerance for certain crimes. Checkpoints are useful in determining whether motorists are capable of operating vehicles safely. (Courtesy of the Florida Highway Patrol, 2008. Retrieved from http://www.flhsmv.gov/fhp/PhotoGallery/2008/images/PG101308.jpg.)

Zero-tolerance policing has its origins during the 1990s in NYC when mayor Giuliani introduced the "Quality of Life Initiative" in which he announced that the New York Police Department (NYPD) would crack down on quality of life issues such as graffiti, panhandling, public urination, and subway turnstile jumping.[57] Mayor Giuliani claimed that concentrating on quality of life issues would create a safer, cleaner, and more prosperous city.

Zero-tolerance policing has been credited with helping the NYPD make a historical reduction in the overall crime rate of the city. This significant reduction in New York's crime rate has been referred to as the New York miracle. William Bratton, former NYPD Police Commissioner, claimed that at the end of 1996, the overall crime rate in NYC had dropped approximately 50% to include a 55% decline in the homicide rate of NYC.[58] However, not everyone agreed that the zero-tolerance policing was responsible for this major decline in NYC's overall crime rate.

There was a significant decline in crime during the mid-1990s in 17 of the 25 largest cities in the United States.[59] Furthermore, "between 1990 and 1996 the crime rate also decreased in 160 of 197 American cities with a population of 100,000 or more."[60] Many criminologists believe that the decrease in the crime can be attributed to a decline in the consumption of crack cocaine during this period of time. It should be noted that Chicago, Los Angeles, Washington, D.C. and San Diego also sustained a major decrease in their crime rate without implementing zero-tolerance policing. These four cities utilized COP and POP to reduce their respective crime rates.[61]

Zero-tolerance policing has been criticized because many critics allege that this police strategy unjustly targets minorities, homeless young people, drunks, and the mentally ill.[62] In addition, zero-tolerance policing has been denounced for using heavy-handed or aggressive tactics while enforcing quality of life issues, which has resulted in hundreds of complaints of police brutality and misconduct against the NYPD. Moreover, zero-tolerance policy or quality of life policing tends to further overburden an overloaded criminal justice system with an influx of misdemeanor arrests. Critics claim that police officers can make better use of their time enforcing more serious types of offenses.

Finally, zero-tolerance policing has been described as a "quick fix" that does not address the underlying causes of crime. Zero-tolerance policing places more of an emphasis on short-term law enforcement and less on long-term strategies.[63] In essence, zero-tolerance policing does not address the underlying causes of crime, but it does provide a useful quick fix for nuisance crimes, such as panhandling and prostitution, in a particular geographical area.

Homeland Security Policing

The traditional goals of policing are to maintain order and prevent crime. Since the events of 9/11, the police mission has also included homeland security, which encompasses antiterrorism and counterterrorism measures.

Over the years, American law enforcement has served as a first responder to critical incidents such as the 1995 Oklahoma City bombing, 9/11, and natural and man-made disasters. Since 9/11 and Hurricane Katrina, American law enforcement has adopted a truly all-hazards approach to its newly acquired homeland security mission. However, the homeland security mission of law enforcement is much more than serving as a first responder to acts of terrorism. State and local law enforcement should be keenly aware of terrorism because the potential targets of terrorists are located within their respective jurisdictions.

Many homeland security pundits strongly believe that American law enforcement is the first line of defense in the war on terrorism; there are approximately 18,000 law enforcement agencies in the United States and, as of 2006, there are approximately 683,396 full-time state, city, municipal, metropolitan, and nonmetropolitan county and other law enforcement officers in the United States. As a result of these numbers, state and local law enforcement are a good resource for gathering intelligence, because they are considered to be our eyes and ears in the war on terrorism.

It is widely believed that the best way for the police to accomplish their homeland security mission is through COP. One assumption of COP is that the local police establish partnerships not only with the public but also with local businesses and various state and municipal institutions that might have an overall interest in the mission of the police agency.[64] This concept is commonly referred to as external partnerships.

Second, a flat organizational structure might ensure more effective terrorist prevention and response.[65] It is quite possible that police officers, either directly or indirectly, might come into contact with potential terrorists as a result of the officer's daily activities such as traffic stops. A flat organizational structure would empower COP officers with the ability to make important decisions during a crisis situation.[66] Moreover, the line officer in the COP paradigm has an advantage due to the fact that the officer has been assigned to a specific geographical area (beat) for a significant amount of time. The officers should be keenly aware of any unusual activity, whether criminal or terrorist, that occurs on their beat. As a result of their daily activity, the COP officers can be an outstanding source of intelligence. Furthermore, the public would ideally place trust in the police, prompting the community to inform the authorities of any suspicious activity.

The National Commission on Terrorist Attacks Upon the United States, otherwise known as the 9/11 Commission, was a bipartisan independent commission created by congressional legislation and approved by President George W. Bush. The commission was chartered to prepare a full and complete account of the circumstances surrounding the 9/11 terrorist attacks, including preparedness for and the immediate response to the attacks. Among its many recommendations, the Commission ordered the improvement of information sharing among federal, state, and local law enforcement.

Before the events of 9/11, information sharing among federal, state, and local law enforcement was problematic. The 9/11 Commission recommended that the FBI be the primary federal law enforcement agency for the dissemination of sensitive information regarding terrorism and homeland security issues. The FBI considers the Joint Terrorism Task Force (JTTF) as its primary means of information sharing. The JTTF is a task force comprised of federal law enforcement agencies such as the U.S. Secret Service; Alcohol, Tobacco, Firearms and Explosives (ATF); and Immigration and Customs Enforcement (ICE) along with various state, county, and local law enforcement agencies. The mission of the JTTF "is to identify and target for prosecution terrorists and terrorist organizations planning or carrying out terrorist acts occurring in or affecting a geographic region and to apprehend individuals committing such acts."[67] The JTTF increases the FBI's resources to prevent terrorist attacks and enhances its ability to collect and share real-time information.[68]

There are approximately 100 FBI JTTFs nationwide, including at least one in each of the FBI's 56 field offices. A total of 65 of these JTTFs were established after 9/11. One of the major problems confronting the JTTF with respect to the dissemination of real-time information is the matter of security clearances. The JTTF relays real-time information to their respective offices; many JTTF supervisors, however, do not possess top secret clearance and as a consequence do not have access to key information. The lack of security clearance has been extremely problematic for the information sharing process. Though the FBI's JTTF concept is not perfect, it has been extremely successful in thwarting numerous terrorist plots against the United States during the past decade.

Another mechanism for information sharing at the federal, state, and local levels has been the creation of fusion centers. The Council of State Governments states the purpose of fusion centers "is to improve the collection, analysis and dissemination of information and intelligence for the purpose of crime and terrorism prevention."[69] During 2009, there were approximately 72 fusion centers around the country and one in just about every state.

Among most jurisdictions, the fusion center is under the command of the state police. In other states, the fusion center is under the control of the state's office of homeland security. In most cases, the fusion center is comprised of public safety, emergency management, law enforcement, the private sector, and the National Guard to provide a bona fide all-hazards approach to homeland security.

The fusion center concept provides local law enforcement the opportunity to request intelligence information on criminals as well as potential terrorists. In addition, the fusion centers have the capability to keep local law enforcement updated with real-time information regarding criminal and terrorist activity within their respective state.

Intelligence-Led Policing

The previous discussion concerning homeland security policing incorporates a consideration of intelligence. This notion provides an introduction to the concept of intelligence-led policing. Intelligence-led policing is a cooperative paradigm that is a "collaborative enterprise based on improved intelligence operations and community-oriented policing and problem solving, which the field has considered beneficial for many years."[70] This notion alludes to the fact that intelligence-led policing involves the salient concepts of both POP and COP. In addition, it also involves the collection of facts and information processing to yield intelligence that influences the rendering of human decisions through time. Given these notions, intelligence-led policing is defined as a "business process for systematically collecting, organizing, analyzing, and utilizing intelligence to guide law enforcement operational and tactical decisions."[71]

Intelligence-led policing integrates the primary concepts of "command and control, community policing, problem-solving policing, and data analysis."[72] This integration contributes to the crafting of preventive mechanisms regarding anticipated trends in crime while concurrently maintaining the privacy of the served citizenry.[73] This approach represents policing as a business model through which a greater understanding of the crime domain is established.[74] This understanding of the crime domain strengthens the ability of humans to make decisions that impact not only the activities of the law enforcement organization, but also of society.

The basic premise of the model involves the following concepts:[75]

- The production of accurate and timely intelligence and analytic products relevant to the operational goals of the agency that describe the nature and extent of problems affecting the jurisdiction.
- The use of these intelligence and analytical products to develop and guide a strategy, operational plan, or course of action that addresses the problems.
- Continuing evaluation, follow-up, and accountability to determine the impact of the strategy or operational plan on the problem, making adjustments as needed.

These concepts illustrate a methodical approach to crafting strategies among law enforcement organizations that are resources utilized to address a variety of crime problems uniquely among communities. These strategies do not appear spontaneously. Instead, they are derived from interaction with society either directly or indirectly. Therefore, the intelligence-led policing paradigm involves a strong capacity to manage and process information, and it involves a two-way communication with the members of society.[76]

The collecting of intelligence ranges vastly from intercepting electronic communications to personal human interactions. Any organization that collects and utilizes data must be mindful of the consequences affiliated with both civil and privacy rights.[77] Collection methods are diverse and include the following methods:[78]

- Open sources
- Community outreach
- Acquisition and analysis of physical evidence
- Interviews and interrogation
- Financial investigations
- Surveillance
- Informants
- Electronic surveillance
- Undercover operations
- The daily interactions that officers have with others

The data gleaned from such activities must be stored and transformed into a format that facilitates appropriate data analysis techniques. These data analysis techniques may be either quantitative or qualitative. Examples of quantitative techniques include the use of statistical analysis for hypothesis testing or to forecast future perspectives of crime, whereas examples of qualitative techniques include the use of historical documents and artifacts or the use of personal case study interviews.

Collecting and analyzing data to support the rendering of human decisions involves the notion that an observable entity is being observed. The analytical aspects of leveraging intelligence often necessitate consideration of the following concepts:[79]

- *Intent:* What is the stated intent of the intelligence target? Has it changed? How might any of the current events or activities influence the stated intent of the target?
- *History:* What has the intelligence target or group done in the past? Often, history can provide insight into future behaviors, methods, and targets. This includes identifying and assessing triggering events from previous attacks or violent behaviors of the intelligence target.
- *Capability:* What capabilities does the target or group have? Have they been trained to execute terrorist attacks or crimes? Do they have critical assets available, including people, munitions, money, documents, and travel to commit the crime?
- *Opportunity:* Are there any unusual or unique opportunities arising that will help facilitate an attack? If so, what kind of access to that opportunity will the intelligence target have? Is there evidence to suggest that planning for an attack or crime to coincide with an opportunity has occurred?
- *Resolve:* Does the intelligence target or group actually has the commitment to execute the attack? Is the intelligence target simply making a threat or does the target actually pose a threat? Are there insights into how the resolve to commit an attack

may be mitigated? Particularly in the case of ideological groups, a critical variable related to "resolve" is learning the characteristics of the leader. If the group has a charismatic leader, then the likelihood increases that the group will act on its intent.

The resources necessary for strongly considering these concepts may exceed those of smaller law enforcement entities. Therefore, analogous with homeland security policing paradigms, intelligence-led policing involves resource sharing and collaboration among factions of law enforcement entities, commercial entities, the public, government agencies, and other entities within the public and private sectors. Within the state of Florida, two examples show the cooperativeness that is involved with intelligence-led policing. The efforts of intelligence-led policing in Citrus County, Florida, are described as follows:[80]

> The program uses intelligence gathering, technology and teamwork to ferret out known criminal elements in the community and use that information to begin surveillance ahead of the commission of a crime. The information can also be used to develop a list of suspects once a crime has been committed. ILP is hitting its stride; the county reduced major crimes by 9 percent in the past year. Sheriff Jeff Dawsy cites this state-of-the-art program as a primary reason for the decrease.

The efforts of New Port Richey, Florida, are described as follows:[81]

> It focuses on agencies gathering intelligence and sharing that information within their departments and with other local, state and federal agencies. It's part homeland security, but also a method of tracking and taking down organized crime. For instance, one county might have two convenience store robberies. A bordering county might have had a rash of four. In intelligence-led policing, these agencies would share information to help catch the crook. The idea is that criminals don't respect or care about county or city lines and that law enforcement will catch more by working together.

With respect to the New Port Richey example, it is estimated that approximately "6 percent of offenders commit 60 percent of crimes."[82] Through using intelligence-led policing, law enforcement anticipates maintaining strong surveillance concerning suspected offenders.[83] The crime-tracking methods of intelligence-led policing allow the local law enforcement organization to target its patrols regarding "where and when crimes are expected to occur."[84]

Other Floridian examples include the implementation of various intelligence-led policing methods in the communities of Sarasota, Hillsborough, Pinellas, and Hernando.[85] After Hillsborough law enforcement implemented intelligence-led policing in 2008, a 25% reduction in crime was observed thereafter.[86]

Intelligence-led policing benefits law enforcement organizations nationally. The state of Oklahoma presents examples from America's heartland. Law enforcement in Oklahoma City, Oklahoma, implements it as a resource through which gang-related crime is combated, deterred, and diminished.[87] The benefit of this program is described as follows: "As a result of that sweep, officers arrested more than 30 known and suspected gang members. They were also able to remove a number of weapons from the streets as well."[88]

During an assessment of the merits and potential implementation of intelligence-led policing, the Oklahoma City Police Department contemplated assigning the civilian populace tasks that were generally conducted by law enforcement personnel.[89] Assignment of civilians to such tasks was considered from the perspective of cost reduction.[90] Another aspect of this type of relationship demonstrates the collaboration between law enforcement and its served community that is essential to the intelligence-led policing paradigm. By establishing and maintaining strong relationships with the citizenry, a two-way communication may be established between the law enforcement organization and its served populace. Furthermore, the citizenry itself may feel and believe that its contribution toward deterring crime and maintaining order is valued by the law enforcement organization, and that its participation is essential in maintaining a safe community.

Some members of the law enforcement community indicate that intelligence-led policing is the "wave of the future."[91] It often represents a form of predictive analysis that incorporates a variety of complex technologies as well as the simplicity of human interaction as methods of collecting data.[92] Examples of this complexity include the use of satellite imagery, artificial intelligence algorithms, database management software, pattern matching software, electronic surveillance equipment, cameras, and myriad other resources (Figures 8.7 and 8.8).

An example of such resources is produced by the IBM Corporation (IBM). IBM produces software and systems that "mine, share and extract intelligence from critical data in order to improve police investigative and prevention programs."[93] In an implementation

			Electricity	Gas	Railways	ICT	Urban water
Infrastructure characteristics	Complexity	Physical					
		Organisational					
		Speed of change					
	Dependence (interconnectedness)	On other infrastructures					
		For other infrastructures					
		Intra-infrastructure					
		ICT control					
	Vulnerability	External impact*					
		Technical/human failure					
		Cyber attacks					
		Terrorist target					
	Market environment	Degree of liberalisation					
		Inadequacy of control					
		Speed of change					
Criticality	Degree of criticality – factors	Scope**					
		Magnitude					
		Effects of time					
	Overall degree of criticality						

Natural hazards, construction work, etc.
**Potential of cascading trans-national effects.*

Figure 8.7 Example of a threat assessment matrix output of intelligence activities. (From Kröger, W., *Reliability Engineering & System Safety*, December 2008. Retrieved from http://www.sciencedirect.com/science/article/pii/S0951832008000744.)

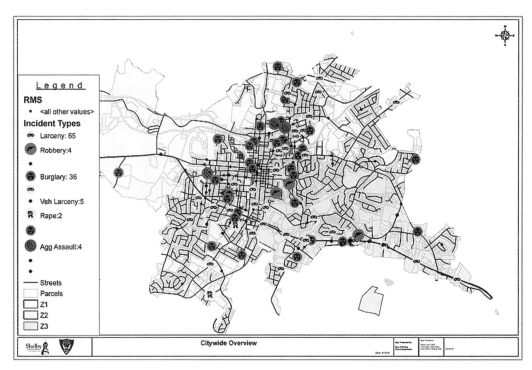

Figure 8.8 Example of information systems software to support intelligence-led policing. (From ESRI, *ArcNews Online*, 2008. Retrieved from http://www.esri.com/news/arcnews/summer08articles/intelligence-led.html.)

taking place in Rochester, Minnesota, IBM is partnering with Alpine Consulting, Inc., to develop Smarter Cities software that discovers and examines patterns in crime for the purposes of bolstering public safety, improving services that are offered to the citizenry, improving risk assessment, and increasing the effectiveness and efficiency of law enforcement.[94] The primary goal of the Rochester Police Department is to "provide more effective police services to the community through the adoption of intelligence-led policing methods."[95]

The use of such software systems is beneficial for intelligence-led policing efforts. Because the software systems are automated and can process data sets significantly faster than could be accomplished manually by humans, less time is required to generate meaningful outputs that law enforcement organizations may use during the course of their investigations. Furthermore, humans are fallible creations and are susceptible to numerous cognitive and physical weaknesses. For example, despite conducting a manual examination of vastly large data sets, a person may not immediately recognize an emerging pattern because of tiredness or human error. Through the use of computerized systems, such a pattern may be discovered quickly without the interjection of human fallibility.

This section has considered the use of intelligence-led policing to influence the rendering of human decisions within the context of law enforcement organizations. However, before any human can render a decision using an intelligence-led paradigm, some form of intelligence output product must exist to provide humans with some knowledge of the problem domain and potential courses of actions. Therefore, the output of intelligence-led policing programs is a catalyst that often influences organizational decisions regarding strategy, tactics, and operations.

The following items are examples of outputs that are generated from various activities that exist within the intelligence-led policing paradigm:[96]

- Summary briefs—incidents and activities, globally or locally, that may have some correlation to threats, particularly if the incidents reflect a trend.
- Threat assessment—a detailed description of threats, targets, the likelihood of an attack against a defined target, and the potential methods of attack.
- Situational awareness reports (i.e., SITREP)—the current status of known threats or changes in the status of known threats.
- Information bulletin—information on new or emerging threats, including threat indicators and methodologies.
- Intelligence assessments—comprehensive analysis, usually of a strategic nature, about a threat.
- Raw intelligence—information that is derived from a source deemed to be reliable but that has not been corroborated or analyzed. Typically, the threat is time critical and potentially severe, hence the dissemination of the information.
- Case intelligence—intelligence related to specific threats, targets, and suspects. Case intelligence is produced and disseminated on a timely basis as facts warrant rather than on a fixed schedule. Dissemination is narrower and goes only to persons who have a demonstrable right to know and need to know the information.

Intelligence-led policing paradigms and activities should not be perceived as replacements or competitors for COP and POP methods. Instead, they should be perceived as complementary paradigms that may strengthen the abilities of law enforcement organizations to accomplish the goals of deterring crime and maintaining societal order. Through the use of any paradigm, regardless of intelligence-led considerations, any law enforcement organization seeks to fulfill these goals. Intelligence-led policing is another resourceful paradigm that provides law enforcement organizations with a systematic method of accomplishing these goals.

Summary

This chapter considers five models of policing that have evolved in the United States for the past several decades. The COP strategy or philosophy has evolved into a very popular model of policing not only in the United States but throughout the entire world. Many countries such as the United Kingdom, Australia, Israel, and India have adopted the COP philosophy to prevent crime and disorder. Even though COP has been extremely popular, the traditional model of policing is still the predominant model of policing in the United States.

Regardless of the model or paradigm employed, the overall goal of any law enforcement organization involves deterring crime and maintaining societal order. Intelligence-led policing, COP, POP, and any of the other policing paradigms contribute toward successfully accomplishing these primary goals. Utilization of these paradigms often increases the effectiveness and efficiency of law enforcement organizations and enables them to better service their respective communities.

Regardless of the size of any law enforcement organization, it is not completely isolated as a functional entity. Within the law enforcement domain, the sharing of resources and information is critical to successfully contribute toward the safety of society. Therefore, fusion centers, task forces, and other collaborative constructs enable law enforcement organizations to improve their ability to address criminal issues.

Collaboration with the public and members of society is also an essential aspect of policing. Within some policing paradigms, the citizenry is a critical component for understanding the acts of crime that impact communities. Law enforcement organizations must maintain flourishing, positive communications with their served communities.

Discussion Questions

1. Describe the traditional style of policing, and explain why many believe that it is a failed strategy for crime prevention.
2. What is community policing, and why is it a good fit for counterterrorism?
3. Zero-tolerance policing has been described as "heavy-handed" policing. In your opinion, why would the police use aggressive tactics to enforce quality of life issues?
4. Explain the JTTF concept, and explain how it affects the information sharing process.
5. Discuss the advantages of local law enforcement utilizing fusion centers in its efforts to prevent crime and terrorism.

References

1. London Metropolitan Police Department. *History of the Metropolitan Police*. Retrieved from http://www.met.police.uk/history/definition.htm
2. Das, D., & Verma, A. (2003). *Police Mission Challenges and Responses*. Lanham, MD: Scarecrow Press.
3. Flynn, D. (1998). *Defining the 'Community' in Community Policing*. Washington, DC: Police Executive Research Forum.
4. Bureau of Justice Assistance (1994). *Understanding Community Policing: A Framework for Action*. Washington, DC: U.S. Department of Justice, Office of Justice Programs.
5. Skogan, W. (1995). Community Participation and Community Policing. Institute for Policy Research, Northwestern University. Retrieved from http://www.ipr.northwestern.edu/publications/policing_papers/caps4.pdf
6. Fleissner, D., & Heinzelmann, F. (1996). *Crime Prevention through Environmental Design and Community Policing*. Washington, DC: National Institute of Justice.
7. Ratcliffe, J. (2008). *Intelligence-led Policing*. Portland, OR: Willan Publishing.
8. Brown, L. (1989). *Community Policing: A Practical Guide for Police Officials*. Washington, DC: National Institute of Justice, U.S. Department of Justice.
9. Ibid.
10. Ibid.
11. Hubert, W., & Murphy, P. (1990). The evolving strategy of police: A minority view. In J. Brandl & D. Barlow (Eds.), *The Police in America* (pp. 26–44). Belmont, CA: Thomson Wadsworth.
12. Kelling, G., & Coles, C. (1996). *Fixing Broken Windows*. New York, NY: Simon and Schuster.
13. Hubert, W., & Murphy, P. (1990). The evolving strategy of police: A minority view. In J. Brandl & D. Barlow (Eds.), *The Police in America* (pp. 26–44). Belmont, CA: Thomson Wadsworth.
14. Eck, J., & Spelman, W. (1987). Who ya gonna call? The police as problem-busters. *Crime & Delinquency, 33*, 31–52.
15. Fleissner, D., & Heinzelmann, F. (1996). *Crime Prevention through Environmental Design and Community Policing* (p. 3). Washington, DC: National Institute of Justice.

16. Fyfe, J., Greene, J., Walsh, W., Wilson, O. W., & McLauren, R. (1997). *Police Administration* (5th ed.). New York, NY: McGraw-Hill.

17. Ibid, p. 551.

18. Stewart, G. (2007). *Community Policing Explained: A Guide for Local Governments* (p. 3). Washington, DC: Office of Community Oriented Policing Services, U.S. Department of Justice. NOTE: There are many definitions for community policing (COP). Perhaps the term is difficult to define since some people regard community policing as a police strategy while others consider COP to be a philosophy.

19. Fuller, J. (2005). *Criminal Justice Mainstream and Crosscurrents* (p. 228). Upper Saddle River, NJ: Pearson-Prentice Hall.

20. Scheider, M. (2008). *Community Policing Nugget: The Purpose of Partnerships* (p. 1). Retrieved from http://www.cops.usdoj.gov/html/dispatch/january_2008/nugget.html

21. Fuller, J. (2005). *Criminal Justice Mainstream and Crosscurrents* (p. 228). Upper Saddle River, NJ: Pearson-Prentice Hall.

22. Ibid.

23. Bureau of Justice Assistance (1994). *Understanding Community Policing: A Framework for Action* (p. 229). Washington, DC: U.S. Department of Justice, Office of Justice Programs.

24. Scheider, M. (2008). *Community Policing Nugget: The Purpose of Partnerships* (p. 1). Retrieved from http://www.cops.usdoj.gov/html/dispatch/january_2008/nugget.html

25. Vitto, G., Walsh, W., & Kunselman, J. (2004). Community policing: The middle manager's perspective. *Police Quarterly*, 6, 1–22.

26. Engel, R. (2002). Patrol officer supervision in the community policing era. *Journal of Criminal Justice, 30,* 51–64.

27. Scheider, M., & Chapman, R. *Community Policing and Terrorism*. Retrieved from http://www.homelandsecurity.org/journal/articles/Scheider-Chapman.html

28. Ibid, p. 1.

29. McGuire, E., & Gantley, M. (2009). Decentralization and geographical accountability. In E. McGuire, & C. Cole (Eds.), *Implementing Community Policing Lessons from 12 Agencies*. (pp. 35–43). Washington, DC: Office of Community Policing Services, U.S. Department of Justice.

30. Bureau of Justice Assistance (1994). *Understanding Community Policing: A Framework for Action*. Washington, DC: U.S. Department of Justice, Office of Justice Programs.

31. Goldstein, H. (1990). *Problem Oriented Policing*. New York, NY: McGraw-Hill.

32. Engel, R. (2002). Patrol officer supervision in the community policing era. *Journal of Criminal Justice, 30,* 51–64.

33. Snipes, J., & Katz, C. (2009). Information and analysis. In E. Maguire & C. Cole (Eds.), *Implementing Community Policing Lessons from 12 Agencies* (pp. 57–63). Washington, DC: Office of Community Oriented Policing Services, U.S. Department of Justice.

34. Sykes, G. (1997). *Community Policing Strategies: Sustaining Citizen Support and Leadership.* Conference held in Dallas, Texas. Co-hosted by Dallas Police Department and University of North Texas.

35. Trojanowicz, R. (1996). *Community Policing Guidelines for Police Chiefs.*

36. Peterson, G. (2004). *Broken Windows*. Retrieved from http://www.crosstalkonline.org/storage/issue-archives/2004/200411/200411-Petersen.pdf

37. Kelling, G., & Wilson, J. Q. (1982). Broken windows: The police and neighborhood safety. In J. Brandl & D. Barlow (Eds.), *The Police in America* (pp. 375–387). Belmont, CA: Thomson Wadsworth.

38. Ibid.

39. Ibid.

40. Archives of Giuliani, R. W. (1998). The *Next Phase of Quality of Life: Creating a More Civil City.* Retrieved from http://www.nyc.gov/html/rwg/html/98a/quality.html

41. Kelling, G., & Wilson, J. Q. (1982). Broken windows: The police and neighborhood safety. In J. Brandl & D. Barlow (Eds.), *The Police in America* (pp. 375–387). Belmont, CA: Thomson Wadsworth.

42. Clark, R. (2002). *Problem Oriented Policing, Case Studies*. National Criminal Justice Reference Services. (Document No. 193801)
43. Ibid.
44. Goldstein, H. (1990). *Problem Oriented Policing*. New York, NY: McGraw-Hill.
45. Ibid.
46. Cordner, G., & Biebel, E. (2003). Research for Practice: Problem Oriented Policing in Practice. *National Institute of Justice, U.S. Department of Justice*. Retrieved from http://www.ncjrs.gov/pdffiles/nij/grants/200518
47. Ibid.
48. Swanson, C., Territo, L., & Taylor, R. (2005). *Police Administration Structures, Processes, and Behavior*. Upper Saddle River, NJ: Pearson-Prentice Hall.
49. Peak, K. (2007). *Justice Administration Police, Courts, and Corrections Management* (5th ed., p. 74). Upper Saddle River, NJ: Pearson-Prentice Hall.
50. Eck, J., & Spelman, W. 1987. Who ya gonna call? The police as problem-busters. *Crime & Delinquency, 33*, 31–52.
51. Ortmeier, P. (2002). *Policing the Community: A Guide for Patrol Operations* (p. 98). Upper Saddle River, NJ: Pearson Prentice Hall.
52. Swanson, C., Territo, L., & Taylor, R. (2005). *Police Administration Structures, Processes, and Behavior*. Upper Saddle River, NJ: Pearson-Prentice Hall.
53. Peak, K. (2007). *Justice Administration Police, Courts, and Corrections Management* (5th ed.). Upper Saddle River, NJ: Pearson Prentice Hall.
54. Oliver, W. (2007). *Homeland Security for Policing* (P. 103). Upper Saddle River, NJ: Pearson Prentice Hall.
55. Walker, S., & Katz, C. (2005). *The Police in America: An Introduction* (5th ed.). New York, NY: McGraw-Hill.
56. Ibid.
57. Archives of Giuliani, R. W. (1998). *The Next Phase of Quality of Life: Creating a More Civil City*. Retrieved from http://www.nyc.gov/html/rwg/html/98a/quality.html
58. Bratton, W. (1996). Cutting crime and restoring order: What Americans can learn from New York's finest. *The Heritage Foundation*. Retrieved from http://www.heritage.org/research/lecture/hl573nbsp-cutting-crime-and-restoring-order
59. Dixon, D. (1999, 14–15 February). *Beyond Zero Tolerance*. Paper presented at the NSW Police Service Conference, University of Sydney, Australia.
60. Marshall, J. (1999). Zero tolerance policing. *Crime & Justice in South Australia, 9*, 1–14.
61. Ibid.
62. Fuller, J. (2005). *Criminal Justice Mainstream and Crosscurrents*. Upper Saddle River, NJ: Pearson-Prentice Hall.
63. Pollard, C. (1997). Zero tolerance: Short-term fix, long-term liability? In N. Dennis (Ed.), *Zero Tolerance: Policing a Free Society* (pp. 44–61). London, England: Institute of Economic Affairs.
64. Friedmann, R., & Cannon, W. (2007). Homeland security and community policing: Competing or complementing public safety policies. *Journal of Homeland Security and Emergency Management, 4*(4), 1–20.
65. Scheider, M., & Chapman, R. *Community Policing and Terrorism*. Retrieved from http://www.homelandsecurity.org/journal/articles/Scheider-Chapman.html
66. Ibid.
67. COPS (2002). *Protecting Your Community from Terrorism: Strategies for Local Law Enforcement. Vol.1: Improving Local-Federal Partnerships. Community Oriented Policing Services* (p. 32). Washington, DC: U.S. Department of Justice.
68. Ibid.
69. The Council of State Governments (2005). *The Impact of Terrorism on State Law Enforcement: Adjusting to New Roles and Changing Conditions* (p. 22). Washington, DC: National Institute of Justice, Office of Justice Programs.

70. U.S. Department of Justice (2005). *Intelligence-led Policing: The New Intelligence Architecture* (p. vii). Washington, DC: Bureau of Justice Assistance.

71. U.S. Department of Justice (2009). *Navigating Your Agency's Path to Intelligence-led Policing* (p. 3). Washington, DC: Bureau of Justice Assistance.

72. Guidetti, R., & Martinelli, T. Intelligence-led policing – A strategic framework. *Police Chief Magazine* (p. 1). Retrieved from http://www.policechiefmagazine.org/magazine/index.cfm?fuseaction=display&article_id=1918&issue_id=102009

73. Ibid.

74. Ibid.

75. Porter, R. (1997). Getting started in intelligence-led policing. In Smith, A., *Intelligence-led Policing: International Perspectives on Policing in the 21st Century*. Lawrenceville, NJ: International Association of Law Enforcement Intelligence Analysts.

76. U.S. Department of Justice. *Intelligence-led Policing: The Integration of Community Policing and Law Enforcement Intelligence*. Retrieved from http://www.cops.usdoj.gov/pdf/e09042536_Chapter_04.pdf

77. U.S. Department of Justice (2009). *Navigating your Agency's Path to Intelligence-led Policing*. Washington, DC: Bureau of Justice Assistance.

78. Ibid.

79. Carter, D. (2009). *Law Enforcement Intelligence: A Guide for State, Local, and Tribal Law Enforcement Agencies* (2nd ed.). Washington, DC: U.S. Department of Justice.

80. Staff writer (2012). Intelligence-led policing program a proactive approach. *Citrus County Chronicle*. Retrieved from http://www.chronicleonline.com/content/intelligence-led-policing-program-proactive-approach

81. Sullivan, E. (2011). New intelligence-led policing strategy strives to stop crime before it happens, not react after. *Tampa Bay Times*. Retrieved from http://www.tampabay.com/news/publicsafety/new-intelligence-led-policing-strategy-strives-to-stop-crime-before-it/1173615

82. Ibid.

83. Ibid.

84. Ibid.

85. Ibid.

86. Ibid.

87. Iwasinski, A. (2011). Intelligence-led policing targets one Oklahoma City neighborhood. *News 9*. Retrieved from http://www.news9.com/story/15171262/intelligent-policing-targets-one-oklahoma-city-neighborhood

88. Ibid.

89. City of Oklahoma City (2008). *Report of a Police Department Management and Manpower Analysis Project*. Retrieved from http://www.okc.gov/police/police_survey.PDF

90. Ibid.

91. Iwasinski, A. (2011). OKC police create intelligence led policing team. *News 9*. Retrieved from http://www.news9.com/story/15030130/okc-police-create-intelligence-led-policing-team?clienttype=printable

92. Carter, D. (2009). *Law Enforcement Intelligence: A Guide for State, Local, and Tribal Law Enforcement Agencies* (2nd ed.). Washington, DC: U.S. Department of Justice.

93. Staff writer (2012). IBM to help Rochester, Minn., police department fight crime. *KTTC News*. Retrieved from http://www.kttc.com/story/16612923/ibm-software-to-help-rochester-police-prevent-crime?clienttype=printable

94. Ibid.

95. Ibid.

96. Carter, D. (2009). *Law Enforcement Intelligence: A Guide for State, Local, and Tribal Law Enforcement Agencies* (2nd ed.). Washington, DC: U.S. Department of Justice.

Patrol Types and Specialized Assignments

9

The police department is not only an agency for crime control and law enforcement, but it is also an important community service agency, which the citizens of the community can come to value highly and from which they should expect prompt and efficient help.[1]

John P. Kenny

Learning Objectives

The objectives of this chapter are to

- Explain special organizational functions and roles
- Describe specialized policing among air, land, and maritime modalities
- Examine the supporting roles of specialized organizations
- Discuss the training of special units
- Cite the benefit of special organizations

Introduction

In his famous work, *Police Administration*, Chief O.W. Wilson divided police activities into what he termed "line" and "staff" functions. The staff functions pertaining to those administrative functions that are necessary to ensure that the day-to-day functions of the agency would continue uninterrupted. The line functions were those activities directly related to the enforcement responsibility of the agency. Wilson further divided line functions into two subcategories: primary and secondary functions. In Wilson's view, primary line functions pertained to activities related to officer patrol, and secondary functions included activities like investigations.[2]

Municipal police patrol is the backbone of United States law enforcement and provides basic crime prevention efforts, law enforcement services, and service assistance to the public. However, contemporary law enforcement requires a variety of specialized and highly technical services that often cannot be effectively delivered by the patrol officer; therefore, many agencies are turning to specialization within their ranks to address the deficiencies and maximize their effectiveness. Specialization allows agencies to direct resources into specific areas to focus on particular problems. Although primarily found at the local level, specialized law enforcement units may also be found at the state and federal levels.

Establishing special units that possess critical expertise and experience has become a priority in many larger departments. These departments normally have the capacity to staff, train, fund, and acquire equipment for an array of specialized units. In smaller departments with limited budgets and equipment, the patrol officer may be required to perform any number of specialized services. In some cases, smaller departments may also seek to secure some specialized services support from state or federal agencies on an as-needed basis.

The increasing use of specialization in law enforcement has both advantages and disadvantages. For many agencies, the positive aspects of specialization offset any disadvantages. Some of the advantages of specialization include the following:

- Increased efficiency
- Better management of key resources
- Very specific task assignments
- Development of expertise
- Esprit de corps
- Flexible work schedules
- Prestige

Some of the disadvantages of specialized units include the following:

- Increased organizational complexity
- Increased coordination and communication requirements
- Increased disconnection from other organizational units
- Reduced focus on overall organizational goals
- Loss of experienced patrol officers to specialized units may have a detrimental effect on the quality of patrol officers remaining in the patrol

The growth of specialized units will likely continue to increase in the future. As more aspects of law enforcement come to demand unique knowledge, skills, and equipment, there will be a commensurate need for specialized units to address those new requirements. This chapter explores various aspects, including duties and responsibilities, of the specialized units commonly found in contemporary police agencies across the United States.

The specialized units presented in this chapter include the following: aviation, bicycle patrol, canine, crime scene investigation, criminal investigations, explosive ordnance (bomb squad), gangs, intelligence, internal affairs, marine patrol, motorcycle, mounted patrol, organized crime/narcotics, and special weapons and tactics (SWAT). Other types of specialized units may also be found within police departments across the United States. In fact, each department determines their specialized needs on the basis of the particular requirements of their jurisdictions and budgetary constraints.

Types of Patrol

Most citizens who come in contact with law enforcement personnel encounter them while they are on patrol. Patrol is, and is intended to be, the most visible element of a law enforcement agency. Especially for local and state-level law enforcement, it is hoped that the clearly marked vehicles patrolling a neighborhood provide the law-abiding citizens with a feeling of security while, at the same time, they deter the potential offender from committing a crime. Patrol dates back to the early period of community enforcement. Before police cruised city streets in patrol cars, officers walked a beat and knew the people on that beat, but foot and automobile are not the only means officers use to patrol their assigned areas.

Figure 9.1 The police officer, walking a beat, is one of the best ways to strengthen department ties with the community. (Courtesy of the City of Woodstock, IL. Retrieved from http://www.woodstockil.gov/index.asp?Type=B_LIST&SEC={B0A473E0-C3CA-4688-A5C8-71D96031CC16}.)

Foot Patrol

It is hard to imagine an earlier form of law enforcement patrol than foot patrol. Over the centuries, night and day watchmen were expected to walk the streets of their communities, alert to dangers, and prepare to raise a cry of alarm. Well into the early twentieth century, cities relied on officers patrolling their beats on foot, often remaining in contact with police headquarters by some remarkably creative means.

In the 1980s, interest in foot patrol increased in many cities in the nation. By the 1990s, foot patrol was considered an important element in community policing. Today, the primary use of foot patrol is limited. Placing an officer on foot patrol limits the area he or she can serve. Although foot patrol is considered costly, it is not without advocates. Research in Philadelphia in 2009 showed that foot patrols reduced violent crime by 23% in high-density cities with a large mix of commercial and residential buildings.[3] One of the major benefits resulting from foot patrol are increased communication, understanding, and cooperation between law enforcement personal and the public (Figure 9.1).

Automobile Patrol

Early in the century, some departments began acquiring automobiles, motorcycles, and bicycles for limited patrol and emergency response needs. Many sources suggest the first

Figure 9.2 The police car has redefined the way law enforcement provides its services. (Courtesy of the State of Florida. Retrieved from http://www.flhsmv.gov/fhp/misc/vehequip/images/Camaro1.jpg.)

use of an automobile in police service in the United States occurred in Akron, Ohio, in 1899 when an electric car patrolled the streets of the city. Other cities soon followed. At least as early as 1903, St. Louis placed into service a "St. Louis," a locally manufactured automobile.

Over the next century, the use of the automobile as transportation for officers on patrol has revolutionized law enforcement. The automobile offers the greatest mobility, widest coverage, and most flexibility of any patrol method. Patrol cars serve many purposes. Patrol vehicles provide the officer not only with a means of transportation, but also serve as a mobile office; transport additional officers, witnesses, and suspects as necessary; transport special equipment, including communication equipment and tactical weapons; provide cover during gun battles; and act as barricades, emergency warning devices, and temporary jails. Officers spend hours in their patrol cars.

Patrol cars are meant to be highly visible. They are usually marked with the department's reflective logo and are equipped with some sort of emergency lighting system. Some departments use rotating halogen lights, whereas others prefer flashing strobes. Many agencies use a combination of both (Figure 9.2).

Motorcycle Patrol

The police motorcycle officer has been an icon in the United States law enforcement for more than a half century. Chief August Vollmer of the Berkeley Police Department in California is credited with organizing the first official police motorcycle patrol in the United States in 1911.[4] However, several police departments used motorcycles before 1911. Harley-Davidson delivered its first police motorcycle to the Detroit Police Department in 1908.[5] In 1909, the Pittsburgh Police Department acquired and put into service five motorcycles.[6]

In the 1920s, state police forces were being established to protect rural areas from crime and to enforce prohibition. The police motorcycle was often selected as the vehicle of choice for that assignment. In 1921, the Washington State Troopers were established with six police motorcycles. Later, in Louisiana, a force of 16 police motorcycle officers patrolled the entire state.[5] Police administrators recognized the value and tactical advantages of police motorcycles early, and over the last several decades, police motorcycle use has spread throughout the United States.

Today, the primary duties of police motorcycle units are traffic-related duties such as enforcement, high congestion traffic control, escorts (parades, funerals, VIP motorcades, etc.), and special event traffic control. The major advantages of police motorcycle use include the following:

- Ability to go many places where police cars cannot
- Ability to maneuver through traffic gridlock with ease
- Ability to respond to dispatched patrol calls as primary officers or backup
- Rapid response (due to mobility) to the scene of high priority calls such as bank alarms, robberies, fires, and shooting calls

Motorcycles also have their disadvantages. Some of the major disadvantages include the following:

- Cannot be used to transport prisoners
- Have limited storage space
- Can be very uncomfortable over long periods
- Offer the rider little or no protection in an accident
- Provide less protection for officers during armed assaults than a police car
- Require restricted use during inclement weather

After weighing the pros and cons, many police agencies continue to find value in the use of motorcycles. Training to become a motorcycle officer is comprehensive and demanding. In most agencies, officers must successfully complete a one- to three-week basic operator's course. In addition, most motorcycle officers are required to receive 8 hours of motorcycle recertification training quarterly. Typical police motorcycle training courses include a closed stress/obstacle course at high and low speeds, braking exercises, and a cross-country course, all designed to force the officer to perform at the highest possible level. Riding a police motorcycle can be a hazardous duty, and the comprehensive training is intended to replicate the frequent split-second situations and adverse street conditions that can cause accidents (Figure 9.3).[7]

Bicycle Patrol

The evolution of police bicycle patrols in the United States is not clearly established. However, as early as 1869, an Illinois sheriff reportedly acquired "boneshaker" bicycles for himself and his deputies. The bicycles were referred to as boneshakers because they were heavy (made of iron and wood) and uncomfortable to ride. The bicycles were also overpriced due to patent license fees. The Illinois experiment was apparently short-lived.[8]

Figure 9.3 Through not used as widely as automobiles, motorcycles continue to play a major role in the enforcement operations of many departments. (Courtesy of the State of Indiana. Retrieved from http://www.in.gov/isp/2626.htm.)

In the late 1880s, the Boston Park Commission Police patrolled on high wheel bicycles. The Newark (NJ) Police Department created a bicycle squad in 1888. In 1892, Orange, New Jersey officers were using modern safety bicycles for patrol and tandem bicycles for quick response to outbreaks and disturbances. By 1894, the beginning of widespread use of bicycles for police patrol in the United States and around the world had begun. In 1894, police departments in Philadelphia, Brooklyn, Cincinnati, and Chicago were using bicycles for patrol.[9]

In 1895, the New York Police Department (NYPD) began its experiment in police bicycle patrol with two bicycle police officers. Within a few months, noting that bicycles increased efficiency and were effective in patrolling and controlling "scorchers" (speeders on bicycles) and runaway horses, a recommendation was made to expand the bicycle squad and make it permanent. Police Commissioner Theodore Roosevelt, who later became the President of the United States, and was a cyclist himself, approved the idea. The NYPD bicycle squad was very successful. In its first year of operation, the 29-member NYPD Bicycle Squad made 1366 arrests.[9]

Although highly effective, police bicycle squads were eventually replaced with motorized vehicles (motorcycles and automobiles). The nature of police work and modes of transportation underwent dramatic changes by the 1920s. Faster response times were required. The police had to deal with the implications of prohibition and a new breed of criminals who used cars capable of increasingly faster speeds to evade the police. For a time, the police patrol bicycle simply became obsolete.

However, since the early 1960s, the use of police bicycle patrols has seen widespread resurgence because of the increased effectiveness of bicycle patrols in highly populated areas. Today, police bicycle patrols have become common again in the era of community policing and increasing crime. Bicycle patrol units are increasingly found in small and large law enforcement agencies as well as on many college and university campuses throughout the United States.

Today's bicycle patrol officers are generally provided training in advanced riding skills, defensive and offensive riding strategies, and general bike maintenance. Officers most often ride mountain bikes. The mountain bikes provide a reliable and safe mode of transportation.

Figure 9.4 First used by police departments in the 1800s, the bicycle has regained a degree of popularity in many departments that have found it provides a unique transportation capability for their officers. (Courtesy of the City of Grapevine, TX. Retrieved from http://www.grapevinetexas .gov/IndividualDepartments/Police/Divisions/UniformOperations.aspx.)

The bicycles are heavy-duty and can withstand being ridden day after day, often over curbs or downstairs, and during inclement weather. Modern police patrol bicycles are equipped with headlamps, reflectors, back racks, and carrying cases. Officers wear safety equipment including headgear. In addition, bicycle officers often wear special uniforms with shorts during the warm seasons and dark fatigue trousers during the cooler seasons (Figure 9.4).

Advantages of police bicycle patrols include the following:[9]

- A police cyclist is often able to travel at least twice as fast as a walking or running officer while expending less energy.
- A bicycle can reach areas inaccessible by motorized vehicles such as trails, difficult terrain, side yards, and alleys.
- Bicycles can also cross traffic gridlock more easily and move more rapidly through large crowds.
- Bicycles are quiet and often go unnoticed, making it easier for officers to observe crimes and apprehend criminals.
- Police cyclists are more approachable to members of the community than officers confined to vehicles, which improves interaction with the public.
- The initial costs and subsequent maintenance of a bicycle are substantially less than those of a patrol car.

Aviation

The NYPD Aviation Unit takes credit for being the oldest airborne law enforcement unit in the world. It was created primarily to combat an increasing menace of reckless pilots known as "barnstormers" who carried paying passengers or performed impromptu air shows over the city.[10] In 1929, the NYPD ended its voluntary aviation unit, which was created in 1918, and replaced it with the first full-time Air Service Division (ASD) with its own aircraft. The unit's first aircraft was a three-seat Loening Commuter Amphibian purchased with funds donated by famed World War I flying ace Rodman Wanamaker. One of the ASD's first notable acts was the rescue of two swimmers who had been carried away by the tide. The water was too rough for landing, so the copilot leaped from the aircraft into the water and both swimmers were towed to shore. The ASD acquired its first helicopter in 1948.[11]

In 1925, the Los Angeles County Sheriff's Department organized a Reserve Aero Squadron, the first of its kind. Utilizing volunteer aviators and aircraft on an "on-call" basis, the effort was highly successful. The volunteers played such an important role in the relief after the earthquake of 1933 that the Sheriff's Department soon obtained an aircraft and established a full-time Aero Detail. In 1955, the Los Angeles County Sheriff's Department began using helicopters throughout its 3200 square miles of responsibility. From the beginning, the helicopters served such vital functions as rescue, transportation, surveillance, command and control, and patrol.

Over the years, airplanes and helicopters have supplemented law enforcement efforts in conjunction with various other types of police units on the ground, in both emergency and nonemergency missions. In 2007, 88% of the police aviation units in the United States had helicopters and 55% of them used airplanes.[12]

Police aviation unit emergency assignments include such activities as

- Searching for suspects
- Search and rescue operations
- Vehicle pursuits
- Aerial rescues
- Medical evacuations ("medevacs")
- Drug interdictions
- Crowd control
- Airborne use of force
- Responding to calls in progress
- Firefighting missions

Nonemergency police aviation roles include the following:

- Prisoner transport
- Administrative transport of personnel/equipment
- Aerial photos/videos for planning and court purposes

Other advantages of police aviation include the ability to cover otherwise impassable areas, removal of officers from dangers on the ground, and a highly visible crime deterrent. Disadvantages of police aviation units include the expense to obtain and operate the aircrafts and noise complaints. Additionally, there is the perception by some that the units are intrusive and create safety issues.

Today, aviation units are found in law enforcement agencies on the local, state, and federal levels, providing a wide range of community services and officer support (Figure 9.5).

Marine Patrol

There are over 25,000 miles of navigable inland waterways in the United States and literally thousands of miles of Pacific, Atlantic, and Gulf coastlines. These waterways and coastlines

Figure 9.5 The Helicopter has proven to be a great asset to local, state, and federal agencies. (Courtesy of the City of Nashville, TN. Retrieved from http://www.police.nashville.gov/bureaus/ fieldops/aviation.asp.)

affect police activities in those jurisdictions and, thereby, create the need for the police to maintain marine patrol units.[13] The basic purpose of marine police units is to conduct law enforcement patrols on the public waters including lakes, ponds, rivers, and jurisdictional tidal waters and enforce marine laws and regulations.

Prior to the terrorist attacks on September 11, 2001, police marine units in the United States were typically used for emergency response capability rather than criminal enforcement action. Aside from drug smugglers, the vast majority of criminals whom police normally encountered rarely used waterways as a mode of transportation. However, twenty-first century terrorism exposed a very large and relatively unprotected area of travel and access to those who might desire to smuggle more than illegal drugs. Today, in addition to more traditional crime concerns, marine law enforcement officers are concerned about waterways being used to smuggle illegal weapons, bombs, and other weapons used by domestic and international terrorists.

Although it is primarily the responsibility of the United States Coast Guard to defend and protect the coastlines and waterways of the United States, the events on 9/11 highlighted the need for more local and state police involvement in marine law enforcement and homeland security (Figure 9.6). Typical day-to-day activities of marine patrols include the following:

- Patrol the public waterways and enforce marine laws and regulations within the agency's jurisdiction
- Board and inspect private and commercial boats for compliance with federal and state commercial vessel laws and regulations, licenses, and permits

Figure 9.6 Marine patrols. (Courtesy of the City of Key Biscayne, FL. Retrieved from http://www.keybiscayne.fl.gov/index.php?submenu=Police&src=gendocs&link=Marine_Patrol&category=Police.)

- Issue warnings, take offense reports, conduct investigations, and write investigative and other reports related to offenses, including sketches, citations, affidavits, and complaints
- Make arrests, work closely with the prosecutor in case preparation, and testify in court as needed
- Respond to and investigate boating accidents and administer first aid to accident victims
- Perform search and rescue missions for lost or distressed mariners
- Assist in traffic control at major waterborne events

Mounted and Equine Patrols

It is unknown when the first horse was used in a police action; however, it is likely that the concept evolved from military antecedents. In 1758, London Bow Street Chief Magistrate Sir John Fielding (half-brother and successor to retired Chief Magistrate Sir Henry Fielding) proposed the establishment of a mounted unit consisting of two riders and two horses to be assigned to the Bow Street Runners. By the time the plan was fully implemented in 1763, the size of the unit had increased to eight. The mission of the mounted unit was crime prevention and criminal apprehension along the roadways leading to London.[14]

By 1805, a more permanent and larger Bow Street Horse Patrol was created with over 50 men and animals, and their duties had expanded to "patrolling main roads up to 20 miles distant of London." By the early 1840s, the mounted unit was found to be highly successful and it became an intrinsic part of the London Metropolitan Police. The mounted officers dressed in red waistcoats and were affectionately known as "Robin Redbreasts." As social disorder and riots increased in London during the nineteenth century, the mounted unit's activities expanded to include crowd control.[14] The London Metropolitan Police maintains a mounted unit today.

In the United States, early mounted police units included the Texas Rangers, which were formally organized during the Texas revolution in 1835. The rangers were created as an auxiliary military unit, but their primary task was to patrol frontier areas of the region. Other early United States mounted units included the Arizona Rangers in 1901 and the New Mexico Mounted Police in 1905.[14]

Many municipal police departments in the United States, using the English model, also established mounted units. The NYPD was the first in 1871. The NYPD mounted unit's primary purpose was to regulate traffic and pursue speeders and reckless drivers. Mounted units followed in San Francisco in 1874 and in Boston in 1883. Although documented history is limited on this subject, it is likely that nearly every police department in the nation used horses at one time or another.[15]

At the federal level, the United States Park Police Horse Mounted Unit is one of the oldest established and continuously operated police equestrian units in the nation. It was established in 1934 with one horse rented from a local stable. As the value of the mounted patrol was proven, the unit was expanded and used to provide police and park services in the Washington Metropolitan Area as well as in New York and San Francisco.[16]

By the 1920s, the use of horses had given way to automobiles, and the number of mounted units began to decline. Police cars could carry more supplies, equipment, and arms while offering protection to officers from the elements. By the start of World War II, the number of police mounted units in the United States had dropped to about 40.[15]

In the 1960s and 1970s, the requirements of effective crowd control methods and high visibility police presence brought renewed interest in and the creation of police mounted units across the nation. Experience showed that mounted units could provide law enforcement with a positive method of crime control and reduction.[17] There are few current statistics on police mounted units. A 1995 survey indicated that there were between 100 and 120 mounted units in the United States, and it appeared that the number of mounted units in the United States was probably increasing.[14]

Clearly, there are some distinct advantages and disadvantages associated with the use of police mounted units. Police mounted patrol limitations include the following:

- Exposure to inclement weather
- Lack of speed over long distances
- Vulnerability of the horse
- Limited carrying capacity
- Inability to dismount and leave horses unattended
- Street "litter"

The street "litter" problem can be eliminated by the use of a horse manure catcher, which is commonly referred to as "diaper" or "bun-bag." Mounted units have proven beneficial where used. Those benefits include the following:

- Mounted police units offer a high visibility police presence. Citizens have a clear view of the rider from considerable distances, and mounted officers have an increased level of visibility to both the criminal element and the community at large.

- They are very effective in riot control and crowd management. In fact, it is generally agreed that an officer on horseback is equal to 10 people on foot in crowd management.
- A horse's size creates an intimidation factor that makes it effective in law enforcement situations.
- From a community relations aspect, officers on horseback offer an exceptional opportunity to interact positively with the people on the street. Persons, especially children, seem naturally attracted to horses.
- Mounted units are particularly effective in patrolling parks, recreation areas, and national borders. In addition, they are also adept at patrolling high crime zones such as busy downtown areas and crowded shopping malls.
- Officers on horseback are valuable in search and rescue efforts in remote areas.
- Mounted units can also operate in close places when required.
- Mounted units reduce police vehicle use, thereby reducing fuel costs and pollutants.
- Officers on horseback offer a touch of pageantry to parades, funerals, and other special events.

Most departments require that mounted unit officers have an unblemished record, and the officers' personalities should be such that they are able to further the department's community relation goals while enforcing the law. Physical guidelines often recommend heights ranging from 5 feet 6 inches to 6 feet 5 inches and weights ranging from 140 to 225 pounds, with about 180 pounds being the optimum. However, with the acceptance of women riders, these guidelines are changing.[15]

Specialized training is required for mounted officers. Before being assigned to any field duties, mounted officers are required to undergo a grueling 4- to 10-week equestrian training program. The local department conducts most mounted unit training, but there are several prominent training centers that offer assistance, located in Chicago, St. Louis, and Detroit, that are under the auspices of the National Park Service.[15] The training covers topics such as basic and advanced equitation skills, tactics, arrest procedures, crowd control tactics, self-defense, equine physiology and psychology, and other equestrian duties a mounted officer could be assigned.

Horses of all breeds are used in police mounted units; however, "grade" (uncertain pedigree) horses are the most common. Geldings are used almost exclusively, but one finds an occasional mare and, very rarely, a stallion. An ideal horse should stand from 15 hands (60 inches) to 16 hands (68 inches) and weigh from 1000 to 1300 pounds. At the time of procurement, horses should be between 2 and 20 years old; most are between 10 and 12 years old. Mounted unit horses are expected to serve from 9 to 13 years. When the horses become unsuited for continued service, they are retired, given away, sold, traded, or euthanatized (Figure 9.7).[15]

Specialized Assignments

Canine

There are ancient accounts of canines protecting their masters and being involved in detective work. However, the first recorded organized police use of canines to patrol in cities for civic protection was in Saint-Malo, France, in the early fourteenth century. In 1899, Ghent,

Figure 9.7 Mounted units have proven beneficial to many agencies. (Courtesy of the Bethlehem, PA Mounted Police. Retrieved from http://www.bethlehem-pa.gov/about/imagegallery/mountedpolice .htm.)

Belgium, became the first European city to establish a police dog training school. Ghent constables used canines to patrol the streets between 10 p.m. and 6 a.m. By 1906, Ghent authorities reported that night crime had all but disappeared. Other European cities followed Ghent's lead. By 1910, more than 600 towns in Germany alone had canine patrols.[18]

Police canines are often referred to as "K-9s," which is a common military/police designation for a dog-assisted unit or team. One of the earliest recorded instances of canine use for police and security purposes in the United States occurred just after the Revolutionary War in 1793. A dog named Nero was acquired for $3.00 by the U.S. Mint in Philadelphia to patrol the enclosed yard overnight along with night guards. Nero was reported to be a "savage brute" and assumed full responsibility for night security in the absence of the night guards.[18]

In 1907, the first United States police department canine program was established in South Orange, New Jersey. A few months later, the NYPD acquired five German Shepherds from Belgium for evaluation. As the canines proved their worth in Orange and New York, numerous other municipal police departments and state law enforcement agencies followed with the creation of dog units.[18] In addition, during World War II, canines were used extensively by the military for scout, sentry (patrol), messenger, and mine detection duties.

Today, the role of the police canine has vastly expanded and become a major asset to law enforcement. Because of their intelligence and formidable powers of smell and hearing, canines are now used as part of a wider strategy in crime prevention and detection. Police canines fall into one of two categories: general-purpose or specialist.

General-purpose canines are generalists in terms of the police roles they play, and they must possess multiple abilities and be very sturdy and intelligent. A specialist canine must possess acute and discriminating scenting powers, because their mission is to exclusively sniff for drugs, explosives, corpses, and traces of petroleum-based substances. It is estimated that there are about 3000 U.S. police agencies using approximately 14,000 canine teams. About 7000 of those are general-purpose dogs used in patrol and the others are used in specialist roles.[18]

Duties of a contemporary police K-9 unit might include any of the following:

- Searching large areas (buildings and open fields) when suspects have eluded police (Police K-9s are trained to intimidate and subdue suspects rather than severely injure or kill.)[19]
- Tracking lost persons
- Crowd control during riots, demonstrations, athletic events, or other special events
- Locating dead bodies (buried or on the surface)
- Detecting illegal drugs, concealed explosives, accelerants, or weapons

Police K-9s perform these and other activities faster, safer, with less labor, and more accurately than officers can alone.[20] In addition, general-purpose police K-9s are trained to defend their handlers against attack.

Police dogs and their handlers attend intensive courses for training, so that they can work together. Training courses vary in length according to the training specialization. Canine handler training generally includes handling techniques, commands, grooming, kennel management, diseases, health, and laws relating to police dogs.

Most of the canine legal issues revolve around the Fourth Amendment right to be free from unreasonable searches and seizures and use of force. In *U.S. v. Place* (1983), the U.S. Supreme Court held that exposure of luggage to a canine sniff in a public area did not constitute a "search" under the Fourth Amendment.[21] The courts have also repeatedly ruled that police dogs are considered reasonable force, not deadly force.[22]

Although various canine breeds are used in police work, the German Shepherd is the most commonly used general-purpose police dog. The combination of their size, controllable aggression, stamina, trainability, and will to work make them an ideal breed. However, numerous other breeds such as Rottweiler, Doberman, and Giant Schnauzer are effectively used for other specialized functions. The average length of service for a police canine is about 7 years.[20] Because police dogs and their handlers work as a team, the dogs often live with their handler's family. Living with the handler's family helps the K-9 to stay friendly and social (Figure 9.8).[19]

Crime Scene Investigation

Crime scene investigation (CSI) units are highly technical units that are responsible for professional processing of crime scenes. The basic goals of CSI units are to document all facets of a crime scene, thereby providing a solid framework for the reconstruction of the crime. CSI units respond to all major crime scenes such as homicides, sexual assaults, kidnappings, and officer-involved shootings to process and document the scenes.

Advances in CSI technologies and, in particular, deoxyribonucleic acid (DNA) analysis have led to dramatic changes in the kinds of evidence collected and how crimes are solved. CSI specialists (crime scene technicians, investigators, or criminalists) work in conjunction with other police officers and detectives on CSIs. CSI units' support allows other responding investigative units to focus their efforts on interviewing involved complainants, witnesses, and victims and to track down known potential leads in a case without undue delay.

Figure 9.8 K-9 units have become common in agencies across the nation. (Courtesy of the State of Massachusetts. Retrieved from http://www.mass.gov/?pageID=eopsterminal&L=5&L0=Hom e&L1=Public+Safety+Agencies&L2=Massachusetts+State+Police&L3=Archived+Massachus etts+State+Police+Stories+of+Interest&L4=Archives+-+MSP+Stories+2006&sid=Eeops&b=term inal content&f=msp_feature_2006_january_msp_feature_tracking_holly&csid=Eeops.)

Using the latest CSI technologies, CSI specialists are directly involved in an array of crime scene activities that may include the following:

- Locating, photographing, documenting, marking, and collecting various types of physical (including biological and digital/electronic) evidence
- Ensuring the chain of custody of evidence is maintained
- Associating persons to the scene of the crime through fingerprints, shoe impressions, hairs, fibers, body fluids, or other evidence
- Taking accurate measurements of the crime scene
- Completing detailed sketches of the crime scene
- Reconstructing the crime scene by taking photographs and video of the crime scene and its surrounding areas

CSI specialists may also be involved in various types of "in-office" examinations, which could not be readily performed at the crime scene, and a variety of other administrative duties. For example, CSI specialists may be involved in requesting further forensic examinations of evidence from other laboratories as well as packaging and shipping of the evidence. CSI specialists may also enter suspect latent fingerprints found at a crime scene into an Automated Fingerprint Identification System (AFIS) to determine any possible matches. The CSI specialist also provides expert court testimony when required.

In recent years, because of the inaccurate portrayal of crime scene technologies in the *CSI* television series and movies, much of the public has developed an unreasonable expectation that most crimes can be solved quickly using sophisticated CSI technologies.

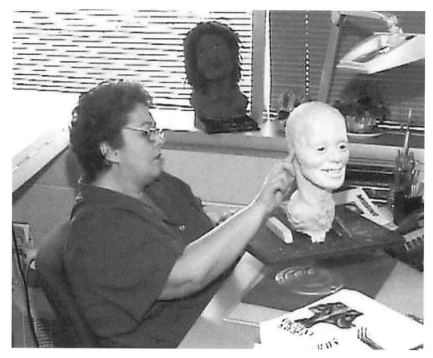

Figure 9.9 Criminal Investigation contains elements of both art and science. Here, attempts are being made to reconstruct facial features on a human skull in support of a homicide investigation. (Courtesy of the State of Georgia. Retrieved from http://www.georgia.gov/00/channel_modifieddate/0,2096,67862954_88103923,00.html.)

This phenomenon is referred to as the "CSI effect." Although much of the CSI technology seen on television is real, the application of the technology is often presented in an unrealistic way. For example, in many of the television programs and movies, a computer instantly matches fingerprints found at a crime scene to those in its database or DNA testing on a show is instant. In reality, it may take days, weeks, or even months for scientists to perform detailed work to complete these tasks or other sophisticated forensic examinations.[23]

The CSI effect phenomenon has now reached courtrooms and classrooms. Universities have seen a dramatic increase in interest in forensic science programs. There are now at least 90 forensic science programs in universities across the nation, and acceptance into some of the graduate programs has become highly competitive. However, it is thought that many students also enter the programs with unreasonable expectations. In addition, prosecutors are facing greater pressure from juries to present more sophisticated forensic evidence in the courtroom. In fact, many jurors expect to see DNA or other scientific evidence in nearly every case. The CSI effect will likely continue to present a formidable challenge to CSI specialists and prosecutors in the future (Figure 9.9).[23]

Criminal Investigations

In 1748, Chief Magistrate Henry Fielding created the first detective unit, the Bow Street Runners, in London, England. The first federal criminal investigators in the United States were agents of the Revenue Cutter Service, an organization authorized by the first Congress in 1790 to combat smuggling. In 1846, detectives were used by the Boston Police

Department and, by 1880, by the NYPD. Today, about 10%–15% of a typical municipal police department consists of detectives.[24] In addition, various types of criminal investigators are found at the county, state, and federal level.

Much like the phenomenon surrounding the public's perception of CSI, there is a mystique associated with the field of criminal investigations. For the public, the term criminal investigations often conjures up the image of "the detective"—the tenacious officer who single-handedly digs out evidence, collects tips from informants, identifies the criminals, tracks them down, and brings them immediately to justice. Like the CSI effect, the mystique surrounding criminal investigations is likely the result of fictional detective stories and the numerous television dramas and feature films that glamorize the detective.

The job of a real-life detective is actually far from glamorous, and most television and movies involving police detectives are far from reality. In fact, television programs and movies distort an assortment of facts surrounding detective work, and they are not a reliable source of facts related to detective work. However, being a detective can actually be interesting and challenging work and, among police professionals, has long been considered a coveted assignment.

In large departments, detectives usually specialize in investigating one type of violation. Detectives are generally assigned multiple cases on a rotating basis and are required to work on those cases until an arrest is made or until the case is dropped. Cases may take months or even years to yield an arrest and may generate an enormous amount of paperwork in the form of investigative and prosecutorial reports. Television programs most often omit these types of grueling details about detective work, because they are not considered exciting enough for viewers.

In major police agencies, criminal investigation divisions are often organized into two major types of crime: violent crimes against persons (such as homicide, rape, sexual assault, and robbery) and crimes against property (such as larcenies, fraud, burglaries, and auto theft). Investigations range from simple to complex and may involve misdemeanors or felonies. In some small departments, where there is no criminal investigations division, the patrol officer may also be required to perform the basic investigative functions. In cases involving major crimes, smaller agencies often request and receive assistance from a county or state investigative unit.

Investigative units are generally staffed with highly talented, knowledgeable, and skilled officers who have had significant experience as patrol officers. Among many other desirable personal characteristics, investigators should be objective, creative, patient, ethical, and tenacious. In addition, investigators must be able to react quickly in response to rapidly changing situations and conditions. Contrary to some popular crime fiction, a police detective is required to work within the boundaries of the law and have the ability to work effectively with the public, other police personnel, and the prosecutor's office.

Duties of criminal investigators vary from agency to agency; however, the following is a list of duties and responsibilities generally associated with criminal investigators:

- Taking citizen complaints about possible criminal activity, obtaining summaries of incidents from officers in charge at crime scenes, or analyzing preliminary investigative reports to determine what additional investigative work is required
- Examining crime scenes or working closely with crime scene investigators to thoroughly identify and collect all evidence
- Taking crime scene photographs and sketching crime scenes

- Properly handling and safeguarding evidence and maintaining the chain of custody
- Using recognized investigative methods and techniques including surveillance, undercover, informants, and other criminal detection methods and techniques to investigate various types of criminal violations
- Identifying and locating witnesses and suspects
- Interviewing and taking oral, written, or recorded statements from complainants, witnesses, and suspects
- Examining records and governmental agency files to find identifying data about suspects such as personal history, arrest history, and outstanding warrants
- Writing affidavits for search and arrest warrants, reports of investigation, and prosecutorial reports
- Executing search warrants
- Serving grand jury or trial court subpoenas
- Arresting and booking suspects
- Preparing and submitting evidence to crime laboratories for examination
- Periodically discussing ongoing criminal cases with the prosecutor
- Testifying before a grand jury or in court
- Disposing of evidence after final judicial action in a case

Explosive Ordnance Disposal (Bomb Squad)

The first municipal police bomb squad in the United States was created by the NYPD. Its primary mission was to deal with bombs used by an organized crime faction in Italian neighborhoods to intimidate immigrant merchants and residents. The NYPD unit celebrated its 100th anniversary in 2003.[25] Because of heightened international terrorism, explosive ordnance units, commonly referred to as bomb squads, have become extremely important to law enforcement.

Both the military and the police have made many advances in bomb squad technology in the last 100 years. The primitive methods and techniques used by early bomb squads have evolved into sophisticated technologies, such as robotics, bomb suits, x-ray equipment, canines, self-contained breathing apparatuses, personal protective equipment, and total containment vessels, allowing technicians to more effectively and safely detect, deactivate, and render safe various types of explosive devices.

Bomb technicians typically respond to all reports involving a possible explosive device. Some of the major responsibilities of an explosive ordnance unit include the following:[26]

- Investigating suspicious packages or devices, bomb threats, or actual bombings
- Locating and deactivating explosive devices
- Disposing of found explosive materials
- Collecting and preserving evidence at bombing scenes
- Conducting post-blast CSIs
- Providing training programs on bomb threat awareness, safety, and explosive device identification
- Providing technical support to special operations such as conducting bomb searches for dignitary protection details

Figure 9.10 EOD unit equipped for action. (From Jernigan, D., 2006, *The FBI Law Enforcement Bulletin*. Retrieved from http://www2.fbi.gov/publications/leb/2006/august2006/aug2006leb .htm.)

Bomb technicians are usually experienced law enforcement officers who undergo intensive training at the Hazardous Devices School, a Federal Bureau of Investigation (FBI)/U.S. Army facility at Redstone Arsenal in Huntsville, Alabama. The course is designed to familiarize officers with the tools and equipment used in this highly specialized field and to provide the officers with the necessary knowledge and skills required to become a bomb technician. Classes in the training program cover such topics as how to recognize, assess, and render safe hazardous devices; decontamination and disposal procedures; basic electronics; fragment analysis; post-blast investigation; protective equipment; and state-of-the-art robotics. In addition, trainees learn about counterterrorism strategies such as how to respond to suicide attacks, large vehicle bombs, weapons of mass destruction, and mortar attacks (Figure 9.10).[27]

Gang Investigations

Contrary to public perception, gangs have been in existence for centuries. The word "thug" dates back to thirteenth century India and refers to roaming gangs of criminals (Thugz).[28] In the United States, a semblance of street gangs emerged on the East Coast after the Revolutionary War around 1793; however, these gangs appeared to involve only youth fighting over local "turf." Serious gang activity appeared in New York City around 1820 in the wake of increased immigration.[29] Other heavily populated areas of the United States such as Los Angeles and Chicago also had early street gang activity.

Since the early nineteenth century, gang activity has spread to all regions of the United States and has become more complex. Today, gangs involve an assortment of groups including street gangs, criminal prison gangs, hate groups, transnational gangs, and numerous others. In 2007, a U.S. Department of Justice survey determined that over 3550 jurisdictions served by local law enforcement agencies (population of 2500 or more) experienced gang problems. The survey also indicated that there were an estimated 788,000 gang members and 27,000 gangs active in the United States.[30]

Historically, gangs claim control over certain territories, engage in various illegal behaviors that usually revolve around money, and use fear, crime, and extortion. Gang members are often volatile, committing acts of violence toward rival gang members or the public for even minor infractions of their code. Common criminal acts committed by gang members often include vandalism, graffiti, illegal drugs, homicide, robbery, assault, burglary, auto theft, and sexual assault. Innocent people are often the victims of drive-by shootings and other types of gang violence.

Gangs represent a danger to the internal security of the United States and a special challenge to law enforcement. During the 1980s and 1990s, it appears that many police agencies across the United States recognized the need to create gang units and be proactive in combating the growing proliferation of gangs and gang crimes, particularly gang involvement in illegal drug trafficking activities.

According to the National Alliance of Gang Investigators Association, there are over 20,000 gang investigators or other related personnel involved in gang law enforcement in the United States (Figure 9.11).[31] Typical gang unit responsibilities include the following:

- Responding to citizen concerns about gang activity
- Gathering intelligence on gangs and gang members and organizing the collected data

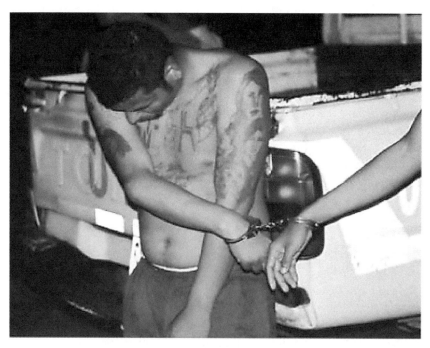

Figure 9.11 Suspected gang member being taken into custody. (Courtesy of the FBI. Retrieved from http://www.fbi.gov/about-us/investigate/vc_majorthefts/gangs/gallery/photo-gallery.)

- Providing training to other field divisions on gang awareness, street gang recognition, and gang investigative techniques
- Assisting in the investigation of gang-related crimes such as illegal narcotics, aggravated assaults, and homicides
- Disrupting and suppressing gang activity through aggressive street-level patrolling

Intelligence Functions

Law enforcement intelligence units are generally charged with collecting, extracting, summarizing, analyzing, and disseminating criminal intelligence information gathered from a variety of sources concerning persons involved in organized crime, terrorist activity, and other multijurisdictional or serial crimes. The unit's synergistic product is intended to provide meaningful and reliable direction to law enforcement decision-makers about complex law enforcement issues, including criminal activities and terrorism, for strategic and tactical planning purposes.

Prior to the 1960s, only a few law enforcement agencies in the United States had intelligence units.[32] However, as early as the 1920s, some United States law enforcement agencies were using the old military "dossier system" of intelligence. The dossier system simply meant that files were kept on known or suspected high-profile criminals.[33] The 1960s ushered in a period of turbulence and unrest in the United States. Because of increases of crime during the 1960s, the federal government recommended that state law enforcement organizations improve or develop intelligence capabilities. It was also recommended that they deter or control civil disorder.[32]

By 1973, law enforcement intelligence activities in the United States had become widespread. Unfortunately, they had also become the subject of high profile and widely publicized civil liberties complaints.[32] Numerous efforts were made to establish stringent governmental regulations, policies, and laws to more effectively control actual or perceived abuses in the criminal intelligence function. However, because of the circumstances, many law enforcement agencies felt compelled to either scale back their law enforcement intelligence operations or eliminate them altogether.[32]

Following the September 11, 2001, terrorist attacks on the United States, another initiative was undertaken to strengthen the nation's intelligence infrastructure, analysis capabilities, and information sharing at all levels of law enforcement. Various types of intelligence units and fusion centers to coordinate the gathering, analysis, and dissemination of information from law enforcement, homeland security, public safety, and other sources of terrorist information were established in many major local and state law enforcement agencies across the United States.[32] Other national intelligence initiatives included the expansion of the FBI's multiagency Joint Terrorism Task Force (JTTF), the creation of the Terrorist Screening Center, and the creation of the National Counterterrorism Center.

Today, even smaller police agencies, those without a formal intelligence unit, usually maintain some type of intelligence capacity. Some departments may simply have a designated officer who serves as the agency's point-of-contact (POC) to receive and disseminate critical intelligence information. In fact, an intelligence unit or POC has almost become a requirement for law enforcement agencies today.

Sworn law enforcement officers and analysts are involved in the law enforcement intelligence process. Intelligence unit sworn officers are often involved in activities that include the following:

- Serving as an agency's liaison with outside law enforcement agencies in receiving and disseminating law enforcement intelligence information
- Identifying, deterring, or detecting activities of active criminals operating within the agency's jurisdiction using various methods and techniques such as surveillance vehicles, visual monitoring equipment, audio monitoring or recording equipment, and undercover officers in accordance with existing state and federal laws
- Developing criminal cases up to the point where actual evidence gathering by the appropriate investigative unit can begin
- Collecting of law enforcement intelligence data from various sources such as informants, police officers, other public employees, field interview/contact cards, offense/incident reports, citizens and crime watch organizations, daily or weekly crime reports, media reports, Internet websites, and other sources
- Making referrals to other jurisdictions when appropriate, such as the FBI in cases involving domestic or international terrorism
- Monitoring and maintaining end-user functionality for outside law enforcement criminal intelligence databases
- Serving as a regional fusion center representative or as a member of a JTTF

In a free society, there are legal limitations on the level of intrusions the government can conduct. In carrying out the law enforcement intelligence mission, the personnel assigned must recognize the delicate balance between individual rights of citizens and the legitimate needs of law enforcement and carry out their duties accordingly.

Organized Crime and Narcotics Investigations

The FBI defines organized crime "as any group having some manner of a formalized structure and whose primary objective is to obtain money through illegal activities."[34] The economic impact of organized crime is staggering. It is estimated that global organized crime reaps $1 trillion a year in illegal profits. Organized crime brings drugs and violence into the nation's communities on an unprecedented scale.[35] In fact, drug trafficking is one the most profitable racketeering activities of organized crime.[36]

Organized crime presents a special challenge to law enforcement. Due to the close connection of organized crime and illegal drug trafficking, numerous police agencies have combined the organized crime and narcotics (OCN) investigation functions into one unit. OCN units are generally responsible for investigating organized crime, felony narcotics cases, intelligence related to such cases, and asset forfeiture. In addition, OCN units also work closely with federal agencies as well as other local and state agencies, including participation in multijurisdictional task forces in combating organized crime and illegal drugs.

Detectives assigned to OCN units are responsible for proactively investigating complex OCN offenses. OCN officers should be highly motivated because, unlike most other detectives who simply follow up on crimes that have already occurred, OCN detectives are often responsible for actually initiating investigations. Cases are initiated based on information received from a variety of sources, including patrol officers, community members, confidential informants, and other law enforcement agencies. In addition to traditional overt criminal investigation methods, OCN detectives may use covert tactics such as physical and electronic surveillance and lengthy undercover assignments to further investigations. Because of the clandestine nature of many OCN investigations, OCN units are often located separately from other police facilities.

Asset forfeiture is an important aspect of many OCN investigations. OCN cases frequently involve asset forfeitures of money, personal property, and real estate, which are used in or are proceeds of criminal activity. An OCN function may include conducting financial investigations to track and account for illicit proceeds. Asset forfeiture represents an important source of financing for OCN crime suppression efforts, because the proceeds from illegal enterprises are equitably shared among the participating agencies.

The following examples are representative of the types of cases an OCN unit might investigate:[37]

- Illegal activities of individuals affiliated with organized crime groups including loansharking, extortion, prostitution, gambling, money laundering, bookmaking, pornography, fraud, alien smuggling, counterfeit goods, theft, public corruption, and racketeering
- Conspiracy
- Narcotics trafficking from street-level sales to wholesale importation and distribution of heroin, cocaine, methamphetamine, LSD (lysergic acid diethylamide), or PCP (phenyl cyclohexyl piperidine)
- Domestic cultivation of marijuana
- Clandestine drug laboratories
- Other violations pertaining to the Racketeering Influenced and Corrupt Organization (RICO) statute

Special Weapons and Tactics

There are numerous highly trained law enforcement units operating under different names across the United States, which are all specially trained to work on high-risk missions that fall outside the abilities of regular patrol officers. Collectively, these units are often referred to as SWAT teams. SWAT is an acronym for special weapons and tactics. The SWAT team concept originated in the late 1960s, because of several high profile sniping incidents against civilians and police officers within the United States. One of the most famous incidents was the Texas Tower Massacre in 1966, where a deranged sniper shot 45 victims on the University of Texas campus.[38] In these incidents, the police were incapable of effectively responding using traditional law enforcement means, and it became obvious very quickly that a new tactic would be required to meet similar challenges in the future.

A forerunner to the present day SWAT concept was created by the Delano Police Department in California in the mid-1960s. Delano created a high-risk team and conducted SWAT-type operations in response to the United Farm Workers uprising led by Cesar Chavez. The high-risk team received training in countersniper, counterforce, and crowd control, but it was not identified as a special weapons or special tactics unit.

Although it touched on the concept and operational guidelines, Delano's action did not actually establish or authorize a SWAT unit;[39] however, it did serve as a predecessor for what was to follow.

The Los Angeles Police Department (LAPD) established what is widely recognized as the first SWAT team in 1967. Their mission was to "provide a ready response to situations that were beyond the capabilities of normally equipped and trained Department personnel." LAPD's first SWAT team consisted of 15 four-officer teams. Team members were volunteers from patrol and other assignments. Most of the volunteers had specialized experience and prior military service. The units were activated monthly for training or when the need for SWAT actually arose. In 1971, the LAPD SWAT personnel were assigned on a full-time basis to the Metropolitan Division. Today, the LAPD SWAT team is recognized worldwide as the premier police tactical unit in law enforcement.[40]

After the success that was achieved by the LAPD SWAT team, the concept continued to grow and spread across the United States. Many police agencies today have some type of "SWAT" team. However, the SWAT concept is very expensive to establish and maintain. In major departments, the SWAT unit is usually a dedicated, 24/7 operation with as many as 60 officers. Costs for equipment, training, and personnel are substantial. Smaller departments often use fewer personnel who perform regular police functions but responds as a SWAT team when the need arises. In addition, to reduce costs further, many municipalities have combined their resources with other departments in the region to form a regional SWAT team. Each municipality has a few trained SWAT members and key pieces of equipment, thus allowing them to form a complete SWAT team when called on to do so.

SWAT teams are called out in high-risk situations requiring specialized equipment or tactical expertise. Some examples of these situations include the following:

- Hostage rescue
- Trapped or isolated officers
- Barricaded suspects
- Arrest of violent or potentially violent suspects
- Service of search warrants on violent or potentially violent suspects
- Searches for armed suspects
- Rapid deployment
- Stakeouts
- VIP protection
- Stakeouts and undercover surveillance
- Civil disorders
- Acts of terrorism
- Other special events

To confront the dangers of the SWAT mission, SWAT team members are equipped with high-tech protective gear and upgraded weapons. Special SWAT equipment includes armored vehicles, stun grenades, assault rifles, submachine guns, night vision gear, body armor, entry tools, an array of nonlethal weapons, and other equipment as circumstances require. SWAT officers are also trained in the use of verbal tactics and negotiations as a vital part of managing special threat situations, with emphasis on trying to resolve crises peacefully through the use of less-than-lethal force.

The SWAT mission requires that officers be versatile and dedicated. SWAT officers are placed in complex, high stress situations and expected to perform in a calm, collected, and intelligent manner. SWAT officers are required to maintain top physical condition, a high level of firearms skill and proficiency, and a demonstrated mastery of tactical knowledge and skills. To maintain such a high state of readiness, SWAT officers train often and regularly.

In fact, authorities recommend that SWAT officers spend about one-quarter of their on-duty time in training. The training is often grueling. Officers, in addition to wearing over 60 pounds of gear, are now being trained to use and carry breathing apparatuses and personal protective equipment to guard against possible exposure to various forms of chemical, biological, or radiological attack carried out by terrorists. An example of the grueling SWAT training requirements are the 2000 hours of specialized training each LAPD SWAT officer underwent in preparation for the 1984 Summer Olympic Games in Los Angeles.[40]

Despite the fact that the shooting of a citizen by a SWAT team is extremely rare, the SWAT concept still has critics.[38] Unfortunately, there have been some high profile SWAT mishaps in recent years. The two most notable mishaps occurred in the 1990s and involved the FBI's Hostage Rescue Team (HRT) at Ruby Ridge, Idaho, and the Branch Davidian Compound near Waco, Texas. At Ruby Ridge, an HRT sniper mistakenly killed the wife of a fugitive. Scores of members of a religious cult died within the walls of the Branch Davidian Compound in Waco when the building caught fire as HRT agents in armored vehicles moved to insert tear gas.

These episodes combined with the increased use of SWAT in serving high-risk search warrants involving drugs have led to calls for reform in the use of SWAT operations. Some critics believe that SWAT teams have become overaggressive and too "militarized" and that there are simply too many SWAT teams, particularly in small departments, which rarely experience the sort of crises that require a SWAT team to resolve. The counterpoint is that recent research indicates that in the cases studied, suspects surrendered to the SWAT officer without gunfire or lethal force 71% of the time. Further, lethal force was used in only 14% of the incidents studied, and the suspect was killed by SWAT officers in less than 1% of the studied cases (Figure 9.12).[41]

Internal Affairs

The mission of law enforcement internal affairs (IA) units is to protect the public trust and to maintain the integrity of the agencies by investigating thoroughly and impartially all observed or reported allegations of police misconduct. In some agencies, the internal affairs function is referred to as the Office of Professional Standards.

Before the late nineteenth and early part of the twentieth centuries, most police misconduct was either ignored or dealt with informally within the agency. The concept of IA units in the United States did not see its origin until the late 1940s and early 1950s. In 1949, LAPD established one of the earliest IA units in the nation.[42] However, it was not until the 1960s with the emergence of civil rights legislation and the resulting civil disobedience that the issues of police brutality and excessive force became matters of serious public concern.

In response to these issues, various congressional committees held hearings and made recommendations for improving police community relations. One of those

Figure 9.12 Training of SWAT personnel. (Courtesy of the City of Lincoln, NE. Retrieved from http://lincoln.ne.gov/city/police/about/swat/swathist.htm.)

recommendations was for police agencies to establish "Internal Affairs" units to investigate allegations of misconduct.[43] Today, major police agencies usually have a separate IA unit for receiving and investigating complaints from citizens against police officers. The unit is often housed separately from other police facilities to reduce the intimidation factor for citizens as well as police officers. In small agencies, the internal affairs tasks often fall to an uninvolved superior officer or detective who ultimately reports to the agency head.

IA investigations involve a variety of allegations such as rudeness or discourtesy, unnecessary or excessive use of force, criminal misconduct, false arrest, racial profiling, intradepartmental misconduct (including equal opportunity employment issues), or other unacceptable behaviors. To maintain public confidence, all complaints against police officers must be investigated fairly and objectively. The results of investigations are forwarded to the agency head or other official for fair and appropriate adjudication and/or sanction.

The IA investigative process may involve an assortment of administrative and investigative duties and the responsibilities include the following:

- Interviewing and taking statements from internal and external complainants for the purpose of identifying officers being accused and obtaining detailed facts surrounding the complaint
- Interviewing accused officers and obtaining responses to accusations
- Responding to scenes where officers have been involved in shootings or discharging firearms as well as other serious incidents; then conducting investigations to determine if the action taken was in accordance with the agency's policies and procedures
- Conducting follow-up investigations to establish facts supporting the complainant or the accused

- Taking photographs, examining medical records, and gathering all available physical evidence
- Scheduling polygraph tests for consenting parties and recording results of exam interpretations for presentation with findings
- Writing reports of investigation
- Testifying at criminal and noncriminal hearings

The "Code of Silence" is a term used to describe the informal prohibition of reporting misconduct of fellow officers and the lack of cooperation from other officers when the accused is a police officer; this presents issues for IA investigators. The phenomenon is neither legal nor a morally justifiable behavior. Unfortunately, it is a part of the police culture in the United States. It likely exists to some extent in virtually every police agency in the nation, and it is an issue every IA investigator must recognize and attempt to overcome.

Another important issue in IA investigations involves statements compelled from law enforcement officers in criminal cases. The landmark U.S. Supreme Court decision on this issue is *Garrity v. New Jersey* (1967). *Garrity* involves the Fifth Amendment (self-incrimination) and the Fourteenth Amendment (due process) issues. The basic thrust of *Garrity* "is that a department member may be compelled to give statements under threat of discipline or discharge, but those statements may not be used in the criminal prosecution of the individual officer."[44] However, anything developed in a criminal investigation may be used in an IA investigation. Therefore, IA and criminal investigations should always be investigated independently. Some agencies investigate both criminal and noncriminal cases simultaneously, while others prefer to complete the criminal investigation first before initiating the noncriminal investigation. In either case, IA investigations are always subordinate to criminal investigations.

Unfortunately, history tells us that police agencies will always be faced with the issue of occasional officer misconduct and corruption. Law enforcement agencies will never be able to eliminate the problem or completely control it. However, agencies can and should be held accountable for how they respond to the issue. It is imperative that the police are proactive in maintaining the public trust and the integrity of the agency. To do so requires a professional and respected IA unit that has the public's full confidence and trust that the police can investigate its own without bias. This can be a very difficult matter in high profile cases involving police corruption or other serious criminal accusations.

Police Bands

When one ponders the concept of policing, the notion of musicianship does not necessarily enter one's thoughts immediately. However, some law enforcement organizations incorporate musical band programs. These units serve a variety of purposes ranging from public performances during holidays to funeral processions. Some police bands may be comprised of only police officers, whereas others may consist of both civilian and police personnel. The use of these units provides methods of community interaction, community service, building goodwill with the public, generating funds to support charities, and improving morale.

One of the oldest police bands is the New York City Police Department Band. This organization was formed in 1901 by members of the police department and eventually became the official band of the city of New York.[45] During modern times, it has performed in the Japanese cities of Tokyo, Fukushima, Sapporo, and Chiba; Hong Kong, China; Quebec City, Canada; and within the United States.[46] Other performances include Macy's Thanksgiving Day parades, the 2008 Giants Super Bowl ceremony, the inaugural ceremony of President Franklin D. Roosevelt, *The Tonight Show* with Jay Leno, and the championship parades for the New York Yankees and the New York Rangers.[47]

Although the New York organization originated during the early twentieth century, it is not the oldest police band in the United States. The Milwaukee Police Band in Wisconsin boasts that it is the "oldest police band in America."[48] This organization was formed in 1897 and continues to prosper during modern times. Its performances have included a variety of venues ranging from appearances with John Philip Sousa to peace officer memorial events.[49] The Milwaukee Police Band is leveraged to facilitate community goodwill and ambassadorship for the city.[50]

The concept of police bands is not limited to the United States. Several nations have bands within their ranks of police. Within the United Kingdom, an example is the Kent Police Band of Great Britain. This organization has performed for the Royal Family and at venues in "America, Germany, Denmark, Norway, Belgium, and France."[51] Other performances included World War I memorial events in France and the unveiling of the National Police Memorial.[52]

Australia also manifests bands among its police organizations. An example is the Victoria Police Band. This organization originated in 1891 and remains a community staple during modern times. Commensurate with the activities of its peers internationally, it also contributes toward morale, goodwill, and ambassadorship. It functions as a "powerful proactive tool for engaging the community and achieving positive contact with all demographics throughout the state."[53]

An example of a Canadian organization is the Ottawa Police Service Pipe Band. This entity serves the purpose of "public relations but even more to contribute to memorials for slain police officers."[54] The performances of this police band are leveraged also for charitable purposes. Through its performances and sales of its affiliated recordings, money is raised for charities including "Children's Hospital of Eastern Ontario, the Children's Wish Foundation, and Big Sisters Big Brothers of Ottawa."[55]

Police bands provide police departments with strong visibility within communities. These bands contribute to stronger community relationships between the law enforcement entity and its served public. Their musical arrangements are diverse and represent an array of pieces including traditional marches and funeral processionals, swing, jazz, country, classical, and popular music. Their venues range from sporting events and holiday performances to funerals and other ceremonies. Because they are utilized for benevolent purposes (e.g., charitable funding, ambassadorship, etc.), they may be leveraged as a form of community service and community policing. Further, they may also serve as recruiting tools through which potential law enforcement candidates are enticed to consider policing careers (Figure 9.13).

Summary

The municipal police patrol function is the backbone of United States law enforcement. Municipal patrols have general law enforcement and crime prevention duties. However, contemporary law enforcement involves an array of ever-increasing complex functions

Figure 9.13 Milwaukee Police Band. (Courtesy of the City of Milwaukee, WI. Retrieved from http://city.milwaukee.gov/police/MPD-Divisions/MPD-Police-Band.htm.)

that cannot be effectively undertaken by police patrol officers. To address these challenges, many law enforcement agencies have turned to specialization. Specialization allows agencies to concentrate workforce resources and equipment on specific needs and problem areas.

In major departments, separate units often exist for each specialized function. The officers assigned to these specialty units are generally experienced field patrol officers who are carefully selected and are often required to undergo lengthy and intensive training before being assigned to specialized field duties. In smaller departments, those without the benefit of specialized units, patrol officers may be required to perform multiple specialized functions and/or seek the assistance of county or state agencies.

Specialized units are important assets to law enforcement. However, there are pros and cons associated with the use of police specialization units, but in most cases, the positive aspects of specialization offset the disadvantages. One of the most important issues involving specialization is the need for each unit, general or specialized, to work effectively together to accomplish the common goal of serving and protecting the public. Law enforcement agencies must always function cohesively as a unit.

This chapter explored various aspects, including duties and responsibilities, of the specialized units most commonly found in contemporary law enforcement agencies across the United States. Specialized units discussed in this chapter included aviation, bicycle patrol, canine, CSIs, criminal investigation, explosive ordnance, gangs, intelligence, internal affairs, marine patrol, motorcycle, mounted patrol, organized crime/narcotics, and SWAT. Other specialized units that may be found in some agencies include dive team, domestic violence, missing persons, recruitment and selection, special victims unit, training, civil process unit, and others. Each agency determines its specialization needs based on the requirements of its communities and available funding.

Discussion Questions

1. List and discuss the major advantages and disadvantages of police specialization.
2. Where was the first police aviation unit created? Why was it created? Discuss how the use of police aviation has changed since it was first established.
3. Explain the demise of police bicycle patrol units.
4. What is the role of canine units in contemporary law enforcement? Do police canines create a police–community relation problem?
5. How do CSI specialists assist other criminal investigators? How has CSI technology changed in recent years? What is the "CSI effect?" What are the implications of the "CSI effect?"
6. Why is there such a mystique associated with the role of police detectives? How have the television and movie industries glamorized and distorted the detective's image? What are the implications of the public's image of police detectives?
7. What are the major responsibilities of an explosive Ordnance unit (bomb squad)?
8. What are typical gang unit responsibilities and duties? Do you know anyone associated with a gang? If so, what gang?
9. Define "law enforcement intelligence." Discuss the state of law enforcement intelligence in contemporary law enforcement. How has it changed since 9/11?
10. What is the police "Code of Silence?" What are its implications to IA investigations?
11. Describe the role of contemporary marine law enforcement. How has the role of marine law enforcement changed since 9/11?
12. What are the major advantages and disadvantages of police motorcycles?
13. Briefly describe the role and historical development of police mounted units.
14. What is the mission of law enforcement OCN units? How do OCN investigative techniques differ from other investigative units?
15. What is a SWAT team? Explain why and where the SWAT concept originated. List five examples of situations requiring SWAT response.

References

1. Kenney, J. P., & Williams, J. B. (1968). *Police Operations: Policies and Procedures*. Illinois: Charles C. Thomas Publishing Company, Springfield.
2. Wilson, O.W., & McLaren, R. C. (1972). *Police Administration*. New York: McGraw-Hill.
3. Komenda, E. D. (Ed.) (December 28, 2011). Harrisburg police foot patrols could be walking away. *The Patriot-News*. Retrieved April 5, 2012, from http://www.pennlive.com/midstate/index.ssf/2011/12/harrisburg_police.html.
4. *Our History*. Retrieved June 19, 2010, from http://www.ci.berkeley.ca.us/police/history/history.html/.
5. Harley Davidson USA. *Police Motorcycles and Harley-Davidson: A Short History*. Retrieved June 18, 2010, from http://www.harley-davidson.com/wcm/Content/Pages/Police_Motorcycles/police_history.jsp.
6. *Police Motorcycle Training*. Retrieved June 19, 2010, from http://www.motorcops.com/police_training/police_survival.asp/.
7. Seattle Police Department. *Motorcycle Unit*. Retrieved June 18, 2010, from http://www.seattle.gov/police/units/traffic/motorcycle.htm/.

8. Dunhan, N. L. (1956). *The Bicycle Era in American History* (p. 119). Cambridge, UK: Harvard University PhD Thesis in History.

9. *The Rise, Fall and Rebirth of Bicycle Police.* Retrieved June 3, 2010, from http://www.ipmba .org/newsletters/ABriefHistoryofPoliceCyCling.pdf/.

10. Solosky, K. J. (2009). *Fixed Wing Aircraft in Law Enforcement.* Retrieved June 19, 2010, from http://www.lawofficer.com/article/patrol/fixed-wing-aircraft-law-enforc.

11. *NYPD Aviation Unit.* Retrieved June 1, 2010, from http://www.pdworks.com/nydp/nydp.html.

12. Bureau of Justice Statistics (2007). *Aviation Units in Large Law Enforcement Agencies, 2007.* Washington, DC: Government Printing Office.

13. Baker, B. M. (2012). *Police Marine Patrol.* Retrieved June 11, 2010, from http://www.careerpo-liceofficer.com/PoliceLinks/police_marine_patrol.html/.

14. Roth, M. Mounted Police Forces: A Comparative History. Presented to the Annual Meeting of the Academy of Criminal Justice Sciences, 1998. Retrieved April 17, 2010, from http://www .emeraldinsight.com/Insight/ViewContentServiet?Filename=/published/emeraldfulltextarticle/ pdf/1810210408.pdf./.

15. Carfield, W. F. (1995). *The Encyclopedia of Police Science* (p. 371). New York, NY: Garland Publishing, Inc.

16. United States Park Police. *Horse Mounted Unit.* Retrieved April 7, 2010, from http://www.nps .gov/uspp/fhorsepage.htm/.

17. *Mounted Patrol.* Retrieved June 14, 2010, from https://ncjrs.gov/app/Search/Abstracts.aspx? id=56002.

18. Chapman, S. G. (1995). *The Encyclopedia of Police Science* (pp. 53). New York, NY: Garland Publishing, Inc.

19. Carson, C. *History of Police Dogs.* Retrieved April 9, 2010, from http://www.ehow.com/ about_5130729_history-police-dogs.html/.

20. *Police Dog Handler.* Retrieved April 9, 2010, from http://www.police-information.co.uk/Docs/ careerinformation/specialistdepts/dogbranch.html.

21. *U. S. v. Place.* Retrieved June 18, 2010, from http://www.caselaw.lp.findlaw.com/cgi-bin/getcase .pl?court=&vol=462&invol=696/.

22. *The Police Dog as an Instrumentality of Force.* Retrieved June 18, 2010, from http://www .uspcak9.com/caselaw/patrol.html.

23. The 'CSI Effect': *Does It Really Exist?* Retrieved June 29, 2010, from http://www.nij.gov/ nij/journals/259/csi-effect.htm.

24. *An Overview of Criminal Investigations.* Retrieved June 13, 2010, from http://www .drtomoconnor.com/3220/3220lect01.htm.

25. Regan, M. P. NYPD celebrates bomb squad's 100th anniversary. *The Associated Press.* Retrieved April 26, 2010, from http://www.policeone.com/SWAT/articles/72782-NYPD-Celebrates-Bomb-Squad-100th-Anniversary.html/.

26. *Bombs and Explosives.* Retrieved April 26, 2010, from http://www.michigan.gov/msp/0,1607,7-123-1593_25680_25798-15951--,00.html.

27. FBI (2004). *Protecting America Against Terrorist Attack.* Retrieved June 8, 2010, from http:// www.fbi.gov/page2/dec04/hds122004.htm/.

28. Carlie, M. K. (2002). *Part 4: Gangs Aren't New.* Retrieved June 8, 2010, from http://www.faculty .missouristate.edu/m/MichaelCarlie/what_I_learned_about/GANGS/they_are_not_new.htm/.

29. Howell, J. C., & Moore, J. P. (2010). History of street gangs in the United States, in *Bureau of Justice Assistance and Office of Juvenile Justice and Delinquency Prevention* (p. 1). *National Gang Center Bulletin.* Washington, DC: Government Printing Office.

30. U. S. Department of Justice, Office of Justice Programs, Office of Juvenile Justice and Delinquency Prevention (2009). *Highlights of the 2007 National Youth Gang Survey.* Washington, DC: Government Printing Office, Retrieved June 8, 2010, from http://www.ncjrs.gov/pdffiles1/ ojjdp/225185.pdf/.

31. *What is NAGIA*. Retrieved June 8, 2010, from http://www.nagia.org/aboutNAGIA.asp

32. Porter, R. M. *Focus on Fusion Centers: A Progress Report*. Statement before the Subcommittee on State, Local, and Private Sector Preparedness and Integration/Committee on Homeland Security and Government Affairs, United States Senate, 2008. Retrieved June 9, 2010, from http://www.hsgac.senate.gov/public/_files/PorterTestimony.pdf/.

33. Carter, D. L. (2004). *Law Enforcement Intelligence: A Guide for State, Local, and Tribal Law Enforcement Agencies* (p. 22). Washington, DC: U. S. Justice Department, Cooperative Agreement #2003-CK-WX-0455.

34. FBI. *Glossary*. Retrieved June 25, 2010, from http://www.fbi.gov/about-us/investigate/organizedcrime/glossary/.

35. FBI. *About Organized Crime*. Retrieved June 16, 2010, from http://www.fbi.gov/about-us/investigate/organizedcrime/overview/.

36. *Organized Crime—Organized Crime Offenses*. Retrieved June 16, 2010, from http://law.jrank.org/pages/11941/Organized-Crime-Organized-crime-offenses.html/.

37. New Jersey State Police. *Special Investigations Unit*. Retrieved April 23, 2010, from http://www.state.nj.us/njsp/divorg/invest/invest.html/.

38. *Police: Special Weapons and Tactics (SWAT) Teams—Bibliography*. Retrieved April 26, 2010, from http://law.jrank.org/pages/1693/Police-Special-Weapons-Tactics-SWAT-teams.html/.

39. *The Birth of SWAT*. Retrieved June 16, 2010, from http:/www.officer.com/publication/printer.jsp?id=50852/.

40. LAPD. *Special Weapons and Tactics*. Retrieved April 26, 2010, from http://www.lapdonline.org/inside_the_lapd/content_basic_view/848/.

41. *The United States S. W.A. T. Program: A History and Overview*. Retrieved June 16, 2010, from http://www.helium.com/item/101114-the-united-states-swat-program-a-history-and-overview/.

42. LAPD. *Internal Affairs Group*. Retrieved June 10, 2010, from http://www.lapdonline.org/internal_affairs_group/.

43. Jolin, A. I., & Gibbons, D. C. (1984). Policing the police: The Portland experience. *Journal of Police Science and Administration, 12*(3), 316.

44. *The Garrity Warning*. Retrieved June 10, 2010, from http://www.njlawman.com/Garrity.htm/.

45. New York City Police Department Police Band. *NYPD Band History*, Retrieved May 15, 2012, from http://www.policeband.org/history.html.

46. Ibid.

47. Ibid.

48. City of Milwaukee. *History of the Milwaukee Police Band*. Retrieved May 15, 2012, from http://city.milwaukee.gov/police/MPD-Divisions/MPD-Police-Band.htm.

49. Ibid.

50. Ibid.

51. Kent Police Band. *About Us*. Retrieved May 16, 2012, from http://www.kentpoliceband.org/id1.html.

52. Ibid.

53. Victoria Police (2012). *Victoria Police Bands*. Retrieved May 16, 2012, from http://www.police.vic.gov.au/content.asp?Document_ID=670.

54. Ottawa Police Service. *OPS Pipe Band*. Retrieved May 16, 2012, from http://www.ottawapolice.ca/en/community/opspipeband/index.aspx.

55. Ibid.

Bibliography

Bennett, C. (2010). The Birth of SWAT. Retrieved June 16, 2010, from http:/www.officer.com/publication/printer.jsp?id=50852/.

Carfield, W. G. (1995). *The Encyclopedia of Police Science*. New York, NY: Garland Publishing Inc.

Investigation

10

When you have eliminated the impossible, whatever remains, however improbable, must be the truth...[1]

Sir Arthur Conan Doyle

Learning Objectives

The objectives of this chapter are to

- Define and explain the definition and concept of investigation
- Explain the concept of evidence
- Describe investigative teams
- Discuss clearance rates
- Recognize that not all crimes are solved

Introduction

For fans of popular detective novels or TV shows, criminal investigation often appears to be a solitary pursuit performed by determined detectives who stop at nothing to "catch the bad guy." Indeed, many police dramas end with the identification of the perpetrator, implying that little work remains.

Of course, this is a completely skewed version of the manner in which real criminal investigations are carried out. In the first place, identifying the suspected criminal is often the easy part. For years, the Federal Bureau of Investigation (FBI) and Organized Crime Units of the New York City Police Department knew who ran the five La Cosa Nostra families in the New York area. It took years, however, to gather sufficient evidence to charge and prosecute members of those organizations.

In addition, investigations are rarely solo endeavors; they require great teamwork on the part of patrol officers, detectives, crime scene technicians, laboratory examiners, prosecutors, and a host of others.

In this chapter, we discuss the manner in which investigations are conducted by the police. To be sure, not every agency carries out investigations in the same way. Large agencies may have evidence technicians whose sole job is to gather evidence at crime scenes, whereas smaller departments may rely on detectives or patrol officers to carry out those same functions. Although some agencies have dedicated forensic laboratories at their disposal, performing all nature of examinations, others may have to submit their evidence to federal or state laboratories. Despite these differences, the definition of criminal investigation remains consistent across agencies.

A criminal investigation is defined as the process of discovering, collecting, preparing, identifying, and presenting evidence to determine what happened and who is responsible. All criminal investigations share common goals. Among these are

- Determining whether a crime has been committed
- Ascertaining who committed the crime
- Apprehending the criminal
- Gathering evidence in a legal way to support prosecution
- Retrieving property
- Preventing further crime through general or specific deterrence
- Assisting victims and providing a sense of justice for community members

Early Advancements in Science, Investigations, and Technology

Science, investigations, and technology have proven essential to effective law enforcement. The basic scientific advancements of the 1800s continued into the 1900s, exploding by the end of the twentieth century with advancements in all aspects of forensic science. Many of the things we take for granted or look to as commonplace in the profession were developed or introduced over the last century. While literature such as Sir Arthur Conan Doyle's *Sherlock Holmes* captured the imagination of countless readers in the late 1800s, real advancements in forensics were also unfolding.

Hans Gross, (1847–1915), a former Austrian magistrate turned criminologist, gained wide recognition as the father of scientific techniques in crime detection. Gross believed that by applying science intelligently, the police could solve most crimes. His major publication, the *Manual for the Examining Magistrate: A System of Criminalistics* had two assumptions. First, the police should be familiar with the psychology of criminal behavior. Second, they should adopt any technical and scientific procedures that might be useful in analyzing a crime scene and its evidence.

In England, many advances in criminal investigation evolved from the London Metropolitan Police. With a distinguished career as an English chemist in the 1830s and 1840s, James Marsh (1794–1846) built a reputation for research advancements and the development of a dependable, simple laboratory test for the identification of minute traces of arsenic. Arsenic had become popular with killers, because it was easy to obtain, simple to use, and difficult to detect at the time.

The Marsh test (or the Marsh arsenic test), involved the testing of given samples of food, fluid, or deceased human tissue by forensic toxicologists from the middle part of the nineteenth century to well into the latter half of the twentieth century. In fact, the test was often used by Mathieu Joseph Bonaventure Orfila (1787–1853), who is often considered the originator of forensic toxicology.

The Marsh test gave investigators an effective and accurate way to detect small amounts of arsenic. The development of this testing method and accompanying apparatus by Marsh helped to promote the scientific advancement of poisoning investigations, and influenced the outcome of several notable murder trials.

Advancements were also occurring in the area of criminal identification at the same time. A Belgian statistician, Lambert Adolphe Quetelet (1796–1874), contended that no two humans were of precisely the same anatomical dimensions. Quetelet wanted to develop a method of human identification that would have far-ranging applications not limited only to the field of crime and justice. Through statistical analysis, Quetelet gained insight into the relationships between crime and other social factors. Among his findings were strong relationships between age and crime, as well as gender and crime. Other influential factors he found included climate, poverty, education, and alcohol consumption. His research findings were published in *Of the Development of the Propensity to Crime*.[2]

Alphonse Bertillon (1853–1914) read the work of Quetelet and developed his own system of identification in Paris in 1880; he named it the Bertillon system of criminal identification.[3] In 1883, widespread attention and acceptance came to Bertillon when the French Surete used his system of body measurements. The death of the Bertillon system began when two unrelated prisoners in Leavenworth Penitentiary had the same Bertillon measurements. Will West and William West had the same Bertillon measurements, the same names, and strikingly similar facial features. The only differences were in their fingerprints. Nevertheless, the Bertillon system survived into the mid-1920s in many American cities, but the complexity of the system, combined with the widespread acceptance of fingerprinting as a means of identification, rendered it obsolete.[4]

The use of fingerprints did not begin in the early 1900s. Historical research reveals that the Chinese used fingerprints for identification as far back as 300 BC. Over the centuries, many contributed to the body of knowledge surrounding fingerprinting including Professor J. E. Purkinje of Breslau, Sir William Herschel, Dr. Henry Faulds, and Sir Francis Galton. Purkinje tried to classify fingerprints as early as 1823. In 1858, Sir William Herschel (1883–1917) began the use of fingerprints in India as seals for agreements.[5] Later, he proposed recording all Indian prisoners' prints in British records as a way to discourage recidivism, though British authorities rejected the idea.

Dr. Henry Faulds' (1843–1930) interest in fingerprinting dated back to the 1870s when he began collecting fingerprints as a hobby. Dr. Faulds is credited with being the first person to recognize the use of fingerprinting for identifying individuals in criminal cases. He also developed a method for lifting latent prints. Sir Francis Galton determined that an individual's prints do not change over his lifetime and that each individual's prints are unique.[6]

As Sir Henry's advances in the use of fingerprinting in the tracking and identification of criminals gained acceptance in England, the Commonwealth, and the United States, similar programs were launched in South America by Juan Vucetich, an Argentine Police Official, and Henry Roscher, a disciple of Dr. Henry Faulds, in Germany. Vucetich is credited with the first positive criminal identification as, in 1892, he was able to extract a set of prints off a door and identify a woman as the primary suspect in a double homicide. Around 1900, Dr. Henry Faulds, William Herschel, and Sir Edward Richard Henry developed a fingerprint classification system that Scotland Yard adopted in 1903.[7] In Germany and South America, Vucetich and Roscher developed systems of fingerprint classification based on the different shapes and patterns in the ridges of fingers.

Henry's System of Fingerprinting Classification was adopted by English-speaking countries, whereas Vucetich's system was utilized in Spanish-speaking countries. Roscher's system was used in his homeland of Germany and also in Japan. Further advancements included that of June 1935, when Dr. E. M. Hudson discovered a method of securing fingerprints from handkerchiefs, cloth, paper, and wood. His method used silver nitrate to change the ordinary salt in a fingerprint to silver chloride.

The Fingerprint Branch at New Scotland Yard (London Metropolitan Police) was created in July 1901 using the Henry System of Fingerprint Classification. In 1903, the New York State Prison system began the first systematic use of fingerprints in the United States for criminals. In 1904, the use of fingerprints began in Leavenworth Federal Penitentiary in Kansas and the St. Louis Police Department. They were assisted by a sergeant from Scotland Yard who had been on duty at the St. Louis World's Fair Exposition guarding the British Display. Sometime after the St. Louis World's Fair, the International Association of Chiefs of Police (IACP) created America's first national fingerprint repository, called the National Bureau of Criminal Identification, located at Leavenworth, Kansas.

In 1924, an Act of Congress directed the creation of a fingerprint identification division to be maintained within the Federal Bureau of Investigation. Forming the nucleus of this new identification division were the fingerprints maintained at the time by the International Association of Chiefs of Police National Bureau of Criminal Identification, and the Department of Justice's Bureau of Criminal Identification.

Today, criminal justice agencies rely on the Automated Fingerprint Identification System (AFIS). The largest AFIS repository in America is operated by the Department of Homeland Security's U.S. Visit Program, which contains over 100 million persons' fingerprints, many in the form of two-finger records. The two-finger records are noncompliant with FBI and Interpol standards but sufficient for positive identification and valuable for forensics, because index fingers and thumbs are the most commonly identified crime scene fingerprints. The largest 10-print AFIS repository in America is the FBI's Integrated Automated Fingerprint Identification System (IAFIS) in Clarksburg, West Virginia. IAFIS has more than 60 million individual computerized fingerprint records (both criminal and civil applicant records).

During this same period, other advancements in criminal investigation were occurring during the early 1900s. Major L. W. Atcherley, who later became Major General Sir L. W. Atcherley of the English Constabulary, developed what became known as the modus operandi system around the late 19th century. This modus operandi system was based upon a 10-point system that included factors such as place of the crime, point of entry, method of entry, tools used in the crime, objects taken, time of the crime, and unusual characteristics of the crime and criminal. Atcherley's assumption was that criminals were creatures of habit and as they committed their crimes, they were inclined to develop, refine, and follow behavior with which they were comfortable. The modus operandi system was embraced by forward-looking departments. Becoming known as the MO, it essentially was an early method of profiling the behaviors of an offender, and is one of the foundational blocks in criminal investigation methods today. Over the next century, advancements occurred in all aspects of criminal investigation including forensics, toxicology, anthropology, and odontology.

Goal of an Investigation

The primary goal of the police in any investigation is to find the truth of the matter under investigation and clear the crime. The definition of clearance can vary from department to department. The FBI's *Crime in the United States*, which is the definitive source of data for crimes reported to the police, states that crimes can be cleared in two ways: (1) through arrest or (2) through exceptional means. In order for a crime to be cleared by arrest, the following three conditions must be met:[8]

1. At least one person must have been arrested.
2. At least one person must have been charged with the commission of the offense.
3. At least one person must have been turned over to the court for prosecution (whether following arrest, court summons, or police notice).

Other conditions impacting investigations must be considered. A case cleared by exceptional means is one where extenuating circumstances prevent the agency from arresting an individual for the crime. In order to meet those criteria, the agency must have completed the following four requirements:[9]

1. Identified the offender
2. Gathered enough evidence to support an arrest, make a charge, and turn over the offender to the court for prosecution
3. Identified the offender's exact location so that the suspect could be taken into custody immediately
4. Encountered a circumstance outside the control of law enforcement that prohibits the agency from arresting, charging, and prosecuting the offender

Instances where a crime is cleared by exceptional means include one where the offender was killed or committed suicide before an arrest could be made. Police departments are often judged by their clearance rates; some criminologists and police executives see this as unfair. For example, between 1961 and 1993, the clearance rates for homicides in the United States declined from 93% to 65%.[10] A cursory reading of this data might indicate that the police became far less effective at investigating homicides. In fact, most criminologists attribute the declining rate of homicide clearance to the fact that during that period, the nature of homicides changed, with many more being committed by strangers rather than acquaintances. Stranger-on-stranger homicides are often very difficult to solve because an obvious suspect is usually not present.

Central to any investigation is the proper gathering and handling of evidence. This is a function that is the responsibility of all participants in the investigation and not merely investigators or detectives. In its simplest sense, evidence is something that is used to prove or disprove a claim. Criminal evidence is that which can be introduced in court to help establish the facts of a case. Both the prosecution and defense use evidence to try to advance their theories of the case. Although most people think of evidence as physical objects, such as guns or bloodstains, it can also take the form of witness testimony; documents, such as letters; and records, such as cellular telephone bills. Increasingly, the police find vast quantities of evidence digitally either through data stored on computer hard drives and disks or on social networking sites, such as Facebook.

In order for evidence to be valid, it must have been legally obtained and properly handled. In order to handle it properly, different types of evidence require different procedures to be followed. In the case of physical evidence, positive chain-of-custody must be maintained from the time evidence is obtained until it is introduced in court. Chain-of-custody consists of both documentation and testimony. The documentation records who had possession of the evidence while in the custody of the police and also shows that the evidence was properly stored in accordance with approved procedures. Chain-of-custody must remain "unbroken," that is, every minute that it was in possession of law enforcement must be documented. The combination of documentation and testimony is used as proof in court that the evidence was not tampered with or altered in any way since its seizure. In addition to an intact chain-of-custody, evidence should have probative value, that is, it should actually be helpful in proving a fact or an issue. Otherwise, it is of little use to the police or prosecution.

Types of Evidence

Physical evidence is any type of tangible evidence usually found at a crime scene or in a search. Some examples include guns, burglary tools, computers, and incriminating documents (Figure 10.1). The theory behind the use of forensic physical evidence was first articulated in the early part of the twentieth century by criminologist Edmond Locard, who became known as the "Sherlock Holmes of France." According to Locard, a criminal always removes something or leaves something at a crime scene that is incriminating; this became known as Locard's principle.

In order to have the greatest probative value, a particular piece of evidence must be linked to the crime. For example, it does little good for the police to have a gun if they cannot show that it was the one used in a murder they are investigating. To that end, they attempt to link physical evidence to a particular crime by comparing unique characteristics of the evidence with something from the crime scene. For example, when a gun is fired, the barrel leaves unique markings on the surface of the bullet. Forensic testing can reveal if a particular gun fired a particular bullet. This can prove to be a crucial piece of evidence if bullets from a body can be conclusively linked to a gun recovered from a suspect.

Humans also possess unique characteristics, which are known as biometrics. The oldest biometric used in law enforcement is the fingerprint.

Perhaps the greatest biometric innovation in the last 50 years has been the introduction of deoxyribonucleic acid (DNA). Nearly microscopic amounts of DNA, which can be found in blood, saliva, hair samples, and other bodily substances, are sufficient for identification purposes. DNA evidence may be found in the locations shown in Table 10.1.

Another type of physical evidence is termed trace evidence, which is nothing more than extremely small items such as hair or fiber. Today, tweezers and vacuum cleaners with filters are every bit as much a part of an evidence kit as crime scene tape.

Evidence can also be exculpatory, that is, it can be used to clear the innocent as well as convict the guilty. DNA has proven to be a godsend for individuals who have been wrongly

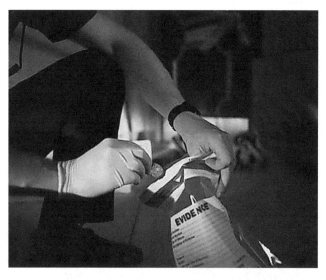

Figure 10.1 An officer collecting evidence. (Courtesy of the FBI, 2006. Retrieved from http://www2.fbi.gov/publications/leb/2006/april2006/april06leb.htm.)

Table 10.1   DNA Evidence

Evidence	Possible Location of DNA on the Evidence	Source of DNA
Baseball bat or similar weapon	Handle, end	Sweat, skin, blood, tissue
Hat, bandana, or mask	Inside	Sweat, hair, dandruff
Eyeglasses	Nose or ear pieces, lens	Sweat, skin
Facial tissue or cotton swab	Surface area	Mucus, blood, sweat, semen
Dirty laundry	Surface area	Blood, sweat, semen, vomit
Toothpick	Tips	Saliva
Used cigarette	Cigarette butt	Saliva
Stamp or envelope	Licked area	Saliva
Tape or ligature	Inside or outside surface	Skin, sweat
Bottle, can, or glass	Sides, mouthpiece	Saliva, sweat
Used condom	Inside or outside surface	Semen, vaginal or rectal cells
Blanket, pillow, or sheet	Surface area	Sweat, hair, semen, urine, saliva
"Through and through" bullet	Outside surface	Blood, tissue
Bite mark	Person's skin or clothing	Saliva
Fingernail or partial fingernail	Scrapings	Blood, tissue, sweat

Source: http://www.dna.gov/basics/evidence_collection/identifying

convicted of crimes. Under the auspices of such initiatives as the Innocence Project, innocent individuals have been released after serving many years in prison for crimes they did not commit.

Before leaving the category of physical evidence, it is important to mention a recent phenomenon that is bedeviling both investigators and prosecutors. The "CSI effect," named after the famous television show *CSI*, describes a situation where juries, conditioned by the popular media, believe that physical evidence can and should be found in every criminal case. Veteran police officers know this is not the case. Environmental conditions degrade evidence, fingerprints are smeared rather than left clearly, and clever criminals ensure that no trace of their presence is left. At present, the CSI effect is proving challenging for law enforcement; whether it will remain so in the future is unknown.

Testimonial evidence includes the recollections and knowledge of witnesses or individuals familiar with the case. Perhaps the greatest skill that an investigator can develop is becoming an effective interviewer. With any investigation, there is usually a variety of individuals who can help the police solve the case. These include witnesses, victims, acquaintances of suspects, informants, undercover agents, and even suspects themselves. Often, of course, those who can help the police the most are also the most reluctant to provide information. This occurs for a variety of reasons—loyalty to the offender, fear of retaliation, or just a desire not "to get involved." As a result, good investigators soon learn to develop superior skills of persuasion. Just as law enforcement personnel must follow procedure when they gather physical evidence, they must also follow rules whenever they conduct interviews. For example, people can refuse to talk to the police. Suspects in custody must be advised of their Miranda rights and will be afforded an attorney if they request one. Additionally, spouses cannot be compelled to testify against each other and communications between individuals and certain professionals including doctors, lawyers, and the clergy are "privileged" and protected from disclosure to the authorities.

One particularly compelling type of testimony, especially in the courtroom, is eyewitness testimony. Nothing is as dramatic as a witness on the stand pointing out the defendant as "the one who did it." Juries tend to believe individuals who "saw it with their own eyes." Unfortunately, recent research indicates that eyewitness testimony is not always credible. Indeed, many of the individuals who have been exonerated by the Innocence Project were convicted on faulty eyewitness testimony. This does not usually occur because people want to lie; instead, they manage to convince themselves that they are correct in their identification. One way that investigators obtain eyewitness testimony is through live lineups where witnesses pick the offender out of a group of other individuals; in order for lineups to be legal, individuals must bear some resemblance to one another (e.g., the same race or roughly the same height). Another way for witnesses to pick out suspects is through the use of a photo spread where a suspect's photo is included among several others; again, the photos must not be so different that the pick of the suspect is a "sure thing." In order to improve the accuracy of eyewitnesses, the U.S. Department of Justice produced *Eyewitness Evidence: A Guide for Law Enforcement* in 1999. Recent research has led to the practice of using an uninterested party to administer the lineup virtually eliminating the possibility of the witness being influenced during the process of viewing the photos.

Another excellent source of information can be coconspirators or acquaintances of perpetrators. Of course, getting them to provide meaningful information can prove difficult. Often an acquaintance must feel that he is obtaining something of value before he will reveal important information.

Informants are generally individuals on the periphery of, or sometimes involved in, criminal activity. They provide information for a variety of reasons (e.g., money, the hope that law enforcement will protect or "go easy on" them, revenge) and are often in a good position to provide information of value. However, they are often reluctant to testify and when they do, skilled defense attorneys can usually damage their credibility by bringing up their unsavory past. As well, informants often try to "play both sides" by providing some information to the police while continuing to engage in criminal activity.

If undercover agents can penetrate an organization, they are generally preferred to informants. As law enforcement officers, undercover agents enjoy better reputations than informants and their credibility is harder to challenge. Undercover agents understand the law and are much less likely to gather evidence that does not pass legal muster. In addition, they can be counted upon to follow the law, and there is no question as to whether or not that they will testify in court.

Finally, one of the best sources of testimonial evidence is the suspect. In a surprising number of cases, suspects confess to their crimes. For a few, this may be done to alleviate guilt, but in most situations, the perpetrator realizes he has been caught and is hoping that his honesty will lead to leniency. Some investigators develop an uncanny ability to interview individuals within the confines of the law in such a way that they develop a reputation for eliciting confessions. In order to keep suspects from recanting their confessions in court and to demonstrate that they followed legal requirements, many agencies today audiotape or videotape suspect interviews. Still others have suspects write out signed statements admitting their guilt and describing the circumstances of the crime.

Often an investigator will ask a suspect to take a polygraph examination to help ascertain his level of honesty (Figure 10.2). Often referred to as a "lie detector," the polygraph in reality measures certain physiological properties, such as blood pressure, pulse, respiration, and galvanic skin response (sweat production), as the interviewee is asked a series

Figure 10.2 Polygraph examination. (Courtesy of the City of Santa Barbara. Retrieved from http://www.santabarbaraca.gov/Government/Departments/Police/Police_Polygraph.htm.)

of questions. The theory behind the polygraph is that lying causes most people distress, which can be measured through their physiological responses. In reality, the best skill that a polygrapher can have is that of being a good interviewer. To that end, investigators often use the polygraph in the hope that a polygrapher's skills will encourage a guilty person to confess. The polygraph is not without controversy. Some claim that its ability to detect "truth" is overrated and that using it for such things as hiring police officers could lead to bad decisions, such as letting in "good liars" and unfairly keeping out individuals who are not guilty of wrongdoing. In general, polygraphs are inadmissible evidence in most states. However, some states allow their admission with stipulation or the agreement of both the prosecution and the defense.

As with false identification, there is always the danger that individuals will confess to crimes they did not commit. Although this may seem incredible, people falsely confess for a variety of reasons. In some cases, they have a mental issue that compels them to admit to something they did not do. In other cases, the interview may have appeared so coercive or stressful that the suspect just wanted to "get it over" and was willing to say anything.

Investigative Team

Investigation is a team effort that requires work by a variety of individuals. An investigation often begins with a call to the police, which is usually answered by a dispatcher. The dispatcher then routes the call to a patrol unit that conducts the initial response. Although the dispatcher is rarely considered part of the investigative team, he or she conducts a valuable service collecting as much information as possible in the earliest stages of the investigation. This can prove especially important if the caller is incapable of making a later statement or becomes deceased.

The first units on the scene are usually patrol officers. Depending on the agency, they may have limited or a lot of involvement in the investigative process. At the very least, they are generally responsible for providing aid to the victim, identifying initial witnesses and securing and protecting the crime scene. They also decide what subsequent personnel (e.g., detectives and crime scene technicians) should be called out. In some agencies, patrol officers are given the responsibility of conducting all investigation of minor matters. In others, especially those with few officers, they may have investigative responsibility for every crime that occurs.

Detectives or investigators are generally involved in both the preliminary and follow-up stages of investigations (Figure 10.3). In many agencies, they serve as the primary investigative personnel and have overall responsibility for all aspects of the case. Each detective usually has a series of cases assigned to him/her, which is referred to as the caseload. It is usually up to the detective to decide what techniques he or she wants to use to solve the case. In some agencies, detectives work in pairs or teams and very often they are assigned to squads that handle one particular type of crime (e.g., robbery/homicide, burglary, property crime). Unlike patrol officers, detectives do not wear uniforms. In addition, they generally have more autonomy than patrol officers in carrying out their assignments.

In some agencies, becoming a detective is a promotion from patrol, whereas in others it is considered a lateral assignment. Nevertheless, many police officers crave an assignment as a detective. For them, the challenge of solving difficult and complex cases is the pinnacle of police work.

Some agencies employ crime scene technicians or criminalists. It is their responsibility to respond to crime scenes and recover evidence. They are usually highly trained and skilled at evidence recovery and provide a great advantage to agencies that can afford them. Some technicians are trained in specialty areas, such as computer forensics, which equips them with highly sought-after skills.

Figure 10.3 An investigative team. (Courtesy of the Joint POW/MIA Accounting Command. Retrieved from http://www.jpac.pacom.mil/index.php?page=press_center&size=90&ind=0&fldr=pressimagearchive&file=2009-06-20.)

In death investigations, the medical examiner or coroner is responsible for determining the cause and manner of death, especially in unusual circumstances. Those with proper training can perform autopsies, which are thorough postmortem examinations that attempt to determine how an individual died. The chief difference between the two positions is that medical examiners are usually medical doctors with specialty training while coroners are elected officials who may or may not have had any medical experience. Many agencies require investigators to attend autopsies; this generally enhances information sharing and allows both parties to have a better understanding of the circumstances surrounding a death.

The prosecutor or district attorney (DA) is usually an elected official whose office is responsible for handling the legal aspects of criminal cases. The DA usually has a number of assistant district attorneys (ADAs) who handle most of the criminal cases. ADAs generally decide what charges to file against an individual; they also present cases before grand juries and represent the government in criminal trials. Investigators must work closely with ADAs, and it is important that professional relationships develop. Smart investigators usually involve ADAs early in a case to ensure that the needs of both the police and the DA's office are met and that matters proceed smoothly.

Every agency has a support staff. Depending on the size of an agency, it may be quite small or comprised of many individuals. Any one of these individuals can enhance or derail an investigation. For example, if the evidence room technician, whose job is to log evidence in and out, fails to document things properly, the chain-of-custody could be broken. Likewise, a good crime analyst can detect patterns in criminal activity, thereby providing the break that could solve a series of serial rapes or burglaries.

Since the 1980s, a trend in investigations has been the task force. Task forces are made up of individuals from a variety of agencies including federal, state, tribal, and local organizations, and their purpose is to leverage the manpower and skills of various departments. Task forces have been formed to address drugs, gangs, and terrorism.

Crime laboratories exist at the local, state, and federal level (Figure 10.4). Some, like the FBI Laboratory, perform a variety of functions while others, like the Bureau of Alcohol,

Figure 10.4 Massachusetts State Police crime laboratory. (Courtesy of the MA Office of Public Safety. Retrieved from http://www.mass.gov/eopss/law-enforce-and-cj/criminal-investig/crime-lab/historymilestones.html.)

Tobacco, Firearms and Explosives and the Drug Enforcement Administration, have a more specialized focus. Agencies submit evidence to these laboratories to determine whether certain evidence is associated with a particular individual or crime.

State and federal specialty units and programs perform a variety of functions to assist and support local investigations. Many states have Bureaus of Criminal Investigation or some other entity that will offer assistance on a variety of cases. Other federal efforts are more narrowly focused. For example, the FBI's Critical Incident Response Group provides expertise in behavioral analysis. Since the attacks of 9/11, every state has developed a state-run fusion center, whose job is to gather and analyze criminal and terrorist intelligence provided by local agencies.

Investigative Process

Every investigation is unique. Given the high number of criminal violations that exist today—serial homicide, transnational organized crime, securities fraud, burglary, embezzlement, drug dealing, and so on—it is impossible to provide a template for every possible investigation. For example, the "crime scene" of a complex white-collar case may consist of a company's ledgers and cancelled checks, which is far different than the site of a murdered body dumped on the side of a highway.

Nevertheless, in this part of the chapter, we will discuss the investigative process in general terms. At all times, one must remember that the goals of all investigations remain consistent with what we outlined at the beginning of the chapter; the means of achieving these goals, however, will differ with each type of investigation. Regardless of what type of crime is involved, there are certain characteristics that are present in any successful investigation.

Perhaps most important, all phases of the investigation must be completely and meticulously documented. All members of the investigative team must be cognizant of the fact that they may be called upon to testify in court many months or even years later. It is essential that they present their testimony in a factually correct and coherent manner. Also, a complete and well-organized case file is essential for a detective to carry out the investigation; without it, he or she will be unable to know what happened or what investigative leads need to be covered. The police today document their investigations in many different ways. Detectives take notes that are later used to construct investigative reports. In addition, logs of most stages of the investigation are maintained and sketches, photographs, videotapes, audiotapes, and other forms of recording are used throughout.

Police officers in general and investigators in particular must display precise attention to detail. Unlike how they are often presented in the movies, investigations are usually laborious and occasionally monotonous. Detectives may find themselves involved in long stakeouts with little action. Crime scene searches can last for hours and even days before anything of value is discovered. Yet, the tiniest and seemingly most inconsequential item may be what ultimately solves the case. One of the largest crime scene searches in history involving an airliner that exploded at an altitude of 30,000 feet is described in Figure 10.5. The crime scene spread out over 800 square miles, each of which had to be

---

A Major Investigation—The Bombing of Pan Am Flight 103

On a cold and ultimately chilling evening just four days before Christmas, [1988,] Pan Am Flight 103 took off from London's Heathrow Airport bound for New York City. Among the 259 passengers and crew were 189 Americans.

They never made it home. Fewer than 40 minutes into the flight, the plane exploded over the sky above Lockerbie, Scotland, killing everyone on board and 11 Scots on the ground.

Until 9/11, it was the world's most lethal act of air terrorism and the largest and most complex act of international terrorism ever investigated by the FBI.

Solving the case required unprecedented international cooperation and many hours of painstaking work. With the midair explosion 30,000 feet up, debris rained down over 845 square miles across Scotland. FBI agents and international investigators combed the countryside on hands and knees looking for clues in virtually every blade of grass, eventually turning up thousands of pieces of evidence. They also traversed the globe, interviewing more than 10,000 individuals in dozens of countries.

Participating in the investigation was an array of international police organizations from such countries as Germany, Austria, Switzerland, and, of course, Great Britain (including Scotland).

Ultimately, forensic specialists from the FBI, the CIA, and elsewhere determined that one of the fragments found on the ground, no bigger than a thumbnail, came from the circuit board of a radio/cassette player. That tiny piece of evidence helped establish that the bomb had been placed inside that radio and tape deck in a piece of luggage. Another small fragment found embedded in a piece of shirt helped identify the type of timer.

This evidence led to two Libyan intelligence operatives. In November 1991, the U.S. and Scotland simultaneously indicted the pair for planting the bomb. On January 31, 2001, after years of working to extradite the men and bring the case to trial, Abdel Basset Ali Al-Megrahi was found guilty of the crime. The codefendant was found not guilty and released.

[T]he Libyan government formally accepted responsibility for the bombing and has agreed to pay nearly $3 billion to the victims' families.

Figure 10.5   The bombing of Pan Am Flight 103. (Courtesy of the FBI, 2003).

painstakingly searched. Ultimately, one of the search teams discovered a circuit board less than an inch square that cracked the case.

Detectives also need to have an innate sense of curiosity and the ability to consider things in an objective manner. One of the worst traits that an investigator can possess is a tendency to jump to conclusions and develop "tunnel vision." In the famous Washington, D.C. sniper case of 2002, the media and the police became convinced that the killer was driving a white van; as a result, the actual killers, who were actually driving a blue Chevrolet Caprice, passed unquestioned through law enforcement roadblocks. In many investigations, multiple hypotheses or theories of the case may develop. Rather than concentrating on one, a good investigator considers each, eliminating the ones that the facts and evidence show to be false. In the words of Sherlock Holmes,[11] quoted at the beginning of this chapter, "… whatever remains, however improbable, must be the truth."

The FBI summarizes the events of locating the D.C. sniper's vehicle as follows:[12]

Just a few hours earlier, at approximately 11:45 p.m., their dark blue 1990 Chevy Caprice— bearing the New Jersey license plate NDA-21Z, which had been widely publicized on the news only hours earlier— had been spotted at a rest stop parking lot off I-70 in Maryland (see Figure 10.6). Within the hour, law enforcement swarmed the scene, setting up a perimeter to check out any movements and make sure there'd be no escape. What evidence experts from the FBI and other police forces found there was both revealing and shocking. The car had a hole cut in the trunk near the license plate (see Figure 10.7) so that shots could be fired from within the vehicle. It was, in effect, a rolling sniper's nest. Also found in the car were:

- The Bushmaster .223-caliber rifle that had been used in each attack
- A rifle's scope for taking aim and a tripod to steady the shots

Figure 10.6 Crime scene location of the D.C. sniper's vehicle. (Courtesy of the FBI, 2007. Retrieved from http://www.fbi.gov/news/stories/2007/october/snipers_102207.)

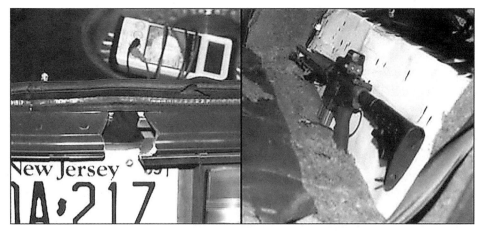

Figure 10.7 Trunk of the D.C. sniper's vehicle. (Courtesy of the FBI, 2007. Retrieved from http://www.fbi.gov/news/stories/2007/october/snipers_102207.)

- A backseat that had the sheet metal removed between the passenger compartment and the trunk, enabling the shooter to get into the trunk from inside the car
- The Chevy Caprice owner's manual with—the FBI Laboratory later detected— written impressions of one of the demand notes
- The digital voice recorder used by both Malvo and Muhammad to make extortion demands
- A laptop stolen from one of the victims containing maps of the shooting sites and getaway routes from some of the crime scenes
- Maps, walkie-talkies, and many more items

Finally, investigative work is certainly not for everyone. Detectives are often exposed to the worst society has to offer; they must be prepared to deal with horrific events and remain under control at all times. Regardless of how "tough" or desensitized one may become, such experiences can and will take a toll. Unfortunately, some in law enforcement deal with this stress in unhealthy ways, such as self-medicating with large amounts of alcohol or taking out frustrations on those they love. Successful investigators develop healthy ways to deal with stress; for example, they may exercise regularly, practice spirituality, and/or, most importantly, develop the ability to keep all things in balance. Recognizing the needs of their personnel, many law enforcement agencies today have employee assistance programs that provide confidential guidance and counseling.

Investigations are processes consisting of numerous phases commencing with a preliminary stage and concluding with a follow-up stage. A prosecutorial phase may occur after the investigation. These concepts are discussed in the following sections.

Preliminary Investigation

As the name implies, the preliminary stage of an investigation begins as soon as a complaint is received or a crime is spotted in progress by the police. This is often a crucial time in the investigation of any case because clues are fresh, witnesses are usually available, and a suspect may still be present. Mark Harrison of the United Kingdom's National Crime and Operations Faculty refers to the period immediately following the commission of a crime as the "golden hour" where the success or failure of an investigation is often determined.[13]

Approaching the Crime Scene

The first police personnel to arrive at the scene of a crime are usually patrol officers. Even before they arrive, they must take steps to initiate the investigation. In the first place, they must arrive safely; it does little good if an officer is involved in an accident on the way to a crime. Perhaps surprisingly, from 2005 to 2007, 54% of officer deaths were traffic fatalities.[14] This means that more officers died in car accidents than they did at the hands of adversaries. Next, officers should prepare themselves mentally for what they might face— they should always assume that a perpetrator is still on the scene unless they know otherwise. Upon arrival, the first officer on the scene must take charge. Initial duties are to render the scene safe and then provide aid to victims who require assistance. Only after this is accomplished can the investigation begin.

First Officers on the Scene

Once the scene has been established as safe and victims have been assisted, the officers have numerous duties that must be accomplished quickly and efficiently. One of their first responsibilities is the identification of witnesses. This must be accomplished quickly because as time passes, witnesses can disappear or decide not to cooperate.

At the same time, the area surrounding the crime must be secured and a protective perimeter must be established. The area where a crime occurred and its surroundings are referred to as the crime scene. It is important that the scene be secured as quickly as possible to prevent contamination of potential evidence. If too many people have access to the scene, they may destroy valuable evidence such as fingerprints, footprints, or tire tracks. Therefore, arriving officers must establish physical barriers such as crime scene tape and post guards. The only individuals allowed entry to the scene should be those who are part of the investigation. To ensure accountability and control, a log of individuals entering the scene should be maintained.

Officers must use discretion when deciding the dimensions of the crime scene. Two of the big factors that are considered are the type of crime and the location of the scene. For example, a homicide where the body was moved would likely require a larger scene than a sexual assault that occurred in one place. A crime in a vehicle will have different dimensions than one that occurred outdoors. As a general rule, it is advisable to start large and gradually reduce the size of the scene to make sure valuable evidence is not lost.

The first officers also need to decide who should be called to the scene. For example, if the case involves a potential murder, obviously the homicide detectives must be summoned. Other personnel, such as crime scene technicians, may be required as well. Summoning others should be accomplished expeditiously to take full advantage of the "golden hour." The arriving officers remain in charge of the scene until they are relieved of their duties by senior personnel.

Initial Steps

Once the scene has been secured and the initial witnesses identified, an initial walk-through/assessment is made. If it has not already been started, documentation begins in earnest. All stages of the initial investigation are detailed and include the use of investigative notes, logs (search, evidence, photo, etc.), videotaping, photographing, and sketching.

Once the detectives arrive, they assume control of the investigation. Usually, a lead detective who will assume responsibility for the case all the way through its prosecution is assigned. Detectives begin to formulate hypotheses of what may have happened and decide upon an appropriate investigative strategy. As the investigation proceeds and more facts become known, hypotheses may change or become discarded and the strategy may evolve.

In the initial stages of the investigation, detectives attempt to identify and locate the perpetrator, identify and interview witnesses or others with information, and obtain evidence. Very often, they will conduct a neighborhood canvass in which they question those who live or work near the crime scene to determine whether they witnessed anything. Detectives also must decide the extent to which a crime scene search is required and carry it out as necessary.

Crime Scene Search

Some crime scenes require a thorough search. This can be a slow, painstaking process, but it must be carried out with utmost care. The police often have only one opportunity to obtain important evidence at a crime scene before it becomes contaminated, and they must make the most of it.

Searches should be well planned and executed in a methodical manner. In some agencies, crime scene technicians or evidence response personnel conduct the actual search. In others, detectives and/or patrol officers perform this function. Logs are kept, inventories of seized items are maintained, evidence is photographed or videotaped, and sketches of the scene and the location of evidence are made (Figure 10.8). In order to ensure efficient and complete searches, some agencies use various search patterns. Search patterns may involve land, maritime, and aviation modalities.

In order to ensure well-organized searches, a single individual should be designated as an inventory control officer. In addition, temporary, fragile, or easily lost evidence should be collected first. Although searches should proceed methodically, those in charge should be mindful of changing conditions that can destroy evidence, such as the appearance of a sudden thunderstorm in an outdoor location.

All recovered evidence should be photographed in its original condition and marked with an officer's initials, the date, the case number, and an individual case identifier. Some types of evidence routinely collected at crime scenes include

- Fingerprints
- Documents
- Shoe and tire impressions
- Tools and tool marks
- Firearms

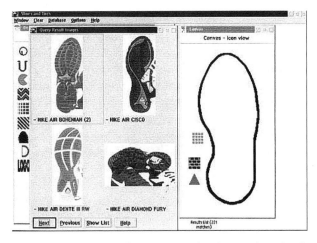

Figure 10.8 The FBI Laboratory uses the automated SoleSearcher database, which contains thousands of outsoles from hundreds of shoe manufacturers, to help identify the brand or manufacturer of shoes when footwear impressions are left behind at a crime scene. (From *Forensic Science Communications*, 2007. Retrieved from http://www2.fbi.gov/hq/lab/fsc/backissu/oct2007/research/2007_10_research01_test2.htm.)

- Glass, soils, and minerals
- Body fluids
- Hairs, fibers, rope, and tape
- Drugs and other contraband
- Computers and electronic media

Once a search has been thoroughly conducted and there is nothing more to be gained by keeping the area under the control of the police, the detective in charge can release the scene.

Follow-Up Investigation

Once all preliminary investigation has been completed, the follow-up investigation begins. During this phase, the detectives employ any number of different investigative techniques depending on the nature of the offense. At this stage, evidence is submitted to forensic laboratories to determine its probative value. Laboratory personnel examine the evidence, write up reports of their findings, and forward the reports and evidence to the submitting agency. If a case proceeds to trial, a laboratory examiner may be called by either the prosecution or defense to testify. Unlike other witnesses, who are allowed to testify only about matters over which they have direct knowledge, forensic examiners can be designated by the court as expert witnesses. This means they are permitted to offer opinions about the examinations they conducted (e.g., a ballistics expert can offer an opinion that a particular bullet was fired by a particular gun).

Some of the other investigative techniques employed in the follow-up stages of an investigation include

- Interviewing witnesses and others with knowledge of the case
- Checking records and databases
- Conducting surveillance
- Utilizing analytical methodologies (e.g., behavioral analysis, geographic profiling, crime analysis, and financial analysis)
- Employing informants
- Initiating undercover operations
- Conducting searches pursuant to obtaining a search warrant
- Obtaining permission to conduct court-authorized wiretaps of telephones and other electronic devices
- Making controlled buys of drugs and other contraband
- Serving of grand jury subpoenas to obtain documents or compel testimony
- Consulting experts with specialized knowledge (e.g., art history experts in the investigation of stolen artwork)
- Working with other law enforcement agencies
- Enlisting cooperation from the public
- Conducting searches on the Internet, including social networking sites
- Utilizing other appropriate investigative techniques specific to the offense (e.g., autopsies)

In some cases, investigations proceed quickly, whereas in others, investigations may take years. For example, in 1964, three civil rights workers were murdered in Neshoba

Figure 10.9   Edgar Ray Killen being escorted by police. (Courtesy of the Associated Press. Retrieved from http://www.usatoday.com/news/nation/2007-02-04-coldcases_x.htm.)

County, Mississippi. In 1967, 7 of 18 defendants were found guilty of federal violations. However, at least one "big fish," Edgar Ray Killen, escaped conviction. Authorities did not give up. Finally, in 2005, some 41 years after the killings, Killen was convicted of manslaughter by the state of Mississippi (Figure 10.9).[15]

As stated at the beginning of the chapter, one of the primary goals of an investigation should be to "clear" the case. However, despite the best efforts of investigators, not all cases can be cleared. Physical evidence may be lacking and witnesses may not exist or may be unwilling to come forward. In addition, many offenses have a statute of limitations, a requirement that legal proceedings based on a particular event must be initiated within a certain period of time or a case cannot be brought. For many crimes in various states, the statute of limitations runs between three and five years. Some crimes, like murder, do not have a statute of limitations.

As a result of a lack of evidence, insufficient investigative resources, or the expiration of the statute of limitations, many cases are never cleared. Often they are closed administratively by an agency. Usually, different types of crimes have different rates of clearance.

If an investigation is successful, the detective will gather sufficient evidence to arrest a suspect and present the case to the DA's office to determine whether charges should be filed and prosecution pursued. This brings the investigation to the prosecutorial phase. It should be noted that an investigator's objective should always be focused on determining the truth of the matter of fact and not simply clearing the crime or making an arrest.

Prosecutorial Phase

Ideally, the investigators and the ADAs will have been working together throughout all phases of the case, but often that is not possible. When the detective believes he or she has sufficient evidence for a successful prosecution, he or she delivers a prosecutorial report to the ADA who will make a decision as to whether to file charges. In some cases, the ADA will present the case to a grand jury to determine whether there is enough evidence to issue an indictment against an individual, compelling him to answer criminal charges. Often, the detective will appear before the grand jury as a witness, outlining the evidence and the facts of the case.

Most criminal cases never go to trial. Instead, charges are dropped or both parties agree to a deal, termed a "plea bargain," where the defendant agrees to plead guilty to reduced charges or the prosecution agrees to seek a reduced penalty in return for not proceeding to trial. If the case does go to trial, the detective will help the ADA prepare the case by submitting the necessary reports and documents from the case file and providing the evidence for introduction in court. Often, the ADA will ask the detectives to conduct additional follow-up investigation, deliver subpoenas, and/or locate witnesses. Some large DA offices have their own staff of investigators who perform these functions. It is likely the detective will also be required to testify during the trial.

Even after a verdict has been rendered, the case may not be over. If convicted, defendants have a right to file appeals, in some cases all the way to the United States Supreme Court. It is not uncommon for a case to be reversed on appeal years after conviction, meaning that a new trial must be conducted. This can prove to be quite difficult for the prosecution insofar as evidence may have disappeared or witnesses may have died or relocated.

Unsolved Investigations and Cold Cases

Although a variety of techniques and resources exist through which investigators may examine criminal cases to solve crimes, many crimes remain unsolved. Examining Nevada crime clearance rates shows statistics that represent this situation. The following observations describe Nevada clearance rates between 1998 and 2010:[16]

- Nationally, about 22% of all Part I crimes that are known to police are cleared by arrest or exceptional means, compared to about 25% in Nevada.
- Since 1998, the national clearance rate for Part I crimes increased about 3%, whereas the clearing rate for these offenses in Nevada increased nearly 14%.
- In 2009, the national clearance rate for murder was far less than Nevada's (67% vs. 80%); however, the clearance rate for rape offenses nationally was noticeably higher than Nevada's (41% vs. 24%).
- In Nevada, clearance rates are higher for violent crimes (43%) than for property crimes (21%).

   The highest clearance rate in the state is for murder (80%) and the lowest is for motor vehicle theft (7%). Within Nevada, the highest clearance rates in 2009 were observed in Esmeralda County (83%) and Mineral County (71%), whereas the lowest clearance rates were observed in Elko County (20%) and Storey County (11%).

Unsolved crimes (i.e., cold cases) exist domestically and internationally. The definition of a cold case (or "historical" cases as they are called in many countries outside the United States) varies from agency to agency. A cold case is defined as "any case whose probative investigative leads have been exhausted."[17] Therefore, cases that are merely months old may be termed as cold cases.[18] Because of the popularity of television programs and public influence, much attention is now directed toward investigations that were initially unsolved.[19]

Cold cases present unique difficulties. Such impediments include lack of evidence, strained resources, ineffective investigation, and the failure of initial efforts to close the case.[20] In recent years, rates of clearance for all types of crime have plummeted.[21] By the late 1980s, the sheer volume of unsolved cases had become an overwhelming problem for many agencies. The promise of technologies, such as DNA and automated fingerprint matching, convinced police administrators that unsolved cases that were neglected might benefit from a fresh perspective.[22] Hence, the cold-case investigation concept was born.[23]

Recent advances in DNA technology are allowing officials to take a fresh look at many of these previously unsolved cases.[24] The creation of the Combined DNA Index System (CODIS) has improved the chances of solving cold cases with DNA.[25] Established and managed by the FBI, CODIS allows DNA profiles to be uploaded into a database and searched against other profiles at the local, state, and national levels.[26] There are two main indices in CODIS: (1) the forensic index, which houses crime scene or evidence DNA samples, and (2) the convicted offender index, which contains profiles for convicted offenders from all 50 states.[27] The CODIS also contains profiles of missing persons and arrestees (if state law permits the collection of arrestee samples).[28]

A 2011 RAND Corporation survey revealed that most agencies do little cold-case work (only about 7%), cold-case funding is tenuous, overall success rates for cold-case investigations are low, agency factors associated with higher clearance rates include level of funding and access to investigative databases.[29] The RAND survey indicated that even when a suspect DNA match was made, about one-third of cases are not filed because of problems with victim cooperation, credibility, or availability of suspects who are deceased or in prison.[30] However, those cases that are prosecuted resulted in convictions and lengthy prison terms more than 90% of the time, and cooperation between police and prosecutors can improve both the efficiency and effectiveness of cold-case investigations.[31] Successful cold-case investigations also provide a sense of relief to the community and closure to the victim's family. In addition, confidence in the judicial system is reinforced.

Throughout history, many unsolved crimes have gained varying levels of notoriety. According to *Time Magazine*, examples of such incidents include[32]

- The British incidents involving the murdering of a prostitute by the unknown assailant known as Jack the Ripper.
- The 1947 murder of actress Elizabeth Short, dubbed the Black Dahlia case.
- Beginning in 1968, the Zodiac killer who terrorized and murdered people in California.
- For about three decades, the Wichita, Kansas BTK killer, who was eventually caught and convicted.

The aforementioned case involving the Zodiac killer, is fascinating. Throughout the duration of his killings, the perpetrator toyed with law enforcement and news agencies by sending encrypted messages, via postal service, that involved a complex set of written alphanumeric characters and symbols. At one point, this criminal "mailed in a piece of bloodied shirt to prove he was who he claimed to be."[33] He also often telephoned to discuss his murderous activities. Despite numerous attempts to decrypt and decipher his messages, he has yet to be identified. Examples of his writings are shown in Figures 10.10 through 10.13.

Figure 10.10 Zodiac writings. (From America's Most Wanted, 2010. Retrieved from http://www .amw.com/features/feature_story_detail.cfm?id=1545.)

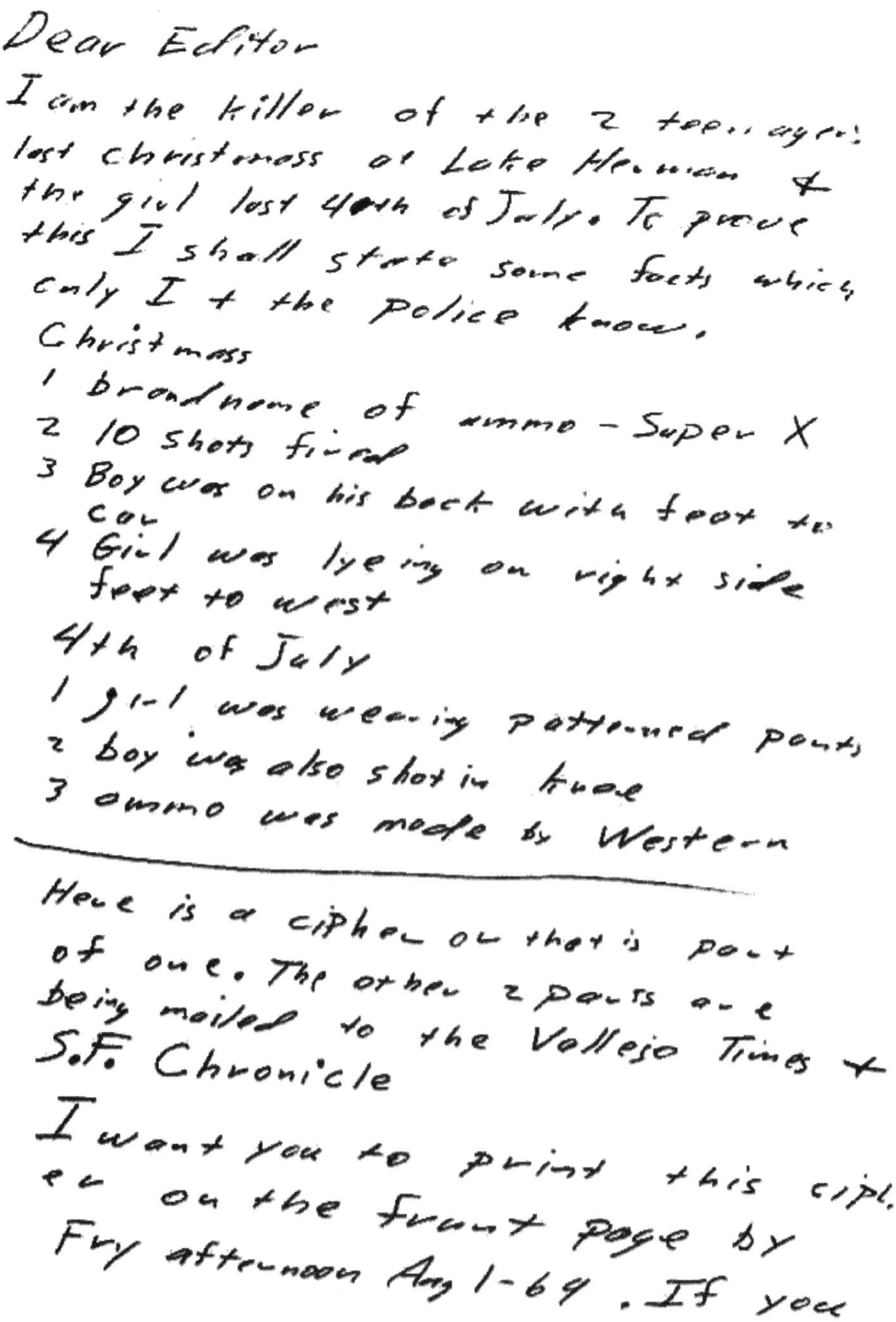
Dear Editor
I am the killer of the 2 teenagers last christmass at Lake Herman & the girl last 4th of July. To prove this I shall state some facts which only I & the police know.
Christmass
1 brandname of ammo - Super X
2 10 shots fired
3 Boy was on his back with feet to car
4 Girl was lyeing on right side feet to west
4th of July
1 girl was wearing patterned pants
2 boy was also shot in knee
3 ammo was made by Western

Here is a cipher or that is part of one. The other 2 parts are being mailed to the Vallejo Times & S.F. Chronicle
I want you to print this cipher on the front page by Fry afternoon Aug 1-69. If you

Figure 10.11 Disturbing writings of the Zodiac. (From America's Most Wanted, 2010. Retrieved from http://www.amw.com/features/feature_story_detail.cfm?id=1545.)

A review of the FBI's Uniform Crime Reports shows differing rates of clearance among each of the states. Although law enforcement agencies make their best efforts to solve crimes, the stark reality is that a variety of factors make it impossible to solve every case.

Figure 10.12   The Zodiac sent this card to taunt news media. (From America's Most Wanted, 2010. Retrieved from http://www.amw.com/features/feature_story_detail.cfm?id=1545.)

Figure 10.13   Front of card sent by the Zodiac killer. (From America's Most Wanted, 2010. Retrieved from http://media.amw.com/multimedia/fileRepository/db/472/142/halloweencard .jpg.)

Summary

Investigations are an integral part of any law enforcement agency. The public must have confidence in the police's ability to solve crimes and bring criminals to justice. Otherwise, the rule of law, the very fabric that binds a society together, disappears. Over the years, the United States has developed a system of law enforcement that is among the best in the world. Although not every crime gets solved, agencies on the federal, state, and local levels continue to evolve into better partners, working together to overcome the many challenges that confront them in the twenty-first century.

A criminal investigation is a legal inquiry. It involves a process of determining what happened and who is responsible. Based on specific evidence, investigators establish proof that a suspect is guilty of committing a crime. For the public, the term "detective" or "criminal investigator" often brings to mind the image of the meticulous individual who single-handedly digs out evidence, collects tips from informants, identifies criminals, tracks them down, and brings them to justice. Although skillful investigators are essential, in reality, it is contributions from the entire police department or agency—teamwork—that result in successful criminal investigations.

Investigations are an integral part of any law enforcement agency. Detectives are generally involved in both the preliminary and follow-up stages of investigations. They perform many functions, for example, photographing, videotaping, and sketching; taking field notes and writing offense and investigative reports; searching crime scenes, identifying and processing physical evidence, interviewing and obtaining information from victims and witnesses; identifying and interrogating suspects; conducting surveillance; executing search warrants; working undercover assignments, working closely with the prosecutor in preparing a case for court; and testifying in court.

Advancements in DNA analysis, together with computer technology, and new investigative databases, have created powerful crime fighting tools for law enforcement and improved the odds of solving new and cold cases. New technologies are taking criminal investigation techniques to the next level and beyond. These emerging technologies are helping to solve crimes that would have been unsolvable just a few years ago. Although recent advances in forensics have been impressive, the continued value of an investigator's careful eye for detail and a sound understanding of human nature is what usually solves a crime.

References

1. Doyle, A. C. (2001). *The Sign of the Four* (p. 42). (Original work published 1890).
2. Beirne, P. (1987). Adolphe Quetelet and the origins of positivist criminology. *American Journal of Sociology, 92*(5): 1140–1169.
3. Rhodes, H. (1956). *Alphonse Bertillon: Father of Scientific Detection*. New York: Abelard-Schuman.
4. Sifakis, C. (1982). *Encyclopedia of American Crime*. New York, NY: Facts On File.
5. Herschel, W. (1916). *The Origin of Fingerpinting*. Oxford: Oxford University Press.
6. Sutherland, E. H. (1924). *Criminology*. Philadelphia, PA: J.B. Lippincott Company.
7. Cole, S. (2002). *Suspect Identities: A History of Fingerprinting and Criminal Identification*. Cambridge: Harvard University Press.
8. Federal Bureau of Investigation (2008). *Crime in the United States, 2007*. Washington, DC: Federal Bureau of Investigation.

9. Ibid.
10. Richardson, D., & Kosa, R. (2001). *Foundation for the Development of a Homicide Clearance Model (Draft)*. Washington, DC: Police Executive Research Forum.
11. Doyle, A. C. (2001). *The Sign of the Four* (p. 42). (Original work published 1890).
12. Federal Bureau of Investigation (2007). *A Byte Out of History: The Beltway Snipers, Part 1*. Retrieved from http://www.fbi.gov/news/stories/2007/october/snipers_102207
13. Foster, R. (2010). High definition survey: Returning to the scene of the crime. *Police Technology*. Retrieved from http://www.police-technology.net/id49.html
14. Halvorson, B. (2010). Police officers not buckling up, fatal crashes rising. *Fox News*. Retrieved from http://www.foxnews.com/leisure/2010/08/04/police-officers-buckling-fatal-crashes-rising/
15. Federal Bureau of Investigation (2007). *A Byte Out of History: Mississippi Burning*. Retrieved from http://www.fbi.gov/news/stories/2007/february/miburn_022607
16. Sakiyama, M., Miethe, T., & Hart, T. (2010). *Clearance Rates in Nevada, 1998–2009*. University of Nevada, Las Vegas. Retrieved from http://www.google.com/url?sa=t&source=web&cd=6&ved=0CDwQFjAF&url=http%3A%2F%2Fwww.unlv.edu%2Fcenters%2Fcrimestats%2FSDBs%2FClearance%2520Rates%2FClearance%2520Rates%2520v4.pdf&rct=j&q=clearance%20rate%20robbery&ei=SkRRTvr0I8TL0QGH--mLBw&usg=AFQjCNGZoWNnmYrgWGFDOdFgeB9VvKdP9A&cad=rja
17. National Institute of Justice (2012). *What is a Cold Case?* Retrieved from http://www.nij.gov/journals/260/what-is-cold-case.htm
18. Ibid.
19. Ibid.
20. Davis, R., Jensen, C., & Kitchens, K. (2011). *Cold Case Investigations: An Analysis of Current Practices and Factors Associated with Successful Outcomes*. Santa Monica, CA: RAND Corporation.
21. Ibid.
22. Ibid.
23. Ibid.
24. National Institute of Justice (2012). *What is a Cold Case?* Retrieved from http://www.nij.gov/journals/260/what-is-cold-case.htm
25. Ibid.
26. Ibid.
27. Ibid.
28. Ibid.
29. Davis, R., Jensen, C., & Kitchens, K. (2011). *Cold Case Investigations: An Analysis of Current Practices and Factors Associated with Successful Outcomes*. Santa Monica, CA: RAND Corporation.
30. Ibid.
31. Ibid.
32. Top 10 unsolved crimes (2012). *Time Magazine*. Retrieved from http://www.time.com/time/specials/packages/article/0,28804,1867198_1867170_1867159,00.html
33. Ibid.

Bibliography

Doyle, A. C. (2001). *The Sign of the Four*. In E. D. Glinert (Ed.), New York, NY: Penguin Classics. (Original work published 1890)

Federal Bureau of Investigation (2003). *A Byte Out of History: Solving a Complex Case of International Terrorism*. Retrieved from http://www.fbi.gov/news/stories/2003/december/panam121903/?searchterm=pan%20am%20103

Federal Bureau of Investigation (2008). *Clearances. Crime in the United States, 2007*. Washington, DC: Federal Bureau of Investigation. Retrieved from http://www2.fbi.gov/ucr/cius2007/offenses/clearances/index.html

Federal Bureau of Investigation (2012). *Integrated Automated Fingerprint Identification System.* Retrieved from http://www.fbi.gov/about-us/cjis/fingerprints_biometrics/iafis

Foster, R. (2012). High definition survey: Returning to the scene of the crime. *Police Technology.* Retrieved from http://www.police-technology.net/id49.html

Hess, K. M., & Orthmann, C. H. (2010). *Criminal Investigation* (9th ed.). Clifton Park, NY: Delmar Cengage Learning.

Law Enforcement Exploring (2010). *Crime Scene Search Study Guide 2010, Part II of II.* Retrieved from http://www.learningforlife.org/exploring/lawenforcement/study/crimescene2.pdf

National Institute of Justice (2001). *Understanding DNA Evidence: A Guide for Victim Service Providers.* Washington, DC: Author. Retrieved from http://www.ojp.usdoj.gov/nij/pubs-sum/BC000657. htm on 10/30/2010

Richardson, D., & Kosa, R. (2001). *Foundation for the Development of a Homicide Clearance Model (Draft).* Washington, DC: Police Executive Research Forum. Retrieved from http://www. policeforum.org/library/homicide/Homicide%20Clearance%20Rates%20-%20Model.pdf

Forensic Science

11

Well, we had nine top forensic pathologists from across the country, who operated as a panel, who looked at all the ballistic evidence, and they came out saying that those bullets did exactly what the Warren Commission said they did.[1]

Louis Stokes

Learning Objectives

The objectives of this chapter are to

- Understand forensic science and its application to law enforcement
- Discuss scientific testing
- Identify the organizational components of forensics
- Understand the responsibilities of forensics

Introduction

Forensic science has not only entered criminal justice, but it has also captured the imagination of citizens across the nation. Although advancements in forensic science over the last 50 years have been astounding, most criminal investigations rely on the efforts and commitments of investigators gathering physical evidence and interviewing witnesses. Fans of television shows like the *CSI* series may believe that law enforcement and science are inextricably linked, which is not necessarily the case as presented by Hollywood.

Forensic crime laboratories are a vital part of the criminal justice system and continue to provide valuable information that assists police in their investigations and courts in their endeavors to determine the guilt or innocence of the parties involved. This is done by way of preservation, collection, analysis of evidence and presentation of results through expert testimony to the courts.

Foundations of Forensic Science

The first recorded description of using scientific principles to solve crimes came in a Chinese book titled *The Washing Away of Wrongs*, which was written in the thirteenth century by Sung Tzu, a pioneer in forensic entomology. Among other cases, Sung described a homicide in which a farmer had been killed by an unknown assailant using a sickle. Sung had all the village farmers lay down their sickles in a row; soon, blow flies were drawn to the one that contained traces of the victim's blood.[2]

Forensic science really began to develop in Europe in the nineteenth century, driven by a desire to see that justice was done in judicial proceedings. Before that time, confessions, oftentimes coerced, and victim statements formed the basis of evidence at criminal trials. Although some tried to follow Sung's lead in the sixteenth century and later, it was in the 1800s that criminologists and jurists truly became convinced that science, with its standards of objectivity and neutrality, could add precision and fairness to investigations. As a result, doctors and scientists began to work with the police to integrate science and crime solving. In Europe and the United States, criminal justice professionals began recognizing the value of science in the struggle against crime and, though often slowly, forensics began to take shape.

Robert Peel's Metropolitan Police Department began making major advancements in what would become known as forensics. Though work had been done in the study of fingerprints, Sir Edward Henry, commissioner of the Metropolitan Police of London, developed his own system in 1896 based on the direction, flow, pattern, and other characteristics in fingerprints. The Henry Classification System became the standard for criminal fingerprinting techniques worldwide. In 1835, Scotland Yard's Henry Goddard became the first person to use physical analysis to connect a bullet to the murder weapon. In 1836, a Scottish chemist named James Marsh developed a chemical test to detect arsenic, which was used during a murder trial.[3]

The Austrian Jurist Dr. Johann (Hans) Baptist Gustav Gross (born Johann Baptist Gustav Gross, 1847–1915) was one of the earliest forensic scientists of modern record. In 1893, Gross published his ground-breaking work, *System Der Kriminalistik* (*Criminal Investigation*). It was the first published work of its kind. Gross went on to publish other important research in the field of criminalistics. He also opened the first criminological institute in the world at the University of Graz, Austria. Considered one of the founders of criminalistics for his research, Gross is also widely credited with coining the term "criminalistics" and regarded as the grandfather of modern criminalistics.[4]

Fiction author Arthur Conan Doyle had a major impact upon capturing the imagination of the public and inspiring early efforts in forensics through his fictional crime-fighting character Sherlock Holmes.

The world's first police crime laboratory, supported and staffed by law enforcement agents, was the small laboratory belonging to Edmund Locard in Lyon, France. Locard studied under Alexandre Lacassagne, a professor of forensic medicine at the University of Lyon, who advocated the use of science in the investigation of crime. According to Locard, three men inspired him to create the crime lab: Lacassagne, Hans Gross, and Arthur Conan Doyle. German criminologist Hans Gross observed failures of criminal investigations based on eyewitnesses and urged the application of scientific analysis to reconstruct a crime. In his textbook, *Criminal Investigation: A Practical Textbook for Magistrates, Police Officers, and Lawyers* (1893), Gross advised police to carefully examine crime scenes for traces of blood and fingerprints and to consult scientists of all specialties for a more accurate recreation of a crime. Arthur Conan Doyle inspired Locard by writing the stories of Sherlock Holmes. Many years later, in a 1929 article in *Revue Internationale de Criminalistique*, Locard credited Doyle as second only to Hans Gross for inspiring techniques of trace evidence analysis.[5] For more than 40 years, Locard worked to advance the field of forensics, developing new and refining existing techniques of scientific investigation.

On the municipal level, throughout the late 1800s and early 1900s, many departments were making advancements in the incorporation of science into law enforcement. In 1916, August Vollmer opened within the Berkeley Police Department in California what many claim to be the first scientific crime laboratory. Vollmer was also an early supporter of the development of the polygraph. He also long believed in the use of both psychiatry and psychology to gain insight into criminal activity and the motivation of criminals.

Sadly, advancements in law enforcement are often fueled by tragedy. High profile crimes such as the St. Valentine's Day Massacre, the murders involving Leopold and Loeb, or the kidnapping and murder of the Lindbergh baby captured the imagination of the public, and in each case, the investigators could have benefited from science.

In the wake of the St. Valentine's Day Massacre, a scientific crime detection laboratory was established by Colonel Calvin H. Goddard. This was a full-service laboratory, patterned partly after a laboratory established earlier by August Vollmer in California and partly after laboratories in several European countries. The laboratory, the country's first independent forensic science crime laboratory, operated under the auspices of the Northwestern University Law School.[6] Colonel Goddard is credited with founding the science of firearms identification.[7]

By 1930, the Federal Bureau of Investigation (FBI) began using outside experts hired for such work on a case-by-case basis. That same year, the Bureau began a criminology library for the use of its agents and support personnel, and it took over the collection and publication of uniform crime statistics from the International Association of Chiefs of Police. In its new agent training program, the Bureau included expert lecturers on subjects like handwriting comparison, typewriting comparison, the taking of fingerprint, fingerprint classification, moulage, ballistics, and similar technical criminological subjects.[8] The FBI had opened its laboratory in Washington, D.C. in 1932.[9]

Early documentation reveals that the silver nitrate process was developed in the 1910s. In 1918, the International Association of Identification (IAI) Conference gave a presentation on this process. Different people were experimenting with it, but its development is historically credited to Dr. Erastus Mead Hudson. In June 1935, Dr. E.M. Hudson, a New York City physician, who had learned about fingerprinting at Scotland Yard, discovered a method of securing fingerprints from handkerchiefs, cloth, paper, and wood. His method used silver nitrate to change the ordinary salt in a fingerprint to silver chloride. By using an iodine gas process, he brought out 500 fingerprints on the ladder used in the Lindbergh kidnapping.[10] In later years, Dr. Hudson did additional research with the New York Police Department, exploring other possible uses for the silver nitrate process, such as recovering latent prints from cloth and gloves.

States also began creating criminal laboratories. In 1936, the Missouri Highway Patrol opened a crime laboratory (Figure 11.1).

Figure 11.1 Forensic investigations often contribute to solving crimes. (Courtesy of the U.S. National Library of Medicine. Retrieved from http://www.nlm.nih.gov/visibleproofs/exhibition/newscience.html.)

Why Science?

For most of us, science enjoys a special distinction. The police and the prosecutors are seen as zealous pursuers of criminals. Defense attorneys are advocates for the accused. Each is seen as having a certain vested interest in the outcome of an investigation. Scientists, on the other hand, are generally perceived to be dispassionate purveyors of the "truth." They run tests, which have been scientifically validated, and make objective reports of their results. In theory, they favor neither the prosecution nor the defense. Science itself is seen as an objective arbiter—we believe that laboratory analyses, such as fingerprint analysis, yield objective results. When a fingerprint examiner testifies that the prints found at a scene match the defendant's, he is saying several things that we hold to be true: (a) fingerprints are unique identifiers (i.e., everyone's is different) and (b) the analysis the examiner performed is sufficiently rigorous and properly performed as to yield a valid and reliable result. In short, we tend to believe a scientist when he or she testifies. As a result, as outlined further, science is afforded a special place in investigations and criminal proceedings.

Forensic Science Defined

Forensic science is the application of established principles of science in a legal setting. For something to be considered a forensic science, it must meet both a scientific and a legal standard. In the first place, the scientific community must recognize the technique as something that is valid. For example, graphologists claim that a person's handwriting reveals much about his personality; however, many studies refute this claim and graphology is generally not allowed to be introduced as evidence at trial.

Many, but not all, forensic science tests attempt to link a particular individual to a specific piece of evidence. For example, it is common today for DNA experts to testify that blood from a crime scene came from a specific individual within a certain margin of error. Underlying this conclusion are several important assumptions. The first involves Locard's Principle of Exchange. Edmond Locard was the director of a crime laboratory in France during the early part of the twentieth century. He articulated a very important principle in forensic science—namely, that when individuals and items come in contact, an exchange is made: A part of each transfers to the other. That means that a perpetrator will leave part of himself, in the form of a footprint, hair, fingerprint, and so on, at the scene of a crime. Likewise, he will carry away something of the scene or the victim. Each can become powerful evidence if retrieved by a skillful investigator.

In the aforementioned example, linking blood to a particular individual also requires other assumptions. We assume that DNA is a unique identifier, that is, the chances of two people having the same DNA are extremely low so low, in fact, that the jury will infer that it has to belong to a particular individual. The second assumption made is that the tests run by the examiner are valid tests, that is, they can properly and accurately measure, test, and compare the recovered evidence against a known sample. The third assumption is that the examiner is qualified to carry out the tests in question and render a scientifically accurate opinion. Examiners generally demonstrate their expertise through their education, training, and experience. In reality, these assumptions are put to the test if the exams performed by the examiner are introduced at trial. At that time, a *voire dire* proceeding takes place at which the examiners must demonstrate their expertise and that the procedures they used to perform the tests are valid.

The second standard for forensic science is a legal one. In some ways, meeting the legal criteria can be more difficult than meeting the scientific one. Judges and legislatures realize that many jurors may not have a good understanding of science. As a result, having an expert explain complex scientific principles may confuse them rather than assist them in determining innocence or guilt. As well, the science must somehow provide insight that helps decide the case; that is, it must have probative value. In addition, scientists are afforded a special position when they testify in court. Unlike other witnesses who testify only to facts they have observed, those offering scientific testimony testify as experts. This means they are also able to offer an opinion about their area of expertise.

For example, a ballistics expert may offer the opinion that a bullet recovered from a victim's body was fired from a specific firearm. This is a very powerful position, which brings with it a substantial degree of responsibility and expertise. As a result, judges must first examine an individual's credentials and the scope of his or her proposed testimony to determine whether the individual should be allowed to testify. This is usually accomplished in a special hearing, called a *voire dire* proceeding, which is often held without the jury present. In a *voire dire* proceeding, the side wishing to call the experts has them explain the type of exam they performed and why they have the expertise (e.g., education, experience) to be considered an expert. The other side has the opportunity to cross-examine the witness and can question either the legitimacy of the science involved or the expert's qualifications. Once both sides have presented their arguments, the judge decides if the expert will be allowed to testify.

Over the years, various rules have been established to help judges decide under what circumstances to allow expert scientific testimony. Each state has its own rules, many of which are modeled after the federal government's standards. It is important to understand that, over time, the rules governing the admissibility of forensic evidence in criminal and civil trials have changed. The police need to be aware of these rules as well as the latest concepts surrounding forensic science as they investigate. After all, it does little good to expend time and energy gathering evidence that has little or no probative value or that legally cannot be introduced at trial.

The primary rules governing expert scientific testimony at trial are contained in Article VII of the Federal Rules of Evidence. Rule 702 governs testimony by experts and states:

> If scientific, technical, or other specialized knowledge will assist the trier of fact to understand the evidence or to determine a fact in issue, a witness qualified as an expert by knowledge, skill, experience, training, or education, may testify thereto in the form of an opinion or otherwise, if (1) the testimony is based upon sufficient facts or data, (2) the testimony is the product of reliable principles and methods, and (3) the witness has applied the principles and methods reliably to the facts of the case.[10]

Rule 702, then, requires a qualified witness to apply recognized principles and methods properly in the examination of evidence. Over the years, various court decisions have interpreted Rule 702 in different ways. Generally, as time has gone on and scientific techniques have improved, the courts have afforded greater scrutiny in deciding whether something qualifies as "science" under the law.

For years, the admissibility of scientific evidence in federal court was judged by the Frye Standard, based on the 1923 case *Frye v. United States*. Basically, *Frye* held that scientific evidence could be introduced in court as long as it was "generally accepted" by the scientific community. This was a rather loose standard, and basically held that as long as other forensic scientists judged a technique to be acceptable, it could be introduced in court. *Frye* preceded the Federal Rules of Evidence; hence, for years it was the sole standard by which scientific evidence admissibility in federal trials was concerned.

After the Rules were enacted, there was still confusion regarding whether the *Frye* Standard met their requirements. In 1993, the U.S. Supreme Court established new rules for the admission of scientific evidence in its ruling in the *Daubert v. Merrell Dow Pharmaceuticals, Inc.* case. The Daubert Standard was much stricter than the Frye Standard. Now, for scientific evidence to be admitted, a judge had to first rule on whether it involved "valid" science. To make this judgment, the Court directed the trial judge to consider the following host of factors:

1. Whether the scientific technique or theory can be (or has been) tested
2. Whether the technique or theory has been subject to peer review and publication
3. The technique's potential rate of error
4. Existence and maintenance of standards controlling the technique's operation
5. Whether the scientific theory or method has attracted widespread acceptance within a relevant scientific community

The Daubert Standard has proven to be a challenge for forensic laboratories. Many defense attorneys, and some scientists, claim that many commonly accepted forensic techniques, such as fingerprint analysis, do not meet the Daubert Standard. The issue is far from settled. In 2009, the highly respected National Academy of Sciences produced a scathing report on the current state of forensic science. Suffice to say, the issue will remain controversial for some time (Table 11.1).

Table 11.1 Forensic Considerations

In 2009, the National Academy of Sciences, a highly respected part of the U.S. scientific community, released a report titled *Strengthening Forensic Science in the United States: A Path Forward*. Despite its somewhat upbeat sounding title, the report was a scathing indictment on the current state of forensic science. The press release accompanying the report stated:

"A congressionally mandated report from the National Research Council finds serious deficiencies in the nation's forensic science system and calls for major reforms and new research. Rigorous and mandatory certification programs for forensic scientists are currently lacking, the report says, as are strong standards and protocols for analyzing and reporting on evidence. And there is a dearth of peer-reviewed, published studies establishing the scientific bases and reliability of many forensic methods. Moreover, many forensic science labs are underfunded, understaffed, and have no effective oversight.

Forensic evidence is often offered in criminal prosecutions and civil litigation to support conclusions about individualization—in other words, to "match" a piece of evidence to a particular person, weapon, or other source. But with the exception of nuclear DNA analysis, the report says, no forensic method has been rigorously shown able to consistently, and with a high degree of certainty, demonstrate a connection between evidence and a specific individual or source. Non-DNA forensic disciplines have important roles, but many need substantial research to validate basic premises and techniques, assess limitations, and discern the sources and magnitude of error, said the committee that wrote the report. Even methods that are too imprecise to identify a specific individual can provide valuable information and help narrow the range of possible suspects or sources."

Evidence, from a forensic viewpoint, is anything that can be used to determine or demonstrate facts that could lead to establishing the truth during the investigation of a crime or an incident. Although physical evidence is often at the center of an investigation, evidence can also be documentary or testimonial. Each type of evidence is supportive and complementary to the other and when combined provide a solid foundation of information used to prosecute or vindicate an individual.

Documentary evidence is described as written observations of events by which ideas are represented on material substance. This type of evidence is furnished in written instruments, inscriptions, and documents of all kinds. Events in a diary, a tag number written on a notepad, or a textbook of scientific facts are all included in documentary evidence. Testimonial evidence is verbal, oath-bearing statements, which can encompass the written word, the spoken word, or the visual word. It is elicited from a witness as communicative evidence. An example of this type of testimony would be a citizen who witnessed a crime. Physical evidence is introduced at a trial, in the form of a physical object, intended to prove a fact in issue based on its physical characteristics. It includes any and all objects that can establish the truth of fact in question. This type of evidence is the most reliable form and includes such items as weapons, drugs, blood, semen, fingerprints, paint, glass, hair, fibers, and so on.[11]

Forensic crime laboratories offer services in multiple areas, which may vary depending on the size and focus of a particular laboratory. For the purposes of simply providing an overview, we outline the services offered by traditional public laboratories.

Physical evidence may be classified as either evidence of individual characteristics, which possess properties that can be attributed to a common source with an extremely high degree of certainty, or evidence of class characteristics, which possess properties that can only be associated with a group and never with a single source (Figure 11.2).[12]

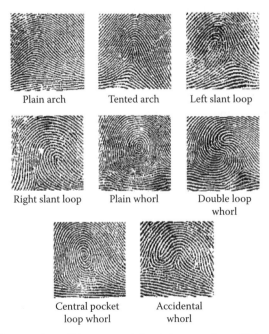

Plain arch   Tented arch   Left slant loop

Right slant loop   Plain whorl   Double loop
                                      whorl

Central pocket   Accidental
loop whorl   whorl

Figure 11.2 Types of fingerprints. (Courtesy of the Arkansas State Crime Laboratory. Retrieved from http://www.state.ar.us/crimelab/printdefi.html.)

Evidence Collection

Patrol officers and investigators routinely collect evidence. Increasingly, large agencies depend on evidence response teams composed of specially trained crime scene technicians or criminalists to gather evidence. Some forms of evidence, such as computers, may require special handling to ensure that valuable information is not disturbed or obliterated. In that case, units staffed by individuals with very special skills, such as one of the FBI's Computer Analysis Response Teams, may respond.

As discussed in Chapters 10, 12, and 13, in order for evidence to be used at trial, it must have been legally obtained and properly maintained. Legally obtained evidence is conceptualized as follows: In the United States, there are strict rules governing the circumstances under which the police are allowed to seize evidence. The general rule governing searches by the police is the Fourth Amendment to the U.S. Constitution.

The Fourth Amendment states: "The right of the people to be secure in their persons, houses, papers, and effects, against unreasonable searches and seizures, shall not be violated, and no warrants shall issue, but upon probable cause, supported by oath or affirmation, and particularly describing the place to be searched, and the persons or things to be seized."[13]

In other words, an officer must obtain a search warrant, where a judge or magistrate has determined that there is probable cause to believe that certain types of evidence will be found at a particular location. Warrants must be timely, that is, the information must be fresh and locations and types of evidence must be specifically identified. Evidence that is improperly seized is subject to the exclusionary rule, which means that it may not be introduced at trial. The courts usually take this one step further—under the fruit of the poison tree doctrine, evidence that is discovered as a result of improperly obtained evidence is itself excluded at trial.

There are many exceptions to the rule for a warrant. For example, if, in the normal course of duty, an officer observes evidence in plain sight, he or she may seize it under the plain view exception. In addition, immediately after an arrest, officers are allowed to search areas where the arrestee may have secreted weapons. Because of their mobile nature, cars are exempt from the warrant requirement, although the police still need to have developed probable cause before the search. There are other exceptions to the warrant requirement as well, usually developed through court cases.

Once evidence has been obtained, it must be properly maintained from the time of its seizure until it is introduced as evidence in court. This positive accountability is called the chain of custody, which is defined as

> The movement and location of real evidence from the time it is obtained to the time it is presented in court. In practical terms, a chain of custody is the documentation and testimony that proves that the evidence has not been altered or tampered within any way since it was obtained. This is necessary to assure both its admissibility in a judicial proceeding and its probative value in any preceding investigation.[14]

The police maintain chain of custody by documenting any time the evidence changes hands or is stored in a secure facility. Like evidence that is improperly obtained, when the chain of custody is "broken," evidence may be excluded from trial. Figure 11.3 shows an evidence bag with chain of custody markings.

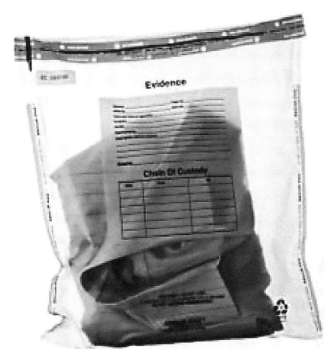

Figure 11.3 Evidence collection bag showing chain of custody entries. (Courtesy of Trevor Owen Limited. Retrieved from http://www.trevorowenltd.com/evidence_collection_bags.htm.)

At the Crime Scene

Evidence is often recovered from a location where a crime has occurred. This is termed the crime scene. A single offense may have several crime scenes. For example, a homicide victim may have been killed at home, transported in a vehicle, and dumped in a vacant lot. In this case, there are at least three crime scenes where valuable evidence may be discovered.

Once a scene has been rendered safe and all victims have been tended to, the primary job of the first responders is to secure and protect the crime scene. This is done by establishing boundaries, such as yellow crime scene tape, and restricting access to the site. It is up to the discretion of responding officers as to how to construct the scene; as a general rule, it is better to start "big" and reduce the size of the scene as situations permit. If a scene is not properly secured and protected, valuable evidence can be lost, trampled, obliterated, or contaminated; when this happens, it becomes useless. Many crime scenes, especially in the case of multiple victims or unusual brutality, may easily become chaotic. It is incumbent upon responding officers to remain calm and protect the scene at all times. However, rendering aid to victims is always the number one priority and takes precedence over evidence collection and preservation.

Those who collect evidence must be precise and meticulous. An entire case may be made with a single drop of blood or strand of hair; it may also be lost if that same evidence is never discovered or destroyed through improper collection techniques. To that end, collectors must be well-trained and cognizant of up-to-the-minute developments in the forensic world, where discoveries are being made daily. As well, each scene is different and will require a different response. Nevertheless, there are certain steps that should be followed at

Table 11.2   Step Summaries

Arriving at the Scene: Initial Response/Prioritization of Efforts
- Safety is the number one priority
- Render emergency care as necessary
- Secure and control persons at the scene
- Secure and protect crime scene
- Document actions and observations

Preliminary Documentation and Evaluation of the Scene
- Conduct scene assessment
- Conduct initial "walk-through" and initial documentation

Processing the Scene
- Determine search team composition
- Establish controls to prevent evidence contamination
- Ensure procedures are in place to complete all necessary documentation
- Formulate collection plan
- Collect, preserve, inventory, package, transport, and submit evidence

Completing and Recording the Crime Scene Investigation
- Conduct debrief
- Perform final survey of scene
- Ensure documentation is complete

every crime scene. The National Institute of Justice authored a book entitled *Crime Scene Investigation: A Guide for Law Enforcement*, which outlines steps that should be followed at each scene. Table 11.2 summarizes these steps.

Once a scene has been secured or protected, the search may begin. Detectives usually do an initial walk-through to gain some understanding of what happened. At this point, they may begin to develop initial hypotheses about what happened. In very large scenes, it may help to employ a particular search pattern. Sample search patterns are shown in Figure 11.4.

What sorts of physical evidence should an officer or investigator expect to find at a crime scene? Common types of evidence include the following:

- Fingerprints
- Shoe and tire impressions
- Bite marks
- Tools and tool marks
- Weapons and ammunition
- Glass, soils, and minerals
- Body fluids (including blood)
- Hairs and fibers
- Rope and tape
- Drugs
- Computers and electronic media

To preserve its integrity, evidence must be properly collected. Of course, different types of evidence require different types of collection, packaging, and preservation. One collects a hair sample differently than a fingerprint. Learning how to collect evidence well takes

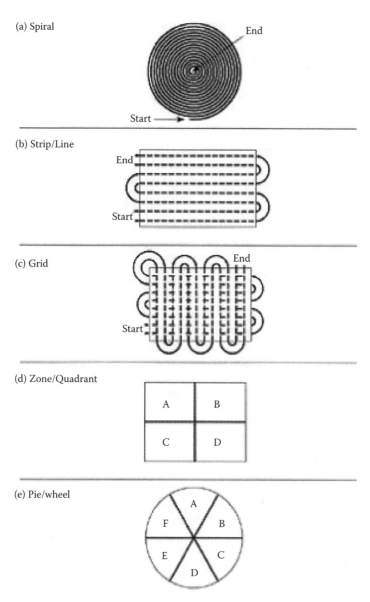

Figure 11.4 Crime scene search patterns.

years of training and experience, and explaining each technique is beyond the scope of this book. Nevertheless, a few rules for evidence collection are as follows:

- Liquid or volatile evidence is to be placed in airtight containers.
- Biological evidence is to be placed in non-airtight containers and allowed to dry.
- Each item must be packaged separately.

When performing actual collection, it is important to remember that safety is the number one priority! Certain types of evidence, such as blood and semen, may contain dangerous diseases, such as hepatitis and HIV. Crime scene personnel must wear the proper protective gear at all times.

Figure 11.5 Investigation of an NYPD crime scene. (From Lauinger, J., 2009, *NY Daily News*. Retrieved from http://articles.nydailynews.com/2009-01-12/local/17914195_1_gun-arrests-shootings-police-precincts.)

It is also important to document all aspects of the crime scene. Evidence must be marked and maintained in accordance with the chain of custody so that it can be properly introduced in court at a later date. Types of documentation include the following:

- Notes
- Logs (search, evidence, photo, etc.)
- Videotaping
- Photographing
- Sketching
- Marking of evidence

A crime scene is depicted in Figure 11.5. Investigations and crime scene searches are often fast-moving events—as a general rule, the longer a case drags on, the less likely it is to be solved. Investigators often refer to the very initial stages of an investigation as the "golden hour," where the success or failure of an investigation is often determined. In short, crime scene personnel need to be quick, thorough, meticulous, and up-to-date on legal and forensic matters. They need to be flexible enough to "shift gears" when the need arises. As one can imagine, this encompasses a substantial range of skills and abilities. It is no wonder that it takes significant experience and years of training to be a good investigator or crime scene technician.

Forensic Laboratory

Once evidence has been collected, in order for it to be tested, it must be submitted to a forensic laboratory, which is a laboratory that is specifically dedicated to examining evidence in criminal and civil cases. In the United States, there are many government and private forensic laboratories. In the public sector, forensic laboratories are often affiliated with a law enforcement agency and are operated at the federal, state, and local levels. The FBI Laboratory, which opened in 1932, is the oldest federal forensic laboratory in the United States. The Drug Enforcement Administration, the Bureau of Alcohol, Tobacco, Firearms and Explosives, the United States Secret Service, and the U.S. Postal Inspectors also operate forensic laboratories on the national level, although their services are available to state, local, and tribal law enforcement agencies as well. Most states also operate crime laboratories, and some large police departments, such as the New York Police Department, operate their own laboratories. The military also operates forensic laboratories (Figure 11.6). Additionally, private laboratories offering various forensic analysis capabilities are available for a fee.

Commonly, law enforcement agencies submit their evidence to any one of the number of government laboratories for analysis. In many cases, these laboratories perform an analysis free of charge for police and sheriffs' departments. Once they have completed their analysis, the examiners prepare a report of their findings, which becomes part of the case file. If necessary, laboratory examiners travel to provide expert testimony on their analyses before grand juries and in trials. Some critics have charged that housing laboratories in law enforcement agencies compromises their independence and predisposes them to favor the prosecution. The National Academy of Sciences is one such critic; it recommends that forensic laboratories cut their ties with law enforcement. Police and sheriffs' departments also have the option of submitting their evidence to private laboratories for testing. This can be quite expensive, but private laboratories often are able to perform tests much more quickly than government ones, which often have a huge backlog of cases to analyze.

Defendants also have the right to have evidence tested by forensic experts, usually in private laboratories. Although the principles of science dictate that both the experts for the prosecution and the defense should arrive at the same conclusions, occasionally this does not happen. What then ensues is a "battle of the experts," where juries have to decide which expert is correct. This often requires them to judge complex scientific principles and techniques, for which the average juror is usually ill prepared.

To standardize proper procedures across forensic laboratories, the American Society of Crime Laboratory Directors (ASCLD) was established after a meeting of 47 crime laboratory directors from around the United States who had been invited to meet with FBI Director Clarence Kelly, FBI Assistant Director Briggs White, and other FBI personnel in Quantico, Virginia. The purpose of the meeting was to open channels of communication between crime laboratories around the country and the FBI. The meeting was well

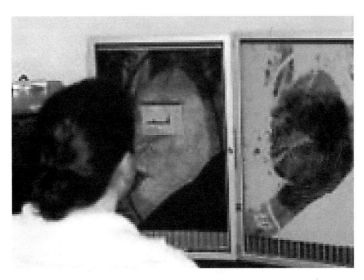

Figure 11.6 Analytical activities. (Courtesy of the FBI. Retrieved from http://www.fbi.gov/about-us/lab/crypt.)

received and led to an agreement that an association of crime laboratory directors should be created. In the spring of 1974, a smaller group of individuals who attended the initial meeting met and began working on an organizational proposal.

In the fall of 1974, a second meeting of laboratory directors was held at Quantico. The participants at this second meeting officially formed the ASCLD.[15] Today, ASCLD is composed of over 600 crime laboratory directors and forensic science managers dedicated to providing excellence in forensic science through leadership and innovation. They represent over 250 local, state, federal, and private crime laboratories in the United States. As of 2011, their membership also included laboratory directors from 23 countries, as well as national and international academic affiliates. As an organization, ASCLD provides leadership in the forensic community as well as assistance to its members by providing information, training, and networking opportunities that are unique to forensic science laboratory management.[16]

One part of ASCLD is the Laboratory Accreditation Board, known as ASCLD/LAB, which has the responsibility of accrediting forensic laboratories. According to its website, the objectives of ASCLD/LAB are as follows:[17]

- To improve the quality of laboratory services provided to the criminal justice system
- To develop and maintain criteria that may be used by a laboratory to assess its level of performance and to strengthen its operation
- To provide an independent, impartial, and objective system by which laboratories can benefit from a total operational review
- To offer to the general public and to users of laboratory services a means of identifying those laboratories that have demonstrated that they meet established standards.

Within a forensic laboratory, there are a myriad of personnel. Forensic examiners are the individuals who actually perform forensic tests. Based on their education, training, and experience, they are judged to have the necessary qualifications to carry out analyses in areas for which they are qualified. At the very least, these individuals possess a bachelor's degree in an area relevant to their forensic assignment. For example, someone who performs serology tests likely has a degree in chemistry, biology, or a related discipline. Often, examiners have advanced degrees, such as an MS or a PhD. Examiners perform the actual forensic tests, write up laboratory reports, and testify as experts when required. Depending on the types of analyses they perform, examiners have to be adept at operating sophisticated scientific instrumentation, including electron microscopes and mass spectrometers and gas chromatographs.

Laboratory technicians assist examiners in handling evidence and setting up tests. Their jobs usually do not require them to have the same level of training, education, or experience required of examiners, but their responsibilities are substantial.

Administrative personnel perform important functions relating to the handling and processing of evidence and the administration of laboratory matters. It bears pointing out that all of these individuals perform critical functions. For example, if a mail room attendant somehow compromises the chain of custody, a crucial piece of evidence could be ruled inadmissible. Therefore, all forensic personnel must understand the seriousness and gravity of their responsibilities (Figure 11.7).

Figure 11.7 Forensic scientist performing duties. (Courtesy of the FBI. Retrieved from http://www2 .fbi.gov/hq/lab/labannual05/labannual05.htm.)

Careers

Numerous career options are available for those who are interested in some area of the forensic sciences.

Forensic Pathologist

A forensic pathologist, also known as a medical examiner, is a trained physician who examines and ultimately determines the cause of death for people who have died unexpectedly, suddenly, or by violent means.

Forensic Toxicologist

Forensic toxicologists are those scientists engaged in the analysis of biological fluids and tissues for drugs and/or poisons; they often interpret the information generated from these analyses in a judicial context.

Forensic Anthropologist

Forensic physical anthropologists specialize in the research and application of techniques used to determine age at death, sex, population affinity, stature, abnormalities and/or pathology, and idiosyncrasies to (usually) modern skeletal material. Forensic anthropologists often work with coroners and medical examiners in the identification of individual skeletons in which the identity of the remains cannot be established by other means.[18]

Forensic Odontologist

Forensic dentists, also known as odontologists, use physical and biological dental evidence to identify human remains and analyze bite marks on a variety of surfaces.

Table 11.3   Laboratory Functional Areas

• Abrasives	• DNA	• Pharmaceuticals
• Adhesives	• Electronic devices	• Polymers
• Anthropology	• Explosives	• Product tampering
• Arson	• Explosives residue	• Questioned documents
• Audio	• Feathers	• Racketeering records
• Bank security dyes	• Fibers	• Rope
• Building materials	• Fingerprints	• Safe insulation
• Bullet jacket alloys	• Firearms	• Sealants
• Caulk	• Forensic facial imaging	• Serial numbers
• Chemical unknowns	• Glass	• Shoe prints
• Computers	• Hair	• Soil
• Controlled substances	• Image analysis	• Tape
• Cordage	• Ink	• Tire treads
• Crime scene surveys	• Lubricants	• Tool marks
• Documentation	• Metallurgy	• Toxicology
• Reconstruction	• Paint	• Video
• Cryptanalysis	• Pepper spray	• Weapons of mass destruction
• Demonstrative evidence		• Wood

Forensic Laboratory Functional Areas

Different forensic laboratories perform different types of analyses, generally within their mission requirements. For example, the Drug Enforcement Administration has a series of regional laboratories whose expertise is testing suspected illegal substances to determine whether they are illicit drugs and the purity of each. Large laboratories, like the FBI Laboratory, which employs over 500 personnel, provide a great many services (see Table 11.3 for a list of examinations performed by the FBI Laboratory). In addition to the forensic examinations listed in the table, the FBI Laboratory also offers special event planning services and runs the Disaster Squad, which assists in fingerprinting deceased persons at mass casualty events. Generally, the functions of most forensic laboratories are divided into three areas of analysis: criminalistics division, analytical division, and bioscience division. Within each of these major divisions are functioning areas of analysis.

Criminalistics Division

The firearms/tool mark section conducts microscopic comparisons of firearms and tool mark evidence. Forensic firearms examinations include items of evidence involving the firing of some type of weapon such as guns, projectiles, cartridge cases, shotgun hulls, pellets and wads, and gunpowder residue on clothing. In addition to these types of examinations, this section restores altered or obliterated serial numbers and examines tool marks and suspect tools. Firearms sections may also be responsible for the operation of the Integrated Ballistics Identification System, which is a cooperative effort with the Bureau of Alcohol, Tobacco, Firearms, and Explosives and the FBI to control violent crimes committed with firearms. Suspected firearms and their test-fired components (projectiles and cartridge cases) along with projectile and cartridge cases recovered as evidence are entered on this computerized database for correlation of possible matches.

The latent fingerprint section examines evidence for the presence or absence of finger-print impressions. When prints are found, they are preserved and compared with known fingerprints to determine the identity of the individual to whom the prints belong. One of the primary tools used in making these comparisons is the automated fingerprint identification system (AFIS), a computer database used to enter known fingerprints and unknown latent (crime scene) prints. The system searches for possible matches and presents candidates from the database to the forensic examiner for individual human examination. It is important to note that the computer does not make the match; instead, the forensic examiner makes the final determination.

The questioned documents section examines documents whose authenticity is questioned, such as checks, wills, and so on. This section also examines burned or torn paper, or paper bearing the imprint of writing. The examinations performed by this section may include identification of erasures, alterations, and indented writing, and ink typewriter, printer, and photocopier examinations. Questioned document examiners also compare suspected writing samples against known writing by an individual. Because everyone is presumed to have a unique style of writing, the examiners can often state that a particular individual wrote a particular document. Some laboratories also have specialized units that examine documents to determine their contents. For example, the FBI Laboratory has the cryptanalyst and racketeering records unit, which decrypts coded documents and examines suspected drug, money laundering, and gambling business records.

The photography unit examines and records physical evidence using procedures that may require the use of highly specialized photographic techniques, such as digital imaging, infrared, ultraviolet, and x-ray photography, to make invisible information visible to the naked eye. This unit also assists other units by preparing photographic exhibits for courtroom presentations.

The polygraph unit utilizes the polygraph, or lie detector, to aid in criminal investigations. This investigative tool is a function of a criminal investigator rather than a forensic science and its operation is conducted by people trained in the techniques of criminal investigation and interrogation. Although the results of polygraph examinations are not generally allowed to be introduced as evidence in criminal trials, the scientific nature of the polygraph makes its placement in a forensic laboratory a logical choice.

The crime scene investigation unit is a specialized unit trained in the recognition, detection, preservation, collection, and transportation of physical evidence. These individuals are dispatched to crime scenes and work in coordination with the case investigators to ensure the crime scene is properly analyzed and all potential physical evidence is collected and preserved for future examinations or presentation in court.

Analytical Division

The analytical division is also sometimes referred to as the chemistry section of a laboratory. This reference is primarily because of the type of instrumentation utilized and chemical processes involved in these types of analysis.

The controlled substance (drug) analysis section classifies and identifies controlled substances such as cannabis (marijuana), pharmaceuticals, and powder material, including cocaine. This section also classifies and identifies miscellaneous substances such as those used in clandestine "illegal" laboratories that manufacture controlled substances.

The definition of a controlled substance is determined by the Controlled Substance Act of 1970 with the following classifications of substances:

Schedule I
- The drug has no medical value accepted by the scientific community
- High potential for abuse
- Highly additive
- Includes marijuana, heroin, MDMA (methylenedioxymethamphetamine), LSD (lysergic acid diethylamide), and mushrooms

Schedule II
- Accepted medical value is present
- High potential for abuse
- Highly additive
- Includes cocaine, methamphetamine, amphetamine, and narcotics

Schedule III
- Accepted medical value is present
- High potential for abuse, but less than Schedule I and II drugs
- Highly addictive but not as addictive as Schedule I and II drugs
- Includes barbiturates such as phenobarbital and steroids

Schedule IV
- Accepted medical value is present
- Low potential for abuse relative to that of Schedule III
- Low potential for addiction relative to that of Schedule III
- Includes benzodiazepines such as diazepam and lorazepam

Schedule V
- Accepted medical value present: antitussive and antidiarrheal
- Low potential for abuse relative to that of Schedule IV
- Low potential for addiction relative to that of Schedule IV
- Includes cough medicines containing less than 200 mg of codeine per 100 ml[19]

The toxicology section examines body fluids to determine the presence of alcohol, drugs, poison, or intoxicating chemicals and also analyzes beverages for ethyl alcohol content. The tests performed include blood alcohol analyses, blood/urine drug screens, beverage alcohol analysis, and miscellaneous analyses. In some laboratories, the implied consent unit will be operated. This unit has the responsibility for calibration of alcohol testing instruments and the training of individuals in the operation of these units. The primary function of these units is to determine if individuals meet minimum legal alcohol standards for intoxication.

The trace evidence section is responsible for the examination and comparison of physical evidence using a variety of microscopic and/or analytical techniques. Types of items examined include paint, glass, plastic footwear, rope, tire impressions (in some laboratories this examination would be placed with the fingerprint section and considered overall impression evidence), gunshot residue, and fire debris. The section also conducts examinations on hair and fiber and conducts fracture matches. Obtaining trace evidence from a crime scene can be a laborious process and is generally done by picking (often with tweezers), lifting, scraping, vacuum sweeping, and combing.

In recent years, this section has become ever more important as trace evidence has assumed a greater role in criminal investigations. For example, in 1982, fiber evidence proved pivotal in the trial of Wayne Williams, who was found guilty of murdering two children in Atlanta, Georgia, but was suspected in the deaths of many more. Through forensic examinations, the prosecution was able to link carpet fibers found on the body of one of Williams's victims to rugs found in his home.

Bioscience Division

The bioscience division performs serological and DNA analysis. Nothing has revolutionized forensic science like the introduction of DNA analysis in the 1980s. Deoxyribonucleic acid (DNA) is considered statistically unique to individuals. In addition, its presence is ubiquitous, being found in the blood and tissue, saliva, spermatozoa, bone marrow, tooth pulp, and hair root cells of humans. In addition, only a very small amount of DNA evidence is required to perform a forensic analysis. DNA has been used to not only convict the guilty but also free the innocent. Since 1992, the Innocence Project, located in New York City at the Benjamin N. Cardozo School of Law at Yeshiva University, has used DNA to exonerate over 300 individuals who were wrongly convicted of crimes; 18 of these individuals were on death row.

The concept of using DNA in a forensic setting was first conceived of by English geneticist Alec Jeffreys in 1985. It was first used in a U.S. trial in Florida in 1986 and, in 1988, the FBI Laboratory became the first public laboratory to offer DNA testing. Today, DNA samples are stored in the Combined DNA Index System (CODIS); using CODIS, DNA samples can be searched against a nationwide database of known offenders and DNA profiles loaded from unsolved crimes.[18] It should be note that although the National Academy of Sciences study discussed in Table 11.1 was critical of many forensic techniques, it offered only praise for DNA analysis, which it found to be scientifically and forensically sound.

The Bioscience section examines items suspected of bearing blood, semen, or saliva. This section performs examinations of items of evidence to collect and identify these stains. The initial analysis is conducted through conventional serological analyses. Stains that are determined to be blood, semen, or saliva are then preserved for additional polymerase chain reaction (PCR), short tandem repeat (STR), DNA analysis. In addition, CODIS is operated through this section. Another area of criminal investigation where DNA has had an unexpected impact is in investigations on "minor crimes." In the past, crimes such a burglary and larceny were not considered serious enough to go through the tedious collection process to secure DNA evidence. With changing technology and routine access to DNA testing, the mindset is changing, resulting in an increase in the rate of property crimes being solved as a result of DNA technology (Figure 11.8).

The services previously listed do not include all of the forensic science services available. In unusual cases, criminal justice officials may seek out the services of specialists in the areas of forensic psychiatry, forensic odontology, forensic engineering, and forensic computer and digital analysis.[20]

Figure 11.8 DNA testing. (Courtesy of the FBI. Retrieved from http://www.fbi.gov/about-us/lab/chem.)

Behavioral Sciences and Forensic Analysis

A broad array of legal issues is considered by forensic psychologists and psychiatrists among "criminal and civil cases and other areas such as family and domestic relations law."[21] Within the context of criminal law, issues such as "competence (e.g., competency to stand trial and to testify, to waive legal representation, or to be executed) and the assessment of mental illness, as it relates to diminished responsibility or innocence by reason of mental illness or defect, are the focus."[22] However, within the context of civil law, these issues may require the assessment of such considerations as "involuntary psychiatric hospitalization, right to refuse treatment, competency to participate in do-not resuscitate decisions, and disability compensation among others."[23] Among family and domestic relations, the range of issues might involve "juvenile delinquency, child custody, parental fitness, domestic abuse, adoption, and foster care."[24]

Summary

Crime laboratories and the forensic sciences have become major benefactors of enormous advances in scientific technology. We have already witnessed the impact that chromatography and spectrophotometry has on forensic methodology, and now DNA technology is a routine analysis that was unknown just 30 years ago. Technology is advancing by leaps and bounds; it is hard to imagine what the next forensic breakthrough will be. As forensic techniques improve and the databases containing identifying information expand, there is no telling how many crimes, both old and new, will be solved. Already, DNA has proven successful at solving "cold" cases that investigators believed would never be cleared. One thing is clear—tomorrow's investigators will have to have an understanding of science in order to carry out their duties. Although no one is expecting police officers to have PhDs in chemistry or biology, they will have to know how science complements the investigative process. Indeed, all people with an interest in criminal justice should be excited about the potential that exists for developing the most exact analysis possible in the pursuit of truth.

References

1. Stokes, L. *Forensic Quotes*. Retrieved May 16, 2012, from http://www.brainyquote.com/quotes/keywords/forensic.html
2. Benecke, M. (2001). A brief history of forensic entomology. *Forensic Science International, 120*, 2–14.
3. Watson, S. (2012). *How Forensic Lab Techniques Work*. Retrieved March 17, 2012, from http://science.howstuffworks.com/forensic-lab-technique1.htm
4. Chisum, W. J., & Turvey, B. E. (2011). *Crime Reconstruction* (2nd ed.). Maryland Heights, MO: Elsevier Academic Press.
5. Stauffer, E. (2004). *Dr. Edmond Locard and Trace Evidence Analysis in Criminalistics in the Early 1900s: How Forensic Sciences Revolve Around Trace Evidence*. Retrieved April 5, 2012, from http://www.swissforensic.org/presentations/assets/aafslocard.pdf
6. The Northwestern University Law School's Scientific Crime Detection Laboratory. *The First American Crime Lab*. Retrieved March 12, 2012, from http://www.gangstersandoutlaws.com/CrimeLab.html
7. Calvin, H. *Goddard Award*. Retrieved March 12, 2012, from http://www.goddardaward.com/
8. Appel, C. (1930). *History of the Bureau of Investigation*. Typecopy by RCU/OPCA, FBI, 2/2002. Retrieved March 12, 2012, from http://www.fbi.gov/about-us/history/highlights-of-history/articles/laboratory
9. Fox, J. F. *The Birth of the FBI's Technical Laboratory: 1924 to 1935*. Retrieved March 12, 2012, http://www.fbi.gov/about-us/history/highlights-of-history/articles/laboratory
10. 111th Congress (2010). *Federal Rules of Evidence, Article VII, Opinions and Expert Testimony, Rule 702, Testimony of Experts*.
11. Cooke, T. G. (1935). New method now develops finger prints left on cloth and other substances. *Fingerprint and Identification Magazine*. Volume 17, Number 3. Retrieved November 21, 2012, from http://www.lindberghkidnappinghoax.com/hudson.pdf
12. Saferstein, R. (2010). *Criminalistics: An Introduction to Forensic Science* (10th ed.). Englewood Cliffs, NJ: Prentice Hall.
13. Fourth Amendment. *United States Constitution, Cornell University*. Retrieved May 17, 2012, from http://www.law.cornell.edu/constitution/fourth_amendment
14. State of California (2011). *California Peace Officers Legal Sourcebook*. Retrieved March 22, 2011, from http://www.cdpr.ca.gov/docs/county/training/hrngofcr/section2-8.pdf
15. *History of the American Society of Crime Laboratory Directors Laboratory Accreditation Board*. Retrieved March 30, 2012, from http://www.ascld-lab.org/about_us/history.html
16. American Society of Crime Laboratory Directors (2010). *Executive Education Digest*. Retrieved March 30, 2012, from http://www.ascld.org/files/2010_ExecDigest.pdf
17. American Society of Crime Laboratory Directors Laboratory Accreditation Board. *Objectives*. Retrieved from http://www.ascld-lab.org/about_us/objectives.html
18. Smiley, J. C. (2008). *Forensic Services Handbook*. Jackson, MS: Mississippi Crime Laboratory.
19. France, D. L. (2012). *Forensic Anthropology: A Brief Review*. Retrieved April 4, 2012, from http://www.wadsworth.com/anthropology_d/special_features/forensics/forensics_index/index.html#head8
20. Saferstein, R. (2010). *Criminalistics: An Introduction to Forensic Science* (10th ed.). Englewood Cliffs, NJ: Prentice Hall.

21. The Federal Bureau of Investigation Laboratory Services. *Frequently Asked Questions (FAQs) on the CODIS Program and the National DNA Index System*. Retrieved on November 21, 2012, from http://www.fbi.gov/about-us/lab/codis/codis-and-ndis-fact-sheet
22. Ibid.
23. Ibid.
24. Ibid.

Bibliography

National Academy of Sciences (2009). "Badly fragmented" forensic science system needs overhaul; evidence to support reliability of many techniques is lacking. Retrieved March 21, 2012, from http://www8.nationalacademies.org/onpinews/newsitem.aspx?RecordID = 12589.

National Institute of Justice (2000). *Crime Scene Investigation: A Guide for Law Enforcement.* Washington, DC: National Institute of Justice.

After Arrest: Taking the Case to Court

12

It is not enough to know that the men applying the standard are honorable and devoted men. This is a government of laws, not of men...It is not without significance that most of the provisions of the Bill of Rights are procedural. It is procedure that spells much of the difference between rule by law and rule by whim or caprice.

William O. Douglas

Learning Objectives

The objectives of this chapter are to

- Discuss the concept of the court
- Describe, in general terms, the court systems in the United States
- Identify the actors within the court environment (e.g., judges, attorneys, and so on)
- Explain the actions of courts
- Compare the roles of law enforcement personnel in relation to court proceedings

Introduction

The concept of the court is quite simple. Generally, a court is a place for resolving criminal and civil disputes. All kinds of transgressions may be considered and argued in courtroom proceedings federally, regionally, and locally. Disputes may involve any act of crime ranging from the smallest infraction of a parking ticket to a heinous crime like murder. Other offenses involving civil issues are also argued in court proceedings. For example, child custody and child support are argued in court settings. If one receives a dissatisfying outcome from court proceedings, then an appeal of the case may be necessary or desirable.

A variety of courts exist, each serving a specific purpose (Figure 12.1). Municipal and justice courts are commonly found in towns and cities, whereas the U.S. Supreme Court represents the highest court within the nation. State courts and federal courts also exist, and the venues of both entities are representative of the types of cases that are argued within their respective settings. Law enforcement entities must be familiar with all forms of courts given the potential for testifying and interacting with them.

Any fan of *Law and Order* knows that making an arrest is only a part of the law enforcement process. The remainder of the process takes place in the court and correctional systems. Although the law enforcement officer focuses on apprehension of persons who break the law, the ultimate goal of law enforcement is conviction and correction of those persons. It is essential that law enforcement officers understand the remainder of the law enforcement process and their role in it. In this chapter, that portion of the process that

Figure 12.1 Delineation of the U.S. federal courts. (Courtesy of the Administrative Office of the U.S. Courts. Retrieved from http://www.uscourts.gov/EducationalResources/FederalCourtBasics/CourtStructure/StructureOfFederalCourts.aspx.)

takes place in the court system is briefly explored. We begin by considering some of the basic concepts underlying this part of the law enforcement process and the various persons who play a role in that process, then conduct a brief overview of the process itself.

Basic Concepts

Some basic concepts must be considered when contemplating the court system, its actors, and the civil and criminal cases that are heard in American courtrooms. These concepts range from the consideration of proper jurisdiction to the characteristics of the argued cases. Every case and hearing are unique, thereby ensuring that daily a complex set of circumstances pervade the justice system.

Jurisdiction

The entire law enforcement process is subject to the requirements of the United States Constitution, including that part of the process that takes place in the court system. Although the requirements are the same throughout the country, the ways in which those requirements are met vary depending on the system in place in the location where the crime occurred and, in many instances, depending on the seriousness of the crime.

The first determination that must be made is which court should handle the charge. Each court can only handle cases within that court's jurisdiction, that is, within the range of cases the court is authorized to handle by the federal or state constitution or the statute creating that court.

A court's jurisdiction is limited in several ways. First, a court may be limited in whether the court can conduct trials or can hear appeals from other courts. Courts that can try a case are referred to as having original jurisdiction. Courts that hear appeals have appellate jurisdiction. Some courts have both types of jurisdiction. In the State of Mississippi, for example, circuit courts can conduct trials in felony criminal prosecutions and civil lawsuits and can also hear appeals from county, justice, and municipal courts and from administrative boards and commissions such as the Workers' Compensation Commission and the Mississippi Department of Employment Security.[1]

Second, as suggested by the description of Mississippi circuit courts, courts are limited in the subject matter of cases they can hear. Courts of general jurisdiction are authorized to hear a wide range of cases. However, even courts of general jurisdiction will have fairly clear parameters drawn on their authority to hear cases. Consider, for example, the courts of the State of Nebraska. According to the Nebraska Judicial Branch:

> District courts hear felony criminal cases, divorce cases, and civil cases involving substantial amounts of money, to name a few.
> County courts handle misdemeanor cases; traffic and municipal ordnance violations; preliminary hearings in felony cases; civil cases involving lesser amounts of money; small claims cases; probate, guardianship, conservatorship, and adoption proceedings.[2]

Other courts are courts of limited jurisdiction, having jurisdiction over specific types of cases. In Maine, for example, the probate court is authorized to probate wills and grant letters testamentary or of administration on the estates, grant leave to adopt children, change the names of persons, and appoint guardians for minors and incapacitated persons.[3] In the federal system, bankruptcy courts are courts of limited jurisdiction.

Federal bankruptcy courts are also courts of exclusive jurisdiction meaning no other court is allowed to hear a type of case allocated exclusively to that court. No bankruptcies can be filed in any state court. They must be filed in the federal bankruptcy courts.[4] In Mississippi, not every county has a county court, but in those that do, the county court has exclusive jurisdiction over juvenile matters.[5] Courts may also have concurrent jurisdiction, that is, they share original jurisdiction with another court. In Maine, the district courts are courts of general jurisdiction with exclusive original jurisdiction over divorces, but concurrent jurisdiction with the superior courts in most other civil lawsuits.[6]

Finally, a court can only take cases that originate within a prescribed geographical area. Texas courts can only take cases from Texas and Iowa courts can only take cases from Iowa. Within states, most courts also have limited geographical jurisdiction. Each state's court system structure is different. For purposes of illustration, we will use the State of Maine system as an example. It has a fairly simple court structure. The first level of courts is the district courts, with courts in each district only able to hear cases from that district.[7] There is also a second level of courts known as the superior courts, each of which has original, general jurisdiction over matter arising in a particular county.[8] The final level is the supreme judicial court, which has final appellate jurisdiction for all cases in the state.

In the federal court system, the court of original (trial) jurisdiction is the district court. Each district court has general jurisdiction of federal civil and criminal cases, but is limited to a particular geographical area. States with small population such as New Hampshire and Idaho constitute one district, whereas Texas, having a larger population, is divided into five districts. The district courts are organized into circuits comprised of courts located in contiguous states. For example, Georgia, Florida, and Alabama, each having a northern, middle, and central district, make up the Fourth Circuit.[9] Each circuit has a court of appeals that has exclusive appellate jurisdiction of appeals from the district courts in its circuit and only appeals from those states (Figure 12.2). Appeals from decisions of the various circuit courts are taken to the United States Supreme Court that has exclusive appellate jurisdiction of appeals from all the circuit courts of appeal throughout the United States and its territories.

The terms "justice court," "district court," "superior court," and "supreme court" are used to designate courts in almost every state. However, they do not necessarily designate the same type of court in each state. In most states, the court of general original jurisdiction bears the title of either district or superior court with the highest appellate court holding the title of Supreme Court, but in New York, the Supreme Court is the primary court of original general jurisdiction, while the highest appellate court is the court of appeals.

For purposes of criminal cases, jurisdiction in state courts is frequently allocated according to whether the case is a felony, misdemeanor, civil violation, or juvenile matter. In some states, the initial proceedings for all matters take place in one court, but that court retains jurisdiction of misdemeanors, while felonies are transferred to another court.

Law enforcement officers should receive special training regarding the jurisdictional requirements for the court system in their law enforcement jurisdiction and quickly become familiar with the particular functions of each of the relevant courts.

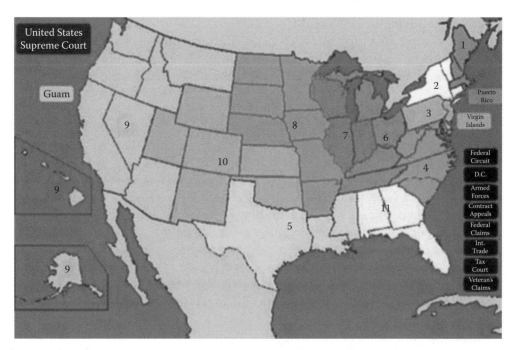

Figure 12.2 Delineation of the U.S. Circuit Court of Appeals. (Courtesy of the FDA. Retrieved from http://www.fda.gov/ICECI/ComplianceManuals/RegulatoryProceduresManual/ucm176577.htm.)

Elements of Crime

Each crime is set forth in a statute or law passed by Congress or a state legislature. Whether or not a person has committed a crime is determined by comparing the facts of the case to the exact language of that law. We looked at one perspective on how laws are interpreted by the courts in Chapter 13. Here we will take another look at the basic statutory interpretation using a slightly more complicated law.

Statutory interpretation is a four-step process, but step three has two parts. First, the facts are gathered. This, of course, is primarily the function of the law enforcement investigator. Often there is a disagreement between law enforcement and the person apprehended for the crime (the "defendant" in court proceedings) over what the applicable facts are. As discussed later in this chapter, each "version" of the facts will be presented to a "fact finder," that is, a judge or a jury, to determine what the facts actually are. Second, a statute is selected that appears to apply to those facts. Third, that statute is broken down into its "elements"; each element is applied to the facts, and that element is analyzed to determine whether the facts satisfy that element. Finally, we reach a conclusion as to whether or not the person has committed the crime. We are not speaking here about whether, assuming a crime has been committed, a particular person has committed that crime. Rather, our concern is whether given a particular set of facts, any crime has been committed.

Thus far, the term "element" has been used without an explanation as to what an element is. Briefly stated, an element is a requirement that must be satisfied in order for a crime to be committed. Most criminal states have four categories of elements:

1. A particular act is required (known to lawyers as the *actus reus*).
2. A particular mental state (*mens rea*) is required, for example, "knowingly," "intentionally," or "willfully."
3. A particular result is required, for example, an injury, death, or property is taken.
4. Particular circumstances are required, for example, "in the nighttime," or "while operating a motor vehicle."

Not all laws require all four (for example, most speeding laws require only the act of driving over the speed limit regardless of whether the driver intended to speed and whether any harm other than the speed itself occurred), but it is helpful to analyze a statute in terms of these four categories.

This is best understood by the use of an example. Here we will use an actual statute entitled "Assault While Hunting." The statute says,

> A person is guilty of assault while hunting if, while in the pursuit of wild game or game birds, he, with criminal negligence, causes bodily injury to another with the use of a dangerous weapon.[10]

This law seems simple enough but it is actually quite complex, as can be seen by breaking the statute down into its elements.

In order to commit the crime of assault while hunting, a person must meet all the requirements of the statute. If a person does not meet those requirements, he or she has not committed that crime, although he or she may have committed another crime with different requirements. For assault while hunting a person must

1. Act: cause
2. State of mind (intent): with criminal negligence

3. Result:
   a. Bodily injury
   b. To another
4. Circumstances:
   a. While hunting
   b. While in the pursuit of wild game or game birds
   c. With the use of a dangerous weapon

If any one of these elements is not met, the crime has not been committed. For example, if a person with criminal negligence causes bodily injury to himself while hunting in pursuit of wild game using a dangerous weapon, the crime has not been committed, because the statute requires injury to another person. Similarly, the crime has not been committed if the person with criminal negligence causes bodily injury to another person while hunting in pursuit of wild game, but not with the use of a dangerous weapon.

This will be clearer if we apply the law to a specific hypothetical set of facts. For example, Joe and his friend, Peter, are preparing to go hunting this weekend. Tonight they have a couple of beers and decide to shoot some target practice—beer cans set up on rocks in the field behind Joe's house. While Peter is setting up the cans he sees a wild turkey and decides to shoot at it. Instead, he drops his rifle with the safety off. It fires and the bullet hits Joe in the arm.

For purposes of this example, we will assume that these facts are true and can be proven in court (or will be accepted as true by both law enforcement and the defendant).

Now we have a set of facts and a statute that has been broken down into its elements. Each of those elements must be applied to the facts. Often law enforcement and the defendant will argue for differing interpretations or the application of the law to the facts. Here, there is no argument that Peter caused (Element 1) bodily injury (Element 3a) to another (Element 3b). Whether he did so with criminal negligence will depend to an extent on exactly how the term "criminal negligence" is defined in the jurisdiction in which this event occurred, but here we will also assume that element (Element 2) is met. It is also likely that all will agree that the gun is a dangerous weapon (Element 4c).

However, even if all this is proven or conceded, Peter cannot yet be found guilty of this particular crime. It must be determined that Peter caused this injury while "hunting" and while "in pursuit of" wild game or birds. Peter is likely to argue that he was not hunting, but target practicing, and not pursuing the turkey, but simply taking advantage of the turkey approaching the practice area. Law enforcement, through its attorney (the prosecutor), will likely argue that once he turned his gun on the turkey, he was no longer practicing but hunting and pursuing the wild bird. Whether the crime was actually committed depends on how the words "hunting" and "pursuing" are interpreted by the courts, a topic discussed in Chapter 13.

The law enforcement officer's role is to meet the following three requirements: (1) understand the elements of crimes with which they are charging defendants, (2) understand what facts are available to meet those elements, and (3) provide evidence that will assist in proving those facts. Often, the evidence will be physical evidence such as fingerprints or statements from witnesses. On many occasions, it is necessary for the law enforcement officer herself to provide testimony as to what she observed or heard as such evidence.

Facts, Evidence, and Proof

Trials are often described as forums in which everyone searches for truth with truth ultimately being attained in the form of a jury verdict. This is the ideal of the American system of justice. However, the jury's verdict is based on the evidence presented to it and that evidence may vary dramatically from what actually happened. Not all evidence is welcomed (admissible) at a trial under the Rules of Evidence, has the same relevance, has the same effectiveness, and is presented in a way that the jury can understand. The goal of each side of a criminal proceeding is to provide evidence that will convince the fact-finder that facts exist that constitute elements of the crime with which the defendant has been charged.

As you can see, facts, evidence, and proof are not the same. The difference between facts, evidence, and proof, and how each of them relates to the case is best seen in the context of the legal underpinnings of the case itself, the elements of the crime with which the defendant is charged as discussed in the previous section of this chapter. Each case involves one or more crimes. Each of these crimes has its own "elements," that is, things that must be proved. In the last section, we saw that the crime of "Assault While Hunting" had particular elements. There we assumed the facts could be proven or would be accepted by both sides. However, in many instances, the facts must be proven through evidence submitted by either the prosecution or the defense. Generally, only evidence that tends to prove or disprove one of those elements is admissible in court. In this context, we can see the importance of the distinction between facts, evidence, and proof.

The *facts* of a case are the bits and pieces that comprise what happened, that is, the event that brought the parties to court, or the particularities of the assault, theft, or other crime. In our hypothetical, we posited certain facts regarding Peter injuring Joe. Some of the facts are likely to be in dispute.

Evidence is something that tends to show, confirm, or verify a fact. It can be testimony such as the driver testifying he looked at the light before he entered the intersection. Not all evidence is equally convincing. Testimony from an uninvolved third party, that is, a school crossing guard, that the light was red or green may be more convincing than the testimony of the driver of either car involved in the accident. A picture taken by a camera set up to track drivers' speed may be even more convincing.

From the lawyer's perspective, evidence is more important than actual facts. Cases must be evaluated and presented based on the evidence available for presentation rather than on the facts the attorney believes to be true. Both the prosecutor and the defense attorney are more concerned about what can be proven than simply what occurred.

Proof is simply whatever evidence is sufficient to convince a jury to accept a fact as true. Thus, a driver's testimony that the light was green when she went through the intersection is proof if it is credible enough for the jury or judge to accept it as a true statement of the facts and is not proof if the jury or judge does not accept it.

The search for evidence begins when the crime is discovered. In some instances, it begins even sooner such as when a law enforcement officer is investigating suspicious behavior to determine whether a crime has been committed. Thus from the start of any investigation, the law enforcement officer should

- Know the elements of the crime and what is needed both theoretically and practically to prove each one of them.
- Develop an investigation plan designed around the elements of the crime.

Figure 12.3 Evidence used during trial proceedings. (Courtesy of the Pennsylvania Office of Attorney General, 2010. Retrieved from http://www.attorneygeneral.gov/press.aspx?id=5462.)

- Be aware of the problems with evidence.
  - Know that no piece of evidence is "proof positive."
  - Know that any piece of evidence can be made to look other than it is.
  - Know that every piece of evidence is influenced by how it came into existence, how it has been handled, and how it has been/is being perceived by the parties, witnesses, attorneys, judge, and jury (each of whom bring their own preconceptions to the courtroom).
  - Know that often the way evidence is presented is as important as what evidence is presented. Be prepared to receive (and seek) guidance from the prosecutorial team (attorney and paralegal) on how you can assist in obtaining, preparing, and presenting the needed evidence.

Evidence becomes proof when it convinces a jury. Regardless of the intrinsic value of the evidence, it is not convincing unless the jury hears or sees it, understands it, and is persuaded by it. When planning what evidence to present and how to present it, the legal team must step out of their normal role and try to assume the role of a juror. This is tricky. It is not enough to say "How would this appear to *me* if *I* were a juror on this case?" The jurors on the case are not likely to have any legal education or the same detailed knowledge of the case that you have (Figure 12.3).

Personnel in the Court Process

As the earlier discussion indicates, the American system of justice assumes two parties interested in the outcome of the criminal charge—the accuser and the accused—presenting evidence and legal arguments to a third, impartial party for a decision on guilt or innocence of the accused. In order to ensure fairness and impartiality, the process is governed by Rules of Procedure and Rules of Evidence that can often seem quite complex both in wording and application. In addition, as we have seen, the process of legal reasoning, the breaking down of a statute into its elements, and applying those elements to the facts can also require education, training, and practice. Thus, although the Sixth Amendment to the Constitution requires a trial in front of an impartial jury,[11] the process by which that trial occurs usually requires participation of persons trained in legal reasoning and the rules governing that process as well as a person who regulates the process according to those rules. This section will discuss the roles of the primary personnel engaged in the court process.[12]

Attorneys

A variety of attorneys represent clients within the justice system. Attorney representation involves both civil and criminal cases and hearings. Both prosecutors and defense attorneys have a fiduciary obligation to provide the highest and best services for their respective clients.

Prosecutors

Although many crimes result in injuries to individual citizens as victims, for example, the person who is injured in an assault or the person whose property is taken in a robbery, many crimes do not involve individual victims. Regardless of who may be considered the victim of a crime, the legal charges are not brought by the victim, but by the governmental entity whose laws have been broken, for example, the City of Detroit, the State of Maine, the United States of America, on behalf of all the citizens of that jurisdiction. The person who makes the formal, legal accusation against the accused on behalf of all the people in a particular jurisdiction is the prosecutor.

The criminal process is intended to seek the best outcome for society. There is a separate civil trial process designed to resolve disputes between citizens. For example, if a driver runs a stop sign and causes another driver injury, the offending driver will be charged in criminal proceedings with the offense of violating the state law regarding stop signs on behalf of the state and may be sued in civil court by the injured driver for incurred medical bills, lost wages, damage to her car, and the like. In the assault while hunting scenario discussed earlier in this chapter, the prosecutor would decide on behalf of the state whether or not to bring a criminal charge. Regardless of the prosecutor's decision, Joe could still sue Peter in civil court for the tort of negligence and recover a money judgment for his damages arising from the incident.

The prosecutor is an officer of the court, usually a lawyer, who represents the interests of all the citizens of a jurisdiction. He is responsible for presenting the government's case against the accused and, within the bounds of the Constitution, laws, and rules, seeking the outcome of the proceeding that best serves the interest of the people of the jurisdiction he represents. Sometimes this can cause conflict between the persons who are actually injured by the crime or the law enforcement officer who investigated the crime and the prosecutor, because the interest of the particular victim or officer is not necessarily the same as the best interest of the society in which a particular crime was committed. For example, the victim of a burglary may be most interested in getting his property back even if that means the burglar gets a lighter sentence than the prosecutor believes is required, or a victim of an assault may want revenge for the injury already done in a matter where the prosecutor is seeking an outcome that will best ensure that the accused does not commit assaults in the future.

Prosecutors hold different titles and are selected differently depending on the jurisdiction in which they serve. In some jurisdictions, prosecutors are elected, while in others, they are appointed by the executive (governor or president). Although they are considered to be officers of the court, they are not members of the judicial branch, but members of the executive branch of the government. The chief prosecutor in state and federal governments is usually the attorney general. In the federal system, each district has a United States Attorney who acts as the prosecutor for that district. Prosecutors in state subdivisions such as counties or prosecutorial districts are referred to as county attorneys or district attorneys. In each jurisdiction, the chief prosecutor often has heavy administrative duties, so the prosecution of most cases is carried out by assistants, also attorneys, who are hired and supervised by the chief prosecutor.

Defense Attorneys

Just as the government has an attorney representing it, the accused may also have an attorney. According to the Sixth Amendment, the accused in any criminal proceeding is entitled to "assistance of counsel in his defense." In most instances, if the accused cannot afford an attorney, one will be appointed to represent her at the government's expense.[13]

It is the defense attorney's responsibility to represent the interest of the accused within the bounds of the Constitution, laws, and rules. Unlike the prosecutor who makes decisions on behalf of the government, the defense attorney must allow the client to make substantive decisions while retaining the responsibility to make those decisions such as whether or not to object to the prosecutor's attempts to enter evidence that are in the particular expertise of the attorney. The attorney cannot make decisions for a client, such as whether or not to plead guilty to a particular charge, even if the attorney believes that the client's decision is not in the client's best interest.

The defense attorney will often assemble a legal team to assist in representing the defendant. Unlike the prosecution, which has law enforcement officers to investigate the facts of a case, the defense attorney will often have to conduct the investigation herself or supervise the defense investigation as it is conducted by private investigators or paralegals.

In most instances, the defense attorney is chosen and paid for by the defendant. When the defendant cannot afford an attorney, one is often appointed for him by the court. The procedure for the appointment of an attorney varies from jurisdiction to jurisdiction. In some jurisdictions, there is a formally established public defender office that handles all court appointments. In others, the court draws from a list of attorneys who have agreed to take court appointments at the court's stated rate of payment. In most cases, the amount paid for court-appointed cases is substantially less than that charged to private clients. Some attorneys also take court-appointed cases on a *pro bono* basis, that is, they do not charge a fee for services. Generally, the court-appointed attorney will also be reimbursed her actual ordinary expenses incurred in the representation, such as copying costs; however, the costs of experts, private investigators, and the like must usually be preapproved by the court on petition by the attorney.

Role of Attorneys

Attorneys have a principal-agent relationship with their clients. They also have other responsibilities and modicums of decorum that influence their behaviors and actions. These attributes range from their argumentation to oaths as officers of the court. Other factors include the educational backgrounds and professional attributes that impact their careers.

Professional Obligations

Although the roles of prosecutors and defense attorneys in the court process differ, there are many commonalities because they are all attorneys. Note, for example, that both are obligated to represent the best interests of their client, whether that client is the citizen of the jurisdiction in which they serve or the individual defendant, with the bounds proscribed by the Constitution, federal and state laws, and the rules of procedure. Both are considered to be officers of the court and bound by their oath as attorneys (Figure 12.4). The particularities of the oath of office for attorneys vary depending on the requirements of the jurisdiction in which they practice. Maine law requires that all attorneys take the following oath:

> You solemnly swear that you will do no falsehood nor consent to the doing of any in court, and that if you know of an intention to commit any, you will give knowledge thereof to the justices of the court or some of them that it may be prevented; you will not wittingly or willingly promote or sue any false, groundless or unlawful suit nor give aid or consent to the same; that you will delay no man for lucre or malice, but will conduct yourself in the office of an attorney within the courts according to the best of your knowledge and discretion, and with all good fidelity, as well as to the courts, as to your clients. So help you God.[14]

Other states specify an obligation to uphold the U.S. Constitution and the constitution of the state in which the attorney practices.

In addition, all attorneys are subject to rules of professional responsibility that govern their behavior. These rules or codes also vary depending on the jurisdiction, but many are modeled after a set of model rules developed by the American Bar Association (ABA).

Figure 12.4 Attorney General Eric Holder administering the oath of office to James Cole, the new deputy attorney general. The deputy attorney general advises and assists the attorney general in formulating and implementing departmental policies and programs and in providing overall supervision and direction to all organizational units of the department. (From Mathers, A., 2011, U.S. Department of Justice. Retrieved from http://www.justice.gov/css-gallery/gallery-jamescole.html.)

The ABA Model Rules govern conduct such as "Candor toward the Tribunal,"[15] "Fairness to Opposing Party and Counsel,"[16] "Impartiality and Decorum of the Tribunal,"[17] and "Trial Publicity."[18] The ABA Model Rules include a special provision for prosecutors that prohibits prosecuting a charge that the prosecutor knows is not supported by probable cause, seeking to obtain from an unrepresented accused a waiver of important pretrial rights, such as the right to a preliminary hearing, and other similar unethical and illegal conduct.[19] Defense attorneys have a well-known obligation to protect the confidentiality of statements made by the client to the attorney during the course of the attorney–client relationship.[20]

Education and Qualifications

Lawyers must be licensed by the jurisdictions in which they practice. This is frequently referred to as being "admitted to the bar," meaning that the person is allowed to cross the bar separating the general public from the area in front of the judge. The procedures and qualifications for admission to the bar are generally established by the highest court in that jurisdiction. According to the U.S. Department of Labor,

> All States require that applicants for admission to the bar pass a written bar examination; most States also require applicants to pass a separate written ethics examination. Lawyers who have been admitted to the bar in one State occasionally may be admitted to the bar in another without taking another examination if they meet the latter jurisdiction's standards of good moral character and a specified period of legal experience. In most cases, however, lawyers must pass the bar examination in each State in which they plan to practice. Federal courts and agencies set their own qualifications for those practicing before or in them. To qualify for the bar examination in most States, an applicant must earn a college degree and graduate from a law school accredited by the ABA or the proper State authorities.[21]

Obtaining a college degree and the law school degree normally takes a total of seven years of full-time study.

Trial Tactics

Attorneys receive very similar education, learning legal reasoning and analysis as it applies to Constitutional law, criminal law, contract law, and the like, but most attorneys develop a degree of specialization. This development can start in law school where some students will participate in clinical programs designed to teach the specific skills and abilities needed to apply the law in a courtroom setting. It is not enough to know the law and the rules. Both the prosecutor and the defense attorney must be able to decide how and when to use the law and the rules to the best advantage for the presentation of their evidence to the jury.

Often, law enforcement officers, witnesses, and defendants are somewhat mystified as to why an attorney makes a particular decision during the course of a proceeding. Most often these decisions are based on considerations of the value of applying a specific rule as a matter of trial tactics. Of course, each attorney will have their own perspective and style, although there are some commonalities.

This is especially true of trial tactics. All attorneys receive roughly the same training and draw their arrows from the same quiver, but each will chose particular tactics and use them in a specific way based on their own style and judgment. It is helpful for law enforcement officers to understand the prosecutor's use of trial tactics. Often a law enforcement officer is frustrated because, after the officer has expended many hours in investigation and gathering of evidence, the prosecutor does not seem to be applying the resulting work to the trial. However, trials are more than just the application of rules of procedure, rules of evidence, statutes, and case law to a set of facts.

Just as important as knowing the rules and law is knowing *how* and *when* to employ them in the context of a particular trial. While knowledge of the rules of evidence will tell the attorney she *can object* to a question or *can ask* a particular question, she must use her judgment to determine *whether* to object and *whether* to ask that question. At each opportunity to object, she must determine the following:

- Whether an objection is likely to succeed because an unsuccessful objection may create a wrong impression in the jury's mind
- Whether repeated objections, even if successful, will cause a jury to think her side has something to hide
- Whether a successful objection will later prejudice her ability to use similar evidence favorable to her case

The above are just a few of many potential ramifications.

Sometimes the attorney makes the best presentation by doing nothing. This is not a comment on the attorney's abilities, but recognition that there are times when the presentation is best enhanced by refraining from action rather than taking action.

As discussed earlier, repeated objections, even if successful, may cause a jury to think her client has something to hide. Here are a few other examples when it is better not to act:

- The witness is rambling and the rambling makes the witness appear incoherent or unreliable.
- The objectionable testimony opens the door to issues on cross-examination that would otherwise be off limits.
- Questioning of a witness is likely to cause confusion on an issue that is fairly clear.
- Questioning of a witness will bore the jury causing the jurors to stop paying attention.
- Questioning of a witness, especially a very young, vulnerable, or distraught witness, will cause the attorney to look like a bully (a characterization that may be transferred to the attorney's client).
- The attorney does not know the answer to the question and the likely answers include answers that will be harmful to the case.

The trial attorney (whether prosecutor or defense attorney) must make tactical use of all available weapons. This can be done only if the case is thoroughly prepared; the facts, law, and rules must all be known and all the evidence must be available in a form that can overcome objections from the other side and be understood by the judge and jury.

Judges

If the prosecution and defense are viewed as two sides each attempting to win a court proceeding similar to two teams on a sporting field, the judge may be viewed as a referee charged with seeing that the rules are obeyed by both teams. Unless the defendant elects to have the judge act as a fact finder and make the final decision of guilty or not guilty, the judge acts only on questions of law, applying the Rules of Procedure and the Rules of Evidence to the proceeding, and instructing the jury on the law that applies to the case. However, unlike referees in games, the judge will seldom make a ruling unless requested to do so by one of the parties. For example, Federal Rule of Evidence 602 requires that a witness only testify as to matters about which the witness has personal knowledge.[22] Should one side ask a witness a question requiring the witness to testify about a matter about which the witness had no personal knowledge, the judge would not invoke the rule unless the other side formally objected to the question.

The procedures for selecting judges, and the qualifications for being a judge, vary from jurisdiction to jurisdiction. In some jurisdictions, such as the federal system, judges are appointed by the chief executive (president or governor) but must be approved by a legislative body (e.g., the Senate). In the federal system, judges receive a lifetime appointment, but some state judges are appointed only for a specific term, for example, 10 years, and must be reappointed to continue service. In other jurisdictions, judges are elected for specific terms and must run for reelection on a regular basis. In some jurisdictions, the judges are appointed, but must submit to a vote by the citizens of a jurisdiction after a number of years in service. Still other jurisdictions have hybrid systems in which some judges are appointed and others elected.[23] Most jurisdictions require that judges be licensed attorneys, but some do not impose this requirement on "lower level" magistrate positions.[24]

Regardless of how they are selected, judges have an obligation to uphold the Constitution, the laws of the United States, and the laws of the jurisdiction in which they serve (Figure 12.5). They must do so impartially, meaning without favoritism for either side (even if their background is that of a prosecutor or a defense attorney). It also means they must set aside their personal preferences, prejudices, and biases. It is not unusual for a judge to rule on a particular matter in a way she would not rule if allowed to act on her own beliefs. As discussed in Chapter 13, judges must follow precedent and decide cases of Constitutional or statutory

Figure 12.5 The attorney general administered the oath of office to EOIR's newly appointed chief immigration judge Brian M. O'Leary at an investiture ceremony at EOIR headquarters. (From Tague, L., 2009, U.S. Department of Justice. Retrieved from http://www.justice.gov/css-gallery/gallery_eoir.html#4.)

interpretation in accordance with the decisions of higher courts, even if they would arrive at a different interpretation if there were no precedents to govern their decision. Similarly, they must apply laws even if they believe the law itself is not a good law.

Trial Jury

As indicated in the previous section, the facts of a case are ultimately determined by a fact finder. In many instances, that fact finder is a jury. All criminal defendants have a right to a trial by an impartial jury under the Sixth Amendment to the Constitution. The rules and procedures governing the selection and operation of a jury are not stated in the Constitution, so those rules and procedures vary from state to state, and sometimes even in different areas of the same state.

In general, the jury is selected from the general body of citizens living in the jurisdiction in which the trial is being held. Citizens are called to jury duty by being selected at random using lists of registered voters, licensed drivers, or similar sources. Although it is often said that a person is entitled to a "jury of peers," this does not mean the jurors have to be of the same gender, race, religion, or other group, but simply that they be fellow citizens of the applicable jurisdiction.

Because the jurors are culled from the entire jurisdiction, the group of citizens from which the jurors are drawn can vary depending on the court in which the trial is being held, even when crimes and trials are held in the same geographic location. For example, a person charged with robbery of a bank may be charged and tried under state law or (in most instances) under federal law. If charged under state law, the court in which the trial takes place is likely to be a county or circuit court and the jury will be drawn from citizens of that county or circuit, whereas if the defendant is charged under federal law, the trial will take place in a federal district court for the district in which the crime was committed, a district that may have vastly different geographical boundaries. Thus, a state trial in Boston, Massachusetts, will draw from a different group of citizens than a federal trial also held in Boston, Massachusetts.

There are few limitations on who can serve on a jury. These limitations will differ from jurisdiction to jurisdiction, but the federal juror qualifications are typical. To be legally qualified for jury service, an individual must

- Be a United States citizen
- Be at least 18 years of age
- Reside primarily in the judicial district for one year
- Be adequately proficient in English
- Have no disqualifying mental or physical condition
- Not currently be subject to felony charges
- Never have been convicted of a felony (unless civil rights have been legally restored)[25]

The role of the jury is to determine the facts of the case. As discussed earlier, the prosecution and the defendant may disagree on what the facts are. Each side will be provided an opportunity to present evidence to the jury. The rules and procedures for presenting that evidence and the jury's role in the evidence production process also varies from jurisdiction to jurisdiction. For example, in some jurisdictions, jury members can take notes, while other jurisdictions prohibit note taking by the jury.

Figure 12.6 Members of a jury. (Courtesy of the Saint Louis, MO 22nd Judicial Circuit Courts. Retrieved from http://www.courts.mo.gov/hosted/circuit22/JuryDuty.htm.)

The jury does not determine the law applicable to a case. The jury members are given ("instructed on") the law by the judge. The jury then determines the facts and decides whether, given those facts, the defendant has committed the crime with which he has been charged. In our assault while hunting example, the judge would read the jury the statute and explain each of the elements. That explanation would include explaining how "criminal negligence," "hunting," and "in pursuit of" are defined and interpreted. The jury must then set aside all personal prejudices and focus only on the evidence presented at the trial. Based on that evidence, the jury determines the facts, applies the law to those facts, and determines whether the defendant has committed the crime (Figure 12.6).

Court Process

Citizens of the United States are granted many rights and protections by the United States Constitution. These rights are primarily found in the Bill of Rights, the first 10 amendments to the Constitution. As discussed in Chapter 13, it is the role of the judicial branch to ensure that the government does not diminish those rights. Many of those rights pertain directly to how defendants are to be treated in the court system itself.

As noted earlier, the Sixth Amendment[26] provides that in all criminal prosecutions, the accused is guaranteed the following six rights: (1) a speedy and public trial, (2) trial by an impartial jury of the state and district wherein the crime shall have been committed, (3) the right to be informed of the nature and cause of the accusation, (4) the right to be confronted with the witnesses against him, (5) the right to have compulsory process for obtaining witnesses in his favor, and (6) the right to an attorney.

The Fifth Amendment[27] includes four stipulations: it (1) requires an indictment by a grand jury in serious cases, (2) prohibits being tried for the same offense twice, (3) prohibits compelling a person in any criminal case to be a witness against himself (the "right to remain silent"), and (4) contains a general prohibition against taking a citizen's life, liberty, or property, without due process of law. The Eighth Amendment[28] prohibits excessive bail, excessive fines, and cruel and unusual punishment.

Although the Constitution guarantees these rights, it does not provide the procedures for seeing that the rights are carried out in the court process. Each state and the federal government must specify the procedures for providing those rights as interpreted by the United States Supreme Court in its court system, and each state has a slightly different way of doing so. Those procedures must provide for all the specific rights listed in the amendments and the general "due process of law" requirement set forth in the Fifth and Fourteenth Amendments.

Some of those procedures are set forth in statutes, but many are found in the Rules of Criminal Procedure[29] promulgated by the court systems. These rules provide the specific procedure for each of the rights provided in the Constitution. For example, Federal Rule of Criminal Procedure 10(a) provides the mechanism for implementing the Sixth Amendment requirement that the accused be "informed of the nature and cause of the accusation":

Rule 10. Arraignment

(a) In General.

An arraignment must be conducted in open court and must consist of:

(1) Ensuring that the defendant has a copy of the indictment or information;
(2) Reading the indictment or information to the defendant or stating to the defendant the substance of the charge; and then
(3) Asking the defendant to plead to the indictment or information.[30]

Similar rules exist governing indictments, grand juries, trials, and the other rights protected by the Constitution.

Because the procedures enacted by each state must provide the protections required by the Constitution as interpreted by the United States Supreme Court, even while they differ in specifics, the basic framework is fairly consistent from state to state. The procedures will also vary within a jurisdiction depending on the seriousness of the crime (usually distinguishing between misdemeanors and felonies), whether the defendant is taken into custody or issued a summons, and other similar factors.

Initial Appearances and Bail

The court process itself begins with an "initial appearance" by the defendant. After a person is arrested, the person must be brought before a magistrate "without unnecessary delay" to be informed of the charges against her and of her right to an attorney, and to have bail set.

What constitutes unnecessary delay depends on whether or not the person is retained in custody after the booking process is complete. In many instances, the arrested person is released by the police with nothing more than instructions on when and where to appear for the initial appearance. It is also not unusual for persons arrested on minor offenses to be released on personal recognizance, that is, on their personal written promise to appear on the date and at the location of the initial appearance. Still others will be released after posting bail established by a bail commissioner or other person authorized by law to set bail, usually based upon a preset amount established for each class of offense.

If a person remains in custody, the initial appearance must occur within a set time, usually 24 hours. One issue addressed at the initial appearance in such cases will be bail. The Eighth Amendment prohibits "excessive" bail. Although the prosecutor and the defense counsel may agree on appropriate bail subject to approval by the judge or magistrate, they often disagree. The court must determine a bail that is appropriate, given the primary purpose of bail, which is to assure the person in custody (who is presumed to be innocent under law) will appear when and where he is required to do so while ensuring the safety of the community. In most jurisdictions, the court is guided in this decision by statutes, rules, or court decisions setting forth the factors that can be or must be considered.[31] Regardless of the amount of bail set, the court can establish conditions of bail such as requiring that the accused not have contact with the victim or witnesses, submit to alcohol or drug tests, turn in their passport, and the like.

Grand Jury Indictments and Preliminary Hearings

The Fifth Amendment requires that all serious criminal charges be brought through indictment by grand jury (Figure 12.7). The other states utilize a preliminary hearing. This is one instance of the judicial branch being given the responsibility for making sure the executive branch is not overreaching in its quest to provide security for citizens, that is, citizens are not put through the ordeal of the full court process merely on the charge of a law enforcement officer or prosecutor. There must be enough evidence available to establish probable cause to believe a crime has been committed and the defendant is the person who committed that crime. Whether there is enough evidence to require that a person endure a trial must be determined by someone other than the prosecutor herself. Unlike other provisions

Figure 12.7 Grand jury session. (From Vasilinda, M., 2009, *Capital News Service*. Retrieved from http://www.flanews.com/?p=5378.)

in the Bill of Rights, the U.S. Supreme Court has held that the grand jury requirement does not extend to the states, but about half the states use a grand jury for serious crimes. Most other states provide for a preliminary hearing for this purpose.

Grand juries are so called only because they are larger (generally 23 jurors) than a trial jury (generally 12 jurors), often referred to as a "petit" jury. The jurors are generally selected from the same pool of citizens as a trial jury, but that is about the only similarity between the two types of juries. A grand jury is usually called into session for a stated period of time. While in session, the grand jury reviews the evidence presented to it by the prosecutor to determine whether there is enough evidence for a person to be tried for a crime. If so, the grand jury issues an indictment, a written accusation charging a person with a crime.

Grand jury proceedings have little resemblance to a trial. They are conducted in secret, the defendant is not present (unless subpoenaed to testify) and there is no opportunity for the defense to present evidence or cross-examine witnesses. The grand jury does have the power to subpoena witnesses, but seldom does so without the direction of the prosecutor even when the grand jury is used to investigate crimes rather than just review the evidence already gathered by law enforcement. Thus, while grand juries are intended to act as an independent check on prosecutorial authority, there is significant doubt as to their effectiveness in this regard.[32] Thus, use of the grand jury, except when required, is diminishing and more cases proceed on an information filed by the prosecutor and a preliminary hearing conducted by the court (Figure 12.8).

Arraignment

As indicated earlier, the arraignment procedure generally entails three prongs as follows: (1) ensuring that the defendant has a copy of the indictment or information, (2) reading the indictment or information to the defendant or stating to the defendant the substance

Easton Police Shooting Grand Jury Investigation

PENNSYLVANIA OFFICE OF ATTORNEY GENERAL

1. Adequate firearms safety facilities must be provided for the unloading, cleaning and loading of all weapons, Cameras should also be installed and maintained in all firearm safety facilities.

2. Regular training should be conducted of all Easton police officers regarding the safe handling of firearms within the Headquarters Building.

3. The Easton Police Department should immediately adopt strict written firearm safety standards.

4. The written firearm safety standards adopted by the Easton Police Department should detail transporting and handling of loaded and unloaded weapons.

5. Specific personnel should be appointed and trained as firearms safety inspectors.

TOM CORBETT ATTORNEY GENERAL

Easton Police Shooting Grand Jury Investigation

PENNSYLVANIA OFFICE OF ATTORNEY GENERAL

6. The Easton Police Department must establish dear standards of conduct, rules and regulations to be adhered to by all Easton police officers.

7. The City of Easton should hire a Chief of Police who is independent of, and without prior affiliation to, the Easton Police Department. This new Chief of Police should be tasked with the reform of the Easton Police Department.

8. The Grand Jury recommends an effort to increase citizen participation in the oversight of the Easton Police Department.

9. The establishment of an internal affairs unit under the direct supervision of the Chief of Police. All allegations of misconduct shall be disclosed to the Mayor.

10. The negligence and errors of judgment of Officer Matthew Renninger in this matter should result in the termination of his employment as an Easton Police Officer.

TOM CORBETT ATTORNEY GENERAL

Figure 12.8 Attorney general findings. (Courtesy of the Pennsylvania Office of Attorney General, 2006. Retrieved from http://www.attorneygeneral.gov/press.aspx?id=1076.)

of the charge, and then (3) asking the defendant to plead to the indictment or information. Revision or reduction of bail may also be addressed during the arraignment. The court generally also sets the schedule for the remaining steps in the process, including establishing when the parties must file motions, complete discovery, and be ready for trial. This schedule is set when the court and the parties have very little information regarding the case, so the schedule may be changed at the request of a party if sufficient reason is shown.

In most cases, a plea of not guilty is entered at the arraignment. If a defendant does not respond to the request for a plea, a plea of not guilty will be entered for him by the court. The defendant may decide to plead guilty or *nolo contendere*. A plea of "nolo" means that the defendant is choosing not to contest the charges and has the effect of a guilty plea for most purposes. If the defendant decides to plead guilty or nolo, the court will address the defendant directly to ensure that the defendant understands the nature of the charge, statutorily mandated minimum and maximum sentences, and that by entering a plea of guilty or nolo, the defendant waives her rights under the Constitution to a trial before a jury, to confront witness, to cross-examine witnesses, to present witnesses, and otherwise defend against the charge.

Most jurisdictions have a rule or statute governing court acceptance of a plea of guilty to a serious offense similar to Rule 11 of the Federal Rules of Criminal Procedure.[33] These rules are designed to require the court to determine that the plea is voluntary and did not result from force, threats, or promises (other than promises in a plea agreement). The court must then have the prosecutor explain what facts would be proven against the defendant if a trial were held to ensure that there is a factual basis for the charge. The court will accept the plea if it is voluntarily made and the prosecutor articulates sufficient facts to meet the elements of the crime.

In some instances, the defendant will be sentenced immediately, especially if there is a plea agreement submitted by the prosecution and the defendant. In many cases, however, sentencing will be delayed in order that a presentence investigation and report be done. The court will use that report as well as arguments by both the prosecution and defense to determine the appropriate sentence for the defendant.

Plea Agreements

Many criminal cases are resolved through plea bargaining. A plea bargain can occur at any point in the court process but usually occur just prior to arraignment or just prior to trial. Plea bargaining is a negotiation process by which the prosecutor and the defense attorney attempt to agree on the appropriate disposition of a criminal case. While in a perfect world one might imagine that all cases would be resolved by trial, this is not practical given the resources available in our court system. It is also not necessarily the best way to resolve doubtful cases. The advantages and disadvantages of plea bargaining has been debated for decades, but the practice remains with us[34] and is formalized in the Federal Rules of Criminal Procedure.[35]

Plea bargaining requires that the prosecutors and defense attorneys each evaluate their case and attempt to obtain the best result for their side given the evidence available, the resources available, the particular defendant involved, and the best interest of their clients. In its simplest form, consider a case in which the most likely sentence for a defendant is 10 years in prison. The prosecutor and defense attorney each believe that there is a 50% chance of a guilty verdict and a 50% chance of a not-guilty verdict. The prosecutor may decide that it is in the best interest of society that the defendant be convicted and receive *some* penalty rather than to take the chance of a not-guilty verdict and there being no penalty. At the same time, the defense attorney may reason that it is better for his client to accept a five-year penalty than to take the risk of a ten-year penalty. The defense attorney would advise his client to plead guilty, rather than take the risk of a trial. Ultimately, the defendant would have to make the decision and authorize his attorney to accept the plea agreement. In most cases, the factors to be considered in determining whether to offer or accept a plea agreement are far more complex than in this example.

Consider also how plea bargaining might work in our assault while hunting example. In our hypothetical case, each party would understand that there is a risk that the terms "hunting" and "pursuit" may be interpreted favorably to the other party. If they are interpreted favorably to the prosecution, Peter will be convicted and, perhaps, fined or serve a short term in jail. If the terms are interpreted favorable to the defense, Peter will not be convicted and will not receive any penalty.[36] However, both parties may agree that under the circumstances, neither result is really in the best interest of society or of Peter, but that both would be better off if Peter took a firearm safety course than if he simply paid a fine. If this were to happen, the prosecutor may agree to delay disposition of the charge until after Peter had taken the course and then agree to dismiss the charge.

In most instances, the court will accept a plea agreement. The court assumes that the prosecutor has zealously represented the public, that the defendant has zealously represented his client, and based on all the factors under consideration arrived at the best resolution of the case. However, the court need not accept the plea agreement. Again, most jurisdictions have a rule or statute governing the procedure by which such agreements are accepted or rejected. Rule 11 of the Federal Rules of Procedure requires a judge to inform a defendant that the court is rejecting the agreement and allow the defendant to withdraw her plea.[37]

It is also possible in some cases for a defendant to enter a conditional plea. A conditional plea is one in which the defendant pleads guilty, but reserves the right to appeal a question of law. Under the federal rules,[38] a conditional plea requires the consent of the prosecutor and approval of the judge, so it arises in most instances through the plea bargaining process. In our hypothetical scenario, Peter might, for example, agree to plead guilty because the trial judge has informed him that the judge interprets "hunting" unfavorably to Peter. However, Peter would reserve the right to appeal to have a higher court interpret the statute. If the higher court agrees with the trial judge, Peter's plea would stay in place, but would be withdrawn if the higher court agreed with the defense's interpretation of "hunting."

In 2012, the Supreme Court ruled in the case of *Missouri v. Frye*[39] that the right to an attorney guaranteed by the Sixth Amendment included the right to competent advice from an attorney during plea negotiations. Frye was charged with driving with a revoked license. The syllabus[40] of the court's opinion summarizes the facts this way:

> Because he had been convicted of the same offense three times before, he was charged, under Missouri law, with a felony carrying a maximum 4-year prison term. The prosecutor sent Frye's counsel a letter, offering two possible plea bargains, including an offer to reduce the charge to a misdemeanor and to recommend, with a guilty plea, a 90-day sentence. Counsel did not convey the offers to Frye, and they expired. Less than a week before Frye's preliminary hearing, he was again arrested for driving with a revoked license. He subsequently pleaded guilty with no underlying plea agreement and was sentenced to three years in prison. Seeking postconviction relief in state court, he alleged that his counsel's failure to inform him of the earlier plea offers denied him the effective assistance of counsel, and he testified that he would have pleaded

guilty to the misdemeanor had he known of the offer. The court denied his motion, but the Missouri appellate court reversed, holding that Frye met both of the requirements for showing a Sixth Amendment violation under *Strickland v. Washington*, 466 U. S. 668. Specifically, the court found that defense counsel had been ineffective in not communicating the plea offers to Frye and concluded that Frye had shown that counsel's deficient performance caused him prejudice because he pleaded guilty to a felony instead of a misdemeanor.[41]

Justice Kennedy noted the "simple reality" that 97% of federal convictions and 94% of state convictions result from guilty pleas, making the plea bargaining process a critical stage of a criminal proceeding. Relying on precedent set in *Montejo v. Louisiana*, 556 U. S. 778, 786, the court held that the Sixth Amendment right to effective assistance of counsel extends to the consideration of plea offers that lapse or rejected. That right applies to "all 'critical' stages of the criminal proceedings," and the Supreme Court held that the right applied to plea bargaining at least to the extent that the defendant be told of any formal offers from a prosecutor. This holding is likely to have a substantial effect on the plea bargaining process and the criminal justice prosecution process in general.

Discovery and Motions

After the arraignment and before trial, the parties to a criminal case may engage in processes known as discovery and motion practice. Discovery is a process whereby the parties exchange evidence prior to trial. This helps avoid "trial by ambush" and may assist the parties in making a more intelligent decision regarding plea agreements. The prosecution in particular is required to provide the defendant with evidence it has available. The prosecution must provide not only the evidence it intends to use at trial—generally evidence that incriminates the defendant (inculpatory evidence)—but also evidence that tends to show the defendant did not commit the crime (exculpatory evidence). The prosecution also has the right to obtain information such as the names and addresses of defense witnesses and test results that the defense intends to use at trial. What discovery is required and the procedure by which it is provided are usually governed by a rule of procedure such as Federal Rule of Criminal Procedure 16.

If either side fails to provide the required discovery, the other side can file a request with the court asking that the judge enforce the rule. This request is referred to as a motion. Motions regarding discovery are some of the most common pretrial motions, together with motions regarding what evidence can and cannot be used at trial. In particular, defendants may file a motion to suppress asking the court to prevent the prosecution from using evidence obtained in violation of the Fourth, Fifth, or Sixth Amendments to the Constitution based on the exclusionary rule developed by the United States Supreme Court as a means of curtailing law enforcement violation of the rights provided by these amendments.

Trial

Once pretrial procedures are completed, the case is ready for trial. Prior to the trial, there may be a pretrial conference attended by the trial judge, the prosecutor, and the defense attorney. At this conference, scheduling of witnesses and other practical procedural matters are addressed. Each side may also file legal memorandum or trial briefs explaining that side's position on issues that may arise during the trial. For example, in our assault while hunting hypothetical, the parties may want to provide the judge with legal argument and case precedent regarding the interpretation of "hunting" and "pursuit." The parties may also file a motion *in limine*, which asks the court to rule in advance on evidentiary issues that will arise during trial. For example, as described below, each attorney will be given the opportunity to make an opening statement to the jury. During that statement, the attorney generally tells the jury what to expect in terms of evidence in the case. The attorney will not want to tell the jury to expect evidence that the judge may exclude under the rules of evidence, so the attorney will ask the court for a ruling in advance.

The trial itself begins with the selection of a jury. The basic composition and selection of the jury pool was previously described in this chapter. The jury usually consists of 12 jurors and one or two alternates selected from the jury pool called into court for that purpose. The first step in the process is for the potential jurors to be "screened" for prejudices and biases. For example, a potential juror who is related to the defendant would likely be considered unable to make an impartial decision. The jurors usually complete a form that provides the parties with some limited information such as their educational background, employment, and employment of close relatives. In some instances, the form may require information pertinent to the issues in a particular case. For example, if the case involves sexual abuse, the form may ask if the juror or a close relative has been the victim of sexual abuse or been accused of sexual abuse.

The information on the form is seldom sufficient for a determination of potential impartiality, so the potential jurors are questioned in a process known as "voir dire." In some jurisdictions, voir dire is conducted by the judge and the attorneys. In others, only the judge asks the questions, but the attorneys can submit questions for voir dire at the pretrial conference.

Based on the responses on the form and to the voir dire questions, attorneys for both side can request that certain jurors be removed from the jury pool through a challenge for cause, that is, the answers to the questions indicate a high probability that the juror will not be able to render an impartial verdict. Since the goal is an impartial jury, there is no limit to the number of challenges that can be made on this basis. However, the court is not required to dismiss a juror from the pool simply because a challenge for cause is made, but must make its own determination as to whether or not the juror is likely to be impartial.

Once jurors challenged for cause have been removed from the jury pool,[42] a number of potential jurors are called forward by a random selection process, sometimes literally by having their numbers drawn from a box. The number of persons called forward exceeds those necessary for the actual juror, because each side is usually allowed a number of peremptory challenges, that is, challenges for which they do not have to give a reason. The number of challenges often depends on the seriousness of the case. The federal rules allow 20 challenges per side in a capital case, 6 prosecutorial and 10 defense challenges in a felony case, and 3 per side in a misdemeanor case.[43] Thus, in order to ensure enough jurors to complete a jury panel in a felony case, 30 jurors would be called forward to allow the 16 challenges, leaving 12 jurors and 2 alternates. The opportunity to exercise challenges usually alternates, so the defense would exercise one challenge, then the prosecution, then the defense would exercise its second challenge, and so on.

Once the jury is selected, the judge gives the jury some preliminary instructions regarding its role in the case, explains the nature of the case, and gives the jury a short statement regarding how the case will be conducted. In cases where there is a reason to fear that the jurors may be influenced by publicity outside the courthouse or that they may be improperly contacted during the course of the trial, the jury may be *sequestered*, meaning they are not allowed to go home but are housed and fed by the court during the course of the trial. Sequestering is not done lightly. It is quite burdensome on jurors, especially in cases that may take weeks or months to complete.

The presentation of the case begins with the prosecutor and the defense each being given an opportunity to make an opening statement. Statements by attorneys at any time during trial are not evidence and the jury is instructed by the court not to consider them as such. However, the opening statement is the first opportunity for the jurors to hear from each side and the closing arguments are the last, so they are important opportunities for the parties to influence the jury's perception of the evidence presented in the case.

In the opening statement, the attorneys do not argue their cases. Rather, they attempt to establish the "theme" of their presentation, explaining to the jury who the parties and witnesses are, what evidence will be presented, and who will present it. Although they do not argue the case, they do take every advantage of the opportunity to engender a favorable view of their side. In some cases, the defense will rely on weaknesses in the prosecution's case rather than present evidence of its own. The opening statement and closing arguments are especially important in these cases, but in every case, both attorneys generally make substantial effort to make the best strategic use of these opportunities.

The prosecution makes the opening statement first. The defense may follow directly after the prosecutor or defer an opening statement until the beginning of the defense's evidence. Generally, the court will establish time limits for statements made by attorneys in the trial. There are rules governing the conduct and content of opening statements and closing arguments, but attorneys are reluctant to make objections during opening statements as it can create a bad impression among the jurors to repeatedly interrupt the other side this early in the proceeding.

After opening statements, the prosecution begins presentation of its evidence. All evidence must be presented through witnesses who can identify and explain the evidence. Often the only evidence presented by a witness will be the testimony of the witness herself. The witness is not allowed to simply talk in a narrative fashion but must answer the question posed to him or her by the prosecutor in her direct examination. When the prosecutor is finished asking the witness questions, the defense attorney may ask questions of the witness in cross-examination. If new matters are raised by the defense's examination, the prosecutor can ask additional questions of the witness.

Either attorney can object to questions considered improper under the Rules of Evidence. The court will generally require the attorney to state the basis for the objection, unless it is obvious. The attorney asking the question is given an opportunity to state why the question is proper. The court will then either sustain the objection and prohibit the question or overrule the objection and allow the question. Often the attorney asking the question will simply withdraw the question or rephrase it so that it is proper under the Rules. Either side may also object to physical evidence such as test results and documents as not being proper under the Rules of Evidence. These objections are handled in the same manner.

The prosecution continues putting on evidence through witnesses until it has completed its case against the defendant, with each witness subject to the same direct and cross-examination process. When it has completed its presentation, the prosecution "rests" its case. At this point, the defense will often make a motion asking the court to dismiss the case on the basis that the prosecution has not entered sufficient evidence on each element of the crime to establish that a crime has been committed by the defendant. The court evaluates the evidence entered by the prosecution in the light most favorable to the prosecution. This motion is seldom granted, but must often be made to preserve the issue for an appeal.

Once the prosecution has completed its case, the defense must decide whether or not it will present evidence. As stated earlier, the defense may rely on weaknesses in the prosecution's case and not present any evidence. If the defense decides to present evidence and an opening statement has not yet been made, it will be made at this point. The defense then calls its witnesses, which are subject to the same direct and cross-examination as the prosecution's witness except that now the defense conducts the direct examination and the prosecution conducts the cross. This distinction can be important because the rules regarding what questions can be asked and how they can be asked are different for direct examination than they are for cross-examination. For example, the rules do not permit leading questions[44] on direct examination, but do permit them on cross-examination.

The defendant may testify in her own defense, but need not. Because the Fifth Amendment prohibits an accused from being forced to testify against herself, the fact that she did not testify cannot be commented upon by the prosecution so as to suggest guilt from the mere fact that she did not testify.

When the defense has completed its case, it too "rests." The prosecution will have the opportunity for rebuttal, that is, to respond to new matters raised by the defense. This is not an opportunity to simply repeat evidence that was presented or should have been presented during the primary presentation (case-in-chief). Similarly, the defense may be given an opportunity for surrebuttal in which the defense can address new matters raised during rebuttal. After all the evidence has been presented by both parties, the defense will generally again make a motion for the charge to be dismissed.

The final step in the presentation of a case is the closing statements of the attorneys. Closing argument provides an opportunity for each party to summarize the evidence they presented, to show how each piece of evidence proves or supports their theory of the case or disproves the other side's theory of the case. As this is the last time the jury will hear from each side, closing arguments, while they are not evidence themselves, can often have a dramatic effect on how the jury views the evidence.[45]

Before the jury considers the evidence, it receives instructions on the law from the judge known as the charge to the jury. The jury then retires to the jury room and deliberates. Generally, a unanimous verdict must be returned. Deliberation can take a substantial amount of time in many cases and the jury may indicate to the judge that it cannot reach a decision. Normally, the judge will reinstruct the jury and require them to continue deliberations. The jury may also send written questions to the judge via the bailiff, if they need clarification of the law or their responsibilities. If the jury cannot reach a verdict, it is a hung jury and the court will declare a mistrial. Because this will not be considered to be a completed trial, the prohibition against being tried twice for the same offense in the Fifth Amendment does not apply, and the prosecution may decide to retry the defendant.

If the jury reaches a not-guilty verdict, they are discharged and the defendant is allowed to go free. If the jury reaches a jury verdict, they may be re-empaneled to consider sentencing in some cases in some jurisdictions. Otherwise they will be discharged. The defendant may be sentenced immediately or sentencing may be delayed pending a presentence investigation and report. If sentencing is delayed, the court will consider whether the defendant should be released pending sentencing or held in custody. The defendant can also appeal the conviction, the sentence, or both, in which case the court will also consider whether the defendant should be released on bail pending a final outcome of his appeal (Figure 12.9).

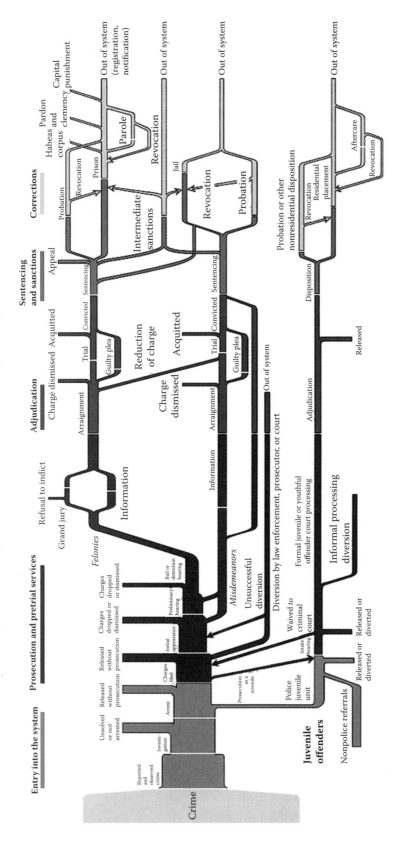

What is the sequence of events in the criminal justice system?

Note: This chart gives a simplified view of caseflow through the criminal justice system. Procedures vary among jurisdictions. The weights of the lines are not intended to show actual size of caseloads.

Figure 12.9 Basic steps of the criminal justice process.[46] (Adapted from *The challenge of crime in a free society*. President's Commission on Law Enforcement and Administration of Justice, 1967 [This revision, a result of the Symposium on the 30th Anniversary of the President's Commission, was prepared by the Bureau of Justice Statistics in 1997].)

Summary

The court systems pervading the United States are complex. A variety of courts exist through which arguments are presented with respect to the resolving of disputes and grievances. These courts may be found locally, regionally, and nationally. Both federal and state entities are represented among these court systems. Courthouses, like the one shown in Figure 12.10, daily host a variety of civil and criminal cases.

The court system involves a variety of agents. Judges, attorneys (serving the defendant and the plaintiff), bailiffs, reporters, witnesses, experts, and administrative personnel may be involved among court proceedings. Within the court system, civil and criminal disputes are heard and argued.

The training of personnel ranges from the earning of law school and undergraduate credentials among attorneys and judges to the specific training regimens for law enforcement personnel that may be mandated by states. In any case, the demeanor and behavior of court officers and personnel must be professional.

Court cases generally involve facts, evidence, and proof. The facts of a case are the bits and pieces that comprise what happened, that is, the event that brought the parties to court, or the particularities of the assault, theft, or other crime. Evidence is something that tends to show, confirm, or verify a fact. It can be testimony such as the driver testifying he looked at the light before he entered the intersection. Not all evidence is equally convincing. Testimony from an uninvolved third party, that is, a school crossing guard, that the light was red or green may be more convincing than the testimony of the driver of either car involved in the accident. A picture taken by a camera set up to track drivers' speed may be even more convincing.

From the lawyer's perspective, evidence is more important than actual facts. Cases must be evaluated and presented based on the evidence available for presentation rather

Figure 12.10 Sumter County, AL courthouse. (Retrieved from http://www.flickr.com/photos/will-jac/5992009744/sizes/l/in/photostream/.)

than on the facts the attorney believes to be true. Both the prosecutor and the defense attorney are more concerned about what can be proven than simply what occurred.

Proof is simply whatever evidence is sufficient to convince a jury to accept a fact as true. Thus, a driver's testimony that the light was green when she went through the intersection is proof if it is credible enough for the jury or judge to accept it as a true statement of the facts and is not proof if the jury or judge does not accept it.

The court process itself begins with an "initial appearance" by the defendant. After a person is arrested, the person must be brought before a magistrate "without unnecessary delay" to be informed of the charges against him or her and of the right to an attorney, and to have bail set.

Grand juries are so called only because they are larger (generally 23 jurors) than a trial jury (generally 12 jurors), often referred to as a "petit" jury. The jurors are generally selected from the same pool of citizens as a trial jury, but that is about the only similarity between the two types of juries. A grand jury is usually called into session for a stated period of time. While in session, the grand jury reviews the evidence presented to it by the prosecutor to determine whether there is enough evidence for a person to be tried for a crime. If so, the grand jury issues an indictment, a written accusation charging a person with a crime.

Other aspects of the American court system include discovery and motions, the potential of plea agreements, and the confining of arrested individuals. Some court proceedings may involve the use of a jury whereas others may have no jury. Regardless of the scenario or characteristics of the court environment, law enforcement personnel must be familiar with the potential of interacting and participating within the court system.

Discussion Questions

1. The American court system involves the presumption of innocence regarding the accused. This perspective is unique from many of those manifested among other court systems globally. Substantively discuss why the American court system differs from its overseas counterparts.
2. This chapter delineated the court process. Draw a diagram that depicts this process with respect to the court system of your respective state. For each stage of the process, provide a discussion that highlights the primary attributes of each stage within the process.
3. Examine the court systems that are present within your locality. Select one of these systems and substantively discuss how it is similar to the model presented within this text, and how it also differs from the model presented within this text.

Notes

1. Circuit courts: About the court. *State of Mississippi Judiciary*. Retrieved from http://www.mssc .state.ms.us/aboutcourts/circuitcourt_about.html. See also Mississippi Code of 1972, Section 9-7-81.
2. Find a trial court. *Nebraska Judicial Branch*. Retrieved from http://supremecourt.ne.gov/public/ find-court.shtml

3. Title 4. *Maine Revised Statutes.* Section 251.

4. Bankruptcy. *United States Courts.* Retrieved from http://www.uscourts.gov/FederalCourts/Bankruptcy.aspx

5. Circuit courts: About the court. *State of Mississippi Judiciary.* Retrieved from http://www.mssc.state.ms.us/aboutcourts/circuitcourt_about.html.

6. Title 4. *Maine Revised Statutes.* Section 152.

7. Title 4. *Maine Revised Statutes.* Sections 151–184.

8. Title 4. *Maine Revised Statutes.* Sections 101–121.

9. *A Map of the Federal Court Districts and Circuits.* Retrieved from http://www.uscourts.gov/uscourts/images/CircuitMap.pdf

10. Title 17-A. *Maine Revised Statutes.* Section §208-A.

11. The Sixth Amendment provides the framework for several aspects of criminal trials including the right to trial by jury, the right to an attorney, and the right to confront witnesses:

    In all criminal prosecutions, the accused shall enjoy the right to a speedy and public trial, by an impartial jury of the State and district wherein the crime shall have been committed, which district shall have been previously ascertained by law, and to be informed of the nature and cause of the accusation; to be confronted with the witnesses against him; to have compulsory process for obtaining witnesses in his favor, and to have the Assistance of Counsel for his defence.
    U.S. Constitution, Amendment VI.

12. Only the primary personnel are discussed here. Most court proceedings will include additional personnel such as

    - A clerk of the court who has official responsibility for maintaining the paperwork involved in the court's files and other tasks.
    - A court stenographer to record the proceeding, taking down everything that is said in the proceeding.
    - Bailiffs or other court officers who assist in maintaining order.

13. See *Gideon v. Wainwright*, 372 U.S. 335 (1963).

14. Title 4. *Maine Revised Statutes.* Section 806. Retrieved from http://www.mainelegislature.org/legis/statutes/4/title4sec806.html

15. *ABA Model Rules of Professional Conduct.* Rule 3.3. Retrieved from http://www.americanbar.org/groups/professional_responsibility/publications/model_rules_of_professional_conduct/model_rules_of_professional_conduct_table_of_contents.html

16. Ibid, Rule 3.4, Fairness to Opposing Party and Counsel.

17. Ibid, Rule 3.5, Impartiality and Decorum of the Tribunal.

18. Ibid, Rule 3.6, Trial Publicity.

19. Ibid, Rule 3.8, Special Responsibilities of a Prosecutor.

20. Ibid, Rule 1.6, Confidentiality of Information

    (a) A lawyer shall not reveal information relating to the representation of a client unless the client gives informed consent, the disclosure is impliedly authorized in order to carry out the representation or the disclosure is permitted by paragraph (b).

    (b) A lawyer may reveal information relating to the representation of a client to the extent the lawyer reasonably believes necessary:

        (1) to prevent reasonably certain death or substantial bodily harm;

        (2) to prevent the client from committing a crime or fraud that is reasonably certain to result in substantial injury to the financial interests or property of another and in furtherance of which the client has used or is using the lawyer's services;

        (3) to prevent, mitigate or rectify substantial injury to the financial interests or property of another that is reasonably certain to result or has resulted from the client's commission of a crime or fraud in furtherance of which the client has used the lawyer's services;

        (4) to secure legal advice about the lawyer's compliance with these Rules;

(5) to establish a claim or defense on behalf of the lawyer in a controversy between the lawyer and the client, to establish a defense to a criminal charge or civil claim against the
lawyer based upon conduct in which the client was involved, or to respond to allegations
in any proceeding concerning the lawyer's representation of the client; or

(6) to comply with other law or a court order.

21. U.S. Bureau of Labor Statistics. Lawyers. *Occupational Outlook Handbook* (2010–2011 ed.).
Retrieved from http://www.bls.gov/oco/ocos272.htm#training

22. Federal Rule of Evidence 602, Lack of Personal Knowledge, states:

> A witness may not testify to a matter unless evidence is introduced sufficient to support a finding
> that the witness has personal knowledge of the matter. Evidence to prove personal knowledge
> may, but need not, consist of the witness' own testimony. This rule is subject to the provisions of
> rule 703, relating to opinion testimony by expert witnesses.

23. For example, in the State of Maine, judges are appointed to the district, superior, and supreme
courts by the governor subject to approval by the state senate, but probate judges are elected.

24. About 40 states allow nonlawyers to hold limited-jurisdiction judgeships according to the
United States Bureau of Labor Statistics. Bureau of Labor Statistics. Judges, Magistrates, and
other Judicial Workers. *Occupational Outlook Handbook* (2010–2011 ed). Retrieved from http://
www.bls.gov/oco/ocos272.htm#training

25. Juror qualifications, exemptions and excuses. *United States Courts*. Retrieved from http://www
.uscourts.gov/FederalCourts/JuryService/JurorQualificaitons.aspx

26. *Supra,* n. 11.

27. "No person shall be held to answer for a capital, or otherwise infamous crime, unless on a pre-
sentment or indictment of a grand jury, except in cases arising in the land or naval forces, or
in the militia, when in actual service in time of war or public danger; nor shall any person be
subject for the same offense to be twice put in jeopardy of life or limb; nor shall be compelled
in any criminal case to be a witness against himself, nor be deprived of life, liberty, or property,
without due process of law; nor shall private property be taken for public use, without just
compensation." U. S. Constitution, Amendment V.

28. "Excessive bail shall not be required, nor excessive fines imposed, nor cruel and unusual punishments inflicted." U. S. Constitution, Amendment VIII.

29. See, for example, *Federal Rules of Criminal Procedure.* Retrieved from http://www.law.cornell
.edu/rules/frcrmp/

30. Ibid, Rule 10.

31. See, for example, Title 15. *Maine Revised Statutes,* Section 1056(4):

> In setting bail, the judicial officer shall, on the basis of an interview with the defendant, informa-
> tion provided by the defendant's attorney and information provided by the attorney for the State
> or an informed law enforcement officer if the attorney for the State is not available and other
> reliable information that can be obtained, take into account the available information concern-
> ing the following:
>
> A. The nature and circumstances of the crime charged;
> B. The nature of the evidence against the defendant; and
> C. The history and characteristics of the defendant, including, but not limited to:
>   (1) The defendant's character and physical and mental condition;
>   (2) The defendant's family ties in the State;
>   (3) The defendant's employment history in the State;
>   (4) The defendant's financial resources;
>   (5) The defendant's length of residence in the community and the defendant's community
>   ties;
>   (6) The defendant's past conduct, including any history relating to drug or alcohol abuse;
>   (7) The defendant's criminal history, if any;
>   (8) The defendant's record concerning appearances at court proceedings;

(9) Whether, at the time of the current offense or arrest, the defendant was on probation, parole or other release pending trial, sentencing, appeal or completion of a sentence for an offense in this jurisdiction or another;

(9-A) Any evidence that the defendant poses a danger to the safety of others in the community;

(10) Any evidence that the defendant has obstructed or attempted to obstruct justice by threatening, injuring or intimidating a victim or a prospective witness, juror, attorney for the State, judge, justice or other officer of the court; and

(11) Whether the defendant has previously violated conditions of release, probation or other court orders, including, but not limited to, violating protection from abuse orders pursuant to Title 19, section 769 or Title 19-A, section 4011.

32. See, for example, FAQs about the grand jury. *American Bar Association*. Retrieved from http://www.abanow.org/2010/03/faqs-about-the-grand-jury-system/

The grand jury is independent in theory, and although the instructions given to the grand jurors inform them they are to use their judgment, the practical realities of the situation mitigate against it.

The grand jury hears only cases brought to it by the prosecutor. The prosecutor decides which witnesses to call. The prosecutor decides which witnesses will receive immunity. The basic questioning is done by the prosecutor on a theory he or she articulates. The grand jury members are generally permitted to ask questions at the end of a witness's testimony. The prosecutor generally decides if he or she has enough evidence to seek an indictment. Occasionally the grand jurors may be asked whether they would like to hear any additional witnesses, but since their job is only to judge what the prosecutor has produced, they rarely ask to do so.

The prosecutor drafts the charges and reads them to the grand jury. There is no requirement that the grand jury be read any instructions on the law, and such instructions are rarely given.

33. Rule 11, Pleas, states:

...

(b) Considering and Accepting a Guilty or Nolo Contendere Plea.

(1) Advising and Questioning the Defendant.

Before the court accepts a plea of guilty or nolo contendere, the defendant may be placed under oath, and the court must address the defendant personally in open court. During this address, the court must inform the defendant of, and determine that the defendant understands, the following:

(A) the government's right, in a prosecution for perjury or false statement, to use against the defendant any statement that the defendant gives under oath;

(B) the right to plead not guilty, or having already so pleaded, to persist in that plea;

(C) the right to a jury trial;

(D) the right to be represented by counsel — and if necessary have the court appoint counsel — at trial and at every other stage of the proceeding;

(E) the right at trial to confront and cross-examine adverse witnesses, to be protected from compelled self-incrimination, to testify and present evidence, and to compel the attendance of witnesses;

(F) the defendant's waiver of these trial rights if the court accepts a plea of guilty or nolo contendere;

(G) the nature of each charge to which the defendant is pleading;

(H) any maximum possible penalty, including imprisonment, fine, and term of supervised release;

(I) any mandatory minimum penalty;

(J) any applicable forfeiture;

(K) the court's authority to order restitution;

(L) the court's obligation to impose a special assessment;

(M) in determining a sentence, the court's obligation to apply calculate the applicable sentencing-guideline range and to consider that range, possible departures under the Sentencing Guidelines, and other sentencing factors under 18 U.S.C. § 3553(a); and

(N) the terms of any plea-agreement provision waiving the right to appeal or to collaterally attack the sentence.

...

> (3) Determining the Factual Basis for a Plea.
>
>   Before entering judgment on a guilty plea, the court must determine that there is a factual basis for the plea.
>
>   Federal Rules of Criminal Procedure, Rule 11.

34. See, for example, Law: Is plea bargaining a cop-out? (1978, August 28). *Time Magazine*. Retrieved from http://www.time.com/time/magazine/article/0,9171,916340,00.html

35. Federal Rule of Criminal Procedure 11(c):

> (c) Plea Agreement Procedure.
>
>   (1) In General. An attorney for the government and the defendant's attorney, or the defendant when proceeding pro se, may discuss and reach a plea agreement. The court must not participate in these discussions. If the defendant pleads guilty or nolo contendere to either a charged offense or a lesser or related offense, the plea agreement may specify that an attorney for the government will:
>
>   (A) not bring, or will move to dismiss, other charges;
>
>   (B) recommend, or agree not to oppose the defendant's request, that a particular sentence or sentencing range is appropriate or that a particular provision of the Sentencing Guidelines, or policy statement, or sentencing factor does or does not apply (such a recommendation or request does not bind the court); or
>
>   (C) agree that a specific sentence or sentencing range is the appropriate disposition of the case, or that a particular provision of the Sentencing Guidelines, or policy statement, or sentencing factor does or does not apply (such a recommendation or request binds the court once the court accepts the plea agreement).
>
>   (2) Disclosing a Plea Agreement. The parties must disclose the plea agreement in open court when the plea is offered, unless the court for good cause allows the parties to disclose the plea agreement in camera.

36. Recall, however, that Joe retains the right to sue Peter in civil court for damages arising from the injury.

37. Federal Rule of Criminal Procedure 11(c):

> (3) Judicial Consideration of a Plea Agreement.
>
>   (A) To the extent the plea agreement is of the type specified in Rule 11(c)(1)(A) or (C), the court may accept the agreement, reject it, or defer a decision until the court has reviewed the presentence report.
>
>   (B) To the extent the plea agreement is of the type specified in Rule 11(c)(1)(B), the court must advise the defendant that the defendant has no right to withdraw the plea if the court does not follow the recommendation or request.
>
> (4) Accepting a Plea Agreement. If the court accepts the plea agreement, it must inform the defendant that to the extent the plea agreement is of the type specified in Rule 11(c)(1)(A) or (C), the agreed disposition will be included in the judgment.
>
> (5) Rejecting a Plea Agreement. If the court rejects a plea agreement containing provisions of the type specified in Rule 11(c)(1)(A) or (C), the court must do the following on the record and in open court (or, for good cause, in camera):
>
>   (A) inform the parties that the court rejects the plea agreement;
>
>   (B) advise the defendant personally that the court is not required to follow the plea agreement and give the defendant an opportunity to withdraw the plea; and
>
>   (C) advise the defendant personally that if the plea is not withdrawn, the court may dispose of the case less favorably toward the defendant than the plea agreement contemplated.

38. Federal Rule of Criminal Procedure 11(c):

> (2) Conditional Plea.
>
>   With the consent of the court and the government, a defendant may enter a conditional plea of guilty or nolo contendere, reserving in writing the right to have an appellate court review an adverse determination of a specified pretrial motion. A defendant who prevails on appeal may then withdraw the plea.

39. *Missouri v Frye*, 566 U.S. 10–444 (2012). [Case No. 10–444. Argued October 31, 2011—Decided March 21, 2012].

40. A syllabus of a Supreme Court opinion is not part of the opinion itself, but is prepared by the Reporter of Decisions for the convenience of the reader and is included at the beginning of the report of the Court's decision.
41. Syllabus. *Missouri v Frye,* 566 U. S. 10–444 (2012), Retrieved from http://www.supremecourt.gov/opinions/11pdf/10-444.pdf
42. Most often the jurors remain seated with the rest of the pool, but their names or numbers are simply removed from selection process.
43. Federal Rule of Criminal Procedure 24.
44. In essence, a leading question is one in which the question contains the answer to the question. "What color was the car?" is not leading. "Was the car blue?" is a leading question.
45. See, for example, Johnny Cochran's famous "If it doesn't fit, you must acquit" statement when arguing the importance of a glove that appeared to be too small for O. J. Simpson's hand. CNN (1995, September 28). *If It Doesn't Fit, You Must Acquit.* Retrieved from http://articles.cnn.com/1995-09-28/us/OJ_daily_9-27_8pm_1_cap-from-two-blocks-robert-heidstra-johnnie-cochran?_s = PM:US
46. As explained in the preceding text, there are many variations on the basic process.

Bibliography

Bureau of Labor Statistics. Judges, Magistrates, and Other Judicial Workers. *Occupational Outlook Handbook* (2010–11 ed.). Retrieved from http://www.bls.gov/oco/ocos272.htm#training
CNN (1995, September 28). *If It Doesn't Fit, You Must Acquit.* Retrieved from http://articles.cnn.com/1995-09-28/us/OJ_daily_9-27_8pm_1_cap-from-two-blocks-robert-heidstra-johnnie-cochran?_s = PM:US

Law Enforcement under the United States Constitution

13

We the People of the United States, in Order to form a more perfect Union, establish Justice, ensure domestic Tranquility, provide for the common defense, promote the general Welfare, and secure the Blessings of Liberty to ourselves and our Posterity, do ordain and establish this Constitution for the United States of America.

The Preamble to the U.S. Constitution

Learning Objectives

The objectives of this chapter are to

- Discuss the historical foundations of the U.S. Constitution
- Understand the amendments that directly affect law enforcement
- Understand that the Constitution represents a foundational basis of societal laws
- Explain why law enforcement personnel must have a strong knowledge of the entirety of the U.S. Constitution
- Explain how the Constitution protects both citizens and law enforcement personnel
- Understand the liberties, freedoms, and securities that are guaranteed by the Constitution
- Understand the balancing of liberty versus security that affects law enforcement

Introduction

The United States Constitution is often referred to as the supreme law of this country. It is, indeed, the source of all of our law; however, it contains very little law. Not counting the amendments, it has barely 4500 words. Constitution Day is September 17, and it commemorates the signing of the document. Jonathan Day (age 26) was the youngest individual to sign the Constitution, and Benjamin Franklin (age 81) was the oldest person to sign the Constitution.[1] Although the assembling of Colonial leaders was primarily to revise the Articles of Confederation, the resulting outcome of the gathering was the drafting of the U.S. Constitution.

From the perspectives of law enforcement and the criminal justice system, the U.S. Constitution represented concepts and ideas that directly contrasted with the paradigms of other foreign governments during the Colonial period. The presumption of innocence was provided within American society for those accused of alleged crimes, and searches and seizures were prohibited unless the obtaining of warrants was properly accomplished. Criminal punishment was neither to be cruel nor unusual. Therefore, the foundations of the American republic were significantly different from those of the monarchial form of government from which the United States originated. These concepts permeate American society during modern times.

The U.S. Constitution is the law of the land. Its scope and magnitude represent a foundational basis for laws that exist at both the local and state levels. The activities of law enforcement organizations and personnel must not conflict with the U.S. Constitution. The Constitution also is an instrument through which the liberties, securities, rights, and freedoms of both society and individuals are protected. Certainly, such protection also encompasses the activities of law enforcement organizations and personnel. Therefore, law enforcement personnel must have a solid understanding and knowledge of not only the amendments that directly affect their duties and services (e.g., the Fourth Amendment), but also the entirety of the Constitution.

The population of the United States is diverse and represents numerous states, commonwealths, cities, towns, and counties (or parishes). Each of these entities manifests its own unique set of laws that necessitates enforcing. Regardless of the location, the activities of law enforcement personnel must be commensurate with local law and federal law. Because the U.S. Constitution is the foundational embodiment of law within America, all laws must be commensurate with its tenets and principles. Therefore, regardless of their location within the United States, law enforcement personnel must perform their duties within the scope and limitations of the Constitution and the laws of their respective localities (Figure 13.1).

The Constitution as the Supreme Law of the United States

The Constitution was not the first attempt by the former British colonies to form a central government after they won separation from England in the Revolutionary War. Each of the 13 colonies viewed itself as a sovereign, separate, and independent entity. They had joined together to win independence from Great Britain and the British monarchy, but did not view themselves as a united country. Yet, it was clear that if they had not worked together, they would likely have fallen prey to another country. In addition to England, Spain and France maintained dominion over large areas of the North and South American continents and could easily conquer each of the 13 colonies if the colonies had not worked together. At the same time, none of the colonies wanted to give up much of their own power and independence. There were many views on how best to balance the need for unity with the desire for independence.

The first attempt to resolve this conflict, the Articles of Confederation, did not work well. It was submitted to the colonies for approval in 1777, even before independence from Great Britain had been won. Despite the colonies' unified stance against Great Britain, there was a great deal of political division among the colonies. Resistance on the part of the individual colonies to giving up power to a central government resulted in a national government with little power. That government consisted only of a one-house legislature.

The national government had very little power. It could only raise an army and navy, enter into treaties and alliances, and act as the group's representative with foreign countries. In essence, it had no power over the internal affairs of the country, but had power only over foreign affairs and national defense. But even this power was limited by the fact that the national government could not enact taxes. It could only request funds to carry out its functions by requesting money from the states. Those requests were often ignored.[2]

The situation did not improve after the war. Each now-independent colony viewed itself as a separate state for all purposes other than those given to the national government

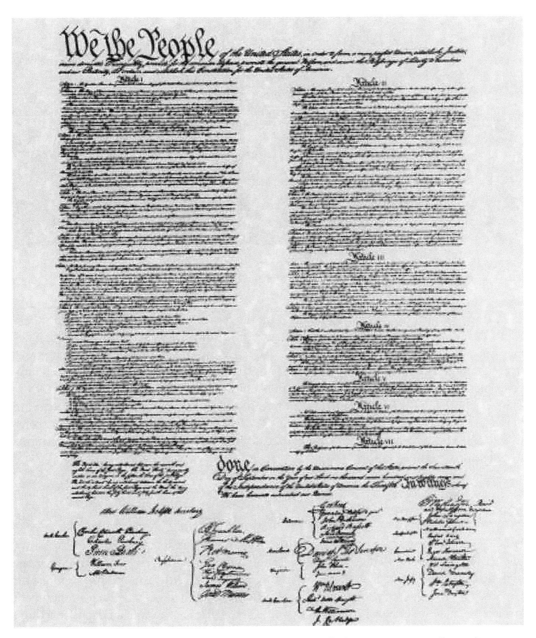

Figure 13.1 The United States Constitution. (Courtesy of The Citizens Foundation for Better Government. Retrieved from http://actnowus.org/full%20text%20constitution.html.)

under the Articles. Each also viewed itself as an independent economic unit in competition with each other state, enacting laws that protected its local businesses and interfering with free trade among the states.

As a result, in 1787, the Continental Congress called for a convention to revise the Articles of Confederation. Only 12 states sent representatives. Although there was still a substantial number of citizens who were satisfied with the Articles because they favored their economic interests, most of the delegates favored substantial change. They soon moved from revising the Articles to working on a whole new structure for the national government.

Figure 13.2 Constitutional Convention. (Courtesy of the U.S. Senate. Retrieved from http://www.senate.gov/artandhistory/history/common/briefing/Constitution_Senate.htm.)

Although most of the delegates agreed on the need for a stronger government, there was little initial agreement on the form that government was to take. Having just won independence from the tyranny of King George III, few were willing to turn significant power over to another centralized government; yet significant power was exactly what that government needed to carry out crucial functions for the common good of the states. While many of the ideals set forth in the Declaration of Independence and the Constitution are derived from a long line of British political philosophers, especially John Locke, the solution to this conflict appears to have emanated in the writings of a Frenchman, Baron de Montesquieu (Figure 13.2).

Separation of Powers

When it comes to law, a government has three basic functions: it makes law, it executes law, and it resolves disputes that arise under the law. Historically, in a true monarchy, the monarch (usually a king or queen) handled all three functions through officials the monarch appointed. The monarch proclaimed a law and then appointed officials such as sheriffs to enforce it. The monarch or his ministers would settle disputes between citizens and those officials regarding the enforcement of the law.

This concentration of power, it was thought, was what led to tyranny such as that experienced by the American colonies under King George III.[3] Baron de Montesquieu argued that tyranny could best be avoided by separating the functions of government, granting the power to perform each of the three functions to separate, equal branches. If done correctly, each of the branches acts as a check and balance against the other.[4]

The United States Constitution as finally issued from the Constitutional Convention and adopted by the states in 1787 incorporates this concept of separation of powers. It allowed the states to give up power to the central, national government necessary for that government to perform the tasks assigned to it for the common good of the states. Because power is shared by the three branches of government, with each providing checks and balances against the other, tyranny can be avoided (Figure 13.3).

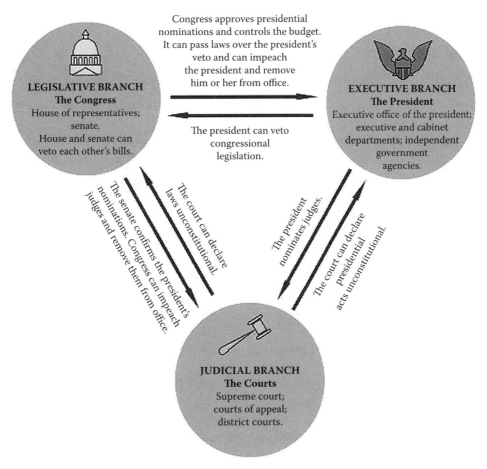

Congress approves presidential nominations and controls the budget. It can pass laws over the president's veto and can impeach the president and remove him or her from office.

LEGISLATIVE BRANCH
The Congress
House of representatives; senate.
House and senate can veto each other's bills.

The president can veto congressional legislation.

EXECUTIVE BRANCH
The President
Executive office of the president; executive and cabinet departments; independent government agencies.

The senate confirms the president's nominations. Congress can impeach judges and remove them from office.

The court can declare laws unconstitutional.

The president nominates judges.

The court can declare presidential acts unconstitutional.

JUDICIAL BRANCH
The Courts
Supreme court; courts of appeal; district courts.

Figure 13.3 Checks and Balances of the U.S. Federal Government. (Courtesy of St. John Fisher College. Retrieved from http://home.sjfc.edu/cals/units/dominick/checks%20and%20balances .htm.)

Understanding the separation of powers and the need for checks and balances is essential to an understanding of the Constitution as it applies to law enforcement. It sets the parameters for the role of the law enforcement officer in our Constitutional system. It also provides the basis for understanding the role of the courts in enforcing Constitutional provisions.

Under our Constitution, the three functions of government relating to law have been separated as suggested by Montesquieu. The power to make laws is granted to the legislative branch, Congress. The power to enforce laws is granted to the executive branch, the President. Finally, the power to resolve disputes regarding the law is given to the judicial branch, ultimately the United States Supreme Court. Each of these functions must be kept separate and independent, with each branch checking the power of the others.

In particular, this reasoning leads to the judicial branch having the power of judicial review, the power to review acts of the legislative branch and the executive branch to determine whether those acts are valid under the Constitution. This power is not specifically set forth in the Constitution but was established by the Supreme Court itself, based on the purpose and structure of the Constitution, in a landmark case known as *Marbury v. Madison*.[5]

The Constitution does not allocate the power to judge the constitutionality of a law passed by the legislative branch or an act of the executive branch to any of the three branches. But if the legislative branch made that decision, there would be no check on the legislature's power to make law, and if the executive branch made that decision, there would be no check on the executive's power. Placing that power in the Supreme Court provides the check and balance intended by the Constitution, because the courts do not have the power to make or execute law.

The judicial branch is charged with checking and balancing the power of the legislative and executive branches. In other words, the courts have a duty to stand between the other branches of the government and our citizens and prevent those branches from overstepping the limits imposed on them by the Constitution.

Of course, most law enforcement officers do not work for the national government. They work for state or local law enforcement agencies. However, each state's government allocates law functions in the same fashion as the allocation in the United States Constitution.

In addition, the United States Constitution is the supreme law of the country. Under our system of federalism, the states retain the right to enact laws and govern their citizens, except when the responsibility for a particular issue is given to the federal (national) government under the Constitution. Therefore, each citizen is subject to the laws of two jurisdictions—the laws of the United States, which apply to everyone, and the laws of the state in which they are located. The same act can be a violation of both federal and state criminal statutes.

However, each state's laws and even each state's constitution are subject to judicial review for compliance with the United States Constitution. The same is true of local governments. For example, the United States Supreme Court recently reviewed a ban on handguns enacted by the City of Chicago. It determined that the ban violated the Second Amendment to the Constitution and was, therefore, invalid.[6]

Bill of Rights

During 1789, James Madison introduced 12 amendments to the First Congress. A total of 10 of these amendments became known as the Bill of Rights. One of these 12 amendments was never ratified, whereas another that considered the issue of "Congressional salaries, was not ratified until 1992, when it became the 27th Amendment."[7] Further, incorporating attributes of the "Virginia Declaration of Rights, the English Bill of Rights, the writings of the Enlightenment, and the rights defined in the Magna Carta, the Bill of Rights contains rights that many today consider to be fundamental to America" (Figure 13.4).[8] According to the U.S federal government, the Bill of Rights may be summarized as follows:[9]

- *The First Amendment*: Provides that Congress make no law respecting an establishment of religion or prohibiting its free exercise. It protects freedom of speech, the press, assembly, and the right to petition the government for a redress of grievances.
- *The Second Amendment*: Gives citizens the right to bear arms.
- *The Third Amendment*: Prohibits the government from quartering troops in private homes, a major grievance during the American Revolution.

Figure 13.4 The Bill of Rights. (Retrieved from http://scdp7.wordpress.com/.)

- *The Fourth Amendment*: Protects citizens from unreasonable search and seizure. The government may not conduct any searches without a warrant, and such warrants must be issued by a judge and based on probable cause.
- *The Fifth Amendment*: Provides that citizens not be subject to criminal prosecution and punishment without due process. Citizens may not be tried on the same set of facts twice and are protected from self-incrimination (the right to remain silent). The amendment also establishes the power of eminent domain, ensuring that private property is not seized for public use without just compensation.

- *The Sixth Amendment*: Assures the right to a speedy trial by a jury of one's peers, to be informed of the crimes with which one is charged, and to confront the witnesses brought by the government. The amendment also provides the accused the right to compel testimony from witnesses and to legal representation.
- *The Seventh Amendment*: Provides that civil cases also be tried by jury.
- *The Eighth Amendment*: Prohibits excessive bail, excessive fines, and cruel and unusual punishments.
- *The Ninth Amendment*: States that the list of rights enumerated in the Constitution is not exhaustive and that the people retain all rights not enumerated.
- *The Tenth Amendment*: Assigns all powers not delegated to the United States, or prohibited to the states, to either the states or to the people.
- *The Fourteenth Amendment*: Guarantees due process among all U.S. citizens.

Enumerated Powers

The U.S. Constitution contains enumerated powers (i.e., expressed powers). The enumerated powers are those powers that are expressly stated within the Constitution. The enumerated powers are represented within the first 18 Congressional powers that are delineated within Article I, Section 8 of the Constitution. Examples of enumerated powers include the power to declare war, to organize the militia, to secure patents and copyrights, and to borrow monies. Specifically, the 18 enumerated powers are given as follows:[10]

1. The Congress shall have power to lay and collect taxes, duties, imposts, and excises, to pay the debts, and to provide for the common defense and general welfare of the United States; but all duties, imposts, and excises shall be uniform throughout the United States;
2. To borrow money on the credit of the United States;
3. To regulate commerce with foreign nations, and among the several states, and with the Indian Tribes;
4. To establish a uniform rule of naturalization and uniform laws on the subject of bankruptcies throughout the United States;
5. To coin money, regulate the value thereof, and of foreign coin, and fix the standard of weights and measures;
6. To provide for the punishment of counterfeiting the securities and current coin of the United States;
7. To establish post offices and post roads;
8. To promote the progress of science and useful arts by securing for limited times to authors and inventors the exclusive right to their respective writings and discoveries;
9. To constitute tribunals inferior to the Supreme Court;
10. To define and punish piracies and felonies committed on the high seas, and offenses against the law of nations;
11. To declare war, grant letters of marque and reprisal, and make rules concerning captures on land and water;
12. To raise and support armies, but no appropriation of money to that use shall be for a longer term than two years;

13. To provide and maintain a navy;
14. To make rules for the government and regulation of the land and naval forces;
15. To provide for calling forth the militia to execute the laws of the union, suppress insurrections, and repel invasions;
16. To provide for organizing, arming, and disciplining the militia, and for governing such part of them as may be employed in the service of the United States, reserving to the states, respectively, the appointment of the officers and the authority of training the militia according to the discipline prescribed by Congress;
17. To exercise exclusive legislation in all cases whatsoever, over such district (not exceeding ten miles square) as may, by cession of particular states, and the acceptance of Congress, become the seat of the government of the United States, and to exercise like authority over all places purchased by the consent of the legislature of the state in which the same shall be, for the erection of forts, magazines, arsenals, dock-yards, and other needful buildings;
18. To make all laws which shall be necessary and proper for carrying into execution the foregoing powers, and all other powers vested by this Constitution in the government of the United States, or in any department or officer thereof.

The enumerated powers have implications for law enforcement. Within these 18 powers are references to the crafting and exercising of various laws. These enumerated powers also necessitate the punishing of offenders (e.g., the punishment of counterfeiters). Law enforcement organizations are responsible for enforcing laws with respect to the goals of maintaining societal order and deterring acts of crime. The expression of the enumerated powers represents a basis for enacting federal law enforcement. Because of federalism and the subjecting of American citizens to both state and federal laws, these enumerated powers also provide a basis for enacting law enforcement among the American states. Further, per the Ninth Amendment and the Tenth Amendment, any powers that are not expressly given to the federal government are retained by the states and the American people.

Such concepts have implications for law enforcement. The 2010 U.S. Census showed that the United States population was 308,745,538.[11] This population is distributed among the various states and territories of the United States. Federal laws affect the entirety of this population. However, only subsets of this population are subject to the various laws of states, cities, towns, counties, and so on. Because states, counties, cities, and towns establish laws that affect their respective populaces, a variety of laws exist throughout the nation. Activities that may be legal within one society may be completely illegal within a different society. Therefore, the policing and enforcing of laws within the United States differs among locations. However, regardless of the crafting and enforcing of such laws, all these laws and their enforcement must be commensurate with the foundational principles established within the U.S. Constitution (Figure 13.5).

Role of Courts

Resolving disputes that arise under laws often necessarily includes the power to interpret the laws so the court also has this power. A classic, simplified example often used to illustrate this point concerns a hypothetical law that states, "No vehicles in the park." The

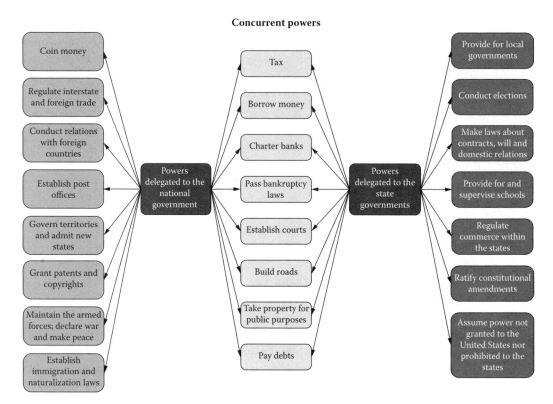

Figure 13.5 Concurrent powers. (Courtesy of St. John Fisher College. Retrieved from http://apgovernment2010.yolasite.com/resources/powers.gif.)

law seems clear enough. It is intended to prevent loud, disruptive, and potentially dangerous vehicles such as all-terrain vehicles from interfering with the quiet enjoyment of the park by families. But what constitutes a "vehicle"? Does the word in this statute apply to motorized wheelchairs? Does it apply to baby carriages? Many laws are written in general language. When the laws are written, the body enacting the laws cannot anticipate every occasion to which they might apply.

The courts cannot simply step in to clarify unclear laws. In this respect, the judicial branch is limited in a way the other two branches of government are not. Both the legislative and executive branches can initiate action. The courts must wait for a dispute to be brought to them.

Let us assume in this case that a law enforcement officer tickets a person with operating a vehicle in the park because the person is pushing a baby carriage. The officer believes he or she is justified in doing so because, to him or her, a baby carriage meets all the requirements of a "vehicle." It has wheels and carries passengers. The person believes the officer is unjustified because the law was not intended to cover baby carriages.

Under our system, the courts are charged with resolving this dispute. They must interpret the language of the law. Once the courts interpret the law, that interpretation becomes part of the law in the sense that from that point on, the words in the law will have the meaning given by the court unless the legislature amends the law to give it another meaning. Notice that while the courts cannot initiate action, that is, they must wait for parties to bring a dispute to them, the courts generally cannot refuse to resolve the dispute once it is brought to court by the parties. It must decide what this law means.

Once the court has decided what the law means, this information can be used by other participants in the legal system to gauge their conduct. In our example, assume the court decides that when it used the term "vehicle" in the law, the legislature intended to cover only motor vehicles. The next time a police officer sees a person pushing a baby carriage in the park, he or she will not summon the person because the officer knows the court will dismiss the charge. If the officer does summon the person, his or her defense attorney will advise the person with some assurance that the charge will be dismissed by the court and the prosecutor may very well refuse to proceed with the charge.

This is because of a principle known as "stare decisis," a Latin term which means "the decision stands." Once a court makes a decision interpreting a law, the decision becomes a precedent. We can be reasonably assured that the court will stand by its decision in future cases and treat like cases similarly. When a new case comes up, the courts will ask whether it is like an earlier case (analogous) or unlike it (distinguishable). Using our vehicle example, we can be quite sure that, if another baby carriage case comes before the court, the court will rule the same as it did in the prior case. Because the court ruled that the law applied only to motorized vehicles, we could also be fairly sure that the court would not apply the law to someone in a nonmotorized wheelchair.

It becomes more difficult to predict what the court would do if an officer summons a person for using a motorized wheelchair. Is a motorized wheelchair more like a baby carriage or more like an all-terrain vehicle? If we look at the reasoning behind the court's interpretation, we may be able to predict its future decisions based on its precedents. If the court ruled that the law did not apply to baby carriages because baby carriages are not loud, disruptive, and polluting while all-terrain vehicles are, then we can predict the court will find the motorized wheelchair to be more like the baby carriage than an all-terrain vehicle and will not interpret the law as applying to motorized wheelchairs. The motorized wheelchair case will be analogous to the baby carriage case and distinguishable from an all-terrain vehicle case. The next section will look more extensively at how courts reason.

How Courts Reason

There are conflicting views on exactly how a court should go about interpreting a law, whether the law is a city ordinance, a state or federal statute, or a provision in the Constitution. One of the more prominent views is "strict constructionism," the position that all laws are to be strictly construed according to their terms. Another believes that this will often lead to foolish results, such as people not being able to use a baby carriage in the park in our example. This view holds that a judge should look to find the meaning of the law in the intent and purpose of the law.

Proponents of each of these views are not unified in exactly how their method should be applied. For example, some strict constructionists take the term "strict construction" to mean that words must be taken to mean exactly what they say and nothing more or less, while others look to the entire text to find the meaning of particular words.

One difficulty is that even strict constructionists must confront occasions when a word in a statute may mean more than one thing. When confronting the need to determine the meaning of a statute, judges do not simply choose the meaning they like best. They apply canons (rules) of construction, standard methods used as guides in determining the meaning of a statute. These canons are subject to the criticism that one canon of construction is often negated or contradicted by another canon.[12] Thus, it may appear that a court is simply choosing the canon that suits a particular interpretation.

There are times when the courts do go beyond the literal meanings of words in a law to determine the meaning of the law. To see how this happens, we will use an analogy—a favorite tool of lawyers and judges. Let us suppose that we are trying to make my favorite meal—my grandmother's meatloaf—from a recipe left by my long-deceased grandmother. We do fine mixing all the ingredients, but then comes the instruction, "put in a pan and bake for 1 hr."

What, we must ask, did she mean by the word "pan"? There are certain contenders that can be eliminated right away using rules of construction. For example, the context of the word "pan" includes the instruction to bake the meatloaf, so we can eliminate frying pans. But even if we modify the word "pan" with "baking," there are many kinds and sizes of baking pans. There is no way to determine the meaning of "pan" here just by taking its literal meaning, since there are several literal senses of the word that could apply.

Trial and error is not a good way to proceed here as we may ruin many meatloaves before hitting upon the correct pan. Nor am I likely to hit upon the correct pan by picking the one I like the best. In fact, I cannot even assume that what I now know as a baking pan was what she knew to be a baking pan or that it even existed at the time she wrote the instruction. However, none of these methods are necessary as there are methods of reasoning that increase the likelihood that we will choose the right pan; that is, we will correctly interpret the instruction.

My grandmother who wrote the recipe is no longer alive, so we cannot ask her. The same is true of most laws and is certainly true of the Constitution. However, we could check other recipes written by her to see if she clarified the term in any of them. This is often the case with laws and the Constitution. Many of the people who wrote and advocated for adoption of the Constitution, known as federalists, wrote works explaining what the Constitution said, what its purposes were, and how it was supposed to function. The primary example of this is a series of writings known as the Federalist Papers. For more modern laws, we can consult the records of the debates and committee hearings as recorded in the Congressional Record for federal statutes and legislative history records for state statutes.

If my grandmother left no other writings, we are still not without recourse. We may, through research, be able to locate writings of other people who had their own recipes for meatloaf in the same era as my grandmother. Reviewing those recipes, we may be able to determine what was generally meant by "pan" in the context of a meatloaf recipe at the time. Again, this approach is often taken by courts when attempting to interpret words in statutes and in the Constitution. In fact, some judges believe it is more important to understand what a provision meant to the general public when it was enacted than to understand what the legislative body intended it to mean. Recent U.S. Supreme Court cases where the Court interpreted the word "militia" in the Second Amendment applied this method.[13]

There are some instances where the meaning of a provision in a law cannot be determined simply by resorting to its factual history. Indeed, some judges believe that the meaning of a provision of law should not be determined *only* by resort to factual history. In such instances, we can look at the purpose of the law to assist in its interpretation. In this illustration, we know that the purpose is to cook a meatloaf so that it is cooked through without drying it out or lessening its taste. We can then look at available pans and determine that the recipe "must" have meant for us to use the one that best suits the purpose. This line of reasoning was used in our "No vehicles in the park" example.

In almost every case where a court has to interpret a law or Constitutional provision, one side or the other will be asking the court to consider the purpose of the provision when interpreting its terms. This is especially true when the court has to deal with circumstances that could not have been foreseen when the provision was written. For example, my grandmother's recipe says to "grease the pan." I know she meant to spread shortening around the inside of the pan to keep the meatloaf from sticking to the pan. But it may not make sense to grease a pan in these days of nonstick pans and sprays. Sometimes it is necessary to adjust the interpretation or application of a law to take into account new circumstances.

We see this at work when a court attempts to apply language from our 1787 Constitution to technological developments such as the Internet and technology that allows for greater intrusion into the privacy of citizens. For example, the Fourth Amendment prohibits unreasonable searches and seizures. The drafters of the Constitution clearly intended to protect "the right of the people to be secure in their persons, houses, papers, and effects," but did not anticipate that one day "papers" would be sent from person to person as electronic communication traveling over the Internet. The court may be able to determine what the framers of the Constitution intended with regard to papers when they adopted the Fourth Amendment. Then the court must determine how that intent applies to concepts and events that the framers never conceived, much less intended (Figure 13.6).

THE U.S. COURT SYSTEM

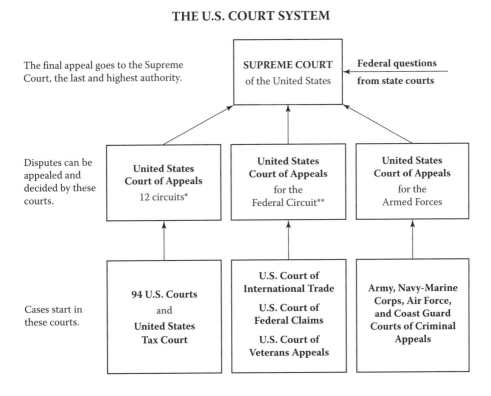

* The 12 regional Courts of Appeals also receive cases from a number of federal agencies.

** The Court of Appeals for the Federal Circuit also receives cases from the International Trade Commission, the Merit Systems Protection Board, the Patent and Trademark Office, and the Board of Contract Appeals.

Figure 13.6 The U.S. court system. (Courtesy of the U.S. Department of State. Retrieved from http://photos.state.gov/libraries/amgov/30145/ejs/1009ejchart.jpg.)

How the Constitution Applies to Law Enforcement

The body of the Constitution sets forth the structure of our government, allocating the powers to make, enforce, and interpret the law. Its application to law enforcement is generally limited to that function. Most of law enforcement's concern with the Constitution lies in the Bill of Rights, the first ten amendments to the Constitution.

These amendments were added to the Constitution in 1791 as part of an agreement to ratify the Constitution itself 4 years earlier. Many people were concerned that the newly formed government would impinge upon the rights of the states and the citizens unless some fundamental rights were enumerated. Thus, the Bill of Rights originally applied only to Congress. The First Amendment starts with the words, "Congress shall make no law." However, the Fourteenth Amendment, ratified in 1868, made them applicable to the states.[14]

Several of the amendments in the Bill of Rights have little application to law enforcement. For example, the Seventh Amendment deals with the right to a jury in civil cases brought under the common law,[15] rather than cases brought by the government against citizens for violation of a criminal statute.

Those amendments that do apply are not laws that law enforcement officers enforce. Unlike criminal statutes, the prohibitions contained in the amendments act as restrictions on the government, restrictions intended to protect stated rights of the citizens. The amendments may best be viewed as laws that must be obeyed by law enforcement officials while enforcing laws enacted by Congress or state legislatures, which laws must themselves be enacted in accordance with the Constitution. Therefore, every law enforcement officer must be well-trained in certain amendments and gain a solid understanding of how they are applied by the courts.

Amendments Most Applicable to Law Enforcement

This section will briefly review the amendments that are most applicable to law enforcement: the First, Fourth, Fifth, Sixth, and Eighth. The Fourteenth Amendment is also important not only because it protects the fundamental rights of citizens from actions of the states, but also because it specifically extends the concept of "due process of law" found in the Fifth Amendment to the states.

As you proceed through these amendments, there is another set of legal categories to keep in mind. Law is often characterized as substantive or procedural. Substantive law is the law that determines the rights and obligations of citizens, states, and government. Procedural law defines the process by which the legal system, including law enforcement, deals with those substantive rights and obligations.

The "due process of law" provisions of the Fifth and Fourteenth Amendments require that the procedural laws, the rules governing the process by which the substantive law is applied, must be fair. The courts have struggled with establishing exactly what constitutes fairness in the day-to-day operation enforcement of criminal law in the legal system, but certain basic concepts are well established. Most of those basic concepts find their source in the Bill of Rights and the courts' interpretation of the amendments examined here. When dealing with constitutional issues, the courts must contend with both the substantive rights protected by the amendments and the procedure by which those rights are implemented.

First Amendment

The First Amendment is most often in the news because of its provisions regarding the press and religion. However, there are provisions that more directly relate to law enforcement. These involve the right of free speech and the right of peaceful assembly. The amendment states, "Congress shall make no law respecting an establishment of religion, or prohibiting the free exercise thereof; or abridging the freedom of speech, or of the press; or the right of the people peaceably to assemble, and to petition the government for a redress of grievances." This amendment provides a good example of how the courts must look beyond the strict meaning of the words in the Constitution.

If taken literally, Congress (and the states as a result of the Fourteenth Amendment) could make *no* laws limiting the freedom of speech and *no* laws limiting where or when people assemble as long as the assembly is peaceful. Yet, we do have such laws, and such laws existed at the time the Constitution was ratified. For example, there are laws requiring those wishing to hold a large assembly to obtain permits, limiting those assemblies to certain times of day, and prohibiting those assemblies in certain places.

The United States Supreme Court acknowledged that freedom of speech is not absolute in *Schenck v. United States*, 249 U.S. 47, 52 (1919).[16] The court interprets the amendment this way, in part, by recognizing the fact that the drafters of the amendment could not have meant to prohibit all laws regarding speech, because at the time of the amendment, it was accepted practice for such laws to exist and be enforced. In the landmark case of *Chaplinsky v. State of New Hampshire*, 315 U.S. 568, 571 (1942)[17], the United States Supreme Court articulated definite and narrowly limited classes of speech which "the prevention and punishment of… [have] never been thought to raise any Constitutional problem." These classes of speech are lewd and obscene speech, libelous speech, and insulting or "fighting" words—those which by their very utterance inflict injury or tend to incite an immediate breach of the peace.

Of most concern to law enforcement are "fighting words," because law enforcement officers are charged with keeping the peace, and "fighting words" are those that tend to incite an immediate breach of the peace. The Supreme Court has made it clear that merely obscene, annoying, or provocative words do not qualify as fighting words. The Court has stated the following:

> Speech is often provocative and challenging…. [But it] is nevertheless protected against censorship or punishment, unless shown likely to produce a clear and present danger of a serious substantive evil that rises far above public inconvenience, annoyance, or unrest.[18]

In addition, the Court ruled that in the context of the First Amendment, "speech" is a synonym for "expression." Thoughts can be expressed with actions as well as speech. When the actions are a substitute for speech, those actions are also protected. For example, a person who burned the American flag in protest as an expression of his opposition to actions being taken by the government is protected by the First Amendment, as in *Texas v. Johnson*, 491 U.S. 397 (1989).

The right of Americans to express their opinion regarding governmental action can have personal ramifications for law enforcement officers, because when law enforcement officers act in their official capacity, they are acting for the government. This means citizens have a right to express their opinions about and *to* law enforcement officers even when those officers are performing their duties. One case puts it this way:

> [T]he freedom of individuals verbally to oppose or challenge police action without thereby risking arrest is one of the principal characteristics by which we distinguish a free nation from a police state.[19]

Even words that might cause others to breach the peace may be protected when directed towards law enforcement officers, since the fact that "police officers have a legal duty to enforce the law is sufficient reason to presume that they will not violate the law."[20] However, the circumstances are important. Words that are directed to inciting others to interfere with an arrest, for example, are not protected.

The First Amendment has sparked numerous debates regarding policing during modern times because of the pervasiveness of recording technologies. The use of cellular telephone cameras and portable recording devices has incited much debate regarding both policing activities and the rights of citizens provided by the First Amendment. Examples of such instances are found among the writings of the American Civil Liberties Union and national news media.

Examples of such incidents involve allegations of police harassment regarding the photographing of Baltimore, Maryland Transit Authority (MTA) "light rail trains."[21] The American Civil Liberties Union (ACLU) highlights incidents in which two photographers legally photographed rail operations. The first incident involves the case of Olev Tamerae. The ACLU summarizes this incident as follows:[22]

> In one incident, which took place on February 20, 2011, an MTA police officer told Olev Tamerae, a photographer visiting Baltimore from Pennsylvania, that it was illegal to photograph rail operations in Maryland, despite the fact that no law prohibits it, and the MTA has no regulation prohibiting such conduct. The officer then demanded Tamerae's identification and issued him a "Warning Notice" documenting the encounter, on which all of his identifying information had been recorded.

The incident involving Tamerae is currently ongoing at the time of this writing. No decisive outcome has been rendered regarding this matter. The second incident involved the case of Christophe Fussell. The ACLU highlights this incident as follows:[23]

> In a separate incident on March 21, 2011, several MTA officers accosted Christopher Fussell, who was photographing the light rail operations at the Cultural Center station while waiting for a train to Penn Station. The three MTA police officers on the scene, one of whom claimed to be a supervisor, recited a litany of misstatements about the law, including that a permit is required to photograph on state property, that persons engaged in photography are required to provide identification to police officers, that "since 9/11 no one is allowed to take pictures of any type of railway conveyance, plane, airport, or anything like that," and that it was illegal for Fussell to record the officers' statements to him. None of these statements is correct. Fussell was detained for more than 30 min, because officers confiscated his fare card, and he was repeatedly threatened with arrest based on his refusal to provide identification, despite the fact that he had not committed any crime.

Such recordings are often used during court proceedings. During 2010, such evidence was used during the trial of law enforcement officer Johannes Mehserle for killing Oscar

Figure 13.7 The last photo Oscar Grant snapped before he was killed by BART officer Johannes Mehserle. The photo depicts Mehserle holding his weapon. (From Miller, C., 2011, Pixiq. Retrieved from http://www.pixiq.com/article/oscar-grant-snapped-a-final-photo-of-cop-who-killed-him.)

Grant in California.[24] Just before his death, Grant photographed Mehserle holding the weapon that was used to kill him. Before his death, Grant stated that he was being abused by Mehserle and gave the photograph to his girlfriend. According to Anthony, "Mehserle drew his Taser on Grant and reholstered it. Then a few minutes later, Mehserle pulled his gun and fired into Grant's back, as the 22-year-old lay face down on a platform."[25] Miller (2011) indicates that Grant was "not resisting" arrest "when he was shot" and that Mehserle was sentenced to a 2-year prison term for "involuntary manslaughter" (Figure 13.7).[26]

The First Amendment provides the freedom of speech through various forms. The use of video incites many debates regarding the photographing and recording of public areas in which expectations of privacy are absent. Such recordings are often used to record the actions of law enforcement personnel during the performance of their duties. Therefore, law enforcement personnel must not only be familiar with the tenets of the U.S. Constitution, but also act in accordance within the limitations of local, state, and federal laws. Failure to do so stains the reputation of law enforcement and erodes public trust in the servants who are sworn to protect society and who are expected to uphold the law. When used within the constraints of the law in a legal fashion, the use of video equipment often shows the short-comings of law enforcement personnel. With respect to the First Amendment, the use of such video, during court proceedings, complements the ability of citizens to "petition the government for a redress of grievances" in conjunction with the freedom of speech.

The U.S. Constitution establishes numerous freedoms and liberties for the citizenry of the United States and provides a basis for establishing a variety of laws among the states and localities of the nation. Law enforcement personnel are expected to uphold and enforce these laws with respect to maintaining order and deterring crime. Within the First Amendment, protections are guaranteed to both law enforcement personnel and the citizenry with respect to airing grievances and exercising the freedom of speech. Therefore, the First Amendment represents a protective mechanism that benefits both law enforcement organizations and the societies that they serve.

Fourth Amendment

The Fourth and Fifth Amendments are applicable to law enforcement on a daily basis as they relate to how evidence can be obtained. The Fourth Amendment states:

> The right of the people to be secure in their persons, houses, papers, and effects, against unreasonable searches and seizures, shall not be violated, and no Warrants shall issue, but upon probable cause, supported by oath or affirmation, and particularly describing the place to be searched, and the persons or things to be seized.

If this language is broken down into its basic elements for purposes of analysis, it becomes evident that there are many aspects that are subject to interpretation:

- The right of the people to be secure in
  - their persons
  - houses
  - papers
  - and effects
- Against unreasonable
  - searches and
  - seizures, shall not be violated, and
- No warrants shall issue,
  - but upon probable cause,
  - supported by oath or affirmation,
  - particularly describing the place to be searched,
  - and the persons or things to be seized.

The amendment does not prohibit all searches, but "unreasonable searches," so that the people can be secure in their persons, houses, papers, and effects. Certainly there can be a great deal of disagreement about what is "unreasonable," but there are also issues that deal with each of the other elements. For example, what does it mean to be secure in one's house? Does the term "house" include an attached garage? An unattached garage? A shed in the backyard? Does being secure in one's house mean government officials cannot hide outside windows and eavesdrop? If so, what is the import now that the government can use technology to eavesdrop from hundreds of yards away or to monitor electronic transmissions? Similar issues involve scanning technologies. An example of the output of such technology is presented within (Figure 13.8).

The courts have three basic approaches to determining the answers to these kinds of questions: the historical approach, the balance of interests approach, and the common law reasoning approach.[27] Each has its counterpart in the approaches we considered in interpreting my grandmother's meatloaf recipe.

The historical approach starts by noting that the Fourth Amendment was designed so that the courts would stand as a bulwark against governmental encroachment for arbitrary and/or capricious reasons under the doctrine of separation of powers. It then looks at what governmental intrusions the Amendment was meant to address and then extrapolates that purpose to present day circumstances.

The balance of interests approach balances the citizens' right to privacy against the need of government to enforce the law. When little government intrusion into the citizens'

Figure 13.8 Scanning imagery. (From Greenberg, A., 2010, *Forbes*. Retrieved from http://www.forbes.com/sites/andygreenberg/2010/08/24/full-body-scan-technology-deployed-in-street-roving-vans/.)

reasonable expectation of privacy is involved, less is needed to justify the intrusion. Thus, in *Terry v. Ohio*, 392 U.S. 1 (1968), the Supreme Court decided a temporary detention to ask for identification required only a reasonable suspicion that the person detained was involved in the commission of a crime, while a full arrest required probable cause.

In addition, the government's need to protect the safety of law enforcement officers allows those officers to perform a quick surface search of the person's outer clothing for weapons if they have reasonable suspicion that the person stopped is armed. Reasonable suspicion must be based on "specific and articulable facts" and not merely upon an officer's hunch. This is often referred to as a "stop and frisk" or a "Terry stop." If the pat-down of the suspect provides specific and articulable facts indicating that the suspect has a weapon, then the officer can reasonably intrude further into the citizen's privacy. Ultimately, the facts available to the officer may constitute probable cause, allowing the officer to arrest the suspect. Probable cause exists where the facts and circumstances within the arresting officers' knowledge and of which they had reasonably trustworthy information are sufficient in themselves to warrant a man of reasonable caution in the belief that an offense has been or is being committed, as in *Draper v. United States*, 358 U.S. 307 (1959). It is important to note that the determination of whether reasonable suspicion or probable cause exists is made based on the information the officer actually had at the time the governmental action was taken. The results of a search cannot be used to justify the search.

The common law reasoning approach requires the courts to look at legal precedent. Disputes over the meaning of the Constitution began shortly after its ratification. Courts would seek the meaning of the Constitution by looking at principles established in court precedents that existed before and at the time of the Constitution's ratification. Later, courts then looked at decisions from cases decided shortly after the ratification of the Constitution for precedent. This process of basing current decisions on precedent continues today. As discussed in the section on how courts reason, this is a process of comparing the facts of the case before the court to the facts of previous cases to determine whether those facts are analogous to the earlier cases or distinguishable from them. If they are analogous, the principle of the earlier case is applied to the case before the court. If they are distinguishable, the court must find other precedent or use another approach to interpreting the law or Constitutional provision.

Numerous Supreme Court rulings have interpreted the Fourth Amendment through the years. The proliferation of modern digital technologies presents various opportunities for invasiveness among locations of American society in which expectations of privacy are present. These considerations have influenced the rendering of judgments and interpretations of the Fourth Amendment during the last 20 years. One case, in which the Supreme Court examined the use of technology among law enforcement agencies, was *Kyllo v. United States*, 533 U.S. 27 (2001). This case involved the use of thermal imaging cameras to examine the dwelling of Danny Kyllo.

Two federal agents, Dan Haas and William Elliott, were suspicious that Kyllo was growing marijuana within his residence. They used a thermal imaging device to examine the amount of heat that was generated within Kyllo's home. During this investigation, thermal imaging was used in conjunction with "electricity bills that were higher than the norm for his area, and informant's tips."[28] A search warrant was obtained from a Federal Magistrate. The outcome of the search yielded the presence of "over 100 marijuana plants growing inside the home," thereby facilitating the indicting of Kyllo for a single "count of manufacturing marijuana."[29]

Kyllo pleaded guilty while retaining his right of appeal. When appealed, the Ninth Circuit Court remanded the case to district court. The district court ruled that the imaging test was nonintrusive because it was incapable of penetrating "walls or windows to reveal conversations or human activities."[30] The warrant was upheld as being valid, and the "denial to suppress the evidence" was affirmed. This decision was appealed.

Upon appeal, the Ninth Circuit Court "initially reversed the conviction, but after withdrawal of the opinion and a change in membership of the court, affirmed the district court's decision."[31] The Ninth Circuit Court indicated that there was no expectation of privacy because no effort was made to conceal the heat that was generated from Kyllo's activities and that the "intimate details" of his life were unrevealed.[32]

The Supreme Court disagreed. The ruling of the Court of Appeals was reversed. This ruling indicated that the imaging device "revealed details of a private home that could not have been previously known without physically entering the house."[33] It was determined that the search occurred in conjunction with the Fourth Amendment and was unreasonable without the issuance of a warrant.

More recently, in January 2012, the Supreme Court ruled on the issue of whether law enforcement can, without a warrant, place global positioning system (GPS) tracking devices on motor vehicles to track a person's movements. In *United States v. Jones*,[34] FBI agents obtained a search warrant permitting them to install a GPS tracking device to Jones's wife's motor vehicle within 10 days and in Washington, D.C. The device was not installed until the eleventh day and in Maryland. The FBI agents then tracked the vehicle's movements for 28 days. Jones was subsequently indicted on drug trafficking conspiracy charges. The trial court suppressed allowed GPS data obtained while the vehicle was parked at Jones's residence, but suppressed data obtained while the vehicle was traveling on the grounds that there was no expectation of privacy when the vehicle was on public streets. Jones was convicted. The D.C. circuit reversed this decision on appeal, concluding that admission of the evidence obtained by warrantless use of the GPS device violated the Fourth Amendment.

The Supreme Court held that the government's attachment of the GPS device to the vehicle constituted a search under the Fourth Amendment. It went on to state that this type of encroachment would have been considered a search within the meaning of the

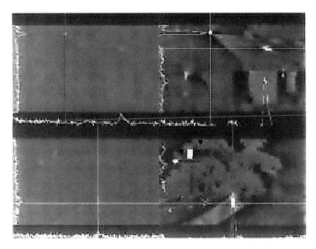

Figure 13.9 Thermal imaging used in the *Kyllo* Case. (Retrieved from http://supreme.justia.com/us/533/27/case.html.)

Amendment at the time it was adopted. Justice Scalia wrote the majority opinion and concluded that "At bottom, the Court must assur[e] preservation of that degree of privacy against government that existed when the Fourth Amendment was adopted" citing the *Kyllo* case as precedent. In the month following the Supreme Court decision in *United States v. Jones*, *USA Today* reported that the FBI had cut back its use of GPS surveillance in order to comply with the decision.[35]

The *Kyllo* and *Jones* cases show that the U.S. Constitution is a protective instrument through which the activities of law enforcement personnel are limited without the proper warrant. It also demonstrates the protections that are afforded to citizens. When performing activities that involve search and seizure, it is of the upmost importance for law enforcement personnel to obtain proper warrants before commencing their activities unless exigent circumstances exist. Without proper warrants, investigations may become unsuccessful. Further, the proper obtaining of warrants protects both U.S. citizens from abusive law enforcement practices and facilitates accountability among law enforcement organizations and personnel (Figure 13.9).

Fifth Amendment

The Fifth Amendment provides several protections to the people of the United States. The most pertinent provision for purposes of the law enforcement officer states:

> No person…shall be compelled in any criminal case to be a witness against himself, nor be deprived of life, liberty, or property, without due process of law.

The amendment itself did not tread new ground. Historically, common law at the time the Fifth Amendment prevented admission of forced confessions primarily based on evidence that such confessions were unreliable; that is, people confessed to crimes they did not commit. However, the Amendment did provide fertile grounds for Constitutional issues. The primary issues have to do with what it means to "be compelled." A confession must have been given voluntarily and not given as a result of promises, threats, or inducements. Compulsion need not be the result of physical coercion.

The term "voluntary" is subject to various interpretations, and courts have often been called upon to decide whether a confession was voluntary. For example, in *Chambers v. Florida*, 309 U.S. 227 (1940), the defendant was subjected to 5 days of prolonged questioning following arrests without warrants and incommunicado detention. In *Ashcraft v. Tennessee*, 322 U.S. 143 (1944), a confession was obtained near the end of a 36-hr period of practically continuous questioning, under powerful electric lights, by relays of officers, experienced investigators, and highly trained lawyers. And in *Ward v. Texas*, 316 U.S. 547 (1942), the confession was obtained from a suspect who had been arrested illegally in one county and brought some 100 miles away to a county where questioning began and who had then been questioned continuously over the course of 3 days while being driven from county to county and being told falsely of a danger of lynching.

Thus, while it is clear that every citizen had a substantive right under the Constitution not to be compelled to be a witness against himself, it became necessary for the Supreme Court to establish procedural rules by which that right could be preserved. The Court did so in *Miranda v. Arizona*, 384 U.S. 436 (1966). The court decided that the government may not use statements resulting from custodial interrogation of the defendant unless it demonstrates the use of procedural safeguards effective to secure the privilege against self-incrimination. The Court went on to provide a statement that, if read to the person being questioned, would help the government establish that such procedural safeguards were in place, a statement now known as the Miranda warning.

There are many misunderstandings about the Miranda warning. Many citizens believe that if they are not given the Miranda warning whenever they are arrested, then they cannot be convicted of the crime for which they were arrested. In reality, the warning does not affect the arrest itself but only the use of statements made by the person arrested. Thus, if the arrest is made on evidence sufficient to gain a conviction without the use of any statements made by the defendant, a conviction can still be obtained. Failure to give the Miranda warning only prevents the use of statements made by the defendant and only if those statements were made as a result of custodial interrogation. Therefore, the Miranda warning must be given before questioning occurs.

Many court cases deal with the question of whether a defendant was actually in custody when a statement was made. A person need not be under arrest in order to be considered to be in law enforcement custody. Many cases also deal with whether a statement was made spontaneously or was the result of law enforcement interrogation.

It is equally misleading to suggest that simply giving the Miranda warning makes any resulting statement by the person being questioned voluntary. A confession obtained near the end of a 36-hour period of practically continuous questioning, under powerful electric lights, by relays of officers, experienced investigators, and highly trained lawyers is still likely to be considered involuntary even if the warning is given. While the person being questioned can waive Miranda rights, that waiver itself must be voluntary (Figure 13.10).

Sixth Amendment

The Sixth Amendment deals primarily with the rights relating to a jury trial. It also states "In all criminal prosecutions, the accused shall enjoy the right ...to have the assistance of counsel for his defense." This is, of course, the right to an attorney included in the Miranda warning, as the right extends from the initial interrogation phase of a

MIRANDA WARNING

1. YOU HAVE THE RIGHT TO REMAIN SILENT.

2. ANYTHING YOU SAY CAN AND WILL BE USED AGAINST YOU IN A COURT OF LAW.

3. YOU HAVE THE RIGHT TO TALK TO A LAWYER AND HAVE HIM PRESENT WITH YOU WHILE YOU ARE BEING QUESTIONED.

4. IF YOU CANNOT AFFORD TO HIRE A LAWYER, ONE WILL BE APPOINTED TO REPRESENT YOU BEFORE ANY QUESTIONING IF YOU WISH.

5. YOU CAN DECIDE AT ANY TIME TO EXERCISE THESE RIGHTS AND NOT ANSWER ANY QUESTIONS OR MAKE ANY STATEMENTS.

WAIVER

DO YOU UNDERSTAND EACH OF THESE RIGHTS I HAVE EXPLAINED TO YOU? HAVING THESE RIGHTS IN MIND, DO YOU WISH TO TALK TO US NOW?

Figure 13.10 Miranda warning carried by law enforcement officers. (Retrieved from http://www.chiefsupply.com/586-Geiger-Miranda-Warning-Card.aspx.)

case through to sentencing and appeal. Some court cases have involved the question of when the right to an attorney applies to a particular aspect of an investigation. For example, the courts have ruled that it does apply to a lineup, but does not apply to the taking of blood, DNA, or writing samples. Many cases involve the issue of whether the defendant knowingly and voluntarily waived their right to an attorney. Finally, there are cases involving the issue of whether the defendant's invocation of the right to an attorney was honored by law enforcement officers. For example, in *Brewer v. Williams*, 430 U.S. 387 (1977), the defendant stated his request for legal counsel several times, but one of the police officers transporting the defendant, who knew that respondent was a former mental patient and was deeply religious, sought to obtain incriminating remarks from the respondent by stating to him during the drive that he felt they should stop and locate the girl's body because her parents were entitled to a Christian burial for the girl who was taken away from them on Christmas Eve. The defendant's conviction based on this evidence was overturned because the police officer had not obeyed the Sixth Amendment of the Constitution.

Eighth Amendment

The Eighth Amendment states, "Excessive bail shall not be required, nor excessive fines imposed, nor cruel and unusual punishments inflicted." Recent important cases involving the Eighth Amendment have dealt with imposition of the death penalty for crimes committed by juveniles[36] and the mentally ill.[37] Of more concern to law enforcement officers, especially corrections officers, on a day-to-day basis is the application of the Eighth Amendment to the use of excessive force. The Supreme Court ruled in the case of *Hudson v. McMillian*, 503 U.S. 1 (1992), that if force is applied maliciously or sadistically, rather than in a good faith effort to maintain or restore discipline, a violation of the Eighth Amendment occurs, even if the resulting injury is minor.

Fourteenth Amendment

The Fourteenth Amendment, Section 1, states:

> All persons born or naturalized in the United States, and subject to the jurisdiction thereof,
> are citizens of the United States and of the state wherein they reside. No state shall make or
> enforce any law which shall abridge the privileges or immunities of citizens of the United
> States; nor shall any state deprive any person of life, liberty, or property, without due process
> of law; nor deny to any person within its jurisdiction the equal protection of the laws.

Such notions are relevant for law enforcement personnel because of the guarantees
of preserving the "privileges or immunities of citizens of the United States." No one may
experience the confiscation of property without the proper implementation of "due process."
Freedom and liberty are afforded to all U.S. citizens with respect to their societal existence,
and all U.S. citizens are afforded equal protection regarding American law.

Such notions are applicable within the context of law enforcement. Because of the
protections that are afforded to citizens within the Fourteenth Amendment, the considerations of due process protect various rights of individuals whom are charged with criminal
offenses (but have not been convicted) from instances of police brutality or the excessive
use of police force while they are in custody. Therefore, law enforcement officers and corrections personnel are disallowed from using any "unreasonable force that amounts to punishment" against such detained or incarcerated individuals.[38]

Remaining Amendments

The remaining amendments also have implications for law enforcement. For example, the
Eighteenth Amendment, which instigated the prohibition of alcohol, but was later repealed
by the Twenty-First Amendment, instigated the use of law enforcement resources to counter instances of bootlegging during the early twentieth century. Another example involves
common law. The Seventh Amendment extends jury trial rights among defendants with
respect to suits involving common law.

The U.S. Constitution is the law of the land. It provides a foundational basis for each of
the laws that exist among each of the American states. It is the duty of law enforcement personnel to enforce these laws within their respective jurisdictions. Therefore, law enforcement personnel must not only familiarize themselves with the dominant amendments that
directly influence the enforcing of laws (e.g., Fourth Amendment), but must have a solid
understanding of the entirety of the U.S. Constitution and the liberties and freedoms that
they are sworn to protect.

Considerations of Evidence

Admissible evidence is "evidence permitted to be introduced at trial," and such evidence "must tend to make more or less probable the existence of some fact material to
the case or some fact otherwise of consequence to making a determination in the case."[39]
Further, evidence that may establish facts used to derive that "some material fact is more
or less probable is also admissible as relevant evidence."[40] Evidence may also be excluded.
"[A]ny evidence gathered as a result of an illegal search, even at a time later than the illegal
search itself, will be excluded from evidence."[41]

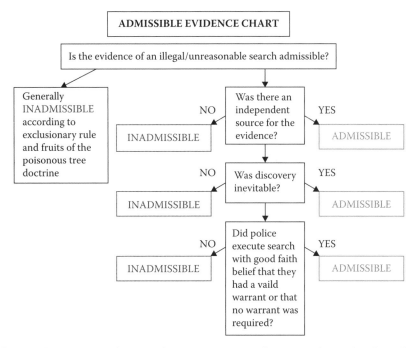

Figure 13.11 Admissible evidence chart. (Courtesy of National Paralegal College, 2007. Retrieved from http://nationalparalegal.edu/conlawcrimproc_public/ProtectionFromSearches &Seizures/ExclusionaryRule.asp.)

If the provisions of the Bill of Rights are to be anything more than platitudes, there must be some mechanism for the courts to enforce those provisions. The mechanism most often used is the exclusionary rule. This rule first applied by the U.S. Supreme Court in federal courts in *Weeks v. United States*, 232 U.S. 383 (1914), provides that the government cannot use illegally obtained evidence in court to obtain a conviction. This rule was extended to state court through the Due Process Clause of the Fourteenth Amendment in *Mapp v. Ohio*, 367 U.S. 643 (1961).

The rule itself is not found in any of the amendments, and exclusion of illegally seized evidence is not considered a Constitutional right. Rather, it is considered a necessary requirement in order to enforce the provisions of the various amendments.[42] It is intended to deter and prevent illegal action on the part of law enforcement officers by removing the incentive to disregard it, *Elkins v. United States,* 319 U.S. 206 (1960). As a result, the courts have carved out certain exclusions and created exceptions when that purpose would not be served, such as when the evidence is illegally obtained by a private individual not acting in concert with law enforcement officials (Figure 13.11).

Issues of Privacy, Security, and Liberty

The founding of the United States was a significant event in Western history. Because of its limits upon government within its Constitution, its application and practices of government represented a limited form of government. Law enforcement agencies are limited by the scope of powers that is granted by the United States Constitution. During the Colonial period, the law enforcement powers of the British Empire were pervasive and invasive, given the existence of a monarchial form of government. However, the establishment of the United States Constitution demonstrated limitations of government through which citizens were, and continue to be, protected from abuses of powers that exist among law enforcement entities.

Obviously, one difference involved the guilt or innocence of someone accused of a crime. Within the American system, the presumption of innocence represented a radically opposite paradigm with respect to the presumptions of guilt that existed among many criminal justice systems. This presumption of innocence continues unabated today. The American system of justice and law enforcement practice necessitates the unequivocal showing of guilt and the convincing of a jury of peers (if a jury trial is necessary). This presumption established a unique approach to law enforcement practices and the workings of the criminal justice system.

This concept also has implications for law enforcement entities and for the criminal justice system. The presumption of innocence and the limitations of government powers (e.g., law enforcement activities) provide security for both the liberties of American society and for those who are accused of crimes. In essence, because of the Constitution, security is embellished regarding the liberties and freedoms that pervade American society. When performing law enforcement activities, such activities must be within the scope and limitation of power granted by the Constitution. Therefore, infringements of liberty, freedom, or security must be contemplated thoroughly during the implementation of any activities that may occur among law enforcement entities. Hence, law enforcement entities must be mindful of the balancing of their activities versus the Constitutional scope of privacy that is granted within society.

This notion may be considered from the perspective of intelligence operations. Among law enforcement entities, a need for obtaining, managing, interpreting, and leveraging information exists to facilitate the rendering of human decisions through time. All law enforcement organizations have varying information requirements, and they have different methods and tools for gathering such information. During the processes of obtaining, managing, interpreting, and leveraging information to generate an intelligence outcome, law enforcement entities must perform their activities and use their resources within the scope of the Constitution.

Modern criminal threats often necessitate the performing of a variety of law enforcement activities that impact liberty, privacy, freedom, and security. For example, as a method of gathering observations, long-term telephone wiretaps may be necessitated to gain knowledge of events, persons, threats, logistics, and any other resources that may facilitate criminal activity. The implementation of such wiretaps necessitates the obtaining of a court order. However, through such wiretaps, the sanctity of privacy is breached during the acts of communication. Despite this breach of privacy, a greater purpose is served: the security of society.

According to a dictionary definition, security is defined as "the quality or state of being secure; freedom from danger; freedom from fear or anxiety; something that secures; measures taken to guard against espionage or sabotage, crime, attack, or escape; or an organization or department whose task is security."[43] According to a dictionary definition, privacy is defined as "the quality or state of being apart from company or observation; freedom from unauthorized intrusion; or a place of seclusion."[44]

Within American society, during the course of investigations, modern law enforcement organizations use a variety of methods and tools to gather, process, and interpret their observations of alleged criminal activities (e.g., wiretaps, electronic information systems, etc.). The use of such methods and tools may breach, in a limited fashion, any perceptions of privacy and liberty that may exist within the domains of individuals and organizations that are investigated. Therefore, additional concepts may be defined: civil liberty and technology. A dictionary definition of civil liberty is "freedom from arbitrary governmental interference (as with the right of free speech) specifically by denial of governmental power and in the United States especially as guaranteed by the Bill of Rights."[45] A dictionary definition of technology is "the practical application of knowledge especially in a particular area."[46]

A consideration of these definitions yields some basic concepts. Based on these definitions, privacy is an inferred function of liberty. Three of the four definitions have freedom as their basic, underlying premise: security, civil liberty, and privacy. Within the context of freedom, a relationship is manifested among security, civil liberty, and privacy. Further, given such definitions, technology is a tool, through which modern functions of intelligence may be facilitated, that contributes toward maintaining security; the provisions of privacy and civil liberty; and the perpetuation of freedom.

An integrative consideration of these definitions may be given to the interpretation of this question. Intelligence functions are necessary for facilitating "preemptive, preventive, and protective" actions associated with security.[47] Such intelligence functions involve "efforts to identify, collect, analyze, and distribute source intelligence information or the resultant warnings from intelligence analysis."[48] Given these notions, with respect to the previous definitions, the gathering of intelligence is a crucial component of ensuring national security and may occur through the use of technology, but the gathering of intelligence must be mindful of the boundaries of privacy.

Taipale provides insight regarding such notions.[49] According to Taipale, one proposition asserts that "concerns about domestic security and civil liberties are often asserted as competing and potentially incompatible policy interests requiring the achievement of some tolerable state of balance" involving the concept of a "zero-sum political game" assuming a "dichotomous rivalry in which security and liberty are traded one for another."[50] Taipale dismisses this notion and indicates that "security and liberty are dual obligations of civil society, and each must be maximized within the constraints imposed by the other," in which "liberty presupposes security, and the point of security is liberty."[51]

Given this notion, Taipale contemplates the words of Benjamin Franklin, regarding security versus liberty, stating that, "Those who would give up essential liberty to purchase a little temporary safety, deserve neither liberty nor safety,'" and considers the presumption "not of tension between the two, but rather of a duality of concern with security on the one hand, and with liberty on the other."[52] Such considerations manifest perplexities regarding the security concerns of gathering of intelligence versus the liberty concerns of privacy. However, any incongruousness regarding the notions of liberty versus security, with respect to the "dual obligation" argument given by Taipale, may be dismissed (Figure 13.12).[53]

Regarding such considerations, various facets of intelligence, technology, and privacy are found among court proceedings. Loundy cites court cases regarding such considerations.[54] Examples include *U.S. v. David* (1991), *U.S. v. Butler* (2001), *U.S. v. Angevine* (2002), *Showengerdt v. U.S.* (1991), and *U.S. v. Scarfo* (2001). Within these cases, examples

Figure 13.12 Society must be mindful of liberty versus security. (Courtesy of The Thomas Jefferson Center. Retrieved from http://www.tjcenter.org/wp-content/uploads/2011/04/GM101120CLR-TSAlineup_.jpg.)

are present of both individual concerns and concerns of national security. Individual concerns are expressed within the cases of *U.S. v. David* (1991), *U.S. v. Butler* (2001), and *U.S. v. Angevine* (2002). The interests of national security are considered within the cases of *Showengerdt v. U.S.* (1991) and *U.S. v. Scarfo* (2001).

Regardless of the unique, separate characteristics of these cases, a common theme connects the situational considerations of privacy, technology, and intelligence. Such situational circumstances are a facet of the perplexities regarding the security concerns of gathering of intelligence versus the liberty concerns of privacy. With respect to modern times, commensurate observations regarding the security concerns of gathering intelligence versus the liberty concerns of privacy are present within contemporary literature.

Diffie and Landau consider the privacy versus security arguments associated with intelligence functions, regarding the surveillance of communications lines.[55] Diffie and Landau introduce the necessities of maintaining national security and consider the permeability of modern "communications infrastructures" concerning the intelligence functions of "wiretapping."[56] Certainly, one must consider arguments regarding intelligence gathering versus privacy from the perspectives of national security and the Patriot Act. Snow and Brooks consider the intelligence function from an ethical perspective.[57] De Rosa considers the issues of privacy and intelligence gathering with respect to the threats and dangers of terrorism.[58] According to De Rosa, propositions that emphasize "privacy and security as inevitably at odds" are both "false and dangerous."[59]

The writings of De Rosa are commensurate with the writings of Taipale, from the perspective of providing security, regarding the basic principles of liberty versus the functions of intelligence. Taiple justifies the "dual obligation," between liberty and security, through observations regarding the potential of current terrorism threats that pose national dangers, with respect to the "constitutional framework of reasonableness."[60] Within this context, Taiple indicates that there is "no inherent policy conflict at all between security and liberty."[61]

According to Taiple, any "strategies that place an unreasonable burden on liberty—for example, demonizing a minority or engendering suspicion of everyone—are not just unacceptable outcomes for liberty, but measures that provide little or no security because they are ineffective at identifying terrorists and they undermine the public cooperation and confidence needed for success."[62] Further, Taiple indicates that "liberty incurs responsibility, and unfettered liberty at the expense of security that can potentially result in catastrophic outcomes impinges not just on collective security, but also on the very foundation of liberty for all individuals and is itself, there, unreasonable."[63] Taiple integrates and justifies these concepts through observing that "effective security strategies—strategies that actually help locate, target, and preempt terrorists before they act without unduly burdening the vast majority of innocent people—are by definition not unreasonable, since individual liberty is not synonymous with permitting plotters to commit terrorist acts free from sanction."[64]

The writings of Taiple imply the necessity of discretion when gathering intelligence versus any transgressions of privacy and liberty.[65] Considerations of tensions, between intelligence functions and privacy, are affiliated with fears regarding the abusing and exploiting of government functions (i.e., intelligence gathering) versus maintaining the boundaries of privacy that are expected among organizations and individuals. Historically, Rosenzweig describes such government abuses and exploitations as "overreactions and overzealousness" and cites examples of such government actions during the U.S. Civil War, World War I, and World War II.[66]

However, Rosenzweig warns against interpreting historical events without sound considerations of the necessities associated with the situational circumstances and indicates that "we may not know for many years whether our current fears were well-founded."[67] Rosenzweig likens the "balance between liberty and security" to the movements of a "pendulum," in that the balance "may be pushed far in one direction by significant events (such as 9/11), but will eventually swing back toward the center, after the catastrophe has ended, the threat has receded, and people have recovered from their initial reaction."[68] Because of the maturing of American society, the balancing of this metaphorical pendulum "is unlikely to swing as far as has happened in the past."[69] Rosenzweig enhances this statement through observations regarding the historical detaining of "over 100,000 Japanese-Americans" versus the modern detaining of "three Americans" during the current terrorism conflict.[70]

Rosenzweig provides salient observations regarding such historical "lessons."[71] According to Rosenzweig, the "power of oversight gives us freedom to grant the government great powers when the need arises, secure in the knowledge that we can restrain their exercise as appropriate," and that "we should not be utterly unwilling to adjust our response to liberty and security for the sake of counterterrorism, since we have the capacity to manage that adjustment and to readjust it as necessary."[72] Given these notions, the relationship between liberty and freedom, with respect to the intelligence function (e.g., intelligence gathering) versus privacy, must be adjusted with respect to the circumstances of catastrophic events and periods of danger that threaten the nation. Tensions and debates will persist regarding the gathering of intelligence versus privacy.

The observations of Rosenzweig are commensurate with the writings of Murphy. According to Murphy, the "argument in favor of abridging liberties through aggressive policing and intelligence collection is that the immediate, asymmetric threat—terrorism like that of al-Qaida—is so grave, and the potential harm so calamitous, that traditional constitutional presumptions in favor of the individual (versus the collective need) must be rethought."[73] Conversely, Murphy also indicates that "if our liberties are curtailed, we lose the values that we are struggling to defend."[74] This dichotomy again shows the tension between government intelligence functions versus the perpetuation of unimpeded liberty.

Given such notions, Murphy describes the situation as one between "principle and prudence" regarding decisions within the context of security functions.[75] With respect to an analogy of government functions, Murphy indicates that a "balance" must be "struck in the allocation of powers among the different branches, so as to create tension between expedience and caution and allow governmental functions—like commerce, foreign affairs, and domestic security—to serve, not oppress, individual liberty and prevent abuses."[76] Based on the writings of Murphy, this "tension between expedience and caution" is an appropriate consideration of intelligence gathering versus privacy.[77]

Digital technology applications represent an intersection between the gathering of intelligence and the infringements of privacy, through which the dichotomy of security versus civil liberty is manifested. According to Taylor et al.[78] and Minow and Cate,[79] a variety of technological applications exist that support the functions of intelligence gathering. The use of such electronic technologies, as methods of gathering intelligence, causes much debate regarding issues of privacy.[80] According to Minow and Cate, data mining is a prominent method, within the intelligence function, that generates such debates regarding privacy.[81]

According to Kudyba and Hoptroff, data mining is the utilizing of the "tools of mathematics and statistical testing" regarding "historical data in order to identify relationships, patterns, or affiliations among variables or sections of variables in that data to gain great insight" within a problem domain.[82] According to McCue, data mining involves seeking "useful relationships" among "information or models, particularly those that can be used to anticipate or predict future events."[83] Given these definitions, two observations are noted regarding data mining: (1) it has strong potential as a tool through which intelligence gathering may occur via the discovery of knowledge, and (2) privacy implications are apparent depending on the types of databases and problem domains examined.

These observations are salient when contemplating the uses of data mining within the problem domain of terrorism. Within the context of the intelligence function, the uses of data mining include the analysis of telephone conversations to determine patterns among sets of data; the analysis of trends and movements among immigration datasets; and the use of statistical tools to forecast the potential of future events occurring given an analysis of historical data sets. Such activities are necessary for both initiatives of antiterrorism and counterterrorism.

Despite the benefits of using digital technologies to perform functions of intelligence gathering, imperfections may exist within such systems that facilitate privacy debates. No system is perfect; various defects impact the use of such systems among intelligence functions. Taylor et al. indicate that data integrity is a significant concern regarding the accuracy and correctness of such information-based tools (e.g., the potential of using the wrong Social Security data to identify people), warn against collecting information unnecessarily, and warn against abuses.[84]

However, within terrorism initiatives, the use of such data gathering methods often may require the investigation of personal, individual data or information regarding organizations, thereby instigating debates regarding issues of privacy. Again, a dichotomy between intelligence gathering activities and issues of privacy is manifested through the implementation of data mining applications. Wilson (p. 18) expresses this dichotomy by posing a straightforward question: "What is the proper balance between the need to detect and remain aware of terrorism activities and the need to protect individual privacy?"[85]

Within the context of gathering intelligence, such a question has influenced numerous responses among acts of legislation, guidelines, and policies. Although a variety of problem domains may be considered regarding the tensions between intelligence gathering and privacy, one perspective involves the considerations associated with the use of digital technologies as instruments of gathering intelligence. The proliferation of such digital technologies has impacted information gathering through an increased capacity to gather, process, interpret, and use intelligence. However, regardless of the situation, Taylor et al. indicate that laws and legislation regarding digital crimes and the gathering of intelligence do not "protect criminals," but "enforce a reasonable person's expectation of privacy."[86]

Taylor et al., from the perspectives of digital technologies and their applications among cyber-based intelligence functions, summarize the salient acts of legislation and policies that demonstrate historically the facilitation of increased powers among intelligence functions.[87] Within their summary, Taylor et al. consider the Fourth Amendment from the perspective of virtual and digital entities.[88] This consideration of the Fourth Amendment highlights the salient characteristics of search and seizure and encompasses discussions of warrantless searches and searching with warrants in relation to digital technology devices (e.g., computers, cellular phones, etc.).[89]

Additional historical considerations regarding the gathering of digital intelligence include "Title III of the Omnibus Crime Control and Safe Streets Act of 1968 and the Pen Registers and Trap and Trace Devices chapter of Title 18."[90] Taylor et al. also consider the Patriot Act from the perspective of cyber-crime and cyber-terrorism and indicate that it is beneficial when "easily and surreptitiously" monitoring communications (both Internet and wireless communications) and provides benefits when securing information, without necessitating warrants, from Internet service providers.[91] Taylor et al. also consider the increased scope and magnitude of intelligence gathering regarding the individual users of technological devices.[92]

The writings of Taylor et al. show a variety of additional laws and acts of legislation that impact the function of intelligence gathering.[93] Other examples include the Communication Assistance for Law Enforcement Act, the Consumer Fraud and Abuse Act, the Economic Espionage Act, the Homeland Security Act, and the Copyright Act. Such acts of legislation, and their associated policies, enhance significantly the ability to gather intelligence and are influenced by the tension between intelligence gathering (i.e., security) and privacy (i.e., liberty).

According to Taylor et al., such influences necessitate guidelines requiring "vastly new training for law enforcement officers, defining the tactical, operational, and legal limits involving intelligence gathering and analysis."[94] Foxman indicates that "Constitutional safeguards are critical" and that "any expanded powers must be continually checked by all branches of government."[95] Foxman also warns against the abuse of increased powers of intelligence and indicates that "legislative oversight" is mandated.[96] Foxman also indicates that "law enforcement authorities must police themselves" regarding the potential of abusing increased capacities within the intelligence function.[97] Given these notions, discretion must be considered heavily regarding the increased scope and magnitude of intelligence gathering functions.

Regardless of any such laws, legal acts, or guidelines, Taylor et al. indicate that any intelligence gathering efforts must remain within their legal limits and within the scope of the Constitution.[98] Although legal limitations must remain within the scope of the Constitution, such legal limitations are dynamic and change with respect to the characteristics of dangers that threaten the nation. In turn, the balance between liberty and security is also impacted via legislation. Again, from the perspective of terrorism, the writings of Wilson express this dichotomy through the posing of a straightforward question: "What is the proper balance between the need to detect and remain aware of terrorism activities and the need to protect individual privacy?"[99]

The arguments of Foxman may be considered regarding this issue.[100] Foxman indicates that the "best way to fashion effective and appropriate security measures is to rely on the constitutional structure that those measures are designed to protect" as a method of facilitating "the right balance between safety and civil liberty."[101] Such a response must be mindful of the effects regarding the tension between intelligence gathering and privacy regarding the shaping of U.S. laws and guidelines through time (Figure 13.13). Therefore, a question may be posed regarding the managing of such tension: How can the tension between intelligence gathering and privacy be managed and best utilized through time, given the historically increased and dynamic capacities of intelligence gathering that result from law and legislation?

Based on the writings of Taylor et al.,[102] Foxman,[103] and Taipale,[104] such a question is answered simply: through discretion. Based on the writings of Taipale, security must be achieved without the abusive compromising of liberty.[105] However, liberty necessitates security (e.g., functions of intelligence) to ensure freedoms (e.g., privacy). Based on the arguments of Taylor et al.,[106] Foxman,[107] Murphy,[108] Taipale,[109] and Rosenzweig,[110] a perfect, solitary combination of laws and legislation versus privacy does not exist through

Figure 13.13 Security vs. liberty. (Retrieved from http://www.frugal-cafe.com/public_html/ frugal-blog/frugal-cafe-blogzone/wp-content/uploads/2011/02/tsa-statue-of-liberty-scan-patdown-political-cartoon.jpg.)

which any form of unanimous consensus may be achieved within American society. Such a combination of laws and legislation versus privacy must be contemplated and weighed regarding the merits of the considered situation, and if passed and ratified, must be implemented with much discretion.

Overall, given the cumulative writings of the aforementioned authors, the inherent tension between intelligence gathering and privacy is manifested through the dynamic balancing between security and civil liberties. Because of the investigative needs of law enforcement regarding various criminal activities, increased functions of security are necessitated that may impact civil liberties, thereby spawning brisk debates regarding the activities of intelligence gathering versus concerns of privacy.

The effects of these events of history were manifested with respect to the tension between intelligence gathering functions versus privacy shaping U.S. laws and guidelines via the periodic expressions and implementations of legislation that increased the scope and magnitude of intelligence gathering functions. Such increases have greatly improved the capacities of intelligence functions to prevent and respond to catastrophic events, but their utilization must be vigilantly managed with discretion to avoid abuse.

Based on the discussions of the aforementioned authors, time presents new challenges that influence the dynamic balance between liberty and security. Although this dynamic balancing will never provide a solution that achieves perfect consensus, an optimal balancing may occur with respect to the attributes of the considered problem domain to provide the furtherance and continuance of the nation. However, such balancing must remain with the scope of the Constitution, and such balancing must be careful to avoid the destruction of the philosophical mechanism that integrates both liberty and security within American society.

Summary

The United States Constitution is the supreme law of the country. It establishes a system of checks and balances by separating the powers of government with regard to law into three branches: the legislative, the executive, and the judicial. The power to make laws is granted to the legislative branch, Congress, and state legislatures. The power to enforce laws is granted to the executive branch, the President, and governors. Finally, the power to resolve disputes regarding the law is given to the judicial branch, including state courts and ultimately the United States Supreme Court. Each of these functions must be kept separate and independent, with each branch checking the power of the others. In particular, this reasoning leads to the judicial branch having the power of judicial review, the power to review the validity of acts of the legislative branch and the executive branch under the Constitution.

The Constitution includes amendments known as the Bill of Rights. Those amendments are not laws that law enforcement officers enforce. Unlike criminal statutes, the prohibitions contained in the amendments act as restrictions on the government, restrictions intended to protect stated rights of the citizens. The amendments may best be viewed as rules that must be obeyed by law enforcement officials while enforcing laws enacted by Congress or state legislatures, which laws must themselves be enacted in accordance with the Constitution. Therefore, every law enforcement officer must be well-trained in certain amendments and gain a solid understanding of how they are applied by the courts.

Law enforcement officers must have a solid understanding of the Fourth, Fifth, and Sixth Amendments as articulated by the courts. They need not memorize every case the courts have decided, but must understand the principles on which those cases are decided and be able to apply those principles in their day-to-day activities. Seldom will a law enforcement officer confront a set of facts that exactly matches those of a particular case. The task of the law enforcement officer is to analyze the circumstances of the matter in which he or she is involved to determine whether they are analogous or distinguishable from precedent cases already decided by the courts. Evidence illegally obtained in violation of the provisions of the Constitution is likely to be refused as evidence for purposes of convicting a person of a crime under the exclusionary rule.

Historically, the U.S. Constitution has represented an antithesis of powers with respect to the powers of foreign law enforcement organizations. Within the American criminal justice system, innocence is presumed and evidence of guilt must be shown unequivocally. The U.S. Constitution also facilitates societal liberties, privacies, and securities. When performing investigations, American law enforcement organizations often perform a variety of activities that may breach perceptions and expectations of privacy, liberty, and security (e.g., wiretaps), but such activities must occur only in accordance with the limitations of law and must be constitutional. Although such activities may be limited infringements, their purpose is to embellish the security of American society. Therefore, from a perspective of law enforcement, a balancing of liberty versus security occurs within American society.

The United States Constitution is the law of the land. It is the foundational basis for the laws that are expressed among the states, commonwealths, counties, parishes, towns, and cities of American society. Although differences of expressed law may occur among localities, thereby necessitating different enforcement activities, all laws and law enforcement activities must be commensurate with the tenets and principles of the United States Constitution.

Notes

1. *Fascinating Facts About the U.S. Constitution* (2011). Retrieved July 9, 2011, from http://www .constitutionfacts.com/?section=constitution&page=fascinatingFacts.cfm.
2. Bond, J. R., & Smith, K. B. (2008). *The Promise and Performance of American Democracy* (8th ed., p. 36). Boston, MA: Thomson-Wadsworth.
3. At this point, Great Britain had a parliament that shared the role of making the laws with the king, but they acted in concert rather than as separate powers from the perspective of the colonies, which had no representation in that Parliament.
4. Manent, P. (1994). *An Intellectual History of Liberalism* (pp. 54–58) (trans. by Rebecca Balinski, Princeton University Press).
5. *Marbury v. Madison*, 5 U.S. (1 Cranch) 137; 2 L. Ed. 60 (1803). Retrieved on October 31, 2012 from http://constitution.org/ussc/005-137a.htm.
6. *McDonald v. Chicago*, 561 U.S. 3025 (2010). Retrieved from http://supreme.justia.com/cases/ federal/us/561/08-1521/.
7. The White House (2011). *The Constitution*. Retrieved July 9, 2011, from http://www.whitehouse .gov/our-government/the-constitution.
8. Ibid.
9. Ibid.
10. *U.S. Constitution—Article I, Section 8*. Retrieved July 12, 2011, from http://www .usconstitution.net/xconst_A1Sec8.html.

11. U.S. Census Bureau (2010). *U.S. Census Bureau Announces 2010 Census Population Counts— Apportionment Count Delivered to President*. Retrieved July 11, 2011, from http://2010.census .gov/news/releases/operations/cb10-cn93.html.

12. Currier, K. A., & Eimermann, T. E. (2009). *Introduction to Law for Paralegals* (4th ed., p. 158). New York. NY: Wolters Kluwer.

13. *District of Columbia v. Heller*, 554 U.S. 570 (2008)

14. Section 1 of the Fourteenth Amendment states, "Section 1. All persons born or naturalized in the United States, and subject to the jurisdiction thereof, are citizens of the United States and of the state wherein they reside. No state shall make or enforce any law which shall abridge the privileges or immunities of citizens of the United States; nor shall any state deprive any person of life, liberty, or property, without due process of law; nor deny to any person within its juris- diction the equal protection of the laws."

15. Common examples of these cases are lawsuits brought by one citizen against another for dam- ages arising from personal injury or breach of contract.

16. Citation of court decisions follows an established format that allows a principle stated by a court to be found by anyone interested in reading the original case. This citation means that the prin- ciple that freedom of speech is not absolute may be found in a case called *Schenck v. United States* that can be found in *United States Reports,* a collection of Supreme Court cases. Specifically, it can be found in volume 249 of those reports. The case starts on page 47 of that volume, but the partic- ular principle, statement, or quote is found on page 52. The case was decided in 1919. Important or "landmark" cases are often referred to simply by the name of one of the parties. Sometimes that name becomes part of law enforcement vernacular such as a "Miranda warning" or a "Terry stop."

17. *Chaplinsky v. State of New Hampshire*, 315 U.S. 568, 572 (1942).

18. *Terminiello v. Chicago*, 337 U.S. 1, 4 (1949).

19. *City of Houston v. Hill*, 482 U.S. 451, 463–64 (1987).

20. *Commonwealth v. Hock*, 696 A.2d 225 (Pa. Super. 1997).

21. American Civil Liberties Union (2011). *ACLU Calls on Maryland Transit Authority to Cease Unconstitutional Harassment of Photographers*. Retrieved July 11, 2011, from http://www.aclu .org/free-speech/aclu-calls-maryland-transit-authority-cease-unconstitutional-harassment- photographers.

22. Ibid.

23. Ibid.

24. Anthony, L. (2010). Grant took picture of Mehserle holding a taser. *ABC News*. Retrieved July 12, 2011, from http://abclocal.go.com/kgo/story?section=news/local/east_bay&id=7487830.

25. Ibid.

26. Miller, C. (2011). *Oscar Grant Snapped a Final Photo of Cop Who Killed Him*. Retrieved July 11, 2011, from http://www.pixiq.com/article/oscar-grant-snapped-a-final-photo-of-cop- who-killed-him.

27. Hubbart, P. A. (2005). *Making Sense of Search and Seizure Law* (pp. 85–108). Philadelphia, PA: Carolina Academic Press.

28. *Kyllo v. United States*, 533 U.S. 27 (2001). *Fourth Amendment Summaries*. Retrieved July 12, 2011, from http://www.fourthamendmentsummaries.com/cases/post_2000_cases.html.

29. Ibid.

30. Ibid.

31. Ibid.

32. Ibid.

33. Ibid.

34. *Unites States v. Jones,* 565 U.S. (2012) [Case No. 10–1259. Argued November 8, 2011—Decided January 23, 2012].

35. Johnson, K. FBI cuts back on GPS surveillance after Supreme Court ruling. *USA Today*, February 7, 2012. Retrieved April 20, 2012, from http://www.usatoday.com/news/washington/ story/2012-02-03/fbi-gps-surveillance-supreme-court-ruling/52992842/1.

36. *Roper v. Simmons*, 543 U.S. 551 (2005).

37. *Atkins v. Virginia*, 536 U.S. 304 (2002).

38. Clark and Clark, LLC (2011). *New Jersey Criminal Defense Attorneys*. Retrieved July 11, 2011, from http://www.csclarklaw.com/your-legal-rights/your-fourteenth-amendment-rights-right-to-due-process.html.

39. National Paralegal College (2007). *The Exclusionary Rule*. Retrieved July 12, 2011, from http://nationalparalegal.edu/conlawcrimproc_public/ProtectionFromSearches&Seizures/ExclusionaryRule.asp.

40. Ibid.

41. Ibid.

42. Hubbart, P. A. (2005). *Making Sense of Search and Seizure Law* (p. 336). Philadelphia, PA: Carolina Academic Press.

43. Security (2010). *Merriam-Webster Dictionary*. Retrieved June 30, 2010, from http://www.merriam-webster.com/dictionary/security.

44. Privacy (2010). *Merriam-Webster Dictionary*. Retrieved June 30, 2010, from http://www.merriam-webster.com/dictionary/privacy.

45. Civil Liberty (2010). *Merriam-Webster Dictionary*. Retrieved June 30, 2010, from http://www.merriam-webster.com/dictionary/civil liberty.

46. Technology (2010). *Merriam-Webster Dictionary*. Retrieved June 30, 2010, from http://www.merriam-webster.com/dictionary/technology.

47. Kamien, D. (Ed.). (2006). *The McGraw-Hill Homeland Security Handbook*. New York, NY: McGraw-Hill Publishing.

48. Ibid.

49. Taipale, K. (2006). Introduction to section 12. In Kamien, D. (Ed.), *The McGraw-Hill Homeland Security Handbook* (pp. 1009–1012). New York, NY: McGraw-Hill Publishing.

50. Ibid.

51. Ibid.

52. Ibid.

53. Ibid.

54. Loundy, D. (2003). *Computer Crime, Information Warfare, and Economic Espionage*. Durham, NC: Carolina Academic Press.

55. Diffie, W., & Landau, S. (2009). Communications surveillance: Privacy and security at risk. *Communications of the ACM*, *52*(11), 42–47.

56. Ibid.

57. Snow, B., & Brooks, C. (2009). Privacy and security: An ethics code for U.S. intelligence officers. *Communications of the ACM*, *52*(8), 30–32.

58. DeRosa, M. (2003). Privacy in the age of terror. *Washington Quarterly*, *26*(3), 27–41.

59. Ibid.

60. Taipale, K. (2006). Introduction to section 12. In Kamien, D. (Ed.), *The McGraw-Hill Homeland Security Handbook* (pp. 1009–1012). New York, NY: McGraw-Hill Publishing.

61. Ibid.

62. Ibid.

63. Ibid.

64. Ibid.

65. Ibid.

66. Rosenzweig, P. (2006). Think about civil liberty and terrorism. In Kamien, D. (Ed.), *The McGraw-Hill Homeland Security Handbook* (pp. 1013–1027). New York, NY: McGraw-Hill Publishing.

67. Ibid.

68. Ibid.

69. Ibid.

70. Ibid.

71. Ibid.

72. Ibid.

73. Murphy, L. (2006). Principled prudence: Civil liberties and the homeland security practitioner. In Kamien, D. (Ed.), *The McGraw-Hill Homeland Security Handbook* (pp. 1045–1061). New York, NY: McGraw-Hill Publishing.

74. Ibid.

75. Ibid.

76. Ibid.

77. Ibid.

78. Taylor, R., Caeti, T., Loper, D., Fritsch, E., & Liederbach, J. (2006). *Digital Crime and Digital Terrorism*. New Jersey, NJ: Pearson Prentice-Hall Publishing.

79. Minow, N., & Cate, F. (2006). Government data mining. In Kamien, D. (Ed.), *The McGraw-Hill Homeland Security Handbook* (pp. 1063–1086). New York, NY: McGraw-Hill Publishing.

80. Ibid.

81. Ibid.

82. Kudyba, S., & Hoptroff, R. (2001). *Data Mining and Business Intelligence: A Guide to Productivity*. Hershey, PA: Idea Publishing.

83. McCue, C. (2007). *Data Mining and Predictive Analysis: Intelligence Gathering and Crime Analysis*. Oxford, UK: Butterworth-Heinemann Publishing.

84. Taylor, R., Caeti, T., Loper, D., Fritsch, E., & Liederbach, J. (2006). *Digital Crime and Digital Terrorism*. New Jersey, NJ: Pearson Prentice-Hall Publishing.

85. Wilson, C. (2007). Computer attacks and cyberterrorism: Vulnerabilities and policy issues for congress. In Linden, E. (Ed.), *Focus on Terrorism: Volume 9* (pp. 1–42). New York, NY: Nova Science Publishers.

86. Taylor, R., Caeti, T., Loper, D., Fritsch, E., & Liederbach, J. (2006). *Digital Crime and Digital Terrorism*. New Jersey, NJ: Pearson Prentice-Hall Publishing.

87. Ibid.

88. Ibid.

89. Ibid.

90. Ibid.

91. Ibid.

92. Ibid.

93. Ibid.

94. Ibid.

95. Foxman, A. (2006). Security and freedom of speech. In Kamien, D. (Ed.), *The McGraw-Hill Homeland Security Handbook* (pp. 1031–1045). New York, NY: McGraw-Hill Publishing.

96. Ibid.

97. Ibid.

98. Taylor, R., Caeti, T., Loper, D., Fritsch, E., & Liederbach, J. (2006). *Digital Crime and Digital Terrorism*. New Jersey, NJ: Pearson Prentice-Hall Publishing.

99. Wilson, C. (2007). Computer attacks and cyberterrorism: Vulnerabilities and policy issues for congress. In Linden, E. (Ed.), *Focus on Terrorism: Volume 9* (pp. 1–42). New York, NY: Nova Science Publishers.

100. Foxman, A. (2006). Security and freedom of speech. In Kamien, D. (Ed.), *The McGraw-Hill Homeland Security Handbook*. (pp. 1031–1045). New York, NY: McGraw-Hill Publishing.

101. Ibid.

102. Taylor, R., Caeti, T., Loper, D., Fritsch, E., & Liederbach, J. (2006). *Digital Crime and Digital Terrorism*. New Jersey, NJ: Pearson Prentice-Hall Publishing.

103. Foxman, A. (2006). Security and freedom of speech. In Kamien, D. (Ed.), *The McGraw-Hill Homeland Security Handbook* (pp. 1031–1045). New York, NY: McGraw-Hill Publishing.

104. Taipale, K. (2006). Introduction to section 12. In Kamien, D. (Ed.), *The McGraw-Hill Homeland Security Handbook* (pp. 1009–1012). New York, NY: McGraw-Hill Publishing.

105. Ibid.

106. Taylor, R., Caeti, T., Loper, D., Fritsch, E., & Liederbach, J. (2006). *Digital Crime and Digital Terrorism*. New Jersey, NJ: Pearson Prentice-Hall Publishing.
107. Foxman, A. (2006). Security and freedom of speech. In Kamien, D. (Ed.), *The McGraw-Hill Homeland Security Handbook* (pp. 1031–1045). New York, NY: McGraw-Hill Publishing.
108. Murphy, L. (2006). Principled prudence: Civil liberties and the homeland security practitioner. In Kamien, D. (Ed.), *The McGraw-Hill Homeland Security Handbook* (pp. 1045–1061). New York, NY: McGraw-Hill Publishing.
109. Taipale, K. (2006). Introduction to section 12. In Kamien, D. (Ed.), *The McGraw-Hill Homeland Security Handbook* (pp. 1009–1012). New York, NY: McGraw-Hill Publishing.
110. Rosenzweig, P. (2006). Think about civil liberty and terrorism. In Kamien, D. (Ed.), *The McGraw-Hill Homeland Security Handbook* (pp. 1013–1027). New York, NY: McGraw-Hill Publishing.

Bibliography

U.S. Constitution (n.d.). *U.S. Constitution—Article I, Section 8*. Retrieved July 12, 2011, from http://www.usconstitution.net/xconst_A1Sec8.html.

Administration and Leadership
Community Support, Recruitment, Selection, Training, and Retention

14

The police administrator is responsible for the organization of his department; for the planning, its functions, services and interrelationships; and for the control of his force to see that its duties are carried out in the most effective way.

O.W. Wilson[1]

Learning Objectives

The objectives of this chapter are to

- Discuss the challenges of police recruiting
- Define the candidate selection process
- Describe the philosophy of police training
- Explain the concept of retention

Introduction

One of the things that never changes in law enforcement is that the system is under constant change. Changes in laws and the interpretation of laws, incorporating new and exciting technologies and applying them within the profession, using innovative strategies to more effectively respond to the challenges of crime, and providing public service all ensure that those in the profession will always serve in an exciting field.

There are over 17,000 law enforcement agencies in the United States. Finding qualified applicants has become an overwhelming task for many of these agencies. Law enforcement as a profession requires officers to undergo extensive training; therefore, the selection of the right candidate is not only efficient for the department but a necessary element for administration. Hiring the wrong person can be expensive for an agency, but also could develop difficult relations between the department itself and the community. Entry-level police officers have a direct relationship with the citizens through the enforcement of traffic laws, patrol, and delivery of services. An employee who is not suited for the nature of the work involved in law enforcement has the potential to cause great harm to a department. It is for these reasons that recruitment and selection should be one of a department's top priorities.

In addition to the need to have better qualified police personnel in order to meet the changing needs of society, accountability of law enforcement is forcing administrators to become more careful in their hiring practices. The increase in the use of many technological devices that are available to the public such as video cameras and phones equipped with cameras and video/audio recording capabilities have created a consequential accountability for law enforcement agencies. Videos can be posted to the web in seconds that become instantly available to the masses.

For individuals seeking a career in law enforcement, there are several factors to take into consideration when researching different agencies. One needs to decide on the professional goals as well as look at the advantages and disadvantages of different characteristics of departments. One of the first factors to consider is whether one wishes to be employed by a local, state, or federal agency. There are several options for each of these levels, and it is advisable to research each carefully. Understanding the minimum physical, educational, and weapons requirements for different positions within each of those levels is important.

Other factors to take into consideration will be the size of the agency. Local departments vary in size across the United States, and present unique opportunities and challenges depending on whether they are small, medium, or large. Crime rates of a jurisdiction also play a major role in the types of work performed for different agencies, so it is important to decide if one wishes to work in an area with high crime rates or a community with lower crime rates. The types of activity engaged in by officers may be limited in smaller communities with lower crime rates. Another factor is the location of the agency under consideration; many officers prefer to work in a community in which they have ties.

Supplementary information needed to research will be the salary and benefits associated with different positions within the agencies. Many departments will provide a job description with salary and other information. In order to gain information about job openings, it is important to employ several different strategies. Networking is one of the best ways to find out about a job. Letting family members, friends, and acquaintances know of an interest in a job in law enforcement can connect an individual with people in the field, which can assist one with the hiring process. Additionally, many college programs include an internship as part of their program. This is an excellent way to create an opportunity in a department while at the same time being able to observe the different types of jobs available in that agency. Agencies themselves largely use colleges as a source of police recruits. Additionally, many open positions may be posted online, particularly by state and federal agencies. The majority of local departments are required to advertise in the local newspaper, which in many instances is also available online.

In 2003, the average entry-level annual salary was $23,400 for small departments and $37,700 for the largest departments. When the size of the department is factored, the average starting salary for all agencies was $35,500. When considering salary options, it is important to factor in other variables. Among the many benefits that are available, about 35% of local departments provided tuition reimbursement and 32% of departments offered education incentive pay. Merit pay and shift differential pay were offered in approximately 21% of local police departments in 2003. Some departments also offer differential pay for special skills and military service. A new skill that a few departments are offering special pay for is being bilingual.[2]

In 2003, there were over 580,000 full-time employees in local police departments.[3] Conditions of the job market in law enforcement are suitable for new recruits. As we discuss later in this chapter, there are individuals resigning and retiring each year, as well as the fact that as long as there is crime, there will always be a need for law enforcement personnel. Not only is there a need to replace officers, but overall employment in law enforcement has been increasing. Local police employment has increased over 27% from 1987 to 2003, and more than 60% of departments hired new officers in the year 2003.[4]

Role of the Law Enforcement Administrator

Leadership is the catalyst in organization and management, especially in a law enforcement organization. For an agency to be effectively operated, it falls upon those in positions of leadership, the department command team, to perform the countless duties, ranging from establishing policy, providing guidance, overseeing budgeting and logistics, recruitment, retention and personnel development and training to strengthening relationships with external constituents that are essential for the agency to operate.[5] Leadership is critical to the success or failure of any law enforcement organization. It falls upon the agency administrator, whether titled a chief, sheriff, or director, to develop a command team and provide that leadership

The nature of law enforcement is that the agency itself develops a personality and reputation. Much of that personality and reputation are shaped by its leaders. One does not have to look hard to find examples of law enforcement administrators whose personalities shaped the identity of their agencies. J. Edgar Hoover, who led the Federal Bureau of Investigation (FBI) for over 40 years, made the term "G Man" a household name in the 1930s and 1940s. The image of his agents, strong and professional, attracted countless numbers to apply for positions in the Bureau.

August Vollmer's forward-thinking approach to agency administration in the early 1900s not only made Berkeley, California, a laboratory for law enforcement innovations, but also served as a launching pad for the next generation of law enforcement administrators and educators, who would continue his legacy. Vollmer's disciples included men such as O.W. Wilson and V.A. Leonard, who both became legendary through the 1940s, 1950s, and 1960s, as leaders in both law enforcement education and administration.

The law enforcement administrator is responsible for the organization of the agency; planning, services, and interrelationships; the control of the agency, and the oversight to ensure the agency works efficiently and effectively. For the law enforcement administrator, the essence of law enforcement leadership is the ability to obtain from each member of the agency the highest quality of service that may be rendered. The law enforcement administrator who fails to gain and maintain the confidence and loyalty of those with whom he or she serves ultimately fails as a leader.[6]

The general track officers follow to reach the pinnacle of being an administrator or executive in a law enforcement organization begins with spending years working through the ranks. The first stages are the first and second line supervisors, commonly holding the ranks of sergeant and lieutenant. These supervisory ranks are critical in the successful operation of any organization; therefore, it is of the utmost importance for the best and brightest officers to move into these positions. It is as field supervisors these officers gain valuable experience in the decision-making processes that are involved in the administration of the department. The law enforcement administrator must depend on the supervisors to implement and enforce the goals and objectives put into place, giving direction to the department as a whole. Choosing the right individuals for these positions can be a pivotal point in the success or failure of an administration.

Law enforcement organizations that choose to reward officers' work with rank find this to be an unwise direction at times. Rank or supervisory positions should be delegated to those individuals who have proven themselves to have an understanding of supervision and are capable of stepping into and growing in the role of supervisor. Many times the final error is made by promoting individuals one step above their capabilities, thereby setting this person up for failure. When this happens, it affects both the officer individually and the overall operation of the organization. Administrators must understand that being a good police officer does not automatically mean one will be a good supervisor.

Moving into the role of administrator in a police organization means the individual must be competent in both the administration of justice and the function of an executive overseeing the operation of an organization. Law enforcement organizations have all the business functions of any other company, requiring people with an understanding of such areas as budgeting, human resources, manpower allocation, purchasing, and equipment needs along with an understanding of how to provide mission-oriented leadership. Because of the multifaceted demands placed upon a law enforcement administrator, specialized training and instruction are critical to their success.

Organizations like the FBI National Academy, Southern Police Institute, International Association of Chiefs of Police, and the association of chiefs of police in each state provide training and assistance such as mentoring programs and policy development assistance, just to name a few, for both the new administrator and the experienced one to meet the challenges of our changing society.

Law enforcement administrators are made aware of such practices as accreditation programs (CALEA), which set standards and best practices for the organization. A successful law enforcement administrator must always remember the words of Robert Peel, which were used to open Chapter 2: "The police are the public and the public are the police; the police being only members of the public who are paid to give full time attention to duties which are incumbent on every citizen in the interests of community welfare and existence."[7] Keeping this in mind, the police should engage citizens within the community to provide both input and feedback as to the goals and objectives of the department; it is the community and its perception of "well being" and "feeling safe" that ultimately determines the success or failure of a public safety organization.

Gaining and Maintaining Public Support

One of the essential roles of the law enforcement administrator is the establishment and sustainment of strong and positive community ties. There is a constant push for professionalism within law enforcement. Today we see more attention brought about by citizens. This is becoming even more apparent in the connection between the media, citizens, and law enforcement agencies. As we see more and more embarrassing moments caught on film involving American officers, communities are demanding that departments and governments have a professional level of accountability while addressing their crime and service problems. While media have often highlighted the negative side of law enforcement in the United States, it is important to note that overall law enforcement has been addressing crime more and more efficiently. Over the last 20 years, we have experienced a stable decrease in both violent and property crime.

If a department is not actively hiring, volunteering is an excellent strategy to begin to make contacts within a department so that when a job does become available, a volunteer/applicant has a "foot in the door." This will give one the opportunity to get to know the job, administrators, and other officers and to be familiar with the expectations of the department.

Personnel Considerations

Law enforcement agencies are comprised of humans; therefore, they are subject to the fallibilities and attributes of human nature. Certainly, because law enforcement agencies are comprised of humans, they are no better than the individuals who comprise their structure, from the lowest rank of patrol officer to the highest ranks of chiefs and sheriffs. Some officers retire after many years of loyal, faithful service, whereas others succumb to temptation and may be relieved for criminal offenses. Others may experience medical issues that necessitate early retirement or a change of careers. Some may realize that policing simply is no longer their preferred occupation and opt to leave the ranks of law enforcement. Others may become suicidal or may die in the line of duty or from natural causes or accidents.

Because of changing city or county demographics or budgetary constraints, some officers may be released because of reduced organizational funding or a decreased need for policing. Some officers may be lured into other professions or vocations because of salary enticements, personal reasons, or benefits. Each of these situations is indicative of turnover among departments and attrition among the ranks of officers throughout the nation.

Regardless of the reason, turnover and attrition exist among law enforcement agencies nationally. For example, the Mobile Police Department (Mobile, Alabama) may be considered a case example of rank losses and attrition. Figure 14.1 shows the quantities of officers who departed the Mobile agency since the end of the twentieth century and during the first decade of the twenty-first century.

This image shows an increase in attrition followed by a decline near the end of the decade. Reasoning for this change involves a consideration of the enticements that are necessary to attract and retain quality personnel. The Mobile Police Department pursued salary increases as a method of attracting and retaining personnel. Through implementing salary increases, the agency became the "county's second-highest paying law enforcement agency for starting salaries, after an average 8% increase."[8] Before implementing this salary increase, the "department shed an average 8% of its force each year for the last 10 years—combined, that accounts for 466 officers, nearly the entire police force."[9] After exercising pay increases,

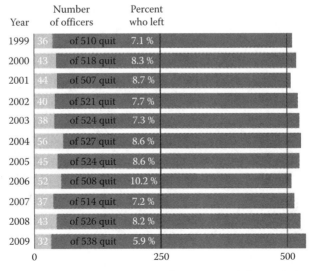

Year	Number of officers	Percent who left
1999	36 of 510 quit	7.1 %
2000	43 of 518 quit	8.3 %
2001	44 of 507 quit	8.7 %
2002	40 of 521 quit	7.7 %
2003	38 of 524 quit	7.3 %
2004	56 of 527 quit	8.6 %
2005	45 of 524 quit	8.6 %
2006	52 of 508 quit	10.2 %
2007	37 of 514 quit	7.2 %
2008	43 of 526 quit	8.2 %
2009	32 of 538 quit	5.9 %

Figure 14.1 Mobile county salary comparison. (Courtesy of the Mobile Police Department. Retrieved from http://blog.al.com/live/2010/01/mobile_police_department_attri.html.)

the department experienced the departure of only 32 officers.[10] Figure 14.2 shows a comparison of the increased salaries compared to the salaries of peer agencies in Mobile.

Another interesting consideration of the Mobile Police Department is that approximately 36% of its personnel have less than 5 years of policing experience, thereby representing a good amount of inexperience among its ranks.[11] Implementing the salary increase was necessary for retaining experienced officers.[12]

Law enforcement agencies have a constant need to identify and recruit quality candidates to replace officers who leave the departments. The case of the Mobile Police Department is not unique within the nation. Turnover and attrition are aspects of policing that all law enforcement organizations will experience at some point in time. Therefore, identifying, recruiting, selecting, training, and retaining quality personnel are paramount factors toward the success of any law enforcement organization. Although these factors are salient characteristics of any law enforcement organization, the organization itself must also have attractiveness to entice people to consider a law enforcement career (Figure 14.3).

	Officer	Corporal	Sergeant	Lieutenant
Mobile	$29,352	$32,400	$35,772	$39,480
Prichard	$20,856	$22,992	$25,344	$27,936
Chickasaw	$26,616	$29,340	$33,960	$37,440
Saraland	$30,900	$34,104	$37,656	$41,556
Citronelle	$28,992	$32,004	$35,328	$38,988
Bayou La Batre	$25,764	$28,440	$31,392	$34,656
Satsuma	$28,092	$31,008	$34,224	$37,776
Mt. Vernon	$25,764	$28,440	$31,392	$34,656
Creola	$22,068	$24,360	$26,892	$29,688
Mobile County Sheriff's Office	$29,352*	$32,400	$37,584	$41,484
*Deputy rank				

Figure 14.2 Mobile County salary comparison. (Courtesy of the Mobile Police Department. Retrieved from http://blog.al.com/live/2010/01/mobile_police_department_attri.html.)

Figure 14.3 North Carolina Highway Patrol recruiting poster. (Courtesy of the North Carolina Department of Public Safety. Retrieved from (http://www.nccrimecontrol.org/index2.cfm? a=000003,000014,000734.)

Recruitment and Selection

Law enforcement agencies are seeking individuals who have various skills, and today's officer needs to have more than just physical ability and weapons skills. Traditionally, physical fitness and the ability to follow orders were the necessary requirements for a career in criminal justice. As society has changed, so has the nature of crime and those who commit offenses. These changes require law enforcement professionals to change as well. Officers need to have physical ability coupled with emotional and intellectual maturity. Interpersonal skills are also necessary for an officer to possess. With an emphasis on community policing that many departments are embracing, the ability of officers to immerse themselves in a diverse community is becoming an invaluable quality.

What are the desired qualities that administrators seek in their law enforcement officers? As addressed earlier, having the requisite physical and weapons ability is no longer the only proficiency that departments are seeking. As society changes, so does the type and level of crime rates in the United States. We have seen an overall decrease in violent and property crime over the past 20 years. However, the nature and type of crimes that our communities are dealing with today are different than what police officers had to deal with 50 years ago. For example, computer crime and escalated levels of terrorism both domestic and international have increased and pose challenges for police officers. The age/crime curve has not varied much over the last 80 years; individuals between the ages 14 and 25 are more likely to be the victim and offender of most crimes. What has changed is the array of individuals themselves. Children are learning how to use computers in preschool, and they are becoming more sophisticated with all types of technology.

To meet the challenges that policing now presents, administrators are looking for officers with a wide range of personal, educational, and social qualities that will help better meet these needs. Personal qualities that are important would include the ability to exercise good judgment, be honest, and have a sense of responsibility.[13] Professionals in the criminal justice field need leadership skills that allow them to guide and direct others. A good leader has the ability to motivate individuals to act. A good officer has the ability to talk to the individuals with whom they come in contact and persuade them to follow orders without the use or threatened use of force. Officers need to possess good decision making skills that allow a person to be able to perceive the consequences of actions of a particular decision and choose a logical course. A good candidate would be able to formulate rational decisions and develop alternative solutions to problems. They would also be able to make quick decisions that will initiate immediate action and feel comfortable defending one's own positions when challenged. An officer must be adaptable. The nature of this job demands dealing with changing situations and a good officer will be able to quickly modify plans based on new information.

A person seeking a career in law enforcement should possess the ability to learn quickly. Additionally, although the requirement of a college education is not necessary in the majority of departments, it does factor in favorably when administrators begin the selection process. The more education and training that one possesses, the better one's chances are of being competitive in the field of criminal justice. A person needs to have the ability to identify important pieces of information. A person should be able to identify strengths and weaknesses as well as identify errors and inaccuracies in written documents. Officers must possess or quickly learn how to write in a coherent and proficient manner.

This would include the ability to deliver effective presentations and persuade others while speaking. It would include the use of correct grammar, spelling, punctuation, and vocabulary when needed. Some departments require a written examination that does not test knowledge of police work but rather measures verbal skills.

Because of the nature of police work, there is a need for individuals to have the ability to complete a task satisfactorily. Many areas of law enforcement require an officer to perform tasks without direct supervision. This creates a situation where an officer must be motivated to complete work that has been started and follow through on tasks. Discipline must be self-imposed when a job is this autonomous.

Communication and listening skills are vital in helping to resolve the majority of cases. An officer should also be able to deal effectively with irate individuals and manage conflict between individuals. The primary goals of law enforcement are to protect and to serve. A recruit must have a personality that leads to a desire and willingness to help others. It is usually only after communication proves unsuccessful that force is used.

Recruitment provides a pool of qualified applicants from whom administrators can select new law enforcement officers. Characteristics of police work such as discretion, authority, variety, ambiguity, and danger distinguish it from what most individuals do for a living. For these reasons, it is important that one understands what the requirements are for specific departments or agencies.

Most agencies have a minimum level of qualifications such as being a U.S. citizen, not having been convicted of a felony, having a valid driver's license, being 21 years of age, and living in the jurisdiction in which the department is located. Beyond these minimum requirements, many departments have additional restrictions or requirements such as height/weight standards, eyesight, hearing, and other medical requirements.[14] Physical requirements exist to ensure that new recruits are physically capable of handling the demands of an intensive training program. Most departments evaluate a candidate's speed, strength, and coordination to figure out if the candidate is in good physical condition. These tests are considered to be necessary because they simulate the conditions an officer may have to face out in the field. Examples of these would be jumping over fences, running, and carrying heavy objects or persons.

State and federal agencies often require extensive background checks including interviews with colleagues, family, friends, and acquaintances. Also police, driving, credit, and military verifications are included in this background check. The purpose of a background check is to determine if there is anything in a person's background that would make him or her unsuitable for work in law enforcement. Candidates are fingerprinted and their fingerprints are run through national, state, and local databases to search for any criminal records.

All references both personal and professional are contacted and interviewed. Previous employers verify past work records, and the financial status of the candidate is reviewed. It is important that a candidate have a good credit check as it shows to the administrator that one is able to live within his or her means and less susceptible to engaging in crimes such as bribery. It also speaks to a level of self-control for the candidate. Most local and state departments and federal agencies use drug testing as a standard screening process. Psychological testing is often administered to determine if a person is emotionally suited for this type of work. The Minnesota Multiphase Personality Inventory 2 or MMPI-2 is the most commonly used test and attempts to measure if someone is prone to unsafe, irresponsible behavior. This test must be interpreted by a qualified psychologist.[15] Polygraph examinations are also used by some agencies.

There is still debate about whether higher education should be a requirement for law enforcement officers at the local level, but many state and federal agencies require varying college degrees or a minimum number of college hours. For example, 81% of local police departments require a high school diploma, while 9% require a 2-year degree or a minimum number of college hours.[16]

The debate is essentially this: Does a formal education make a better police officer? Proponents of higher education claim that a college education for a police officer creates an employee that is less biased and less likely to use force when compared to officers who do not have a college education. Many believe that college graduates will be more mature and flexible, and therefore more able to develop an appropriate response to a challenging situation. The argument against departments having a higher education requirement is that it will disqualify potentially good officers. Those with college degrees may be less likely to apply for jobs in law enforcement based on pay and job conditions. Those with higher levels of education may be more likely to suffer job dissatisfaction when having to perform tasks such as issuing traffic tickets and performing ID checks. There is also the controversy that the real skills that an officer must gain knowledge of are only learned on the job and cannot be taught in a classroom. Despite the controversy that surrounds this topic, trends show that more and more departments require and prefer recruits that have degrees.

Local departments use a variety of screening methods for recruit applications. Almost all departments use a personal interview, with 98% stating that they used them in 2003. The majority of departments also used medical exams (85%), drug tests (73%), and psychological testing (67%) for screening. Additionally, over 80% of departments used some form of physical ability test and more than half used polygraph exams. Lastly, over 50% of departments conducted credit checks of potential employees.[17]

Finding the right person to hire is very important for police administrators. Finding the best fit between the candidate and agency can be cost-effective, efficient, and promote goodwill between the department and the community. When the wrong person is hired, it can be damaging for an agency's reputation and may also become a legal liability. Negligent-hiring lawsuits are becoming more and more common. These cases involve law enforcement supervisors being held liable for negligence in hiring individuals who are unqualified and unsuited for this type of work. These cases are usually brought against a department that has not established adequate, professional hiring practices (Figure 14.4).[18]

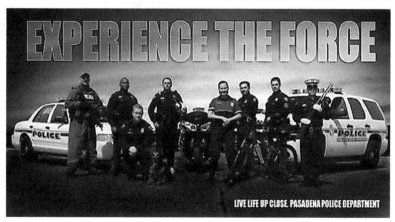

Figure 14.4 Pasadena Police Department recruiting poster. (Courtesy of the City of Pasadena, TX. Retrieved from http://www.ci.pasadena.tx.us/default.aspx?name=pol.personnel_training.)

Recruitment Challenges

There are several factors that create challenges in recruiting qualified applicants. There is a shortage of potential applicants because demographically baby boomers are retiring, and there are a limited number of replacements available. There is also a problem with attracting individuals into the field because of negativity surrounding the job. Because of media stories highlighting some of the more intense incidents between law enforcement and the public, there has been a negative connotation surrounding this career choice. There is also the battle caused with overcoming the misconception that a career in law enforcement is going to be as exciting and interesting as what is depicted in fictional television. Beyond fictional portrayals, we are also seeing an increase in reality television shows that only show the most exciting 15 minutes of an 8-hour shift. This is coupled with the fact that many persons who would normally be interested in a service-oriented job like law enforcement have been siphoned away by the military since September 11, 2001. These factors combined have led to unique challenges in recruitment.

Another consideration of recruiting involves the motivations of the recruit. Many enter the law enforcement domain solely because of financial and economic reasons. In such cases, personnel may leave after only a few months or years necessitating a replacement candidate. Their job performance may be impacted because of such personal motivations. Their service may not envision a long-term period.

In other instances, the recruit may be motivated by an unequivocal desire and commitment to serve the local community without regard to the attractiveness of salary or of organizational benefits. This scenario may demonstrate recruits that possess the capacity to render selfless contributions to community service. Such individuals view their law enforcement occupations as a calling and not just as a job in which financial incentives and other benefits are the primary considerations and motivations. Figure 14.5 shows a vintage recruitment poster enticing individuals to consider the calling of law enforcement.

Figure 14.5 Vintage Detroit police recruiting advertisement. (Retrieved from http://pifdetroit.tumblr.com/post/7702919716/blankkhaos-detroit-police-recruitment-poster.)

Recruitment of Minority Groups and Women

Recruitment of minority groups and women has become a major consideration for many departments. Some departments are being forced to correct disparities in the hiring of these two groups. Targeted recruitment of racial and ethnic minorities, women, and other protected groups should occur in departments that do not have appropriate representation. In the past, women have been more restricted in employment in law enforcement because of physical requirements. As a result, we are beginning to see the physical requirements being altered to reflect differences in sex and age.

The racial and ethnic minority composition of law enforcement departments in the United States in 2003 was 23.6% of full-time sworn offices. In 2000, the figure was 22.6%. Looking at the two largest minority groups, blacks made up 11.7% of local police officers and Hispanics made up a little over 9%. The percentage of women in this male-dominated profession was 11.3% in 2003, which represented less than a 1% increase from 2000.[19]

A more important motive to actively recruit minorities and women is to improve community relations. To be effective in a community and develop trust among its members, it is important that the department reflect the same diversity that the community does. Having a diverse department will help strengthen relationships and communication with minority groups because racial minority officers often bring with them a unique understanding of minority communities. The same is true for ethnic minorities. When an officer is bilingual, he or she possesses the ability to communicate with residents of a community and to provide a better understanding of the cultural values and norms of that community. For example, there are certain cultural expectations of a Hispanic community in which reporting criminal victimization will be lower when compared to non-Hispanic populations. Understanding this difference could lead an officer to provide useful feedback to the agency in better preparing and executing community policing efforts. These officers could also facilitate the connection between the department and the community.

Women have been shown to perform just as well as men in police work and are actually measured to perform better when it comes to use of force. In particular, women are more likely to be able to handle a situation without the use of excessive force. Women may also bring better relationships between the department and the community in regard to community-oriented policing. There are specific crimes in which women can be instrumental such as an agency's response to domestic violence.[20] There is, however, the problem of women being accepted into law enforcement in general by fellow officers. For years, law enforcement has been a gender-segregated profession, and in many agencies that culture still exists.

Some models exist through which the recruiting of females and minorities may be embellished. One model is identified as a collaborative model in which community participation and awareness contributes toward the recruiting effort. Figure 14.6 shows the components of this model.

This model aims to bolster the efforts of law enforcement agencies and their respective governments in increasing departmental diversity. Specifically, the model emphasizes community collaboration and mobilization to "increase the number of minorities who both apply and are selected for police positions."[21] The stages of the model encompass three primary areas: (1) community recruiting issues, (2) stakeholder action planning, and (3) implementing, monitoring, and evaluating.

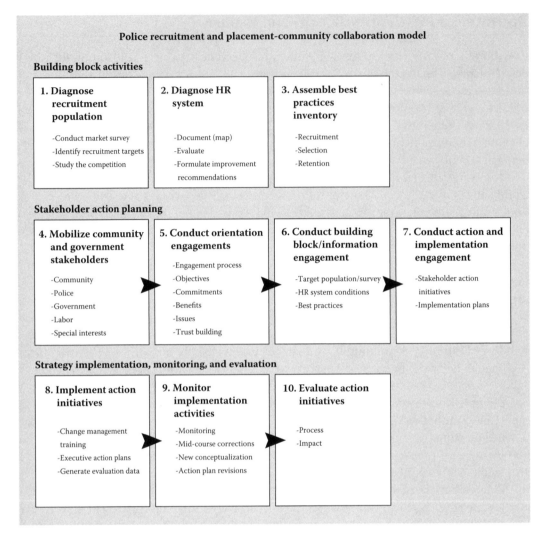

Figure 14.6 Police recruitment and placement-community collaboration model. (Courtesy of *Police Chief Magazine*. Retrieved from http://www.policechiefmagazine.org/magazine/issues/32004/pdfs/MinorityRecruitment.pdf.)

The first stage of the model examines the characteristics of the community in which the recruiting effort is exercised. This stage is critical for generating a foundational understanding of the market characteristics from which potential recruits may be identified.[22] This stage demonstrates an "assembly of a body of data on the most important characteristics of the recruitment-age and prerecruitment-age population" to focus recruiting initiatives toward recruiting candidates who are "most likely to seek a career in policing and can serve as a foundation for designing and implementing recruitment strategies."[23] This action is accomplished through a surveying of the market population to determine its characteristics and to determine which people may be strong candidates for policing employment.[24]

Although an understanding of the market population and potential candidates is necessary within the recruiting effort, the internal human resources systems of the law enforcement agency must also be considered during recruiting initiatives. During the initial stage, human resources systems must be leveraged with respect to internal policies and hiring procedures that impact the recruiting and selecting mechanisms within the organization.[25] Leveraging the human resources system of the organization facilitates the identification of the "strengths and weaknesses of jurisdictional and agency recruitment and selection policies and practices" regarding potential barriers that affect organizational hiring.[26]

Further, consideration of the human resources system must also accommodate a "goal of identifying a series of profiles, including the following: recruitment and selection attrition, adverse impact, and turnover and retention."[27] Such profiles are used to generate a stronger recruiting process and to identify improvement areas within the context of human resources.[28] These profiles are used to track the progress of applicants throughout the recruitment and selection process by maintaining statistics regarding "number of applicants, the number of applicants that appear for the initial step of the testing process, the number that survive each subsequent step in the selection process, the number that become eligible for appointment, and the number selected."[29] Grouping and stratification of data should encompass "race, gender, and other descriptors of local significance so that the evaluation can lead to specific recommendations for improvement in the process."[30]

Adverse impact profiling is used to identify process factors that may impede minority recruiting and selecting and involves constructs that detail the race, ethnicity, and sex of candidates during each stage of the model. Such data is essential when defining the potency of diversification efforts within the law enforcement agency.[31] These same characteristics are applied to both sworn and nonsworn personnel within the department to examine attributes of attrition and turnover within the organization.[32] By understanding such facets of the organization, recruiting efforts may be tailored within the targeted population and improvements may be generated within the organization itself regarding its "personnel policies and practices."[33]

The second stage of the model involves stakeholder action planning. Stakeholders are defined as individuals who have a vested interest in the success of the recruitment and selection initiative. Stakeholders may "influence the outcome, positively or negatively, in the development of strategies to address police agency recruitment and selection objectives."[34] Feedback from stakeholders is essential when considering the ramifications of community involvement and engagement during the processes of recruiting and selecting. Interaction between the law enforcement organization and the community should be mutually beneficial and interactive, thereby representing a collaborative relationship. Within the context of this relationship, the members of the community believe that their opinions are valued by the law enforcement organization.

The primary goal of this relationship involves familiarizing stakeholders with the "recruitment issues and needs that confront the police agency," in order to define and develop "responses to the issues and needs, and promote stakeholder ownership and commitment to implementing the responses."[35] This stage of the model culminates in the crafting of an action plan through which recruiting and selecting initiatives may be exercised both efficiently and effectively.

The third and final stage of the model involves implementing, monitoring, and evaluating the action plan. This stage involves active participation by both the community and the law enforcement organization. Collaboration between the law enforcement organization and community members encompasses "clear information with regard to the plan's objectives, task definitions, staffing, timetables, and the evolving nature of plans, generally."[36]

The implementation of the action plan involves monitoring throughout its entirety. The use of monitoring may provide an understanding of any changes within the community or unanticipated issues that affect the potential of the recruiting and selecting processes.[37] Evaluation is a tool through which a law enforcement organization may "measure the degree to which objectives have been achieved" with respect to determining whether increases of "minority recruitment and selection" are occurring.[38] Further, evaluation should also occur regarding the recruiting and selecting process itself. By examining the process itself, law enforcement organizations may improve the methods through which recruiting and selecting occur. Identifying shortcomings, rectifying defects, and improving these processes improves the ability of the law enforcement agency to conduct any future recruiting and selecting initiatives.

This model is not unique to any certain law enforcement organization. It may be applied to small agencies as well as larger organizations. It may be tailored and crafted to suit the needs of practically any law enforcement organization that pursues a diversity initiative through time. It also demonstrates a valuing of the society that is served by the organization through its collaborative facets. It also presents an opportunity to refine organizational hiring practices and policies.

Further, this model also represents a systematic, methodical approach to hiring. It provides a logical foundation through which a specific market may be identified and targeted for acquiring new personnel within the law enforcement organization. Because it may be tailored to the characteristics of the served population, this model embellishes the ability of law enforcement organizations to implement recruitment and selection activities that emphasize the acquisition of females and minorities.

Police Training

Training is a key element in any successful law enforcement agency. Training has to be not only ongoing, but also embraced as a necessary element of the law enforcement function. Training is not just about professional or tactical proficiency. It is a function of training to help the individual officer realize the importance of the impression he or she makes upon the public.[39]

Most officers have a probationary period of 6 to 18 months. During this time, the officer must complete training at the academy. The average number of hours that officers must complete is 628 hours in the academy and an average of 328 hours in field training.[40]

The characteristics of training academies are not static throughout the nation. Some states and localities have extremely stringent requirements for candidates, whereas others may be considerably easier to satisfy. For example, applicants for a full-time law enforcement position in Mississippi must satisfy a course training regimen consisting of a minimum of 400 hours of training.[41] However, in the neighboring state of Alabama, law enforcement basic training consists of a minimum of 480 hours.[42] Throughout the nation, states have varying requirements and training programs for admitting candidates into the domain of law enforcement. Within the state of California, the South Bay Regional Public Safety Training Consortium facilitates a minimum of 880 hours of training.[43] The Southern Arizona Law Enforcement Training Center facilitates a minimum 640-hour training regimen.[44] Similar differences exist when comparing training requirements for both part-time and full-time officers among the remainder of the states.

Academies are typically run by the state or a local agency that serve several jurisdictions. During classroom training, cadets learn search and seizure laws, laws surrounding arrest and interrogations, and constitutional law. Cadets learn how to work with various service agencies in the community, how to administer first aid, and how to manage crisis intervention. Tactical skills instruction teaches cadets how to arrest a suspect, the use of weapons and investigative techniques such as how to secure a crime scene, and how to conduct interviews of witnesses. During this process, instructors teach and evaluate the recruit's performance. These evaluations along with progress reports are sent to police administrators.

Once admitted to the police academy, cadets are required to participate in a vigorous physical fitness program. During this training, progress is measured and a physical fitness test is administered. The exact measurement of the physical fitness test will vary by academy, sex, and age of the cadet. Being physically fit is an important aspect of policing because law enforcement officers must be physically capable of performing their duties and handling the stress associated with this job. Physical fitness has been determined to be an occupational qualification that predicts job performance.

The physical fitness requirements differ among states. Within Arizona, "A typical physical fitness routine for recruits includes an up to four mile run at a 10 minute per mile pace, 20 to 40 sit-ups or crunches, 20 to 40 push-ups, 10 to 20 chin-ups, and 10 to 20 dips."[45] The entry-level requirements in Florida at the beginning of the police academy program consist of demonstrating the ability to complete at least 15 push-ups and 25 sit-ups within 1 minute, and complete a 1.5 mile run within 18 minutes.[46] Similar differences exist throughout the nation.

Field training is the second major learning requirement for new recruits. The officer is paired with an experienced police officer. This experienced officer is tasked with teaching the "rookie" officer practical information that translates to street policing. They will handle real situations and not simulations as the experienced officer transmits information that helps the officer police in that particular community. A community is comprised of a diverse group of individuals, and the real situation can rarely be captured in a classroom or in the academy. It is this field training that allows for "hands-on" experience without pushing new officers out on their own before they are prepared.

Certain skills can only be learned through experience. For example, discretion is used by law enforcement and is learned on the job. During field training, more experienced officers show and teach "rookie" officers when and how to use discretion. Discretion is a difficult area to teach and administer because many situations that police find themselves in are tense, dangerous, and demand immediate reactions. There is no time to consult a supervisor, and the consequences of any given decision could be a person's reputation, their freedom, or their lives. For these reasons, it becomes very important that officers make wise, intelligent, and compassionate decisions.

During field training, the "rookie" will ride with a field-training officer for a period of time, and this officer will send periodic reports to the chief or top administrator. After completing field training, officers will continue to ride with other officers until their official training or probationary period is over. Once an officer has successfully completed this probationary period, the officer is a full member of the police department.

The development of the officer is not just a responsibility of the academy or of the field training officer. Continual development of personnel is one of the most important responsibilities of a first-line supervisor. The first-line supervisor is expected to provide continuous on-the-job training (OJT) to their subordinates so that they can fulfill their duties in the most effective and efficient manner possible and in compliance with all agency regulations and procedures.

Throughout an officer's career, there will be a certain amount of continuing education credits that will be required to remain certified or licensed. These may include instruction from a criminal justice approach or training on new techniques, legislation, or compliances. Approximately 24 of these hours will be state mandated and 23 hours will be departmental in-service training.[47]

Through experiencing the rigors of an academy, bonding occurs among the participating individuals. A sense of belonging and brotherhood is crafted through time. Participants learn to operate as teams, and to administer the use of discretion when rendering decisions as individuals. Participants learn to recognize situations that may become increasingly dangerous, and learn the basics of officer safety. Certainly, candidates are trained in the essentials of marksmanship and self-defense.

Police academies exist to provide individuals who are capable of rendering public service mentally and physically. Although differences exist among training regimens nationally, an overall goal of police training is to produce graduates who are capable of contributing successfully to the policing goals of deterring crime and maintaining societal order. Training academies also serve as tools through which weak or uncommitted candidates may be eliminated during periods of stressfulness and evaluation thereby generating graduates of some quality and dedication.

Performance Reviews

Performance reviews are a common aspect of most any profession or vocation. They may be administered periodically ranging anywhere from monthly or quarterly to annual periods. These reviews encompass a review of the individual by a supervisor and may incorporate peer commentaries regarding the performance of the individual. In addition to performance reviews by supervisors many departments have implemented a practice of the supervisor being evaluated by the subordinate. This evaluation provides the administration valuable insights as to how the rank and file view the supervisors and if the goals and objectives of the administration are being implemented at the first and second line supervisory levels of the organization.

Performance reviews serve as a tool through which the behavior and job performance of officers may be tuned and adjusted through time to correct any defects and to improve the performance of the officer. When a new officer enters a law enforcement agency, some performance reviews may occur at the end of a probationary period to determine the strengths and weaknesses of the new employee. Performance reviews may be affiliated with promotion potential or recommendations for specialized training programs.

Further, performance reviews may involve the specification of goals and objectives that must be satisfied during a targeted period of time. In such cases, the reviewed officer and supervisor collaboratively identify specific goals and objectives that should be accomplished (e.g., completion of continuing education, physical fitness improvements, etc.) within a specific period of time. Completing the identified goals and objectives facilitates a sense of accomplishment and successfulness. Such accomplishments may be useful when personnel are reviewed for pay increases or organizational accolades (Figure 14.7).

Performance reviews may be viewed as mutually beneficial for both the reviewing organization and the individual being reviewed. Shortcomings may be identified and corrected, thereby potentially improving the efficiency and effectiveness of the officer. Reviewed

Figure 14.7 One of the major responsibilities of law enforcement leadership is the establishment of a positive officer recognition program. Here, Officer Kelly Rouse (left) is receiving the Officer of the Year award from University of Charleston Police Chief Jack Rinchich (right), the President of the Police Hall of Fame and the National President of the National Association of Chiefs of Police, as well as the National Chaplain. (From *Berea Online*, 2012. Retrieved from http://bereaonline.com/?p=9283.)

personnel may gain a better understanding of how their functions, roles, and responsibilities contribute toward the overall workings of their group and organization. If one is experiencing difficulty in the assigned position, performance reviews may be useful in determining whether the officer may be better suited for a different job responsibility or a different organizational component.

Performance reviews generally occur as a component of the performance management process (PMP). This process is indicative of a cyclic construct that shows the "achievement of performance goals within a specific time frame."[48] Included within the PMP are the establishing of performance goals, "performance review systems, performance monitoring, and personnel development."[49] Using this type of system contributes toward the crafting of an organizational culture that emphasizes performance as an aspect of personnel motivation and the achieving of defined goals.[50]

The PMP is cyclic and repeats itself through time periodically. It involves defining and understanding of personnel and organizational goals and objectives that must be achieved through time. A discussion of whether the goals and objectives from the preceding were satisfied may also be incorporated within the discussions between the reviewer and the individual being reviewed. In many cases, performance reviews incorporate commentaries and feedback from the person being reviewed to highlight any ancillary concerns or clarifications of discussions. Some personnel may be allowed to write self-assessments to enhance performance reviews. Such self-assessments may justify the behaviors and actions of personnel during the review period.

Performance reviews may be mutually agreed upon by the supervisor and reviewed personnel. They may also be forwarded upwards throughout the organizational hierarchy for further review and approval. Supervisors, the reviewed personnel, and human resources departments may retain copies of personnel reviews. Finalization of performance reviews signifies a mutual understanding and approval of all associated parties that participate in the review process.

After finalization, personnel experience the next review period in which they attempt to satisfy the goals and objectives that were established during the review discussions that occurred between the reviewer and the personnel being reviewed. Once the review period expires, the supervisor and reviewed personnel again meet to discuss the performance that occurred during the reviewed period. This event represents the beginning of the PMP again within its next cyclic iteration. Figure 14.8 shows the cyclic attributes of the PMP.

Performance reviews may alleviate factors that contribute toward job dissatisfaction and burnout among officers. Reviewed officers may have an opportunity to voice their concerns and aspirations. During reviews, both the organization and officer may discuss issues of satisfaction or dissatisfaction. Through such interaction, discussions may occur regarding future expectations and responsibilities. These discussions may counter problematic issues or issues that may become problematic in time.

Performance reviews show levels of improvement or degradation of performance through time that may contribute toward decisions regarding personnel retention. Retaining quality personnel is beneficial for any organization. Through the use of performance reviews, law enforcement agencies may determine which individuals show promise for promotion and additional responsibilities, may be better suited for different responsibilities or tasks within the organization, or may need to seek other professions or vocations.

Performance reviews may also contribute toward the retaining of officers among law enforcement agencies. Because of the mutual understanding of goals and objectives between

Figure 14.8 Performance management process. (Courtesy of George Washington University, 2010. Retrieved from http://www.gwu.edu/hr/manual/performance/evaluations.html.)

the organization and its personnel, individuals have an understanding of exactly what is required of them during the reviewed period. They understand what constitutes success or failure within the context of employment. They understand the available opportunities for career growth and progression within the organization and can judge whether they are progressing satisfactorily toward any ultimate goals. These considerations contribute toward open and mutual communication between the reviewed officer and the law enforcement agency. Through such communication and the establishing of objectives and goals mutually, personnel may experience fewer difficulties and have greater opportunities to avoid problems organizationally and with respect to any performance expectations. As a result, personnel may be inclined to remain employed by the law enforcement agency.

Retention of Police Officers

In 2003, 61% of local police departments had at least one officer leave their department either through retirement, resignation, or dismissal.[51] Because the process of recruiting and training of police officers is so expensive and time consuming, it is important to retain those officers that have been selected for employment. Retaining employees is not only cost effective but beneficial for the department. An agency that has low turnover rates will be a department that has stable and well-organized administration. When a department is unable to keep officers, the department becomes inefficient and incapable of meeting the community's needs. There will be a disruption in services, lower quality of those services, and an increased probability of being sued for mistakes. For these reasons, it is important to take into consideration that it is not only the cost of sending a recruit to the academy and the pay associated with field training, but the costs that are involved in lawsuits and unsteady community relations that are the results of an unstable police department.

When there is a high turnover rate in a department, there are also the costs of crime to the community. When a department is unable to function properly and respond to crime, then crime rates will begin to escalate. Even when there are candidates to replace those more experienced officers who are retiring or resigning, there is a learning curve that must be met. It takes time for an officer to learn the skills needed to be proficient on the "street," and during the interim there can be resultant problems for the agency.

The majority of separations for departments are a result of individuals resigning. In 2003, there were over 16,000 resignations compared to 9000 retirements and approximately 2600 dismissals.[52] Some factors that contribute to high turnover rates include low pay and working conditions. Across the U.S., there is little conformity in salaries among police departments. Salary is usually dependent upon the size of the department and its ability to pay. Other salary factors are cost of living in an area and comparable pay scales of neighboring departments. Typically, a department is set up on a pay scale with a starting salary for new hires with an increase in pay after six months. After this initial pay increase, raises are given each year until the officer reaches the top pay for the position that he or she holds. After reaching the top salary, which typically occurs after 3 to 5 years, the only way to increase one's pay is to be promoted to a different position. There is a starting and top salary for each rank or position within the department.

In addition to salary, fringe benefits are important and may include medical, dental, vision, and life insurance. Other incentives include vacation pay and sick leave. Supplementary benefits that can help with retention of experienced officers would be deferred compensation, incentive pay for college education, tuition reimbursement, retirement funds, and a pension plan. These along with promotional opportunities can be useful in retaining quality officers.

There are also ways to address problems with a department and look at the underlying causes for a high turnover rate. Women are more likely to leave a department that tolerates sexual harassment. Having "zero tolerance" for this behavior can go a long way in recruiting and retaining female officers. Police departments that experience high levels of sexual harassment tend to be resistant to change. Male officers in these departments are less accepting of the increasing number of female officers in a male-dominated profession. There is an overall reluctance of administrators to deal with sexual harassment in their departments, and there is pressure for women who want to be accepted in the career to not report incidents. The best way to deal with this problem and how it relates to the retention of female officers is prevention. Education, rules, and policies in the department are a positive way to address this problem.

An added major source of officer attrition is stress and in particular long-term stress that leads to burnout. The inherent nature of the job of policing has high stress situations that occur with almost every shift. Law enforcement as a career is partly controlling and resolving conflict between citizens of their community. Many situations can be volatile and unpredictable. Crime rates are higher in cities with a larger population. This may be a contributing factor for higher levels of stress, burnout, and resignation among officers. In 2003, almost every local police department that had a population of 50,000 or more residents had officers leave, whereas less than half of departments had a separation with a population of fewer than 2500 residents.[53] There are also demands built into the job that cause stress such as job performance within the department, relationships with the community, relationships with the media, and relationships with political entities.

Stress is a condition where the demands placed on a person create a reaction. This reaction may be physical and/or emotional. Many people choose a career in law enforcement in order to have a level of stress and excitement in their lives. There are many situations that a law enforcement officer faces that could be considered positive stress or excitement. These episodes may be short and intense and not result in an excessive amount of stress for the individual. Continual stress, however, can lead to more consequences for a person because it can cause physical and emotional problems. Long-term stress can lead to a crisis for the police officer that may lead to burnout.

For the police officer, change and uncertainty may be a major work stressor. Officers who are responding to a call have no idea how that situation is going to unfold. The uncertainty of the situation can create heightened levels of anxiety and adrenaline. When dealing with the public, a conversation with a citizen can quickly turn from a calm exchange to a highly intense situation that could lead to a life-threatening situation. There are several factors that are out of the control of the officer such as how that person is going to behave, and if an arrest does happen, whether that offender be successfully prosecuted. Shift work can also be a stressor for some police officers. Working different shifts, day and night or more than 8 hours at a time can cause a form of physical stress.[54]

Overall, police officers can suffer mental and physical problems similar to military personnel such as posttraumatic stress disorder or PTSD. Symptoms from this disorder will include extreme fatigue, disinterest, cynicism, and a diminished sex drive.[55] All these symptoms created from their work environment can translate into problems with family and home life. Problems at home can lead to an additional source of stress for the officer.

Inherent in the job of law enforcement is isolation and the expectations of the public for individuals to live and behave at such a high standard, and these factors can cause additional stress. For example, many hours are spent alone on patrol which can lead to stress. There is also the fact that officers are constantly dealing with the criminal element of our society. These are individuals that often lack the self control to follow the rules of society and sometimes what we consider human decency. Officers in many jurisdictions are continually exposed to violence, and individuals who lie and are cruel to one another, to children, and to the elderly. These working conditions can lead to circumstances in which these stressors invade other areas of the officer's life.

High levels of stress can lead to burnout. An officer is burned out when they no longer have a desire to meet the conditions of their job. They tend to lack enthusiasm and overall interest in the job and other people. There is the resultant decrease in job performance, motivation, and commitment to the job.[56] While job burnout is a negative condition for the officer to experience, it also has consequences for the department. When a department has apathetic officers, there is the potential that they will not deliver quality services, and worse yet, the office may not react in an appropriate way to a stressful situation. The worst scenario would be an officer that is disinterested in his or her job reacting inappropriately in a life-threatening situation.

Many departments recognize the stress that is inherent in the job and take steps to help officers effectively deal with job stress. While these programs are a step in the right direction, it is ultimately up to the officer to recognize stressors of the job and take steps to manage these pressures. There are several activities that individuals can engage in to help reduce stress, such as maintaining a healthy lifestyle that includes exercise and a healthy diet. Long-term stress that is not addressed can lead to physical ailments, dependence on drugs and alcohol, depression, marriage problems, and, in the worst case, suicide.

The classic signs and symptoms of burnout include the following:

- Chronic negativism
- Cynicism
- Anger
- Second-guessing oneself and others
- Lateness
- Incomplete projects
- A decay in the quality of work performed on the job
- A resentment of supervisors, even clients
- Extramarital affairs
- Increased risk taking
- A sense of desperation that life is slipping away
- A general dissatisfaction with life, family, career
- The desire to relocate geographically
- The desire to change careers
- The desire to divorce
- Increased alcohol and/or tobacco use
- Depression
- Panic attacks
- A fear of aging
- Dressing and acting much younger
- A sense of foreshortened future

::Surviving Stress::
(Retreat for Law Enforcement)

"Surviving stress" -Stress is a common part of our daily lives and how we deal with stress determines, in many ways, the quality of our lives. Law enforcement officers experience higher levels and more unique types of stress than the rest of society. There are things officers are exposed to that are difficult to understand and process. Being in charge of our stress is the key to not letting it control our lives. Depending on the time, amount, duration and intensity of stress, we all reach a critical limit that differs for each individual. We want to work towards avoiding the stress taking control of our lives. We will talk about the kinds of stress we face and the impact of that stress and ways to do self-care and weather the storms of stress (specific to law enforcement officers) that is out of our control and learn to rely on God's strength so that we can increase our lifespan and quality of life. This retreat is designed for law enforcement officers (and spouses) and will be led by LAPD Chaplain Father Mike McCullough and Alhambra PD Chaplain Dr. Mary Glenn who have a combination of 47 years in law enforcement chaplaincy.

Date: October 2–3, 2010 (Saturday am through Sunday lunch) **Limited to 25 participants.**
Location: The Desert Refuge for Peace Officers in Joshua Tree, CA **Website:** http://www.drpo.org/
Cost: $25 suggested donation, plus costs for own hotel room
For more info and/or to register: DesertRefugeforPeaceOfficer@gmail.com Father Mike McCullough (323) 298-7174

Figure 14.9 Advertisement for Officer Stress Survival Event. Stress is one of the major health concerns for law enforcement personnel. (Courtesy of the LAPD. Retrieved from http://lapd. com/events/surviving_stress_retreat_for_law_enforcement/.)

In the most extreme variations, stress and burnout may be associated with suicidal, even homicidal, thoughts. Reducing stress and personnel revitalization are essential components of policing. Often, counseling sessions and various sequestering of personnel may occur to address such issues. Figure 14.9 presents a sample advertisement for such a retreat.

Role and Development of Field Training Officers, First-Line Supervisors, and the Command Team

It is hard to imagine a law enforcement agency operating effectively without a solid command team composed of field training officers, first-line supervisors, and a command team. Field training officers play an essential role in the development of new officers. They work directly to train new officers so that each is prepared to function as a single beat officer at the conclusion of their training cycle.

First-line police supervisors, often titled sergeants and lieutenants, provide the supervision of police employees who are directly involved with the day-to-day delivery of police services. First-line supervisors and field training officers have the greatest impact on the organizational culture of a law enforcement agency. Despite this, many departments fail to expend any significant effort towards influencing the attitudes of these individuals, thereby managing the culture of their agencies. If a first-line supervisor displays a negative attitude, he will likely infect an entire squad of officers, causing declining morale and low productivity.

The command team is composed of personnel including the chief and assistant chiefs and administrative support staff. It falls to the command team to ensure that the agency is running efficiently and effectively.

Human Resources Contexts

The recruiting, selecting, training, and maintaining of officers and other law enforcement personnel are functions of human resources management. The most precious assets of any organization are the people who comprise its ranks. This notion is recognized by most law enforcement agencies through investments in specific human resource or personnel departments. Generally, these departments exist to design organizational systems formally towards a purpose of ensuring the "effective and efficient use of human talent to accomplish organizational goals."[57]

Three facets of human resources management affect law enforcement organizations: (1) strategic, (2) administrative, and (3) operational.[58] The strategic aspect emphasizes the value of humans with respect to a long-term organizational perspective. In this case, career planning and progression may incorporate long-term, achievable goals and objectives that new officers may strive to attain through time. For example, one may desire to work their way upwards through the existing ranks of hierarchy to assume a leadership position. Administrative and operational facets address the daily personnel issues of law enforcement organizations ranging from compliance with organizational policies and procedure to mentorship programs for new officers. For example, new officers may be paired with experienced officers who can mentor and guide their progress within the law enforcement organization.

An example of incorporate human resources management functions is manifested within the Delaware State Police. A primary human resources management goal of the Delaware State Police is to design and manage "formal systems to ensure the effective and efficient use of human talent to accomplish the organization's goals. The procurement of organizational objectives requires focusing on tasks and concerns relative to staffing, compensation and employee benefits, health and wellness, employee development, labor/management relations and equal employment opportunities/affirmative action compliance."[59] Within its human resources section, the Delaware State Police oversees activities that are associated with the following endeavors, policies, and programs:

- Contract negotiations
- Handling grievances and lawsuits
- Sworn and civilian hiring
- Administering the performance appraisal system
- Recruitment and retention of Delaware State Police employees
- Employee assistance program
- Administration of the random drug testing program
- Equal employment opportunity complaints
- Family Medical Leave Act
- Workman's compensation
- Payroll and benefits
- Military deployments
- Maintenance of employee's personnel files
- Pension applications

Human resources or personnel departments enhance the ability of law enforcement agencies to perform a variety of functions that range from prospecting communities to identifying potential officer recruits to tracking career progression and performance throughout the duration of employment. These departments also may perform a variety of statistical functions to determine strengths, weaknesses, opportunities, and threats that may exist within the departmental workforce or among the recruiting base within its served population.

Human resources or personnel departments may be useful when determining whether interventions are necessary among police personnel to counter destructive behaviors or to counter other potential problems. Tools exist through which law enforcement agencies may "monitor officers whose behavior places departments at risk, erodes public confidence, increases liability, and undermines effectiveness."[60] One such tool is the risk analysis management system (RAMS). The RAMS mechanism provides an ability to track officer performance internally, determine which officers may be classified as "at risk" personnel, intervene during the onset of problematic issues to potentially yield a "positive and constructive solution," and potentially reduce the dangers of legal actions that may be directed against a department.[61]

Using these types of human resources tools provide law enforcement agencies with the potential abilities to reduce turnover, affect attrition, and avoid adverse outcomes of lawsuits. Rectifying aberrant human behavior may contribute toward the retaining of personnel and increased satisfaction of employment with the law enforcement organization. Retaining such personnel does not incur the costs of recruiting, training, and seasoning new officers, and ensures that a loss of experiential knowledge does not occur within the law enforcement agency.

Humans are the most important facet of any law enforcement organization. Humans possess knowledge that is acquired through time and experience. Humans form relationships within the agency and externally within the community. Experienced offers may serve as role models and mentors for newer officers. Humans uniquely contribute toward the sum of the whole of any organization. Given these notions, law enforcement agencies must be mindful of the importance of human resources management regarding their initiatives of recruiting, selecting, training, and maintaining personnel.

Other Administrative and Command Responsibilities

As we have stated, the law enforcement administrator is responsible for everything that does and does not occur within the agency. While the law enforcement administrator has the responsibility for what occurs, this does not necessarily mean they have the resources or the authority to control all dimensions of the agency. Planning, budgeting, directing, controlling, developing departmental policies and procedures, and performing public or community relations all fall within the scope of administrative responsibilities. Facets of controlling, leading, organizing, planning, and coordinating are essential within the context of leading and managing law enforcement organizations. It is the wise administrator who can balance these duties and responsibilities effectively while maintaining both agency and community support.

Summary

A career in law enforcement can be exciting and fulfilling. As with any career, it is important to conduct proper research and to understand the qualifications for the job. This may lead to the need for physical and educational training before one fills out the first application. Law enforcement jobs require extensive training that will be an investment by the department that chooses to employ an individual. Understanding the factors associated with job satisfaction and job burnout will help one make that investment a sound one.

Policing is a benevolent occupation. Some may serve for decades whereas others may serve only a few weeks or months. Regardless, those who enter the ranks of policing are generally motivated by a commitment to serve others and to faithfully render public service. Maintaining societal order and deterring crime are responsibilities that are shared among all law enforcement agencies and officers.

Law enforcement organizations must be mindful that their employees must have some amount of satisfaction. Although a desire to serve and commitment to public service are paramount aspects of the policing profession, other motivators include competitive salaries and benefits versus the endangerments of the occupation and its responsibilities. Even police officers must accumulate retirement savings and pay their monthly bills ranging from mortgages to car payments.

Recruiting and selecting candidates are continuous considerations of all law enforcement agencies. Regardless of organizational size, individuals will leave departments because of numerous reasons ranging from other job opportunities to death and from occupational burnout to medical reasons. Therefore, replacement officers are a consideration of all law enforcement entities. Using a systematic, methodical approach that incorporates community participation and feedback actively embellishes the ability of law enforcement agencies to recruit and select candidates for potential employment.

Training academies exist throughout the nation to provide well-trained graduates that contribute toward the goals of deterring crime and maintaining societal order. Although the concepts taught in law enforcement training academies are similar, differences exist throughout the nation. Law enforcement academies generally emphasize officer safety, academics, physical fitness, self-defense, road safety, and marksmanship. However, differences exist regarding an understanding of different state laws, physical fitness requirements, and the quantities of hours that are mandated for officer certifications among the states.

Performance reviews must be viewed as positive events that are mutually beneficial for both the law enforcement organization and the reviewed officer. Performance reviews provide a method of identifying and addressing issues of concern for both the law enforcement agency and the reviewed officer. Performance reviews may contribute toward long-term career decisions and the conferring of accolades. Further, performance reviews may be used to identify issues that may potentially contribute toward occupational burnout or job dissatisfaction among officers.

Retaining quality personnel is a concern of all law enforcement agencies. When a department is unable to keep officers, the department becomes inefficient and incapable of meeting the community's needs. There will be a disruption in services, lower quality of those services, and an increased probability of being sued for mistakes. Retaining employees is not only cost–effective, but also beneficial for the department. An agency that has low turnover rates will be a department that has a stable and well-organized administration.

Humans are the basic element of any organization, and represent the most precious of organizational assets. This concept is a foundational principle of human resources management. Three facets of human resources management affect law enforcement organizations: (1) strategic, (2) administrative, and (3) operational. The strategic aspect emphasizes the value of humans with respect to a long-term organizational perspective. Administrative

Figure 14.10 Much of the activities of law enforcement personnel are non-crime related. (From Forman, J., 2009, *The News-Herald.* Retrieved from http://www.news-herald.com/articles/2009/10/02/news/nh1484868.txt#photo2.)

and operational facets address the daily personnel issues of law enforcement organizations ranging from compliance with organizational policies and procedure to mentorship programs for new officers.

Members of the general public form perceptions of law enforcement agencies based on their own direct and indirect experiences. Therefore, law enforcement organizations must attempt to field the best quality officers daily. Investments must be made not only towards recruiting and selecting quality candidates, but also for maintaining and retaining quality personnel through time (Figure 14.10).

Discussion Questions

1. Recruiting, selecting, training, and maintaining officers are relevant aspects of human resources management among law enforcement organizations. Define each of these terms and discuss how your local law enforcement agency implements these activities.

2. All law enforcement organizations must be concerned with officer burnout and job dissatisfaction. Define both of these terms. Discuss how your local law enforcement agency attempts to counter the effects of burnout and the methods it uses to improve job satisfaction.

3. Certification requirements differ among the individual states regarding entry into the law enforcement domain. Determine the certification requirements that exist for your state. Compare and contrast your certification requirements to those of your neighboring states. What similarities and differences exist?

4. Most organizations conduct performance reviews of their personnel annually. Determine the frequency and type of performance reviews that are used by your

local law enforcement agency. Based on your findings, how does your local law enforcement agency use performance reviews to support career progression, personnel retention, and departmental accolades?

5. The primary functions of management are controlling, leading, organizing, planning, and coordinating. Please define each of these terms and discuss examples of how they are exercised within your local law enforcement organization. Further, from a long-term, strategic perspective, what are some of the effects of each of these items?

References

1. Wilson, O. W. (1963). *Police Administration*. New York, NY: McGraw-Hill.
2. U.S. Department of Justice (2003). *Local Police Departments*. Retrieved May 16, 2010, from http://bjs.ojp.usdoj.gov/content/pub/pdf/lpd03.pdf
3. Ibid.
4. Ibid.
5. Leonard, V. A., & Harry, M. (1978). *Police Organization and Management* (5th ed.). Mineola, NY: The Foundation Press.
6. Wilson, O. W. (1963). *Police Administration*. New York, NY: McGraw-Hill.
7. Peel, R. (2012). Police quotes. *BrainyQuote*. Retrieved March 29, 2012, from http://www.brainyquote.com/quotes/keywords/police_9.html
8. Kramer, J. (2010). Mobile Police Department attrition hits 10-year low. *Press-Register*. Retrieved March 29, 2012, from http://blog.al.com/live/2010/01/mobile_police_department_attri.html
9. Ibid.
10. Ibid.
11. Ibid.
12. Ibid.
13. Hess, K. (2006). *Introduction to Law Enforcement and Criminal Justice*. Stamford, Cambridge: Delmar Cengage Learning.
14. Federal Bureau of Investigation (2010). *Careers*. Retrieved June 30, 2010, from http://www.fbijobs.gov/1261.asp
15. Hess, K. (2006). *Introduction to Law Enforcement and Criminal Justice*. Stamford, Cambridge: Delmar Cengage Learning.
16. Gaines, L., & Miller, R. (2011). *Criminal Justice in Action*. Stamford, Cambridge.
17. U.S. Department of Justice (2003). *Local Police Departments*. Retrieved May 28, 2010, from http://bjs.ojp.usdoj.gov/content/pub/pdf/lpd03.pdf
18. Hess, K. (2006). *Introduction to Law Enforcement and Criminal Justice*. Stamford, Cambridge.
19. U.S. Department of Justice (2003). *Local Police Departments*. Retrieved May 28, 2010, from http://bjs.ojp.usdoj.gov/content/pub/pdf/lpd03.pdf
20. Hess, K. (2006). *Introduction to Law Enforcement and Criminal Justice*. Stamford, Cambridge.
21. Tangel, W. Minority recruitment: A working model. *The Police Chief*. Retrieved March 2, 2012, from http://www.policechiefmagazine.org/magazine/index.cfm?fuseaction=display&article_id=254&issue_id=32004
22. Ibid.
23. Ibid.
24. Ibid.
25. Ibid.
26. Ibid.
27. Ibid.
28. Ibid.

29. Ibid.
30. Ibid.
31. Ibid.
32. Ibid.
33. Ibid.
34. Ibid.
35. Ibid.
36. Ibid.
37. Ibid.
38. Ibid.
39. Wilson, O.W. (1963). *Police Administration*. New York, NY: McGraw-Hill.
40. U.S. Department of Justice (2003). *Local Police Departments*. Retrieved May 28, 2010, from http://bjs.ojp.usdoj.gov/content/pub/pdf/lpd03.pdf
41. Welcome to the MSU police department. *Mississippi State University*. Retrieved March 29, 2012, from http://www.police.msstate.edu/welcome
42. South Bay Regional Public Safety Training Consortium. *Basic Training*. Northeast Alabama Law Enforcement Academy. Retrieved March 29, 2012, from http://lea.jsu.edu/
43. *Basic Police Academy #115*. Retrieved March 29, 2012, from http://www.theacademy.ca.gov/flyer_details/node/3234
44. *Basic Training*. Southern Arizona Law Enforcement Training Center. Retrieved March 29, 2012, from http://cms3.tucsonaz.gov/police/basic-training
45. Arizona Law Enforcement Academy (2012). *Physical Fitness Preparation Guide*, ALEA/Phoenix police department. Retrieved March 29, 2012, from http://www.google.com/url?sa=t&rct=j&q=arizona%20law%20enforcement%20physical%20fitness&source=web&cd=1&ved=0CCQQFjAA&url=http%3A%2F%2Fwww.glendaleaz.com%2Fpolice%2Fupload%2Falea%2520physical%2520fitness%2520guide%25202003color.pdf&ei=9Z13T_TqN8fqtgf83tmODw&usg=AFQjCNFwDWokQB4mZc_hK8bUMBvTRWBQGQ&cad=rja
46. *Orlando Police Department Police Recruiting*. Orlando Police Department. Retrieved March 29, 2012, from http://www.cityoforlando.net/police/misc/recruiting_pat_test.htm
47. U.S. Department of Justice (2003). *Local Police Departments*. Retrieved May 28, 2010, from http://bjs.ojp.usdoj.gov/content/pub/pdf/lpd03.pdf
48. Battacharyya, D. (2011). *Performance Management Systems and Strategies*. Noida, India: Pearson.
49. Ibid.
50. Ibid.
51. U.S. Department of Justice (2003). *Local Police Departments*. Retrieved May 28, 2010, from http://bjs.ojp.usdoj.gov/content/pub/pdf/lpd03.pdf
52. Ibid.
53. Ibid.
54. Hess, K. (2006). *Introduction to Law Enforcement and Criminal Justice*. Stamford, Cambridge.
55. Ibid.
56. Bennett, W., & Hess, K. (2007). *Management and Supervision in Law Enforcement*. Stamford, Cambridge.
57. *Human Resources Management at KCKCC*. Kansas City Kansas Community College. Retrieved March 29, 2012, from http://www.kckcc.edu/services/employment/humanResources ManagementAtKCKCC
58. Ibid.
59. *Delaware State Police Human Resources Section*. State of Delaware. Retrieved March 29, 2012, from http://dsp.delaware.gov/human%20resources.shtml

60. *Early Warning and Intervention Systems*. Police Foundation. Retrieved March 29, 2012, from http://www.policefoundation.org/docs/prof_services.html#pcr
61. *Features and Benefits*. Risk Analysis Management System. Retrieved March 29, 2012, from http://www.policefoundation.org/docs/rq_benefits.html

Bibliography

Tangel, W. Minority recruitment: A working model. *The Police Chief*. Retrieved March 29, 2012, from http://www.policechiefmagazine.org/magazine/index.cfm?fuseaction=display&article_id=254&issue_id=32004

The Future of Law Enforcement and Its Changing Role 15

Prediction is very difficult, especially about the future.

Niels Bohr

Learning Objectives

The objectives of this chapter are to

- Discuss trends that may affect the future of law enforcement
- Understand technologies that may affect the future of law enforcement
- Explain the concept of emerging technologies
- Understand the ramifications that emerging technologies and other factors will have on policing

Introduction

The law enforcement profession has evolved throughout the ages. What began as the "cop on the beat" turned into the era of professional policing in the first half of the twentieth century. Today, we are surrounded by a smorgasbord of policing philosophies: Some agencies claim to do community policing while others say they are guided by the COMPSTAT accountability model. Still others insist that their policing philosophy is intelligence led.

The focus of this chapter is not on the present but on the future—where is law enforcement headed? In particular, what skills will the police professional of tomorrow need to successfully navigate the uncertain waters of the twenty-first century? To understand that, we need to have some idea of the future that awaits us. In particular, there are five major areas that deserve consideration:

1. Technological trends
2. Demographic trends
3. Economic and social trends
4 Crime trends
5. Emerging technologies

Once these have been examined, we will discuss the type of law enforcement agency that can best meet the challenges of the future. To be sure, Niels Bohr's admonition at the beginning of the chapter deserves special attention. No one can predict the future with certainty; therefore, although some of the trends we discuss will no doubt come to pass, others may not. Readers should feel free to use their own judgment to construct the "futures" they think may emerge. Better still, readers should decide the sort of agency and law enforcement professional that can best serve their community.

Technological Trends

Perhaps the most important thing to understand about technology is the amazing rate at which it is developing. Just a few short years ago, if a bird was "tweeting," it was making a chirping sound. Likewise, a "Facebook" was literally a book full of photographs. If you are under the age of 30, things that you take for granted—personal computers, high definition television, and "downloading"—were not around when your parents were growing up. It is difficult to remember that it took mankind fewer than 70 years to go from the Wright Brothers to walking on the moon.

One thing that seems certain about technology is the rate at which it is progressing is not even and orderly. Instead, new innovations keep being developed faster and faster. Noted author and inventor Ray Kurzweil calls this the "law of accelerating returns," which he describes as follows:

> An analysis of the history of technology shows that technological change is exponential, contrary to the common-sense "intuitive linear" view. So we won't experience 100 years of progress in the 21st century—it will be more like 20,000 years of progress (at today's rate).[1]

Since the 1960s, computers have doubled in power every 18 months or so. This has become so consistent that it has now become known as "Moore's law," named after computer scientist Gordon Moore who first expressed it in the 1960s. In order for this to happen, computer technology will need to continue to evolve. In fact, scientists today are talking about quantum computing where computers will literally use atoms and molecules as hardware. Should this come to pass, imagine your computer in 10 years, you probably will not need a keyboard to access it; instead, it will use a linguistic user interface where you will communicate via spoken commands and it will respond likewise. In fact, your computer may not be housed in a box or laptop—it may be sewn into your clothing and like today's mobile computing devices handle all your communications.

Eventually, your computer may be able to "think" more like a human being; many scientists today are excited about the possibility of artificial intelligence (AI) where computers achieve, or closely mimic, human thought. Given the speed at which computers perform mathematical computations and search functions, if they develop the capacity to "think," how long will it be until they develop the ability for "superhuman" thought? Months? Days? Minutes? What happens if computers become smarter than humans? The answer is that no one really knows. Scientists have given this moment a name, the Technological Singularity. It is that point that all future prediction becomes meaningless, because so much is unknowable. Although many engineers and scientists are excited about the possibility of supersmart computers, others are not so sure this will be a good thing. Silicon Valley pioneer Bill Joy, who is himself a computer scientist, wrote a famous article in *Wired* magazine in 2000 where he warned that powerful twenty-first century technologies, such as AI, could make human beings an "endangered species."[2]

Whatever happens, one forecast seems all but certain: in the future, computers and computer chips will be small, cheap, and everywhere. Radio frequency identification (RFID) chips are small devices used today to store data and track movements. Usually, they are embedded in an object and when scanned by special instruments can reveal a whole host of data. Pet owners use them today to "mark" their animals. Experts have suggested that they could be embedded in humans to store important medical information or when equipped with global positioning system (GPS) used to keep track of children, those with mental defects, or even criminals on probation or parole.

Many of the technologies that are being developed today that may have use for the police of the future are being developed for the military. Consider, for example, the unmanned aerial vehicles (UAVs) that today patrol the battlefields of Afghanistan and Iraq. Could they someday be used by law enforcement for surveillance duties or traffic enforcement? There seems to be nothing to suggest that this could not happen.

Another potential technological benefit for law enforcement currently being developed for the military is augmented reality (AR), where images and data are superimposed digitally over live action. One current use of AR, familiar to most people, is the yellow or orange first-down line that is superimposed on the field during televised football games. Imagine SWAT teams outfitted with portable, wearable AR gear that allows them to look at a building with its schematic layout or the location of a perpetrator revealed.

Technology is also making us a transparent society, where virtually everything we do has the potential to be gazed upon by others. Consider the vast number of cameras that record all aspects of our life. Anytime we shop at a convenience store, purchase gasoline, enter a school or mall, or even walk along the streets of a city, there are cameras capturing all of our movements. Anyone with a cellular telephone is a potential photojournalist able to capture important events as they unfold. Additionally, anytime we use a cell phone, we give away our approximate location. Every time we use our customer cards at the grocery store to receive discounts, we are telling the storeowners a great deal about ourselves—what we eat, how much beer we drink, whether we smoke, and so on. This is information that many would pay dearly for; in fact, many do because several retailers sell our personal information to data warehouses like LexisNexis.

If this is what is going on in the present, what will happen in the future? Some have claimed that privacy is, for all intents and purposes, disappearing. This will certainly become an issue for law enforcement, which is entrusted with enforcing the law while maintaining individual civil rights.

These are but a few of the technologies that will likely emerge in the next several years. Others include nanotechnology or the manipulation of matter at the atomic level. Some believe that future manufacturing will occur through nanotechnology. Instead of big factories, we will build things from the bottom up, manipulating and replicating cells in the same way that nature "grows" a flower. Likewise, cybernetics, or marrying human beings with robotic machinery, could provide a great tactical advantage to law enforcement engaged in activities like gathering evidence or making highly risky arrests; the days of a real "Robocop" may not be far off.

Recent technologies have affected American lifestyles professionally and personally. During recent years, a variety of technologies have emerged that may be of use among law enforcement organizations. Figure 15.1 depicts estimated times of technological adoption within society. The development, testing, and introduction of technologies require various amounts of time. Although new technologies may be emerging during the current time, it may be years before they are ready and accepted for use among law enforcement entities and within society.

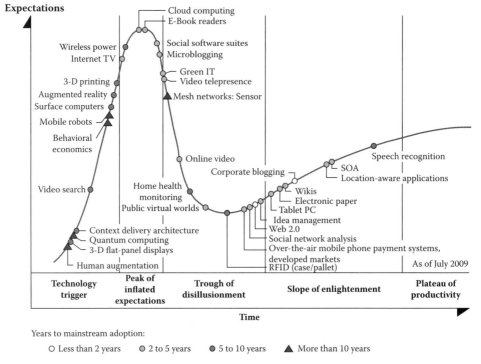

Figure 15.1 Technological adoption periods. (Courtesy of Gartner, Inc., 2009. Retrieved from http://www.gartner.com/resources/169700/169747/gartners_hype_cycle_special_169747.pdf.)

Demographic Trends

The U.S. Census Bureau contains a plethora of data sets regarding American demographics. Law enforcement agencies are tasked with a tremendous responsibility regarding maintaining order and deterring crime within American society. Figure 15.2 shows current demographic facets of American society regarding the sex and age characteristics of the population.

Another demographic trend affecting the population also influences border incidents. Although American law enforcement attempts to stem the tide of illegal aliens within the boundaries of the United States, it is undeniable that such individuals affect American society. Historically, border crossing incidents have fluctuated in accordance with governmental policies and the scope and magnitude of policing and law enforcement initiatives. Figure 15.3 shows the historical trends of American border apprehensions.

These two diagrams may be considered from the perspectives of law enforcement and policing. Policing is a "people" business; that will not change in the future. What will change, however, is the demographic makeup of the world law enforcement will face. Census experts claim there are three trends that especially bear watching in the United States:

1. Immigration is at very high levels and will likely continue at high levels into the future.
2. The birthrate of native-born Americans is decreasing.
3. The population on average is getting older.

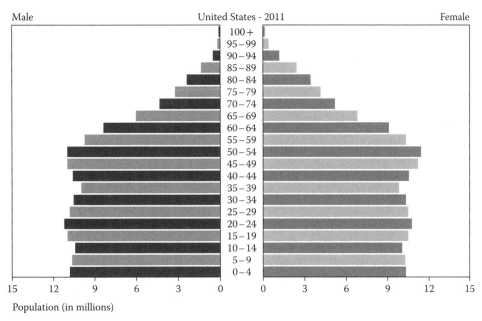

Figure 15.2 American age distributions vs. population. (Courtesy of the U.S. Census Bureau. Retrieved from http://www.census.gov/population/international/data/idb/country.php.)

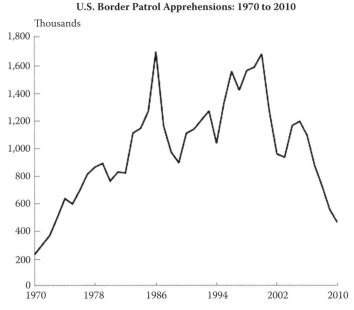

Figure 15.3 American border apprehensions between 1970 and 2010. (Courtesy of the U.S. Department of Homeland Security, 2011. Retrieved from http://www.dhs.gov/xlibrary/assets/statistics/publications/ois-apprehensions-fs-2005-2010.pdf.)

The population of the world continues to grow and will likely reach 8 billion by the year 2025.[3] However, only a small amount of that growth will occur in the United States and North America. Both India and China will be big winners in the population race; however, much of the growth will occur in areas of the world that can least afford to support the population they already have, such as the Middle East and Sub-Saharan Africa. This will put great pressure on young people from those countries to immigrate to areas of the world that can support them, including both the United States and Europe. Despite this trend, some countries, particularly those in Eastern Europe, are in danger of seeing their populations decline.[4]

Another factor that will enhance pressure for immigration concerns the declining birthrate of native-born residents in the United States. People are choosing to have fewer children. In order to meet the labor needs of the future, workers will have to come from somewhere. Many experts feel that the only way to make up for this shortfall is by allowing high rates of immigration.

America is a country of immigrants; indeed, immigrant population brings new, diverse ideas. Criminological research, in fact, suggests that first-generation immigrants are generally better behaved than the native-born population. However, immigrant groups can bring challenges as well. Many come from countries with a history of corrupt law enforcement; consequently, they distrust the police and are often not willing to report crimes or assist law enforcement efforts. As well, some things that are acceptable in their countries of origin, such as striking women and children, may be considered crimes in the United States. Finally, new types of criminality including transnational organized crime as personified by groups like Mara Salvatrucha (MS-13) and the Russian Mafia are even today providing great challenges to the police.

Thanks to better lifestyles and improved medical care, Americans are living longer and healthier. This is occurring at a time when a large portion of the U.S. population, the so-called Baby Boomers, is entering its senior years. This means the police will be confronted with a much larger senior population than ever before. There are both positives and negatives in this situation. In the first place, seniors tend to feel vulnerable and thus tend to have very favorable impressions of the police, who they count upon to protect them. This can help law enforcement in multiple ways. In addition, the elderly on average vote in far greater numbers than their younger counterparts. As such, the police can count on support at the ballot box, where ever-important budgets and other issues are often decided. Additionally, some savvy law enforcement managers will use the seniors in their jurisdiction as volunteers, thereby obtaining free labor.

The elderly, however, bring their own challenges. They often fall victim to scams and frauds. Today, many con artists have figured out that they do not have to meet with victims individually; instead, they can use the Internet and e-mail to perpetrate their crimes. Another relatively new phenomenon that will increasingly occupy the time of law enforcement is elder abuse, where uncaring family members or unscrupulous caregivers take advantage of those who cannot protect themselves. Finally, out of loneliness, some seniors call 911 because they know someone will respond to their needs, even if no crime has been committed. This can waste valuable law enforcement resources; some police managers have successfully used volunteers to reach out to their elderly population to reduce the number of "unfounded" 911 calls.

Such characteristics of demographic change have implications for law enforcement. Certainly, appropriate resources will be necessary to accommodate the changing needs and wants of society through time. Law enforcement must also adapt and respond to changes in criminal activity through time. Further, because law enforcement personnel are representative of their served societies, demographic changes may occur among departments through time. Table 15.1 shows the anticipated demographic changes that may impact society during the coming years.

Table 15.1 American Demographic Trends—Present, Past, and Future Estimates

Demographic Indicators	2011	1995	2005	2015	2025
Population					
Midyear population (in thousands)	311,051.00	266,278.00	295,753.00	322,371.00	351,353.00
Growth rate (percent)	0.90	(NA)	0.9	0.90	0.80
Fertility					
Total fertility rate (births per woman)	2.10	(NA)	(NA)	2.10	2.10
Crude birth rate (per 1000 population)	14.00	(NA)	14.00	14.00	13.00
Births (in thousands)	4258.00	(NA)	4138	4381.00	4585.00
Mortality					
Life expectancy at birth (years)	78.00	(NA)	(NA)	79.00	80.00
Infant mortality rate (per 1000 births)	6.00	(NA)	(NA)	6.00	5.00
Under 5 mortality rate (per 1000 births)	7.00	(NA)	(NA)	7.00	6.00
Crude death rate (per 1000 population)	8.00	(NA)	8.00	8.00	9.00
Deaths (in thousands)	2607.00	(NA)	2449.00	2711.00	3057.00
Migration					
Net migration rate (per 1000 population)	4.00	(NA)	3.00	4.00	4.00
Net number of migrants (in thousands)	1120.00	(NA)	979.00	1183.00	1349.00

Source: Courtesy of the U.S. Census Bureau. Retrieved from http://www.census.gov/population/international/data/idb/country.php.

Economic and Social Trends

Extreme economic change can lead to political instability; this, in turn, can bring on crime, terrorism, and general disorder.[5] As this book goes to press, the world appears to be slowly recovering from the greatest economic recession since the Great Depression of the 1930s; at this point, it is anybody's guess as to when or if total recovery is in our future.

One thing is certain—the world is integrated economically in ways it has never been before. Since the 1990s, a phenomenon known as globalization has been at work, resulting in open economic markets and the movement of people and ideas across what used to be impenetrable boundaries. During the Cold War, we lived in a bipolar world, where capitalism and communism competed against one another, and the major powers attempted to extend their spheres of influence to nonaligned countries. This led to a relative stalemate—the Western democracies traded among themselves as did the nations that labored under communist rule.

By the early 1990s, however, the Soviet Union had collapsed under the weight of its enormous and inefficient bureaucracy; countries that once were part of the Soviet Union, such as Georgia and the Ukraine, gained their independence. It appeared that the great socialist experiment that embraced communism turned increasingly to capitalism. Some, such as China, did not totally abandon all communist ideas. Perhaps the best way to describe the economies of these countries today is limited capitalism with a great deal of state control.

As countries began to trade with one another in earnest, tariffs and trade barriers began to disappear. Different countries established partnerships, such as the European Union, to try to maximize the influence they had on the rest of the world.

While this was happening, the Internet greatly enhanced communications across countries; people could communicate and share ideas as never before. All of this led to a great deal of interconnectivity and dependence. Some countries, such as China and India, became the suppliers of goods and services to the rest of the world, whereas others, like the United States, became consumers buying what other countries had to offer. For a variety of reasons, this came crashing down by the late 2000s. Because all countries were connected by globalization, the pain that was felt by one was shared by all.

Four countries today appear to be emerging as economic leaders: Brazil, Russia, India, and China, known collectively as the BRICs. Each has something to offer—abundant resources, cheap labor, and/or an educated work force—that leads experts to suggest that they will be global economic leaders by the mid part of the twenty-first century.

There is every reason to believe that at least some of the BRICs will not be content to remain only economic leaders. For the last several years, China has increased its military budget; in 2009, this increase equaled almost 15%. It has also changed the types of weapons it buys, leading some to conclude that China intends to become a military superpower.[6] This notion is meaningful within the context of intelligence analysis.

During 2011, China launched its first aircraft carrier. This ship, originally named the *Varyag*, was initially purchased as a Soviet relic of the Cold War and its stated purpose was to be a "floating casino in Macau." However, its stated purpose is unfulfilled. Instead, it is now a warship within the Chinese Navy. Other observations of increases and improvements within the Chinese Navy include

> The PLA (People's Liberation Army) has invested heavily in submarines. It is believed to be close to deploying the world's first "carrier-killer" ballistic missile, designed to sink aircraft carriers while they are maneuvering at sea up to 1500 km (930 miles) offshore, and it is building its own stealth fighter aircraft along with advanced carrier-based aircraft built from Russian designs. All of these can target U.S. bases, U.S. ships, and U.S. carriers in Asia. They will make it much more dangerous for U.S. carrier fleets to operate close to China's coast, pushing them out further offshore.[7]

The strengthening of Chinese military power has significant economic and political ramifications regarding the balance of power within the Pacific region. During recent years, numerous international disputes have occurred between China and neighboring nations and regions regarding maritime territories. Disputed areas involve regions near Japan, the Philippines, and Vietnam. Furthermore, because of an improved Chinese military capacity, some nations may question the potential of the United States to remain as an effective protector and mediator within the region.

Such modernization is not unnoticed within the American intelligence community. These events will influence future American policies within the Pacific regions. Furthermore, should any hostilities occur, military police units will be components of forces that are routed and deployed within affected regions. Within the context of intelligence analysis, the Chinese improvements and modernization will present hearty challenges that may affect the United States and its allies.

Globalization has also led to some other unforeseen and unfortunate consequences. For one thing, it allows terrorist groups like al-Qaeda to communicate, share information, and recruit members with relative ease. No longer constrained by geography and physical boundaries, small groups can cause much greater damage than ever before. Terrorists are not the only threat; prior to the globalized world, the existence of transnational criminal organizations, such as MS-13, with members traveling freely between a dozen countries, would have been unthinkable.

The interconnected world expands the span of even small-time crooks. Today, a "phisher" in Russia can steal the identities of citizens in Kansas with relative ease. Traditional jurisdictional boundaries, however, remain just as they were in the twentieth century. To date, law enforcement has not developed a good way to deal with cyber criminals. Figure 15.4 depicts a conceptual framework of cyber crime regarding its global characteristics.

Globalization is also a social and cultural phenomenon. Many law enforcement agencies claim to do community policing, but just what does "community" mean in the age of the Internet? Historically, one's community was defined by physical boundaries. People associated and communicated with their neighbors. Today, however, communications are virtually ubiquitous—people can associate with whomever they choose as long as the other person has a computer and Internet access. A person's community is no longer just his neighborhood; it can encompass the entire world. How will police departments deal with this new reality? Some have already established a presence on the web with blogs and websites, still others have begun to embrace Twitter and other means of social networking. Where this is all headed is still unclear, but it seems fairly certain that those most comfortable with new technologies, usually the most junior members of the organization, will lead the way.

Crime Trends

We have already mentioned some of the crime trends that we expect to see in the twenty-first century. Criminals will increasingly make use of the globalized world to engage in more transnational crime or crime that extends across national boundaries. Today, there is a virtual civil war raging in Mexico involving rival drug cartels, and the Mexican government has sworn to end their influence. The violence that has resulted has been unprecedented—beheadings and mass executions have become common and the cartels have gained access to military grade weapons that can wreak havoc. Experts worry that the Mexican violence will inevitably spread to the United States where Mexican gangs already operate in large numbers. Local U.S. law enforcement on the Mexican border and even the federal Border Patrol are likely unequipped to deal with an adversary that acts more like an army than it does a gang.

In many countries, public corruption is a way of life. Politicians and civil servants are routinely bribed and the rule of law is virtually nonexistent. As the world continues to shrink, the influence of corruption will inevitably extend to the United States. Already some U.S. companies are faced with the difficult choice of abetting this activity if they want to do business in certain parts of the world. This is a dangerous and slippery slope because

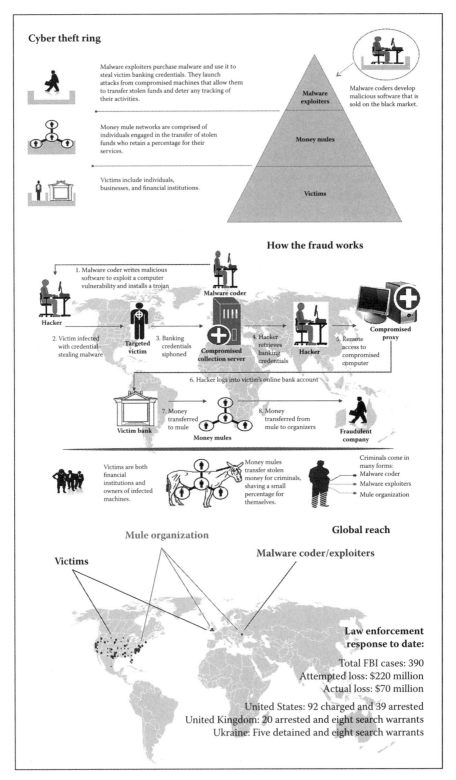

Figure 15.4 The concept of cyber crime. (Courtesy of the FBI, 2010. Retrieved from http://www.fbi.gov/news/stories/2010/october/cyber-banking-fraud.)

corruption begets corruption, and the likelihood that it will spread is great, unless it is effectively and efficiently dealt with by the United States. Despite the emergence of "new" types of criminality, it is unlikely that traditional crime such as murder, robbery, rape, and theft will disappear. Most parts of the United States have enjoyed a decline in crime in recent years. Although this is a welcome trend, most criminologists and law enforcement personnel believe it is only a matter of time before it begins to inch up again.

One of the new types of crime, one that most jurisdictions gave little thought to prior to September 11, 2001, is terrorism. As a result of those attacks, America realized just how vulnerable it was and continues to be. Of course, terrorism is nothing new; it has been around in one form or another since ancient times. However, up until 9/11, it was generally considered to be the responsibility of federal agencies such as the Federal Bureau of Investigation (FBI). After the attacks, a new phrase entered the law enforcement vocabulary—homeland security. Now, every department, large and small, realizes it has a role to play in protecting the nation. Some agencies, such as the New York City and Los Angeles Police Departments, have gone so far as to station personnel overseas in the hopes of enhancing intelligence and getting an "early warning" about future attacks. Although most agencies lack the resources to do likewise, many are adopting a more international perspective in the realization that what happens in faraway lands increasingly affects us here at home.

Another form of crime, which is increasing with the advent and proliferation of technology, is cyber crime. This form of crime is conducted via the use of electronic media. Because cyber crime occurs within the virtual domain, perpetrators may reside anywhere geographically and possess the capacity to attack targets remotely over great physical distances. Through the use of numerous servers and software to conceal transactions and physical locations, cyber crime represents a criminal activity that is often completely anonymous.

As the world becomes more "wired," the amount and sophistication of cyber crime will only increase. Identity theft will continue and complicated and intricate schemes to defraud and steal will no doubt proliferate. Cyber criminality is already a huge challenge to law enforcement, one that is barely addressed in many areas. Until and unless the police become better able to handle this growing challenge, it will quickly spin out of control.

Recent examples of cyber crime show the scope and magnitude of financial losses that may be incurred from virtual criminal activities. During 2011, a Brooklyn, New York man, Jonathan Oliveras, admitted his guilt involving a fraudulent credit card operation within the East Coast of the United States:[8]

> Oliveras admitted to managing a scheme to purchase stolen credit card account information through the Internet from individuals believed to be in Russia. Oliveras also admitted to distributing the purchased information to individuals in the New York, New Jersey and Washington, D.C., metropolitan areas so that it could be used to make fraudulent purchases. In pleading guilty, Oliveras admitted to illegally possessing information from 2341 stolen credit card accounts as well as equipment to put that information onto counterfeit credit cards. According to information presented in court, companies have reported to the government more than 4400 fraudulent charges totaling $770,674 on accounts illegally possessed by Oliveras. Oliveras also possessed 409 gift, debit, or credit cards used as part of the scheme, which had a total stored value of $42,688.[9]

Such financial amounts are significant and affect many entities ranging from the stakeholders of the defrauded institutions to the actual owners of the stolen credit card numbers. These types of crime are not uncommon during modern times and may be perpetrated with varying levels of complexity. Furthermore, some types of virtual crime parallel physical crime. For example, one can steal money physically as well as electronically via computer networks. The former case may leave some type of evidence through which the perpetrator may be apprehended, whereas the latter may be completely untraceable.

Cyber crime presents an enigma for modern investigators because many instances of virtual criminal activity defy Locard's principle. Simply, Locard's principle expresses the notion that if two entities come into contact with each other, then an exchange of attributes occurs between the two objects. For example, within the physical world, criminals may leave behind some evidence of their activity (e.g., fingerprints, footprints) within a crime scene, and may experience the transfer of some of the attributes of the crime scene onto their physical person (e.g., soil). However, within the intangible, virtual world of cyber crime, such an exchange does not necessarily occur, thereby increasing the complexity and difficulty of potentially solving cyber crimes.

The Internet, commercial intranets, and government networks increasingly connect geographic locations of the physical world through the intangible realms of cyberspace and virtual domains. Such interconnectedness presents a continuously increasing array or target opportunities for virtual crime. Similarly, such increased connectedness provides opportunities for perpetrators to gain access to these virtual domains. Because of the growth of networked environments, increases in cyber crime may be anticipated during the coming years.

Emerging Technologies

Modern technologies are the result of cascading efforts and serendipitous events through time. An old adage states that necessity is the mother of invention. This notion is true—practically all technologies are nothing more than tools through which humans attempt to solve some problematic issue. Furthermore, such technologies are often resources through which the efficiency and effectiveness of human activities and pursuits are improved through time. This section highlights the potential of emerging technologies within the context of law enforcement.

Biometrics

Biometric research may influence future applications of technologies among policing domains. The term biometrics is defined as the "measurement and analysis of unique physical or behavioral characteristics (as fingerprint or voice patterns) especially as a means of verifying personal identity."[10] Through the introduction of faster computing devices with greater memory capacities and the maturing of biometric algorithms, the ability to quickly identify individuals, based on their physical attributes, is improved.

Miles and Cohn consider the use of biometric identification and tracking of prisoners within military brig settings of the U.S. Navy:[11]

> Under the manual system of tracking inmate movements, the corrections specialists failed to note a prisoner's non-arrival in all 12 test grabs. Under the manual system, it took corrections specialists an average of 43 minutes to notice an out-of-place prisoner. In half the cases, more than 1 hour passed before the corrections specialists realized the situation. Once the computer

tracking system was introduced, however, the average time it took for staff to notice a non-arriving inmate dropped to 17 minutes. In only 1 of 10 cases did more than 1 hour pass.[12]

According to Wagstaff, uses of biometric resources encompass "iris and fingerprint biometric technology, manages electronic key cabinets, secures airlock portals, catalogues inmate property storage, monitors visitor appointments, conducts criminal record checks, integrates key access policies" and are implemented among 25 prison environments within the United States.[13] The application of data mining may be applicable within the context of biometric resources, because it facilitates the examining of data sets to identify various patterns that may otherwise remain unnoticed by humans.[14]

These outcomes are not the only concerns associated with biometric technologies. Others are hygienic. Some may object to the sharing of physical devices because of hygiene concerns.[15] Because physical scanning devices are shared among incarceration environments, the potential of spreading diseases must not be ignored.

Another consideration of biometric devices involves the physical characteristics of humans. Jabbar indicates that differences among the physical attributes of humans demonstrate varying complexities regarding biometric data. Jabbar maintains that obtaining a "good" scanned iris image, taken from the human eye, may be difficult. For example, "people having heavy eyelids have a hard time holding them apart" during the scanning of iris data."[16]

The application of biometric technologies is imperfect. Regardless, improvements of biometric resources are being pursued during modern times. Although such systems currently demonstrate varying amounts of imperfection, technological improvements may mature biometric systems to benefit future law enforcement organizations.[17] Figure 15.5 shows a biometric system that may be useful for law enforcement entities.

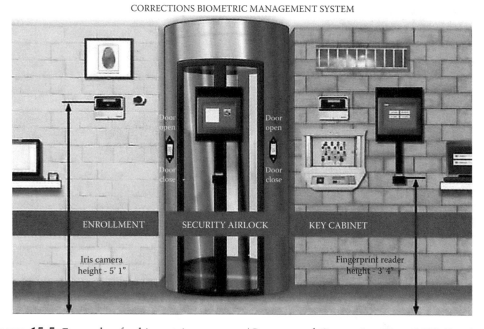

Figure 15.5 Example of a biometrics system. (Courtesy of CorrectionsOne, 2010. Retrieved from http://www.correctionsone.com/police-technology/investigation/biometrics-identification/articles/2189110-Biometric-prison-management-Technology-of-the-future/.)

Simulation Technologies

Simulation is defined as the "imitative representation of the functioning of one system or process by means of the functioning of another."[18] Although many simulations may involve manual processes and physical resources, modern simulations are often conducted through the use of digital resources and automated computer systems (Figure 15.6). A variety of simulation resources exist to enhance police training, and other simulation systems are being developed through which future training environments may be strengthened.

According to *Police Magazine*, an example of a simulation environment is the

> ... [Advanced System Architecture for Urban Live Training (ASAULT)], consisting of cameras, speakers, smoke generators, high fidelity indoor tracking and computer systems plus sophisticated exercise control and debriefing application programs. In addition, it will supply 24 MILES Individual Weapons System (MILES IWS) kits that will be worn by trainees. Cubic's ASAULT is used for creating scenarios, gathering sensor data and controlling systems in the facility and the MILES After Action Review System (MAARS) is used to create debriefing sessions after an exercise.[19]

The use of simulation technologies attempts to provide realistic training scenarios in police training environments. Simulation systems, enhanced with virtual reality, present the opportunity to craft training environments that may improve the realism of training

Figure 15.6 Police training simulation system. (From Griffith, D., *Police Magazine*, 2009. Retrieved from http://www.policemag.com/Channel/Technology/Articles/2009/04/Virtual-Reality-Training.aspx.)

scenarios. During the preceding decades, advancements in virtual reality, computer software, and computer hardware have vastly improved realism.

Among some of these training simulations, the realism of training scenarios is accomplished through the use of spectral imagery in which holographic images are projected within the training setting. In some cases, such holograms may not be interactive. However, as technology progresses, it is anticipated that future training environments may incorporate interactive holograms to further improve the realism of training regimens and scenarios.[20] Among police environments, the use of these types of simulation systems and virtual reality integrations is increasing and will continue to spread among local, state, and federal agencies. Future training regimens may incorporate significantly more realism among all police training initiatives ranging from patrol scenarios to marksmanship.[21]

Artificial Intelligence

AI is the attempt to generate computing devices that emulate human behaviors and characteristics. Domains of AI are diverse and encompass a variety of applications. Prominent AI endeavors include the recognition of patterns, rendering decisions, learning systems, and prediction. Although AI is employed among a variety of commercial settings, it is finding new applications within the domain of policing and intelligence analysis.

A significant example involves the functions of the National Security Agency (NSA). Bamford indicates that AI may be used eventually to detect deception and "one area of study is to attempt to determine if people are lying simply by watching their behavior and listening to them speak."[22] Human cues of deception involve changes of verb tense and facial expressions.[23] Through the use of advanced analytical techniques, systems may eventually be developed that significantly improve the ability to detect deception during conversations or questioning.

Another potential application of AI involves the improvement of the intelligence analysis function via the parsing of massive sets of data. For example, "evidence from different online sources and databases, and how particle swarm intelligence—inspired by the behavior of flocks of birds—could probe information shared by groups on social networks."[24] This type of parsing and integrating of data sets may decrease the time necessary to conduct analytical functions of identifying patterns and connecting relationships (that may not be obvious) among large sets of data ranging from fraud analytics to social network connections.[25]

One project, conducted by the Artificial Intelligence Laboratory (AIL) of the University of Arizona, is investigating the potential use of detecting deception through the use of data mining methods. This experimental system assists in the verification of personal identities. In this instance, an "automated detection algorithm using string comparison techniques" was applied against a database that contained "a taxonomy of criminal identity deception" involving "different deception characteristics in different identity attributes."[26] The outcomes of initial experimentation showed that the "proposed algorithm correctly detected 94% of deceptive criminal identities" among test cases.[27]

These types of AI systems are currently experimental. However, considering the maturation of technology, deception systems may become valuable assets among law enforcement organizations. A sample of the type of output that is generated from the AIL experimental system is displayed in Figure 15.7.

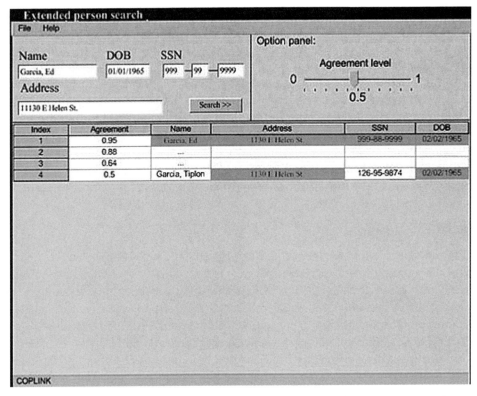

Figure 15.7 Example of software output—artificial intelligence deception system. (Courtesy of the University of Arizona. Retrieved from http://ai.arizona.edu/research/coplink/deception .asp#screen.)

Future uses of technology may also benefit the police environment managerially. The use of AI software is beginning to influence hiring decisions within law enforcement organizations. An example of this use of AI involves the application of BrainMaker software to detect potential misconduct among law enforcement personnel within the Chicago Police Department (CPD). A synopsis of this study is given as follows:

> After BrainMaker studied the records of the 12,500 current officers (records that included such information as age, education, sex, race, number of traffic accidents, reports of lost weapons or badges, marital status, performance reports, and frequency of sick leaves) the neural network produced a list of 91 at-risk men and women. Of those 91 people, nearly half were found to be already enrolled in a counseling program founded by the personnel department to help officers guilty of misconduct. The I.A.D. now intends to make the neural network a supplement to the counseling program because, as Deputy Superintendent Raymond Risely said, the sheer size of the Chicago police force makes it "pretty much impossible for all at-risk individuals to be identified [by supervisors]."[28]

Participating in the BrainMaker research was voluntary and held no punitive measures for individuals who were identified as misbehavior risks. Because of the controversial basis of the program, the use of the BrainMaker application was terminated. Although the CPD no longer implements the use of neural networks to identify potential misbehavior risks, other law enforcement agencies may opt to implement similar software packages within their personnel departments. In the future, such applications of AI may eventually become a routine component of hiring and retention among law enforcement agencies.[29]

Data Mining

Data mining involves the discovery of knowledge from data sets as forms of data and pattern analysis.[30] The primary goal of data mining is to understand large amounts of data in some domain.[31] In simple terms, data mining explores the potential relationships among vast sets of data to determine the presence of patterns (Figure 15.8). Although manual processing may be used against these data sets, manual methods require large amounts of time (ranging into years and decades); the use of data mining software may reduce these processing times to mere days or weeks. In some cases, depending upon the solvability of the context, manual solutions and explorations of potential data relationships may be impossible to generate.

Data mining supplements the investigative capacity of law enforcement organizations. Because data mining software is automated, fewer personnel are necessary to examine large sets of data. Furthermore, because data mining involves specific algorithms that serve unique purposes, patterns that may not be obvious may be readily identified. Current uses of data mining within the context of law enforcement are widespread. Examinations of border crossing transactions, reported incidents of crime, telephone records, criminal histories, financial transaction histories, fraud analytics, and social networks are all candidate domains for data mining applications.[32]

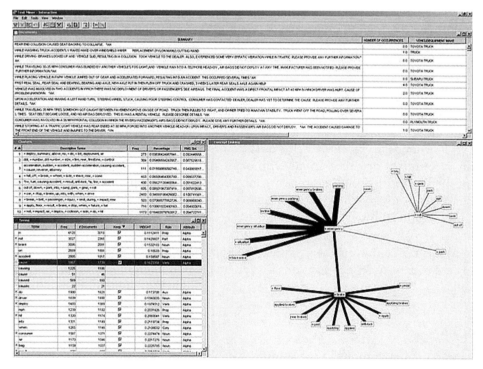

Figure 15.8 Sample output of data mining software. (Courtesy of SAS. Retrieved from http://www.sas.com/industry/travel/pricing-revenue-opt.html.)

Border security contexts of data mining are within the realm of American intelligence analysis. According to Westphal data mining is used to examine a variety of border characteristics involving arrivals and departures affecting American borders. When considering land borders, data mining algorithms may be used to identify relationships among data sets consisting of hour of the day, day of the week, date of a border-crossing transaction, points of entry, lane clusters, responsible inspectors, cities and states, and vehicle identification numbers. When considering the quantities of individuals and vehicles that cross U.S. borders annually, these attributes of data quickly become quite vast through time. Because of such gargantuan data sets, manual processing becomes impractical. Therefore, software must be leveraged to parse data and to explore potential relationships among sets of data.[33]

Although data mining is certainly beneficial during modern times, its potential for bolstering the efforts of law enforcement agencies may improve the efficiency and effectiveness of future law enforcement operations and initiatives. This notion is not unnoticed by the American federal government. During 2009, an initiative was undertaken to facilitate the "gathering, documenting, processing, analyzing, and sharing of information about terrorism-related suspicious activities."[34] Through the mining of such data, patterns may be identified that are indicative of potential terrorist activities and operations. Furthermore, through the mining of such data, potential targets may be identified. Because of the identification of such patterns, law enforcement agencies may act accordingly to safeguard target locations.

Data mining involves also serves as a predictive resource. It is used to explore existing sets of data that represent historical transactions through time. The establishment and identification of historical patterns and trends may be used to forecast potential future events that may impact policing decisions. For example, a law enforcement agency may examine crime reports that were collected during the preceding decade to project the potential amount and type of criminal offenses that it may encounter during future periods. Leaders and managers of law enforcement agencies then need to accommodate the hiring of additional personnel to counter potential increases in crime that were identified within the data mining processes. However, if decreases in crime are projected, reductions of personnel within the police agency may be mandated during future periods.

Regardless of its application, data mining provides a tool through which law enforcement organizations may identify patterns that potentially exist regarding historical observations of criminal or other events. Although the identification of such patterns and relationships assists law enforcement organizations in rendering public service, the generation of such items is insufficient to enact or influence future policies among law enforcement organizations. Instead, humans must use the results of data mining initiatives to render decisions regarding policy and initiatives. Although data mining is a useful tool through which law enforcement activities are conducted, it is the human who must use the tool of data mining to render decisions that are in the best interests of society.

Summary

No one can predict or foretell the future with complete accuracy and certainty. However, one can estimate and forecast future events and situations. Law enforcement is no exception to this notion. Only time will be the judge of the impacts of demographic, sociological, economic, and technological developments that occur in the future. Regardless, two notions are highly likely to occur among all future generations: (1) law enforcement personnel and organizations will continue to deter crime and maintain order within society, and (2) crime has always pervaded society, currently affects society, and will continue to do so in the future.

Policing has matured throughout history. It is still maturing with respect to the types of technologies that are implemented among law enforcement settings. Human nature never changes; the temptation that lured Cain to slay Abel remains common during modern times. Certainly, such temptations shall influence future generations.

Social influences will impact future generations of policing. The demographic characteristics of American society are anticipated to change through time. The society that is manifested within America today will be a thing of the past relatively soon, and changed demographics may be indicative of altered perceptions of policy, policing, enforcement, and politics during the future. Certainly, these considerations will affect law enforcement organizations.

Historically, crime has occurred in physical environments. Investigations have emphasized the physical attributes of criminal offenses and the resources that were necessary to close cases. However, the advent and proliferation of digital technologies has introduced a virtual world in which cyber crime has become prevalent. This new environment presents a variety of challenges for law enforcement agencies given the intangibility of virtual crime. Agencies must adapt and develop new resources to counter events of digital crime.

Humans and human nature are relatively static entities. However, technology changes through time. Manual methods of information processing have been replaced with automated technologies that supplement the activities of law enforcement organizations. In modern times, computerized technologies support a variety of law enforcement functions ranging from digital communications networks to the applications of data mining. New inventions and technological advancements will similarly affect the environments and functions of future law enforcement organizations.

Discussion Questions

1. Consider the historical crimes that have impacted your locality. Perform some research and determine the primary forms and quantities of criminal events that have affected your community and law enforcement organization. Based on your findings, perform some form of forecasting to determine what quantities and types of crime may exist over a five-year period. Based on these outcomes, what recommendations would you offer for your law enforcement organization?

2. Consider the demographics of your locality. Perform some research and determine what demographic characteristics are exhibited by your community. Most cities have long-term strategic plans to accommodate future conditions of growth. Examine the strategic plan for your city and forecast what types of demographic issues may impact the future of policing within your locality.

3. Economic conditions have affected crime and policing historically. Based up the continuous growth of globalism, determine how crime and policing have changed within

American society over the last three decades. Given your outcomes, consider how globalism will affect American crime and policing during the coming decade.

4. Technology changes quickly over time. Perform some research and determine five emerging technologies that you believe will be useful resources within the context of policing and law enforcement during the upcoming decade. Justify your responses with a substantive discussion of each technology and its potential merits within the policing and law enforcement contexts.

References

1. Kurzweil, R. (2001). The Law of Accelerating Returns. Kurzweil: Accelerating Intelligence. Retrieved from http://www.kurzweilai.net/the-law-of-accelerating-returns
2. Joy, B. (2000). Why the Future Doesn't Need Us. Wired. Retrieved from http://www.wired.com/wired/archive/8.04/joy.html
3. National Intelligence Council (2008). *Global Trends 2025: A Transformed World.* Retrieved from http://www.dni.gov/nic/PDF_2025/2025_Global_Trends_Final_Report.pdf
4. Ibid.
5. Ibid.
6. Spencer, R. (2009). China to increase defense spending by 15 percent. *The Telegraph.* Retrieved from http://www.telegraph.co.uk/news/worldnews/asia/china/4936931/China-to-increase-defence-spending-by-15-per-cent.html
7. British Broadcasting Corporation (2011). *China's First Aircraft Carrier Starts 'Sea Trials.'* Retrieved from http://www.bbc.co.uk/news/world-asia-pacific-14470882
8. U.S. Department of Justice (2011). *Brooklyn Man Pleads Guilty to Online Identity Theft Involving More Than $700,000 in Reported Fraud.* Retrieved from http://www.cybercrime.gov/OliverasPlea.pdf
9. Ibid.
10. Biometrics (2011). *Merriam-Webster Dictionary.* Retrieved from http://www.merriam-webster.com/dictionary/biometrics
11. Miles, C., & Cohn, J. (2006). Tracking Prisoners in Jail with Biometrics: An Experiment in a Navy Brig. National Institute of Justice. Retrieved from http://www.nij.gov/journals/253/tracking.html
12. Ibid.
13. Wagstaff, E. (2010). Biometric Prison Management: Technology of the Future. Corrections One. Retrieved from http://www.correctionsone.com/police-technology/investigation/biometrics-identification/articles/2189110-Biometric-prison-management-Technology-of-the-future/
14. Ibid.
15. Jabbar, S. (2011). *Face Recognition Systems for Facility Access.* Retrieved from http://snajsoft.com/2011/01/03/face-recognition-systems-for-facility-access/
16. Ibid.
17. Miles, C., & Cohn, J. (2006). Tracking Prisoners in Jail with Biometrics: An Experiment in a Navy Brig. National Institute of Justice. Retrieved from http://www.nij.gov/journals/253/tracking.html
18. Simulation (2011). *Merriam-Webster Dictionary.* Retrieved from http://www.merriam-webster.com/dictionary/simulation
19. Cubic equips college with 'tactical village.' (2011). *Police Magazine* (p. 5). Retrieved from http://www.policemag.com/Channel/technology/News/2011/04/19/Cubic-Equips-College-with-Tactical-Village.aspx

20. Stuart, W. (2008). What Role Will Technology Play in the Future of Law Enforcement Firearms Training Facilities? The future of realistic training. Huntington Beach Police Department. Retrieved from http://www.google.com/url?sa=t&source=web&cd=9&ved=0CFEQFjAI& url=http%3A%2F%2Flibcat.post.ca.gov%2Fdbtw-wpd%2Fdocuments%2Fcc%2F42-stuart .pdf&rct=j&q=holographic%20training%20simulation%20police&ei=vL5hTsKVOsnIgQfCwr TACg&usg=AFAFQjCNEoQAlw5kMmDxGnHKi8nfiZDunQ&cad=rja

21. Griffith, D. (2009). Virtual reality training. *Police Magazine*. Retrieved from http://www .policemag.com/Channel/Technology/Articles/2009/04/Virtual-Reality-Training.aspx

22. Bamford, J. (2009). The new thought police: The NSA wants to know how you think—maybe even what you think. *Public Broadcasting Service*. Retrieved from http://www.pbs.org/wgbh/ nova/military/nsa-police.html

23. Ibid.

24. Heath, N. (2008). *UK Police Enlists Artificial Intelligence in Fight Against Crime*. Retrieved from http://www.zdnetasia.com/uk-police-enlists-artificial-intelligence-in-fight-against-crime- 62048038.htm

25. Ibid.

26. Data Warehousing—Coplink/Border Safety/RISC (2011). University of Arizona. Retrieved from http://ai.arizona.edu/research/coplink/deception.asp#screen

27. Ibid.

28. Neural network red-flags police officers with potential for misconduct (2011). *California Scientific*. Retrieved from http://www.calsci.com/Police.html

29. Ibid.

30. Han, J., Kamber, M., & Pei, J. (2012). *Data Mining: Concepts and Techniques* (3rd ed.). Waltham, MA: Morgan-Kaufman—Elsevier Publishing.

31. Cios, K., Pedrycz, W., Swiniarski, R., & Kurgan, L. (2007). *Data Mining: A Knowledge Discovery Approach*. New York, NY: Springer Publishing.

32. Westphal, C. (2009). *Data Mining for Intelligence, Fraud, and Criminal Detection: Advanced Analytics and Information Sharing Technologies*. Boca Raton, FL: CRC Press.

33. Nationwide SAR Initiative (2011). U.S. Department of Justice. Retrieved from http://nsi .ncirc.gov/

Index

A